THE WESTMINSTER CHRONICLE
1381 - 1394

OXFORD MEDIEVAL TEXTS

General Editors

C. N. L. BROOKE   D. E. GREENWAY

M. WINTERBOTTOM

THE WESTMINSTER CHRONICLE
1381-1394

EDITED AND TRANSLATED

BY

the late L. C. HECTOR

Formerly a Principal Assistant Keeper of Public Records

and

BARBARA F. HARVEY

Fellow of Somerville College, Oxford

CLARENDON PRESS · OXFORD
1982

Oxford University Press, Walton Street, Oxford OX2 6DP

London Glasgow New York Toronto
Delhi Bombay Calcutta Madras Karachi
Kuala Lumpur Singapore Hong Kong Tokyo
Nairobi Dar es Salaam Cape Town
Melbourne Auckland

and associate companies in
Beirut Berlin Ibadan Mexico City

Published in the United States by
Oxford University Press, New York

British Library Cataloguing in Publication Data

The Westminster Chronicle, 1381-1394.
 — (Oxford medieval texts)
 1. Great Britain — History — 1381-1394
 I. Hector, L. C.   II. Harvey, Barbara, F.
 942   DA130

ISBN 0-19-822255-6

Typeset by Anne Joshua Associates, Oxford
Printed in Great Britain
at the University Press, Oxford
by Eric Buckley
Printer to the University

PREFACE

I must first say how responsibility for this volume has been
divided between its two editors. Mr. Hector began work on
the Westminster Chronicle in 1946. In 1962, with the text
(though not the full critical apparatus) complete and a third
of the translation in its final form, he felt unable to continue.
With his ready concurrence the General Editors of the Series
invited me to complete the edition. Subsequently, at my
entreaty, and to the great benefit of all who will use this
volume, Mr. Hector agreed to complete the translation of the
Chronicle and the critical apparatus of the text, when other
work to which he was committed should permit. The edition
then became a joint enterprise in which my part was to be
the Introduction and the general historical notes, and in the
volume now published these are my work. Mr. Hector completed his part in 1973, and all the regrettable delay since
then has been my own. Owing to Mr. Hector's death in 1977,
the final preparation of the whole volume for the Press has
fallen to me, and I am also responsible for the collation of
the Chronicle with other sources where this has seemed
necessary. It is my hope that all this has been done in ways
that will enhance the reader's enjoyment of and profit from
the text of the Chronicle and the translation, the vital com-
ponents of the volume. In the discussion of authorship in the
Introduction I am greatly indebted to correspondence with
Mr. Hector over the years, but must accept entire responsibility for the views expressed here.

On behalf of both editors I thank the Master and Fellows
of Corpus Christi College, Cambridge, for permission to publish the unique text of the Westminster Chronicle, C.C.C.C.
MS. 197A, pp. 130–210, together with a photograph of
p. 178, in this new edition, and I am personally indebted to
Dr. R. I. Page, Librarian, and to Mrs. J. Rolfe, Assistant
Librarian, for facilitating my work on the manuscript.

I gladly acknowledge help received at the University Library, Cambridge, the Bodleian Library, Oxford, the University Library, Edinburgh, the British Library, and the Public Record Office, London. Muniments of Westminster Abbey are cited with the permission of the Dean and Chapter of Westminster. The extent of my own debt to the Dean and Chapter, to Mr. H. M. Nixon, Librarian, and to Mr. N. H. MacMichael, Keeper of the Muniments, for the freedom of the Muniment Room will be clear from the Introduction and footnotes. I am also indebted for help to Dr. Pierre Chaplais, Professor C. R. Cheney, Mrs. Consuelo Dutschke, Mrs. S. M. Hall, Dr. G. L. Harriss, Dr. J. R. L. Highfield, Dr. N. R. Ker, Professor M. D. Legge, Dr. M. B. Parkes, Mr. Andrew Prescott, Professor R. H. Rouse, and Mr. John Taylor. To Professor Legge, who helped most generously with the final scrutiny of the French portions of the text and with the translation, I am especially indebted. In the early stages of his work Mr. Hector received some help from Professor A. A. M. Duncan. No one whom I have mentioned, however, is to be identified with any particular views expressed in the Introduction or elsewhere.

An edition so long in preparation does not survive to see publication without incurring debts of a special kind to the friends who prevent collapse on the way. In this connection Mr. Hector would have wished to thank, as I do, Dr. Roy Hunnisett, of the Public Record Office, and Professor Christopher Brooke. Professor Brooke's interest in the Chronicle extends over a longer period than my own. It is a pleasure to me to salute the memory of Professor V. H. Galbraith, the General Editor who first discussed with me the possibility that I might work on the Chronicle, and to thank Professor May McKisack for encouragement in the early stages.

Finally, it falls to me to express, though I cannot hope to do so adequately, what this volume owes to the present General Editors: to Professor Brooke, again, for reading the final typescript and advising on many points; to Dr. Diana Greenway, for her meticulous care over every detail of a large volume; and to Dr. Michael Winterbottom, for his scrutiny of the Latin text and translation and indispensable suggestions for their correction and improvement.

8 February 1980   B. F. H.

CONTENTS

C.C.C.C. MS. 197A, p. 178   *frontispiece*

ABBREVIATIONS   ix

INTRODUCTION   xiii

  The Manuscript   xiv

  The Chronicle   xxii
    (i) Authorship and Date   xxii
   (ii) Sources   xliii
  (iii) Value   lviii
      Diplomatic History   lviii
      English Politics   lxiii
      London Affairs   lxvi
      The Peasants' Revolt   lxix
      The King   lxxii

  Previous Edition   lxxv

  Note on Editing   lxxv

THE WESTMINSTER CHRONICLE   1

APPENDIX   522

CONCORDANCE   529

INDEX OF QUOTATIONS AND ALLUSIONS   533

GENERAL INDEX   534

ABBREVIATIONS

Anon. Chron.	The Anonimalle Chronicle, 1333 to 1381, ed. V. H. Galbraith (Manchester, 1927).
B.E.C.	Bibliothèque de l'École des Chartes.
Bellamy, *Law of Treason*	J. G. Bellamy, The Law of Treason in England in the Later Middle Ages (Cambridge, 1970).
B.I.H.R.	Bulletin of the Institute of Historical Research.
B.L.	British Library, London.
Bower	Johannis de Fordun Scotichronicon cum supplementis et continuatione Walteri Boweri, ed. W. Goodall (2 vols., Edinburgh, 1959).
B.R.U.O.	A. B. Emden, A Biographical Register of the University of Oxford to A.D. 1500 (3 vols., Oxford, 1957-9).
Cal. Ch. R.	Calendar of Charter Rolls.
Cal. Cl. R.	Calendar of Close Rolls.
Cal. Fine R.	Calendar of Fine Rolls.
Cal. Inq. p.m.	Calendar of Inquisitions post mortem.
Cal. Papal Letters	Calendar of Entries in the Papal Registers relating to Great Britain and Ireland: Papal Letters (1198-1492), ed. W. H. Bliss and J. A. Twemlow (14 vols., London, 1893-1960).
Cal. Pat. R.	Calendar of Patent Rolls.
Carte	T. Carte, Catalogue des Rolles Gascons, Normans et François (2 vols., London, 1743).
C.C.C.C.	Corpus Christi College, Cambridge.
C.U.L.	Cambridge University Library.
D.N.B.	Dictionary of National Biography.
E.H.R.	English Historical Review.
Expeditions by Henry, earl of Derby	Expeditions to Prussia and the Holy Land made by Henry, earl of Derby, 1390-1, 1392-3, ed. L. Toulmin Smith (Camden Soc., n.s., lii, 1894).
Favent	Historia siue Narracio de Modo et Forma Mirabilis Parliamenti apud Westmonasterium anno Domini millesimo ccclxxxvi per Thomam Fauent Clericum indictata, ed. M. McKisack (Camden Miscellany, xiv, 1926, pp. 1-27).
Flete	The History of Westminster Abbey by John Flete, ed. J. Armitage Robinson (Cambridge, 1909).
Fordun	Johannis de Fordun Chronica Gentis Scotorum, ed. W. F. Skene (2 vols., Edinburgh, 1871-2).

Froissart, *Chroniques*	*Œuvres de Froissart*, ed. Kervyn de Lettenhove: *Chroniques* (25 vols., Brussels, 1870–7).
G.E.C.	G. E. Cokayne, *The Complete Peerage*, ed. V. Gibbs, H. A. Doubleday, *et al.* (13 vols. in 14, London, 1910–59).
Higden	*Polychronicon Ranulphi Higden Monachi Cestrensis*, ed. C. Babington (vols. i–ii) and J. R. Lumby (vols. iii–ix) (R.S., 1865–86).
Knighton, *Chronicon*	*Chronicon Henrici Knighton vel Cnitthon, monachi Leycestrensis*, ed. J. R. Lumby (2 vols., R.S., 1889–95).
Letter Book H	*Calendar of Letter Books preserved among the Archives of the Corporation of the City of London at the Guildhall: Letter Book H, circa A.D. 1375–1399*, ed. R. R. Sharpe (London, 1907).
Liber Niger Quaternus	Westminster Abbey Muniments, Book no. 1 (a cartulary).
Mirot and Déprez, in *B.E.C.*, lx	L. Mirot and E. Déprez, 'Les Ambassades Anglaises pendant la Guerre de Cent Ans', part ii, in *Bibliothèque de l'École des Chartes*, lx (1899), pp. 177–214.
Monks	E. H. Pearce, *The Monks of Westminster* (Cambridge, 1916).
MSS. of Westminster Abbey	J. Armitage Robinson and M. R. James, *The Manuscripts of Westminster Abbey* (Cambridge, 1909).
Palmer	J. J. N. Palmer, *England, France and Christendom, 1377–99* (London, 1972).
P.B.A.	*Proceedings of the British Academy.*
Perroy	E. Perroy, *L'Angleterre et le grand schisme d'Occident: étude sur la politique religieuse de l'Angleterre sous Richard II (1378–1399)* (Paris, 1933).
P.R.O.	Public Record Office, London.
Reign of Richard II	*The Reign of Richard II: Essays in Honour of May McKisack*, ed. F. R. H. Du Boulay and C. M. Barron (London, 1971).
Réville	A. Réville, *Le Soulèvement des travailleurs d'Angleterre en 1381* (Paris, 1898).
Riley, *Memorials*	*Memorials of London and London Life, in the xiiith, xivth and xvth Centuries*, ed. H. T. Riley (London, 1868).
R.P.	*Rotuli Parliamentorum.*
R.S.	Rolls Series.
Rot. Scot.	*Potuli Scotiae* (2 vols., Record Commission, 1814–19).
Russell, *English Intervention*	P. E. Russell, *The English Intervention in Spain and Portugal in the time of Edward III and Richard II* (Oxford, 1955).

Rymer, *Foedera*	T. Rymer, *Foedera, Conventiones, Literae, etc.* (15 vols., London, 1704–1713).
Speculum Historiale	*Ricardi de Cirencestria Speculum Historiale de Gestis Regum Angliae*, ed. J. E. B. Mayor (2 vols., R.S., 1863–9).
S.R.	*Statutes of the Realm.*
Taylor, *Hidgen*	J. Taylor, *The Universal Chronicle of Ranulf Higden* (Oxford, 1966).
Tout, *Chapters*	T. F. Tout, *Chapters in the Administrative History of Mediaeval England* (6 vols., Manchester, 1920–33).
Valois	N. Valois, *La France et le grand schisme d'Occident* (Paris, 4 vols., 1896–1902).
V.C.H.	*Victoria History of the Counties of England.*
Vita Ricardi Secundi	*Historia Vitae et Regni Ricardi Secundi*, ed. G. B. Stow, Jr. (University of Pennsylvania, 1977).
W	W.A.M. 12227.
W.A.M.	Westminster Abbey Muniments.
Walsingham, *Hist. Ang.*	*Thome Walsingham Quondam Monachi Sancti Albani, Historia Anglicana*, ed. H. T. Riley (2 vols., R.S., 1863–4).

INTRODUCTION

The reign of Richard II has been studied for a period comparable in length with that separating his accession from the death of King Alfred, but even now, when so much attention is rightly ·given to its institutional framework — to the administrative system, social structure, and European context of Richard's England — interest still focuses on the character and aspirations of the king himself, as it did when Tudor polemicists began the long scrutiny.[1] While this remains true, the chronicles of the reign will hold pride of place among the sources, for the king is observed in them as nowhere else. The voices of Knighton, Walsingham, and the Monk of Evesham are not, of course, substitutes for Richard II's own, which we so rarely hear, but they reveal more of the man than the Close or Patent Rolls, the plea rolls, or the accounts of ambassadors. Among the chronicles, that written at Westminster Abbey is of singular interest, for Richard II was known at Westminster as at no other house in the kingdom. Any assessment of him must take into account what is said here or have plausible reasons for setting it aside.

As though to match the complexity of the events which it relates, the Westminster Chronicle presents its readers with knotty problems of dating and authorship, and these must now be examined. A synopsis of the conclusions which are reached in the following pages may be found useful.

Two monks shared unequally in the writing of the Westminster Chronicle for the years 1381 to 1394. One composed a narrative for the first three years; the other took over as an independent author at the end of 1383. The whole of the unique manuscript is in the hand of the second author. He introduced alterations and additions into the narrative for the years 1381 to 1383, for, though dependent on his

---

[1] For the Tudor interest in Richard II see M. Aston, 'Richard II and the Wars of the Roses', in *Reign of Richard II*, pp. 280 ff.

text, he felt free to change it; and whether composing or transcribing, he left on these pages the mark of his own idiosyncratic Latin. But he was not the creator of the narrative for these early years in the full sense of the word, and over parts of the way he was a mere copyist. His original intention may have been to go as far as October 1388 but no further, and he may have paused in his work at that point. The ensuing narrative is less well ordered and less substantial than the narrative to the autumn of 1388 and represents an earlier stage of composition. These suggestions do not resolve all the difficulties posed by the text and manuscript, but others seem to resolve fewer. In the following account, the author of the Chronicle from the end of 1383 will be referred to as the Monk of Westminster.

The Manuscript

The unique manuscript is now part of Corpus Christi College, Cambridge, MS. 197A, a codex containing several distinct items which was given to the College by Archbishop Parker.[1] The most considerable of these, apart from the Chronicle itself, is a copy made in the sixteenth century, no doubt for Parker himself, of Robert Ciboule's *Tractatus* and other extracts relating to the trial of Joan of Arc and her rehabilitation. These occupy pp. 1–78 according to Parker's own pagination, but with a description and figures of a Jewish coin in Beza's New Testament interposed at p. 37. There follow (pp. 85–106) transcripts, also in sixteenth-century hands, of records directly relating to the martyrdom of Richard Scrope in 1405 or that might be considered relevant to it by one of his admirers. These items show that

[1] See M. R. James, *A Descriptive Catalogue of the Manuscripts in the Library of Corpus Christi College, Cambridge* (2 vols., Cambridge, 1909–12), i. 472–5. The final item listed here, the 8th-century fragments of the Gospels of St. John and St. Luke, has been rebound separately and is now C.C.C.C., 197B. C.C.C.C., 197A is entirely of paper. The first item in the present volume, a 16th-century transcript of the epistle of King Alfred to Waerfrith, bishop of Worcester, though a Parker MS., did not, it appears, belong to the original codex. It was not paginated by Parker or included in his brief index to C.C.C.C., 197A; nor is it listed in Thomas James's catalogue or William Stanley's. See Thomas James, *Ecloga Oxonio-Cantabrigiensis* (London, 1600), i, p. 81, no. 152; William Stanley, *Catalogus Librorum Manuscriptorum in Bibliotheca Collegii Corporis Christi in Cantabrigia* . . . (London, 1722), p. 40.

C.C.C.C., 197A was put together late: the Westminster Chronicle survives in a setting that tells us little or nothing about the history of the manuscript between the 1390s and the time of Archbishop Parker. C.C.C.C., 197A, pp. 109-10, however, deserve comment. They are a single sheet, apparently of the same paper as the quires on which the Chronicle is written but separated from the latter by a sheet with a different watermark. On p. 109 a distich on the kings of England from William I to Richard II is followed by the text of Edward I's letter to the abbot and convent of Westminster in 1291, enclosing two letters recording the submission to him of the claimants to the throne of Scotland in that year for inclusion in the Abbey's chronicles.[1] This page may be in the same hand as C.C.C.C., 197A, pp. 111-210 but is not part of the Chronicle, and indeed the sheet does not belong to its quires. Page 110, in a different hand, contains a fragment of an account of a large household ('nostre messone') covering the period 9 July to 12 August in a year which is not given; however, some names mentioned in the fragment occur in official records of the 1380s and 1390s.[2] It has not been possible to identify the household.

The Westminster Chronicle was written as a continuation of three other works that were themselves continuations of a *Polychronicon* of Ranulph Higden ending in 1327. These works, which precede the Westminster Chronicle in C.C.C.C., 197A and together with the Chronicle form a single item in it, are: Higden's own continuation of the *Polychronicon* to 1344; an anonymous continuation from 1346 to 1348; and John of Malvern's continuation from 1348 to 1381. Archbishop Parker paginated the items in his codex continuously, and in this edition references to the manuscript will be given by his pages; no contemporary folio numbers exist. The three items together occupy pp. 111-210 of the codex; the Westminster Chronicle begins near the lower margin of p. 130.

---

[1] For these letters, see Rymer, *Foedera*, ii. 529-30; and for C.C.C.C., 197A, p. 109, J. Armitage Robinson, 'An unrecognised Westminster Chronicle, 1381-94', in *P.B.A.*, iii (1907-8), 78.

[2] I owe this point to Dr. G. L. Harriss, who kindly scrutinized the text of this fragment for me.

The chronicle of John of Malvern, a monk and later (from 1395) prior of Worcester Cathedral Priory, was a popular work, and copies of it are quite common, but only in C.C.C.C., 197A is the author identified. Under the year 1344 the following entry occurs:[1]

Hic revera Ranulphus monachus Cestren' suas cronicas terminavit . . . concludens vero suum opus in septem libellulis, ad exemplum primi Opificis cuncta condentis. Post hunc scripsit quidam monachus Wygorn' Johannes Malverne, quasi duorum annorum omittens tempora; forsan in hiis nil gestu comendabile peractum fuerat, quod pennarum postularet labores. Quare sic procedit . . .

The opening words of the chronicle for 1346 follow.

The unknown author of these words was mistaken in thinking that Malvern's own work began with the entries for 1346. The chronicle for the years 1346 to 1348 was used by John de Reading, himself a monk of Westminster, and since Reading died in 1368 or 1369, but Malvern occurs as prior of Worcester as late as 1407, it is unlikely that Malvern was the author: his chronicle began in 1348 ('gravis et magna mortalitas').[2] It ended with the death of Thomas Hatfield, bishop of Durham ('senex multorum dierum'). Hatfield died in May 1381, but Malvern believed that he died in March. Whether it occurred in March or in May, Hatfield's death did not precede but followed the next event noticed in C.C.C.C., 197A — the destruction of Rochester Bridge at the beginning of February 1381.[3] This small disturbance in the chronological order of the entries for 1381 betrays the passage from the work of one writer to that of another: it is with the destruction of Rochester Bridge that our chronicle begins.

C.C.C.C., 197A, pp. 111–210 is of paper having a fine

---

[1] C.C.C.C., 197A, p. 112; cf. *Higden*, ix, pp. vii–viii.

[2] For the text see ibid., viii. 355–406; and for comment, G. B. Stow, 'Thomas Walsingham, John Malvern and the *Vita Ricardi Secundi*, 1377–1381: a Reassessment', in *Mediaeval Studies*, xxxix (1977), 490–7, correcting Taylor, *Higden* (Oxford, 1966), pp. 122–3. The latter work, however, is indispensable for an understanding of the *Polychronicon* tradition. For the improbability of Malvern's authorship of the continuation for the years 1346–8, see *Chronica Johannis de Reading et Anonymi Cantuariensis, 1346–1367*, ed. J. Tait (Manchester, 1914), p. 44 n., and for the crucial passages, ibid., p. 105. This continuation was also used by the author of the *Eulogium Historiarum*, a work completed in the 1360s (ed. F. S. Haydon (R.S., 3 vols., 1858–63), iii. 212–13).

[3] C.C.C.C., 197A, p. 130; below, p. 2.

watermark of a pomegranate with four leaves.[1] The fact
that the design occurs on all the sheets used for the
Chronicle suggests that all the paper needed for the work
was purchased on a single occasion, and if this inference is
correct it follows — and other evidence points to this
conclusion — that composition of the Chronicle was well
advanced before transcription on to the quires now making
up this part of C.C.C.C., 197A was begun. The make-up of
the quires is irregular but does not, even so, reflect the
change of authorship in 1381: the Westminster Chronicle
begins on the third bifolium of the second quire and ends
on the verso of the penultimate leaf of the fifth.[2] The final
page is entirely filled with text, but the final sheet of the
quire to which it belongs is blank. From this latter circumstance it is a fair inference that we have the complete text
of the Chronicle. The hand is distinctive, the work of a
writer who liked to vary the form of individual letters and
try out new practices: sometimes, for example, but not
invariably, he wrote capital 'H' and capital 'L' with a
divided top; and he wrote the letter 'a' and the letter 'g'
each in two different ways. Perhaps the same attitude of
mind explains his adoption towards the end of the Chronicle of the spelling 'aput' in preference to 'apud'; he

[1] Probably no. 7400 in C. M. Briquet, *Les Filigranes*, ed. A. Stevenson (4 vols.,
Amsterdam, 1968); examples occurring over the period 1366–83 are noted here.
A watermark of the same design is one of three found on the day-account book of
the steward of the abbot of Westminster's household which happens to survive
for the years 1371–3 (P.R.O., S.C. 6/1261/6, part i). This is the account book
'of some English person of distinction' referred to in J. Hunter, 'Specimens of
marks used by the early manufacturers of paper . . .', in *Archaeologia*, xxxvii
(1857), 451–2, where the mark is drawn. The abbot's steward bought his paper in
small quantities, a quire at a time. The steward at the time was Br. John Lakingheath.

[2] Probable collation of bifolia: i⁴, ii⁸, iii⁷, iv², v⁶. In q. i the text runs without
a break from leaf 3 (MS. pp. 115–16) to leaf 5 (pp. 117–18); leaf 4, therefore,
was eliminated in the course of the transcription of the quire. Q. ii, leaf 16 was
lost after the writing of the MS. but before Parker paginated the codex. His
pagination runs from q. ii, leaf 15 (pp. 153–4) to q. iii, leaf 1 (pp. 155–6) without
a break; but there is a break in the text at this point. The catchword on MS., p.
154 is not contemporary, and pp. 153–4 were not originally the final leaf of a
quire. The text runs from q. iv, leaf 3 (MS., pp. 187–8) to q. v, leaf 1 (pp. 189–
90) without a break, and q. iv, leaf 1 is held by a guard. Q. iv, leaf 4, therefore,
was eliminated in the course of transcription.

encountered the new spelling in a written source which he transcribed at this point.[1] The size of the hand varies as the text passes from Latin to French and back again: the French hand is smaller than the Latin and fills less of the interlinear space. The Latin hand itself shows a readiness to experiment. For example, the hand used for the account of the quarrel between the archbishop of Canterbury and the bishop of Exeter in 1384, which apparently represents a single stint of copying, is characterized by accentuation of downward strokes and failure to join all the strokes in each letter and has a more broken appearance than that in the rest of the manuscript.[2] This readiness to experiment makes it difficult to be quite certain that the whole manuscript is the work of the same writer, but the occurrence throughout of certain basic characteristics, some of which are themselves idiosyncratic, makes this conclusion highly probable. The margins are justified throughout. Each new year of grace is written in arabics in the left-hand or right-hand margin, in a contemporary hand, from the beginning of the manuscript, and from the beginning of Richard II's reign (C.C.C.C., 197A, p. 126) the regnal year (in roman figures) is added. From p. 127, the year of grace and the regnal year are written in roman figures in the upper margin of the recto of each leaf; some of these dates have been trimmed off. The regnal years in, respectively, the right-hand and left-hand margins of pp. 127 and 128 appear to be in a later hand.

In copying the continuations of the *Polychronicon* from 1327, the Monk at first left some initial capital letters to be done later, by an expert hand: the guide letters for the illuminator can still be seen. At this stage, therefore, he saw the manuscript as the final fair copy of the projected work. From near the beginning of the narrative of Richard II's reign, he began to write all the capitals himself as he went along. This change took effect on C.C.C.C., 197A, p. 128. An afterthought on p. 126 may have precipitated it. On this page,

---

[1] C.C.C.C., 197A, pp. 199 (from 'octavo die Augusti') ff., but four cases of 'apud' occur on MS., p. 200. See below, pp. 454 ff. For the source in question, see below, p. xlv, no. 25. The spelling 'aput' occurs on C.C.C.C., 197A, p. 109, for which see above, p. xv.

[2] MS., p. 144; below, pp. 84–6.

Malvern's chronicle reaches the end of Edward III's reign and the narrative of Richard II's reign begins. Originally a space marked the transition from the one reign to the other. Subsequently, however, a decision was made to add the encomium on Edward III from Walsingham's *Short History*, and this addition filled all the space in the text and much of the bottom margin of p. 126 beside.[1] The addition put an end to hopes that no fairer copy of p. 126 and the quire to which it belonged would be needed. The abandonment on p. 128 of the plan to have elaborate capital letters suggests that the addition was made soon after the transcription of p. 126: Walsingham's work, it seems, came to hand at this very time.

Despite this early decline in the status of the manuscript, the writing continues to be smooth and the appearance of the manuscript neat for some pages after p. 128 and well into the Westminster Chronicle. On p. 138, however, a long passage describing the end of Bishop Despenser's crusade in 1383 was first much corrected and amended on the page and then cancelled, to be transcribed again, considerably altered, on p. 139.[2] From the top of p. 141 the whole appearance of the manuscript subtly changes: the writing becomes in however small degree less smooth and the number of lines to a page increases, as though the general appearance of the page now matters less. Changes of ink show that the writer's copying stints were now shorter than they had been. From appearances we should conclude that C.C.C.C., 197A, pp. 111-40 were copied in a short period of time from an exemplar the whole of which existed before the writer put pen to paper, but that thereafter he wrote discontinuously, copying a text that was still to some extent in process of creation.

---

[1] For the encomium in C.C.C.C., 197A, see *Higden*, ix, pp. viii-ix; and for Walsingham's final text, *Hist. Ang.*, i. 327-8. The two versions are not identical, but Westminster's dependence on Walsingham for the encomium, other versions of which found their way into other continuations of the *Polychronicon*, is clear enough. The Westminster version probably preserves for us one of Walsingham's early drafts of the passage. Versions of the *Short History* and the *Chronica Majora* were in circulation by 1392 and probably before that date; see *Vita Ricardi Secundi*, pp. 13 ff.

[2] Below, pp. 46-50; and for the discarded version see pp. 522-6.

Pp. 138–41, in the second quire of C.C.C.C., 197A, are critical to an understanding of the relationship between the Monk of Westminster and his text, for not earlier than p. 138 or later than p. 141 he ceased to be dependent on the work of another and became himself the author of the Chronicle. The evidence for divided authorship is mainly textual and will be considered later. Here will be noted the features of the manuscript which seem to identify the scribe as at first in a subordinate role but subsequently the author himself. In copying the account of the quarrel between the duke of Lancaster and the earl of Northumberland in the aftermath of the Peasants' Revolt, the scribe was twice unable to make sense of his text. In one place he wrote 'aulicū' (a meaningless word in the context), where his exemplar perhaps had 'amicissimi'; and a few words later he wrote 'interne mente diligen'', where the correct reading may have been 'interveniente diligencia'.[1] In this part of the work there are few marginal corrections or afterthoughts. Increasingly from 1384,[2] the marginalia are the work of an author who was still thinking about his text — refining its style, adding to its contents, and so on; and small alterations designed to achieve the *mot juste* are now quite frequently interlined or written on the line over erasures. These alterations and additions, which appear to be in the same hand as the main text, mean that the manuscript is now an autograph. Occasionally, though not often, a passage is ill adjusted to the space allotted to it: it is too long or too short, and this must mean that it was composed and inserted after this point in the manuscript had been reached and passed. From time to time directions are given to the scribe who, it was envisaged, would eventually recopy the whole.

Yet even now the manuscript does not, as a rule, represent a first draft. Changes in ink and the regularity of the hand show that most of it was still written in stints too long to have been the extempore work of an author composing as he went along. Marginal additions to the text are always

---

[1] C.C.C.C., 197A, p. 134; below, p. 20. For the subject-matter of this paragraph I am particularly indebted to Mr. Hector, who also drew my attention to some of the idiosyncrasies of style in the early pages of the Chronicle.

[2] Below, pp. 56 ff.

neatly done and evidently well thought out in advance. Some of them may represent, not afterthoughts, but passages on separate slips of paper or parchment which were accidentally overlooked in transcription. Changes of ink suggest that several marginal entries were added in the course of the next stint of transcribing. Above all, the text itself points to the conclusion that the manuscript is not a first draft: it is so well ordered as to make it certain that the Monk had in fact toiled hard before these pages of C.C.C.C., 197A were written. More than once he refers in the body of the text to a later passage: within limits, he knew what was coming.[1] But he never revised the work as a whole, and a few glaring inconsistencies have survived in consequence.[2]

The collation of the quires suggests that the Monk may once have intended to carry his narrative down to the autumn of 1388 but no further. He finished a quire of seven bifolia with an entry for 1 August 1388[3] and then made up a quire of only two bifolia; this took him as far as the beginning of April 1389 and Urban VI's bull *Salvator noster.*[4] A change in the character of the writing is noticeable at the top of the recto of the third leaf of this quire (C.C.C.C., 197A, p. 187). On the previous leaf (pp. 185–6), the Monk was still evidently copying a well-considered draft. Page 187 has much more the appearance of a page composed as the author went along. The break comes soon after entries describing the death of Sir Thomas Trivet at the end of the first week of October 1388, and the release from custody at the same time of the knights and clerks detained since the end of the Merciless Parliament.[5] This may have been the point at which the narrative was intended to stop.

---

[1] Below, pp. 92, 102, 138, 146, 190.

[2] See, for example, the references to Archbishop Nevill, below, pp. 342–4, 492.

[3] C.C.C.C., 197A, p. 182; below, p. 344. It is possible that the original quire was of eight bifolia and that one was eliminated.

[4] C.C.C.C., 197A, p. 188; below, p. 386. C.C.C.C., 197A, pp. 187–8 were in fact the 3rd leaf of the original quire, the 4th having been eliminated in the course of transcription; but this does not affect the argument.

[5] Below, p. 370.

The Chronicle

(i) *Authorship and Date*

Since the publication in 1907 of Dean Armitage Robinson's essay on the Westminster Chronicle, it has not been in doubt that it was written at Westminster Abbey.[1] The provenance of the work explains not only its interest in the affairs of the Abbey but also some of its other distinctive features. The interest in and knowledge of Thomas of Woodstock, earl of Gloucester, and Eleanor de Bohun, his wife, are to be expected in a chronicle written in a house to which each was a benefactor and where each was to be buried.[2] Nor is it surprising that a chronicle written at the very hub of official life should be exceptionally well informed about the minutiae of diplomatic intercourse and the councils and parliaments of the period. Since glancing blows are administered to contemporary society in both parts of the work, it is tempting to conclude that these rather radical views reflect, not personal idiosyncrasy, but the temper of the monastic community as a whole.[3] Notices — some unusually detailed — of the weather, the skies, and of natural and supernatural phenomena occur throughout and may similarly reflect a common interest of the monks of Westminster at this time.[4]

The participation of two writers in the Chronicle cannot be proved: it is, however, the best way of explaining otherwise puzzling features of the text. The evidence is chiefly that of style: mannerisms occur in the chronicle for 1381 to 1383 that are not found later. The first author liked to give dates according to the Roman calendar.[5] If dating by reference to the feast-day of a saint, he preferred rather obscure saints or saints who appear infrequently in dating clauses of the period: St. Basilides and St. Cyrinus, St. Milburga, St. Processus, and St. Martinianus — all occur in

---

[1] Armitage Robinson, in *P.B.A.*, iii (1907), 1 ff.

[2] B. Harvey, *Westminster Abbey and its Estates in the Middle Ages* (Oxford, 1977), pp. 380, 397. But note that Thomas of Woodstock is first mentioned on MS., p. 139.

[3] e.g., below, pp. 22, 518 (comments on, respectively, the death of the earl of Suffolk in 1381 and the Anglo-French peace proposals of 1394).

[4] Below, pp. 2, 26-8, 122-4, 232, 344, 444, 508.

[5] Below, pp. 2, 22, 26, etc.

these early pages of the Chronicle.[1] Place-names are sometimes pretentiously latinized. 'Fons Clericorum' (Clerkenwell), 'Planus Campus' (Smithfield), and 'Combusta Silva'
(Brentwood), occur in the account of the Peasants' Revolt.[2]
St. Albans is referred to on one occasion as 'civitas Vero-
lamia', and the Londoners as 'Trinoventani'.[3] Classical words
— '*stratoris* officium', for example, and '*senatus* London' '[4] —
are sometimes preferred to a vocabulary that would have
been more familiar to fourteenth-century readers. In sum,
this part of the Chronicle has a precious quality that is
missing from the pedestrian prose of the later part.[5] Taken
with the pointers in the manuscript that its scribe's role
changed in the course of the transcription, these idiosyncrasies of style may perhaps convince us that two writers
had a hand in the work. The first of these had a capacity for
invention that the second lacked or judged inappropriate
in a chronicler, and he was readier to sacrifice truth for
dramatic effect. The flight of priors into sanctuary at Westminster in the aftermath of the Peasants' Revolt was surely
a fantasy — one prior, perhaps, and one malevolent body of
canons in the background, but not several of each:[6] so too
the outrageous statement that the rite of taking the Cross was
unknown in England before 1383 and recorded only at
Westminster Abbey;[7] and the statement that Bishop Despenser was dumbfounded at his arraignment in parliament is
dramatically satisfying but quite untrue.[8]

Where exactly did the break in authorship come? The
cancelled passage relating to Despenser's crusade on C.C.C.C.,
197A, p. 138 and the revised version on p. 139 contain
clues.[9] There was a need to explain how it was that in the
early autumn of 1383 Despenser was stripped of his gains in
Flanders — just recounted at length — and left without
reinforcements from England. The first version divided the

---

[1] Below, pp. 4, 24, 28. Note, however, W.A.M. 29711, an acquittance of 1345,
which uses the feast of St. Processus and St. Martinianus in its dating clause.

[2] Below, pp. 4, 10, 12. But note also below, p. 504 ('strata piscaria').

[3] Below, pp. 14, 20.   [4] Below, pp. 22, 24.

[5] Note, however, the archaism 'portitor privati sigilli', occurring in both parts
of the work (pp. 50, 210, 392, 524).

[6] Below, p. 18.   [7] Below, p. 32 and n.

[8] Below, p. 52 and n.   [9] Below, pp. 46-8, 522-4.

blame between the bishop's treacherous lieutenants, the duke of Lancaster, who, though encamped on the Kentish coast throughout September, failed to respond to the bishop's personal appeal for help, and a king who smiled on the bishop when they met but did nothing. According to the second version, the duke of Lancaster and Thomas of Wood-stock, earl of Buckingham, his brother, on hearing towards the end of August how badly things were going in Flanders, warned the king, who was in the north, of the danger and took up position on the Kentish coast. They expected that the king would join them there, ready to face the king of France. The king came to London, but his council, called to consider what should be done, prevented him from taking the decisive action that he would have preferred, and, in the event, nothing was done. The second version is not only lacking in the malice of the first towards Lancaster: it is better informed and much more convincing. Thomas of Woodstock, the one person mentioned in it but not in the first version, was perhaps the chronicler's source at this point.

The date 'septimo kalendas Novembres' seems to betray our first writer. It occurs in the middle of the cancelled passage on p. 138, which must, if we are right, have been his work in the first instance. The latest echo of his voice is in the phrase 'ultimum vite sue vale', a euphemism for 'death' in the description of the pestilence at the end of 1383.[1] Two other circumstances suggest that the change in authorship occurred about this time but not earlier.

The Monk of Westminster was interested in the mayor of London, his election, and his conduct when in office. He made a point of noticing the election on 12 or 13 October each year, and sometimes appended a short account of the outstanding events of the ensuing mayoralty.[2] In the chronicle that he took over, however, the whole of John Northampton's stormy mayoralty from 1381 to 1383 and his defeat by Brembre in the election of 13 October 1383 had passed with scarcely a notice. Without some knowledge of these events, his readers would not understand why Northampton was arrested in February 1384 and much else in the history of the ensuing period. Therefore, it is suggested,

[1] Below, p. 56. [2] Below, pp. 60-2, 100-2, 136 etc.

the Monk inserted a retrospective account as a preliminary
to the story of the arrest, introducing it with the words:
'hoc anno erat quidam major in civitate London' Johannes
Northampton' nomine'.[1] Though Northampton ceased to be
mayor in October 1383, he could be said to have been mayor
'this year' from the standpoint of next February, for the
chroniclers' year ended on 24 March. Yet by the Monk's
own standards of rigorous adherence to a chronological order
the passage is oddly placed: its position suggests that when
he took over the composition of the Chronicle, the narrative
was already past October 1383, and with it the opportunity
of mentioning Northampton's defeat in its proper place.
Similarly, the notice of the capture by Spaniards of sixteen
English clerics in the Mediterranean in December 1383 is
inserted out of place, in the narrative for the early months
of 1384.[2] Here perhaps the Monk was making a contribution
of his own to the narrative which he had taken over. These
passages occur on, respectively, C.C.C.C., 197A, pp. 141 and
142, just past the point where the appearance of the manuscript seems to reflect a change in the conditions under
which it was written.[3]

Who then was responsible for cancelling the passage on
p. 138 and composing the revised version on p. 139? Was it
the first author, still actively involved in the Chronicle and
at hand to revise the text almost as soon as it was written?
Or did the Monk of Westminster anticipate the larger role of
independent author that he was soon to play and drastically
alter his inherited text? The alterations included not only
major ones of substance but also small stylistic changes, such
as an author will make but not a scribe. A marginal entry on
p. 138, once very likely containing the gist of the amended
version subsequently transcribed on p. 139, has been erased:
the hand that wrote it cannot be identified. But all the
corrections and additions on p. 138 that can now be read
appear to be in the same hand as the text itself: they were
the work of the Monk. And the very magnitude of the
changes of substance effected in the revision does perhaps
mean that a fresh mind had been brought to bear on the
passage. Quite probably the Monk of Westminster was

[1] Below, pp. 58-60.   [2] Below, p. 64.   [3] Above, p. xix.

himself responsible for altering the account of the end of Despenser's crusade. This conclusion is of some importance, reflecting as it does on his attitude to the first author's work: it was not a sacrosanct text, but one that could be altered, and other changes may have been made that have left no trace in C.C.C.C., 197A. Indeed, a hypothesis of this kind is needed if we are to explain how so much of the Monk's indifferent Latin and some of his unusual forms crept into these pages: he used the first writer's text but was not enslaved to it.

Every reader of the Westminster Chronicle must be impressed by its strictly ordered chronology, particularly evinced in the work of the Monk of Westminster himself down to the end of 1388. Digressions which take us outside this framework are dexterously inserted in the main narrative at the point indicated by the opening or closing date of the sequence of events to which they relate. This ordered structure must be deemed a work of art needing some little trial and error before it could be achieved.

From the end of 1388, however, unaccustomed lapses — the insertion of a written source out of strict sequence,[1] repetitious entries,[2] egregious errors of dating,[3] and so on — betray the fact that this part of the narrative has not been as thoroughly revised as the preceding part; and the relatively small scale of the chronicle for these years suggests an author who was pressed for time or perhaps just bored with his task. To this extent the evidence of the text corroborates that of the collation of quires: this suggests that the chronicle from the closing months of 1388 may represent an afterthought on the part of the Monk. One passage, indeed, may give rise to the suspicion that this part of the Chronicle is the work of a different author, for under the year 1390 we are told how, after Richard II's coronation in 1377, he was carried from the Abbey to the Palace of Westminster by 'a certain knight, Sir Simon Burley'.[4] Would the Monk himself have referred in this inconsequential way to the hapless Burley, whose trial is treated at such length in the earlier narrative? The answer must be that an author capable, as the Monk was,

---

[1] Below, pp. 416–18, 430. [2] Below, pp. 452, 474.
[3] Below, pp. 378, 454, 484 etc. [4] Below, pp. 414–16.

of giving his readers two accounts of the Merciless Parliament without, it seems, feeling the slightest embarrassment at the inconsistencies between the two was capable of anything.[1] Moreover, the author of the chronicle from the end of 1388 does in fact draw on the earlier narrative and assume that his readers will know of it: in his account of the iniquities of John Paule, under the year 1392, for example, he assumes that his readers will know of the arrest of Robert Tresilian in the sanctuary of the Abbey early in 1388.[2] There is really no need to postulate a second break in authorship.

The author of the chronicle for 1381 to 1383 wrote as a continuator of John of Malvern's chronicle, a work that was probably finished soon after its terminal date in 1381.[3] Internal evidence suggests that this part of the Westminster Chronicle was not completed before the late 1380s, if as soon. Jean de Vienne's expedition to Scotland, which took place in May 1385, is placed in the winter of 1383 to 1384.[4] To make such a mistake the chronicler must have been at some little remove from the early summer of 1385 as well as the winter of 1383 to 1384. If, however, as seems likely, this author was Br. Richard Cirencester, the *terminus ante quem* is probably Richard's departure overseas at the end of 1391.[5]

The Monk of Westminster himself had but a hazy recollection of some of the events of 1385. Having noticed the re-election of Nicholas Brembre as mayor of London for the second time, on 13 October 1385, he summarizes three ordinances which were, he says, 'very soon' enacted by Brembre on the advice of the aldermen. The ordinances in question were enacted between July and September 1384: they belong to the first year of the mayoralty, not to the third.[6] The Monk renders them rather freely, as though he had heard the gist but seen no full text. One, regulating the inflammatory matter of elections to the mayoralty, can hardly have been kept out of the conversation when the leading citizens of London paid their customary visit to the

---

[1] Below, pp. xlviii, 234 ff.   [2] Below, pp. 496–8.

[3] Stow, *Mediaeval Studies*, xxxix (1977), 495–6; *Vita Ricardi*, p. 11.

[4] Below, p. 56.   [5] Below, p. xxxiii.

[6] Below, p. 136 and n. Note also the anachronistic reference to Thomas Usk as 'sheriff's clerk' *s. a.* 1384 (below, p. 90 and n.).

Abbey on 13 October 1384, the feast of St. Edward the Confessor,[1] for in it were enacted the very rules that — as many thought and as the Monk himself hints — Brembre and his supporters flouted in order to bring about his re-election for the first time that very day. When the Monk wrote this passage, it had become rather difficult to distinguish one crowded year of Brembre's mayoralty from another.

Very nearly half the Monk's chronicle is devoted to the successive crises of the years 1386 to 1388. A short tale related under January 1386 shows that he conceived of his account of these years as a dramatic whole. A man of religion in Lombardy had predicted that in the course of the next three years the English nation would be punished for its evil life by famine and pestilence, but would then be the happiest of all kingdoms.[2] This story prepared his readers for the testing events to come, though not, of course, for their precise nature. The whole of the narrative of these years was written after the king's assumption of his majority in May 1389 and very likely quite a long time after that event. This fact, implicit in the range and balance of the account as a whole, is made explicit in a passage occurring under February 1386.[3] Here, after noticing certain marriages between English men of rank and countrywomen of Anne of Bohemia for whom, it is implied, the king provided dowries, the Monk reflects on the open-handed generosity of the king 'in his early years': he gave away all the property annexed to the Crown and much, too, of the Exchequer's revenues; in consequence he had to tax the common people. If only, the Monk adds, the king would relieve the complaining poor, he would reap great benefit. The king of this passage was out of his tutelage and doing badly; 1386 was now part of his youthful past.

Whenever the Monk wrote his account of the years 1386 to 1388, his narrative for the early months of 1389 was probably not written before 1393. We are told that a great council held on 20 January 1389 persuaded the king to confer the dukedom of Ireland on his uncle, the duke of Gloucester.[4] In fact Gloucester never became duke of Ireland. In April

[1] See below, p. lvi.
[2] Below, pp. 156–8.
[3] Below, pp. 160–2.
[4] Below, p. 378 and n.

1392, however, he was appointed the king's lieutenant in Ireland. The reference to him under January 1389 probably represents a confused recollection of that later appointment, and the Monk's very confusion suggests that even the real event — Gloucester's appointment as lieutenant in Ireland in April 1392 — had to some extent receded into the past when he wrote; this seems to take us at least into 1393. The erroneous statement that Sir Henry Percy became seneschal of Aquitaine in the summer of 1389 is not likely to have been written before Percy's later assumption of office in the duchy was itself to some extent in the past; Percy in fact became the duke of Lancaster's lieutenant there in the course of 1393.[1] But the reference under February 1389 to the quarrel between the monks of Westminster and the canons of St. Stephen's Chapel in the Palace of Westminster as a matter still in lively contention must have been written before this *cause célèbre* was finally compromised in August 1394.[2] Here, at the beginning of 1389 in his narrative and on C.C.C.C., 197A, p. 187, the Monk was writing not less than three, or more than four, years after the event.

The narrative for five years is compressed into the remaining twenty-three pages of the manuscript and here, too, the Monk's memory played tricks that would have been impossible without some lapse of time. He thought that the ordinance of the parliament of November to December 1391 on papal provisions had been enacted in the parliament of November to December 1390.[3] Yet not even the most remarkable lapse of these pages — the misdating of Anne of Bohemia's funeral in Westminster Abbey in 1394 — need mean that a long interval separated the event and the notice of it in the Chronicle.[4] The unflattering reference to the mode of life of Br. Alexander Bache occasioned by the notice of Bache's consecration as bishop on 8 May 1390 was written before Bache's death in August or September 1394, for the Monk tells us that he was still, at the time of writing, the king's confessor.[5] When the Monk ended his Chronicle, with the narrative for 1394, the duke of Gloucester had lost ground politically but had probably not yet taken up a

[1] Below, p. 402 and n.   [2] Below, p. 380.   [3] Below, p. 454 and n.
[4] Below, p. 520 and n.   [5] Below, p. 434.

position openly hostile to the ideas of Richard II and John of Gaunt on peace with France: the Monk saw him as one who weakly connived at the wicked ambitions of his brother.[1] Unfortunately, Gloucester's last years lie so much in the shadows that we have, even so, no *terminus ante quem* more exact than the summer of 1397: he was arrested on 11 July.[2]

Textual evidence suggests, therefore, that the Westminster Chronicle was not begun before the late 1380s, if as early. Most of the narrative for the years 1386 to 1394 was composed not less than three years after the event and quite possibly later than this; but the Chronicle was finished by the summer of 1397, if not earlier. Very tentatively we must now take into account the authorship of the Chronicle and the evidence of the unique manuscript. Their witness does not enable us to say when the Monk composed whatever pre-liminary drafts underlie the work that he finally copied into C.C.C.C., 197A, but it suggests that he was at work on this more advanced stage in or after 1392.[3] If so, the reader's sense that he wrote his account of the crises of 1386 to 1388 with hindsight is understandable: when he included a refer-ence to the king's extravagant 'early years' in his narrative for 1386, he was writing some six years after the event and perhaps three years after Richard's assumption of his majority.

To some extent the collection of material for a chronicle of this kind can be distinguished, as a stage in the work, from composition. A change in the quality of the Chronicle towards the end of 1385 is relevant. Although the narrative for the years 1381 to 1385 includes some passages the loss of which would have impoverished our understanding of the period, it is thin in comparison to the sequel. By 1386, but not much earlier than this, someone at Westminster had

[1] Below, p. 518.

[2] *Annales Ricardi Secundi*, ed. H. T. Riley (R.S., 1866), pp. 203 ff. On the story in *Chronicque de la Traïson et Mort de Richart Deux Roy Dengleterre*, ed. B. Williams (London, 1846), pp. 1 ff., see now J. J. N. Palmer, 'The Authorship, Date and Historical Value of the French Chronicles on the Lancastrian Revolu-tion': II, in *Bulletin of the John Rylands Library*, lxi (1978-9), pp. 398 ff. On the breach between Gloucester and Lancaster see also *Eulogium Historiarum*, iii. 369; but the chronology of the Continuator at this point is unsure.

[3] Below, pp. xxxiii–iv.

begun the systematic collection of material covering a wide range of topics for a history of his own times, and it is only sensible to conclude that this person was the first of our two authors. The preparatory work underlying the narrative for 1381 to 1385 was, in comparison, desultory and amateur, the role of memory and even invention correspondingly large. But equally some of the imperfections of the later pages of the Chronicle reflect the fact that the preparatory collection of material had been rather sketchy.

By the 1380s, the earliest term for the beginning of the composition of the Westminster Chronicle, the monks of Westminster could look back on a long tradition of writing or compiling chronicles. From 1265, when the continuation of the *Flores Historiarum* was moved from St. Albans to Westminster, until the death of John de Reading in 1368 or 1369, the tradition was never interrupted for more than a year or two.[1] At the time of Reading's death, Br. Richard Cirencester had been a monk of Westminster for some fourteen years. He entered the monastery not later than 1354 to 1355, in which year he is mentioned as a novice. Seven years later, in 1361 to 1362, he said his first Mass, and since monks of Westminster were now normally ordained as soon as they reached the canonical age, he was probably twenty-four years old or thereabouts at the time. As a young man he spent a brief period at Oxford, and it must have been after he left the university in 1365 that he began his *Speculum Historiale de Gestis Regum Angliae*.[2] This was not a chronicle of near contemporary events, such as John de Reading had written, and indeed not a chronicle at all, but a historical work delving into the remote past — a work at once very ambitious and wholly derivative. In the second book, which ends with

[1] On the Westminster *Flores*, see A. Gransden, *Historical Writing in England, c.550 to c.1307* (London, 1974), pp. 420, 453 ff.; for Reading's chronicle, *Chronica Johannis de Reading et Anonymi Cantuariensis, 1346–1367*, ed. Tait; and Taylor, *Higden*, pp. 112–13. Some MSS. of the continuation of the *Polychronicon*, described by Taylor as 'D' and extending to 1379, seem to have a connection with Westminster Abbey and may point to activity in the scriptorium there in the 1380s; see ibid., pp. 116–17.

[2] Ed. J. E. B. Mayor, 2 vols., R.S., 1863–9. For Cirencester's career, see *Monks*, p. 100; and B. F. Harvey, 'The Monks of Westminster and the University of Oxford', in *Reign of Richard II*, pp. 121 n., 124, 125, 126.

the death of Ethelred I in 871, and again in the fourth book, extending to 1066, Richard Cirencester cites Higden's *Polychronicon*.[1] The purchase of a copy of the *Polychronicon* recorded in the account of the conventual treasurers in 1375 to 1376 may have been made to facilitate his work.[2] He was precentor at the time: he held the office customarily given at Westminster to bookish monks. In the fourth book of the *Speculum Historiale*, Cirencester refers to the attacks of 'moderni' on the privilege of sanctuary at Westminster.[3] Such a reference would have been apt at any point in the last quarter of the fourteenth century. Cirencester goes on, however, to point out that the privilege of sanctuary at Westminster extended even to those guilty of an offence against the king's majesty. This was the very point at issue when the monks of Westminster were called upon to defend their privilege before the king at Kennington in April 1388,[4] and it seems likely that the controversies of the late 1380s were in Cirencester's mind when he penned this passage. If so, only a short interval of time may have separated the composition of the fourth book and the commencement of the Westminster Chronicle; the Chronicle was probably begun in the late 1380s or early 1390s. At the end of the fourth book of the *Speculum Historiale* a fifth, which should begin with the reign of William I, is promised, but this book does not survive and may never have been written.[5]

Did Richard Cirencester have a hand in the Chronicle? Three of the tricks of style found in the narrative for the years 1381 to 1383 — a liking for classical words[6] and for the Roman calendar,[7] and the habit of latinizing

---

[1] *Speculum Historiale*, i. 204; ii. 335.

[2] 'In j libro vocato Policronicl' empto, iiij li.' (W.A.M. 19867). For the suggestion that Bodleian Library, Oxford, MS. Bodley 341 (containing Higden's *Polychronicon* to 1327 and the *Historia Alexandri Magni regis Macedoniae de Proeliis* of the Archpresbyter Leo) had a Westminster connection, see Taylor, *Higden*, p. 122 n. The suspicious circumstance is a note at the end of the *Polychronicon* (fo. 135): 'reliqua de isto Edwardo iij.º vide infra in papero in fine libri': i.e. it is suggested that C.C.C.C., 197A, pp. 111–210, containing the unique text of the Westminster Chronicle, once belonged to this volume. The hand that wrote this note in MS. Bodley 341 does not seem to occur in C.C.C.C., 197A, pp. 111–210.

[3] *Speculum Historiale*, ii. 249–50.　　　　　　　　　　　　[4] Below, p. 324.

[5] *Speculum Historiale*, ii. 337.

[6] e.g., 'trinepos'; 'vaticinium'; 'tetrarchia'; 'causidicus' (ibid., i. 295; ii. 120, 194, 212).　　　　　　　　　[7] Ibid., i. 160, 167, 329; ii. 49, 56, etc.

place-names[1] — are present also in the *Speculum Historiale*, and this work includes an account of St. Milburga, one of the saints whose feasts are used, rather unusually for the period, to date events in the Chronicle for the years 1381 to 1383.[2] The case is not proven, for, after all, other monks of Westminster may have modelled their style on that of Cirencester. Yet it does seem likely that Cirencester was in fact the first of our two authors. If so, it follows that it was Cirencester who, in or shortly before 1386, with the *Speculum Historiale* still not advanced beyond the Anglo-Saxon period, began to collect material for a history of his own times. But since Cirencester lived until 1400, we have to ask why he abandoned the Westminster Chronicle so soon after its inception, and how it was that — so it seems — he was not at hand when his work was copied into C.C.C.C., 197A, to advise the scribe: for unless we are to conclude — and this is not impossible — that the scribe (the Monk of Westminster) did not realize that 'aulicū' and 'interne mente diligen'' were strange readings, it seems to follow that the first author was not at hand to be consulted about them when they were copied onto p. 134 of the manuscript.[3] The answer to the second of these questions may also be the answer to the first, and it is perhaps to be found in Cirencester's departure on pilgrimage to Rome and other holy places at the end of 1391.[4] If so, we have an approximate date for the transcription of the early part of C.C.C.C., 197A, pp. 111 ff., a date having an interest not confined to the history of the manuscript. The appearance of the manuscript suggests that, when the Monk began to write C.C.C.C., 197A, much of his own chronicle for the years 1384 to 1394 was still in process of creation, in the sense that the author was still refining the presentation of his work.[5] If, therefore, he began the work of transcription

---

[1] e.g., 'Insula Vituli Marini' (Selsey); 'Ovium Insula' (Sheppey); 'Pons Belli' (alias Stamford Bridge) (ibid., i. 197, 307; ii. 299).

[2] Ibid., ii. 330; and see above, p. xxii. Note also Cirencester's account of St. Denys (ii. 332-3) and the date according to this saint's feast which occurs below (p. 20). [3] Above, p. xx.

[4] Abbot Colchester's licence for the pilgrimage is dated 21 Dec. 1391 (W.A.M. 6663). The next day Colchester himself departed for Rome (below, p. 484). Cirencester no doubt accompanied him. He had returned to Westminster by Mar. 1393, when he had 3 days in the infirmary (W.A.M. 19378).

[5] Above, p. xx.

in or about 1392, the main part of the Chronicle was put into the form which has come down to us in or after 1392.

The second author, whom we have called the Monk of Westminster, was responsible for most of the well-informed political narrative for which the Chronicle is famous, and an identification, if it is to convince, must be compatible with the views expressed here. In the early part of the Monk's work the king is often shown in a damaging light. It was on his orders, for example, that twenty-five prisoners were executed in 1384 without trial.[1] The next year he drew his sword on Archbishop Courtenay and nearly ran him through.[2] His questions to the judges in 1387 were a cause of harm to others.[3] Although the Monk regretted the violence and loss of life attending the rise to power of the Appellants and even at one or two points offered his readers a grain of salt for their propaganda, the very scale on which he used this propaganda argues a degree of sympathy with the Appellant cause: to some extent he made their charges of miscounsel and misgovernment against the king his own. When, as happens only a little later in the Chronicle, the glimpses we have of the king become mainly favourable, the Monk's underlying attitude to some of the policies with which he was identified is still often critical. Nevertheless, he wishes Richard II well and offers criticism more in sorrow than in anger.

The Monk was keenly interested in the diplomacy of his times, though probably not himself a participant.[4] The solemnity of the events recorded in the Chronicle is relieved in the margin by a number of extraordinarily vigorous caricatures. Some of these are probably intended to be *nota* signs. If these are the Monk's own work, he had some little talent as an artist. He was a poor Latinist, often guilty of grammatical errors and quite incapable of fine writing; when attempting this he could lapse into absurdity — as for

[1] Below, p. 98.

[2] Below, p. 116. The king was restrained by Thomas of Woodstock and two others, and Thomas was probably the Monk's source for the tale. Cf. below, p. 138.

[3] Below, p. 202. The comment, following the text of the questions, is probably the Monk's own. On the derivative character of his main narrative of the crisis of 1387–8, see below, pp. lii–iv.

[4] Below, pp. lix–lx.

example, in his account of the summons of Londoners to York in 1392.[1] He was, moreover, an inattentive scribe, capable of omitting long passages even when he was copying a narrative of which he was himself the author.[2] He may have begun to compose in the late 1380s and may not have put down his pen before 1397; but it is quite possible that he began after 1390 and finished earlier. The shorter the time of composition, the more likely it is that the author held no major office in the monastery while he was at work. A private chamber would have eased the problem of the safe-keeping of the materials which must have accumulated against the making of the fair copy that has come down to us. Most of the literary references in his work, though not quite all,[3] are scriptural. He uses 'return of writ' in a non-technical sense[4] but shows acquaintance with the thirty-ninth decretal letter ascribed to Pope Clement[5] and perhaps with the canon law on the judgement of a pope.[6] Walsingham's influence may explain the epitome of the year's weather which the Monk gives, uniquely, for 1387.[7] Did he pen this entry fresh from reading a version of the *Chronica Majora* or the *Short History*? Finally, the Monk was sententious and given to platitudes.[8]

This specification hardly fits two of the monks whose names have long been canvassed in the search for the author of the Westminster Chronicle — Thomas Merks and William Sudbury. Merks is one of the most elusive of the monks of Westminster of this period.[9] He entered the house *c.*1376, perhaps as a mature recruit — there is at any rate no evidence

---

[1] Below, p. 492. One characteristic of the Monk's Latin, the habit of giving impersonal verbs personal constructions, may help to identify other works by the same author, if any exist. For examples see below, pp. 52, 86, 102, 116, etc. (I am indebted for the grammatical point to Dr. M. Winterbottom.) Note also the Monk's habit of tautology.

[2] For examples see below, pp. 312, 342. Cf. R. Vaughan, *Matthew Paris* (Cambridge, 1958), p. 130.

[3] See below, p. 190.   [4] Below, p. 494.

[5] Below, p. 138 and n.   [6] Below, p. 106 and n.

[7] Below, p. 204.   [8] Below, pp. 108, 162, 444, etc.

[9] For his career see *Monks*, p. 116; *B.R.U.O.*, ii. 1263–4; *Reign of Richard II*, p. 116; *Formularies which bear on the History of Oxford, c.1204–1420*, ed. H. E. Salter, W. A. Pantin, and H. G. Richardson, vol. i (Oxford Historical Soc., n.s., iv, 1942), 195 ff. A Richard Merk of Tolleshunt Major (Essex) is mentioned in a deed of 1386 (W.A.M. 1011).

that he said his first Mass as a monk. He never held office in the monastery, and his career is utterly obscure until, *c.*1388, he went to Oxford: there, *c.*1395, he incepted as a doctor of Theology. Was it in these years or before his profession at Westminster that he became known to the king? Richard II took him to Ireland in 1394 and chose him for the see of Carlisle in 1396,[1] at a juncture in his reign when we should expect only those whom the king knew well and whom he trusted to receive promotion. Merks's intervention on Richard's behalf at the deposition is recorded in some chronicles of that event. In his ensuing retirement, part of which he spent at Oxford, he composed his only known surviving work — a treatise on the *dictamen.*[2] It is not impossible that one holding the Monk's critical view of Richard II at an earlier point in the reign should have won the king's confidence and promotion to a bishopric in 1396. But Merks's residence at Oxford and, more particularly, the direction of mental energy this implies in the very years when the Monk was certainly absorbed in his chronicle seem to rule him out. Moreover, the Monk was singularly uninterested in theology: though he had a plain man's abhorrence of John Wycliffe's preaching and the pernicious doctrines of the Lollards, he sheds scarcely any light on the latter and none on the former.[3] Further, the treatise on the *dictamen* seems to exclude Merks: whatever else the Monk wrote, we may doubt whether it was a treatise on the *dictamen* or, if he wrote such a work, that it would have enjoyed the success implied in its survival today in six manuscripts.

William Sudbury entered the monastery in 1373.[4] He was the son of Henry Sudbury, a skinner of London — one of three children all of whom entered religion.[5] An exceptionally

---

[1] i.e. in time for his provision to the see on 4 Jan. 1397.

[2] For which see N. Denholm-Young, 'The Cursus in England', in *Oxford Essays in Medieval History presented to H. E. Salter* (Oxford, 1934), p. 100 and references given there; see also ibid., p. 81. I have used the copy in Bodleian Library, Oxford, MS. Selden Supra, 65, fos. 111–125[v]. [3] Below, pp. 106, 326, 330.

[4] For his career, see *Monks*, p. 113; *B.R.U.O.*, iii. 1813; *Reign of Richard II*, p. 121 and n.

[5] *Calendar of Wills proved and enrolled in the Court of Husting, London, A.D. 1258–A.D. 1688*, ed. R. R. Sharpe (2 vols., London, 1889–90), ii. 225. See also below, p. 34 n.

able young man, he was sent to Oxford almost at once and before his ordination; this probably took place in 1376 or 1377. He was admitted B.Th. in 1382 but continued a member of Gloucester College for five more years. It must have been during his Oxford years that he wrote the treatise on the coronation regalia which Richard Cirencester included in the *Speculum Historiale* and which was indeed composed for that purpose.[1] He held no office in the monastery before 1391 and none between 1393 and 1400 or in the four years preceding his death in 1415. But as a graduate he was a natural choice if the Abbey needed a spokesman or if there was a difficult letter to be written. In 1389, for example, he composed the letter in which Richard II petitioned Urban VI for a confirmation of the Abbey's privileges,[2] and in 1391 to 1392 he represented the monks at an important hearing of their case against the canons of St. Stephen's, Westminster, before the king, at Windsor — one of several occasions when he appeared for the monks in that cause.[3] Nor did his status as a graduate save him from the humdrum tasks that anyone could have done; so, in 1388, together with Richard Cirencester and two others, he drew up an elaborate inventory of the Abbey's vestry.[4] It was perhaps the distraction of jobs such as these that he had in mind when, in the introduction to his index of the works of St. Thomas Aquinas, he wrote feelingly of the loss of uninterrupted time for study that he suffered on his return from Oxford.[5] Certainly his work on the index was long-drawn-out: it was begun in 1382 but not completed until 1403.[6] Sudbury's works included, in addition to the treatise on the regalia, a treatise on the authenticity of the relic of the Precious Blood of Christ

[1] *Speculum Historiale*, ii. 26 ff.

[2] *Liber Niger Quaternus*, fo. 88. The text does not survive.

[3] W.A.M. 19876; *Monks*, p. 113. The hearing at Windsor in 1391-2 is not mentioned in the Chronicle.

[4] J. Wickham Legg, 'On An Inventory of the Vestry in Westminster Abbey taken in 1388', in *Archaeologia*, lii (1890), 195 ff. The inventory was made by Sudbury, Cirencester, Br. John Breynte, and Br. Ralph Tonworthe.

[5] London, B.L., Royal MS. 9.F.iv, fo. 174^r; see T. Käppeli, 'Die Tabula des Wilhelm Sudbery, O.S.B., zu den Werken des hl. Thomas von Aquino', in *Theologische Quartalschrift*, cxv (1934), 75 ff.

[6] B.L. Royal MS. 9.F.iv, fo. 174^r; *Theologische Quartalschrift*, cxv. 75-7. Sudbury says here that he worked on the index for 16 years in the cloister — i.e. after his return to Westminster in 1387.

given to Westminster Abbey by Henry III;[1] and he was almost
certainly the author of the treatise on the privilege of sanctuary at Westminster which precedes the treatise on the
Precious Blood in the unique manuscript.[2]

The Abbey's dispute with St. Stephen's, the privilege of
sanctuary, its claim to the coronation regalia — the Monk
touches more than once on all these themes. But this need
not mean that he and William Sudbury were one and the
same person, for these were matters of high concern to every
patriotic monk of the house. The Monk's treatment of
the origins of the dispute with St. Stephen's is simpler than
we should expect from Sudbury's pen;[3] of the regalia and
the sanctuary he writes loyally but not as an expert — there is
no echo of Sudbury's laboured treatment of these topics,
at once scholastic and antiquarian, in the pages of the
Chronicle. Sudbury's Latin does not share the characteristics
of the Monk's: it is more accurate, confident, and economi-
cal. Though for many years Sudbury was free of the cares of
office, it so happened that in 1392 to 1393, when the Monk
was probably hard at work on the Chronicle, he was both
conventual treasurer and treasurer of Queen Eleanor of
Castile's manors and must have been a very busy man.
Finally, he lived too long for our purpose.

In his quest for the author of the Chronicle, Armitage
Robinson considered only one other name, that of Br. John
Lakingheath, and he was tempted to identify the chronicler
with Lakingheath.[4]

John Lakingheath is first mentioned at Westminster in
1362 to 1363, when he was steward of Abbot Litlington's
household. Even in the exceptional decades following the
Black Death, this position would not have been held by one
who was in any sense a novice. We can therefore assume that
Lakingheath entered the monastery not later than the mid-
1350s. From 1362 until 1392, he was never out of office,
and for most of these years he held the more demanding
offices: he was conventual treasurer, treasurer of Queen

---

[1] Longleat, Wilts., Marquis of Bath MS. 38, fos. 256^V-308. For which see
Historical Manuscripts Commission, Third Report, Appendix, p. 182.

[2] Ibid., fos. 9 ff.   [3] Below, pp. 378-82.

[4] *P.B.A.*, iii (1907-8), 76-7. For Lakingheath's career see *Monks*, pp. 106-7.

Eleanor's foundation, and so on. The valuation of the monastic obediences that he made before relinquishing the treasurer's office in 1392, in order to discover what each could contribute to the New Work,[1] shows that finance was not just the care that happened often to be thrust upon him but also his real *métier*. In the vacancy following Nicholas Litlington's death on 29 November 1386, Richard II tried to bring about Lakingheath's election;[2] in his already long and crowded life at Westminster, Lakingheath had, no doubt, come to the king's notice many times. The monks refused the request, and it is easy to see why: as the man who had been doing so much of the work for so long, Lakingheath was just the kind of person whom electors pass over. But from 1387 until his death early in 1396, he enjoyed a pension of £4 a year and quite possibly a private chamber.[3] He held no office after 1392. The reason may have been ill health. At all events, a physician was summoned to see him at about this time.[4] Armitage Robinson pointed to Lakingheath's importance in the life of the community, to his opportune death at about the time when our chronicler ceased to write, and to passages in the chronicle evincing, as he believed, a particular interest in the Abbey's treasure and its finances.

There is in fact no reference to the Abbey's income or expenditure in the Westminster Chronicle, excepting only whatever is implied in a note of its loss of temporalities in 1383 and 1384.[5] The treasure (in which we must include the regalia) is mentioned several times;[6] but this must have been a source of pride to every right-thinking member of the community at Westminster — these references tell us nothing in particular about the chronicler. Surprisingly, Armitage Robinson did not point to the chronicler's detailed account

[1] Liber Niger Quaternus, fos. 85ᵛ, 140.

[2] For this episode see *Reign of Richard II*, p. 108 and n. Were the monks emboldened by the eclipse of Richard II's authority since the appointment of a continual council on 19 Nov.? A solitary reference to Lakingheath as the agent for a payment of money to the keeper of the wardrobe occurs on the Issue Roll for 1383 (P.R.O., E. 403/499, 13 Nov.).

[3] W.A.M. 19874 ff.; *Monks*, p. 107.

[4] Between 29 Sept. 1392 and 28 Sept. 1393 (W.A.M. 19378). No period of residence in the infirmary is recorded, and this makes it seem very likely indeed that Lakingheath had a private chamber.

[5] Below, p. 38.   [6] Below, pp. 90, 154-6, 372, etc.

of proceedings in the parliament at Salisbury in 1384 and while it was in session; Lakingheath attended this parliament as one of Abbot Litlington's proxies.[1] Even so, Lakingheath is an unlikely candidate for the authorship of the Chronicle. Ironically, what seems to exclude him is the chronicler's very reference to Richard II's efforts on his behalf in 1386.[2] The king's three messages urging the election of Lakingheath are reported in the common form of such requests: the monks were to look upon him as a person 'merito commendata'. Yet it hardly seems likely that the author who chose to record this episode — according to the evidence of the rest of his chronicle a self-effacing man — was himself the abbot *manqué*.

If none of these three — Merks, Sudbury, and Lakingheath — was the author of the chronicle for 1383 to 1394, it by no means follows that none influenced the work. In a community such as that at Westminster, the breadth of experience and range of activity of the individual monk became in a sense the possession of all; had this not been the case, the identification of the author would not be so difficult. The monk who fashioned the chronicle for these years from all the resources to hand may have been one whose claims Armitage Robinson overlooked: Br. Richard Exeter.

Exeter entered the monastery in 1358 or 1359, and from the fact that he said his first Mass in 1361, we should probably conclude that he entered at the age of 21 or 22.[3] When he died, forty years later, Thomas Exeter, his brother, and another relative named John Exeter, received some of his chattels.[4] The name tells us nothing, therefore, about Br. Richard's immediate origins: by the time of his entry into religion it had become the family surname. Exeter spent at least a year and possibly as many as five at Oxford,[5]

---

[1] W.A.M. 19870. The other proxy was Br. John Stow. For this parliament see below, pp. 66 ff. Note also that Lakingheath was one of the conventual treasurers at the time of the purchase of the *Polychronicon* referred to above (p. xxxii).

[2] Below, p. 176. [3] For his career, see *Monks*, pp. 101-2.

[4] W.A.M. 6603. His brother and brother's wife attended the funeral.

[5] A residence of 52 weeks at Oxford is recorded for him in the account of the conventual treasurers for 28 Sept. 1375 to 28 Sept. 1376 (W.A.M. 19867), but there is a gap in the accounts between 1372 and 1375 and between 1376 and 1378. (The statement in *Reign of Richard II*, p. 121 n. that he is known to have been in Oxford in 1372-3 is incorrect.) Was Br. Robert Exeter, prior of Holy Trinity,

and it was presumably his status as a university man that ensured his election as prior in 1377, for he had no previous experience of monastic office. Five years later he resigned the office. From that time until his death late in 1396 or early in 1397 he enjoyed a pension of £2. 13s. 4d. per annum,[1] and throughout this period he probably occupied the spacious quarters described in the inventory of his goods made after his death; these comprised a hall, buttery, kitchen, chamber, and study.[2] Other entries in the inventory confirm the impression that Exeter followed a life of his own in retirement. The possession of 21 plates, 23 potagers, and 24 saucers suggests a man given to hospitality; his silver seal, gold signet, and clerk (described as 'comensalis'), a busy man with affairs to transact outside the monastery — one who had, no doubt, many occasions for wearing the best frock, fur-lined tunics, and London cloak that are also listed among Exeter's effects.

Exeter's reasons for resigning the priorship passed unrecorded. Perhaps the trials of the office proved too much for an essentially bookish nature; and Exeter's experience of handling the magnificent library of Cardinal Langham when it reached Westminster in 1378 may have stirred scholarly ambitions that could not be satisfied in the prior's office.[3] In retirement he gratified his tastes as a bibliophile, and he died possessed of a veritable library of his own. According to the inventory, there were in his study the following works:

Hostiensis in summa; prima pars Hostiensis in lectura; Rationale divinorum;[4] Polychronicon cum libro Marci

---

Aldgate, 1391–1408, and one of the executors of the will of Eleanor, duchess of Gloucester (d. 1399), a relative? See *Testamenta Vetusta*, ed. N. H. Nicholas (2 vols., London, 1826), i. 149; *V.C.H. London*, i. 474; and below, p. 494.

[1] W.A.M. 19870 ff.; *Monks*, p. 102. He died between Michaelmas 1396 and Easter 1397.

[2] W.A.M. 6603. A serious illness between 28 Sept. 1386 and 28 Sept. 1387 is indicated by the infirmarer's outlay of £1. 6s. 8d. on medicines for him during that period (W.A.M. 19370).

[3] W.A.M. 6604.

[4] Willelmus Durandus, *Rationale divinorum officiorum*. Cardinal Langham's library included 'tercium et quartum scriptum Durandi' (*MSS. of Westminster Abbey*, p. 6). I am greatly indebted to Professor R. H. Rouse for his generous help in identifying the works in Exeter's library.

Pauli; apparatus Pauli super Clementinas;[1] Bromyerd, bonus;[2] Bellum Troianum[3] cum multis tractatibus; Scholastica Historia;[4] Dignus de regulis juris;[5] Excerpta de viciis et virtutibus;[6] mappa Anglie; mappa maris; mappa Scotie.

A so-called 'liber de jocondio amoris', possibly a metrical romance, was being copied for him at the time of his death, and his executors paid 18*d*. for the work; the paper for which they paid 5*s*. to one Thomas Gervys may have been needed for this.[7] His executors also paid for the binding of a work of John Maudith, the Oxford astronomer. The book which they retrieved from Clandon, in Surrey, was probably one that Exeter had lent to a friend there.

The contents of Richard Exeter's library suggest that during his long retirement he had cultivated an interest in canon law and been in demand as a preacher. The former interest is compatible with what we know of the Monk of Westminster; and the moralist in the Monk may well have been nourished on sermons. Yet his works of reference in the canon law and the works which he may have used as a preacher are less remarkable in a collection of this period than the historical items in the list. In particular, the copy of the *Polychronicon*, bound, it seems likely, with a copy of Francesco Pipino's work on Marco Polo,[8] is of singular

---

[1] Paulus Liazari, *Lectura super Clementinis.*

[2] Johannes Bromyard, *Opus Trivium ex tribus legibus, divina, canonica et civili*, also known as *Distincciones Bromyard*; revised and expanded as *Summa Praedicantium.*

[3] Guido de Columna, *Historia de Troia.*

[4] By Petrus Comestor. Exeter took charge of Langham's copy of this work when it reached Westminster (W.A.M. 6604).

[5] Dinus de Mugello, *Super titulum Sexti de regulis iuris.*

[6] Probably extracts (which may have been from one of the English versions) of the *Somme le Roi* of Lorens d'Orléans. For this work see P. Meyer, 'Notice sur le MS. Bibi. Nat. Fr. 13304 renfermant les trois premières parties de la *Somme le Roi*', in *Romania*, xxiii (1894), 449–55; and *The Book of Vices and Virtues*, ed. W. N. Francis (Early English Text Society, orig. ser., ccxvii).

[7] A London draper named Thomas Gerveys is mentioned in 1396 (*Cal. Cl. R. 1396–9*, p. 61).

[8] *Marci Pauli de Venetiis de conditionibus et consuetudinibus orientalium regionum*. I am greatly indebted to Mrs. Consuelo Dutschke for the information that the Pipino version of 'Marco Polo' occurs with a text of the *Polychronicon* in the following MSS.: C.U.L. Dd. i. 17; ibid., Dd. viii. 7 (but the Pipino text here is a fragment); London, B.L., Royal MS. 14. C. xiii (a Norwich codex); and Oxford, Bodleian Library, MS. Digby 196 (a 15th-century MS. containing

interest. Exetei possessed three maps, each a rather unusual acquisition for the period and each potentially of use to the author of the Westminster Chronicle. He was interested in astronomy. He sometimes used paper in preference to parchment. In the years when the Chronicle was in hand, he enjoyed considerable leisure and spacious quarters. As a former prior of Westminster he would have had contacts and friendships outside the cloister beyond those available to an ordinary monk and such as it is easy to believe our chronicler enjoyed. He lived long enough to have written the Chronicle, but not too long. Quite possibly he was the Monk of Westminster.

(ii) *Sources*

The Chronicle is more heavily indebted to written sources between 1386 and 1394 than in the earlier part of the work, and this is not surprising, for it was not until 1386, or perhaps towards the end of 1385, that the deliberate collection of material for a contemporary chronicle was begun. Further, the way in which written sources are used changes in the course of the narrative for 1386, and the change ensures that such sources become not only more important but also more conspicuous. The first author wove such texts as he possessed into his narrative, and the second, the Monk of Westminster, began by following this example. But the formidable texts relating to the appointment of a continual council in November 1386 were too much for the Monk's powers of assimilation: these he transcribed in full, and this now became his usual, though still not his invariable, practice. Moreover, he took the risk of copying these texts and some others directly from his source on to the pages of C.C.C.C., 197A without trying out the passages in his antecedent drafts. From time to time, but notably in his account of the Merciless Parliament, this practice dislocated his narrative and occasioned rare pieces of extempore composition to repair

excerpts from both works). C.U.L. Dd. i. 17 also contains Guido de Columna, *Historia de Troia*, and several other historical works. Its text of the *Polychronicon* ends with Bk. viii. *cap.* 2 ('ad Angliam recesserunt verum male'). It is a composite volume, not originally a single one; the *Polychronicon* and the Pipino text can never have been consecutive items.

the damage.[1] In the Chronicle considered as a whole, the following texts were used in one or other of these ways:

1. Records relating to the Abbey's dispute with St. Stephen's Chapel, Westminster, in and after 1376 (below, p. 380).

2. Urban VI's bull empowering nuncios to grant the indulgences and privileges of the crusade in Castile, 1383 (p. 164).

3. Letter about Bishop Despenser's crusade, 17 to 25 May 1383 (pp. 38-40).

4. Letter from Robert II, king of the Scots, to Richard II, 14 December 1383 (pp. 54-6).

5. Account of the affair of the Carmelite friar, 1384 (pp. 68-80).

6. Thomas Usk's appeal of John of Northampton and three others, 1384 (pp. 90-2).

7. List of the slain in the Battle of Aljubarrota, 14 August 1385 (p. 132).

8. Account of Richard II's campaign in Scotland, July to August 1385 (pp. 124, 126-30).

9. Account of events in, around, and off Calais in September and October 1385 (pp. 134-6).

10. Note on the council's appeal to parliament for a subsidy, December 1385 (p. 148).

11. (i) Letters patent of 19 November 1386 containing the commission of the continual council appointed in the parliament of October to November 1386 (pp. 166-74).

(ii) The statute on the above commission (pp. 174-6).

12. Accounts of the first and second naval expeditions of the earl of Arundel, March to April and May 1387 (pp. 180-4).

13. Richard II's questions to his judges, 25 August 1387 (pp. 196-202).

14. Narrative of events from 11 November 1387 to 18 January 1388, originating in the circle of the Appellants (pp. 208-34).

15. Texts relating to the parliament of 3 February to

[1] See below, p. li. Of the sources in the following list, nos. 11, 13, 15, 19, 20 and 22-6 were almost certainly copied by the Monk as he went along; and the same may be true of some others.

3 June 1388 (the Merciless Parliament):

(i) Appeal against the five principal accused (pp. 236-68).

(ii) Articles of impeachment against Sir Simon Burley and three others (pp. 268-78).

(iii) The 'Process' of the parliament (pp. 280-96).

(iv) Petitions forming the basis of the pardons granted at the end of the parliament and of the exceptions to these, also of the declaration that the acts of the parliament were irreversible (pp. 296-306).

(v) Oath taken by Lords and Commons at the conclusion of the parliament (p. 306).

16. Arguments advanced by the monks of Westminster before Richard II in support of the Abbey's privilege of sanctuary, 18 April 1388 (pp. 324-6).

17. Account of the Battle of Otterburn, August 1388 (pp. 346-50).

18. Account of the expedition of the earl of Arundel to La Rochelle, June to September 1388 (pp. 350-2).

19. Roll of the Commons' petitions in the parliament at Cambridge, September to October 1388, with the king's reply to the petition on liveries (pp. 356-68).

20. Statute of this parliament on provisors (12 Richard II, *cap.* 15), with introductory sentence (p. 430).

21. The council's instructions to the English envoys negotiating with the French at Leulingham, January 1389 (p. 376).

22. Urban VI's bull *Salvator noster*, 8 April 1389 (pp. 384-90).

23. Statute on pardons for homicide, 1390 (13 Richard II, 2, *cap.* 1) (pp. 416-18).

24. Second Statute of Provisors, 1390 (13 Richard II, 2, *caps.* 2-3) (pp. 418-30).

25. Account of the earl of Derby's crusade to Prussia, August to October 1390 (pp. 444-8).

26. Texts relating to the mission of Boniface IX's envoy, the abbot of Nonantola, to England in 1391:

(i) Letter of Boniface IX to Richard II, 14 April (pp. 458-60).

(ii) Message delivered by the envoy (pp. 462-8).

(iii) Letter of Richard II to Boniface IX, 30 July 1391 (pp. 468–72).

27. Account of the deaths of Sir John Clanvow and Sir William Nevill, October 1391 (p. 480).

28. Royal writ summoning the mayor, sheriffs, and aldermen of the City of London to Nottingham, 29 May 1392 (pp. 492–4).

29. The reply to no. 28 (p. 494).

30. Text of the terms offered to the City by the king, probably on 21 August 1392 (pp. 506–8).

Much of the Chronicle's value derives from the parliamentary items in this list, and in particular from the text described as the 'Process' of the Merciless Parliament (15. iii above). The official record of a late fourteenth-century parliament was the roll, made up by the clerk of parliament and kept with the records of Chancery, to which department the clerk of parliament belonged. This roll was not made in a moment: it was a compilation behind which lay a fastidious process of selection from the available material. The clerk also saw to the drafting and enrolment of statutes enacted in parliament, and the time-consuming nature of this work helps to explain why a considerable interval sometimes elapsed between the end of parliament and the publication of its statutes in the shires.[1] His draft often followed verbatim the roll of the common petitions which was itself sometimes the longest section in the roll of parliament in this period.

It is likely that the abbot of Westminster attended or sent proxies to all but three of the parliaments which met in the years covered by the Chronicle.[2] John Scarle, the clerk of parliament for at least ten of the thirteen years covered by the Chronicle (1384 to 1394), was a pensioner of the Abbey:

---

[1] For a case in point see below, p. 482 and n. On the subject-matter of this paragraph see Tout, *Chapters*, iii. 447–8; G. Edwards, *The Second Century of the English Parliament* (Oxford, 1979), Chs. 4–5.

[2] He was excused attendance in the parliaments of 6 Oct. 1382, 3 Nov. 1391, and 27 Jan. 1394. He was a trier of petitions in the parliaments of 3 Nov. 1381, 7 May 1382, 23 Feb. 1383, 26 Oct. 1383, 20 Oct. 1385, 1 Oct. 1386, 3 Feb. 1388, 12 Nov. 1390. For his attendance at the parliament of Sept.–Oct. 1388 see below, p. 354 n.

throughout this period and for much longer he received a
pension of £2 13s. 4d. per annum.[1] The Commons sometimes
met within the monastic precinct. The Monk of Westminster
was as well placed as any chronicler could be to acquire
copies of the parliamentary records mentioned in the preceding paragraph. But how exactly did he come by the
'Process' of the Merciless Parliament, and what indeed is this
text?

The 'Process' is a narrative of proceedings in the parliament and of its judgements, written in French — 'after the
manner of those employed in the king's service about the
court at Westminster'.[2] In common with the version of events
enrolled in the Rolls of Parliament, the 'Process' focuses our
attention on judicial proceedings: it is not much interested in
the general business of the realm, of which, even in this
parliament, some was transacted. Yet there are differences
between the 'Process' and the Rolls of Parliament.[3] The
author of the 'Process' was more confused than the compiler
of the official version about legal details or less adept at
explaining anomalies away. So, for example, he says that
Brembre was both appealed by the Lords and impeached by
the Commons; but the latter makes the Commons say that
but for the Appeal they would have impeached Brembre.
The author of the 'Process' apparently committed the egregious blunder of assigning the events which occurred between
Monday, 2 March and Friday, 6 March inclusive to the previous week; and his account of proceedings against Nevill,
de Vere, Pole, and Tresilian on 3 to 5 February is altogether
less particular than that in the Rolls of Parliament. But he
is more careful than the author or authors of the official
version to record the king's presence or absence from proceedings in parliament, who presided in the king's absence,
and who pronounced the judgements and sentences of the
parliament. His account of Nicholas Brembre's trial and the
later trials in the Merciless Parliament is more particular than
that in the Rolls of Parliament, and here he recorded some

[1] W.A.M. 19865 ff. This payment to Scarle began in 1370. See also Tout,
Chapters, iii. 448 n.
[2] Below, pp. 278-80.
[3] For what follows see below, pp. 278-96, and *R.P.*, iii. 228-52.

details, such as the continuance of proceedings against Simon Burley on 17 March, despite Burley's enfeebled state, that were discreditable to those responsible. His description of the proceedings against Thomas Rushock, which makes them sound less neat, more fumbling, than those enshrined in the official version, has the ring of truth;[1] so too his account of disagreement among the Lords Temporal on 27 February — correctly 5 March — as the trial of the judges reached its climax.[2] Yet we are a long way from the frank, circumstantial account of the disagreements behind the scenes in the Merciless Parliament, particularly during Simon Burley's trial, that is to be found later in the Chronicle, in the Monk of Westminster's own account of proceedings, and in Favent's chronicle.[3] Here in fact is a version of events less circumspect than the official version but still reticently biased, as that is, towards the cause of the Appellants and their friends. If its language is that of the king's servants, its sentiments are not on the whole those of the king's friends.

A single source provided the Monk with his text of the 'Process' (15. iii in the above list), the commission of appointment of the continual council of 1386 (11. i), the statute in which this was enacted (11. ii), the king's questions to the judges in 1387 (13), the Appeal against the five principal accused (15. i), the articles of impeachment against Burley etc., and the other acts of the Merciless Parliament which he transcribed (15. ii, iv). As far as we know this source does not survive. However, one analogous to it does, and this source — now W.A.M. 12227 — sheds light on the identity of the source used by the Monk of Westminster.

W.A.M. 12227 (in this edition, *W*) is a parchment roll of seven membranes sewn end to end, in accordance with the practice of Chancery. Two stitching holes at the top of the first membrane seem to show that the complete roll does not survive. The extant membranes contain the following

---

[1] Below, pp. 284-6, 292-4. The order of events in the 'Process', which puts Rushock's impeachment *before* the judgement against the judges and lawyers on 28 Feb. (correctly, 6 Mar.), may be correct: it makes better sense than the opposite order, implied in *R.P.*, iii. 240-1, of the presence and absence of the lords spiritual at the several episodes of the day. See, however, below, p. 316.

[2] Below, p. 284.

[3] Below, p. 328; *Favent*, p. 21.

texts relating to the Merciless Parliament or cited in the course of its proceedings, in the following order:

(i) The articles of the impeachment of Simon Burley and others, with the preamble, as in the Rolls of Parliament, iii. 241.

(ii) The petitions for pardon, ending with that on behalf of Londoners.

(iii) The commission of the continual council appointed on 19 November 1386, as recited in the first petition.

(iv) The statute on the commission.

(v) The 'Process' of the parliament.

On the dorse of membrane 2 is an entry in a different, cursive hand, summarizing, though in Latin and not in the English of the original, the confession of Thomas of Woodstock, duke of Gloucester, before William Rickhill in 1397.[1] From this entry we should perhaps conclude that *W* was in fact made for the appeal against Gloucester. A note at the end of the text of the 'Process' in *W* shows what it was that was copied for this purpose. Both here and in the Westminster Chronicle,[2] the 'Process' ends with the words: 'et ensi fina le parlement'. In *W*, however, two words follow: 'Burton. Explicit'. These words may refer only to the 'Process', the last item on the recto of *W*. It is more likely, however, that they refer to the entire roll which was written as a continuous whole. 'Burton' was, almost certainly, John Burton, keeper of the rolls of Chancery between 1386 and 1394.[3] It appears, therefore, that *W* was copied from a roll of the proceedings of the Merciless Parliament made by John Burton or for him; the original and the now missing membranes of *W* no doubt included the articles of the Appeal against the five principal accused. If so, the 'Process' common to *W* and the Westminster Chronicle is of singular interest. As a text of Chancery origin it was probably available to the clerk of parliament when he made up the official roll and if so could have been used for the narrative of events in which the articles of the Appeal and those of the impeachment of Burley and his fellow accused are there set. If that is so, however, we may find in the differences between the

---

[1] Cf. *R.P.*, iii. 378–9.   [2] Below, p. 296.
[3] See Tout, *Chapters*, iii. 450.

'Process' and the official narrative points to which the clerk
of parliament and those in whose shadow he worked attached
particular importance. Those responsible for making up the
official roll did not like unambiguous references to the king's
absence from the solemn proceedings of the parliament; they
wanted the account of Rushock's trial to read smoothly;
and above all they were determined to suppress most of the
details of the legal wrangle that erupted during the trials of
Brembre, Blake, and Burley.

W was not itself the Monk's source. In his source, the
'Process', with which W concludes, was evidently the third
item, following the articles of the impeachment.[1] Moreover,
collation of the Monk's text and W brings to light words and
phrases which are in the former and therefore, presumably,
in his source, but not in W.[2] But the Monk's text and W were
closely related, and one passage seems to show that they
derived the 'Process' from a common source. After the
conclusion of Nicholas Brembre's trial, on Thursday, 20
February 1388, judicial proceedings in the Merciless Parliament were suspended for ten days; then, on Monday, 2
March, proceedings began against Robert Bealknap, C. J.,
and the other judges and lawyers arraigned with him.[3]
After recording the events of 20 February, the Monk's text
reads: 'Et le Lundy et le jour de Mars lors proschein monseignur Robert Beleknapp, monseignur Johan Holte . . .
feurent arrayne en plein parlement.'[4] The Monday and
Tuesday after Thursday, 20 February 1388 were 24 and 25
February. Thus the text of the 'Process' in the Chronicle
advances the initiation of proceedings against the judges by
one week. Not one error but two were thus perpetrated, for
the judges were not in fact brought into parliament on two
consecutive days at this juncture. Tuesday, the morrow of
their first appearance, was devoted to the beginning of the
proceedings against John Blake and Thomas Usk, who received judgement in parliament on the following day.[5] The
Monk's text is, however, correct in all particulars except the
initial date: after noting the arraignment of the judges in
parliament 'le Lundy et le jour de Mars lors proschein', it

---

[1] Below, pp. 278–80. [2] e.g., below, pp. 282, 286, 292.
[3] R.P., iii. 238. [4] Below, p. 284. [5] R.P., iii. 240.

faithfully records that 'le Maresdy proschein' Blake and Usk
were arraigned and that they received judgement 'Meskerdy
apres'. He was the victim, not of a real misunderstanding of
the chronology of proceedings at this point, but of scribal
error: where his text has 'le Lundy et le jour de Mars lors
proschein', the correct reading was: 'le Lundy le seconde
jour de Mars lors proschein'. The mistake was, almost certainly, in the text of the 'Process' which was copied into
W, for in W the correct reading — 'le Lundy le seconde jour
de Marcz lors proschein' — is written partly over an erasure.
From this it seems likely that the Monk's text of the 'Process'
and that in W were derived from the same source. If we are
right, this was a roll of the proceedings of the Merciless
Parliament made by or for John Burton, keeper of the rolls
of Chancery. The Monk probably obtained this source at the
hands of John Scarle.

The Monk transferred the contents of his copy of Burton's
roll straight on to the pages of C.C.C.C., 197A without
considering with due care where exactly in his narrative the
several parts belonged. His account of the Merciless Parliament was, in consequence, deranged. He began his own narrative of the parliament on C.C.C.C., 197A, p. 165, with an
account of events on 3 February,[1] proceeded, appropriately
enough, to give the text of the articles of the Appeal rehearsed in parliament that day, but then transcribed several
other items which happened to follow in his Chancery source
at that point, among them the 'Process' which covers the
entire life of the parliament down to 3 June, before resuming
his own narrative of the parliament on C.C.C.C., 197A, p.
178 at the exact point (3 February) where he left off. To
justify the return to February, he cobbled together a few
lines on changes in the judiciary at that time which he had
not previously noticed.[2]

Several of the Chronicle's sources were of a propagandist
nature: they represented attempts by individuals or by the
government of the day or its opponents to influence opinion

---

[1] Below, pp. 234–6.

[2] Below, pp. 306–8, and Frontispiece. The passage of cobbling is in a less
regular hand than the ensuing narrative of the parliament and seems to represent
extempore composition. See also p. 318 n.

through select information. The most ambitious of these (no. 14 in the above list), is there described as a 'narrative of events from 11 November 1387 to 18 January 1388, originating in the circle of the Appellants'. The description itself is a little ambitious, for this text is not self-evidently one of the Chronicle's sources, and the reasons for believing in its existence need to be set out.

At three points in his narrative of events in the period in question, the Monk of Westminster betrays the fact that he is drawing on a written source, and in each case the tell-tale sign is a lapse into the first person in a passage intended to be in *oratio obliqua*. He stumbles in this way in the course of reporting the reply of Gloucester, Arundel, and Warwick to the intermediaries sent by the king on 14 November; and the same thing happens in the case of the reply of Robert de Vere's men to a message from the earl of Arundel and the other lords in his company near Witney on 20 December, and in the speech of the bishop of Ely to the assembled representatives of the London gilds on 18 January.[1] A close reading of the Chronicle suggests that the entire narrative of events from the failure of Gloucester and Arundel to appear before the king on 11 November down to the meeting on 18 January is indebted to a text written from the standpoint of the Appellants and designed to represent their conduct during this period in a favourable light. Into this text, it is suggested, the Monk introduced some short pieces of narrative of his own and some comments, particularly on the expulsion from the household of the king's favoured servants and courtiers on 1 and 2 January[2] and on the meeting at the Guildhall on 18 January, that were far from sympathetic towards the Appellants. But from 11 November to 31 December he is probably following his source very closely and is not the author, in the full sense of the word, of the political comment that is woven into the narrative between these dates. Very likely his source was guilty of the lapses from *oratio obliqua* into the first person noted above. The derivative character of the Chronicle for the period 11 November to 31 December 1387 is betrayed by its tone. In other parts of his work the Monk of Westminster reveals

---

[1] Below, pp. 210, 222, 232–4.   [2] Below, pp. 228–32.

himself as, though critical of Richard II, well disposed
towards him, and his sympathy for the Appellants is never
undiscriminating. Moreover, in respect both of the king and
of the Appellants, we have to piece together his view before
discovering what it is: his judgements are given piecemeal
and, except where the liberties of the Church are concerned,
they are moderate, often reticent. By contrast, the narrative
for the period 11 November to 31 December amounts to a
piece of sustained advocacy for the Appellant cause which
cleverly excuses every questionable act of its principals:
the refusal to obey the king's summons on 11 November, the
muster at Haringay two days later, the resort to arms against
de Vere — who, after all, went to Chester on the king's
business — and so on.[1] Not even the proposal to dethrone the
king, itself, no doubt, notorious at the time, is shirked: rather
a candid confession of it is used to great advantage, as
Warwick scotches the idea with a moving speech on the king's
claim to the loyalty of those who have done him homage and
fealty.[2]

As the argument is pointed, so is the language coloured.
Ambushes prepared by Sir Thomas Trivet for Gloucester,
Arundel, and Warwick on 17 November are described in
terms at once inflated and opaque, as though to prevent the
reader from knowing exactly what the puny threat to their
security had been.[3] 'Insanum consilium' turned the king
against the Appellants; 'viri cordati' flocked to their support
when de Vere fled; and in the king's household the Appellants found 'superflui' whose 'numerositas' they pruned.[4]
The author of these pages knew what the Appellants said to
the king in their private interview with him in the Tower on
30 December and that this included some matters not made
public.[5] Finally, the Monk was twice tempted to improve his
text by substituting in one place 'nec' for 'aut' and in another
'enervacio' for 'suppeditacio', but in neither case did he
delete or erase the original reading: he was perhaps inhibited

[1] Below, pp. 208, 210, 220-2.
[2] Below, p. 218.   [3] Below, p. 212.
[4] Below, pp. 216, 224, 228. For 'viri cordati' see also pp. 376, 488.
[5] Below, pp. 226-8. Cf. p. 220, where the author knows what the Appellants
said to each other when they arrested Robert Pinchbeck and Richard Skelton at
the beginning of the campaign of Radcot Bridge.

by respect for a written source; and indeed the variant readings may have been in his source.[1]

The meeting at the Guildhall on 18 January was the last considerable event before the opening of the Merciless Parliament on 3 February. If we are right, therefore, the Monk had at his disposal and largely used a defence of the actions of the Appellants from their first defiance of the king on 11 November down to the initiation of judicial proceedings — of a kind — against the so-called traitors from whom they claimed to be saving the king. We are reminded of the protestation (probably in French) presented to the king by the duke of Gloucester on 13 February, purporting to show that all that the Appellants and their friends had done, from the assembly under arms on 13 November until the day when the protestation was presented, had been done for the honour of God and the honour of the king and of the realm, etc.[2] Such a document, one supposes, would not have been written in a moment or without trial and error and the discarding of drafts. Quite possibly the Monk's source belongs to the period of gestation. It was, it seems, in Latin, and this suggests that it was made for an official or semi-official purpose. The prominence given in the narrative to the earl of Warwick — today the most elusive of the five Appellants but here twice represented as their leader — is a clue to the provenance of the source: our text may have been written by a member of the earl's household.

The authors of the Westminster Chronicle were not only well provided with written sources: they encountered face to face many of the actors in the scenes which they described. Both facts reflect the exceptional variety and range of their monastery's contacts with the outside world. The Abbey owed most of these to its fame as a sanctuary, centre of pilgrimage, and — most important of the three — place of resort for visitors to London and the royal court and to the hospitable way of life of its abbot and obedientiaries. The Abbey's *Customary*, put together *c.*1270 but still in use in the time of Abbot Litlington and Abbot Colchester, recognized the

---

[1] Below, pp. 222, 228. Cf. p. 68 (where also the Monk was following a written source).

[2] *R.P.*, iii. 237, 244.

tyranny of really distinguished visitors: normally the sacrist,
the official who showed the relics to visitors to the church,
was to speak to the latter 'breviter . . . quasi in silencio';
but he was permitted to address the king, the queen, bishops,
abbots of the Order, and the greater earls 'manifeste'.[1]
We cannot be sure that the French envoys to Scotland
visiting the Abbey in 1384 on their way north heard what
was said to them, for they were mere diplomats, not entitled
to be addressed 'manifeste'.[2] As a king in exile, Leo VI of
Armenia probably did better in 1386, when Richard II took
him to see the relics and the regalia at Westminster. It was no
doubt from the conversation on this occasion and again a
fortnight later, when Leo came for the consecration of a
bishop, that the full inwardness of his discussions with the
king at Eltham became known to the monks.[3]

It was Richard II's practice to visit St. Edward's shrine
at a critical turn of events, and the Chronicle records such
visits on 15 June 1381, before the king's meeting with the
rebels at Smithfield;[4] on 10 November 1387, when he was
accompanied by Archbishop Nevill, Robert de Vere, and
Michael de la Pole;[5] and on 21 August 1392, the day on
which Richard received the submission of the City of
London.[6] He liked to worship in the monastic church on
the feast of the translation of St. Edward the Confessor
(13 October) and on the patronal festivals of St. Peter and
St. Paul and sometimes came on other feast-days beside
these. In 1388 the feast of St. Peter in Cathedra brought him
to the Abbey on 22 February, two days after the condemnation of Nicholas Brembre.[7] Evidently the duke of Gloucester
had similar feelings towards the Abbey and its saints, for he
presented some magnificent gifts to the church on the eve
of his abortive departure for Prussia in 1391.[8] The foundation

---

[1] *Customary of the Benedictine Monasteries of Saint Augustine, Canterbury,
and St. Peter, Westminster*, ed. E. M. Thompson (2 vols., Henry Bradshaw Soc.,
xxiii, xxviii, 1902, 1904), ii. 51–2. These rules applied if another monk was
present.   [2] Below, p. 90.
[3] Below, pp. 154–6.   [4] Below, pp. 8–10.
[5] Below, pp. 206–8.   [6] Below, p. 506.
[7] Below, p. 314; see also pp. 450, 508–10. Visits from Richard II on the feast
of St. Edward's translation in 1391 and 1393 are recorded in other sources
(W.A.M. 19648, 19651).
[8] Below, p. 480.

deed of an anniversary for Gloucester and his wife — a document not likely to have been sealed in their absence — is
dated 1 December 1387.[1] Gloucester's act in arresting
Tresilian within the bounds of the sanctuary was, then, a
wound inflicted on the monks by a friend, even a brother,
and on 15 May 1388, when the main judicial business of the
Merciless Parliament was at an end, Gloucester came to make
his peace with the abbot.[2] He just missed the funerals of
James Berners and John Salisbury, who were executed on
12 May and buried in the chapel of St. John the Baptist in
the Abbey.[3] John of Gaunt, lacking a town house after the
sack of the Savoy, stayed from time to time at La Neyte,
the abbot's house near the Abbey: he was there at the time
of Brembre's election to the mayoralty in 1383;[4] for the
second parliament of 1384;[5] and probably for the first of
1390.[6]

By the end of the fourteenth century, the chamberlain of
Westminster was in the habit of entertaining the mayor,
sheriffs, and other leading citizens of London on the feast of
St. Edward, which happened also to be, in most years, the
day of the mayoral election.[7] This was by no means the only
occasion when the monks were at home to their neighbours
in the City: visits by Londoners, among whom tenants of
the Abbey are specifically mentioned, seem to have been
customary on the feast of St. Peter and St. Paul (29 June)
and that of St. Peter in Chains (1 August); and in 1383, not

[1] W.A.M. 9474*, for which see *Archaeologia*, lii (1890), 284-5.
[2] Below, p. 332; and for the arrest of Tresilian within the sanctuary, see
p. 310. For Gloucester's estrangement from the monks at some point between
this episode and his departure on crusade in 1391, see pp. 380-2, 480 n.
[3] Below, p. 332.
[4] *A Book of London English 1384-1425*, ed. R. W. Chambers and M. Daunt
(Oxford, 1931), p. 28, where 'The Neyte' is the abbot of Westminster's house. See
also M. Sharp, 'A fragmentary household account of John of Gaunt', in *B.I.H.R.*,
xiii (1935-6), 156.
[5] W.A.M. 4761*; *B.I.H.R.*, xiii (1935-6), 156-7.
[6] Cf. the following entry in the account of the steward of the household for
28 Sept. 1389 to 28 Sept. 1390: 'Item, dat' cursori ducis Lancastr' portanti
literas apud le Hyde pro manerio de la Neyte erga parliamentum iijs. iiijd.'
(W.A.M. 24540).
[7] W.A.M. 18729-33. See also W.A.M. 25307-15, vouchers recording the
expenses of (unidentified) monastic officials on the entertainment of royal
officials *temp.* Richard II.

for the first time or the last, they came on the anniversary
of Edward III and Philippa of Hainault (21 June).[1] When,
therefore, William Essex, the London draper who was
accused with John Northampton in 1384, entered sanctuary
at Westminster, he found himself in familiar surroundings.[2]
If the Abbey under Nicholas Litlington and William Colchester no longer gave livery or fees with the open-handed
generosity of an earlier age, it nevertheless had a few retainers
in key positions. One of these was Mr. Thomas Southam,
papal sub-collector in England, who received ten yards of
cloth, with furs, annually throughout the period covered by
the Chronicle.[3] Robert Bealknap had been in happier days a
pensioner of the Abbey.[4]

How did the two authors of the Chronicle use these exceptional opportunities for hearing about contemporary history
from those who made it? Should we imagine them jotting
down what they were told, against the day when it would
be needed? Or were they content to rely on memory to
retrieve the information when the time came? It seems clear
that the Monk of Westminster, though a diligent researcher
who set great store by written sources, also relied greatly on
memory — his own and other people's — and the role of
memory was certainly not less in the chronicle which he took
over. The Monk's memory was well stocked but apt to play
tricks. Such a trick must explain, for example, a serious error
in his account of Richard II's final settlement with the City
of London in 1392.[5] In the end, on 19 September, Richard
restored the City's liberties without exception 'until further
order'. But the Monk says that the king made three exceptions on this occasion, and these he rehearses in detail. Very
likely Richard did threaten to revoke the liberties in question
at an earlier stage in the negotiations, and the Monk seems

---

[1] W.A.M. 18731.   [2] Below, p. 94.
[3] W.A.M. 19868 ff. The livery to Southam is first recorded in 1378-9. See also
J. R. Maddicott, *Law and Lordship: Royal Justices as Retainers in Thirteenth-
and Fourteenth-Century England (Past and Present* Supplement, 4, 1978), p. 76.
    [4] Bealknap received a fee of 20s. per annum from the abbot from 1371 to
1384 and possibly for a longer period (W.A.M. 24515 ff.). For the pension of
John Scarle, clerk in Chancery 1384-94, see above, pp. xlvi-vii.
    [5] Below, pp. 506-8 and nn. See also the words 'secundum quosdam' with
which the Monk twice buttresses his narrative of earlier stages in the quarrel
(pp. 496, 502).

to have possessed a text setting out these interim proposals in terms sympathetic to the king. When he composed the Chronicle for 1392 he forgot that the king did not finally carry out his threats — of this final settlement he had no note. Relying perhaps on the recollections of some of the participants, the Monk quite often gives a well-informed report on the substance of diplomatic negotiations — those, for example, between John of Gaunt and Juan I of Castile, in 1387 and 1388[1] — but is mistaken about details; and we can sympathize with his difficulty in remembering which had been the acts of the parliament of November 1390 and which those of the parliament which met exactly a year later.[2]

(iii) *Value*

The Westminster Chronicle must have been described as 'well informed' more frequently than any other chronicle of the period, and the compliment is paid not only to its dense, well-ordered narrative of events at home and abroad, but also to the intimate knowledge which its authors, especially the Monk of Westminster, seem to have possessed of what people thought and felt and said about those events at the time. The following evaluation will not, it is hoped, seriously undermine the high repute of the work. It will, however, take into account the fact that it was composed after some little lapse of time from the events recorded in it and the extent to which each author relied on memory.

Diplomatic History

The weight given to the diplomatic history of the period and the detailed treatment of this theme are remarkable by any standards. Quite frequently we are told the names of the English envoys serving on the several missions of the period, when they went overseas ('crossed to Calais') and when they returned. The Monk of Westminster liked to record the reaction of king and council to diplomatic manœuvres in France, Flanders, and the Spanish peninsula, and he traced an intimate connection between English diplomacy and domestic politics in the 1380s and 1390s: Richard II's supposed intention to relinquish English claims to sovereignty

---

[1] Below, p. 194 and n.   [2] Below, p. 454 and n.

in Aquitaine was one of the occasions of the Appellants' rising in 1387;[1] and when a few years later John of Gaunt supported the French demand that Richard II relinquish his rights in Aquitaine, and Thomas of Woodstock acquiesced in the proposal, Thomas's weakness brought on his own political decline.[2]

In one or two cases the particularity of the information is explained quite simply by the fact that the writer was a monk of Westminster. In March 1382 the English envoys to France made their report at a council to which the abbot of Westminster had been summoned and at which, presumably, he was present.[3] The Monk's dossier on the abbot of Nonantola's mission to England in 1391 was probably sent to the Abbey by a government anxious to publish its own view of the case: Walsingham seems to have enjoyed the same facility at St. Albans.[4] But the diplomatic entries as a whole cannot be explained in this way: they suggest very strongly that the Monk (who was responsible for most of them if not for all) drew on the knowledge and experience of one or more of the envoys of the period, or that he himself served on embassies; and both explanations could, of course, be true. It is unlikely that the Monk had more than a minor role in the solemn embassies of the period, for no monk of Westminster is named in the surviving procurations for these; but even a minor role, in the retinue, perhaps, of one of the appointed envoys, would have given him not only first-hand experience of the diplomatic scene but also access to otherwise confidential documents. Which is the correct inference?

If the substance rather than the detail of the diplomatic entries is considered, it becomes clear that the Monk wrote of English diplomacy as an outsider, not a participant — an interested and well-informed observer, but a mere observer

---

[1] Below, p. 204.   [2] Below, p. 518.

[3] Below, p. 24; but see also p. lxi. The abbot was Nicholas Litlington. William Colchester, Litlington's successor, is described as a royal councillor in a French source in 1396 and may have been sworn of the council by that date and perhaps considerably earlier. See *Anglo-Norman Letters and Petitions*, ed. M. D. Legge (Oxford, 1941), p. 240. It is to be noted that the chronicler continues to be unusually knowledgeable about diplomatic affairs and the response to them at home in 1392, when Colchester was at the papal curia: he had other sources of information.

[4] Below, p. 462 n.

none the less. His viewpoint is usually that of a man who stayed at home. His account of Anglo-French negotiations in the early months of 1391, for example, is centred on the council and not at Calais and betrays no little confusion about the course and content of the negotiations.[1] It is hard to believe that his thoroughly muddled account of the Gascon mission to England at the end of 1390 (which he misdates) and its consequences was written by one acquainted at first hand with the bundle of diplomatic questions involved.[2]

Though not himself a participant, the Monk, clearly, was acquainted with some who were. His account of the Anglo-French negotiations at Calais in the summer of 1384 is based on the report of an eye-witness who observed that the French expressed themselves 'pompose' and dwelt on irrelevancies.[3] His summary of the truce of Leulingham of 1389 goes beyond the published text and is probably based on oral report.[4] He had probably not seen a copy of the protocol of the conference at Leulingham in July 1390, for he did not summarize its contents, but evidently someone had told him of its existence.[5] As a rule he was able to discover the names of some of the envoys serving on missions, if not of all, and when the missions effectively began and ended; and on a few occasions he lists an envoy who is not named in the main procuration of the embassy.[6] Who were the key witnesses on whom he relied?

On general grounds — their connections with the Abbey — and for specific reasons, we must include John of Gaunt and Thomas of Woodstock and members of their respective households in the list. For example, it was probably from someone serving in Gaunt's retinue, if not from Gaunt himself, that the Monk heard of his visit to the king at Eltham on 1 February 1384 — the only precise date given in the passage in question — to report on the current Anglo-French negotiations.[7] One or two entries in the Chronicle suggest that John Gilbert, bishop successively of Bangor,

[1] Below, pp. 456–8 nn.
[2] Below, p. 484 and n.
[3] Below, p. 88.
[4] Below, p. 398 and n.
[5] Below, p. 436.
[6] For examples see below, pp. 374 and 514; see also p. 28.
[7] Below, pp. 56–8.

Hereford, and St. David's and a much used diplomat, was a source of information. Gilbert is one of the only two envoys named in the notice of the Anglo-French negotiations early in 1382.[1] He is one of the envoys who did in fact set out for Calais 'about the end of June' 1384,[2] and in later passages the Monk twice refers to the bishop, who was a Dominican, rather informally as 'Brother Gilbert'.[3] The Monk's notice of negotiations early in 1386 suggests that his informant was Walter Skirlaw, bishop of 'Chester', or the Chancery official, Mr. Richard Ronhale, or someone travelling with one or other of these envoys: their known dates for this mission tally with the Monk's.[4] In November 1388, however, Skirlaw and Ronhale crossed to Calais a week or more after the date given by the Monk (5 December). His informant on this occasion may have been Mr. John Sheppey or one of Sheppey's companions.[5]

No connection between the envoys just mentioned and the Abbey has come to light — not even in Gilbert's case can one be proved. It is in fact likely that the Monk's informants served in the retinues of these principal envoys. Was it perhaps in this way that Br. Thomas Merks came to the notice of Richard II and prepared himself for the role of a fully fledged ambassador that was entrusted to him in the Anglo-German negotiations of 1397, just after the Monk put down his pen?[6]

It is now possible to evaluate the famous passages relating to English sovereignty in Aquitaine referred to above. Is it true, in the first place, that as early as 1387 Richard II entertained a proposal, favoured by some of his counsellors, that he do homage to the king of France for Aquitaine? According to the Monk of Westminster the rumour that he was prepared to pay this price for peace with France or even — for on this point the writer is confused — for a truce, was one of the occasions of the Appellants' rising.[7] The Monk

---

[1] Below, p. 24.   [2] Below, p. 88 and n.   [3] Below, pp. 382, 402.
[4] Below, p. 160 and n. For Skirlaw and Ronhale see P. Chaplais, 'English Diplomatic Documents, 1377-99', in *Reign of Richard II*, p. 35.
[5] Below, p. 374 and n. Sheppey (the only envoy in the Monk's list who is not named in the procuration) is the only one, except Devereux, whose accounts do not indicate a later crossing, and the Monk himself tells us that Devereux crossed later.   [6] Rymer, *Foedera*, vii. 858.   [7] Below, p. 204.

does not report the proposal unsympathetically — on the contrary, he points out that unless the king were to make peace, he could not avoid taxing his people. But the passage as a whole is clearly indebted to propaganda on behalf of the Appellants. Quite possibly its catalogue of reasons for the rising of the Appellants was taken from the source which supplied the Monk with most of his narrative for the period 11 November 1387 to 18 January 1388.[1] The passage was written not less than two years after the event and probably after a considerably longer interval. It is full of hindsight. When the king's principal counsellors were appealed of treason in the Merciless Parliament in 1388, such a proposal was not mentioned.[2] We cannot rely on the Monk's testimony.

The demand that Richard II relinquish his claim to sovereign rights in Aquitaine was put forward by the French at Amiens in the spring of 1392.[3] John of Gaunt, the principal English envoy who was met by the king on his return, brought this and other French proposals before a council at Stamford in May of that year and before parliament in January 1394.[4] It is in his account of the latter occasion that the Monk seems to portray Gaunt as, not simply the mouthpiece of the proposed settlement with France, but a committed proponent who had his own selfish reasons for wishing to see a treaty on these lines sealed, and he mentions the common report that Thomas of Woodstock was bribed into acquiescence in Gaunt's 'perversissima intencio'. No such treaty was sealed. The passage is important, first, because it seems to catch the mood of the political nation which rejected it, and, secondly, for its portrayal of the duke of Gloucester as his brother's dupe. This interpretation of Gloucester's attitude is very different from that of Sir Richard Stury, which found its way into the pages of Froissart.[5] Stury, one of Richard II's chamber knights, believed that Gloucester connived at Gaunt's ambitions in Aquitaine because he was anxious to see Gaunt removed from the English scene, and he expressed this view to

---

[1] For which see above, pp. lii–iv.   [2] But cf. *Palmer*, pp. 117–18.
[3] Cf. below, p. 486, where the Monk notes the conference in question but locates it at St. Omer.
[4] Below, pp. 490, 516–18.   [5] Froissart, *Chroniques*, xv. 165–6.

Froissart as he emerged from further discussions in council in 1395. The Monk's account may have been written two or even three years after the event; it was certainly not written contemporaneously. The Monk is consistently hostile to Gaunt, who may indeed be described as the anti-hero of the work. This in fact is precisely the kind of passage in the Monk's work that we do well to treat circumspectly.

English Politics

Our knowledge of the political history of Richard II's reign would be the poorer at many points had the Westminster Chronicle never been written. We should lack, for example, the best account that survives of the parliament at Salisbury in 1384,[1] the unique text of the common petition underlying the Statute of Cambridge,[2] and an account of the council at Stamford in May 1392 that is evidently based on the report of an eye-witness.[3] But the most important pages in the Chronicle under this head are those devoted to the rise to power of the Appellants in 1387 and their triumph in the Merciless Parliament the following year.[4]

Throughout these pages, the Monk's standpoint is that of someone observing the political scene from London and Westminster, and, except where he draws directly on propaganda supplied by the Appellants, he is poorly informed about events at a distance from the capital: he did not know, for example, the dates and correct sequence of the councils held by Richard II on his 'gyration' in 1387.[5] His main informant on the Appellant movement as a whole was no doubt the duke of Gloucester. Certainly Gloucester's intimacy at the Abbey lends authority to the story of the chance meeting between himself and the archbishop of Dublin in October 1387 that precipitated the Appellants' first act of disobedience to the king;[6] and it is probably Gloucester's voice that we hear in the apology for the rising to which this story is the epilogue. From 11 November 1387 to 18 January 1388, however, the Monk's narrative is indebted, if we are right, to a text originating in the circle of the earl of Warwick

---

[1] Below, pp. 66 ff.
[2] Below, pp. 356 ff.
[3] Below, pp. 488–90.
[4] Below, pp. 204 ff.
[5] Below, p. 186 and nn.
[6] Below, p. 206.

and written soon after the conclusion of the events which it describes. This narrative includes one of the best-known passages in the entire chronicle: the account of the armed encounter between the Appellants and Robert de Vere on 20 December 1387.[1]

The final article of the Appeal against de Vere presented in parliament on 3 February 1388 (Article 39) accused him of displaying the royal banner at Radcot Bridge in the company of forces which had marched with him across England from Lancashire, Cheshire, and Wales.[2] This is the earliest surviving account of his encounter with the Appellants, and it probably explains how it is that the brief campaign has come to be known as that of Radcot Bridge, despite the uncertain witness of the chronicles on this point. The Monk places the main engagement, not at Radcot Bridge, but between a point north of Stow-on-the-Wold and Witney;[3] de Vere had large numbers in his company when he reached Radcot Bridge, but he came there as a fugitive — a man already beaten. This, it appears, was the version of events current in the circle of the earl of Warwick. The Monk probably put this part of his chronicle into its final form not less than four or five years after the event. But even if we date his account of the campaign by this, the time of final compilation, and not by the date when his source was composed, his is still one of the earliest narratives of the episode. The only notice of the campaign that was certainly written earlier, a very short account in the register of Henry de Wakefield, bishop of Worcester, agrees with the Monk in bringing de Vere to Radcot Bridge as a fugitive.[4] Knighton, writing at much the same time as the Monk, places the main engagement at Radcot Bridge: according to his account, the hero of the occasion was Henry, earl of Derby, who had

[1] Below, p. 220 ff. For indispensable comment see J. N. L. Myres, 'The Campaign of Radcot Bridge in December 1387', in *E.H.R.*, xlii (1927), 20 ff.

[2] Below, p. 268.

[3] Cf. Myres, art. cit., p. 24, where the Monk's account is understood as locating the engagement *at* Witney. The actual site of the encounter described by the Monk was probably, as Dr. Myres suggests, Burford.

[4] R. G. Davies, 'Some notes from the register of Henry de Wakefield, bishop of Worcester, on the political crisis of 1386–1388', in *E.H.R.*, lxxxvi (1971), 557; and for the suggestion that the note was written in the summer of 1388, see ibid., p. 549. Wakefield had connections with the duke of Gloucester.

occupied the bridge in anticipation of de Vere's arrival.[1]
Knighton here no doubt expresses the tradition which St.
Mary's Abbey, Leicester, received from Derby himself, its
patron. Of two versions of events, each indebted to a source
from among the Appellants, which is to be believed? Article
39 of the Appeal must mean that the main engagement on
20 December was at Radcot Bridge. But the conflicting testi-
monies of the participants in these events are evidence that
the division which opened in the ranks of the Appellants
before the Merciless Parliament was over was in existence
from very nearly the beginning of their enterprise.[2]

The Monk includes two accounts of the Merciless Parliament in his chronicle. One of these is not his own work but
a product of Chancery, of great value for the light it sheds on
the mentality of those who finally put together that other
product of Chancery — the official version of events in the
Rolls of Parliament.[3] The Monk's own narrative of the parliament was probably composed later than Thomas Favent's,
than which it is less rhetorical, less vivid, more substantial,
and much better informed about procedure.[4] It is a particularly important source for the trial of Nicholas Brembre and
that of Simon Burley, both of which are described with a
frankness entirely lacking in the official version. But for the
Monk we should not know of the decision of a committee of
twelve Lords of parliament on 19 February that Brembre
was accused of nothing meriting death, or of the counter-
move of his accusers who appealed to representatives of city
gilds and to the City authorities to support his condemnation.[5] He corroborates Favent's testimony that the king tried
to save Burley's life; but he did not know or did not care to
record the division that opened in the ranks of the Appellants
themselves at this juncture.[6] Above all, he hits off the

---

[1] *Chronicon*, ii. 252; and for the date of this work, V. H. Galbraith, 'The
chronicle of Henry Knighton', in *Fritz Saxl, 1890–1948*, ed. D. J. Gordon
(London, 1957), pp. 136 ff.

[2] Cf. K. B. McFarlane, *Lancastrian Kings and Lollard Knights* (Oxford, 1972),
pp. 31–2.

[3] Below, pp. 280 ff.; and see above, pp. xlvii–l.

[4] Below, pp. 308 ff.; *Favent, passim*.

[5] Below, pp. 310, 312–14; cf. *Favent*, p. 17.

[6] Below, pp. 328–30; cf. *Favent*, p. 21.

character of these proceedings well — their mood so much more savage, their ordering so much more a matter of improvisation than the official version would have us believe. His attempts to rationalize what he or his informants observed often have the ring of truth. For example, on 12 March Simon Burley attempted to respond to the charges against him in detail before submitting to the requirement that he enter a comprehensive plea of 'Guilty' or 'Not Guilty' to the charge as a whole, and the denial of the right to respond was a severe setback to his chances of a fair trial. But it was also the case that his very readiness to respond incriminated him, since, though rebutting most of the accusations, he admitted their truth in one or two particulars. Burley, it seems, realized this and in some confusion ceased to respond even as the right to do so was formally denied to him. The Monk's description of the scene at this juncture is a just and penetrating piece of observation.[1]

The Chronicle is our principal narrative source for the transaction of the general business of the realm in the Merciless Parliament. It records, for example, the authorization by Lords and Commons on 21 February of a naval expedition and the appointment of the earl of Arundel to the command,[2] and the decision on 20 April to appoint ambassadors to treat with the Flemings and with the Prussian towns of the German Hanse.[3]

London Affairs

In the 1380s the politics of the City of London were disordered to a degree not experienced since the 1260s, a revolutionary decade.[4] For a short time, and perhaps uniquely in the City's history, the victualling and non-victualling gilds ranged themselves in opposing camps, and their mutual hostility, fed on the non-victualling side by London's chronic anxiety about food supplies, sharpened every occasion on which a gild interest was at stake. At the same time, the mutual distrust of the small artisan and trader, on the one hand, and the substantial London capitalist on the

---

[1] Below, p. 318. [2] Below, p. 314. [3] Below, p. 330.
[4] On the subject-matter of this paragraph, see R. Bird, *The Turbulent London of Richard II* (London, 1949), *passim*.

other, obstinately refused to die down after its sensational airing during the Peasants' Revolt. These areas of conflict overlapped but did not coincide, and to this circumstance is owing much of the confusion of the City's domestic politics in this decade.

The Monk of Westminster, taking over as he did a chronicle in which London's internal dissensions at the time of the Revolt had been barely mentioned, blamed the mayoralty of John Northampton (1381 to 1383) for the lamentable divisions of the ensuing years.[1] His vivid account of Northampton's trial before the council at Reading in 1384 is evidence of a connection between Northampton and John of Gaunt. When the king, exasperated with Northampton's demeanour, was about to proceed to judgement, Northampton questioned the propriety of his doing so in Gaunt's absence: he flaunted his own connection with Gaunt — whatever form that took — and humiliated the young king with a hint of his dependence on his uncle.[2] Just how pointed the insult to Richard II was depends on the veracity of an earlier passage in the Chronicle. The first writer says here that on a visit to the king at Kennington in February 1382 for the confirmation of their liberties, the mayor, who was John Northampton, and citizens of London expressed the wish that they might have only one king; and the next day John of Gaunt left London in haste.[3] On the face of it an unlikely story. Yet it is just possible that Northampton's insult to the king in 1384 played on their common recollection of this earlier episode.

The reference to an attempt on Gaunt's part to obtain Northampton's release at the end of the second parliament of 1385 is well founded, despite the touch of incoherence in what the Monk says at this point.[4] The episode occasioned the exchange of letters between Gaunt and the City authorities several months later which is preserved in the City's own records. The description of Brembre's election as mayor in 1383 and that of his re-election in 1384 afford rare insight into the City's electoral processes at this time.[5]

---

[1] Below, p. 404.   [2] Below, p. 92.
[3] Below, p. 24.   [4] Below, pp. 148–50 and n.
[5] Below, pp. 60–2, 100–2.

Yet neither in respect of the early 1380s nor of later years was the Monk quite as well informed about the City's internal affairs as might be expected of one with his exceptional opportunities for learning. He did not know of or, if he knew of it, care to record the vain appeal of Northampton and his supporters to John of Gaunt (then residing in the abbot's house at La Neyte) to set aside Brembre's election in 1383;[1] and he attributed ordinances enacted during Brembre's first year to his third year.[2] He rightly admired Adam Bamme's success in mitigating the consequences of dearth in the winter of 1390 to 1391 but did not mention and may not have known of or remembered Bamme's most striking measure, the use of £400 from the orphan fund for the purchase of corn.[3] Not a little of the importance of his account of Richard II's quarrel with the City in 1392 stems from the fact that he mistook interim peace proposals for the king's final terms to the Londoners and recorded them in detail.[4] For the rank and file members of the gilds the Monk felt little sympathy, deeming their testimony against Brembre in the Merciless Parliament but 'verba superflua'.[5] He was contemptuous of the willingness, as he believed, of the mercers, the goldsmiths, and the drapers in 1388 to breach the cherished judicial privileges of the City, if only they could bring down Nicholas Exton.[6] Himself a member of a privileged body, the Monk found such behaviour incomprehensible.

The Monk comes into his own as a chronicler of the City's affairs in his account of the crisis of 1387 to 1388. He records six appeals to the City, or attempts to woo opinion there, on the part of the king or the Appellants between 28 October 1387 and 19 February 1388, and in each case he is an indispensable authority — in some cases the only authority — for the episode in question. On the first occasion, on 28 October 1387, the king, through Alexander Nevill and Michael de la Pole, solicited the support of the mayor,

---

[1] Cf. *Book of London English, 1384-1425*, ed. Chambers and Daunt, p. 28.
[2] Below, p. 136 and n.   [3] Below, p. 474 and n.
[4] Below, pp. 506-8 and n.; cf. C. M. Barron, 'The Quarrel of Richard II with London, 1392-7', in *Reign of Richard II*, pp. 191-2 and n.
[5] Below, p. 312.   [6] Below, pp. 334-6 and n.

Nicholas Exton, and the citizens of London, in terms that
must have reminded a worried citizenry of the daunting
oaths of allegiance extracted from its members only a few
weeks earlier, in the last days of Nicholas Brembre's mayoralty.[1] A fortnight later, on 10 November, the king, with
Tresilian, Pole, and Robert de Vere, came from Sheen to
take up residence in his palace at Westminster and was
received at the Abbey *en route*.[2] The Monk's source for
the king's approach to Londoners on 28 October was, then,
authoritative, and we may suggest that the fulsome promise
of support for Richard that he puts into the mouths of
the Londoners on this occasion echoed the very words
in which the foolhardy Tresilian and Pole made their report
to a credulous king. The next four episodes span the period
from 28 November 1387 to 18 January 1388. They belong
to the period for which the Monk's narrative as a whole
is probably indebted to a text originating in the circle of
the Appellants.[3] The partisan character of his source is
perhaps betrayed by a phrase in his account of the Appellants' attendance at Guildhall on 30 December, in the aftermath of Radcot Bridge. There, he says, they explained 'under
what legal forms'[4] they had done what they had done. The
confidence that the recent activities of the Appellants were
covered by 'legal forms' suggests a partisan source. By contrast, the Monk's account of the Appellants' attempt on 17
and 18 January to restore peace to the gilds by arranging for
complaints to be heard by a tribunal which included themselves breaks away from its text to explain how it was that a
deafening silence greeted the proposal: the citizens feared
that the members of the tribunal were not as impartial as
they should have been.

The Peasants' Revolt
The pages devoted to the Peasants' Revolt contain the most
ambitious and lively piece of composition in the entire

[1] Below, p. 206. For the oaths see below, pp. 233, 264.
[2] Below, pp. 206-8.
[3] Below, p. 216 (where the episode of 28 Nov. is assigned to 30 Nov.); p. 224
(in late Dec. the citizens parry the king's attempt to requisition accommodation);
p. 226 (30 Dec.); pp. 232-4 (17-18 Jan.).
[4] 'Sub qua forma'. For this phrase see also below, pp. 400, 456.

chronicle.[1] Here indeed is a *tour de force* — an apparently circumstantial account of the Revolt in London which exculpates Londoners. The rebels who ran amok in London between 13 and 15 June 1381 were 'rurales rustici' from Kent and Essex, 'servi', a 'rustica manus'; the point is reiterated too often for us to doubt its importance to the chronicler. But there was, of course, a risk that the commons of the City would join in, and it was fear of provoking them that kept the City authorities in a state of dithering uncertainty while London was looted and fired around them.[2] The chronicler has written what amounts to an apology for the aldermen whose failure to act decisively against the rebels later brought on their heads a charge of being accomplices in the Revolt. Though we know, as he must have done, that others beside 'rustici' participated in the violence in London, his description of the fearful yet well-intentioned indecision of the City authorities at this time rings true.

The chronicler's insight, like the art of these pages considered as a whole, reflects the distance of several years separating him from the events he described: there had been time for reflection. But equally, there had been time to forget, and this no doubt explains the gaps in his narrative — most conspicuously in the case of Thursday, 13 June, when he had nothing to relate before the late afternoon.[3] His narrative lacked details such as the sack of Southwark and

[1] Below, pp. 2–18. I am much indebted to Mr. Andrew Prescott, who generously allowed me to read two unpublished papers, one on the reliability of the Westminster Chronicle and the Anonimalle Chronicle as sources for the Peasants' Revolt in London, and the other on the suppression of the Revolt. The responsibility for the opinions expressed in the following paragraphs is entirely my own. For the Revolt in London see now Caroline Barron, *Revolt in London: 11th to 15th June 1381* (London: Museum of London, 1981) and references given there. For Londoners accused of complicity in the Revolt, see *R.P.*, iii. 112, 113; *Calendar of Plea and Memoranda Rolls . . . of the City of London, A.D. 1364–81*, ed. A. H. Thomas (Cambridge, 1929), pp. 288–91. M. Honeybourne, *A Sketch Map of London under Richard II* (London Topographical Soc., no. 93, 1960) is indispensable.

[2] Below, p. 8.

[3] Below, p. 4. Cf. *Anon. Chron.*, pp. 140–1. The differences between the Monk's account of events on 13 June and that of the Anonimalle writer are among the cogent reasons for regarding the two sources as independent of each other. This point is expounded in the 1st of the 2 papers by Mr. Prescott mentioned in n. 1 above. But cf. *Anon. Chron.*, pp. xlii–iii; V. H. Galbraith, 'Thoughts about the Peasants' Revolt', in *Reign of Richard II*, p. 50.

the Temple that were known to some other chroniclers writing at a distance from the capital. At three points, however, he gratified his preference for giving not only the date but also the time of day, if he could: the Palace of the Savoy was attacked at about 4 p.m. on 13 June; the priory of St. John at Clerkenwell at dusk the same day, and after that Robert Hales's manor at Highbury; and Archbishop Sudbury and his fellow victims were executed at Tower Hill at 11 a.m. on 14 June.

According to the Anonimalle Chronicle, Londoners set parts of the Savoy on fire before the arrival of rebels from the country who systematically sacked and fired the contents.[1] It is this latter work of thorough destruction that our chronicler places in the late afternoon of 13 June. If he is right, he lends support to Walsingham's belief that the rebels, once in the City, took some time to decide on their next move. Walsingham relates much wooing of the populace of London and discussion of plans early on 13 June, and then, when the sun was very high and had grown warm, an agreement between the men of Kent and Essex and lower-class Londoners to attack the Savoy.[2] This indecision, and the orgies of drinking which Walsingham also describes, may well have delayed the departure of the main body of rebels for the western suburbs until the afternoon. Anyone familiar with medieval reckonings of time will know that the 'twilight' to which the chronicler assigns the attack on Clerkenwell could be long drawn out. He means us to understand that the event took place very late in the evening of 13 June and was the work of rebels who had moved on Clerkenwell from the Savoy and who went on to destroy the manor house at Highbury at an hour which he does not describe but which seems to belong in his account to Thursday, 13 June rather than Friday, the 14th.[3] Highbury was in fact destroyed on 14 June.[4] This correction, however, leaves the sequence of

[1] *Anon. Chron.*, pp. 141-2.

[2] *Hist. Ang.*, i. 456-7. The abortive meeting between the king and rebels arranged, according to the Anonimalle chronicler, for Prime [sunrise?] on 12 June should probably be placed on 13 June (*Anon. Chron.*, pp. 138-40; cf. Froissart, *Chroniques*, ix. 398-9).   [3] Below, p. 4.

[4] *Réville*, pp. 195, 204, 210; Walsingham, *Hist. Ang.*, i. 467; C. Oman, *The Great Revolt of 1381* (Oxford, 1969), p. 211.

events as given in the Chronicle — the attacks on the Savoy, Clerkenwell, and Highbury — unshaken, and if the events occurred in this sequence it may also be true that all three outrages were the work of a body of rebels who had come via the City of London.

The chronicler tells us not only that the execution of Archbishop Sudbury and others on Tower Hill on 14 June took place at 11 a.m., but also that the rebels entered the Tower while Richard II's meeting with the rebels at Mile End was in progress.[1] The second detail may seem to conflict with the account of the executions in the Anonimalle Chronicle. Here the executions occur after the meeting at Mile End and in consequence of the permission there given to the rebels to take all who were traitors to the king.[2] The same story is enrolled in the Letter Book of the City of London:[3] it was what the authorities wished people to believe about the executions. It is possible that the executions followed on the pretext of some rash words of the king at Mile End and yet took place before the main crowd of rebels gathered there had dispersed. Whether Sudbury's executioners had come hotfoot from Mile End or were a separate group of rebels seizing the chance offered by the king's absence to gain entry to the Tower, the meeting at Mile End, which, says Anonimalle, was arranged for 7 a.m.,[4] begins to seem a protracted affair, and this is the value of our chronicler's time for the executions. By his silence he corrects the Anonimalle writer in one other particular, for if, as the latter says, the heads of the victims on Tower Hill were carried by their triumphant executioners even to the shrine of St. Edward the Confessor in Westminster Abbey,[5] our chronicler would not have omitted the sacrilegious detail.

The King

Richard II has the unusual distinction among English kings of having executed his most successful stratagem at the age of

---

[1] Below, p. 6.   [2] *Anon. Chron.*, p. 145.

[3] Riley, *Memorials*, pp. 449–50; R. B. Dobson, *The Peasants' Revolt of 1381* (London, 1970), p. 210. Cf. McFarlane, *Lancastrian Kings and Lollard Knights*, p. 18.

[4] See below, p. 6 n.; but cf. G. Kriehn, 'Studies in the sources of the social revolt in 1381', in *American Historical Review*, vii (1901–2), 279 n.

[5] *Anon. Chron.*, p. 145.

fourteen. The occasion was his meeting with the rebels at
Smithfield on 15 June 1381, and the Westminster Chronicle
is one of our sources for this high moment.[1] Richard is seen
to advantage in the Chronicle on other occasions beside this
one: at a critical point in the course of the Merciless Parliament, for example, he made peace between his uncles,
Gloucester and York; and he acted with great prudence on
assuming his majority in 1389.[2] Nearly all these later
successes, however — which were, in the nature of things, less
sensational than the king's triumph at Smithfield — occurred
in or after 1388. Similarly, the king's character as seen
through the eyes of the Monk takes a turn for the better at
about the same time. The early Richard, though capable of
a calm demeanour in trying circumstances,[3] is apt to lose his
temper and self-control,[4] abuses Lancaster, and is even considered by some to plot against him,[5] contemplates the
murder of Gloucester,[6] lusts for glory,[7] and goes into a huff
when thwarted.[8] The later Richard puts up patiently with the
changes effected in his household by the Appellants,[9] is of a
mild and kindly nature,[10] consents to a reconciliation with
the Appellants,[11] and instead of losing his temper — as we
may suspect the early Richard would have done — when
Lancaster asks him to pardon John Northampton, allows
himself to be persuaded, making only a hesitant reference to
the possibility of other pardons much nearer his heart.[12]
Though given to pomp and ceremony, he is a humane king,
alarmed by the danger of jousting with unrebated lances.[13]
The later Richard behaves like a real person; the early
Richard more resembles a caricature. The later Richard
behaves with considerable circumspection; the early Richard
needs the tutelage which he receives in such abundance.

The apparent progression in the king's character and
behaviour is laid bare within the compass of the Monk of
Westminster's work and owes little or nothing to the change

[1] Below, pp. 10–12.   [2] Below, pp. 328, 392.
[3] Below, p. 114. For sagacity on an earlier occasion, see p. 54.
[4] Below, pp. 68, 92, 116.   [5] Below, pp. 110, 130.
[6] Below, p. 184.   [7] Below, p. 138.
[8] Below, p. 186.   [9] Below, p. 232.
[10] Below, p. 502; cf. p. 328.   [11] Below, pp. 406–8.
[12] Below, p. 440.   [13] Below, p. 436.

of authorship occurring, if we are right, c.1383. It is explained in part by the Monk's own changing circumstances in
relation to his subject. To state the obvious, he was further
removed in time from the king's early years than from the
later: his early pages are perhaps more indebted to other
people's reminiscences than to his own observation. Almost
certainly, however, some change in the king himself underlies
the contrast between the violent-tempered boy of the Monk's
early pages and the mild young man of the later; if not, how
was it that memory and observation picked out such different things? Was the change in fact of the kind that a plain
reading of the Chronicle would suggest? At this point we do
well to remember the Monk's limitations as a writer — he was
honest but not profound, energetic but incapable of finesse —
and the possibility of deception in some of the forms of
behaviour which he had occasion to describe. If unbridled
temper in the nature of things always betrays itself for what
it is, a mild and kindly manner can cloak subtle purpose,
devious contrivance, and low cunning. When Richard II,
showing what the Monk describes as characteristic mildness
and good will, intervened to pacify York and Gloucester in
the Merciless Parliament, he was intent upon saving his friend
Simon Burley, whom York wished to spare but Gloucester
to condemn;[1] and when, in 1392, the mild and kindly king,
yielding to the pleas of his prostrate queen, pardoned the
citizens of London for offences the nature of which may
have been not much easier for some of them to understand
than for ourselves, the price of his mercy was to be a fine in
the enormous sum of £40,000 and a ceremonial reception for
the king on a scale calculated to empty scores of well-lined
purses.[2] Without doubt, Richard was quite as vainglorious as
he had ever been. What he had perhaps learnt from the
calamitous events of the winter of 1387 to 1388 was the
necessity of often dissembling, proceeding adroitly, and
biding his time.[3] Arguably, the conventions of the chronicler's
art made it difficult for the Monk to impute attitudes such as
these to a royal subject, even if he correctly identified them;
or adjectives like 'clemens' and 'benignus' may themselves

---

[1] Below, p. 328.   [2] Below, pp. 502–4.
[3] Cf. A. Steel, *Richard II* (Cambridge, 1941), pp. 174 ff.

have been conventional descriptions of kingly virtue. But it is hard to believe that inhibitions of the former kind or the need to conform to literary convention weighed heavily with a chronicler who had already revealed so much about the king that was to his discredit and, of its kind, quite sensational. More likely, the Monk failed to understand the new and quieter Richard II. If the king did indeed put on new ways at about this time, it is a measure of his success that they to some extent deceived the chronicler better placed than any other for observing them. As a witness to the most difficult of all the topics demanding attention in Richard II's reign — the character of the king himself — the Monk of Westminster was rich in material but a little naïve in judgement. On that note this appraisal of his work may well end, for the combination of strength and weakness is characteristic of the whole.

Previous Edition

The Westminster Chronicle was edited by J. R. Lumby in 1886, in the ninth and final volume of his edition of the *Polychronicon* and as an appendix to the latter.[1] Lumby, however, attributed the work to John of Malvern, whose continuation of the *Polychronicon* to 1381 precedes the Chronicle in the unique MS. His edition, at the time a major contribution to the historical literature of the late fourteenth century, does not conform to modern editorial conventions and standards of accuracy, and it has long been recognized that a replacement is needed.

Note on Editing

The Monk of Westminster's Latin was singularly prone to error, but in this edition few of his mistakes have been corrected in the text and some have been passed in silence, without even a caution to the reader in a footnote. To do otherwise would have been to print a cluttered text, quite unnecessarily burdened with critical apparatus. The following pairs of words, in each case occasionally run together in the manuscript, are printed separately: *de difficili, de facili, de*

---

[1] *Higden,* ix.

novo, fide digno, in dies, in vanum, post futuris, sui ipsius, una cum. Ex inde, written thus in the manuscript, is printed as one word.

In the French text abbreviations have been extended, as far as possible, in accordance with what appear to be the conventions of the passage in question. Since the Monk was a copyist in these portions of his work, and since neither he himself nor the scribes whose work he copied achieved consistency, the conventions change from time to time and there are variants even within the space of a single extract. The reader will find, for example, *qe* and *que*, *qi*, and *qui*; and sometimes *qe* or *que* in the nominative form, sometimes not.

Throughout the volume, *i* and *u* have been used as vowels, *j* and *v* as consonants. Punctuation and capital letters have been modernized. Conjectural emendations to the text, unless otherwise attributed, are the work of Mr. Hector. Italics denote marginal captions or marginal numerals in the manuscript. Except where otherwise stated in the apparatus, marginalia in the manuscript appear to be in the main hand. Only those containing substance not found in the main text have been translated. The dates in the margins of the edition are editorial; the page references in the margin of the text are to the manuscript.

In the collation with other texts, variant spellings which can be deemed to lie wholly within the competence of a scribe normally pass unnoticed. Occasionally, however, such variants, or the common use of an unusual spelling, may help to establish the relationship between the Monk's text and his source or a related source. In these cases mere differences of spelling are noted. For example, both the Monk and *W*, the source of much of his account of the Merciless Parliament, used the forms *comines* and *cominalte* from time to time, in preference to *comunes* and *comunalte*, and in these cases the agreement between the two is noted. (The abbreviated form *cõẽs* has been extended in every case as *comunes*.)

Even when scribal variants are ignored, there remain many points at which the Monk's version of official and semi-official documents differs from others in existence, and these versions severally from each other. Some pages in the text printed below are burdened, therefore, with many textual notes. It may be urged on behalf of this critical apparatus that it demonstrates a noteworthy feature of Richard II's England, namely the lack in both Church and State of the idea of a single, authoritative text of official documents. This lack may not have passed unnoticed by those who, appealed or impeached of treason in the Merciless Parliament, struggled to answer written charges 'point by point'; and it was not without influence on their fate.

In the Introduction, '1375 to 1376', etc., denotes the year of account, beginning on 29 September.

B. F. H.

CHRONICON WESTMONASTERIENSE
1381-1394

CHRONICON WESTMONASTERIENSE
1381–1394

1381
p. 130
Isto anno circa Purificacionem beate Marie dirupta fuit magna pars pontis Roucestr'; fuerat quidem glacies inmensa, que postmodum tepido aere resoluta mole suarum parcium ponti incumbencium pontem confregit. Dominus de Latymer vitam relinquens temporalem mundo valefecit; hic denique per dominum Robertum Halys invitatus ad epulas de equo volens descendere subita paralisi raptus sermonem perdidit et mortem invenit.[1]

Ignobilis turba rusticorum surrexit. Eodem anno pridie Idus Junii coadunata fuit maxima multitudo ruralium Estsexie pariter et Cancie;[2] et hii quidem qui de Cancia per plures

p. 131
partes Cancie uti rabidissimi canes discurrentes / plurimorum domos et maneria solotenus diruerunt, nonnullos decapitaverunt, et quosque sibi occurrentes qui de eorum contubernio non fuerant ut eis adhererent et cum eis in defensionem regis Ricardi*a* interposito juramento constringebant, pretendentes se defensuros regem et regni commoditatem contra suos traditores. Quare concrescente eorum turba longe lateque debachabantur, magistrum Simonem de Sudbur' tunc archiepiscopum pariter et Anglie cancellarium proditorem esse asserentes et morte dignissimum; unde ad manerium suum de Lambhuth' descendentes libros, vestes, mappas, et plura alia inibi relicta igne combusserunt; dolia vino referta confregerunt et hauserunt, et quod vini fuerat relictum in terram effuderunt; singula coquine vasa adinvicem collidentes fregerunt; et ista perpetrantes velud de re laudabili plaudentes 'A revelle! A revelle!' exclamarunt.

a Supply irent *or some such word (Winterbottom).*

[1] William, Lord Latimer, died on 28 May 1381 (*Cal. Inq. p.m.*, xv. 375–84).

[2] The narrative of the Peasants' Revolt begins on the day when the main body of rebels from Kent gathered at Blackheath and that from Essex approached London north of the river. The first recorded act of open violence in Kent occurred on 2 June, at Lesnes, and that in Essex on 30 May or a little earlier, at

THE WESTMINSTER CHRONICLE
1381–1394

About the feast of the Purification of the Blessed Virgin 1381 [2 February] this year a great part of Rochester Bridge was destroyed. Ice had formed in vast quantities; and when it broke up, with the onset of milder weather, the massive pressure of the floes which had composed it wrecked the bridge. Lord Latimer made his farewell to the world and departed this earthly life: he had been asked to dinner by Sir Robert Hales and was about to dismount from his horse when he was seized by paralysis and parted with speech before meeting with death.[1]

Rising of the peasant rabble. On 12 June in this same year the peasants of Essex and Kent gathered together in very large numbers.[2] In Kent they behaved like the maddest of mad dogs, and ran wild over much of the county, razing to the ground the manors and houses of many landowners, beheading some people, and forcing everybody they met who was not of their fellowship into sworn association with themselves in the defence of King Richard, since they held themselves out as champions of the king and the welfare of the kingdom against those who were betraying them. In a throng thus growing ever denser they went rampaging far and wide, declaring that Master Simon Sudbury, at that time archbishop and also chancellor of England, was a traitor and that he richly deserved to die. Swooping upon his manor of Lambeth they set fire to most of its abandoned contents, including books, clothes, and linen; stove in wine-barrels and drained them, pouring what wine was left on to the floor; banged together and smashed all the kitchenware; and all the while accompanied this behaviour, as if in self-congratulation on some praiseworthy feat, with shouts of 'A revel! A revel!'

Brentwood; the general amnesty and the charters of pardon granted later in the year reckoned the time of the insurrection from 1 May. On the following account of events in and around London between 12 and 15 June, see above, pp. lxix–lxxii.

Acta. Acta sunt hec pridie Idus Junii, die videlicet Basilidis et Cirini, que dies tunc erat vigilia Corporis Christi. Interea archiepiscopus, manibus se querencium comprehendi timens, in regium fugit palacium, deinde ad regem in Turrim London'.

In crastino vero agrestis illa societas totum[a] stimulata in rabiem hora quasi quarta post nonam hospicium ducis vocatum le Savoye invaserunt, omnes clausuras disrumpentes, nichil quod preciosum erat parcentes quin illud aut igne combusserunt aut in Thamense flumen demergendum projecerunt.[1] Cerneres ibidem rem nostris seculis insolitam, nam dum preciosissima cernerent, tractarent, et colligerent, non audebat rustica manus preciosa furtivis manibus surripere, quia si quis in aliquo furto fuerat deprehensus, sine processu sive judicio ad mortem rapiebatur decapitandus.[2] Nec ista facientes saciati fuerunt vindicta quin ignem in pluribus locis inmittentes tam speciosum locum, tam insigne hospicium, in cineres redigerent. Super hoc in sequente noctis crepusculo ad locum Sancti Johannis de Fonte Clericorum pergentes quosque sibi resistentes interfecerunt universasque domos igne consumpserunt, set et manerium de Hybury, quod noviter construxerat Robertus Hales, tunc temporis loci prior et Anglie thesaurarius,[b][3] et aliorum maneria flammis voracibus delenda tradiderunt.

Ista ergo videntes tam archiepiscopus quam thesaurarius Anglie, et ex talibus principiis deteriores fines aucupantes et de vita sua desperantes, in Turri London' cum rege latuerunt. Tandem hoc cernens illa turbulenta et tumultuosa turba ruralium petiverunt ut rex ad eos accederet, tanquam colloquium habituri cum rege et pro regni negocio tractaturi; set metuentes tam archipresul quam thesaurarius ne regi et regno cederet in dampnum si illa furens turba postulata optineret non permiserunt regem ad eos accedere; unde cumulato furore agitati ad Turrim London' impetuose accesserunt et dicte[c] Turris minabantur ruinam nisi ad eos

[a] *Sic MS.*   [b] *MS.* thesaurararius.   [c] *MS.* dicti.

[1] Cf. *Anon. Chron.*, pp. 141–2, and *Réville*, pp. 199, 201–4, 211, both implicating men from the City and its environs as well as rebels from the country in the sack of the duke of Lancaster's palace of the Savoy and particularly its precincts.

Proceedings. Such was the story of 12 June, the feast of
SS. Basilides and Cyrinus, and that year the Eve of Corpus
Christi. Meanwhile the archbishop, fearful of falling into the
hands of those who were searching for him, fled to the royal
palace, later joining the king in the Tower of London.

About four in the afternoon on the following day the
peasantry, wrought up to a state of sheer frenzy, attacked the
duke's palace of the Savoy, where they burst through every
barrier and spared no article of value from destruction either
by burning or by being flung out to sink in the Thames.[1]
A spectacle was to be seen there that is not familiar in our
day: with priceless objects in full view and under their hands
as they assembled them, the yokel band did not dare to pur-
loin any of the valuables, since everybody caught in any act
of theft was haled away, without trial or judgement, to death
by beheading.[2] Their thirst for vengeance unsatisfied by what
they had so far done, they now started a fire at several points
and reduced to ashes all the beauty of that noble dwelling.
After this, as the evening twilight drew on, they made their
way to the priory of St. John at Clerkenwell and killing
everybody who offered any opposition burned down the
entire structure, going on to consign to destruction in the
ravening flames the manor of Highbury, just built by Robert
Hales, the then prior of St. John and treasurer of England,[3]
and manors belonging to other people besides.

Prepared, after witnessing these events, to see such a beginning followed by even worse consequences, and in despair for
their lives, the archbishop and the treasurer lay low in the
Tower of London with the king. When at length they became
aware of this, the riotous and disorderly mob of peasants demanded that the king should meet them, since they intended
to have conversations with him and to discuss affairs of state;
but the archbishop and the treasurer alike were afraid that
it would be to the detriment of king and kingdom if the
frenzied crowd got their way, and refused to let the king go
to them; whereupon they, spurred on by heightened fury,
rushed to the Tower, which they threatened to demolish

[2] Cf. Walsingham, *Hist. Ang.*, i. 457; Knighton, *Chronicon*, ii. 135.
[3] In fact Highbury was attacked early on 14 June.

1381 rex accederet suis peticionibus satisfacturus. Videns igitur rex eorum insultum ac improbam eorum audaciam annuit peticioni eorum, perrexitque ad locum qui Anglice vocatur Mile Ende,[1] ubi illa aggrestis multitudo congregata instantissime postulavit a rege sibi omnimodam libertatem donari et cujuscumque delicti contracti racione illius commocionis seu alicujus alterius rei usque ad illud tempus concedi indulgenciam. Timens rex ne, si postulata non concederet, ex negacione proveniret detrimentum, furentis vulgi cessit precibus, optatam eis annuens libertatem forisfactorumque indulgenciam.

Interea dum ista agerentur,[2] pars funesta villani cetus ad Turrim London' accessit extraxitque archipresulem et thesaurarium et quendam fratrem Minorem, cirurgicum domini ducis Lancastr',[3] et in Monte Turris adductos et quendam Johannem Leeg, clavigerum regium, et alium ibidem decollarunt.[4]

Acta. Facta fuit hec decollacio xviij. Kalendas Julii hora xj. Tandem capud archipresulis et ceterorum in palis figentes per diversos London' vicos portarunt tanquam de ingenti victoria gratulantes, ipsaque capita super pontem London' ponebant; sacratum capud archiepiscopi in medio et eminenciori loco fixerunt, et ut specialius a ceteris capitibus agnosceretur capellam rubeam super capud cum clavo fixerunt.[5]

Nec in hiis malis quemlibet eorum furor mitigatus a cede retraxit, set eciam transierunt per ripas Thamensis fluminis, quo Flandrenses maxime morantur,[6] omnes Flandrenses repertos sine judicio et sine causa decollaverunt: videres enim congeries corporum in plateis et per loca diversa truncos occisorum jacere. Taliter hunc diem consumpserunt, solum

---

[1] The meeting was arranged for 7 a.m. ('vii del knolle') on 14 June (*Anon. Chron.*, pp. 142-3). For the charters of manumission and general pardon granted at this meeting and subsequently, see Rymer, *Foedera*, vii. 317-18; Walsingham, *Hist. Ang.*, i. 467; and B. Harvey, 'Draft Letters Patent of Manumission and Pardon for the men of Somerset in 1381', in *E.H.R.*, lxxx (1964), 89-91.

[2] See above, p. lxxii.

[3] Br. William Appleton (*Anon. Chron.*, p. 145; see also *John of Gaunt's Register, 1379-1383*, ed. E. C. Lodge and R. Somerville (Camden 3rd Ser., lvi-vii), i. 72, 557; and *Cal. Pat. R., 1381-1385*, p. 16).

[4] Legg had taken a prominent part in enforcing the poll-tax of 1380-1

unless the king came to them prepared to satisfy their claims. 1381
In view of their aggressive temper and their gross effrontery,
the king fell in with their request and went to the place
known as Mile End,[1] where the assembled throng of rustics
insistently demanded of him that they should be given every
kind of liberty and an amnesty for all offences committed
up to that time, whether in connection with the insurrection
or not. Fearing that if he did not give in to these demands
mischief would follow from his refusal, the king bowed to
the importunity of the raging mob and agreed to give them
the liberty they wanted and to remit the forfeitures they
had incurred.

While these events were going forward,[2] a sinister section
of the horde of serfs moved on to the Tower of London,
from which they dragged out the archbishop, the treasurer,
and a Friar Minor who was surgeon to the duke of Lancaster,[3]
brought them to Tower Hill, and there beheaded them,
together with a royal sergeant at arms, named John Legg, and
another victim.[4]

Proceedings. These executions took place on 14 June, at
eleven o'clock. The heads of the archbishop and the rest
were stuck on poles and carried through the city streets, as
if in triumph after some great victory, before being set up
on London Bridge. The hallowed head of the archbishop
they set in the middle and higher than the others and to
make it specially recognizable among them they nailed on it a
scarlet cap.[5]

Despite all this mischief there was none of them in whom
the abatement of his frenzy induced any revulsion from
slaughter. Roaming through the district bordering the River
Thames where, for the most part, the Flemings live,[6] they
beheaded without judgement or trial all the Flemings they
found; so that mounds of corpses were to be seen in the
streets and various spots were littered with the headless
bodies of the slain. In this way they passed the entire day,

(Knighton, *Chronicon*, ii. 130; *Cal. Fine R., 1377-83*, p. 250). The other victim
was Richard Somenour of Stepney, and he is the 'juror' mentioned in *Anon.
Chron.*, p. 145; cf. Riley, *Memorials*, p. 450.
[5] Cf. D. Wilkins, *Concilia Magnae Britanniae et Hiberniae* (4 vols., London,
1737), iii. 153; *Vita Ricardi Secundi*, p. 65.   [6] i.e. Cheapside.

1381 neci Flandrensium vacantes.* Doluit interea rex, et consilium maxime in tali temporis articulo periit a sapiente;[1] set et tota civitas London' in seipsa confusa et aliquantulum, ut a multis putabatur, in seipsam divisa quid ageret non[a] cernebat. Egre namque tolleravit aggrestis turbe tumultuacionem et invasionem, tum in occisione civium, tum in consumpcione sine recompensacione victualium, tum in destruccione edium; rusticorum aggressionibus resistere cupiens obstare non valebat[b] vel audebat; formidabat quidem ⟨ne⟩[c] si invalescentibus servis resisterent, communes tanquam suorum fautores cum servis contra reliquos civium insurgerent, sicque tota civitas in seipsa divisa deperiret. Quievit igitur civitas, sue salutis dubia, rerum gestarum exitum cum formidine expectans.

p. 132   *Acta.* In crastino quippe, que dies sabbati erat,[2] sepe nominata turba more solito omnes penes quos ira movebantur diligenti indagacione inquirebant, apprehensos decapitabant: inter[d] quos quendam Ricardum Ymmeworthe, senescallum de marchalsie ad ecclesiam Westm' causa sue salutis confugientem et columpnas feretri amplexantem violenter a tam sacrato loco extraxerunt et extractum sine aliquo judicii processu decollaverunt in medio Chepe.[3] Set Sanctus Edwardus irrogatam sibi injuriam citissime vindicavit in sue sanctitatis exaltacionem et regni consolacionem.

Rex venit ad Westmonasterium. Nam post horam ejusdem diei nonam rex in tanta rerum turbine concomitantibus dominis et militibus cum multo civium equitatu ad Westmonasterium causa oracionis accessit, divinum ad feretrum predicti regis imploraturus auxilium ubi humanum omnino defuit consilium: unde accedenti propius porte monasterii

---

*Attende quod isto die nitebantur erarium regium spoliare apud Westm' in the margin.[4]

---

[a] *Interlined.*   [b] MS. valens.   [c] MS. om.   [d] in quos *deleted before* this word.

---

[1] Cf. Jer. xviii. 18.   [2] 15 June.
[3] The chronicler lends no support to the belief, soon current, that this violation of sanctuary took place in the king's presence; cf. *Réville*, p. 212.
[4] Cf. P.R.O., E. 403/484, 1 Aug., implying that rebels attacked the treasury of

bent only on the massacre of the Flemings.* Meanwhile 1381
the king was in deep distress, and it was at this moment, if
ever, that 'counsel perished from the wise'.[1] The whole of
London, the prey of internal confusion and, as many thought,
of some degree of internal dissension, was without a clear
view of what was to be done. While the city resented the
lawlessness and aggression of the peasant mob manifested
in the murder of citizens, the unrequited consumption of
foodstuffs, and the destruction of buildings, and yearned to
resist the encroachments of the yokels, it lacked both the
power and the courage to oppose them: it was, indeed, feared
that if resistance were offered to the growing strength of the
serfs, the city's lower orders might champion their own class
and join the serfs in rising against the rest of the citizens
and that in this way the entire city, divided against itself,
would be ruined. And so the city remained inert, doubtful
of its own safety and fearfully awaiting the outcome of events.

Proceedings. On the following day, which was Saturday,[2]
the mob continued, in a manner by now familiar, their
thorough search for those against whom their wrath was
directed. Those they caught they beheaded, among them
Richard Imworth, steward of the Marshalsea, who had fled
for safety to the church of Westminster and was clinging to
the columns of the shrine when he was forcibly dragged away
from that holy spot, to be later beheaded, without any judicial process, in the middle of Cheap.[3] But St. Edward, to the
exaltation of his sainthood and the comfort of the realm,
was swift indeed to avenge the wrong offered to him.

The king visits Westminster. The political whirlwind
was at its height when, in the afternoon of the same day,
the king, accompanied by lords and knights and a large
body of mounted citizens, proceeded to Westminster for
his devotions, to supplicate at the shrine of the sainted king
for divine aid where human counsel was altogether wanting.
As he approached the monastery gate the convent set out in

*Note that it was on this day that they attempted to plunder the royal treasury
at Westminster *in the margin.*[4]

the wardrobe in the precinct of Westminster Abbey and damaged plea rolls and
other records there.

1381 conventus processionaliter ibat in obviam. Rexque equo continuo descendens flexis genibus crucem que ante conventum ferebatur devote cum lacrimis osculatus est, dein ad feretrum gloriosi regis Edwardi accessit, moram ibidem in oracione protrahendo. Videres ibidem dominos, milites, armigeros, aliosque innumeros pia devocione contendere quis ante alium sanctorum reliquiis ibidem repositis prius offerret, quis profusius lacrimas in oracione profunderet.[a] Nec defuit devotis oratoribus meritis sui Sancti regis Edwardi divinum presidium: surgentes ab oracione singuli quandam spem et confortacionem boni eventus conceperunt, sicque animati iterum ad civitatem equitarunt et ad locum qui Planus Campus vocitatur perrexerunt colloquium habituri cum duce villane turbe. Is enim cum innumera rusticorum multitudine ibidem regium prestolabatur adventum ut a rege emendaciorem optineret de libertate cartam; displicuerat enim eis carta per regem primitus concessa. Accessit igitur rex cum suis, et assistente majore London' Willelmo Walworth' fit a Waltero[b] Tegulatore duce prefate multitudinis cum rege de relaxacione servitutis tractacio;[1] set nephandus dux, dum plura pro rusticorum libertate haberet colloquia, nullum quem debebat[c] regie majestati exhibebat honorem set pocius capite operto, vultu minaci, verbis audacissimis, in facie[d] regis aggressus est. Sermonem ejus, temeritatem improbam et temerariam improbitatem cernens ipse major[e] in hoc potissime consistere quod nullam regi ut subditum decuit prebebat reverenciam, talem intulit affatum. 'Cur', inquit, 'regi tuo nullam exhibes reverenciam?' At ille indignanter verbum assumens, 'Nullus', inquit, 'regi per me ministrabitur honor.' Subintulit major, 'Et ego te arresto.' Et ille extracto cultello majorem nitebatur percutere; unde major in ipsum irruens gladio perforavit, aliusque armiger qui affuerat,[2] apprehenso capite iniqui ducis, ad terram de equo dejecit.[3] Ceciditque virtus spes et fiducia rusticorum;

---

[a] Nota devocio *[sic]* in the margin.   [b] *Marginal correction from* Johanne.
[c] *MS.* debebatur.   [d] *Sic MS.; recte* in faciem? *(Winterbottom).*   [e] *Three letters have been cancelled after this word.*

[1] Cf. *Anon. Chron.*, p. 147.
[2] Ralph Standyche (Knighton, *Chronicon*, ii. 137).

procession to meet him. The king at once dismounted, and 1381
was in tears as he knelt and reverently kissed the cross borne
before the convent. Going to the shrine of the glorious King
Edward, he spent some time there in prayer. Lords, knights,
esquires, and countless others were to be seen competing in
their reverence and devotion for the distinction of being first
to make oblation to the relics of the saints deposited there
and of being most prodigal of the tears that accompanied
their prayers. Nor, through the merits of his royal saint, did
God's protection fail the devout suppliants: every man, as
he rose from prayer, took fresh heart and fresh hope of a
happy outcome. Thus inspired, they rode away again to the
city and on to a place called Smithfield for a conference
with the leader of the servile mob, who, with an uncountable
crowd of peasants, was waiting there for the king's coming in
order to obtain from him a revised charter of liberty, since
the one first granted by the king had not given satisfaction.
The king and his party came up; and William Walworth, the
mayor of London, was in attendance when Walter Tiler, the
leader of the crowd, opened with the king a discussion about
the emancipation of the serfs.[1] As the conversation about the
peasants' freedom developed, their unspeakable leader showed
for the king's majesty none of the deference he ought to
have done: on the contrary, he advanced upon the king with
his head covered, his looks threatening, and his language
bold in the extreme. Observing that his manner of speech,
his villainous recklessness and his reckless villainy chiefly
took the form of failure to pay to the king the respect proper
in a subject, the mayor put a word in. 'Why', he asked, 'do
you show no respect to your king?' 'The king is going to get
no deference from me', was the scornful reply. The mayor
retorted 'I arrest you.' The other now drew a dagger and tried
to stab the mayor, who darted at him and ran him through
with his sword. A squire who stood by[2] seized the rascally
leader's head and flung him from his horse to the ground.[3]
All the heart, hope, and confidence now went out of the

[3] A passage compatible with a knowledge of but hesitation in accepting the
tradition that the rebel leader was not in fact killed by the blow that felled
him to the ground; for the macabre story see *Anon. Chron.*, p. 149.

1381   et exclamante tota servili[a] turma 'Occiditur primicerius
noster!' respondit rex. 'Silete!' inquit. 'Ego sum vester rex,
vester dux, vester primicerius; et si qui ex vobis michi
adherent, exeant statim in campum.'[1] Interea strenuus ille
major citissimo gressu equitavit in urbem, jubens omnes et
singulos quatinus arma caperent[b] et in regis defensionem
quam cito possent in campos transirent. Paruit statim majoris
imperiis generosa civitatis communitas et ad arma ruens nunc
per unam portam nunc per aliam turmatim egrediens in
campum in regis auxilium citissime currunt, rusticamque
multitudinem undique circumvallantes eorum minabantur
internicionem: igitur videntes se undique circumseptos armatorum manu ac mortis imminere periculum arma, fustes,
arcus, sagittas, et queque defensiva proicientes corruerunt
in terram, regis clemenciam pariter postulantes ne reos
puniret suppliciis dignos set pocius demerentibus misericordiam impertiret. Tandem concessit rex indignis indulgenciam, civilis sanguinis effusionem abhorrens, et jussit ut
unusquisque ad sua remearet ipsa nocte, comminans unumquemque infra urbis menia repertum penam capitalem
subiturum. Optenta tali modo regia benignitate recessit turba
illa paulatim diminuta dum unusquisque ad sua revertitur.

Post hec et alia hujus tempestatis tormina, convocat rex
omnem suam miliciam, et circumdatus manu armata in partes
Estsexie proficiscitur rebelles castigaturus:[2] per hos enim
qui Estsaxiam inhabitant juxta villam que Combusta Silva
nominatur et villulas circumjacentes inchoata fuerat ista
civilis turbacio; quare[c] non obstante regia indulgencia iterato
adunati resurgere statuerunt, set rex eos invadens plurimos
occidit, in rubetis, in segetibus, corpora occisorum relinquens. E quibus plurimi erant suspensi et plures eorum
videntes ex eorum rebellione provenire incomodum in abdita
silvarum fugerunt. Castigatis ad unguem[3] ipsis partibus hujus

_____

    [a] MS. servilis.   [b] MS. capere.   [c] Sic MS.; recte qua? (Winterbottom).

    [1] i.e. into Clerkenwell Fields (ibid., p. 148; see also Riley, *Memorials*, p. 451).
    [2] The king was in Essex between 22 June and 8 July (W. H. B. Bird, 'The
Peasant Rising of 1381; the King's Itinerary', in *E.H.R.*, xxxi (1916), 125; see also
Riley, op. cit., p. 452). The fighting described by the chronicler took place at
Billericay on 28 June, and the rebels were routed, not by the king in person, but
by Thomas earl of Buckingham and Sir Thomas Percy (Walsingham, *Hist. Ang.*, ii.
18–19).

peasants; and the cry 'Our captain is killed!' was raised by the 1381 entire company of serfs. The king answered it. 'Quiet!' he said. 'I am your king, your leader, your captain. Those among you who support me are to go out at once into the open country.'[1] Meanwhile the zealous mayor rode off at full gallop to the city, ordering one and all to take up arms and go as quickly as they could into the fields to defend the king. The staunch commons of the city obeyed their mayor's commands without hesitation: springing to arms they set out in companies through one city gate after another and sped rapidly to the king's assistance in the fields, where they completely encircled the assembled peasants and threatened their annihilation. Seeing themselves hemmed in on every side by armed force and mortal danger looming over them, the peasants threw away their weapons — staves, bows and arrows, and all their means of defence — and flung themselves to the ground, imploring the king's mercy and begging that he would not visit their guilt with the punishment it had earned but accord them a clemency they had ill deserved. His distaste for civil bloodshed at length secured for them an unmerited forbearance from the king, who ordered that they must all go home that very night and added the threat that every man of them found inside the city walls would suffer the extreme penalty. Having won this generous concession from the king, the mob withdrew, gradually dwindling as individuals went back to their homes.

With the end of these and other convulsions of this time of storm, the king summoned the whole of the country's chivalry and, escorted by an armed force, set out for Essex to punish the insurgents:[2] for it was by the Essex population of the neighbourhood of Brentwood and the surrounding villages that the domestic upheaval had been begun; and notwithstanding the king's amnesty they had again started to congregate, determined to renew the insurrection. But an attack by the king destroyed them in great numbers and left thicket and cornfield strewn with the bodies of the dead. Many of the rebels were hanged; and still more, seeing that the rising had turned out disastrously for them, went into hiding in the woods. Having put the finishing touches to his chastisement[3]

---

[3] An echo of the words rather than the sense of Horace, *Ars Poetica*, 294.

1381 commocionis fautoribus revertitur rex London', quo paululum moratus transivit ad civitatem Verolamiam quosdam ibidem dissidiosos castigaturus. Quo adveniente et in monas-
p. 133 terio / Sancti Albani moram trahente suggestum fuerat[a] per abbatem loci ejusdem et per priorem quod plures et nobiliores de villa huic commocioni assensum prebuerunt et proposuerunt destruxisse funditus monasterium; quare suspensi fuerunt nobiliores ville ejusdem, unde plures doluerunt.[1] Interea capitur in villa Coventr' quidam Johannes Balne, presbiter presbiterali per omnia indignus caractere, et ad villam Sancti Albani adducitur. Hic enim predicabat per villas diversas Anglie ea que vulgum in hanc conjuracionem summe stimularent;[2] quare productus coram judice, nil quantum ad hoc quod talia predicaverat que plebem commoverent negans, morti addictus, suspensus et distractus est et postea in quatuor partes divisus:[3] ejus capud super portam de Ludgate est affixum. Videres tunc regium justiciarium ubique residere et de hujusmodi conspiratoribus inquirere et quoscumque reos sine dilacione suspensioni adjudicare. Tunc furce erigebantur ubi prius non erant, quia dampnatorum corporibus non sufficiebant jam erecte. Multi hujuscemodi[b] commocionis conscii fugiebant ne comprehensi cum aliis [c]amaram mortem[c] subirent. Horruit vulgus videre tot corpora visui solis exponi suspendio, doluitque videre indigenas quasi exules natale solum relinquere. Nec in hiis penis reis inflictis quoquomodo mansuescere videbatur regie censure rigor set magis [d]in sontum[d] penas aggravari; quare plurimis visum est quod in consimili eventu pocius regia benignitas uti deberet clemencia quam vindicta, et videntes penis dignissimi quod superhabundaret gracia ubi habundavit delictum[4] suis conjuracionibus imponerent

[a] Sic MS. [b] MS. hujuscemode. [c–c] amaram mortem Winterbottom; amara morte MS. [d–d] MS. insontum.

[1] Cf. Walsingham's better-informed hint that the majores among the convicted townsmen were not executed but imprisoned (Hist. Ang., ii. 31–9; Gesta Abbatum Monasterii Sancti Albani (ed. H. T. Riley, 3 vols., R.S., 1867–9), iii. 347–54; and see Cal. Pat. R., 1381–5, p. 125). The king was at St. Albans from 12 to 20 July; judicial proceedings began on 13 July.
[2] i.e. Wycliffite doctrines; see below, p. 28. For a more exact account of Ball's teaching see Walsingham, Hist. Ang., ii. 32; see also Fasciculi Zizaniorum Magistri Johannis Wyclif cum tritico, ed. W. W. Shirley (R.S., 1858), p. 273.

of the districts which had fomented the revolt, the king 1381
returned to London, and after a short pause went on to the
town of St. Albans to punish certain disaffected elements
there. Upon his arrival it was reported to him by the abbot
and the prior, during his stay in the monastery of St. Albans,
that several townsfolk of the upper class had countenanced
the revolt and had planned the complete destruction of the
monastery. This led to the hanging of prominent inhabitants
of the town, which caused widespread dismay.[1] In the meantime John Ball, a priest in every respect unworthy of the
priestly style, was arrested at Coventry and brought to St.
Albans. He had preached up and down the towns of England
doctrines peculiarly designed to incite the masses into joining
the conspiracy.[2] He was accordingly put on trial before a
judge; and as he did not deny having preached matter calculated to stir up the populace he was condemned to death,
being hanged and drawn and afterwards quartered.[3] His head
was stuck up over Ludgate. The royal judges were now everywhere to be seen in session, inquiring into the activities of the
conspirators and giving the guilty short shrift. Gibbets rose
where none had been before, since existing ones were too few
for the bodies of the condemned. Many who had been privy
to the insurrection took to flight to avoid sharing the arrest
and bitter fate suffered by others. The populace shuddered
at the spectacle of so many gibbeted bodies exposed to the
light of day, and were distressed to see men of native stock
quitting, as it were for exile, the soil of their birth. Despite
all the retribution thus visited on the guilty the severity of
the royal displeasure seemed to be in no way mitigated but
rather to be directed with increased harshness towards the
punishment of offenders, so that it was widely thought that
in the circumstances the king's generous nature ought to
exercise leniency rather than vindictiveness, when those who
richly deserved punishment, seeing that 'where sin abounded,
grace did much more abound',[4] would put an end to their

[3] Ball was tried before Tresilian on 13 July and executed in the king's presence
two days later (Walsingham, *Hist. Ang.*, ii. 32-4). The following description of
judicial proceedings relates to those before commissioners of oyer and terminer
and other extraordinary commissioners and in the King's Bench between late
June and the beginning of Nov. 1381; see *Cal. Pat. R., 1381-5*, pp. 23, 69-71,
79-80; *Cal. Cl. R., 1381-5*, pp. 7-8, 85.   [4] Romans v. 20.

1381 terminum; econtrario nonnulli in cumulum dampnorum conspiratores penarum tormenta cumulare summe justicie decretum esse dicebant, ut dum hii condigna pro factis gustarent supplicia consimilibus essent in exemplum talia non agendi. Set dum harum racionum in pendulo maneret sentencia, manus vindex adeo extensa est quod truncus ligneus cum securi in medio Chepe positus erat in expedicionem amputacionis capitum dampnatorum; nam pro qualitate maleficii discreta dampnacionis subiere decreta, unde alii patibulis affixi sunt, alii decollati, alii distracti, alii horum tormentorum cumulo puniti.[1] Amicis quoque Flandrensium qui secus Tamenses ripas lares fovebant, qui eciam campestris turbe manibus neci tradebantur, pro eorum voto interfectores[a] suorum carorum animadverti[b] concessum est, in tantum quod uxoribus interfectorum occisores maritorum largita est decollandi potestas. Dum ergo pena[c] reorum corporibus non parceret set in dies magis cresceret in malorum interitum, ceperunt plurimi corde indurescere et in conjuracionis fomentum animum revocare, et congregati in silvarum saltibus per adveniencium incrementum eorum conventicula augebantur; nullum enim senciebant remedium quo diri leti declinarent incursum, quare magis elegerunt collatis viribus persequencium gladiis magnanimiter interire quam avide taxacionis servituti colla subicere seu patibulorum jugulo vitam terminare. Tacitus interea subintravit huic errori error per omnia pejor, qui civilis discidii scintillas magis obtegeret quam extingueret. Plurimi namque cernentes nullorum misereri quos conjuracionis macula aliquo modo infecerat, hiis singulis erga quos canescentis odii malicia movebantur tanti maleficii crimen imponebant, ut vel tali objeccionis titulo diu affectatam in hos quos oderant explerent vindictam. Sceleris itaque accusatus horum trium

---

[a] Recte ⟨in⟩ interfectores *(Winterbottom)*.   [b] *Sic MS.*   [c] *MS.* plena.

---

[1] Hanging was the normal form of execution for capital offences other than treason under the common law; if used in cases of treason — and many who paid the penalty in 1381 were condemned as traitors — it was aggravated by drawing. Beheading, a swifter and surer penalty, was not a normal common-law form of execution. See J. Bellamy, *Crime and Public Order in England in the later Middle Ages* (London, 1973), pp. 186 ff. The commission to William Walworth and others to punish rebels in the City of London sanctioned beheading (*Réville*, pp. 234-5).

plotting. On the other hand there were some who maintained that for the conspirators to pile up the torments of
punishment until they equalled the havoc they had piled so
high was a decision of supreme justice, since as long as they
experienced the penalties appropriate to their behaviour
they served as a warning to the like-minded not to imitate
it. While the issue between these arguments was still in the
balance, the hand of vengeance reached out so far that a
wooden block and an axe were set in the middle of Cheap
for the speedier beheading of the condemned, since the
sentences passed on them varied with the nature of their
misdeeds, so that some were hanged, some beheaded, some
drawn, and some punished by a combination of these
sufferings.[1] The friends of those Flemish dwellers along
Thames-side who had been put to death at the hands
of the peasant mob were, at their own request, permitted
to carry out the punishment of those who had slaughtered
their dear ones; and indeed the wives of victims were given
authority to behead their husbands' murderers. With retribution, so far from sparing the bodies of the guilty, growing
daily more intent on the destruction of wrongdoers, there
were many who began to harden their hearts and to pluck
up courage to hatch fresh plots. In the forest glades where
they foregathered their companies were constantly swollen
by new arrivals: feeling, as they did, that there was no
means of warding off the grim fate which bore down upon
them, they naturally preferred to unite their efforts and die
like men upon the swords of their pursuers rather than bow
their necks to the slavery imposed by a rapacious taxation
or end their lives in the hangman's noose. Beside this
mistaken notion there meanwhile silently crept in another,
in every respect more mischievous, which served rather to
cover up than to extinguish the sparks of domestic faction.
Observing that no pity was shown to anybody to whom the
taint of conspiracy in any way attached, many people
began to charge with this grave offence all those towards
whom some hoary grudge had made them ill disposed,
exploiting even this ground for denunciation in order
to wreak their long-cherished vengeance upon those they
hated. The accused was obliged to submit to one of three

1381 alterum subire cogebatur: aut enim seipsum uti innocentem purgabat duodene decreto; aut ut convictus infami adjudicabatur suspendio; aut ut cicius mortem evaderet onere gravissime mulcte depressus perfidi accusatoris satisfecit per singula voto. Taliter effrenata cupiditas oportunitatem captans ex tempore exquisitis fraudibus non solum mirum lucrandi adinvenit compendium set et invidie sue solacium plurimorum exterminium per *commocionis pretextum* insontes mulctans aut dampnans. Set talia exequi parum erat videre secularium versucias, cum pari tergiversacione vaga quorundam religiosorum levitas utpote sedicionis reos incusaret proprios ea tempestate prelatos. Virus hujus dampnosi criminis adeo canonicorum animos invaserat quod nonnulli eorum priores accusatorum instancia cogebantur Westmonasterium fugere ad asilum.[1] Miserum erat intueri zeli voto faventibus penis servum dominum accusare, civem in sibi conterminum insurgere, uxorem dampnare maritum, domine ancillam minari, et subditos disruptis tollerancie frenis suos inordinate calumpniare rectores. Horum in cumulum accessit malorum tanti nephas diuturnitas nec finem captans ex tempore. Perpendens igitur regalis clemencia ex cupiditatis adinvencionibus tocius civilitatis imminere jac-

p. 134 turam, provido / sensatorum consilio decrevit quod deinceps nullus pretacti facinoris accusatus aliter legalium penarum tormenta subiret nisi prius trium duodenarum sentencia dampnaretur;[2] concessit insuper rex ex sua pietate munifica universales indulgencias conjuracionis obnoxiis, ipsius commocionis dumtaxat exceptis auctoribus pariter et aliis quos cedis aut incendiorum[b] labes multipharie resperserat.[3]

Nonis Augusti accitis tocius Anglie magnatibus rex tenuit consilium suum Radyngie;[4] in quo fuit electus cancellarius

a–a MS. commociones pretextu.   *b* MS. incendiarum.

---

[1] See above, p. xxiii.

[2] Cf. Walsingham, *Hist. Ang.*, ii. 35-6, and *Gesta Abbatum Monasterii Sancti Albani*, ed. Riley, iii. 348-9, where the use of three successive juries in securing verdicts against rebels is attributed to Tresilian at St. Albans. In attaint procedure a jury of 24 persons pronounced on the verdict first given by a jury of 12.

[3] A reference to the pardons granted in the parliament of Nov. 1381 (*R.P.*, iii. 103, 111-13; cf. ibid., p. 139; *Cal. Pat. R., 1381-5*, pp. 272, 297-8).

[4] The council was summoned on 26 July for 4 Aug., a Sunday (P.R.O., E. 403/484, 30 July).

necessities: he might establish his innocence by the verdict 1381
of a jury; or he might be convicted and condemned to the
ignominy of the gallows; or, to secure at an earlier stage his
escape from execution, he might gratify to the full the
desires of his perjured accuser by accepting the burden of a
crushingly heavy money payment. In this way uncontrolled
greed, with well-timed opportunism, used all the refinements
of chicanery to blackmail the innocent or secure their condemnation, and so hit upon not only a wonderful short cut
to riches but also a salve for envy in the destruction of
large numbers of people on the pretext of their complicity
in the revolt. It was too little to see seculars do such things:
with the same abandonment of principle the fickle light-
mindedness of certain men of religion brought accusations
of sedition against their own prelates at that time. The
poison of this pernicious vice had penetrated so deep into
the minds of canons that there were some of their priors
who were forced by the zeal of their accusers to take
refuge at Westminster.[1] With penalties so favourable to the
aspirations of jealousy it was saddening to see the servant
accusing his master, the citizen rising up against his neigh-
bour, the wife convicting her husband, the maid threatening
her mistress; and subordinates bursting the restraints of
self-control and making monstrous charges against their
superiors. The crowning addition to these evils was the long
continuance of such iniquity, to which time brought no
end. In view, therefore, of the fact that the ingenuities of
greed threatened the overthrow of the entire body politic,
the king acted on the discerning advice of shrewd counsellors and mercifully decreed that henceforward nobody
accused of the crime should suffer the rigour of the
penalties prescribed by law without having been first
condemned by the verdicts of three juries;[2] in his liberality
and sympathy he further granted general pardons to those
who lay open to the charge of conspiracy, excepting only
the authors of the actual revolt and those who were heavily
marked by the stains of murder and arson.[3]

On 5 August the king held at Reading a council to which
all the leading men of the country were summoned.[4]
William Courtenay, bishop of London, was appointed

1381 Anglie dominus Willelmus Courteneye episcopus London', et thesaurarius dominus Hugo Segrave miles. Fuerat eodem mense Oxon' fervens hominum mortalitas et London' subsequenter set maxime puerorum et puellarum.

Dissensio inter ducem Lancastr' et comitem de Northumbrelond'. Circa festum Sancti Dionisii celebravit rex consilium suum in castro de Berkhampstede ad pacificandum ducem Lancastr' et comitem Northumbr': hii quidem ex certis causis amicissimi[a] ante ferales inimici effecti sunt.[1] Quare studuit rex [b]interveniente diligencia[b] magnatorum animos ira retortos ad rectitudinem unitatis et pacis revocare, ne dissidencium dominorum invalescente rancore nondum penitus sopite conjuracionis scintille in destructivas tocius regni succrescerent flammas: set casso labore fatigata dominorum sedulitate in equa vel in majori inimicicia discesserunt. Subsequenter comes prenominatus London' accessit et Londoniensium captans benevolenciam interveniente juramento civis effectus est; nec sine causa irarum, namque incendia que dudum Londoniensium animos contra pretactum ducem in inmensum calefacere⟨n⟩t ex inito federe sumebant argumentum.[c] Metuens igitur[d] dux magnanimitatem comitis et inter hunc et Trinoventanos firmatas amicicias ad parliamentum apud Westmonasterium die Lune post festum Omnium Sanctorum celebratum in fortitudine quingentorum armatorum accessit;[2] cujus facti racione Londonienses singulas urbis sue portas robustissima manu armatorum custodierunt in quarumcumque venellarum introitu ex transverso positis repagulatoriis ne quis ex parte prescripti ducis fraudulencius intraret dampnum civitati allaturus. Intuens rex ex accidentibus imperii sui pacem verisimiliter posse infirmari, solempni in pleno parliamento prohibuit edicto ne quivis ex alterutra parte armatus ad

---

[a] MS. aulicū. *The scribe was perhaps faced with a contracted form of* amicissimi. *(Mr. Hector acknowledged help from the Revd. S. T. Collins at this point. B.F.H.)* [b-b] MS. interne mente diligen'. [c] *Recte* augmentum? [d] rex *deleted after this word.*

---

[1] The council was summoned on 3 Sept. for 6 Oct. (P.R.O., E. 403/484, 3 Sept.). For the quarrel between John of Gaunt, duke of Lancaster, and Henry Percy, earl of Northumberland, which was precipitated by Percy's refusal of

chancellor and Sir Hugh Segrave treasurer. In the same month there flared up, first at Oxford and later in London, an outbreak of plague which chiefly affected boys and girls.

Discord between the duke of Lancaster and the earl of Northumberland. About the feast of St. Denis [9 October] the king held a council at Berkhampstead Castle to reconcile the duke of Lancaster and the earl of Northumberland, who, from having been close friends, had for particular reasons become deadly enemies.[1] The king therefore sought by interposing the efforts of his magnates to recall hearts warped by passion to the proper courses of harmony and peace, lest intensified ill-feeling between the estranged nobles should cause the sparks of sedition, still smouldering, to be fanned into a blaze which would destroy the whole of England: but when the assiduity of the councillors had been exhausted in vain endeavour the two disputants departed in undiminished, or even increased, hostility. The earl now visited London and made a bid for the goodwill of the inhabitants by taking the oath and becoming a citizen, providing thereby further occasion for strife, for the burning resentment which had long and intensely inflamed the hearts of the Londoners against the duke took fresh substance from the alliance thus concluded. Fearful of the earl's mettlesome spirit and of the friendship cemented between him and the people of London, the duke was therefore supported by 500 armed men when he attended the parliament held at Westminster on Monday after All Saints [4 November];[2] this prompted the Londoners to set a powerful armed guard over each of the city gates and to erect barriers across the entrances of every lane to prevent anybody on the duke's side from gaining admittance by false pretences and inflicting some harm upon the city. Observing that the peace of his domains might well be prejudiced by what was happening, the king issued a solemn injunction in full parliament ordering that no member of either side should come armed

hospitality to Lancaster, the king's lieutenant in the march towards Scotland, on the latter's progress south from Berwick-upon-Tweed in June 1381, see S. Armitage-Smith, *John of Gaunt* (London, 1904), pp. 252-9.

[2] Percy also brought armed retainers to this parliament (*R.P.*, iii. 98; Walsingham, *Hist. Ang.*, ii. 44).

1381 parliamentum accederet.[1] Tandem illius odii propositis articulis et tante discordie causis manifestatis pax renovatur inter eosdem.

Durante adhuc parliamento Thomas Ufford comes South-folchie subito cadens ad gradus introitus hostii capelle Sancti Stephani xv°. Kalendas Octobres[a] vitam terminavit.[2] Non frustra, uti reor, cecidit tam nobilis illius temporis articulo; exemplum enim fuerat extantibus dominis umbratilem mundi non magnipendere gloriam nec ex subditorum loculis in suum comodum coacervare pecuniam dum inopinate[b] mortis accessu, ut is, extimplo possent e mundo auferri.

Venit regina. Modicum ante Natale Domini soror imperatoris Dovorr' applicuit, cui fuit obvius dux Lancastr', quam honestissime receptam usque ad castrum de Ledys perduxit, ubi per totum Natale morata est. Infra hujus Natalis dies nocte media inter festum Sancti Stephani et festum Sancti Johannis Evangeliste obiit comes Marchie in oris Hibernicis.[3] Huic per regem tocius Hibernie fuerat commissa tutela ut armorum virtute rebellium insolenciam refrenaret. Erat is gestu maturus, affatu suavis, regno fidelis, et in rebus
1382 agendis summa prudencia fultus. Decimo octavo die mensis Januarii cum summo honore Londoniensium civium recepta fuit soror predicti imperatoris et ad Westmonasterium cum ingenti gloria perducta, stratoris officium gerentibus dominis .[c][4] Residebat enim in uno dextrario. Que terciodecimo Kalendas Februarii in ecclesia Westmon' regi desponsata est et in die sancti Vincencii proximo subsequente per manus domini Willelmi Courteneye archiepiscopi in reginam coronabatur. Desponsacionis peragebat solempnia episcopus London',[5] quare archiepiscopus indignatus, licet injuste,

---

[a] *Sic MS.; recte* Marcii.   [b] MS. inopinati.   [c] *A blank 6 cm. long has been left here in the MS.*

[1] The order was made in the king's name on 6 Nov.; the formal proceedings of parliament had not yet begun. On that day they were further adjourned for three days for the settlement of the quarrel. On 9 Nov. Percy apologized to Lancaster in parliament (*Anon. Chron.*, pp. 155–6; *R.P.*, iii. 98; *John of Gaunt's Register, 1379–83*, ii. 1243). Cf. below, p. 408.

[2] *William* de Ufford, earl of Suffolk, died on 15 Feb. 1382, the 15th of the Kalends of March (*Cal. Inq. p.m.*, xv. 599 ff.). The parliament of Nov. 1381 was then in its second session.

[3] Edmund Mortimer, earl of March, died at Cork on 27 Dec. 1381, having

to the parliament.[1] After the details of the feud had been 1381
paraded and the origins of this great quarrel brought to light,
peace was at last restored between them.

On 17 September, while the parliament was still in session,
Thomas Ufford, earl of Suffolk, suddenly collapsed at the
entrance door of St. Stephen's chapel and brought his life to
a close.[2] The passing of so illustrious a figure at such a
moment was not, I think, in vain, since it was a warning to
the nobles of the day not to set great store by the shadowy
glories of earth or to amass for their own ends wealth from
the pockets of the people while by the coming of death when
they least expected it they might, like him, be snatched in
a trice from the world.

Arrival of the queen. Shortly before Christmas the
emperor's sister landed at Dover, to be met by the duke of
Lancaster, who received her with great courtesy and conducted her to Leeds castle, where she stayed over Christmas.
During this Christmas season, on the night between the feasts
of St. Stephen [26 December] and St. John the Evangelist
[27 December], the earl of March died in Ireland.[3] Entrusted
by the king with the charge of all Ireland, to keep the effrontery of rebellion in check by his military prowess, he was a
man of accomplished manner and easy address, loyal to his
country and sustained in his conduct of affairs by a super-
lative statesmanship. On 18 January the emperor's sister 1382
was received with signal honour by the citizens of London
and, seated upon a charger, was escorted with great pomp to
Westminster, the office of marshal being discharged by   .[4]
On 20 January she was married to the king in the church
of Westminster, and on St. Vincent's Day [22 January]
following was crowned queen at the hands of the archbishop,
William Courtenay. The bishop of London[5] conducted the
marriage service, to the resentment (unjustifiable though it
was) of the archbishop, who officiated at the coronation

been lieutenant in Ireland since 22 Oct. 1379 (ibid., nos. 534 ff.; *G.E.C.*, viii.
447–8).
    [4] MS. blank. On the mood in London on the occasion of the royal wedding,
see also *Calendar of Select Pleas and Memoranda of the City of London, 1381–
1412*, ed. A. H. Thomas (Cambridge, 1932), p. 3.
    [5] Robert Braybrooke, bishop of London, 1382–1404. For Braybrooke's
part in negotiating the Anglo-Bohemian marriage alliance, see *Perroy*, pp. 153–5.

1382 coronacionis sacra complevit quamquam pallium a papa nondum optinuerat.[1] De ista regina sic quidam scripsit metrice:

Digna frui manna datur Anglis nobilis Anna;
set scrutantibus verum videbatur non dari set pocius emi, nam non *modicam pecuniam* refundebat rex Anglie pro tantilla carnis porcione.[2]

In festo Milburge Virginis senatus London' una cum majore ejusdem civitatis et aliquibus de quocumque artificio pro carta sue libertatis venerunt ad regem in manerio de Kenyngton' tunc moram trahentem: numerus eorum erat quasi sexcenti. Regiam majestatem deprecabantur quatinus libertates et privilegia que antea sibi concessa fuerant ipse ratificaret, postulantes insuper ut unum solum haberent regem, asserentes se sub uno tantum subesse velle. Quare dux Lancastr' pavescens in crastino, videlicet in die Sancti Mathie Apostoli, circa horam nonam a civitate summa cum festinacione diffugit, primitus a rege optenta licencia.

Circa ista tempora venerunt de Calesia ambassiatores, scilicet dominus Johannes Coboham et episcopus Hereford-ensis, quandam condicionalem concordiam secum afferentes inter Anglos et Francos; habitisque responsis redierunt.[3]

p. 135 Eodem tempore / capte fuerunt decem naves diversis victuali-bus onuste, que directe fuerant versus castrum de Chire-bourgh' per Normannos, et alie due naves juxta Calesiam lanis onuste. Venerunt ambassiatores prefati et succincta Gallorum responsa manifestarunt in concilio celebrato apud West-monasterium in crastino Annunciacionis beate Marie, ad quod vocati fuerunt per regias literas abbas Westmon' et alii priores de London'.

Bellum inter Gaunt et Bruges.[4] In die Invencionis sancte

---

a-a MS. modica pecunia.

[1] Courtenay received the pallium on 6 May.

[2] Anne of Bohemia's dower was fixed at £4,500 (*Cal. Pat. R., 1381-5,* pp. 125-6; see also ibid., pp. 157, 159, 192 etc.). Richard II also promised to lend Wenceslas of Bohemia 80,000 florins (*c.*£12,000), of which sum the greater part was delivered by the end of Jan. 1382 (P.R.O., E. 403/484, 31 May; ibid., 487, 9 and 21 Dec., 30 Jan.; Rymer, *Foedera,* vii. 301-2).

[3] The end of the first and the beginning of the second of the embassies of those empowered on 16 Dec. 1381 to treat with the French; John Gilbert, bishop of Hereford, returned to London on 27 Feb. 1382 and left again on 26 May

ceremony in spite of not having yet received the pallium 1382
from the pope.[1] About this queen somebody wrote the verse:
> Worthy to enjoy manna,
> To Englishmen is given the noble Anna;

but to those with an eye for the facts it seemed that she
represented a purchase rather than a gift, since the English
king laid out no small sum to secure this tiny scrap of
humanity.[2]

On the feast of St. Milburga the Virgin [23 February] the
aldermen of London, together with the mayor and members
of all the city crafts, forming a party of about 600, visited
the king, who was then staying at the manor of Kennington,
to obtain a charter of liberties. After petitioning his majesty
to confirm the liberties and privileges which had been theirs
by previous grants, they further requested that they might
have only one king, declaring that they wished to be the
subjects of one man alone. This so alarmed the duke of
Lancaster that at about noon on the following day (which
was the feast of St. Matthias the apostle [24 February])
he left the city in a great hurry, after first taking leave of the
king.

About this time Sir John Cobham and the bishop of Hereford arrived from their mission to Calais, bringing with them
a conditional agreement between the English and the French;
they were given a reply and returned.[3] Ships captured during
this period comprised ten with mixed cargoes of foodstuffs,
destined by the men of Normandy for Cherbourg castle, and
two others, laden with wool, taken near Calais. The envoys
came and reported the answers of the French in concise form
at a council held at Westminster on the morrow of the
Annunciation [26 March], to which were summoned by
royal writ the abbot of Westminster and also certain London
priors.

Battle between Ghent and Bruges.[4] On the day of the

(Rymer, *Foedera*, vii. 338-9; Mirot and Déprez, in *B.E.C.*, lx, pp. 204-5, nos.
457-9). See also below, p. 28 and n.

[4] The battle was that between the men of Ghent and the forces of Louis de
Mâle, count of Flanders, at Beverhoutsveld on 3 May 1382; it gave the former
control, not only of Bruges, as the chronicler implies, but of much of northern
Flanders beside. For Flemish affairs in this period, see F. Quicke, *Les Pays-Bas à
la veille de la période bourguignonne (1356-1384)* (Brussels, 1947), pp. 297 ff.

1382 Crucis cives de Gaunt, inextinguibili odio contra villanos de Bruges succensi, civile bellum inter eos jamdudum inceptum sub lamentabili invasione continuarunt; et hoc modo. Antiqua Brugencium consuetudo fuerat et religiosissime sine quavis intermissione servata quod in die Invencionis sancte Crucis tota civitas in unum conveniret singulique artifices cum summa devocione et facta processione solempni sanguinem Crucifixi miraculose obtentum deferebant; cujus ritus observanciam ut devotissimi imitatores jam observabant, prefate jam consuetudini[a] comite Flandren', quare agebatur solempnitas illa ingenti leticia velud a gente iminentis periculi penitus ignara. Interea illi de Gaunt, uti pervigiles bellatores nichil[b] segniter agentes, studebant quomodo eos vincerent: et oportunitatem habentes ex tempore constitutis certis infidus quidam Philippus Hartefeld'[1] filius Jacobi Hartefeld' civitatem invasit. Quod comes cum suis considerantes ad arma convolarunt, et rem gladiis agentes ex incognitis insidiis circumvallati oppressi sunt. Agnoscens comes adversarios triumphare de suis fugam cum aliquibus iniit sue vite solum in hoc consulens. Devictis hostibus resistentibus persecuti sunt ceteros fugientes in urbem de Bruges; queque gladio consumebant nulli sexui parcentes, Anglicis mercatoribus dumtaxat exceptis. Sicque eis de inimicis gloriosus pro tempore cessit triumphus.

Terremotus. Duodecimo Kalendas Junii fuit terremotus ingens, non universalis set particularis, utputa circa oras maris et fluminum, hora post nonam; cujus vi ceciderunt templorum pinnacula[2] et concussa sunt volta ecclesiarum. Isto die terminatum fuit parliamentum apud Westmonasterium.[3] In crastino hujus terremotus hora diei xij^ma. visus est circulus nigerrimus et nebulosus et inmensus et latus circa solem. Nono Kalendas ejusdem mensis diluculo diei iteratus fuerat terremotus, non tamen adeo

---

[a] Supply assistente *or some such word.*   [b] *The letter* s *has been expunged after this word.*

---

[1] *Rewaert* of Ghent since Jan. 1382.   [2] Cf. Matt. iv. 5.
[3] Writs of expenses for this parliament, which assembled on 7 May 1382, were not issued until 22 May.

Invention of the Holy Cross [3 May] the citizens of Ghent, 1382 who burned with an unquenchable hatred for the towns-people of Bruges, made an onslaught which carried a calamitous stage further the long-standing civil war between the towns. This is how it happened. It was an ancient custom of the people of Bruges, and one scrupulously and uninterruptedly observed, that on the day of the Invention of the Holy Cross the whole city should assemble and the members of every craft should form a ceremonial procession in which was borne with extreme reverence the miraculously vouchsafed blood of the Crucified. With faithful adherence to tradition they were now celebrating this ceremony, which was attended on this occasion by the count of Flanders; and the ritual was being conducted with the great rejoicing natural in a people wholly unconscious of impending danger. The men of Ghent, like the watchful campaigners they were, were meanwhile far from idle but were meditating the means for their defeat. The holy season gave them their chance; and a treacherous character called Philip van Artevelde,[1] the son of James van Artevelde, made his dispositions and launched an attack on Bruges. In face of this assault the count and his men flew to arms and began to fight it out, but owing to an unsuspected ambush they were surrounded and overborne. Recognizing that the enemy had the upper hand of his own troops, the count, with thought in this crisis only for his own survival, took to flight with some companions. When all resistance by the Brugeois had been overcome, the fleeing remnants were pursued into Bruges, where the entire city was put to the sword without distinction of sex and only the English merchants were spared. So, for the moment, a resounding triumph over their enemies went to the men of Ghent.

Earthquake. On 21 May, an hour after noon, there was a great earthquake, which was not felt everywhere but only locally, as, for example, in maritime and riverside areas; it was violent enough to bring down the 'pinnacles of temples'[2] and to shake the vaulting of churches. This was the day on which the parliament at Westminster came to an end.[3] At the twelfth hour of the day following this earthquake a very dark hazy ring of enormous width appeared round the sun; and early in the morning of the 24th of May the earthquake

1382 vehemens fuerat sicut die Mercurii precedente.

In die Processi et Martiniani reversus est episcopus Here-fordens', Robertus Aston', dominus Johannes Devrose, de partibus transmarinis, et Ricardus Stury, magister Johannes Shepeye.[1] Quarto Idus Julii[2] dominus Ricardus Scrop' remotus fuit ab officio cancellarie. Eodem tempore fuit epidemia London' set maxime puellarum et puerorum. Episcopus London' fuit cancellarius effectus secundo die mensis Augusti in consilio tento apud Wodestoke.[3] In quindena sancti Michaelis fuit parliamentum celebratum London', in quo post multas multorum altercaciones fuit concessum regi ex parte laicorum una quintadecima,[4] set clerus tunc nichil concessit. Quarto Nonas Octobres[5] obiit London' Isabella comitissa de Bedeforde et filia regis Edwardi tercii, que apud Fratres Minores London' sepulta est.

Circa festum Sancti Edmundi Regis, congregatis episcopis et cleri multitudine apud Oxon' per archiepiscopum Cantuar' pro heresis examinacione de qua superius fit mencio,[6] concessum fuit regi dimidia decima dum cederet in usus regni magis necessarios; asserebant enim quod decime actenus concesse pocius cedebant in comodum inimicorum quam regni, quod concludebant ex expedicione facta in Hispanniam per comitem de Cantebrigia, que fuit circa festum Sancti Johannis Baptiste anno Domini M⁰. CCC.lxxxj⁰.[7] Et ista congregacio fuit quasi sinodus.

Circa idem tempus reversus est comes Cantubrigie de oris Hispannicis dissoluto matrimonio inter ejus filium et filiam regis Portugalie.[8] In ista expedicione congregato alterutro

---

[1] The end of the second embassy of those empowered on 16 Dec. 1381 to treat with the French; John Gilbert, bishop of Hereford, in fact returned on 29 June (Mirot and Déprez, in *B.E.C.*, lx, pp. 204-5 (nos. 457-9); and see above, p. 24 n.). Robert Aston is not named in the procuration.

[2] Correctly, 11 July.

[3] Robert Braybrooke, bishop of London, was appointed chancellor on 9 Sept. 1382 and did not receive the seal until 20 Sept. (*Cal. Cl. R., 1381-5*, pp. 214-15).

[4] For some of the antecedent debate see *R.P.*, iii. 134. Parliament in fact assembled on 6 Oct.

[5] Correctly, 5 Oct. (*Cal. Cl. R., 1381-1385*, p. 186).

[6] i.e. the Wycliffite heresy; see above, p. 14 and n.

[7] Convocation met at St. Frideswide's, Oxford, on 18 Nov. and granted a half-tenth on 26 Nov. (Wilkins, *Concilia*, iii. 172; *Cal. Fine R., 1377-83*, p. 346). In referring to its synodical character, as he does in his next sentence, the Monk likens this meeting to a provincial council in the full canonical sense: it was not a

was repeated, but with less violence than on the Wednesday 1382 before.

On the day of SS. Processus and Martinianus [2 July] the bishop of Hereford, Robert Aston, and Sir John Devereux returned from overseas; as also did Richard Sturry and Master John Sheppey.[1] On 12 July[2] Sir Richard Scrope was removed from the chancellorship. At this time there was an epidemic in London, but chiefly among boys and girls. The bishop of London was appointed chancellor on 2 August at a council held at Woodstock.[3] On the quinzaine of Michaelmas [13 October] a parliament was held in London, in which, after a great deal of wrangling in which many people joined, the king was granted a lay subsidy of a fifteenth;[4] but the clergy granted nothing on this occasion. On 4 October[5] Isabel countess of Bedford, daughter of Edward III, died in London; she was buried at the Greyfriars there.

About the feast of St. Edmund the King [20 November], at an assembly of bishops and many clergy convened at Oxford by the archbishop of Canterbury to examine the heresy of which mention is made above,[6] the king was granted a half-tenth on condition that it should be applied to the more pressing national purposes; for it was maintained that tenths hitherto granted had been applied to the interests of its enemies rather than to those of the nation, this being an inference drawn from the expedition to Spain undertaken by the earl of Cambridge at Midsummer 1381.[7] This assembly was in the nature of a synod.

It was at about this time that the earl of Cambridge returned from Spain following the dissolution of the marriage between his son and the daughter of the king of Portugal.[8] In

---

mere taxing assembly. By 1382 the distinction was becoming blurred. See E. W. Kemp, *Counsel and Consent* (London, 1961), p. 108; and for the offensive against the Wycliffite heresy at this council, K. B. McFarlane, *John Wycliffe and the Beginnings of English Nonconformity* (London, 1952), pp. 112-13. For the earl of Cambridge's expedition to Portugal see Russell, *English Intervention*, pp. 305 ff.

[8] The earl of Cambridge was in England by 24 Nov. 1382. The short-lived betrothal of his son, Edward, to the Infanta Beatriz, was dissolved in accordance with the terms of the Treaty of Badajoz between Castile and Portugal, in Aug. 1382 (Russell, op. cit., pp. 337-8, 343 n.). The chronicler mentions this treaty in his next sentence and hints at the possibility that the English were tricked by it: the parties to the treaty did not in fact inform the earl of Cambridge until it was completed.

1382 exercitu, videlicet Anglorum et Hispannorum, reformata est pax inter regem Hispannie et Portugalie. Dixerat enim rex Hispannie quod nollet pugnare contra Anglos et precipue contra filium nobilissimi regis Edwardi tercii: nescitur an amore an fraude hec dixerat. Sicque Angli ex bello innocenter in Angliam sunt reversi.

Cruciata. Instante hoc tempore papa Urbanus direxit bullas suas episcopo Northwycen' ut virtute illarum litterarum insurgeret contra Gallos tanquam adversus scismaticos et in eorum devastacionem erigeret crucem, concedens eandem indulgenciam omnibus et singulis hanc expedicionem adjuvantibus vel in eadem personaliter euntibus que conceditur ad Terram Sanctam peregrinantibus.[1]

Hiis temporibus venerunt nuncii in Angliam de tribus civitatibus Flandrie, petentes a rege expensas per eos factas per avum suum regem Edwardum iij.[a] circa obsidionem Calesie;[2] petiverunt eciam multa alia: de quibus peticionibus attonitum fuit consilium regis. Venerunt insuper quidam episcopus et quidam miles, cancellarius regis Portugalie,[3] duci Lancastr' missi quatinus dirigeret auxilium fratri suo comiti Cantubrigie; set dum ista fierent concordati sunt reges, ut pretactum est. Hiisdem temporibus innumera multitudo Gallorum intrarunt fines orientales Flandrensium et villas de Gravenyng, Dunkyrke, et Neuport et alias villas, assistente rege Francie et [b]vexillum suum[b] erigente. Circiter

p. 136 festum Sancte Katerine / optentis partibus orientalibus Flandrie rex Francie t⟨ristissim⟩um[c] bellum commisit cum duce civium de Gaunt, scilicet Philippo Hartefeld', et ipsum fraude Flandren' circumventum devicit et ita villam de

---

[a] *Written above the line.*   [b-b] *MS.* vexillam suam.   [c] *MS.* t[i]um.

---

[1] The bulls were *Dudum cum vinea Dei* (23 Mar. 1381), *Dudum cum filii Belial* (25 Mar. 1381) and *Dignum censemus* (15 May 1382), all addressed to Henry Despenser, bishop of Norwich. They did not empower Despenser to do more than preach a crusade against the Clementists and grant indulgences for it; Despenser, however, interpreted them as a commission to himself to lead such a crusade in person, and this is also the chronicler's interpretation. The bulls were published on 17 Sept. 1382. See M. Aston, 'The impeachment of Bishop Despenser', in *B.I.H.R.*, xxxviii (1965), 127 ff.

[2] Correctly, the siege of Tournai, 1340, for which see H. S. Lucas, *The Low Countries and the Hundred Years' War, 1326–1347* (Michigan, 1929), pp. 408 ff. The Monk refers to the embassy led by William de Coudenberghe, from the cities

the course of this expedition, when both sides, English and 1382 Spanish, had their armies in the field, peace was restored between the kings of Spain and Portugal, the former having declared that he would not fight against Englishmen, and certainly not against the son of the illustrious Edward III: whether this was said out of friendly feeling or duplicity is not known. The English accordingly came home unblooded from the wars.

Crusade. During this period Pope Urban addressed to the bishop of Norwich bulls empowering him to rise in arms against the French as schismatics, to effect whose overthrow he was to raise the Cross, granting to everybody who aided the expedition or personally accompanied it the same indulgence as is given to those who go on pilgrimage to the Holy Land.[1]

At this time there arrived in England envoys from three Flemish cities with a request to the king for payment of the charges incurred by them through his grandfather, king Edward III, in connection with the siege of Calais.[2] They also made numerous other demands, causing thereby considerable surprise to the king's council. Other arrivals were a bishop and a knight who was chancellor to the king of Portugal;[3] they had been sent to the duke of Lancaster to get him to dispatch help to his brother, the earl of Cambridge, but while this was happening the kings had come to terms, as is stated above. During this same period an enormous French army, with which the king of France, flying the royal standard, was present, advanced into the eastern territories of the Flemings and into Gravelines, Dunkirk, Nieuport, and other towns. After gaining possession of the eastern districts of Flanders, the king of France engaged about St. Katherine's Day [25 November] in a tragic battle with Philip van Artevelde, the commander of the Gantois, and on the defeat of his adversary, who had been made the dupe of Flemish treachery,

of Ghent, Bruges, and Ypres, which came to England in Oct. 1382. For the conditions which this embassy laid down for an Anglo-Flemish alliance see *Perroy*, p. 175.

[3] The chancellor of Portugal, Lourenço Anes Fogaça, was in fact accompanied by William Bettenham, squire to Sir William Beauchamp, constable of the English army in Portugal. The two were in England in Sept. 1382 (Russell, op. cit., p. 335 and n.).

1382 Bruges et de Ip⟨re⟩s occupavit.[1] Interim rex Anglie metuens ville de Caleys imminere periculum tum propter paucitatem victualium tum propter defectum bellatorum undique victualia collecta cum multitudine armatorum Calesiam transmisit ville[a] in tutelam.

Per duos dies et tres noctes ante festum Sancti Thome Apostoli indesinens erat inundacio pluviarum, unde per diversas partes Anglie in tantum augebatur aquarum discursus ut exinde sequeretur frugum et aliarum rerum inmensum detrimentum. In die predicti Apostoli episcopus Northwycensis sumpsit crucem pariter et erexit in ecclesia Sancti Pauli super gradus ante ostium chori, peragente solempnia episcopo Londoniensi. Ipso die clara fuit et sine nube temperies, aliquod felix auspicium offerens. Et quia invisa fuit et incognita Anglis ista solempnitas, ubique in omni ecclesia cathedrali scrutatus est episcopus formam tanti facti, set nullibi reperiens solum in ecclesia Westmonasterii plenissimam hujus observacionis invenit formam.[2]

Rex tenuit Natale apud Westmonasterium. Proposuerat ipsum tenuisse ⟨apud⟩[b] Wyndeshoram, set impediebatur aquarum inmensitate. Et prefata pluvia tanta crevit aquarum inmensitas in pluribus locis inopinate quod demersit greges ovium et armenta diversa pecudum, et in adeo se levavit in altum quod homines vite sue consulentes solaria altissima domorum, quidam arborum cacumina, petiverunt. Egit rex in sceptris pariter et regina in ecclesia Westmon' in die Natalis inter solempnia missarum.

1383 Finitis diebus Nataliciis in multis hastiludiis, tenuit rex consilium suum ibidem; in quo regi erat concessum[c] altera dimidia decima ex parte cleri sub ista condicione, quod rex bella pararet adversum eos qui magis contra regnum instabant:[3]

---

[a] MS. villam. [b] MS. om. [c] Sic MS.; cf. above, p. 28 and below, pp. 320, 524.

---

[1] A reference to the battle of Roosebeke, 27 Nov. 1382, for which see R. Vaughan, *Philip the Bold* (London, 1962), pp. 25-7, and Quicke, *Les Pays-Bas à la veille de la période bourguignonne*, pp. 342-3. Charles VI of France entered Bruges in the aftermath of the battle; Ypres, however, capitulated a few days before it.

[2] If so, the bishop found what he wanted in the monks' Pontifical or in their Manuale; but he could have found versions of the rite for the taking of the Cross at several cathedral churches in England. See J. A. Brundage, ' "Cruce Signari": the Rite for Taking the Cross in England', in *Traditio*, xxii (1966), 289 ff. (I am

occupied the towns of Bruges and Ypres.[1] Meanwhile, appre- 1382
hensive of the danger threatening Calais through the scantiness
of its food supplies and the inadequacy of its garrison, the
king of England assembled provisions from every source and
sent them, together with a numerous armed force, to Calais
for the defence of the town.

For two days and three nights before the feast of St.
Thomas the Apostle [21 December] there was a ceaseless
downpour of rain, causing such overflowing of streams and
rivers in various parts of England that incalculable damage
resulted to crops and other property. On St. Thomas' Day
the bishop of Norwich took the Cross and set it up in St.
Paul's on the steps before the entrance to the choir, the ceremony being conducted by the bishop of London. Clear and
cloudless weather on the day itself provided a sort of happy
omen. As the ceremony had not hitherto been seen in England, where it was unknown, the bishop searched all the
cathedrals for the form of service, without, however, finding it until in the church of Westminster he came upon a
statement of the ritual in full detail.[2]

The king kept Christmas at Westminster. He had meant to
keep it at Windsor, but was prevented by the vast extent of
the floods. Owing to the rain such enormous expanses of
water had spread without warning over various parts of the
country that whole flocks of sheep and herds of cattle of all
kinds were drowned, the floods rising to such a height that
in self-preservation people took to the uppermost rooms in
their houses or, in some cases, to the tops of trees. At Mass in
the church of Westminster on Christmas Day the king (and
the queen too) took part in full regalia.

The Christmas season having ended with a great deal of 1383
jousting, the king held a council at Westminster at which he
was granted a second half-tenth on the part of the clergy
with the stipulation that he should prepare for military action
against those by whom the country was hardest pressed:[3]

indebted to Dr. Paul Hyams for this reference.) The chronicler was, of course,
mistaken in his belief that the ceremony had never been seen before in England.

[3] The grant was made by the prorogued session of the Canterbury convocation
at Blackfriars, London, on 21 Jan. 1383 (*Cal. Fine R., 1377-83*, p. 346). A great
council was held at Westminster soon after Epiphany (6 Jan.) 1383 (*R.P.*, iii.
144).

1383 timebant ne dux Lancastr', qui semper Hyberorum aspiravit ad regnum, optentis pecuniis illuc omni expedicione transiret et non contra Gallos, ex quorum rebellione majus regno inminebat periculum.

Nocte sequente inmediate festum Scolastice Virginis comes de Notyngham etate xx. annorum vitam terminavit et apud Fratres Carmelitas sepulturam possedit.[1]

De mense Februarii obiit abbas de Bello.[2] Hic missarum peractis misteriis dum diceret illud evangelium 'In principio',[3] et pervenisset ad illud ubi dicitur. 'Et verbum caro factum est',[4] juxta cor langore percussus clamitabat 'Domine, miserere mei', unde accurrentes ministri eum confortare nitebantur; set dum nil in hoc valerent in stratu suo eum reposuerunt, ubi statim doloris angustia prevalente corpus sine spiritu reliquid. De cujus morte plurimi summum merorem trahebant; fuerat enim sub habitu monachico belliger insignis, patriam et conterminos littoraque maris ab invasionibus piratarum strenuissime servans. Huic successit dominus Johannes Craneforde[5] monachus ejusdem monasterii.

Secundo die mensis Februarii tenuit rex parliamentum suum apud Westmonasterium et de mense Marcii.[6] In quo parliamento proposuit negocium suum episcopus Northwycen' super crucis assumpcione contra Robertum antipapam, offerens[a] se in ea expedicione profecturis stipendia anualia collaturum;[b] a tempore enim quo bulle indulgenciales per papam sibi fuerant transmisse statim per diversas partes Anglie certos collectores et penitenciarios,[c] qui et populum de confessis criminibus absolverent et pecunias sub spe

---

[a] The letter s has been expunged after this word.   [b] A marginal entry has been erased.   [c] Supply miserat or some such verb.

[1] Cf. Cal. Inq. p.m., xv. 819 ff. If the chronicler gives the age of John de Mowbray, earl of Nottingham, correctly, he was born in 1362 or 1363; the only certain fact is that he was born not later than 13 Aug. 1365 (Cal. Pat. R., 1367–70, p. 236; see also G.E.C., ix. 780–1, and below, p. 62). He was created earl in 1377.

[2] Haymo de Offynton, abbot of Battle, was dead by 18 Feb. 1383 (Cal. Pat. R., 1381–1385, p. 225). The chronicler's close knowledge of this event is no doubt explained by the fact that Br. William Sudbury of Westminster had a brother, named John, who was a monk of Battle Abbey; see Cal. of Wills proved and enrolled in the Court of Husting, London, A.D. 1258–A.D. 1688, ed. Sharpe,

it was feared that if the duke of Lancaster, who was constant 1383
in his aspiration to the Spanish kingship, once laid hold of
these funds he would speedily be off to Spain instead of
against the French, from whose resistance greater peril
loomed over the realm.

During the night following the feast of St. Scholastica
the Virgin [10 February] the earl of Nottingham brought his
life to a close at the age of twenty years; he was buried at
the Whitefriars [London].[1]

In February the abbot of Battle died.[2] After celebrating
the solemnities of the Mass he was reading the Gospel 'In the
beginning',[3] and had just reached the passage which runs
'And the Word was made flesh',[4] when he was stricken by an
internal malady and cried out 'Lord have mercy on me!' The
attendant ministers rushed up and tried to relieve him, but
their efforts proving of no avail they put him to bed, where
the anguish of his sufferings at once became overwhelming
and the breath left his body. His death was the occasion of
deep and widespread regret, for beneath his monkish habit
he was a soldier of mark and the stout defender of home,
neighbours, and coast against the attacks of pirates. He was
succeeded by John Craneforde,[5] a monk of the same house.

On 2 February the king held at Westminster a parliament
which continued into March.[6] In this parliament the bishop
of Norwich submitted his proposals for action to follow his
taking of the Cross against Robert the antipope, offering
to pay yearly wages to those who set out with his expedition;
for immediately on his receipt from the pope of the bulls
empowering him to grant indulgences he had sent collectors
and penitentiaries through various parts of England to give
absolution to the people for the sins they confessed and to

---

ii. 225. The ensuing passage refers to Offynton's part in repulsing the French from
Winchelsea in 1377 (cf. Walsingham, *Hist. Ang.*, i. 341-2).
    [3] John i.1, the opening words of the last Gospel of the Mass.   [4] Ibid., 14.
    [5] *Alias* John Crane. He had been elected by 20 Mar. 1383 (*Cal. Pat. R., 1381-
1385*, p. 236).
    [6] Parliament met on 23 Feb. 1383; writs *de expensis* were issued on 10 Mar.
For the controversy in this parliament over the bishop of Norwich's proffer of a
'crusade' against the adherents of Clement VII (Robert of Geneva) in Flanders
(i.e. against the French forces there), see *R.P.*, iii. 147-8, and Aston, in *B.I.H.R.*,
xxxviii (1965), 137 ff.

1383 obtinende indulgencie collatas[a] congregarent; unde inumera summa pecuniarum per suos tales ministros sibi fuit allata. Set dominorum invidia diu ei resistens dicebat quod accideret de ejus transitu Anglie sicut contigit de Neapoli: dicebant enim in consimili casu Neapolim fuisse pape rebellem,[b] unde misso duce et exercitu pro parte pape capta fuit civitas et ex hoc hucusque in potestatem pape redacta.[1] Conformi modo aiebant jus quod rex Anglie habuerat in Francia posse de facili deperire si is episcopus sub colore assumpte crucis Franciam bellorum virtute subjugaret, precipue cum videretur pocius in causa ecclesie quam in causa regis eam optinuisse. Hiis aliisque suasionibus iniquo zelo ducti nitebantur plurimi dominorum ejus transitum impedire; quapropter communitas regni, videns inerciam dominorum in multis preactis expedicionibus regno fuisse nocivam, parti episcopi favebant, insistentibus pro eo maxime [c]duo filii comitis Devonie et milites, videlicet Philippus et Petrus[c] de Courteneye. Qua de re dux Lancastr' indignacione permotus dicebat quedam verba, quorum verborum racione rumore in vulgo divulgato communitas cepit commoveri;[2] quod cum ad aures ducis venisset, cum paucis, equis ascensis, ad alias aufugit partes. Sicque remansit parliamenti negocium aliquantulum indecisum. Post hoc factus est dominus Michael de Pole cancellarius Anglie episcopo London' amoto.[3]

De mense Marcii transmissi sunt in Angliam captivi longa / captivitate in Hispannia detenti, dominus le Sparra, Johannes Harpedene et Johannes Cossons milites.[4]

p. 137

---

[a] MS. collate.   [b] MS. rebellis.   [c-c] Sic MS.

[1] A reference to the winning of Naples by Charles of Durazzo from Joanna I in 1381, immediately following his investment with the kingdom of Sicily by Urban VI. The argument was serviceable for root-and-branch opponents of the projected crusade against the French; some lords, however, now supported this scheme and disputed only the wisdom of appointing the bishop as commander of the English forces. For Neapolitan affairs in this period, see M. Rothbarth, *Urban VI und Neapel* (Berlin and Leipzig, 1913), pp. 36 ff.; E. G. Léonard, *Les Angevins de Naples* (Paris, 1954), pp. 462 ff.; and see also below, p. 100 and n. Interest in them at Westminster Abbey dated from the time of Cardinal Langham's residence at Avignon (W.A.M. 9238).

[2] The main cause of Lancaster's irritation was, no doubt, the rejection, implicit in parliament's acceptance of Bishop Despenser's proffer, of his own proffer of a 'crusade' against schismatic Castile. See Aston, art. cit., pp. 135 ff.

gather the money contributed in the hope of winning indul- 1383
gence, and as a result untold sums had been brought in to
him by these agents of his. He met, however, with prolonged
opposition from the ill-will of the lords, who argued that the
consequences for England of his venture abroad would be
those which occurred in the case of Naples. They told how in
similar circumstances Naples had been in resistance to the
pope so that a commander was dispatched with forces on the
pope's behalf, the city was captured, and from that day forward brought under the pope's control.[1] The rights the king
of England had in France, they said, might easily be extin-
guished in a similar fashion if the bishop, in ostensible
consequence of having taken the Cross, were to subdue
France by military action, especially as he would seem to
have made his conquests in the Church's cause rather than
the king's. With these and other arguments many of the
lords strove, from motives of base jealousy, to obstruct the
bishop's expedition; which caused the commons, who had
observed how often in past ventures the apathy of the nobles
had damaged the country's interests, to side with the bishop;
the two sons of the earl of Devon, Sir Philip and Sir Peter
Courtenay, being particularly emphatic in his support. The
duke of Lancaster was profoundly irritated by this and let
fall certain remarks whose effect, when gossip had noised
them abroad, was to set the commons in a ferment.[2] When
news of this reached the duke's ears, he took horse with a
few companions and made his escape to other regions. The
business of the parliament thus remained to some extent
unsettled. Sir Michael de la Pole now became chancellor of
England on the removal from that office of the bishop of
London.[3]

During March the Sire de Lesparre, Sir John Harpeden,
and Sir John Cossons were sent back to England after long
captivity in Spain.[4]

[3] Braybrooke resigned the seal on 10 Mar. 1383 and Pole received it on 13
Mar.

[4] For the first-named in this list, Florimund de Lesparre, a lord of Médoc in
Gascony, see Russell, *English Intervention*, pp. 224 n., 345–7. He reached
England well before Mar. 1383, bearing peace proposals from Juan I of Castile,
his captor since 1377. For the capture of Sir John Harpeden by a Castilian fleet
off la Rochelle in 1372, see below, p. 152 and n.

1383   Septimo^a decimo die Aprilis episcopus Northwycen' in
ecclesia Westmon' accepit vexillum crucis ac illud ipsemet
portavit aliquantulum extra monasterium; processitque cum
infinita multitudine ad Sanctum Paulum. Decantata ibidem
missa solempni continuavit iter suum postmodum versus
mare. Illo quoque die abbas et conventus Westmon' perdiderunt sua temporalia, et abhinc usque festum Apostolorum Petri et Pauli anno revoluto in manu regis fuerunt;
mediantibus tamen amicis nichil inde percepit. Perdiderunt
namque eorum temporalia quia prosecuti sunt jus eorum in
curia Romana contra decanum et collegium Sancti Stephani
situatum infra palacium regis contra prohibicionem regis.[1]

In festo Sancte Trinitatis applicuit episcopus Northwycen'
cum capitaneis suis Cales',[2] ubi per dies Lune et Martis usque
ad horam nonam recreacionis causa prestolans ad villam de
Gravenyng equitarunt, et dispositis aciebus die Mercurii
magnanimi insultu peracto villam optinuerunt, et alias villas,
Dunkyrk, Neuport, *b*Boreburgh', Poperyng' et Lumbard*b*
cum adjacentibus municionibus in suam potestatem redi-
gerunt.*c*3 Vicesimo quinto die mensis Maii, dum episcopus
et sui in villa de Dunkyrk armis exuti se recrearent, post
horam diei nonam venerunt gens numerosa Flandrensium et
Francorum in armatis cuneis optime dispositi, vexillis et

---

*a This paragraph is written in the top margin of the MS. and is here inserted in
what seems to be its proper place. It is of interest that the addition was made
before the insertion of the regnal year and the year of grace on the right-hand
edge of this margin.   b–b Boreburgh', Poperyng' et Lumbard' Winterbottom;
MS. Boreburgh' et Poperyng', Lumbard'.   c Sic MS.; cf. below, p. 128.*

[1] The Abbey's dispute with St. Stephen's Chapel, Westminster, had been discussed in parliament in Mar. 1380 and, on the failure of the ensuing attempt at
compromise, remitted to Chancery. The monks then took the case to Rome,
where judgement was given in their favour on 26 July 1381. Further pleading
followed there on the refusal of the dean and canons of St. Stephen's to compen-
sate the monks for the expenses incurred in this litigation, and on 15 May 1383
the dean and canons were excommunicated by Urban VI. Richard II's writ of
prohibition in this phase of the proceedings is dated 30 Mar. 1383, and this is the
prohibition referred to in the text; but a general prohibition of proceedings
against St. Stephen's had been issued on 8 Dec. 1377, and Edward III had issued
a writ of prohibition in the case between the Abbey and the Chapel on 18 Feb.
1377. The temporalities were restored on 30 June 1384. See W.A.M. 18437,
18447; ibid., Bk. 12, fos. 31 ff.; *Cal. Pat. R., 1381–5*, p. 437; and for the grounds
of the dispute, below, p. 380 and n.
[2] For the letter on which the following account of events in Flanders between

On 17 April the bishop of Norwich received the standard 1383
of the Cross in the church of Westminster and himself carried
it for some little distance after leaving the abbey, whence
he made his way, attended by a vast number of people, in
procession to St. Paul's. Here a solemn Mass was sung; the
bishop then resumed his journey towards the coast. It was
on this day that the abbot and convent of Westminster lost
their temporalities, which from then until the feast of SS.
Peter and Paul [29 June] in the following year remained in
the king's hands, though owing to the intervention of friends
the king took no profit from them. The reason for their
losing their temporalities was that in contravention of the
king's prohibition they prosecuted a claim in the court of
Rome against the dean and college of St. Stephen within the
royal palace.[1]

The bishop of Norwich landed at Calais with his commanders on Trinity Sunday [17 May];[2] after waiting there
throughout the Monday and until noon on the Tuesday to
rest themselves they rode on to Gravelines. On the Wednesday
they made their dispositions and at the end of a spirited
assault had gained possession of the town, going on to bring
under their control the towns of Dunkirk, Nieuport, Bourbourg, Poperinghe and Lombartzyde with their satellite
fortresses.[3] On the afternoon of 25 May, while the bishop
and his troops, stripped of their arms, were resting in the
town of Dunkirk, a numerous body of Flemings and Frenchmen, efficiently drawn up in armed squadrons and their ranks
everywhere crammed with banners and lances, appeared at a

17 and 25 May is based, and which it cites verbatim at several points, see W. A.
Pantin, 'A Medieval Treatise on Letter-Writing, with examples, from the Rylands
Latin MS. 394', *Bulletin of the John Rylands Library*, xiii (1929), 359-61. The
author was, almost certainly, Bishop Despenser himself; see *Perroy*, p. 190 n. The
recipient may have been Abbot Nicholas de Litlington of Westminster: Litlington
was a member of the Despenser family and is known to have given quite frequent
hospitality to the bishop at an earlier date (P.R.O., S.C. 1/1261/6, part i, fos.
3, 4, 37^V, 43, 61^V).

[3] Bourbourg surrendered on 20 May, a few hours before Gravelines fell; the
English entered Dunkirk on 24-5 May (*Bulletin of the John Rylands Library*,
xiii (1929), 360-1). The chronology of the campaign after the battle before
Dunkirk on 25 May is less certain; Poperinghe did not fall until 9 June (*Istore et
Croniques de Flandres*, ed. Kervyn de Lettenhove (Académie Royale des
Sciences, des Lettres et des Beaux-Arts de Belgique, 1879-80), ii. 294).

1383 lanceis undique stipati, vix per miliare a villa distantes; quorum numerus ad xxviij. milia hominum ad minus extendebat. Factoque in exercitu Anglorum ingenti buccinarum et tubarum sonitu strepitu et clamore cursum est ad arma, et catervatim villam exeuntes bellum viriliter aggressi sunt. Conjunctisque aciebus fit fragor lancearum, disrumpuntur cassides, solvuntur laquei, et totus campus sonuit a fremitu occisorum, fugientesque adversarios armati equites insecuntur. Traduntur neci ad numerum x. milium ad minus, per totam patriam in fossis segetibus et planiciebus dispersi. Quo finito ad vexilla cunctis reparantibus 'Te Deum laudamus' humiliter genuflexi decantarunt, Altissimo pro victoria illis celitus concessa gracias exsolventes; ympnoque finito accidit mirabile,[a] enim tonitruum et grandissonum terribileque fulmen et nebula densissima super loca ad que inimici fugientes divertebant apparuerunt, aeris serenitatem auramque lenem super exercitum Anglorum Domino ostendente. In quibus omnibus pauci aut nulli de Anglis neci succubuerunt.

Prope festum Sancti Johannis Baptiste missum fuit per consilium regium episcopo predicto ad inquirendum de eodem an vellet habere comitem de Arundell' in suum adjutorium qui vicem gereret regiam; set per eum responsum est quod noluit.[b1] Promiserat is comes invenire certum numerum armatorum propriis expensis ut sic saltem transfretaret. Circa eadem tempora quidam Parys civis London', qui dudum tutor maris constitutus fuerat,[c2] in flumine Secana cepit decem naves de Hispannis, occisis in eisdem quampluribus Januensibus et Hiberis.

Mense Junii Scoti invaserunt pariter et ceperunt quoddam castrum fortissimum Johannis Montacu militis et seneschalli regis.[3] Postmodum scientes quia illud diu tenere non possent

[a] *Some adjective ending in -bile seems to have dropped out through homoeoteleuton with* mirabile.   [b] Circa eadem tempora quidam Paris civis London' qui dudum tutor maris *deleted after this word.*   [c] naves de Hispannis occisis *deleted after this word.*

[1] Cf. Despenser's denial at his trial that he had refused to acquiesce in the appointment of a lieutenant (*R.P.*, iii. 154-5). For the secular leadership of the crusade see also Aston, in *B.I.H.R.*, xxxviii(1965), 131 ff.

[2] Robert Parys, a cofferer of London, and 3 others had undertaken the defence of the sea between Winchelsea and Berwick-upon-Tweed from 24 May 1383 until

distance of barely a mile from the town; their total reached 1383 at least 28,000 men. In the English army bugles and trumpets blared and amid hubbub and shouting there was a rush to arms; and company after company sallied out of the town and swept gallantly into battle. As the opposing lines met with a clash of lances, helmets were shivered and lacings burst; the whole field echoed with the screams of the fallen and cavalry pressed the pursuit of their fleeing enemies. The victims of the slaughter, scattered in ditch, cornfield, and plain over the entire countryside, numbered at least 10,000. When the battle was over, there was a general rally to the standards by the English who humbly knelt and sang a Te Deum in thanks to the Most High for the victory vouchsafed to them from Heaven. As the hymn ended a miracle took place: over the regions for which their fleeing enemies were making, thunder pealed deafeningly and appalling lightning and murky cloud appeared, while above the English army the Lord provided tranquil weather and a gentle breeze. In all this fighting few or none of the English lost their lives.

Towards Midsummer Day a message was sent to the bishop by the king's council asking whether he wished to have the assistance of the earl of Arundel, who would represent the king: his reply was that he did not.[1] The earl had undertaken to find at his own cost a specified number of armed men in order that on these terms, at least, he might make the crossing. About the same period a citizen of London named Parys, who had some time before been made warden of the sea,[2] captured ten Spanish ships in the Seine, inflicting great slaughter on the Genoese and Spaniards aboard them.

In June the Scots attacked and captured a castle of very great strength belonging to Sir John Montague, the king's steward.[3] Knowing that they could not hold it long, they

---

29 Sept. 1384 (*Cal. Pat. R., 1381–5*, p. 278).

[3] Wark Castle. Anglo-Scottish relations should have been regulated by the truce of Nov. 1380, extended on 18 June 1381 until 2 Feb. 1384 (Rymer, *Foedera*, vii. 312–14). For the background see J. Campbell, 'England, Scotland and the Hundred Years War in the Fourteenth Century', in *Europe in the Late Middle Ages*, ed. J. R. Hale, J. R. L. Highfield, and B. Smalley (London, 1965), pp. 207 ff.

1383 castrum combusserunt et diruerunt et quandam villam concremaverunt.[1] Quare aliqui armigeri de partibus borealibus Scociam intraverunt et villas incenderunt, inmensam de bestiis predam captantes; quare adjudicatum fuit per ducem Lancastr'[2] quod armigeri predicti deberent Scotis reddi, qui nolentes injuste manibus adversariorum suorum tradi coadunata multitudine armatorum inter montes de Chiveot latuerunt. Prope festum sancti Johannis Baptiste in tractatu circa Scotos et Anglos capta est treuga usque ad festum Purificacionis beate Marie proximo securiturum.[3]

De mense Maii pariter et Junii peregrinabantur rex et regina versus Dominam de Walsyngham: transivitque per abbaciam de Buria, ubi electum per conventum in presencia sua fecit installari provisore interim in carcere de Wyndeshore detento.[4] Deinde transivit Northwycum, deinde ad villam Eliensem; quo dum rex moram traheret inmensa facta fuerant tonitrua et dies usque ad mediam diem tenebris obumbrata. Contigit ipso die quod quidam miles regis, nomine Jacobus Beernes, regi summe familiaris,[5] ictu fulminis cecus efficeretur in presencia regis et quasi extra mentem positus. Ob hoc rex jussit clerum processionaliter ad tumbam Sancte Ethelthrethe Virginis devotissime pergere quatinus interveniente populi devota oracione excecatus visum recuperaret. Factum est, ipso milite in ecclesiam ducto et coram feretro tante virginis collocato. Videbatur militi quod raptus fuerat ante judicem a quo condempnandus fuerat nisi interventi fuissent pro eo et predicta virgo et Sanctus Johannes Evangelista, set horum intercessionibus plene sanitati restitutus est.

Peragratis partibus Northfolchie, rex versus partes boreales iter arripuit et ad Notyngham veniens tenuit ibidem consilium per tres dies; ad quod consilium tantum fuerunt cancellarius, thesaurarius, dux Lancastr', comes Cantebrigie,

[1] Roxburgh. For this episode see Froissart, *Chroniques*, x. 291.

[2] Warden of the marches towards Scotland (and the king's principal representative there) and a conservator of the truce (*Rot. Scot.*, ii. 51-2).

[3] The truce of Muirhouse, concluded on 12 July 1383; it reaffirmed the terminating date of the truce of 1381 (Rymer, *Foedera*, vii. 403-4).

[4] The elect was John de Timworth; the provisor, Edmund de Brounfeld. Timworth's election had received the royal assent in Jan. 1379, but Urban VI provided Edmund de Brounfeld, who obtained possession of the Abbey later that year; the king then ordered Brounfeld's arrest (*Cal. Pat. R., 1377-81*, pp. 317,

afterwards fired and demolished it, and also burned down a 1383 town.[1] This prompted certain northern squires to enter Scotland, where they set towns on fire and seized vast plunder in cattle. The duke of Lancaster[2] consequently held that these squires ought to be surrendered to the Scots, but they, declining to be unjustly delivered into the hands of their enemies, formed an armed band and went into hiding in the Cheviot Hills. Towards Midsummer, in the course of negotiations dealing with Anglo-Scottish relations, a truce was made until the feast of the Purification of the Virgin [2 February] next following.[3]

During May and June the king and queen were on a pilgrimage to Our Lady of Walsingham, travelling by way of the abbey of Bury, where the king caused to be installed in his presence the abbot elected by the convent. The appointee provided by the pope was meanwhile confined in prison at Windsor.[4] The king passed on to Norwich and subsequently to Ely. While he was staying here there was immensely heavy thunder and until high noon the daylight was blotted out by darkness. On this particular day the king was present when one of his knights, Sir James Berners, who was on terms of the closest intimacy with him,[5] happened to be struck by lightning, which left him blind and half crazed. The king therefore gave orders that the clergy should go in reverent procession to the tomb of St. Etheldreda the Virgin so that through the people's devout prayers of intercession the blinded man might recover his sight. This was done; and the knight was led into the church and set in front of the shrine of the great virgin. The knight had a vision that he had been haled before a judge by whom he was certain to be condemned unless she and St. John the Evangelist should intercede for him; but through their intervention he was restored to complete health.

After traversing Norfolk the king took the road to the north; and on arriving at Nottingham held there a council, lasting three days, which was attended only by the chancellor, the treasurer, the duke of Lancaster, the earl of Cambridge,

418, 420). Timworth seems to have obtained papal confirmation of his election by the end of June 1383, but at great cost (ibid., *1381–5*, p. 300; *1389–92*, p. 45).   [5] Cf. *R.P.*, iii. 243.

1383 et custos privati sigilli; domini vero de partibus noluerunt ibidem venire. Sicque de villa de Notyngham transivit Eboracum, ubi a civibus cum multo honore et plurimis muneribus receptus est. Sub hiis diebus magna epidemia invasit partes Northfolchie, set solum regnabat pestis illa in homines et feminas infra etatis vij^{tem}. et xxij. annorum. Cessit officio suo Johannes Devrose, scilicet a custodia Cales'.[1]

De mense Junii obsedit episcopus cum suis et Ganensibus villam de Ipres quasi per octo septimanas, et modicum profecit.[2] Quibus expletis soluta obsidione jussit omnes voce preconia non vadiatos ad Angliam repedare: fuerunt quasi innumerabiles ibidem pedestres et inermes qui audita strage prefata inibi recenter peracta lucri causa avidius ad prefatum episcopum confluebant, / nullatenus tamen voluerunt sub^a alicujus ducis regimine gubernari. Secessit episcopus cum suis in partes illas quas primo ingressus est, scilicet Borbourgh, Poperyng', et Gravenyng'. Nec mora; fama predicante aures episcopi insonuit quod rex Francie cum ingenti exercitu ad partes illas disposuerat confestim^b accedere. Proposuit dictus episcopus Deo disponente primam aciem dicti regis quadam nocte furtive invadere et depopulare antequam ad fines illos propius approximaret, quare vocatis militibus, scilicet Thoma Tryvet, Willelmo Elmham, et Willelmo Faryndon', quorum consilio astrictus erat actus bellicos peragere, illi noluerunt consentire ad quod providus ille episcopus cum assensu domini Hugonis de Calveleye pro meliori excogitavit in animo percomplere. Igitur rex Francie cum inumera multitudine armatorum in partes Flandren' descendit et quoddam municipium ^cde Bo⟨ur⟩bourgh^c quasi in fine mensis Septembris[3] gravibus insultibus invasit, in quo recepti erant milites prefati cum aliis valentibus militibus strenuis et bellicosis. Primo insultu hostes eorum valide protriverunt; set postmodum

p. 138

---

^a *Interlined.*   ^b *Written over an erasure.*   ^{c-c} *Added in the margin after* municipium, *which ends a line.*

[1] William Beauchamp, his successor, was appointed on 15 Sept. 1383 (*Carte*, ii. 144). Devereux had been keeper since 17 Jan. 1380 (ibid., p. 130).

[2] The siege of Ypres began on 9 June and was abandoned on 10 Aug. (*Perroy*, pp. 193–6; cf. *Istore et Croniques de Flandres*, ii. 294–306). On leaving Ypres, Trivet, Elmham, and Faringdon, captains in Despenser's army, withdrew to Bourbourg; Despenser himself, as the chronicler notes, with Calveley, another of his captains, marched for a time against the French but then withdrew to

and the keeper of the privy seal, since the nobles from 1383 the remoter districts declined to make the journey. From Nottingham he passed on to York, where he was welcomed by the citizens with signal honour and numerous gifts. During this period a great epidemic attacked Norfolk, but this pestilence held sway only over persons between the ages of seven and twenty-two years. John Devereux retired from his office as keeper of Calais.[1]

In June the bishop, with his own men and forces from Ghent, laid siege to Ypres, but after eight weeks he had made little progress.[2] At the end of that time he raised the siege and caused the heralds to proclaim his orders that all who were not in receipt of official wages should return to England: for there were with the army countless persons with neither horses nor weapons who, on learning of the great execution recently done in those parts, had flocked to the bishop, the more eagerly because their motive was profit, but who were wholly disinclined to be subject to the control of any commander. The bishop now withdrew his men to the neighbourhood of Bourbourg, Poperinghe, and Gravelines into which he had first marched. Almost at once there was borne to his ears by the voice of rumour the news that the king of France planned an immediate move into the area with a huge army. The bishop proposed, subject to the determination of God, to steal upon the French king's van one night and to deliver a devastating attack on it before he approached any closer. He accordingly summoned the knights — Thomas Trivet, William Elmham, and William Faringdon — whom he was obliged to consult about the conduct of military operations, but they refused their consent to what the far-sighted bishop, with the agreement of Sir Hugh Calveley, had worked out in his mind as the best plan to carry out in the circumstances. So the king of France came down upon Flanders with an untold host under arms, and towards the end of September[3] launched a series of heavy attacks upon a town — Bourbourg — in which the knights named, together with other stalwarts of their order, all stout warriors, had established themselves. At the first onset they heavily repulsed the enemy; but they

Gravelines (R.P., iii. 155-6; Walsingham, *Hist. Ang.*, ii. 99-100).

[3] Correctly, in the 2nd week of Sept.

1383 muneribus laqueati opidum reddiderunt regi Francie, interveniente juramento[a] quod arma non portarent contra regem
p. 139 Francie quousque personaliter fuissent in Anglia:[1] / et taliter
isti milites egerunt ut vita sua, immo bonis suis temporalibus,
fruerentur. Profecto istud dampnabile factum numquam ab
Anglicis militibus gestum esse cognoscimus, ut cicius temporalia lucra et momentanea contenderent servare quam
bonam famam sibi accumulare que universis bonis fortuitis
preminet et precellit. Nonne illud prophete vaticinium eis
possumus adaptare: 'Erubesce, Sydon; ait mare'?[2] Nonne
factum istorum militum in perpetuam ignominiam Anglicis
in posterum redundabit? Utique; et utinam quod numquam
fuisset hec[b] pecunia pro qua tanto dedecore se involverent,
ut tam vili pacto villas domino regi virtute bellica conquisitas
sic de facili redderent in manus inimicorum suorum. Receperunt namque isti milites pro hiis et aliis inter se xxviij. milia
francorum.[3] Interea dum hec infeliciter gererentur vidit episcopus suos non recte agere; recepit se cum suis in opidum de
Gravenyngg', cui adhesit dominus Hugo de Calveleye; cogita-
bant enim hii predictum fortilicium contra suos adversarios
aliquamdiu tenere, set ob defectum hominum armorum et
victualium (nec sperabant de succursu) illud funditus destruxerunt,[c] prout inter ipsos et Francos extitit concordatum.[4]
Illi vero in Angliam repedarunt; venerunt Francigene[d] et
reedificaverunt illud forcius quam umquam fuit et pro presidio
tenent illud. Ganenses namque deserta obsidione ville de
Ipres, quam ipsi cum episcopo et suis quasi per duos menses
obsederunt, paulo post[5] quandam villam ceperunt vocatam
Audonard, in qua inmensos thesauros et vina in magna copia
invenerunt; cujus spoliis ditati relictis ibidem capitaneis ad
tuicionem ville predicte mox ad propria sunt reversi.

---

[a] *A word was interlined here but subsequently erased.*   [b] *Interlined.*
[c] Illi vero in Angliam repedarunt *deleted after this word.*   [d] *MS.* Frangene.

[1] i.e. in return for bribes Despenser's captains agreed to take the English forces
home. The treaty with the French was the centre-piece of the ensuing impeachment; see *R.P.*, iii. 156–8, and below, p. 50. Froissart (*Chroniques*, x. 269–70)
places the agreement to surrender Bourbourg on 14 Sept. The passage borne on
the remaining three-quarters of p. 138 of the MS. has been struck out. It is
printed below, pp. 522–6.   [2] Isa. xxiii. 4.
[3] Cf. *R.P.*, iii. 157, where sums amounting to 13,000 francs are specified, but
Trivet is accused of receiving, additionally, 'diverses grantz sommes de monoie'.

were subsequently lured by bribes into surrendering the town 1383
to the king of France, taking an oath that they would not
bear arms against him until after their actual arrival in
England.[1] Their motive in acting in this way was to enjoy
their lives — or rather their worldly goods. We are aware of
no occasion when this infamous thing has been done by
knights of England, that they should sooner strive to preserve
this world's ephemeral riches than to lay up for themselves
that good name which outshines and surpasses all fortune's
favours. Can we not apply to them the words of the prophet,
'Be thou ashamed, O Zidon, for the sea hath spoken'?[2] Will
not the action of these knights redound to the everlasting
future humiliation of Englishmen? It will indeed; and would
that that money had never been for which they involved
themselves in dishonour so great and by so shabby a bargain
tamely surrendered into the hands of the king's enemies
towns won for him by valour in war. Between them they
received, for this and other services, the sum of 28,000 francs.[3]
While these sorry doings were afoot, the bishop, observing
the misconduct of his associates, ensconced himself and his
troops in the town of Gravelines; and to him Sir Hugh Calveley
attached himself. The two of them meditated holding this
fortress for some time against the enemy, but owing to their
lack of men, arms, and food supplies (and they had no hope
of relief), they demolished it completely in accordance with
an agreement with the French.[4] The English now returned
home; and the French came in and, having rebuilt the fortress
in greater strength than ever, at present hold the place as a
garrison town. The Gantois abandoned the siege of Ypres,
which in company with the bishop and his forces they had
been investing for about two months, and a little later[5]
captured a town called Oudenarde, in which they found
untold treasure and wine galore. Enriched by its spoils they
shortly afterwards returned to their homes, leaving behind
them certain commanders to safeguard the town.

[4] Cf. Walsingham, *Hist. Ang.*, ii. 103, and *Vita Ricardi Secundi*, p. 79. The
agreement was mentioned at Despenser's trial (*R.P.*, iii. 156). Despenser returned
to England in Oct. 1383; Gravelines was garrisoned by the French towards the
end of Nov. (*Istore et Croniques de Flandres*, ii. 344; *Perroy*, p. 200).

[5] By 12 Sept. (*Croniques de Franche, D'Engleterre, de Flandres, de Lile et
especialment de Tournay*, ed. A. Hocquet (Mons, 1938), p. 261).

1383   Dux Lancastr' et comes Bukyngham frater suus circa
xxiiij. diem Augusti, audientes quod rex Francie versus partes
nostras descendit cum tanta multitudine armatorum, de quo
literis suis premunierunt regem, profecti sunt in Canciam et
ibi morati sunt juxta litus maris usque post festum sancti
Michaelis cum suo toto retenemento: putabant isti domini
quod rex exercitum suum celeriter congregaret ac cum
celeritate possibili ad dimicandum cum rege Francie omissis
ceteris impiger festinaret. Rex vero existens in partibus
borealibus,[1] postquam fama ad eum pervenit quod rex
Francie venisset prope terram suam cum ingenti exercitu,
nulla mora protracta celeriter cum paucis venit London'
circa festum Exaltacionis sancte Crucis, convocatoque super
isto suo consilio responsum est quod rex non potuit habere
tam brevi tempore, scilicet per unam septimanam vel duas,
exercitum preparatum nec esset honorificum regi in lato
campo coram tota potencia regis Francie comparere nisi
nobili apparatu; et hoc esset sumptuosum nec habetur in
erario regio ad complendum ea que affectat.[2] Et sic sua
intencio isto modo fuit frustrata.

Parliamentum. Septimo Kalendas Novembres tenuit rex
suum parliamentum apud Westmonasterium, et duravit usque
vigiliam Sancte Katerine. In quo concesserunt viri ecclesiastici unam decimam et laici unam quintamdecimam, sub
ista forma, quod si rex haberet pacem cum Francigenis et
Scotis tunc perciperet medietatem decime una cum medietate
quintedecime concesse et non plus, sin autem, plene concessis
gauderet.[3]

Tractatus. Circa ista tempora misit rex Francie domino
regi Anglie[a] ut transmitteret aliquos de suis apud Cales' ad
tractandum inter eos de pace. Super ista missione mirantur
plurimi quod rex Francie[b] loqueretur de pace ex quo de

---

[a] *Interlined.*   [b] *The letter* d *has been expunged after this word.*

[1] At Daventry (Walsingham, *Hist. Ang.*, ii. 103).

[2] Lancaster's appointment on 12 Sept. as commander in Flanders and France
and the procuration to treat with the French issued in his favour on the same day
may express decisions of this council; if so the king's return from the north must
be put a little before 14 Sept. See Rymer, *Foedera*, vii. 408–11; and on the whole
passage, above, p. xxiv.

[3] In fact parliament granted a half-fifteenth, payable by 20 Jan. 1384, and
promised to grant another half by 29 May, if peace was not made with France

About 24 August the duke of Lancaster and the earl of 1383
Buckingham, his brother, hearing that the king of France was
bearing down upon our territory with so numerous an armed
force, warned the king by letter and set out for Kent, where
they remained with their entire retinue on the coast until
after Michaelmas: they thought that the king would quickly
assemble his army and to the neglect of everything else would
hurry with all possible speed and energy to fight it out with
the king of France. The king was in the north;[1] and upon the
arrival there of reports that the king of France had appeared
with a huge army near his territory he lost no time but came
quickly with a small escort to London, which he reached
about Holy Cross Day [14 September]. A meeting of the
council, called to consider the situation, produced the reply
that it was impossible in so short a time as a week or two for
the king to have an army ready; that it would be undignified
for him to appear in the open field, facing the full might of
the king of France, except in majestic array; that this would
be expensive; and that the royal treasury did not contain the
means to fulfil his aim.[2] In this way, then, his purpose was
thwarted.

Parliament. On 26 October the king held at Westminster
a parliament which lasted until St. Katherine's Eve [24 Nov-
ember] and in which the clergy granted a tenth and the laity
a fifteenth, with the condition that if the king made peace
with the French and the Scots he was to receive half, and no
more, of the tenth and half of the fifteenth thus granted;
otherwise he was to enjoy the grant in full.[3]

Negotiations. At about this time the king of France sent
to the king of England suggesting the dispatch of English
envoys to Calais to conduct negotiations for peace between
them. Many people were surprised, over this, that the king of
France should be talking of peace when he had unwontedly

(*R.P.*, iii. 151). On 2 Dec. the southern convocation granted a half-tenth, payable
by 1 Mar. 1384, and on 23 Jan. 1384 the northern convocation granted a half-
tenth, payable by 24 Apr.; evidently similar promises for the future accompanied
these grants. See *Cal. Fine R., 1383–91*, pp.. 31, 44–5. The king claimed the conditional half-fifteenth and half-tenth at the parliament of Apr.–May 1384 (below,
p. 82).

Writs *de expensis* for the parliament of 26 Oct. 1383 were not issued until
26 Nov.

1383 nostris manum superiorem insolito more modicum antea reportavit. Diriguntur tamen pro parte nostra ad tractandum cum Francigenis, *a*scilicet dux Lancastr',*a* episcopus Herefordensis, magister Walterus Skyrlowe doctor legum et portitor privati sigilli, magister Johannes Shepeye doctor legum, et dominus Willelmus Nevyle miles;[1] qui de mense Novembris venerunt Cales' et fuerunt ibi per totum tempus Natale et diu post.

Scoti rebellant. Incepto parliamento quasi in principio Novembris invaserunt Scoti partes Northumbranas, homines occiderunt, spoliarunt, et totam patriam more hostili crudeliter consumentes dampnis gravissimis incolas affligebant; propter quod consilio regis super hujusmodi consulto concorditer ordinatum est ut domini habentes terras et redditus illinc ea*b* a talibus invasionibus de cetero custodirent, illi vero cum suis eo pacto ab omni tallagio seu imposicione prorsus deinceps fierent inmunes.[2] Unde super hoc ordinavit consilium predictum viros prospicuos et nobiles qui custodiam patrie seu plage predicte pre ceteris primaciam optinerent,*c* scilicet Eboracensem archiepiscopum, episcopum Caerlien', dominum de Nevyle, dominum Fitz Watre, dominum Ricardum Scrop', immo et comitem de Northumbrelond', cum aliis inibi in patria sibi adjunctis, dansque eis plenam potestatem ea faciendi que ad regni regisque comodum et honorem cedere. poterunt in futuro quousque ea duxerit revocanda.[3]

*De militibus qui erant cum episcopo Northwy⟨censi⟩.*d *in Flandria.* Interim durante parliamento coram rege*e* et proceribus terre adducti sunt milites prefati, qui dudum in Flandria villas regi Anglie adquisitas accepta pecunia suis adversariis reddiderunt, et super premissis*f* requisiti quare

---

a–a MS. dux Lancastr' scilicet; *and* scilicet *is interlined.*   *b* MS. inserts vero; *Winterbottom om.*   *c* *A small erasure follows.*   *d* *The final letters of this word have been lost through wear and tear at the edge of the MS.*   *e* *Interlined.*   *f* MS. premissa.

[1] John Holland, the king's half-brother, Thomas Percy, and William Beauchamp also served on this embassy. Beauchamp's service terminated on 7 Jan. 1384, on his appointment as captain of Calais; the main delegation returned to England at the beginning of Feb. 1384 (P.R.O., E. 364/17, m. 53; and see below, p. 58 and n.
[2] Cf. *R.P.*, iii. 161, 200.
[3] On 12 Dec. 1383, Henry Percy, earl of Northumberland, and John Nevill

gained the upper hand of our troops shortly before. Our 1383 representatives were, however, sent to treat with the French; they were the duke of Lancaster, the bishop of Hereford, Master Walter Skirlaw, LL.D., keeper of the privy seal, Master John Sheppey, LL.D., and Sir William Nevill.[1] They reached Calais in November and remained there over the whole of the Christmas season and for a long time after.

The Scots renew hostilities. About the beginning of November, when the parliament had just opened, the Scots attacked Northumberland, slaughtering and pillaging and by a ruthlessly hostile devastation of the entire countryside inflicting very severe damage on the inhabitants. This led, after discussion of the matter in the king's council, to a unanimously approved order that the owners of lands and rents in those parts should for the future defend them against aggression of this sort and that on this condition they and their dependants should henceforward be exempt from all tallage or other taxation.[2] The council thereupon designated certain persons of rank and prominence who were to have the keeping of the countryside and to enjoy the foremost position in the region concerned, namely the archbishop of York, the bishop of Carlisle, Lord Nevill, Lord FitzWalter, Sir Richard Scrope, and also the earl of Northumberland, together with other local gentry who were associated with them, giving them full power to do whatever might tend in the future to the profit and honour of the king and the kingdom, until the council should see fit to rescind its grant.[3]

The knights who were with the bishop of Norwich in Flanders. Meanwhile the knights who in Flanders some time before had been bribed into surrendering to the enemy towns won for the king were brought, during this parliament, before him and the leading men of the land and questioned about the reasons for their conduct and about the authority

of Raby, were appointed wardens of the marches towards Scotland and, with Thomas Percy, took over the East March. On 12 Jan., Walter FitzWalter and Scrope, with Roger Clifford, were appointed wardens of the West March, and a little later Scrope became keeper of Carlisle castle (*Rot. Scot.*, ii. 57-9; R. L. Storey, 'Wardens of the Marches of England towards Scotland, 1377-1489', in *E.H.R.*, lxxii (1957), 597, 611). The first 2 persons named by the Monk received no formal commission at this time.

1383 sic fecerunt aut*a* qua potestate absque cognicione et licencia domini regis seu locum*b* tenentis ibidem ad tam*c* facinus prorumpere presumebant.*d* Set quia ad objecta congruum non

p. 140 dederunt responsum adjudicati sunt ad / custodiam*e* in Turrim London'.[1] Thomas vero Tryvet ilico posuit se in graciam regis et liberis gaudebat habenis; alii vero mediantibus eorum amicis regi fine facto (quoniam pecunia solvit omnia istis diebus) reconciliati sunt et libertati pristine restituti.

Circa finem vero parliamenti sic allocutus est cancellarius Anglie episcopo Northwycen*f* coram rege et regni magnatibus:[2]

'Domine episcope, vos habetis gladium vestrum delatum coram vobis ubilibet sicut dominus temporalis. Deponatis gladium vestrum, quia ob hoc offenditur rex, et ceteri domini temporales inde gravi murmure conqueruntur; habeatis eciam vos de cetero secundum quod episcopus deceat se habere. Preterea, domine episcope, ad peticionem communitatum prout desiderastis rex prefecit vos gubernatorem guerrarum suarum per unum annum integre duraturum ad debellandum viriliter hostes suos ubicumque contingerent vobis occurrere, magna summa pecunie proinde a rege accepta; finaliterque promisistis premissa indilate servare. At nunc medietate anni fere transacta promissum relinquitis incompletum, thesauroque terre sine expedicione absumpto status guerrarum quasi in nichilum adduxistis.'

Episcopus vero ad hec quodammodo stupefactus excusabile responsum ad objecta minime protulit set sicut homo undique suis inimicis vallatus, dispendium evitare non valens, ea que potuit amittere, scilicet temporalia sua, ab eo quantocius erant ablata et in manu regis protinus sequestrata.[3] Rex

---

a Interlined.   *b* MS. loci.   *c* Corrected from tantum, but no adjective added.   *d* This word and attemptabant are both marginal corrections for an erased audebant which was itself interlined.   *e* Interlined. Two or three words, probably in a later hand, have been erased in the top margin of MS. p. 140. *f* Domino episcopo deleted after this word.

[1] Of Bishop Despenser's captains, William Elmham, Henry Ferriers, Robert Fitz Ralph, and Thomas Trivet were imprisoned (R.P., iii. 158).
[2] Except for its opening words, the following speech is a summary of the first part of the chancellor's first arraignment of Despenser in the parliament of Oct.-Nov. 1383; the bishop's sword and temporal mode of life were themes of the second arraignment on 24 Nov. (R.P., iii. 153-4, 156). The summary omits one of the charges against Despenser, namely that he had failed to carry out promises relating to the secular leadership of the crusade that were the condition

by which, without the knowledge or leave of the king or his 1383
lieutenant there, they had presumed to launch out into such
action. Upon their failure to make any adequate reply to the
charges against them, they were ordered into confinement in
the Tower of London;[1] but Thomas Trivet threw himself
then and there upon the king's mercy and was allowed to go
free, while others, having through the intervention of friends
effected a composition with the king (since money is a
universal solvent nowadays), made their peace and were
restored to their original liberty.

Towards the close of the parliament the chancellor, in the
presence of the king and the great men of the kingdom,
addressed the following words to the bishop of Norwich.[2]

'My lord bishop, you have your sword borne before you
everywhere like a temporal lord. Lay aside that sword of
yours; its presence is an affront to the king, and the rest of
the temporal lords are loud in their murmurs of complaint
about it: and for the future conduct yourself according to
what is proper for a bishop. Furthermore, my lord bishop, at
the petition of the commons and in conformity with your
own desire the king advanced you to the control of military
operations on his behalf for one whole year, to wage vigorous
war upon his enemies wherever they might chance to cross
your path, and you received from the king a large sum of
money for this purpose. Lastly you undertook to carry out
the project without delay. Yet now, with almost half the year
gone, you leave your undertaking unfulfilled; with the
country's treasure drained away and no expedition in being,
you have brought the military situation to virtual ruin.'

Somewhat dazed by this attack, the bishop failed to offer
any excuses by way of reply to the charges, but like a man
hemmed in by his enemies on every side, and powerless to
avoid some sacrifice, he found taken from him without
further ado all that was his to lose — his temporalities, which
were forthwith seized into the king's hands.[3] The king,

of the king's acceptance of his proffer. See also T. F. T. Plucknett, 'State Trials
under Richard II', in *T.R.H.S.*, 5th ser., ii (1952), 162-3, and Aston, in *B.I.H.R.*,
xxxviii (1965), 128 ff.

[3] In fact the bishop spoke twice at length in his own defence. Judgement was
given on 24 Nov. 1383, but writs giving effect to the confiscation of temporalities
did not issue until 6 Feb. 1384 (*R.P.*, iii. 154-6; *Cal. Fine R., 1383-91*, p. 33).

1383 vero consolatus est episcopum et hortatus est eum ne ullatenus expavescat, protestans quod satis favorabilis sibi
existeret quicquid ibidem protunc extitit judicatum. Acta
sunt hec, ut dicebatur, feria vj^{ta}. proxima ante finem parliamenti, litera dominicalis D.

Item in isto parliamento inter regem et dominos temporales
magna dissencio est exorta; nam prout eis videbatur rex
insano consilio adherebat et propter hoc bonum regimen
circa se non admisit; unde nitebantur totum onus guber-
nacionis supra se assumere. Allegabant enim quod predecessores sui reges nobilissimi temporibus retroactis dominorum
consilio regebantur, et quamdiu illorum gubernacio fuerat^a
acceptata regnum Anglie magnificis prosperitatibus affluebat.
Rex vero, contrarium senciens, dixit se nolle illorum consilio
regi^b vel duci solummodo, set per suum consilium, scilicet
per viros electos et probatos de regno, placuit sibi modeste
et tractabiliter gubernari. Et licet ad hec domini excan-
descentes multipliciter essent moti, egit tamen rex in isto
casu multum sagaciter et prudenter, videlicet ne forsan^c sub
dominorum regimine aliquid mali acciderit illorum negli-
gencie communitas imputaret ac sic divisi status regni diversimode turbarentur.^{d} Igitur ut premissa consulcius possit
rex pacificare primo dominorum insolenciam aliqualiter
rigide reprehendit ut inferiorum animos ab ipso quodammodo elongatos verbis persuasibilibus^e ad suum imperium
expedicius revocaret.

Ordinatum est in isto parliamento quod causas et negocia
tam beneficialia quam prophana in curia Romana prosequentes per breve regis ad prosecucionem suorum adversariorum utlagati possent in banco domini regis per procuratorem
de cetero comparere, quod eis antea non licebat.[1]

Quarto decimo die Decembris[2] misit rex Scocie domino

---

^{a} MS. fuerit. ^{b} Interlined; rei deleted. ^{c} Recte ⟨si⟩ forsan (Winterbottom). ^{d} MS. turbaretur. ^{e} MS. persuabilibus.

---

[1] A reference to statute 7 Richard II, cap. 14 (S.R., ii. 35, and cf. R.P., iii.
159).
[2] i.e. after the breakdown of negotiations during the late parliament for an
extension of the current Anglo-Scottish truce, due to expire on 2 Feb. (R.P.,
iii. 149–50; Walsingham, Hist. Ang., ii. 109).

however, consoled the bishop and urged him not to lose 1383 ·
heart, declaring that he himself remained well disposed, whatever might have been the judgement of parliament on the
present occasion. These proceedings took place, it was said,
on the Friday before the parliament ended [20 November],
the dominical letter being D.

In the course of this parliament a serious quarrel arose
between the king and the lords temporal, because, as it
seemed to them, he clung to unsound policies and for this
reason excluded wholesome guidance from his entourage;
they therefore strove to take the full burden of control upon
themselves. They maintained that in former times the most
illustrious of his royal predecessors had been ruled by the
advice of their lords, and for as long as the control of those
lords had been accepted the realm of England was a land of
plenty and brilliant prosperity. The king, however, was of the
opposite way of thinking: he said that he was unwilling to be
ruled or led exclusively by their advice, but he was content
to accept with all deference and docility the guidance of his
council, composed as it was of the kingdom's picked and
tested men.

Although this created a considerable stir of indignation
among the lords, the king acted in this situation with great
shrewdness and discernment to prevent the possibility that
under the rule of the lords some mishap might occur which
the commons would ascribe to their negligence, and that the
estates of the realm, thus sundered, would be thrown into
every kind of turmoil. With a view, therefore, to the most
judicious means of keeping the peace he began by rebuking
the effrontery of the lords with a certain sternness so that
by the use of winning language he might the more readily
recall to his dominion the hearts of the less exalted classes
which were in some degree estranged from him.

It was ordered in this parliament that those who, through
prosecuting pleas and other business in the court of Rome in
connection with either benefices or secular matters, were
outlawed by the king's writ at the suit of their opponents
might henceforward appear in the King's Bench by attorney,
which had not previously been permissible.[1]

On 14 December[2] the king of Scotland sent to the king of

1383 regi Anglie quandam literam humillimam et devotam, excusans se super transgressione suorum in partibus borealibus regni Anglie nuper commissa, recitando quod homines nostri de marchia quam plura dampna eis per prius nequiter intulerunt, propter quod quidam de suis ipso inconsulto et sine ejus licencia surrexerunt et injuriam vindicarunt. Affectabat tamen, quicquid sit actum, treugas inter nos firmatas libenter servari*a* ac dampna ex utraque parte facta bona mediacione per visum virorum nobilium de consensu utriusque partis electorum previa discrecione efficaciter compensari.*b* Set quicquid dictus rex nobis per suas literas misit,*c* certum est quod dominus Johannes de Vienna de Francia miles nominatissimus fovebat in Scocia per totam hyemem de Francigenis quinque milia hominum armatorum, ac de die in dies turmatim de Francia ad eum venerunt;[1] nec Scoti ab inceptis destiterunt quin ad xx*ti*. miliaria et amplius in terra Anglie predas agebant, occidendo, comburendo, captivando, villas et castra eciam spoliando. Illam oportunitatem habuerunt protunc quia predicti domini nuper ad custodiam dicte patrie deputati noluerunt movere arma contra eos donec treuga inter eos capta foret elapsa. Rex tenuit Natale apud Eltham in multis hastiludiis et aliis jocundis solaciis consuetis.

Pestilencia. Circa ista tempora fuit magna pestilencia in Cancia et aliis pluribus locis Anglie, nonnullos ad ultimum vite sue vale deducens, neque sexui vel etati quoquomodo pepercit.

1384 De mense Januarii[2] vacante custodia castri Dovorr' per mortem domini Roberti de Assheton' militis rex contulit illam domino Simoni de Burle, ad cujus introitum rogavit eum esse; cui consenciens rex xviij. die ejusdem mensis versus Dovorr' profectus est. Quo peracto rediit rex ad manerium suum de Eltham penultimo die Januarii et ibidem tenuit festum Purificacionis beate Marie. Ad quem primo die

---

a MS. servare. *b MS.* compensare. *c MS.* miserit.

[1] Cf. below, p. 120, where the expedition of Jean de Vienne to Scotland is correctly placed in the early summer of 1385. In the summer of 1383 Charles VI had engaged to send 1,000 men to Scotland before May 1384 if England and Scotland should be at war (Campbell, in *Europe in the Late Middle Ages*, ed. Hale, Highfield, and Smalley, p. 208).

[2] On 5 Jan. (*Cal. Pat. R., 1381–5*, pp. 366–7).

England an extremely humble and dutiful letter, excusing 1383
himself over the offences recently committed in the North
of England by his subjects in a detailed statement that our
countrymen in the marches had wrongfully inflicted very
extensive damage on them in the first place, and that for this
reason certain of his subjects, without consulting him and
without his leave, had risen up and avenged the outrage. But,
despite what had happened, his own aim was that the truce
between us should be willingly maintained and that after
honest mediation the damage done on either side should,
with sound judgement to lead the way, be effectively re-
dressed by view of men of rank chosen with the consent of
both parties. Yet whatever the message the Scottish king sent
us in his letter, it is certain that throughout the winter a very
celebrated French knight, Sire Jean de Vienne, maintained in
Scotland 5,000 French men-at-arms and that new arrivals
from France reached him in companies daily.[1] Nor did any
pause in their activities keep the Scots from conducting, to
a depth of twenty miles and more inside English territory,
cattle-raids accompanied by fire and slaughter, the carrying
off of prisoners, and the sack of towns and even of castles.
They were given the opportunity to do so at this time because
the English noblemen lately appointed to the defence of that
countryside were unwilling to take military action against
them until after the expiry of the truce concluded between
the parties. The king kept Christmas at Eltham with a great
deal of jousting and other pleasant diversions of the usual
kinds.

Plague. At about this time there was a great plague in Kent
and several other districts of England which in no way spared
either age or sex and brought some people to the last leave-
taking of their lives.

In the course of January[2] the king conferred the keeper- 1384
ship of Dover Castle, vacant through the death of Sir Robert
Ashton, on Sir Simon Burley, who requested the king's
attendance at his entry upon his duties. The king agreed, and
set out for Dover on 18 January. The formalities over, the
king returned on 30 January to his manor of Eltham, where
he kept the feast of the Purification [2 February]. The duke
of Lancaster visited him on 1 February to report the full

Februarii dux Lancastr' accessit, referens / sibi totam medullam tractatus inter ipsos et Francigenas habiti. Venerunt eciam tunc temporis London' omnes qui ex parte nostra erant Cales' causa tractatus, narrantes quod pro meliori capta fuit una treuga tam per mare quam per terram inter nos et Gallos usque proximum festum sancti Michaelis, ut interim ambo regna consulcius et caucius deliberarent se super articulis concordie tactis in prenominato tractatu.[1]

Circa ista tempora Scoti cum ingenti multitudine obsederunt castrum de Laoghmaban, in quo fuit quidam Scoticus ad fidem Anglorum conversus qui custodi castri predicti optulit se illud custodire cum xx. hominibus cum illis victualibus jam habitis in illo xx. diebus, eo pacto quod ipse medio tempore laboraret pro habendo succursum. Ipse vero ut vecors id renuit facere. Unde quinto die Februarii[a2] custos predictus tanquam infidelis et ingratus reddidit eis castrum predictum: Scoti namque ilico intrantes illud solotenus destruxerunt, compatriotam suum predictum membratim discerpserunt, lapides itaque castri predicti in flumen[b] Loogh, ne deinceps pro reparacione dicti castri aliquatenus deservirent, nequiter projecerunt, demum consumptis omnibus structuris castri supradicti ad sua salvi et incolumes sunt regressi. Cujus facti fama ocius pervenit ad regem, qui celeriter super hoc sumpto consilio propter impotenciam nostrorum ibidem in partibus existencium nec resistere tante multitudini valencium ducem Lancastr' et dominum Thomam comitem Bukyngham fratrem ejusdem ducis cum aliis potentibus ad compescendam Scottorum audaciam destinare curabat; qui de mense Marcii iter arripientes xxiiij. die ejusdem mensis apud Novum Castrum super Tyne cum eorum exercitu salvi pervenerunt.[3]

Hoc[c] anno erat quidam major in civitate London'

[a] tanquam *deleted after this word.* [b] *Sic MS.; recte* aquam. *But apparently the chronicler understood the next word as a proper name.* [c] j[a] *in the margin but damaged by trimming.*

[1] The truce of Leulingham, 26 Jan. 1384, for which see Rymer, *Foedera*, vii. 418–21; it was to last until 1 Oct. 1384, and a date for the resumption of negotiations was agreed. For the return of the English envoys in the first week of

inwardness of the negotiations conducted between his 1384 party and the French. It was at this time too that all the persons who had represented us in the negotiations at Calais arrived in London and announced that they had improved the situation by arranging a truce on land and sea between us and the French until the following Michaelmas so that both kingdoms might meanwhile give more informed and careful consideration to the articles of final agreement discussed in the negotiations.[1]

The Scots about this time laid siege in very great strength to the castle of Lochmaben, in which there was a Scotsman who had transferred his allegiance to the English and who made an offer to the keeper of the castle that given twenty men and the food supplies already in it he would hold it for twenty days, provided that in the meantime the keeper exerted himself to get help. This the keeper cravenly refused to do, and showed his want both of loyalty and of gratitude by surrendering the castle on 5 February to the Scots, who upon their entry razed it forthwith to the ground and tore their fellow countryman limb from limb.[2] In their spite they threw the very stones of the castle into the loch to prevent them from being of the slightest use for future repairs; and at last, when the castle buildings had all been demolished, they returned safe and sound to their homes. News of these events soon reached the king, who, after swift consultation, took steps, in view of the weakness of our countrymen in the area, who were unable to oppose numbers so great, to dispatch the duke of Lancaster and Thomas earl of Buckingham his brother, with powerful support, to curb the insolence of the Scots. Having set out earlier in the month they arrived safely with their forces at Newcastle upon Tyne on 24 March.[3]

This year the city of London had a mayor, John 1383

Feb. see also P.R.O., E. 364/17, mm., 56-6ᵛ; ibid., 364/18, m. 60; and Mirot and Déprez, in *B.E.C.*, lx, p. 206 (nos. 469-70). Cf. above, p. 50.

[2] Cf. *Fordun*, i. 383, where the date given for the capture of Lochmaben is 4 Feb. The keeper of the castle, Alexander de Fetherstanhalgh, was later accused of misprision of treason (*Cal. of Documents relating to Scotland*, ed. J. Bain (4 vols., 1881-8), iv, pp. 73-4; *Cal. Cl. R. 1381-5*, p. 370).

[3] Cf. *Rot. Scot.*, ii. 60-1.

1383 Johannes Northampton' nomine:[1] hic in officio suo per duos
ferme[a] annos rigide se habuit, nam piscarios in civitate
London' dure et acerbe afflixit, et digne, ut aliqui judicabant,
quia omnis generis pisces carius quam necessitas pro tempore
exposcebat semper indefesse vendebant. Unde propter ista,
immo et propter alias iniquas consuetudines quas jugiter in
vendicione piscium observabant, major predictus curiam
eorum destruxit, recentes pisces eis vendere interdixit nisi
ad mare vellent transire et inde pisces afferre ac eo foro
vendere quo extranei vendere voluerunt. Ad hec enim communitas civitatis multipliciter applaudebat; videns namque
major predictus hoc communitati valde placere apposuit[b]
uberiorem diligenciam adhibere, scilicet ut communitas
predicta deinceps meliori foro eorum victualia emerent
quam antea fecerunt, ordinavit extraneos venire cum piscibus
et eos in plateis stare, ac cuicumque voluerint pisces vendere
libere permisit. Placuit enim primo ista ordinacio universis
civitatis predicte, set cum vellet alias artes ejusdem civitatis
super eorum transgressionibus eciam justificare eorumque
pravas consuetudines in melius transmutare et errata corrigere, aliqua vero[c] temptavit emendare que ad finem effectualem perducere propter maliciam partis adverse prout voluit
non valebat; quare inter ipsum majorem et quasdam artes
civitatis predicte[d] grave[e] dissencionis materia[f] est suborta,
et percrebuit in tantum quod multi ex eis[g] qui primo fortiter
tenuerunt cum eo, amicicie vinculo procul abjecto, diver-
tentes ab eo noluerunt ejus imperio ulterius[h] obedire.
Tandem adveniente die quo ad novi majoris eleccionem
procederent, aliqui clamabant 'Northampton!', ipsum affectantes ut ante in eorum majorem habere, alii vero contrarium
sencientes ipsum respuerunt et dominum Nicholaum Brembre

---

[a] Interlined.   [b] Recte disposuit?   [c] Interlined.   [d] discordia suscitata
deleted after this word.   [e] Sic MS.; cf. below, p. 84.   [f] inter eos deleted
after this word.   [g] Interlined.   [h] Interlined.

---

[1] John Northampton, a draper, was elected mayor for the first time on 13 Oct.
1381 and re-elected on 13 Oct. 1382. There follows a summary of ordinances of
the mayor and aldermen and common council of 28 June and 18 July 1382,
which restricted London fishmongers to the sale of fish caught in their own
vessels and of perishable kinds of salt-water fish purchased from non-citizen
wholesalers within the City. The surrender of charters required of the fishmongers
at this time had the effect of depriving them of the right of pleading in all matters

Northampton by name,[1] who over a period of about two 1383
years behaved in his office with a certain severity, subjecting
the city fishmongers to sore vexations — and properly, in
some people's opinion, since they regularly and tirelessly
sold fish of all kinds more dearly than the need of the
moment demanded. Because of this, and because, too, of
other improper practices which they consistently followed in
the sale of fish, the mayor abolished their court and prohibited their selling fresh fish unless they were prepared to
go to the sea, bring the fish from there, and sell it at the same
market price as strangers were willing to sell at. The commons of the city strongly approved this action; and the
mayor, observing the satisfaction it had given, now brought
enhanced attention to bear in order that in future the commons should buy their food more cheaply than they had
hitherto done. He ordered that strangers should come with
their fish and take up their stand in the city streets, where
they were freely permitted to sell their wares to whomsoever
they wished. At the outset this ordinance pleased everybody
in the city, but when the mayor wanted also to execute
justice upon other city crafts for their misdeeds, to alter their
improper practices for the better, and to correct their errors,
and when he tried to introduce certain reforms which,
through the ill-will of the opposing party, he was unable to
carry through to the successful conclusion he desired, occasions arose for serious disagreement between the mayor and
some of the city crafts and multiplied to such a degree that
many of those who had at first strongly supported him cast
off the ties of friendship and fell away, refusing to submit
any longer to his authority. When in due course the day came
for them to proceed to the choice of a new mayor, there
were some who, with shouts of 'Northampton!', expressed
their desire to have him for their mayor as before, but there
were others of the opposite way of thinking who would
have none of him and assiduously demanded the election

concerning their trade in their own courts, and this is the meaning of the Monk's
statement that Northampton 'abolished their court'. See *Letter Book H*, pp. 190
ff.; cf. *R.P.*, iii. 141-3; statute 6 Richard II, i, *caps.* 10-11 (*S.R.*, ii. 28). On the
following passage see also above, pp. xxiv-v, and for the background, Bird, *Turbulent London of Richard II*, pp. 63 ff.

1383 in eorum majorem attencius pecierunt: et sic aliquamdiu invicem disceptantes demum dominum N. Brembre rege favente in majorem London', licet non habuit vota singulorum, erat tamen assumptus.[1] Qui cum arte sua[a] piscaria tam viriliter stetit quod piscarii sicut ante omnis generis pisces more solito vendiderunt. Extraneos eciam in eorum stacionibus pisces vendere permisit set eis pisces scindere penitus interdixit.

1384 Septimo die Februarii prandente comite de Notyngham[2] cum predicto J. Northampton' rogavit eum comes prefatus ut post prandium veniret [b]cum suis[b] ad Fratres Carmelitas, exhibendo sibi honorem eo quod dies aniversarii fratris sui nuper ibidem sepulti in proximo inminebat. Annuit ipse et venit cum cccc[tis]. circiter viris de diversis artibus congregatis: major vero London' non habuit secum in sua comitiva ultra xl. viros. In redeundo quoque major obviavit Northampton', querens ab eo ad quid tanta turba eo tempore erat vallatus; at ille retulit sibi causam, dicens quod omnes qui erant cum illo protunc minime invitavit, immo gratis absque sui noticia ad eum confluebant. Alii namque indignati dixerunt illam fuisse causam quare tot et tales sibi protunc ascivit, scilicet ut tumultum et sedicionem in populo suscitaret; unde per sediciosos orta dissencione non obstante ejus multitudine Northampton' interfectus ibidem fuisset nisi major eum cicius arrestasset. Demum postea facta de illo relacione domino regi, scilicet quomodo nitebatur civitatem London' cameram suam diversimode perturbare et nisi alibi sit pro tempore quam in civitate prefata timendum est quod ipse erit causa destruccionis civitatis predicte; quare super ista suggestione rex jussit eum mitti in castrum de Corf, ut ibi in custodia

---

[a] Written above sicut, deleted.   [b-b] Interlined.

[1] Brembre (a grocer, not a fishmonger), was elected on 13 Oct. 1383. The Monk refers to ordinances of 11 Dec. 1383 removing many of the restrictions imposed on victuallers during Northampton's mayoralty and to another of 31 July 1384 specifically relating to fishmongers. The former ordinance gave effect to a statute of the recent parliament. The reference to a concession to non-citizen fishmongers is the Monk's own. To sell fish 'cut up' was to retail it in small quantities. See R.P., iii. 160, 161–2; statute 7 Richard II, cap. 11 (S.R., ii. 34); Letter Book H, pp. 222, 243–4.

of Sir Nicholas Brembre. After some time spent in dispute 1383
between the factions Sir Nicholas Brembre, despite his not
having universal support, was with the king's approval
adopted as mayor of London.[1] So resolutely did he range
himself alongside his fellow fishmongers that they sold fish of
all kinds in accordance with their former habitual practice.
He allowed strangers, too, to sell fish in the places allotted to
them, but prohibited them absolutely from cutting it up.

On 7 February the earl of Nottingham[2] was at dinner 1384
with John Northampton and asked him to bring his friends
after dinner to the Whitefriars, where the earl's brother
had been buried not long before; he paid him this compliment because his brother's anniversary was close at hand.
Northampton accepted, and arrived in the company of some
400 persons brought together from various city trades; while
the mayor of London had with him an escort of no more
than forty men. On the way back the mayor fell in with
Northampton and asked him why, on an occasion like the
present, he was surrounded by so great a crowd: Northampton offered his reasons, explaining that by no means all
those now with him were there by his invitation; indeed it
was of their own free will and without his being privy to it
that they flocked round him. On the other side there were
angry suggestions that his real purpose in attaching to
himself persons of such a type and in such numbers at
this time was to stir up riot and disaffection among the
populace. This led, through the agency of disorderly
elements, to the outbreak of a quarrel, and despite the
numbers with him Northampton would have been killed
on the spot if the mayor had not been quick to arrest him.
A report on the affair was subsequently made to the king,
pointing out that Northampton was endeavouring to
create disturbances of various kinds in the city of London,
which was the king's special home, and that unless he was
lodged elsewhere for a time than in the city there was reason
to fear that he would cause its undoing. In pursuance of
this suggestion the king ordered that Northampton should
be sent to Corfe castle, to be kept in custody there until

---

[2] Thomas de Mowbray, earl of Nottingham, 1383-99. For his brother's death
the previous year see above, p. 34 and n.

1384 teneretur ad tempus quousque ipse super quibusdam sibi impositis eciam[a] potuerit se purgare.[1]

De suto⟨re⟩. Preterea xj°. die Februarii quidam sutor[2] spiritu diabolico agitatus, ut volunt quidam, discurrebat per plateas civitatis commovens populum assurgere in majorem, asserens majorem velle omnes adherentes J. Northampton' in frusta delere, innuens per hoc ut illi subito et inopinate majorem extinguerent. Set Deus justus et misericors noluit quod tanta sedicio in tam populosa civitate foret exorta ut pretextu unius persone unus forsan extingueret alium, immo

p. 142 pro meliori / disposuit ut unus cicius moreretur quam tantorum sanguis innoxius funderetur. Propter quod sutor predictus fuit captus et coram omnibus valencioribus de civitate de mendacio convictus morti fuit legittime adjudicatus; cujus capud super portam de Neugate jubente senatu erat affixum. Verumptamen de predicto sutore dixerunt quidam eum fuisse bone vite utpote jejuniis et oracionibus multipliciter insistentem, pia loca et sacra devote et sepius visitantem, nec erat intencionis sue ut verba sua quempiam moverent offendere tante civitatis majorem: unde concludebant eum fore male peremptum, ac mors sua [b]verisimile est[b] in posterum ut[c] gravem expeteret ulcionem. Confestim major predictus sumpto sano consilio artes civitatis adinvicem discordantes quas potuit cum omni diligencia pacificavit.

1383 Hoc anno mense Decembris circa festum Natalis Domini Hispani Angligenis opido infesti clericos Anglicos et bene promotos de Roma versus Neapolim proficiscentes numero xvj. in mari Mediterraneo ceperunt et captos secum in

1384 Hispanniam adduxerunt. Item de mense Marcii quinque naves ex ipsis armatorum agmine sufficienter onuste naves nostras tendentes versus Burdegal' pro vino quindecim ex eis ceperunt; quod facile potuissent tum quia separatim et non gregatim se marinis periculis exposuerunt tum quia sine

---

[a] *Interlined.*   [b-b] *Interlined.*   [c] *Interlined.*

[1] On his arrest (which took place in Fleet Street) on 7 Feb., Northampton was taken to Brembre's house; the writ ordering his committal to Corfe castle is dated 9 Feb. 1384 (*Cal. Cl. R., 1381–5*, p. 369). Cf. *The Peasants' Rising and the Lollards*, ed. E. Powell and G. M. Trevelyan (London, 1899), pp. 35, 37–8, and Bird, op. cit., pp. 138–9.

[2] John Constantyn (*Letter Book H*, p. 231; *Cal. Pat. R., 1381–5*, p. 391).

he should be able to clear himself of certain charges against 1384 him.[1]

The cordwainer. On 11 February a cordwainer,[2] excited, as some will have it, by a spirit sent from the Devil, careered through the streets of London urging the populace to rise against the mayor, whom he declared to be bent on smashing all those who supported John Northampton, and whom he thereby meant to imply they should suddenly surprise and destroy. A righteous and merciful God, however, unwilling that the emergence of serious sedition in the densely populated city should lead, because of a single individual, to people's destroying one another, ordained a better course for events in choosing rather that one man should die than that the innocent blood of the many should be spilled. And so the cordwainer was arrested, and upon his conviction before all the leading citizens of spreading false statements, he was condemned to death in conformity with the law. By order of the court of aldermen his head was set above Newgate. There were nevertheless some people who said of this cordwainer that he was a man of godly life, who applied himself habitually to prayer and fasting and was regular and reverent in his attendance at places of devotion and at the celebration of the Mass, and that it was no part of his intention that his language should prompt anyone to an outrage against the mayor of that great city; from which they argued that he had been wrongly made away with and that in time to come a stern revenge would probably be exacted for his death. On good advice the mayor now set industriously to work to appease those he could of the city crafts which were in conflict with each other.

In December of this year, about Christmas time, the 1383 Spaniards, bitterly hostile to the English, captured in the Mediterranean sixteen very exalted members of the English clergy on their way from Rome to Naples, and carried off their prisoners with them to Spain. Then in March five of 1384 their ships, with their due complement of armed troops aboard them, captured fifteen out of our vessels bound for Bordeaux to fetch wine. This they were easily able to do, first because the English ships exposed themselves to the hazards of the sea separately instead of in convoy, and

1384 presidio et tutela virorum armorum incaute mare*a* intrabant. Papa vero tunc temporis et diu antea traxit moram Neapol', unde duxit originem.[1]

Hoc anno tercio die Aprilis[2] dux Lancastr', comes de Bukyngham, et alii domini de Anglia cum ingenti exercitu Scociam intrabant, dampna quam plurima Scoticis inferebant, et longe majora fecissent nisi dux Lancastr' eos impedivisset; nam abbaciam de Meuros funditus destruxissent nisi ipse prohibuisset eo quod ibi hospitatus fuisset quando in Scociam causa tuicionis fugisset tempore turbacionis plebeiorum. Item villam de Edenburgh ceperunt, et illam voraci flamma consumpsissent nisi dux Lancastr' contrarium senciens illam redempcioni exponere judicasset;[3] et ab hinc usque ad aquam de Forth que mare Scoticum nuncupatur procedentes modicum dampnum quodammodo nostris hostibus inferebant. Multi quoque tam homines quam eorum equi propter caristiam et raritatem victualium in illo itinere perierunt. Demum inter eos capto consilio nondum quindena completa postquam Scociam intrassent omnes domini cum suis in Angliam sunt reversi. Comes vero de Northumberland' non sine invidia multorum custodiam marchie et eorundem finium super se solus recepit.[4]

Parliamentum. Preterea xxix^mo. die Aprilis rex Anglie apud Sar' tenuit parliamentum, et duravit usque xxvij^m. diem mensis Maii; in quo aliqua in sui principio emanarunt miranda. Primo*b* quia tam viri ecclesiastici quam domini temporales inter se mirabiliter adversantes effectum parliamenti pene frustrabant; set dux Lancastr' superveniens[5] eos in multa verborum facundia minas intermiscens pacificavit. Secundo*c* de verbis comitis Arundell', nam cunctis audientibus in pleno parliamento et rege presente dixit hec verba sive consimilia:

---

a Interlined.   *b* j. *in the margin.*   *c* ij. *in the margin.*

[1] Urban VI was at Naples from 10 Nov. 1383 to 16 June 1384, when he left for Nocera (*Cronicon Siculum incerti authoris*, ed. J. de Blasiis (Società Napoletana di Storia Patria: Monumenti Storici, 1887), pp. 52–3).

[2] For the date cf. *Bower*, ii. 398; Knighton, *Chronicon*, ii. 203; and Walsingham, *Hist. Ang.*, ii. 111. 'Hoc anno' refers to the marginal date '1384' opposite this entry: the chronicler's year has just changed.

[3] So too *Bower*, loc. cit.

secondly because they were rash enough to put to sea 1384 without the protection and safeguard afforded by men-at-arms. At this time, as for a long period before it, the pope was staying at Naples, from which he derived his origin.[1]

On 3 April[2] this year the duke of Lancaster, the earl of Buckingham, and other English nobles marched with a huge army into Scotland. They inflicted very extensive damage on the Scots and would have wrought far greater havoc had not the duke of Lancaster prevented them, since they would have completely demolished the abbey of Melrose if the duke had not forbidden it on account of his having been entertained there when he fled for safety into Scotland at the time of the popular disturbance. Edinburgh was captured, and would have been devoured by fire if the duke had not been of the opposite way of thinking and ruled that the town should be held to ransom.[3] From here they advanced to the Firth of Forth, otherwise called the Scottish Sea, contriving to inflict some slight damage on our enemy. Both men and horses died in large numbers on the march owing to the dearth and scarcity of food. Eventually, after consultation among themselves, all the nobles returned with their troops to England less than a fortnight after they had entered Scotland. The earl of Northumberland, not without widespread ill-feeling, assumed sole charge of the march and the adjoining territory.[4]

Parliament. On 29 April the king held at Salisbury a parliament which lasted until 27 May. Some remarkable events in its opening stages subsequently came to light. In the first place, churchmen and temporal lords alike, by their astonishing squabbles among themselves, almost nullified the effect of the parliament, but the duke of Lancaster made his appearance[5] and in a speech compounded of eloquence and threats reduced them to calm. Secondly there was the language of the earl of Arundel, who in full parliament made in the hearing of everybody present, including the king, the following speech or something like it.

---

[4] A reference to the agreement of 23 Apr. 1384 between Lancaster and Northumberland, whereby the latter became in effect sole warden of the marches towards Scotland (*Rot. Scot.*, ii. 62; Storey, in *E.H.R.*, lxxii (1957), 597–8).

[5] He did so after 9 May. For this parliament see *R.P.*, iii. 166 ff.

1384 'Domini[a] mei, vos scitis quod omne regnum carens provida gubernacione in periculo destruccionis consistit, et res jam est in aperto, quia, ut nostis, regnum istud a diu propter malum regimen cepit languescere ac modo fere tabescit, et nisi cicius appositis sibi remediis succurratur ac de tempestuosa voragine qua involvitur celerius relevetur, profecto timendum est ne in brevi maxima incomoda et graves jacturas sustineat ac omnino deficiat, sublata omni potestate (quod absit) in posterum succurrendi.'

Ad hec verba excanduit rex et totus versus in furorem ac torvo vultu comitem predictum respiciens dixit ei: 'Quod si tu michi imponas, et mei culpa sit ut malum regimen habeatur in regno, in faciem tuam mentiris. Vadas ad diabolum!' Quo audito tacuerunt omnes, nec fuit unus de astantibus qui loqui audebat. Tunc dux Lancastr' rupto silencio in suorum prolacione sermonum sagaciter dictum comitis interpretatus est, sic quod furor regis destitit mitigatus.

De fratre Carmelita. Tercio[b] de quodam fratre Carmelita,[1] qui quodam stimulo fatuitatis ductus ad curiam regis accessit ea intencione ut ducem Lancastr' accusaret, [c]scilicet quod ipse dux Lancastr' dolose et proditorie mortem regis[c] machinatus sit. Igitur postquam frater iste quadam die coram rege in camera comitis Oxon'[d] missam celebrasset optentaque licencia dicendi ea que sibi placuisset domino regi, super hujusmodi re frater predictus ducem Lancastr' instanter impeciit, et tam acriter processit quod rex sine examinacione ducem predictum juberet occidi; set alii nobiles domino regi astantes[e] id fieri omnino negabant, asserentes iniquum fore ut quispiam sine judicio[f] condempnaretur.

---

[a] ⟨Pro⟩lacionis *in the margin opposite this passage.*   [b] iij. *in the margin.*
[c-c] *Written over an erasure.*   [d] *Written over an erasure. The original word was longer.*   [e] *The words* aliter assistentes *are written above this word, which has not been deleted.*   [f] *The words* aliter responsione *are written above this word, which has not been deleted.*

---

[1] Br. John Latimer, an Irishman. The Monk's use of a written source or sources in the following account seems to be betrayed by marginal notes amplifying or correcting information given in the main text which is nevertheless left unaltered. The main source was probably a narrative of events based on the testimony of the keeper of the gaol of Salisbury castle, whom the following pages tend to

'You are aware, my lords, that any kingdom in which 1384 prudent government is lacking stands in peril of destruction; and the fact is now being illustrated before your eyes, since this country, which, as you know, began long ago through bad government to lose strength, is at present almost in a state of decay. Unless remedies are promptly applied for its relief and it is speedily rescued from the stormy whirlpool in which it is engulfed, there is reason to fear that it will very soon suffer enormous setbacks and crippling losses, leading to its total collapse and the removal (which God forbid!) of all power to come subsequently to its aid.'

White with the passion which, at these words, pervaded his whole being, the king scowled at the earl. 'If it is to my charge', he said, 'that you would lay this, and it is supposed to be my fault that there is misgovernment in the kingdom, you lie in your teeth. You can go to the Devil!' A complete hush followed as these words were heard, and there was nobody among the company who dared to speak. Then the duke of Lancaster broke the silence and delivered a speech in which he skilfully glossed the earl's remarks, so that the king's anger was assuaged.

The Carmelite friar. Thirdly there was the affair of the Carmelite friar[1] who, prompted by some idiotic impulse, came to court with the object of accusing the duke of Lancaster himself of a crafty and treasonable plot against the king's life. And so one day, after the friar had celebrated Mass, attended by the king, in the apartment of the earl of Oxford, he obtained leave to say to the king what he thought fit and set up an insistent attack on the duke, running on so relentlessly that the king gave orders for the duke to be put to death without further investigation; but the nobles in attendance on him flatly refused to allow this to happen, declaring that it was wrong for anybody to be condemned without trial.

exculpate from blame and whose inner thoughts are at one point laid bare. It is of interest that the mortally injured friar thought that the keeper would understand Latin (below, p. 78). The 'statement by Sir John Clanvow' referred to in the text may have been a written deposition.

1384 ^aHiis quoque auditis rex velud sapiens secundum consilium eorum se protunc facturum promisit.^a Et ulterius^b interrogavit sepedictum fratrem an foret aliquis hujus rei conscius vel ipse solus novit. Ad quem frater respondit: 'Immo dominus le Souche[1] plenam noticiam habet hujus materie; et bene cognosco me moriturum pro ista causa.' Cui iterum ait rex: 'Sume tibi^c parcamenum et facias duas billas indentatas continentes omnia que volueris obicere contra aliquam personam et tradas michi unam, et alteram habebis penes te; et tunc sciemus quid super hujusmodi faciemus.'* Set frater quodammodo confusus erat eo quod dux Lancastr' ad objecta sibi imposita respondere deberet. Igitur secundum quod dominus J. Clanvowe predixerat[2] statim simulavit furorem, exuit se capa sua et calciamentis suis eaque per fenestram eiciebat, ac ea que furiosi sunt ipse per omnia agebat. Rex itaque hec videns jussit eum interim custodiri donec deliberaret se cum suo consilio quid secum agere deberet.† Erant tunc presentes tam

---

* *In the margin and damaged at the edge:* ⟨R⟩evera iste due bille postea secundum quod ⟨di⟩ctus frater jacendo in lecto suo dictavit ⟨er⟩ant confecte et in pleno parliamento ⟨ex⟩hibite et perlecte; in quibus vero fatebatur ⟨ex⟩presse dominum le Souche totam materiam dicte ⟨pro⟩dicionis ad plenum scivisse; insuper et ⟨a⟩ffirmavit in billis predictis communitatem London' et Coventrensem dicte prodicioni eciam ⟨co⟩nsensisse.

† *In the bottom margin:* Illo quoque die quo frater ducem Lancastr' de prodicione accusaverat de consensu tocius parliamenti solempnis processio haberetur cum una missa pro statu universalis ecclesie et prosperitate regis et regni; unde episcopi et alii de clero usque post lapsum hore none in cimiterio cathedralis ecclesie regem jugiter expectabant, set eo die propter tardacionem regis missa et processio fuerunt omisse. Qua de causa dux Lancastr' ad regem accessit; quem videns frater dixit regi: 'Ecce adest ille nequam proditor! Irrue in illum et prives eum vita; alioquin in posterum interficiet te.' Dux vero ad hec stabat stupefactus, set postquam innotuit sibi de hiis que frater de illo predicabat resumpto spiritu cepit se coram rege de sibi impositis excusare, in tantum quod rex eum pro excusato habebat. Rex vero repletus furore fratrem jussit occidi, at dux ne ita fieret regem obnixe rogavit; cujus prece rex destitit mitigatus versus fratrem predictum, secundum quosdam.

---

^{a–a} *Written over an erasure. Two short passages in the ensuing text were inadvertently transposed in the course of transcription but are here printed in the correct order, itself indicated in the MS. See L. C. Hector, 'An alleged hysterical outburst of Richard II', E.H.R., lxviii (1953), pp. 62–5.*   ^b *Interlined.*   ^c *Interlined.*

After listening to them the king wisely undertook to act in 1384
the present situation in conformity with their advice. He then
proceeded to ask the friar whether there was anybody else
who was privy to this matter or whether he alone knew of it.
To this the friar replied: 'No; Lord la Zouche[1] has full knowledge of the affair; and I am well aware that this thing will be
the death of me.' The king went on: 'Take some parchment
and draw up two indented bills containing all the charges you
wish to prefer against anybody; hand one to me and keep the
other in your own possession; and then we shall know what
we are going to do about this.'* The friar, however, was
somewhat disconcerted by the prospect of the duke's replying
to the charges brought against him. He therefore, according
to a statement by Sir John Clanvow,[2] immediately shammed
insanity, stripping off his cloak and his shoes and throwing
them out of the window and generally exhibiting the
behaviour characteristic of a maniac. On seeing this the king
ordered him to be kept in custody pending consideration by
himself and his council of what should be done with him.†

* *In the margin:* These two bills were in fact afterwards drawn up from a statement made by the friar as he lay in his bed and were produced and read in full
parliament. In them the friar expressly declared that Lord la Zouche had had full
knowledge of the whole substance of the treason, to which, moreover, he asserted
that the commons of London and Coventry had also given their consent.

† *In the bottom margin:* On the day on which the friar accused the duke of
Lancaster of treason, there was to have been, by common consent of the parliament, a solemn procession, with a Mass, for the whole state of the catholic
Church and the welfare of the king and the kingdom. The bishops and the other
clergy went on waiting in the cathedral precincts for the king until past noon,
when, owing to the king's lateness, the Mass and procession were abandoned for
the day. The duke of Lancaster accordingly went to the king, to whom, at sight
of the duke, the friar exclaimed 'Here he comes, the scoundrelly traitor! Set upon
him and have his life, or the time will come when he will take yours.' The duke
halted in astonishment at this, but by the time he had learned of the friar's statements about him, he had recovered his breath and set about clearing himself
before the king of the charges against him, and to such purpose that he was
exonerated in the eyes of the king, who, in the rage that filled him, now ordered
the friar to be put to death. The duke, however, pleaded strenuously that this
should not be done; and as a result of his entreaties the king's anger with the
friar was appeased, according to some people.

[1] William, Lord la Zouche (of Harringworth), for whom see *G.E.C.*, xii (2),
pp. 942-3.
[2] A knight of the chamber, for whom see McFarlane, *Lancastrian Kings and
Lollard Knights*, pp. 165-6.

1384 seneschallus, dominus J. de Monte Acuto, quam camerarius, dominus S. de Burle, qui accipientes fratrem predictum tradiderunt ipsum custodi castri Sar' ad custodiendum, set antequam pervenerunt ad portam regie*[a]* mansionis occurrit eis dominus J. de Holand' cum aliis militibus,* protestans quod faceret eum recognoscere illum qui induxit eum talia predicare, et sic in presencia dictorum officiariorum ipsum assumentes in decretam sibi cameram adduxerunt ac misso fune ultra trabem illius camere manus predicti fratris

p. 143 post terga ligabant et ipsum per funem sursum / trahebant*[b]* lapidemque ponderis duorum modiorum frumenti*[c]* ad ejus pedes appendebant et sic eum mobiliter in aere cum tali pena et tormento pendere fecerunt. Tandem venerunt ad eum imperantes ut fateretur quis consuluit eum talia pronunciare, set ille velud Christi servus omnia predicta sibi imposita paciencer sustinuit, asserens illos in vanum circa hujusmodi laborare; propter quod*[d]* illi in majorem insaniam prolapsi ipsum per partes domus predicte nequiter impellebant, nunc ipsum deprimendo et nunc elevando non modicum ipsius corpusculum variis contusionibus*[e]* affligebant. Nichilominus inter hec famulus Dei inmobilis permanebat nec voluntati eorum propter ista cedebat, set spiritum forciorem assumens eorum malicias in omnibus deridebat. Nec ista facientes adhuc eis satisfecerunt quin eciam copiosum ignem subtus eum fecerunt ut ejus incendio et fumo dupplici pena illum contererent: nec sic vincitur, set ista pacientissime tolleravit. Illi vero in eorum maliciis persistentes et iniquitatem super iniquitatem apponentes*[f]* quemdam alium lapidem ponderis unius modii frumenti simul circa ejus virgam et testiculos appendebant; nec multo post*[g]* dominus P. de C. super dictum lapidem ascendit et super eum stetit ac cum violencia pedum suorum simul cum ponderositate sui corporis valide nervos et venas protendit in tantum quod lapis ille super quem

*P. Courteneye, J. Holand', S. Burle, W. Elmham, T. Murreus, H. Grene *in the margin.*[1]

[a] MS. regii.   *[b]* j. *in the margin.*   *[c]* Interlined.   *[d]* ij. *in the margin.*
[e] MS. contunsionibus.   *[f]* iij. *in the margin.*   *[g]* iiij. *in the margin.*

[1] Of those named, Holland was the king's half-brother, and Morieux, like Burley, a knight of the chamber (Tout, *Chapters*, iv. 345). For the connections

Among those present were the steward, Sir John Montague, 1384
and the chamberlain, Sir Simon Burley, who took the friar
and handed him over for safe custody to the keeper of
Salisbury castle, but before they reached the gate of the
royal lodging they were met by a party of knights,* among
them Sir John Holland, who vowed that he would make the
friar confess who had prevailed upon him to tell his story.
They accordingly laid hold of him, in the presence of the
royal officers, and took him to the room assigned to him,
where they passed a rope over a beam, tied the friar's hands
behind him, and, hanging from his feet a stone weighing as
much as two bushels of wheat, hauled him up by the rope so
as to make him dangle, suffering torturing pain, in mid air.
At long last they came up to him, demanding that he should
confess who had instructed him to make his statement, but
he bore his ill usage with the patience of a servant of Christ
and declared that they were wasting their efforts. At this
they proceeded to yet crazier excesses and brutally swung
him to every corner of the room, alternately bearing him
down and tossing him high and adding no little, through
bruises of various kinds, to the distress of his frail body.
Yet amid all this the servant of God remained steadfast and,
far from bowing to their will because of it, adopted a more
resolute spirit and mocked their spite throughout. Not yet
satisfied with what they were doing, they went on to light
a big fire beneath him to harass him with the twofold
torment of heat and smoke: yet even so he remained
undefeated and endured it all with the utmost patience.
In stubborn continuation of their vicious conduct they added
outrage to outrage, suspending from his genitals a second
stone, as heavy as a bushel of wheat, upon which Sir Philip
Courtenay shortly afterwards climbed and stood; and the
weight of his body, coupled with the stamping of his feet,
violently wrenched sinews and veins to such an extent

* Philip Courtenay, John Holland, Simon Burley, William Elmham, Thomas
Morieux, Henry Green *in the margin.* [1]

---

of Green and Morieux with Lancaster see *John of Gaunt's Register, 1379–1383*,
ed. Lodge and Somerville, i, p. 7; ibid., nos. 107, 155, 543, and ii, nos. 982,
1009-10, 1113; and on the list as a whole, Tout, op. cit., iii. 392 n.

1384 stetit ita erat depressus ut lapis ille et alius qui erat ad pedes
ejus appensus insimul offenderent, ex quorum collisione
divisus est lapis ille *in duas partes* qui circa ejus verenda
fuit appensus: et revera gravior fuit sibi ista pena quam
omnia precedencia que fuerunt sibi illata, quia ista causabat
ejus mortem, prout infra dicetur. Premissa tamen eis minime
sufficiebant. Set quid? Deposuerunt[b] eum tunc ac pedes suos
et tibias usque ad genua diu in igne violenter jacere fecerunt,
nam dominus W. Elmham tam ponderose super lumbos
predicti fratris sedebat quod vis retrahendi pedes suos ab
igne penitus ab eo erat ablata; qua[c] de causa ex ignis
adustione et incendio plures rime torride in ejus pedibus
et tibiis usque in diem sue sepulture cunctis intuentibus
apparebant. Ad ultimum[d] vero cogebant eum super ejus
dorsum jacere et in os suum opertum lintheo fundebant
aquam calidam ad mensuram trium lagenarum et amplius,
monentes eum sepius inter ista ut fateretur quisnam esset
ille qui illum adversus tam magnum dominum tanta et talia
proponere procuravit, set ille injuriis et tormentis afflictus[e]
multipliciter et attritus ad illorum interrogata respondere
non curavit. Putabant enim isti milites predictum fratrem
ab aliquo magno fore subornatum, et ideo ipsum talia
supplicia sive cruciatus subire cogebant ut *saltem aliquando*
metu pene ipsum eis cicius revelaret; set supervacue laborabant. Igitur appropinquante noctis umbraculo custos castri
predicti *annuentibus militibus* secundum quod sibi erat
primitus imperatum accepit fratrem predictum et leves
compedes super eum posuit, et timens ne forsan experi-
mentis uteretur in tuto loco tamen honesto *castri predicti*
ipsum reclusit et ei quantum licuit in esculentis poculentis
et lectisterniis nocte illa habundantissime ministravit.

Rex namque postquam predictus frater a suis conspectibus
esset subtractus incontinenti misit pro domino le Souche
ut ceteris postpositis ilico veniret ad eum; qui audito nuncio
nulla mora protracta, licet aliquali infirmitate esset gravatus,
statim accinxit se ad iter et infra paucos dies pervenit ad

---

a–a Interlined.   *b* v. *in the margin.*   *c* vj. *in the margin.*   *d* vij. *in the
margin.*   *e Interlined.*   *f–f Interlined. A word has been erased in the margin.*
g–g In the margin but marked for insertion at this point.   *h–h Interlined.*

that the stone he stood on dipped low enough to collide 1384 with the one attached to the friar's feet and to split in two with the impact. This torture was undoubtedly more serious in its effect on the friar than all the ill treatment previously dealt him, since it was this which brought about his death, as will be made clear below. But what they had already done was not enough for the knights. Need I elaborate? They now took him down and forced his feet and the whole length of his shins up to the knees to rest for some time on the fire, while Sir William Elmham sat so heavily astride his loins that he was deprived of all power to draw his feet back from the flames; with the result that through the scorching and burning of the fire a number of heat-cracks were plainly visible on his feet and shins until the day of his burial. Finally they made him lie on his back and poured over his face, which they covered with a sheet, three gallons or more of hot water, pressing him repeatedly the while to confess who it was who had arranged for him to prefer so serious a charge against such a great noble; but the friar, sorely distressed and exhausted as he was by his wrongs and sufferings, did not trouble to answer their questions. The knights thought, of course, that he had been suborned by some prominent person, and forced him to undergo these ordeals and tortures so that sooner or later the fear of pain would speed his disclosure of his principal's name: but their efforts were in vain. As dusk approached, the keeper of the castle, without opposition from the knights, took charge of the friar in accordance with his original orders and put light shackles on him, and for fear that he might resort to witchcraft locked him up in safe but decent quarters in the castle, supplying him as lavishly as was permissible with food, drink, and bedding for the night.

When the friar had been removed from sight, the king immediately sent for Lord la Zouche, ordering him to neglect everything else and come at once. On receipt of this message Lord la Zouche lost no time, in spite of being handicapped by an illness of some kind, in preparing for the journey, and within a few days entered the

1384 regem. *Dux itaque Lancastr' audiens ipsum fore penes dominum regem graviter accusatum celeriter accessit ad eum et ipsum super hujusmodi infamia splendide excusavit, sic quod rex ipsum postmodum pro excusato habebat.*
Supervenit eciam ad eum dominus le Souche et dicta predicti fratris reprobavit, dicens se nullatenus de tali prodicione umquam scivisse; et hoc optulit se duello probare contra quemlibet sibi contradicere volentem. Quid plura? Tanta enim instancia penes regem et alios dominos tunc presentes instetit quod ab hujusmodi impeticione totaliter extitit absolutus.[1]

Decurso igitur noctis spacio facto mane prefatus castri custos perrexit ad locum ubi frater predictus jacebat et invenit eum gravi infirmitate oppressum, nam vene et nervi ejus virilis virge ceperunt introrsus putrescere ac corpus ejus totum ita erat diversis suppliciis conquassatum quod eum sine magna pena movere non posset; unde custos prelibatus misericordia motus ipsum in eminenciorem locum fecit adduci, *compedes suos deposuit,* et ibi pro eo stravit lectum satis honestum atque alia sibi neccessaria sufficienter providit. Audivit namque frater predictus de adventu domini le Souche; vocavit ad se custodem castri et dixit ei: 'Amore Dei et beate Virginis Marie hoc unum rogo facias pro me, si placet, et habebis c. solidos tibi eo pacto fideliter persolutos: procures cum diligencia quod cum domino le Souche possem habere secretum colloquium per aliquod tempus, et habebis sine dubio quod promisi.' Cui custos: 'Temptabo, si possem, implere desiderium tuum.' Et discedens ab eo venit ad curiam regis; ac eundo versus curiam cogitabat intra se quod de hujusmodi possit de facili imminere periculum si hoc esset factum absque sciencia domini regis. Igitur accessit ad seneschallum et camerarium domini regis et eis negocium ex ordine totum pandit; qui accedentes ad regem et eidem retulerunt ea que a prefato custode audierunt, eo interim presencialiter existente. Rex vero quesivit ab eo qualiter frater se habuit (nesciebat enim quod talibus gravissimis

---

[a–a] *Cancelled and enclosed within the syllables* Va . . . cat.   [b–b] *Deleted;* ⟨va⟩cat *repeated after these words.*   [c–c] *In the margin but marked for insertion at this point.*

king's presence[. Hearing of the grave accusations that had 1384
been made against him, the duke of Lancaster hurried to the
king and disposed so brilliantly of the slur upon him that the
king thenceforward regarded him as cleared. Lord la Zouche
himself arrived later] and rebutted the friar's story, declaring
that he had never had the slightest knowledge of the treason
and offering proof by battle against anybody who was prepared to gainsay him. Need I say more? He urged his case
with such earnestness upon the king and the other nobles
present that he was completely absolved from the charge
against him.[1]

The night had run its course and morning had come when
the keeper of Salisbury castle made his way to the place
where the friar lay, to find him seriously ill. The veins and
sinews of his member had begun to fester internally, and his
whole body was so shattered by his various ordeals that he
could not be moved without great pain; and out of pity for
him the keeper had him taken to less humble quarters,
removing his shackles and making up a reasonably decent
bed for him and otherwise providing adequately for his
needs. When the friar heard of the arrival of Lord la Zouche
he called the keeper of the castle to him and said: 'There is
one thing that I beg you, for the love of God and the blessed
Virgin Mary, to do for me, if you will; and if you agree you
shall have 100*s*. paid to you without fail. Take care to
arrange for me to have some time in private conversation
with Lord la Zouche, and there will be no doubt of your
having what I promised you.' 'If I can,' replied the keeper,
'I will try to carry out your wish'; and leaving the friar he set
off for the royal court. On the way there it occurred to him
privately that an affair of this kind might easily spell danger
if it was carried through without the king's knowledge. He
accordingly approached the king's steward and his chamberlain and revealed the whole business to them from beginning
to end; whereupon they went to the king and with the keeper
standing by reported what they had heard from him. The
king asked him how the friar was (being unaware of the

---

[1] Cf. Walsingham, *Hist. Ang.*, ii. 114, describing a formal hearing of the charge
against la Zouche in parliament — a version supported by the Monk's marginal
note on p. 78 below.

1384 questionibus fuisset expositus), set postquam scivisset quomodo stetit cum eo anxiosos gemitus pectoris ab ymo suspirando eduxit. Demum tamen^a concessit rex ut frater ille cum prefato domino le Souche colloquio frueretur, sub ista tamen forma quod aliqui ex suis in quibus multum confidebat in fenestris vel aliis locis propinquis residentes possent audire ea que sibi voluerit ea parte referre.

Nec mora; venit ad sepedictum fratrem dominus le Souche et quidam secretarii domini regis cum eo,* qui steterunt juxta eum et inquirentes ab eo instanter an aliud quam bonum scivisset de predicto domino le Souche; quibus ipse dixit: 'Scio ipsum esse valentem dominum et fidelem, nam profecto aliud quam bonum nescio de illo proferre.' Mox respiciens custodem castri dixit Latine: 'Nonne dixi tibi etc.?', innuens per hoc quod^b si cum predicto domino in secreto potuisset^c colloquium habuisse, c. solidos eidem dedisset. Post hec vero cepit graviter languescere ac spiritu consolacionis procul abjecto neque cibum neque potum gustare curavit: tandem invalescente infirmitate causante putrefaccione nervorum et venarum ob nimiam lesionem eorundem, ut premittitur, ac urgente mortis stimulo post aliquot dies frater predictus ab hac instabili luce migravit et in pace quievit. Igitur publicata morte supradicti fratris postquam ad aures ducis Lancastr' fama de ejus morte pervenit, non rectis oculis predictum castri custodem aspexit sicut antea,† nam fratre vivente

---

*In the bottom margin: Veneruntque cum domino le Souche ad fratrem prefatum sex milites domini regis, tres milites ducis Lancastr', et tres milites de parliamento, qui coram rege et toto parliamento dicta fratris quasi referendarii proponebant, asserentes ipsum palam dixisse quod suggestione diabolica talia contra prefatos dominos predicavit: propter quod in pleno parliamento ad peticionem domini le Souche, favente ad hoc potissime duce Lancastr', statutum fuit assensu^d omnium procerum tunc ibidem existencium quod tales dominorum delatores nisi juste et juridice ea probaverint que eis objecerint penam traccionis et suspensionis incurrerent indilate.

†In the margin: Vera est ista litera secundum quosdam; alii vero contrarium affirmant, asserentes ducem Lancastr' vitam fratris predicti habere salvam libencius voluisse.

---

^{a} Interlined. ^{b} Interlined. ^{c} Written above posset, which has been underlined. ^{d} Interlined.

extremely severe examination to which he had been sub- 1384
jected), and on learning how matters stood with him gave
expression to his concern with groans and gasps fetched from
the very depths of his being. In the end, however, he agreed
that the friar should have his interview with Lord la Zouche,
with the proviso that some greatly trusted persons in his own
service should be posted in the windows or somewhere else
close by, where they could hear the things he would want
reported to him in connection with the affair.

Without loss of time Lord la Zouche visited the friar, and
with him went certain persons in the king's confidence,*
who stood over him and pressed the question whether he
knew anything but good of Lord la Zouche. He replied:
'I know him for a worthy and loyal gentleman; indeed I
cannot advance anything but good about him.' Then, looking
round at the keeper of the castle, he said, in Latin, 'Didn't
I tell you . . .?', referring to the fact that if he could have had
a private conversation with Lord la Zouche he would have
given the keeper 100s. After this he began to be seriously
ill, and putting the spirit of comfort far from him did not
even trouble to touch food or drink: and at length, his disorder gaining in intensity with the progressive decomposition
of sinews and veins following upon the extensive damage
done to them, as described above, and the prickings of death
becoming more insistent, a few days later he passed from this
world's fickle light and rested in peace. When the friar's death
was made known, and reports of it reached the ears of the
duke of Lancaster, he began, in marked contrast with his
former manner, to look askance at the keeper of the castle,†

* *In the bottom margin:* Lord la Zouche was accompanied on this visit to the
friar by six knights in the king's service, three in that of the duke of Lancaster,
and three representing the parliament, who, acting as a kind of official reporters,
laid before the king and the whole parliament what the friar said. They declared
that he had openly stated that it was at the Devil's prompting that he had spoken
as he had against the nobles concerned. It was accordingly decreed in full parliament, at the petition of Lord la Zouche, particularly strongly supported by the
duke of Lancaster, with the assent of all the nobles present, that similar informers
against the nobility, unless they proved their accusations fairly and in legal form,
should forthwith incur the penalty of drawing and hanging.

† *In the margin:* This, according to some, is the true account; but there are
others who maintain the contrary and declare that the duke of Lancaster would
have been very glad to see the friar's life saved.

1384 sub ejus custodia familiarius secum conferre solebat, set
p. 144 nunc mutata facie causam mortis sue et culpam / sibi
imponere contendebat, sub isto tamen colore ut illi qui
causam mortis dederunt immunes ab ejus nece penitus
viderentur; quia dixerunt illum nequaquam mori propter
illa que sibi intulerunt set pocius propter carcerales penas
quas sub ejus custodia jugiter sustinuit illum obire et dece-
dere oportebat.[1] Ad hec custos castri, videns illos velle contra
se omnimodo prevalere ac illum sic falsissime illaqueare,
confestim ad seneschallum et camerarium domini regis cum
aliis suis amicis accessit et totum processum eis narravit.
Qui videntes ejus innocenciam ipsum ad regem induxerunt
et coram eo illum fore immunem de predicti fratris morte
evidenter extitit declaratum ac ab hujusmodi impeticione
pro absoluto ab omnibus habebatur. Tunc ejus emuli per-
pendentes istam viam fore eis preclusam aliam invenire
sollicite laborabant in salvacionem ipsorum; et quia frater
predictus odiosam prodicionem super alios seminabat nec
probare valebat quod impie proponebat, de consilio cujusdam jurisperiti dignum estimabant ipsum consimilem penam
sustinere quam alii procurabat. Igitur[a] penam talionis
sentencialiter super eum dictabant, et accipientes illius
cadaver opertum pallio ponebant super cratem, cui cum[b]
funibus ligabant; deinde trahi illud fecerunt per plateas
civitatis predicte ac postremo ad instanciam fratrum permiserunt illud sepeliri in cimiterio Sancti Martini juxta
civitatem predictam; ubi ad laudem Dei diu postea resplen-
duit lux inmensa.

Interim[c] isti per communitatem electi pro communi
utilitate regni[d] de veniendo ad parliamentum graviter sunt
conquesti super potentes homines in partibus dominantes,

---

[a] *Interlined.* [b] *Interlined.* [c] Nota de signis *in the margin.* [d] *Interlined.*

[1] A charge the more plausible because John Homes, keeper of the gaol of Salisbury castle, was at this time indicted for the ill-treatment of prisoners in his
charge: in Trinity Term 1384 he pleaded 'Not Guilty' in the King's Bench to
allegations that he had caused the deaths of 4 named prisoners by confining them
in the stocks for 17 days in conditions of extreme cold, in Dec. 1383. He was
dismissed to mainprise and subsequently, in Trinity Term 1399, produced royal
letters patent of pardon dated 8 March 1399 (P.R.O., K.B. 27/493, Rex, rot. 12).
(I am indebted to Mr. Hector for this reference.) Was this charge pressed by some
who wished to inculpate Homes in the death of the friar?

with whom, while the friar was still alive and in his 1384
charge, he had been in the habit of friendly conversation.
Now, however, with a complete change of front, he was
at pains to saddle the keeper with the responsibility and
blame for the friar's death, putting such a complexion on
matters that those who had actually dealt the cause of
death were made to appear wholly blameless of his
murder; since they maintained that it was certainly not
because of what they had done to him that he had died
but that he must have succumbed to the hardships to
which he had been continuously subjected as a prisoner in
the keeper's charge.[1] Perceiving that they intended by all
means to get the better of him and to implicate him in
a grossly false accusation, the keeper thereupon went,
accompanied by friends, to the king's steward and the
chamberlain and told them the whole story. They, seeing
his innocence, took him to the king, in whose presence a
declaration was made in the clearest terms that the
keeper was not responsible for the friar's death, and he
was held by everybody to be quit of any charge of
causing it. Thereupon his adversaries, in view of the fact
that that road was barred to them, set anxiously to work
to find another that would lead to their own preserva-
tion; and since the friar had aspersed others with his
accusations of heinous treason and had been unable to
substantiate his wicked assertions, they decided, after
taking legal advice, that it would be fitting for him to
suffer a similar penalty to that which he had tried to
bring about for someone else. They therefore invoked the
law of retaliation to pronounce sentence upon him; and
taking his corpse, covered with a pall, they put it on a
hurdle, to which they tied it with ropes, and caused it to
be drawn through the streets of Salisbury. At the request
of the friars they finally allowed it to be buried in the
churchyard of St. Martin near the city, where, to the
glory of God, a great light shone long afterwards.

In the meantime those who had been elected by the
commons to attend the parliament to promote the general
welfare of the kingdom complained bitterly about the
tyranny of certain locally powerful persons who, furnished

1384 scilicet quomodo per dominos regni signis quasi ornamentis diversis prediti ac eorundem favore protecti et profecto ex hoc nimis elati pauperes et inopes in patria minus juste opprimunt ac confundunt legesque pro communi utilitate regni editas ac eciam promulgatas conantur evertere, ipsorum eciam subtilitatibus ac amicicia dominorum freti non permittunt eas suam rectitudinem tenere; unde digne et juste arbitrabantur eos fore generali statuto in posterum cohercendos ne illorum fraus et versucia in detrimentum regni ulterius invalescat. Ad hec dux Lancastr' respondit, dicens illud nimis generaliter fuisse locutum, asserens ulterius illud et hujusmodi consimilia specietenus oportunum fore proferre, quia quilibet dominus satis sufficiens est et potens suos ad se pertinentes pro talibus excessibus corrigere et punire. Nam in rebus temporalibus et seculari potencia post regem dixit se ceteris regni dominis precellere: si quis igitur suorum sibi in aliquo pertinencium in hujusmodi inventus fuerit[a] culpabilis sive reus et ad ejus noticiam pervenire contigerit, talem subibit penam[b] quod ceteris ad committenda similia timorem incuciet: hoc idem respondebat pro fratribus suis, comitibus videlicet Cantebrig' et Bukyngham'. Illi vero per communitatem regni electi hec audientes — quod nullum foret in hujusmodi datum[c] remedium — tacuerunt.

Rex autem cum suo consilio ardenter instabat erga clerum et populum ut ab eis pecunias extorqueret. Post multa vero consilia et sermocinaciones pro et contra clerus concessit ei dictam medietatem decime que supra in alio parliamento sub condicione fuerat eidem concessa: simili modo fecerunt sibi et laici de sua quintadecima.[1] Set rex hiis concessis non contentus dixit se velle exercere illam gravissimam inquisicionem contra usurpatores corone vocatam trailbaston'[2] nisi ampliora vellent sibi concedere; quo audito et habito

---

[a] *Interlined.*   [b] *Interlined.*   [c] *MS.* dare.

[1] The southern convocation, sitting at Salisbury, granted a half-tenth on 31 May, payable by 1 Nov. (*Cal. Fine R., 1383–91*, p. 59). Parliament granted a half-fifteenth, payable by 29 Sept., and promised another half-fifteenth by 25 March 1385 if peace had not been made with France or Scotland and provided the clergy also made a further grant (*R.P.*, iii. 167–8; cf. ibid., p. 185). There is, however, no record that the clergy made any promise for 1385. See also above, p. 48 and n.

[2] For other uses of 'trailbaston' in this sense see below, pp. 406 and 443; and for the strict application of the word, ibid., p. 383 n.

with badges (taking various forms of embellishment) by 1384
lords of the realm and sheltered by their favour, and having
in natural consequence an exaggerated conceit of themselves,
unjustly oppressed and dismayed the poor and helpless of
their neighbourhoods, trying to overthrow laws passed and
published for the common weal of the realm, and, in full
reliance on their own smartness and the friendship of their
lords, refusing to allow those laws to hold to their straight
course. The commons, therefore, rightly and properly
thought that these men should for the future be brought
under control by a general statute to prevent their deceit
and chicanery from becoming too rampant for the well-
being of the kingdom. This was answered by the duke of
Lancaster, who said that the complaint was expressed in too
general terms, and added that now was the time for this and
kindred subjects to be brought forward with full particulars,
since every lord was competent and well able to correct and
punish his own dependants for such outrages. In temporal
matters and worldly power, he said, he himself, after the
king, surpassed the rest of the lords of the realm, and if any
of the people in any way dependent on him should be found
guilty or chargeable in this respect and it should happen to
come to his own knowledge, the offender would suffer such
punishment as would strike into the hearts of the rest a terror
of committing similar misdeeds: and on behalf of his
brothers, the earls of Cambridge and Buckingham, his answer
was the same. The representatives of the commons of the
realm, hearing this as a statement that no remedy was going
to be provided in this matter, were reduced to silence.

Abetted by his council, the king made urgent appeals to
the clergy and the laity in an endeavour to wring funds from
them. After much consultation and speech-making, for and
against, the clergy granted him the half-tenth that had been
conditionally granted to him in the preceding parliament, and
the laity did likewise in regard to their fifteenth.[1] The king,
however, was not satisfied with these grants and said that
unless they were prepared to increase them he was minded
to set on foot that formidable inquisition, directed against
usurpers of the royal prerogative, known as 'trailbaston'.[2]
On hearing this the clergy, after conferring about it, granted

1384 super hoc consilio clerus concessit sibi aliam medietatem unius decime ac laici modo consimili concesserunt sibi unam aliam medietatem quintedecime, secundum illud, 'sicut tenebre ejus ita et lumen ejus'.[1] Constat namque istis diebus fere in ecclesia Dei omnia luminaria fore extincta, quod dolendum est, quia premaxime tenebre obnubilant ejus superficiem usquequaque, nec est aliquis jam qui disponat se exurgere et stare ex adverso pro ecclesia Dei. Facti sunt ejus prelati sicut 'canes muti non valentes latrare'.[2] Propter hoc timendum est (quod absit) ne super viros ecclesiasticos taliter sublimatos veniat repentina calamitas, dolor inmensus, angustia intollerabilis, et miseria lacrimosa.

Quo in tempore[3] inter archiepiscopum Cantuar' et episcopum Exonien' grave[a] dissencionis materia hoc modo fuit exorta. Disposuit enim prefatus archiepiscopus suam provinciam visitare, et primo in Devonia suam visitacionem incepit, venitque ad ecclesiam cathedralem Exon'. Canonici vero ejusdem ecclesie contra suum episcopum aliqua obiciebant; quare archiepiscopus misit pro memorato episcopo ut veniret ad eum et ad objecta responderet ac in aliis prout decet suam visitacionem subiret. Set antequam archiepiscopi nuncius pervenit ad episcopum, ejus ministri ipsum interceperunt, cognita vero causa pro qua venerat literas quas archiepiscopus predicto episcopo direxerat per eundem ipsum deglutire fecerunt.[4] Archiepiscopus namque videns suum nuncium ita contemptibiliter dehonestatum totus ira incaluit ac in episcopum prelibatum graves censuras dictavit. [b]Familiares quidam dicti archiepiscopi cum quibusdam aliis[b] in quasdam nundinas ingressi quendam scutiferum prefati episcopi ibidem inventum summitates sive aculeos solutarium suorum masticare et deglutire coegerunt, [c]set non comedit licet comedere fuisset coactus.[c] Istis ridiculis sic[d]

---

[a] Sic MS.; cf. above, p. 60.
words occupy approximately half.
marked for insertion at this point.

[b-b] *Written over an erasure of which these*
[c-c] *In the margin over an erasure, but*
[d] *Interlined.*

---

[1] Ps. cxxxviii. 12 (cxxxix. 12).   [2] Cf. Isa. lvi. 10.
[3] The visitation of the diocese of Exeter, the occasion of the quarrel about metropolitan jurisdiction between William Courtenay, archbishop of Canterbury, and Thomas de Brantingham, bishop of Exeter, which the Monk now relates, began on 7 Mar. 1384. Brantingham, having on 18 Mar. forbidden his subjects to

him a second half-tenth, and the laity similarly granted a 1384
further half-fifteenth, bearing out the text that 'darkness
and light are both alike'.[1] It is generally agreed that nowadays
almost all the lamps have gone out in the Church of God,
more is the pity, since the darkness that on every side
shadows her face is great indeed and there is none now inclined to bestir himself and make a stand for God's Church.
Her prelates have become like 'dumb dogs that cannot bark'.[2]
There is therefore ground for the fear (which I pray may not
be realized) that sudden disaster, limitless sorrow, insupportable anguish, and tears of wretchedness will be the lot of
churchmen who have reached eminence in conditions like
these.

At about this time[3] the occasion for a serious quarrel
between the archbishop of Canterbury and the bishop of
Exeter came about in the following circumstances. The archbishop, having decided to conduct a visitation of his province,
began it in Devon and arrived at Exeter Cathedral. Here the
canons made certain charges against their bishop; whom the
archbishop accordingly summoned to come and reply to
them and to submit, as was proper, to the visitation in all
other respects. Before, however, the archbishop's messenger
could reach the bishop he was intercepted by some of the
latter's officers, who, on learning his errand, made him
swallow the letters the archbishop had addressed to the
bishop.[4] On seeing his messenger thus treated with humiliat-
ing disdain the archbishop, ablaze with anger, pronounced
a severe censure of the bishop. Certain members of the
archbishop's household, in company with some other people,
now attended a fair, and finding there one of the bishop's
squires they forced him to chew and swallow the tips of his
own shoes; but he did not eat them, in spite of the compulsion put upon him to do so. At the end of this mischievous

obey the archbishop, submitted on 2 July. See *Register of Thomas de Brantyng-
ham, bishop of Exeter (A.D. 1370–1394)*, ed. F. C. Hingeston-Randolph (2 vols.,
London, 1901–6), ii. pp. xiii ff.; ibid., i. 530 ff.

[4] Cf. ibid., ii, p. xviii. On 25 Mar. commissaries carrying the archbishop's
citation of the bishop to answer the *detecta* of his dean and chapter against him,
having been refused access to the bishop at his manor of Clyst, took refuge at
Topsham, where one of their squires was forced by three of the bishop's squires
to tear up the citation and swallow the seal.

1384 ex utraque parte nequiter peractis majoris odii fomitem inter
illos cicius suscitavit; unde sepedictus episcopus senciens se
gravatum perrexit Sar' et illic episcopos parliamenti causa congregatos alloquitur, exponens eis qualiter in aliquibus dictus
archiepiscopus in sua visitacione modum excessit, et si in hujusmodi debuerit resistere eorum consilio uti vellet. Cui episcopi
dixerunt: 'Nos reputamus te ita potentem in tua diocesi sicut
archiepiscopum. Igitur defende te ab eo meliori modo quo
poteris. Nos vero, cum prefatus archiepiscopus gracia visitandi
ad ecclesias nostras contigerit declinare, faciemus prout nobis
melius *ea parte* videbitur expedire.' Postquam vero dictus
episcopus cognovit voluntatem eorum misit archiepiscopo
viros prospicuos et genere preclaros quorum mediacione et
industria pax inter illos reformata est. Archiepiscopus voti
compos effectus ulterius in visitacione sua processit.

  Parliamentum finitur apud Sar'. Finito vero parliamento
predicto[1] rex pro majori tempore estatis cum regina et sua
familia per loca diversa in australibus partibus moram traxit.

  Interim mense Junii Scoti cum multitudine gravi Angliam
intraverunt et more solito ceperunt insolencius agere: terram
namque Northumbranam rapinis et incendiis vastaverunt,
prede eciam rapaci et cedi pestifere continue vacaverunt,
et profecto multo majora dampna ibi fecissent nisi archiepiscopus Eboracensis, episcopus Dunelmensis, et episcopus
Carlion' cum aliis dominis in patria eis celerius occurrissent;
qui cum eis inierunt tractatum, et pacem a festo Nativitatis
Sancti Johannis Baptiste usque festum sancti Michaelis[b]
optinuerunt treuga firmata.[2]

  Item xx°. die Junii apud Oxon' quidam frater Carmelita,
eo quod in predicacione sua publice asseruit prefatum
p. 145 fratrem Carmelitam nuper apud / Sar' enormiter occisum[3]
nepharie fuisse peremptum ac martirizatum, per suum pro-
vincialem fuit perpetuo carceri condempnatus; restitutus
est tamen postea pristine libertati.

---

a–a Interlined.   *b This word is followed by an erasure.*

---

[1] On 27 May (above, p. 66).
[2] A truce, to last until 1 Oct., was concluded at Ayton on 7 July 1384. The
English deputies beside John Fordham, bishop of Durham, were in fact John
Nevill of Raby, and John Waltham, sub-dean of York (Rymer, *Foedera*, vii.
434–5).   [3] See above, pp. 72 ff.

foolery on each side greater ill-will than ever was rapidly kindled between them; and the bishop, feeling himself aggrieved, went to Salisbury, where he spoke to the bishops who had assembled for the parliament, describing to them how in the conduct of his visitation the arch- bishop had in some respects overstepped the mark, and wishing to profit by their advice about whether in this situation he ought to resist. The bishops replied: 'We regard you as being, within your own diocese, as powerful as the archbishop; so defend yourself against him in the best way you can. For our part, when the archbishop happens to make a halt at our churches with a view to visitation, we shall do what seems to us most expedient in the circumstances.' After thus ascertaining their temper the bishop of Exeter sent to the archbishop some prominent persons of illustrious family, through whose efforts at mediation peace was restored between them. The archbishop, having got his way, went on with his visitation.

The Salisbury parliament concluded. When the parlia- ment came to an end,[1] for the greater part of the summer the king spent his time at various places in the south with the queen and his household.

Meanwhile the Scots entered England during June in formidable numbers and began to behave with their usual insolence, devastating the Northumbrian countryside with fire and pillage and devoting themselves unremittingly to insatiable rapine and foul murder. Indeed they would have done far greater damage there if the archbishop of York and the bishops of Durham and Carlisle with other lords of the district had not been quick to meet them and, after entering into a parley with them, to secure peace from Midsummer Day until Michaelmas by con- cluding a truce.[2]

At Oxford on 20 June a Carmelite friar, who had publicly stated in a sermon that the Carmelite lately done to death with such brutality at Salisbury[3] had been iniquitously made away with and martyred, was con- demned by his provincial to life imprisonment, but he was afterwards restored to his former liberty.

1384 Preterea in ista estate tanta erat siccitas ita ut fluvii et fontes perhenni cursu de terra scaturientes, immo (quod magis mirabile videbatur) eciam putei altissimi siccarentur; et duravit ista siccitas usque festum Nativitatis beate Marie; et ab hinc usque festum Purificacionis ejusdem Virginis continuo, exceptis paucis diebus, pluebat. Grossa vero animalia in ista estate quamplurima pro aque penuria perierunt.

Tractatus. Circa finem mensis Junii dux Lancastr' et comes Bukyngham frater suus, dominus Thomas Percy miles et alii superius nominati ad tractandum de pace cum Francigenis versus Cales' iter arripuerunt, qui ibidem circa principium mensis Julii applicuerunt.[1] Diu namque ibidem Francigenas expectabant: demum postquam ad locum destinatum insimul convenissent, pompose Gallici sunt locuti ac semper in extraneis materiis dormientes, ea vero que pacis sunt quasi parvipensa penitus neglexerunt, sicque omni die caute et callide in eorum versuciis permanentes tempus consumendo usque circa festum Sancti Mathei Evangeliste. Interim tamen fuit tractatum de quadam treuga inter nos et illos firmanda, que duraret usque in primum diem mensis Maii, prout in suo loco infra dicetur.[2]

Item de mense Julii apud castrum Arundell' fiebant solempnes nupcie celebrate, nam dominus Thomas Mombray comes Notyngham desponsavit filiam Ricardi comitis Arundell' ibidem;[3] et duravit ista solempnitas per unam septimanam et amplius; ac omnibus intrare volentibus sive exire libere patebat introitus et egressus. Hiis nupciis interfuerunt rex et regina cum tota eorum familia; quos omnes comes predictus leta fronte suscepit et secundum statum cujuslibet eorum unumquemque remuneravit.

Quo in tempore venerunt in Angliam duo viri valentes de Francia, unus clericus et alter miles,[4] cum paucis eorum

---

[1] Lancaster and Buckingham, who were given power to treat on 27 May 1384, were accompanied on this embassy by John Holland, Mr. Raymond Guilhem du Puy, Walter Skirlaw, John Gilbert, Thomas Percy, and John Sheppey. Holland, Gilbert, and Sheppey set out on 30 June; Percy and Skirlaw on 11 and 15 June respectively. The negotiations took place at Boulogne. See P.R.O., E. 364/17, mm. 54[V], 57[V]; ibid., 364/18, m. 60; and Mirot and Déprez, in *B.E.C.*, lx, p. 206 (no. 473). See also above, p. 50 and n.

[2] Below, p. 98. For the French tactics in the negotiations at Boulogne see also *Palmer*, p. 51.

During this summer there was so great a drought that 1384 streams and springs which normally gushed from the ground in ceaseless flow, and indeed, as seemed yet more remarkable, even the deepest wells, all dried up. The drought lasted until the Nativity of the Virgin [8 September]; and from then until the Purification [2 February 1385], with the exception of a few days, it rained continuously. In the course of the summer the larger cattle died in very great numbers through the shortage of water.

Negotiations. About the end of June the duke of Lancaster, his brother the earl of Buckingham, Sir Thomas Percy, and the others named above set out for Calais to conduct peace negotiations with the French, and landed there about the beginning of July.[1] They spent a long time at Calais waiting for the French, and when at last they met at the place appointed, the French adopted a consequential tone, continually dwelling on irrelevant subjects and neglecting entirely, as if they cared little about them, those which bore on peace. In this way, by a wary and artful persistence day after day in their wiles, they took up the time until St. Matthew's Day [21 September]. Meanwhile, however, negotiations went on for the conclusion of a truce between them and ourselves, to last until 1 May, as will be recounted below in its proper place.[2]

During July a wedding ceremony took place at Arundel castle, where Thomas Mowbray, earl of Nottingham, married the daughter of Richard, earl of Arundel.[3] The festivities lasted for a week or more, and all who wished to enter or leave were free to come and go. The wedding was attended by the king and queen with their entire household; all received a smiling welcome from the earl, who gave each of them a present according to his rank.

It was at this time that there arrived in England two personages from France, one a cleric and the other a knight,[4]

[3] She was Elizabeth, widow of Sir William de Montague (*G.E.C.*, ix. 604; see also *Cal. Pat. R., 1388–92*, p. 16).

[4] Guychard Maresey, knight, and Mr. Peter Frisevell, clerk. The purpose of their mission was to tell the Scots of the truce of Leulingham of Jan. 1384 between England and France, and their safe-conduct lasted from 13 Feb. to 1 June 1384 (Rymer, *Foedera*, vii. 423; Campbell, in *Europe in the Late Middle Ages*, ed. Hale, Highfield, and Smalley, p. 209).

1384 domesticis, et salvo conductu usque Scociam per medium
Anglie transierunt et ab hinc usque ad australes partes Anglie
pervagantes tam in exeundo quam in redeundo omnia secreta
regni que optabant videre libere aspexerunt, in tantum quod
regalia regis et regine apud Westmonasterium reposita rege
mandante sunt eciam liquido contemplati.

Circa festum Sancte Margarete quidam Londonienses
ceperunt Thomam Husk' clericum vicecomitis London' et
precipuum J. Northampton',[1] qui plura que in civitate facere
proponebat redigebat in scriptis, missusque in carcerem, in
quo aliquamdiu erat detentus ea de causa ut secreta J.
Northampton' revelaret: qui videns viam evadendi sibi fore
preclusam ac illos quibus antea coherebat carcerali custodie
deputari nec sibi posse in aliquo suffragari, caute votis
illorum cessit quos protunc noverat prevalere. Satagebat
namque astu et arte illorum amiciciam sibi attrahere quos
proculdubio ante capitales hostes sibi fuisse bene cognovit.
Unde major London' eum recepit in graciam, licet confessus
fuerit proditorem fuisse civitatis predicte, liberatusque de
carcere in domo majoris manebat eo mandante,[2] ubi interim
contra J. Northampton' multa enormia et sinistra in diversis
articulis recitavit et eum super hujusmodi appellavit ac in
scriptis redegit. Interea amici J. Northampton' vivaciter
laborabant erga regem et ejus consilium pro ipsius libera-
cione; propter quod dominus rex xviij. die Augusti apud
Radyng' consilium celebrare decrevit, ad quod tam prelati
ecclesie quam proceres regni confestim jussu regis venerunt.[3]
Accessit autem ad dictum consilium major London' cum
senioribus et valencioribus dicte civitatis, et adduxit secum
Thomam Husk predictum, qui stans coram rege et toto
consilio dixit: 'Ego, T.H., proditor civitatis London' et tocius
regni Anglie, scienter scripsi ea et celavi que J. Northampton'

---

[1] The letters patent naming persons to arrest Usk are dated 6 Aug. 1384 (*Cal. Pat. R., 1381–5*, p. 500). Usk was appointed under-sheriff of London and Midd. in Sept. or Oct. 1387 (*Letter Book H*, pp. 316–17).

[2] Cf. *Cal. Cl. R., 1381–5*, p. 476.

[3] The council was summoned for 17 Aug. (*Letter Book H*, pp. 245–6; cf. *Cal. Cl. R., 1381–5*, p. 470). For Usk's appeal see *Book of London English, 1384–1425*, ed. Chambers and Daunt, pp. 22–31. It embraced, in addition to Northampton, 3 of his supporters — William Essex, John More, and Richard Northbury — but only Northampton was tried at the council at Reading. The charge on this occasion was probably of misprision and, not, as the Monk implies (below, p. 96),

with a few members of their households. They passed through 1384
England under safe-conduct to Scotland and from there
travelled back to the south of England, being free to observe,
on both the outward and the return journeys, all they wanted
to see of the secrets of the kingdom — so much so that by the
king's orders they were even given an unrestricted view of his
and the queen's regalia kept at Westminster.

About St. Margaret's Day [20 July] some Londoners
arrested Thomas Usk, sometime clerk of the sheriff of
London and secretary to John Northampton,[1] many of
whose projects for action in the city he had taken down in
writing. He was lodged in prison and kept there for some
time with the intention that he should disclose Northampton's
secrets. Seeing that the way of escape was barred to him and
that those to whom he had formerly clung had been clapped
into prison and were unable at all to help him, he prudently
bowed to the wishes of those whom he knew to be now in
the ascendant, and set shrewdly and craftily to work to win
the friendship of those whom earlier, without a doubt, he
had clearly recognized to be his chief enemies. As a result,
in spite of his being a self-confessed betrayer of the city of
London, he was taken into favour by the mayor, on whose
orders he was released from prison and lodged in the mayor's
own house,[2] where in sundry articles he rehearsed a large
number of outrages and crimes imputed to John Northampton, formally accusing him of them and setting them down
in writing. Northampton's friends were meanwhile actively
at work upon the king and council to secure his release; and
in consequence the king determined to hold a council at
Reading on 18 August, to which the dignitaries of the Church
and the great lords of the realm made haste to come at the
king's command.[3] The council was also attended by the
mayor of London, accompanied by aldermen and leading
citizens, and with him he brought Thomas Usk, who, standing forward before the king and the whole council, said 'I,
Thomas Usk, traitor to the city of London and to the whole
realm of England, wittingly wrote down and kept secret the

of treason itself (Bellamy, *Law of Treason*, p. 152). In the English version of the
appeal the words 'I appele etc.' occur at the end of each article; even so it is likely
that the Monk wrote with a text of the appeal before him.

1384 cum suis fautoribus in destruccionem et enervacionem civitatis predicte proposuit ordinare.' Sicque ibidem seriatim in diversis articulis mala non pauca et odiosa contra J. Northampton' et suos complices sine erubescencia publicavit ac eum super eisdem articulis appellavit; et ad quemlibet articulum sic incepit: 'Ego, T.H., proditor etc.' Et econtra J. Northampton' constanter negavit ea que sibi obiciebat, vocansque eum in presencia regis falsum ribaldum morteque dignum;^{a} et quod falsum sibi imposuit manu propria optulit se probare duello. In hoc vero J. Northampton' nimis limites suos transcendit, quia reverenciam domini regis, ut in talibus decuit, non excepit. Nichilominus rex de sua gracia speciali concessit sibi annuatim de suis redditibus centum marcas refundi: nec propter hoc^b regi, ut debuit, est regraciatus.^{c} Igitur rex videns eum aliqualiter obstinatum dixit: 'Faciamus finem istius controversie et eamus ad judicium secundum comperta et probata.' Cui J. Northampton' sic intulit: 'Spero, domine mi rex, quod in absencia ducis Lancastr' avunculi vestri non vultis ^{d}ad judicium procedere neque^d in ista causa pro tribunali sedere.'$^{e\,1}$ Quo audito rex ira totus incaluit, dicens se fore satis habilem tam ipsum quam ducem Lancastr' judicare. 'Cognosces namque', ^{f}dixit rex,^{f} 'quod ero judex tuus sua absencia non obstante.' Confestim vero jussit eum trahi et suspendi ac omnia bona sua eciam confiscari: verum est quod omnia bona sua mobilia propter hoc erant confiscata, non tamen bona sua inmobilia, ut inferius clare patebit.^{2} Sicque J. Northampton' propter tria premissa ac propter incompositos mores vitam suam turpi morte finaliter termin⟨a⟩sset nisi domina regina ibi casualiter extitisset ac pro ejus vita ne moreretur domino regi provoluta humiliter supplicasset; cujus interventu rex concessit sibi vitam set jussit eum tamen perpetuo carceri mancipari.^{3} Demum

---

^{a} j. in the margin. ^{b} A short erasure, covered by a dash, follows. ^{c} ij. in the margin. $^{d-d}$ Added in the margin. ^{e} iij. in the margin. $^{f-f}$ Interlined.

---

^{1} Cf. Walsingham (*Hist. Ang.*, ii. 116), who says that Northampton referred to Lancaster as his lord. See also above, p. lxvii.

^{2} Cf. below, pp. 150, 184; but the Monk probably refers to matter on the now missing leaf of the MS.

^{3} Northampton was sentenced on 20 Aug. 1384 to perpetual imprisonment and forfeiture of goods (*Cal. Cl. R., 1381–5*, p. 478; *Cal. Pat. R., 1381–5*, p. 470).

things which John Northampton with his supporters proposed 1384
to ordain to the overthrow and enfeeblement of the city.'
And so, in a series of articles, he unblushingly announced a
succession of misdeeds, both numerous and heinous, imputed
to Northampton and his confederates, and formally appealed
him upon these articles, beginning as he came to each article,
with the words 'I, Thomas Usk, traitor etc.' On his part
Northampton steadily denied Usk's charges against him,
calling him, in the king's presence, a lying rascal and a gallows-
bird; that his accusations against himself were false he offered
to prove by his own hand in duel. In saying this, however,
Northampton exceeded proper bounds, since he did not, as in
such a case he should have done, save the king's reverence.
None the less the king, in the exercise of his special grace,
granted him a repayment of 100 marks yearly from his rents,
but in return for this he did not thank the king as he ought to
have. The king, seeing that he was somewhat stubborn,
exclaimed 'Let us put an end to this argument and proceed to
judgement in accordance with the facts found and proved.'
'I hope, my lord king', said Northampton, 'that you do not
mean to proceed to judgement or to exercise jurisdiction in
the absence of your uncle the duke of Lancaster.'[1] When he
heard this the king flared up and asserted that he was competent to sit in judgement on Northampton and on the duke
of Lancaster as well. 'You will find out', he said, 'that notwithstanding his absence I am going to be your judge'; and
forthwith ordered Northampton to be drawn and hanged and
all his goods to be forfeited too; and it is a fact that in pursuance of this judgement all his movable goods were confiscated, but not his immovable ones, as will plainly appear below.[2]
Northampton would thus have brought his life to an ignominious close, as a result of his three blunders and his undisciplined
behaviour, but for the chance presence of the queen, who in
a plea for his life threw herself at the king's feet and humbly
begged that Northampton should not die. Through her intercession the king granted him his life but ordered that he
should be committed to lifelong imprisonment.[3] So eventually

The threat of a capital sentence went beyond the usual penalty for misprision and
beyond the competence of the council, which could not make a judgement of life
or limb (Bellamy, op. cit., pp. 151, 223-4).

1384 J. Northampton' sic a mortis interitu graciose ereptus ad castrum de Corf' celeriter est adductus, ubi prius erat carcerali custodie deputatus. Finito consilio unusquisque remeavit ad propria.

Non multum post inter Londonienses (quod dolendum · est) gravis discordia est exorta quia divulgatum erat apud eos quod J. Northampton', J. More vicecomes tunc London', Ricardus Nortbury et Willelmus Estsex', quondam magni in civitate predicta, cum suis complicibus mortem magnorum tam in civitate quam extra (ne dicam regis seu aliorum illustrium) proditorie affectarunt et quantum in eis fuit nequiter procurarunt;* propter quod capti sunt J. More et R. Northbury et missi in custodiam.[1] Relatum est eciam quod isti ad excitandam sedicionem in civitate London' multipliciter laborabant, et ideo erant capti. Set W. Estsex' longe ante causa refugii ad Westmonasterium caute transivit.[2]

p. 146   Vicesimo nono die Augusti clerici London' apud Skynnereswell' fecerunt quendam ludum valde sumptuosum; duravitque quinque diebus.[3]

Circa principium mensis Septembris J. Northampton' de castro Corf' eductus transmissus est in Turrim London'.[4] Quo in tempore misit rex pro justiciariis suis et jurisperitis ut sine dilacione ulteriori vij. die Septembris se apud Westmonasterium ejus conspectui presentarent ad procedendum juridice contra predictos super tam notoriis criminibus et excessibus publice appellatos ac eciam notorie diffamatos. Principalis vero judex regis, nomine Robertus Tresilian, timuit in hujusmodi causa sentenciare; dicebat enim illorum judicium majori London' tantummodo pertinere, at quia isti

---

* Licet ista fuerunt eisdem imposita tamen non erant omnino vera, ut patet inferius per processum *in the margin*.

[1] The king ordered the arrest of More and Northbury on 20 Aug. The two submitted themselves to the king's grace at a council at Westminster on 5 Sept., when their goods were forfeit and they themselves sent in custody to Windsor castle. Almost at once they were brought to the Tower of London for the trial described by the Monk; the charge on this occasion was treason. See *Cal. Cl. R., 1381-5*, pp. 474-5, 478, 481-2; *Cal. Pat. R., 1381-5*, p. 470. More had been sheriff since 21 Sept. 1383 (*Letter Book H*, p. 218).

[2] Cf. *Letter Book H*, p. 304. The king ordered the arrest of Essex on 20 Aug. (*Cal. Cl. R., 1381-5*, pp. 474-5; cf. *Cal. Pat. R., 1381-5*, p. 500).

[3] See also below, p. 476; and for the importance of these references to plays of

Northampton, snatched from doom by an act of grace, was 1384
expeditiously conveyed to Corfe castle, where he had been
lodged in prison before. The council over, everyone returned
home.

Shortly after this a serious and regrettable controversy
broke out among the Londoners following a report that John
Northampton, John More, then sheriff of London, Richard
Northbury, and William Essex, who had formerly been
prominent in the city, with their accomplices, had treasonably
aimed at, and had done their wicked worst to contrive, the
deaths of important persons in the city and outside it, not
to speak of the king or other eminent people.* More and
Northbury were accordingly arrested and placed in confinement.[1] There was also a story that these two had made
numerous efforts of various kinds to stir up sedition in the
city and this was the reason for their arrest. Essex, however,
had long before this prudently removed himself to Westminster in search of refuge.[2]

On 29 August the clerks of London performed at Skinners
Well a lavishly produced play, which lasted five days.[3]

About the beginning of September John Northampton
was removed from Corfe castle and transferred to the Tower
of London.[4] At the same time the king sent for his justices
and law officers, ordering them without further delay to
make their appearance before him at Westminster on 7
September, ready to proceed judicially against the persons
named above whom public accusation and popular scandal
charged with flagrant crimes and outrages. The king's chief
justice, Robert Tresilian, hesitated to pronounce in a case of
this nature; he said that judgement on the accused was a
matter for the mayor of London alone, but inasmuch as

* Though these were the charges against them, they were not altogether true,
as appears from the proceedings reported below *in the margin.*

clerks at Skinners Well, near Clerkenwell, E. K. Chambers, *The Mediaeval Stage*
(2 vols., Oxford, 1903), ii. 380–1; W. O. Hassall, 'Plays at Clerkenwell', *Modern
Language Rev.*, xxxiii (1938), 564–7. For Skinners Well see J. E. B. Gover,
A. Mawer, and F. M. Stenton, *The Place-Names of Middlesex* (English Place-Name
Society, xviii, 1942), p. 95.
    [4] The mandate to the constable and lieutenant of Corfe castle to deliver
Northampton is dated 3 Sept. 1384 (*Cal. Cl. R., 1381–5*, p. 477; ibid., p. 478).

1384 predicti, scilicet J. Northampton' et ejus socii, fuerunt super prodicione appellati[1] ac eciam indictati necessario eorum bona tam mobilia quam inmobilia confiscarentur si contigerit eos propter hujusmodi crimina ad mortem in judicio condempnari. Igitur decimo die Septembris[2] in Turri London' coram domino Johanne de Monte Acuto senescallo domini regis presentibus eciam duobus justiciariis, scilicet Robertus[a] Tresilian et Robertus[b] Beleknap', tres illorum fuerunt producti et super sibi impositis examinati. Ea illis illata fatebantur esse vera, se tamen totaliter in regis graciam posuerunt; et hoc ideo fecerunt quia propter subornacionem in hominibus patrie confidere non audebant; unde dominus Johannes de Monte Acuto senescallus domini regis, ut prefertur, tulit sentenciam super eos et adjudicavit eos trahi et suspendi. Mox dominus Michael de Poole cancellarius domini regis concionem intravit, et patefacta sunt ei singula que circa eos erant acta et quomodo erant confessi ea que sibi imponebantur, unde rite fuerant adjudicati trahi et suspendi. Tunc cancellarius cunctis audientibus dixit: 'Licet isti propter scelera commissa mortem subire celeriter debuissent, tamen quia regie gracie se ultro dederunt rex concedit eis vitam tantum de sua gracia speciali; nichilominus tamen vult quod usque ad beneplacitum suum in locis securis interim custodiantur donec, si videatur expedire, eis graciam facere duxerit ampliorem.' Confestim ne isti tres insimul aliquibus solaciis congauderent missi sunt ad tres partes Anglie adinvicem satis remote distantes, scilicet R. Northbury ad castrum Corf' in australi parte Anglie[c] situatum, J. More ad castrum de Notyngham in boreali parte situatum, et J. Northampton' ad castrum de Tyntagel in Cornubia situatum, ut ibi in custodia morarentur.[3] Hec autem omnia sibi fieri procurarunt eorum emuli piscarii, ut dicebatur, quia per illos stetit quod ars et curia eorum erant destructe.[4]

[a] *Sic MS.*   [b] *Sic MS.*   [c] *Interlined.*

---

[1] The Monk's first intimation that More, Northbury, and Essex were appealed by Usk. The trial, however, was begun by indictment.

[2] Correctly, 12 Sept. See *Letter Book H*, pp. 264–6; and for the commission to the justices, *Cal. Pat. R., 1381–5*, p. 503.

Northampton and his associates were appealed,[1] and 1384 actually indicted, for treason, their goods, movable and immovable, would inevitably be forfeit if it turned out that judgement of death was passed upon them for their crimes. And so, at the Tower of London on 10 September,[2] three of them were brought before Sir John Montague, the king's steward (two justices, Robert Tresilian and Robert Bealknap, being also present) and examined on the charges against them. They confessed to the truth of the accusations, but cast themselves entirely on the king's mercy, doing so because on account of subornation they dared not trust to a jury. Sir John Montague, the king's steward, as before mentioned, accordingly passed sentence on them and condemned them to be drawn and hanged. Presently Sir Michael de la Pole, the king's chancellor, joined the gathering and was informed of the action taken about them and the way in which they had confessed to the charges so that they had been duly condemned to drawing and hanging. Then, while everybody listened, the chancellor spoke: 'Although, for the crimes they have committed, these men ought to suffer death out of hand, yet, since they have voluntarily submitted themselves to the royal mercy, the king, of his special grace, grants them their lives; it is his will, however, that they shall be kept during his pleasure in places of safety until, if it seems expedient, he thinks fit to show them increased mercy.' To prevent their enjoying mutual comfort the three of them were promptly dispatched to three parts of England at some distance from each other, Northbury to Corfe castle in the south, More to Nottingham castle in the north, and Northampton to Tintagel castle in Cornwall, there to remain in confinement.[3] It was their enemies the fishmongers, so it was said, who contrived their fate for them, because it was to them that the fall of the fishmongers' craft and of their court was due.[4]

---

[3] On 26 Sept. these sentences were reduced, in each case, to 10 years' imprisonment in prisons at least 100 miles from London; but assurance was given that even after their release Northampton, More, and Northbury would not come within 100 miles of the City (*Cal. Pat. R., 1381–5*, p. 464; see also *Letter Book H*, p. 279). [4] Above, p. 60 and n.

1384   Item circa festum Exaltacionis sancte ⟨Crucis⟩*a* obiit
dominus Willelmus de Wyndeshore, miles strenuus et
bellicosus ac multis diviciis opulentus quas sibi virtute
sua bellica adquisivit.[1]

Item xix. die Septembris ad instanciam cujusdam
valetti domini regis summo mane de Neugate xxv. viri
sunt educti et apud Foule Oke in Cancia erant
decapitati. (Distat autem locus parum a civitate London'
versus Canciam.) Erant namque quinque illorum
presbiteri, qui alta voce gementes et querelantes contra
ecclesiam Dei eo quod sine processu sive examinacione
et sine judicio quodammodo ita turpiter morerentur.
Retulit namque domino regi prefatus valettus quod
violenter sunt eum depredati et quod erant notorii
et latrones ac eciam valde astuti predones; quare rex
jussit eos occidi ordine judiciario pretermisso.[2]

Circa festum vero Sancti Mathei Evangeliste dux
Lancastr', comes de Bukyngham frater suus, et alii qui
causa tractatus cum Francigenis missi fuerant Calesiis
redierunt et effectus tocius tractatus fideliter domino regi
et ejus consilio intimarunt, affirmantes pro vero quod
secundum intellectum eorum plus placuit votis Francorum bellum habere quam pacem; nichilominus tamen
quandam treugam tam per terram quam per mare inter
nos et eos cum adherentibus usque in principium mensis
Maii proximo sequentis consenserunt firmari, si volu-
erimus acceptare ac interim, si nobis visum fuerit, eciam
cum illis de pace tractare. Placuit enim omnibus dictam
treugam ratam habere; unde protinus ad Francigenas ex
parte nostra directis nunciis inter nos et illos usque
idem tempus et cum adherentibus est treuga firmata.[3]

Quo in tempore in Apulea apud Tarentum obiit dux

---

a MS. om.

---

[1] Windsor, husband of Alice Perrers, was formerly the king's lieutenant in
Ireland (*G.E.C.*, xii. 877–89; *D.N.B.*, xxi. 648–50). He died on 15 Sept. 1384
(*Cal. Inq. p.m.*, xvi. 162 ff.).

[2] Cf. below, p. 248. For the suggestion that 'Foul Oak' was the name of a
gibbet see *Favent*, p. 5 n.

[3] This, the truce of Boulogne, was to be effective from various dates (according
to the place) between 16 Oct. and 15 Nov. 1384 until 1 May 1385; it included the

About Holy Cross Day [14 September] the death 1384 occurred of Sir William Windsor, a sturdy warrior-knight and a rich man by reason of the abundant wealth that his military prowess had won him.[1]

At dawn on 19 September, at the instance of one of the king's yeomen, twenty-five prisoners were brought out of Newgate and beheaded at Foul Oak in Kent. (The place is a short distance from London on the road into Kent.) Five of them were priests, who raised shrill wails of complaint against the Church of God because they were to die thus ignominiously without trial or examination or any sort of judgement. The yeoman having informed the king that they had robbed him with violence and that they were a byword as thieves and cunning footpads, the king ordered them to be put to death and the normal judicial procedure dispensed with.[2]

The duke of Lancaster, his brother the earl of Buckingham, and the others who had been sent to treat with the French returned from Calais about St. Matthew's Day [21 September] and made to the king and his council a faithful report of the result of their negotiations, stating that so far as they could gather there was no doubt that it suited the wishes of the French better to have war than peace; the French had nevertheless agreed to the conclusion of a truce between us and themselves, including their allies, to be operative on both land and sea until the beginning of the following May, if we were willing to accept it and to go on in the meantime, if we thought fit, to discuss peace with them. Everybody was content that the truce should be confirmed; envoys were accordingly sent at once to the French on our behalf and a truce for the period specified was concluded between us and them, including their allies.[3]

The duke of Anjou died at this time at Taranto in

Scots (Rymer, *Foedera*, vii. 438–43). For the identity of the English envoys see above, p. 88 n.; those whose accounts survive returned after 21 Sept. The decision to confirm the truce was made at a council in London on 11 Oct. (P.R.O., E. 403/502, 15 July; ibid., 505, 11 Oct.).

1384   Andegavie;[1] qui a duobus annis elapsis cum ingenti exercitu
Alpes pertransiens venit Italiam eo animo ut Romam, immo
et papam cum omnibus suis pariter destrueret, quod facile
potuisset si ceptum iter forsitan tenuisset. Set comes Salmo[2]
eum ab hoc proposito pie inflexit, ne hoc scelus committeret
ipsum est multis racionibus et monitis allocutus, asserens
illum locum fore sanctissimum ac per totum sanguine sanctorum martirum dedicatum atque multa sanctorum corpora
ibi quiescere dinoscuntur humata; ob quorum reverenciam
consuluit eum ne quicquam[a] mali faceret illi loco nec personis
in eo habitantibus set ceptum iter versus Apuleam recto
tramite tenere sibi suasit illis dimissis in pace, quoniam adversus clericos et presbiteros dimicare magis dedecus quam
honor sibi potuit applaudere. Dux vero annuit votis suis et
continuo flexo itinere versus Apuleam tendit quo principaliter ire disposuit, et cito post ibi, ut est supra relatum,
diem clausit extremum. Item circa idem tempus in Minori
Britannia obiit ducissa ejusdem, soror domini regis ex parte
matris.[3]

Scoti vero, treugis elapsis [b]inter nos et illos initis,[b] parum
vel modicum curantes de treuga que inter nos et Francigenas
cum eorum adherentibus extitit firmata plagam Northumbranam invaserunt et pene eam destructam et desolatam
rapinis et incendiis reddiderunt.[4]

Verumptamen quia xij^{mo}. die Octobris seniores et valenciores civitatis London' ad novi majoris eleccionem solebant
procedere,[5] dominus Nicholaus Brembre, qui fuit major anno
transacto, voluit precavere ne in hujusmodi eleccione foret

---

[a] *The words* vel aliquid *are written above this word, which has not been
deleted.*   [b-b] *Added in the margin but marked for insertion at this point.*

---

[1] Louis I, duke of Anjou and claimant to the throne of Naples and Sicily
and that of Jerusalem, died at Bari on 20/21 Sept. 1384. The main purpose
of his Italian expedition of 1382, to which the Monk now refers, was the rescue
of his stepmother, Joanna I of Naples, the prisoner, as he believed, of Charles of
Durazzo; he did not know that she was already dead. The rivalry of the Angevin
and Hungarian claimants to Naples and Sicily was caught up in the larger issue
of the papal schism. Louis I had been invested with the kingdom of Sicily by
Clement VII; Charles of Durazzo, by Urban VI. In forbearing to attack Rome,
where Urban could have offered little opposition, Louis I was disappointing his
Clementist allies, the better to pursue his own ambitions further south. For the
campaign see *Valois*, ii. 38–49, and Léonard, *Les Angevins de Naples*, pp. 466–7.

Apulia.[1] Two years before he had crossed the Alps into Italy 1384
with a huge army, bent on the destruction of Rome, and
indeed of the pope and his entire following likewise, which
he might easily have accomplished if he had happened to
hold to the course he had started on. But Count Salmo[2] vir-
tuously dissuaded him from his purpose, putting to him a
number of arguments and warnings against committing this
crime, and pointing out that Rome was a pre-eminently
hallowed spot, consecrated through and through by the
blood of holy martyrs, and the bodies of many saints were
well known to rest in burial there; he charged him, out of
reverence for them, to do no harm to the place or to those
who dwelt there, but to leave them in peace and continue
by the direct route the march to Apulia he had begun, since
war on priests and clergy would involve more discredit than
honour could condone in him. The duke agreed to do as
Salmo wished, and at once struck off to Apulia, his chief
objective, where shortly afterwards, as is reported above,
he ended his days. At about the same time the king's uterine
sister died in Brittany, of which she was duchess.[3]

Upon the expiry of the truce entered into between ourselves and them, the Scots, paying little or no heed to the
truce concluded between us and the French, including their
allies, attacked Northumbria and reduced it almost to rack
and ruin with fire and pillage.[4]

It being the custom for the aldermen and leading citizens
of London to proceed on 12 October to the election of a new
mayor,[5] Sir Nicholas Brembre, the mayor of the year just
past, was anxious to guard against the outbreak of any dispute

[2] Probably a reference to Amadeus VI, count of Savoy; if so the sentiments
attributed to him are inappropriate. See Valois, op. cit., ii. 49 and n.
[3] Joan Holland, daughter of Thomas Holland, earl of Kent (d. 1360) and
Joan, his wife, who subsequently married Edward, prince of Wales (the Black
Prince), died in Nov. 1384. In 1366 she married John IV, duke of Brittany, for
whom see below, p. 188 n.
[4] The current Anglo-Scottish truce expired on 1 Oct. 1384; the truce of
Boulogne was to take effect in Scotland on 24 Oct., but the above passage is not
the only evidence that it was not observed by the Marchers (Rymer, *Foedera*,
vii. 442; Campbell, in *Europe in the Late Middle Ages*, ed. Hale, Highfield, and
Smalley, p. 209; and see above, p. 86 n.).
[5] Cf. *R.P.*, iii. 226. The customary date was 13 Oct. Brembre's rival, Nicholas
Twyford, was a goldsmith. See also Bird, *Turbulent London of Richard II*, p. 69.

1384 aliqua discordia sive perturbacio suscitata; in cameris apud Gyldehall' clam abscondit viros armatos sub ista condicione quod si aliqua dissencio sive discordia fieri contigerit in ipsa eleccione statim exirent ad compescendum rebelles et discordes, ut saltem metu pene incarceracionis se a tumultu et verborum loquacitate inordinata penitus abstinerent et ad concordiam ac unitatem prorsus redirent. Quid plura? Convenerunt predicti valentes in unum pro eleccione novi majoris facienda apud Gyldehalle; una pars civitatis fortiter acclamabat 'Tuyford'! Tuyford'!', affectans illum in eorum majorem habere; altera vero pars econtrario senciebat, que eciam clamando prevaluit 'Brembre! Brembre!' Sicque facta inter eos dissencione protinus ad nutum domini N. Brembre comparuerunt dicti armati coram illis*[a]* qui aderant in*[b]* concione ut sediciosos sedarent; quibus visis fugerunt illi qui clamabant 'Tuyford''. Porro sedata tempestate / valenciores civitatis qui remanserant predictum dominum N. Brembre iterato in eorum majorem concorditer assumpserunt; quo facto N. Brembre cum predicto cuneo armatorum perrexit in vicum qui vocatur Chepe ad inquirendum et investigandum si qui pacis perturbatores forent inibi congregati; postea in alios vicos ea de causa transivit ut si quos tales sediciosos inveniret eos in exemplum aliorum apud Neugate ad tempus in vinculis custodiret. Isto modo fuit predicta eleccio celebrata: tamen licet aliqui illam prout audebant impugnaverint, nichilominus per totum annum deinceps stetit major rege precipue annuente.

p. 147

Parliamentum. Duodecimo die Novembris tenuit rex parliamentum apud Westmonasterium, in quo more solito petuntur subsidia domino regi concedi pro defensione regni precipue. Tandem post magnam super hoc deliberacionem concesse sunt sibi a clero due decime ac due quintedecime a populo laicali eo pacto quod dominus rex manu robusta transiret in Franciam anno sequenti, alias non haberet nisi medietatem omnium concessorum.[1] (Postea, quia transivit in Scociam, prout inferius describetur, accepit omnia sibi concessa

---

[a] Interlined.   [b] MS. in in.

---

[1] For the lay grant see *R.P.*, iii. 185. The clerical grant was made by the two convocations in Dec. 1384 and Jan. 1385 respectively and consisted of a single tenth, payable in two instalments (*Cal. Fine R., 1383–91*, pp. 75, 95, 97). The

or rioting on this occasion and secretly concealed a number 1384
of armed men in the rooms of the Guildhall on the understanding that if any controversy or quarrelling should occur
during the election they were at once to come out and quell
the unruly and quarrelsome elements, in order that fear of
the pains of imprisonment, if nothing else, might effectually
restrain them from riot and undue talkativeness and make
them revert directly to unity and concord. Need I say more?
The leading citizens assembled at the Guildhall to make their
choice of a new mayor; one city faction raised vigorous cries
of 'Twyford! Twyford!', eager to have him for their mayor;
but the other faction held contrary views and shouted them
down with 'Brembre! Brembre!' Disagreement between them
having been thus established, the armed men, at a signal from
Sir Nicholas Brembre, immediately made their appearance in
the gathering to quell the disorderly; and at sight of them
those who were shouting 'Twyford' took to flight. When the
storm had subsided, those of the leading citizens who remained proceeded to re-elect Sir Nicholas Brembre to the
mayoralty; this done, Brembre went with the armed party
into Cheap in quest of any disturbers of the peace who might
have gathered there, afterwards passing on into other streets,
so that any disorderly persons he might find should be
clapped in irons at Newgate for a time as an example to
others. Such was the way in which this election was held;
yet though there were some people who, as far as they
dared, called it in question, Brembre none the less remained
mayor throughout the ensuing year, with the especial
approval of the king.

Parliament. The king held a parliament at Westminster on
12 November, in which the usual request was made for the
grant of subsidies to him, especially for the defence of the
realm. After close consideration of the matter grants were
at length made of two tenths by the clergy and two fifteenths
by the laity, on the understanding that the king should cross
to France in force during the coming year; otherwise he was
to have only half of the total grants.[1] (He eventually received
the whole amount, and the condition was waived, because

king had declared his intention of leading an expedition to France in March 1382
at a great council (*R.P.*, iii. 122; and see Aston, in *B.I.H.R.*, xxxviii. 138-41).

1384 condicione rejecta.)[1] In isto vero parliamento pro comodo regni nichil utile fuit actum, quia domini temporales, quibus competit loqui pro statu et comodo regni, adinvicem adversantes semper eo tempore discordes fuere, ac eo finito in discordia recesserunt. Durante parliamento Scoti dolose ceperunt castrum de Berewyk', et licet comes Northumberlond, custos castri predicti, erat tunc London' causa parliamenti, prout a rege habuit in mandatis, non potuit excusari quin domini temporales et precipue dux Lancâstr' decernebant ipsum juste debere predictum castrum suis propriis expensis tantummodo recuperare, quia propter sui defectum illud erat amissum, et nisi fuerit infra certum tempus recuperatum decreverunt illum et omnia bona sua mobilia et inmobilia subjacere regie voluntati.[2] Accepit namque comes prèdictus pro custodia dicti castri annuatim a rege quingentas marcas.[3] Qui videns a rege aliud subsidium non posse habere celer accinxit se ad iter et venit Berewycum, ubi invenit suos stipendiarios graves insultus in dies hostibus castellanis et dampna cotidiana[a] inferre; set propter fort⟨it⟩udinem loci contra eos minime prevaluerunt. Prefatus vero comes considerans quod dicti castri recuperacio sine majori potencia virorum armorum fuisset omnino sibi impossibilis, unde super hoc librato consilio ad evitandum majus malum et pro meliori emit illud a Scotis duobus milibus marcarum, sub ista condicione adjecta quod Scoti possent libere in Scociam cum suis redire: quod et factum est.

Duellum.[b] Ultimo die Novembris in palacio domini regis apud Westmonasterium factum est duellum inter Johannem Walshe Anglicum defendentem et quendam Navarrium vocatum Martigo appellantem,[4] prevaluitque Anglicus. Et quia

---

[a] Interlined.   [b] This caption, which replaces bellum (deleted), is in a later hand.

[1] pp. 124 ff.

[2] Judgement against the earl of Northumberland was given on 14 Dec. 1384, but on 17 Feb. 1385 he was pardoned (Walsingham, Hist. Ang., ii. 118; Calendar of Documents relating to Scotland, ed. Bain, iv. 333). He had been appointed keeper of Berwick-upon-Tweed for 6 months from 1 Aug. 1384 (Storey, in E.H.R., lxxii (1957), 598). For the capture of Berwick, which the Scots effected by bribing the earl's deputy there, see Walsingham, loc. cit., and Fordun, i. 382.

[3] Northumberland was in fact promised £4,000 on his appointment.

he made an expedition to Scotland, as will be narrated 1384 below.)[1] But nothing which furthered the interests of the kingdom was done in this parliament, because the lords temporal, whose business it is to speak up for the condition and welfare of the realm, were mutually antagonistic and at this time perpetually at odds; and when the parliament was over they departed in discord. While this parliament was still in being the Scots captured Berwick castle by means of a ruse; and though the earl of Northumberland, the keeper of the castle, was at the time in London for the parliament in obedience to a command received from the king, no excuse availed to prevent the lords temporal, among whom the duke of Lancaster was conspicuous, from deciding that he was in justice bound to recover the castle at his own sole expense, on the ground that it was by his default that it had been lost; and if it was not recovered within a specified time they ruled that he and all his property, movable and immovable, would be at the disposal of the king.[2] For the keeping of the castle the earl received 500 marks a year from the king,[3] from whom he saw that he could get no further assistance. He therefore quickly prepared himself for the road, and on reaching Berwick found his hired troops daily delivering heavy assaults on the enemy in the castle and daily inflicting losses on them, but failing completely, owing to the strength of the place, to overcome them. Deciding that without a more powerful force of men at arms the recovery of the castle would be wholly impossible, the earl calculated his policy and, in order at once to avoid a worse calamity and to improve the situation, bought the castle back from the Scots for 2,000 marks, the bargain having attached to it a condition that the Scots and their followers should be allowed to return unhindered to Scotland; which is what in fact happened.

Duel. On the last day of November a duel was fought in the king's palace at Westminster between an English defendant, John Walsh, and a Navarrese appellant named Martigo,[4] in

---

[4] The accuser is named by Knighton as Martyletto de Vynelef (*Chronicon*, ii. 204). The occasion of the duel was an insult offered by Walsh to his accuser's wife (Walsingham, *Hist. Ang.*, ii. 117-18). Walsh was victualler at Cherbourg (*Cal. Cl. R. 1381-5*, p. 633).

1384 predictus Martigo appellavit prefatum Johannem de prodicione, constabularius et marescallus Anglie ex officio
adjudicarunt ipsum trahi et suspendi. Et ne tales appellaciones in ista terra nimis in posterum multiplicarentur, rex
cessit judicio reo lato.

Quartodecimo die Decembris fuit finis parliamenti, et
unusquisque velud in discordia ad propria remeavit. Rex
vero tenuit suum Natale apud Wyndeshoram. Et in die Sancti
Stephani magister Johannes Wyclyf subito[a] arreptus paralisi
diem clausit extremum;[1] qui multa heretica et perversa in
ecclesia Dei, ut placeret hominibus non Deo, nequiter
seminavit.

1385 Item[b] circa principium Januarii certificatum fuit domino
pape quod sui cardinales, immo quidam eorum, conspirarunt
in ejus mortem, accusantes eum de heresi et de aliis
criminibus majoribus que si contra eum fuissent probata
merito deponeretur ac eciam juxta canones, si ea defendere
temere voluerit, sinodi judicio moreretur.[2] Set dominus
papa scivit a talibus criminibus se fore inmunem; sex cardinales quos precipue hujusmodi faccionis habuit suspectos
incarceravit et eos ut vera faterentur gravissimis tormentis
exposuit; inter quos fuit quidam cardinalis Anglicus,
quondam monachus Northwycen';[3] qui professus est se de
hujusmodi conspiracione perante scivisse, unde papa valde
contra eum ira commotus quia sibi minime indicavit, tam
eum quam alios omni honore ordine et dignitate privavit;
demum fecit eos in arto loco ad tempus recludi.

Verumptamen quia de isto papa Urbano vj.[c] hic fit mencio,
aliqua de illo tangam hic quasi recapitulando pauca que
supra erant omissa.[4] Constat namque reginam Neapolitanam
primo de istius pape promocione multum gaudere eo quod
unus de sua patria dignus poterat repperiri qui regeret
ecclesiam[d] universalem, et misit ei literas regraciatorias quibus

---

[a] Interlined.   [b] De papa hic plus in the margin in a fifteenth-century hand.
[c] This numeral has been added above the name.   [d] MS. ecclesia.

[1] Wycliffe was taken ill on 28 Dec. 1384 and died on 31 Dec.
[2] For the teaching of the canonists on the judgement of a pope, see B. Tierney,
Foundations of the Conciliar Theory (Cambridge, 1955), pp. 56 ff., 212 ff. The
crucial text is Gratian, *Decretum*, Dist. 40 c.6.
[3] Adam Easton, cardinal-priest of St. Cecilia. For the identity of the other

which the Englishman was victorious. Martigo having appealed 1384
Walsh of treason, the constable and the marshal of England,
in the exercise of their function, condemned him to be drawn
and hanged. In order to discourage any untoward increase
in the future numbers of such appeals in this country, the
king acquiesced in the judgement passed on the defeated
party.

The parliament came to an end on 14 December, and it
was in something like dissension that everybody returned
home. The king kept Christmas at Windsor. On St. Stephen's
Day [26 December] Master John Wycliffe was suddenly
seized by paralysis and ended his days.[1] With the aim of
pleasing men rather than God, he had sinfully spread a
number of heretical and wrong-headed doctrines in God's
Church.

About the beginning of January the pope was assured that 1385
his cardinals, or rather some of them, had plotted to bring
about his death by accusing him of heresy and other serious
crimes for which, if they were proved against him, he would
merit deposition and even, according to the canons, death
by judgement of a synod if he were so rash as to seek to
defend his conduct.[2] The pope, however, who knew himself
to be invulnerable to these charges, threw into prison the six
cardinals he particularly suspected of conspiracy and subjected them to the severest of tortures to make them confess
the truth. Among them was an Englishman, a former monk
of Norwich,[3] who admitted that he had had prior knowledge
of the plot. The pope was therefore furiously angry with him
for having failed to inform him, and stripped him and the
others alike of all their honours, orders, and dignities before
shutting them up for the moment in close confinement.

Now that mention of Pope Urban VI has cropped up, I
will deal here with some facts about him by way of summarizing a few matters omitted above.[4] There is no doubt that the
queen of Naples was at first very pleased about his advancement, in that a fellow-countryman was to be found who was
worthy to govern the universal Church; and she sent him an

cardinals see C. Eubel and G. Van Gulik, *Hierarchia Catholica Medii Aevi* (3 vols.,
Regensburg, 1898–1910), i. 22–3. See also on this episode Walsingham, *Hist.
Ang.*, ii. 122–5; *Valois*, ii. 112–17 and references cited there. [4] p. 100.

1385   evidenter poterat deprehendi qualem affeccionem erga eum
gerebat; fuit eciam postea manifestius declaratum, nam
rebellantibus contra eum suis cardinalibus peciit ipse ab ea
quoddam subsidium virorum armatorum ut per illos suos
valeat confundere inimicos.[1] Statim ipsa concessit, et misit
sibi centum viros in armis strenuos et in bellicis congressibus
valde expertos: quod postquam innotuit Roberto Gebenensi
Romani papatus intrusori mox ad predictam reginam clam
accessit factisque ei quibusdam mediacionibus familiariter
ab ea fuit acceptus ac demum in suam partem illam allexit,
ita ut papam Urbanum sperneret et protinus ipsum
Gebenensem pro vero papa penitus acceptaret. Statimque
misit predicta regina ad papam Urbanum quatinus ut sibi
mitteret dictos viros bellicosos quos sibi in sui auxilium
nuperrime destinavit: confestim ipse illos remisit. Ecce quam
leviter potest quis mulierum animos inmutare! Nec mirum,
quia[a] inconstancia eas excusat. Quo cognito papa Urbanus
sepius monuit prefatam reginam ut relicto scismate ad verum
Christi vicarium in terris se tempestive converteret, et nisi
voluerit ad ecclesie unitatem redire procederet contra eam
juridice ad privacionem regni Neapolitani pro perpetuo:
set illa nulla suasione aut monicione vellet a suo proposito
declinare, affirmans semper dictum Gebenensem verum esse
papam. Mox papa Urbanus facto processu contra prefatam
reginam deposuit eandem et Carolum de Pace filium regis
Hungarie in regem Neapolitanum solempniter coronavit.[2]
Aliqui domini tamen illius regni contra eum rebellantes
numquam illum pro eorum domino recipere voluerunt.
Papa quoque Urbanus fecit predictum Carolum jurare ad
tenendum certas convenciones inter illos initas antequam
vellet sibi tradere insignia regalia; quas tamen postea observare
neglexit. Papa Urbanus habens quendam consanguineum cui

---

[a] eas *deleted after this word.*

[1] A reference to the secession of cardinals from the court of Urban VI (who
was a Neapolitan) in June and July 1378. At this juncture Joanna I of Naples is
said to have provided Urban not only with 100 men at arms but also with 200
lances. Only a little later, however, she was won over by the dissident cardinals,
and in Nov. 1378 she formally declared her support for Clement VII ('Robert of
Geneva'). She was deposed by Urban VI in the summer of 1380, but between her
first defection from his cause and that event she renewed her adherence, though

appreciative letter from which could be very clearly deduced 1385
the fondness she entertained for him — a fondness that was
later yet more obviously manifested, for when his cardinals
revolted against him and he asked her for armed assistance to
enable him to discomfit his enemies, she at once agreed and
sent him a hundred stalwart men at arms with considerable
experience of combat.[1] As soon as this became known to
Robert of Geneva, the usurper of the Roman papacy, he
made secret approaches to the queen, and when his intermediaries had done their work was welcomed by her in
friendly fashion, eventually enticing her over to his side, so
that she rejected Pope Urban and without hesitation or
reserve accepted the Genevan as the true pope. She now sent
to Pope Urban demanding the return of the troops she had
so recently dispatched to him; and he promptly sent them
back. How easily women's minds can be altered! And no
wonder, when their fickleness is an excuse for them. After
learning what had happened, Pope Urban repeatedly warned
the queen to abandon her state of schism and effect her
timely conversion to Christ's true vicar on earth: unless she
agreed to return to the unity of the Church, he would insti-
tute judicial proceedings to deprive her for ever of the
monarchy of Naples. But no persuasion or warning could
induce her to turn from her purpose, and she persistently
declared that the Genevan was the true pope. Pope Urban
therefore soon afterwards instituted proceedings against her,
and, having deposed her, solemnly crowned as king of Naples
Charles the Peacemaker, son of the king of Hungary.[2] Some
of the Neapolitan nobles, however, revolted against him
and refused to accept him as their sovereign. Before he would
hand over to Charles the insignia of kingship, Pope Urban
made him swear to keep certain agreements entered into
between them, but Charles subsequently omitted to honour
them. Pope Urban had a kinsman on whom, to the indignation
of Charles when he heard of it, he bestowed the lordship

very briefly — an episode which the Monk omits. See *Valois*, i. 74-8, 159-60,
177-80; Léonard, *Les Angevins de Naples*, pp. 454-8.
    [2] Urban VI invested Charles of Durazzo, called 'the Peacemaker', with the
kingdom of Sicily on 1 June 1381 and crowned him the following day. Charles
was the son of Lewis, duke of Durazzo (d. 1362), whom the Monk confuses with
Lewis the Great, king of Hungary (d. 1382).

1385 contulit dominium de Capua, quod dictus Carolus tunc in
sua manu tenebat;[1] quo audito rex Carolus iratus versus
papam Urbanum, et cognita incarceracione dictorum
cardinalium apud castrum de Nusceryn venit cum multitudine pugnatorum et papam in eodem castro obsedit.[2]
Papa vero ipsum excommunicavit, inhabilitavit ac demum
p. 148 regno / Neapolitano privavit; ob quam causam rex Carolus
eum acrius infestavit, ponens obsidium circa castrum predictum undique ne fuge subsidium inde haberet. Papa itaque
bene vidit se non posse manus regis Caroli sine succursu
aliquorum magnorum evadere; misit latenter ad valentes
dominos regni Neapolitani, videlicet Jacobum de Sancto
Severino et Raymundum de Balsio filium comitis Nolani,[3]
ut illum sic inclusum succurrerent sub benediccione paterna;
cui responderunt se fore paratos sibi in omnibus obedire
tanquam spirituales filii merito tanto patri, presertim si
prout incepit contra Carolum processum privacionis voluerit
continuare. Ad hec papa applaudens promisit eis dictum
processum contra prefatum Carolum se velle debite finire
prout incepit, vita comite si contigerit eum ad aliquem
locum tutum venire.[a]

Cum vero infausta infortunia quandoque evitari non
possint, igitur xiij^{mo}. et xiiij^{mo}. diebus Februarii in Carniprivio
et in Magna Aula Westmon' tenuit rex hastiludia: ultima
quoque nocte eorundem a quibusdam dominis, ut dicebatur,
rege ad hoc favente fuit conspiratum in necem ducis
Lancastr', set ipse caute de hujusmodi premunitus paucis
secum comitantibus clam aufugit.[4] Causa namque quare
ipsum voluerunt interfecisse fuit ista, ut quidam assertive
volunt. Parum ante in quodam consilio tactum fuit de

---

[a] Plus anno 1386 *in the margin, in a fifteenth-century hand. Cf. below,*
p. 162.

[1] A misinformed or disingenuous account. As a condition of his investiture
with the kingdom of Sicily, Charles of Durazzo promised to ratify the grant of
Capua and other territories to the pope's nephew, Francis Prignano, but he
delayed to do so (*Valois*, ii. 9, 65–6).
[2] The siege began on 31 Jan. 1385. On 15 Jan. the pope had excommunicated
Charles of Durazzo and released his subjects from their obedience; at the end of
Feb. he launched a crusade against him. See *Cronicon Siculum*, ed. J. de Blasiis,
pp. 55–6; H. Simonsfeld, 'Analekten zur Papst-und-Konziliengeschichte im
14 und 15 Jahrhundert', *Abhandlungen der Historischen Classe der Königlich*

of Capua, then in Charles's hands.[1] On learning of the im- 1385
prisonment of the cardinals at the castle of Nocera, Charles
marched there with a large fighting force and besieged the
pope in the castle.[2] The pope excommunicated and incapaci-
tated him, and finally deprived him of the kingdom of
Naples; which caused Charles to intensify his attack and to
mount a blockade all round the castle to prevent the pope
from resorting to flight. Realizing that unless powerful
people came to the rescue he could not escape the clutches
of King Charles, the pope sent secretly to two prominent
Neapolitan nobles, Giacopo de San Severino and Reimundello de Balsio, son of the count of Nola,[3] a request that
under his paternal blessing they would relieve his present
confinement. They replied that they were ready to give him
in all things the obedience properly due from sons in the
spirit to a father of his greatness, and especially so if he was
willing to go on as he had started with proceedings for
Charles's deprivation. Thoroughly approving their reply, the
pope assured them that if it turned out that he reached some
place of safety with his life he was prepared to carry through
to their due conclusion, as he had begun them, the proceedings against Charles.

Untoward incidents are sometimes unavoidable; and so it
was that when, during Lent, the king held a tournament in
Westminster Hall on 13 and 14 February, a plot was hatched
on the concluding night by some of the nobles (with the
king's approval, it was said) to murder the duke of Lancaster;
but he was wary enough to get warning of this and
unobtrusively made his escape with a few companions.[4] The
reason for this desire to kill him was, as some people affirm,
the following. At a recent council there had been discussion

Bayerischen Akademie der Wissenschaften, xx (1893), 38–41. The Monk here omits
the chequered course of events between the first breach between Urban VI and
Charles of Durazzo, occasioned by the former's ambitions for his nephew, and the
siege of Nocera; later, he refers to an episode belonging to this period — the brief
captivity of the pope at Aversa in 1383. See below, p. 162; and *Valois*, ii. 9 ff.

[3] Both partisans of the Angevin cause — i.e. that of the enemies of Charles of
Durazzo — in Naples, but it was Thomas de San Severino who, with Reimundello
de Balsio and others, helped in Urban's escape from Nocera in July 1385 (*Cronicon Siculum*, pp. 58, 60–1; *Valois*, ii. 114–15; see also below, p. 140 and n.).

[4] Cf. Walsingham, *Hist. Ang.*, ii. 126; and for comment, Aston, in *B.I.H.R.*,
xxxviii (1965), 141.

1385   regni gubernacione regisque regimine et quid foret expedicius regi facere pro utilitate regni sequenti autumpno;
dux vero Lancastr' prout ipse senciebat dicebat magis
utile fore pro comodo regni quod rex cum exercitu suo
transiret in Franciam ut ibi manu armata hostes suos
viriliter debellaret pocius quam daret eis facultatem
veniendi in terram istam et nos non sine gravi dampno et
jactura continuo infestarent. Ad hec quidam de consilio
contrarium sencientes ducis consilium improbant et
violenter impugnant, asserentes non esse sanum regem
maria transmeare neque terram Francorum intrare certis
de causis, set pocius in terra propria securius residere,
illam ab inimicorum morsibus defendendo, quam ad
exteras provincias inconsulte transire, nil gloriosum sue
fame addendo. Placuit istud universis de consilio excepto
duce Lancastr' et fratribus suis,[1] qui propter hoc indignati
continuo de consilio exierunt; insuper dux Lancastr'
protestatus est se neque suos auxilium domino regi velle
impendere nisi in Franciam disposuerit se transire, quod
quidem verbum tam regi quam toti ejus consilio valde
displicuit, unde propter. hoc arbitrantes eum neque regi
neque regno fore fidelem. Tamen isti domini temporales
ducem Lancastr' propter ejus magnam potenciam, pruden-
ciam commendabilem et suum ingenium tam preclarum
semper timebant; ideo licet aliquod sinistrum scivissent de
illo non tamen audebant in lucem producere; unde, ut
predictum est, aliqui illorum ipsum occulte perimere
satagebant.

Item xxiiij[to]. die Februarii dux Lancastr' armatorum
comitiva stipatus nocte apud Shene venit ad regem,
dimissa prius sua turba armatorum citra flumen Thamense,
transitoque flumine dimisit ibi quosdam de suis qui usque
ad reditum suum cymbam taliter custodirent ne illam
interim quispiam occuparet; accessitque ad portam eciam
et ibi dimisit quosdam de suis qui usque ad suum
regressum introitum et exitum quibuscumque negarent.
Demum loricatus ingressus est cum paucis ad regem, cui,
ut decuit, facta debita veneracione satis dure et aspere est

---

[1] Edmund of Langley, earl of Cambridge, later duke of York, and Thomas of
Woodstock, earl of Buckingham, later duke of Gloucester.

about the administration of the kingdom and the task of guid-
ing the king and about the action it would be most expedient
for the king to take during the following autumn in the
interests of the realm. The duke of Lancaster gave it as his
opinion that it would best serve those interests for the king
to cross with his army to France and crush his enemies by
force resolutely applied there rather than afford them the
opportunity of entering English territory and delivering a
swift attack, with heavy loss and damage to us. At this
certain members of the council, who took a contrary view,
expressed their disapproval of the duke's advice in a violent
onslaught, contending that there were good reasons why it
was not sound policy for the king to cross the sea or enter
France: he ought to remain in the security of his own country,
defending it from the nibbling attacks of his enemies, rather
than make an unconsidered excursion into foreign parts,
adding thereby no lustre to his reputation. This argument
appealed to all the council except the duke of Lancaster and
his brothers,[1] who in consequence promptly walked out in
high dudgeon, the duke further vowing that neither he nor
his dependants would give the king any assistance unless he
meant to cross to France. These words gave great displeasure
both to the king and to the whole council, who because of
them judged him to be wanting in loyalty to king and kingdom
alike. Yet these temporal lords went in constant fear of the
duke of Lancaster because of his great power, his admirable
judgement, and his brilliant mind; and so, though they had
learned something ugly about him, they did not dare to bring
it out into the light of day, and some of them, as is stated above,
busied themselves about removing him by underhand means.

On the night of 24 February the duke of Lancaster, closely
escorted by an armed guard, paid a visit to the king at Sheen.
Leaving the bulk of his force on this side of the Thames, he
crossed the river and detached some of his men to guard the
boat until his return and prevent anyone's taking possession
of it in the meantime; he then proceeded to the gate and
there too left some of his men to stop everyone from going in
or out until his own reappearance. Finally, wearing a breast-
plate, he made his way into the king's presence and, having
made to him the bow which propriety demanded, began by

1385 eum primitus allocutus, increpans eum quod tam diu tam malos consiliarios secum retinuit, finaliter ipsum consulens tales ab eo penitus amovere ac de cetero viris sanioris consilii adherere; nam inhonestum est regem in suo regno, cum sit dominus omnium, se privato homicidio vindicare, cum ipse sit supra legem, cujus est posse vitam tribuere et membra eciam, et si voluerit ea tollere potest ad nutum. Igitur eo amplius ac necessario convenit tam excellentem personam bonos consiliarios et fideles circa se habere, quorum sano consilio semper se ab illicitis abstineret et ea que recta sunt illis mediantibus ferventi animo jugiter agere minime formidaret. Cui rex mollia verba et suavia benigne refudit, asserens indubitanter ea que antea minus juste sunt gesta operam daret deinceps in melius reformare. Demum dux Lancastr' petita licencia excusavit se de non veniendo ad eum in posterum sicut antea solebat, quia illic quosdam videbat ei assidue adherere qui libencius vellent eum vita privare; statimque a rege discessit et ea nocte cum suis venit ad villam de Todenham, ubi parumper quievit, deinde festinus accessit ad castrum suum de Herteford', ubi secure cum suis*a* statuit commanere. Mater quidem regis de hiis cerciorata nimio dolore et stupore turbata celeriter festinavit ad regem, suadens ei semper discordias suorum nobilium evitare, presertim ducis Lancastr' et fratrum suorum, qui patrui ei existunt. Igitur ad ejus suasum vj^{to}. die Marcii venit Westmon' cum magna militum comitiva. Mater regis confestim accessit ad ducem Lancastr' et ita eum inflexit quod eum ad regem adduxit; cujus eciam mediacione protinus sunt*b* adinvicem concordati. Remisit eciam dux Lancastr' ad rogatum domini regis iracundiam suam quam erga quosdam dominos regi familiares gerebat; et fuerunt hii comes Sar', comes Oxon' et comes Notyngham.[1] Aliique fuerunt qui nondum potuerunt ab eo protunc remissionis*c* graciam optinere.

a Interlined.   *b Interlined.*   *c Interlined.*

---

[1] Cf. below, p. 124, where Lancaster's formal reconciliation with the earls is put later in the year.

speaking to him with some harshness and severity, reproach-
ing him with having kept such bad counsellors about him for
so long, and ended by advising him to get rid of them altogether and to cling in future to men of sounder judgement:
it was, he said, shameful for a king in his own kingdom,
where he was lord of all, to avenge himself by means of
private murder when he was himself above the law and had
the power to vouchsafe life and limb with a nod, or, if he
were so minded, to take them away. All the more, then, was
it necessarily right and proper that a person so pre-eminent
should have about him good and loyal advisers, by whose
sage counsel he might forbear lawless action and with whom
as his instruments he need not be afraid to do always and
enthusiastically what was right. The king answered him
amiably, giving him, in mild and soothing language, a positive
assurance that he would see to it that in future there should
be improvement and reform in those respects in which there
had been injustices in the past. Finally the duke begged leave
to be excused henceforward from attending the king as he
had habitually done in the past, because he saw that the
king's company was sedulously cultivated by certain persons
who would cheerfully rob him of his life. With this he left
the king and arrived that night at Tottenham with his party,
pressing on from there, after a short rest, to his castle at
Hertford, where he decided to stay in safety with his
followers. When she was informed of these events the king's
mother was very much shocked and distressed and hurried
without loss of time to the king, whom she urged always to
avoid quarrelling with his nobles and especially with his
uncles, the duke of Lancaster and his brothers. As a result of
her persuasion the king came on 6 March to Westminster,
escorted by a large number of knights. His mother made
haste to visit the duke of Lancaster and influenced him to
such purpose that she took him with her to the king; and
through her good offices harmony was soon restored between
them. At the king's request the duke dropped the resentment
he had nursed against some of the nobles who were intimate
with the king. These were the earls of Salisbury, Oxford, and
Nottingham:[1] there were others who were not yet able to win
from him the favour of forgiveness.

1385 Incontinenti[1] postea apud Westmonasterium consilio celebrato archiepiscopus Cantuar' aliique ecclesiarum prelati, ac de dominis temporalibus aliqui, de istis consiliariis circa regem conversantibus graviter sunt conquesti eo quod induxerunt regem assentire interfeccioni ducis Lancastr' tam crudeliter in privato, tum[a] quia fuit res mali exempli tum quia[b] sequeretur ex hoc quod quandocumque rex versus magnam sive mediocrem personam cor sive animum gestierat odiosum, consimili modo forsitan illam (quod absit) mandaret occidi, ut sic per hoc leges et consuetudines approbate[c] lesionem non modicam paterentur, rixe lites jurgia contenciones, dissenciones et cetera talia in regno (quod absit) ubique forsitan nascerentur. Igitur abstinendum est a talibus sceleribus in futurum ne propter hujusmodi illicita deterioracio regni fieri manifeste contingat. Ista verba sive consimilia archiepiscopus Cantuar' retulit regi ex parte dominorum tunc ibidem existencium; quibus auditis rex iratus versus archiepiscopum ilico surrexit et minas ei intulit. Illo namque die comedit rex cum majore London': finito prandio rex flumen Thamense intravit et inter palacium suum et Lambheth' archiepiscopum habuit obvium, venerat enim prefatus archiepiscopus ad regem sub salvo conductu comitis de Bukyngham. Demum recitata materia quam ante prandium archiepiscopus fuerat prosecutus rex extracto ense archiepiscopum ilico perfodisset nisi comes Bukyngham, dominus Johannes Deveroys[2] et dominus Thomas Tryvet[3] eidem fortiter restitissent; quibus rex iratus, igitur de scapha regis propter metum in cymbam archiepiscopi statim prosiliebant et sic ab eo protunc in discordia recesserunt.

Item xxiij°. die Marcii tractatores pacis ex parte nostra omnes excepto duce Lancastr' Cales' transierunt; qui circa finem mensis Aprilis redierunt absque pacis effectu.[4] Item p. 149 xv. die Aprilis obiit dominus / Robertus Stanton' Cestren'

---

[a] Interlined.   [b] Interlined.   [c] MS. approbatas.

[1] On the subject-matter of this paragraph cf. Walsingham, *Hist. Ang.*, ii. 128 and *Vita Ricardi Secundi*, p. 86.

[2] A distinguished soldier, councillor, and diplomat, for whom see Tout, *Chapters*, iii. 328, 344; ibid., iv. 205.

[3] A knight of the chamber, for whom see also below, p. 228.

[4] For earlier stages in the negotiations see above, pp. 88, 98. The Monk's

At[1] a council held very soon after this at Westminster the 1385
archbishop of Canterbury and other leading churchmen, and
some of the temporal lords, were bitter in their complaints
against those councillors who moved in the king's immediate
circle for having induced him to countenance the duke of
Lancaster's being callously murdered in secret, in the first
place because it set a bad example, and secondly because the
consequence would be that whenever the king bore any
grudge or ill will against somebody, great or humble, he
might perhaps (though God forbid that he should) order
that person's death by like means, with the result that
accepted laws and customs would thereby suffer grave injury and everywhere in the kingdom there might spring up
(which Heaven forfend) wrangles, disputes, brawls, strife and
discord, and so on. Crimes of this kind must therefore in
future be shunned, to prevent the decline of the realm,
through these lawless courses, from becoming an unmistakable
fact. It was in these or some such words that the archbishop addressed the king on behalf of the lords present on
this occasion; and on hearing them the king, enraged with the
archbishop, leapt to his feet with a volley of threats at him.
On the same day the king dined in the company of the mayor
of London and when the meal was over embarked on the
Thames. Between his palace and Lambeth he met the archbishop, who had come to visit him under safe-conduct of the
earl of Buckingham. Eventually, after a repetition of the
theme which the archbishop had pursued before dinner, the
king drew his sword and would have run the archbishop
through on the spot if he had not been stoutly resisted by the
earl of Buckingham, Sir John Devereux,[2] and Sir Thomas
Trivet,[3] with whom he was so angry that in their fear they
jumped from his barge into the archbishop's boat. It was
therefore in discord that on this occasion they parted company with the king.

All our representatives in the peace negotiations, except
the duke of Lancaster, crossed to Calais on 23 March; they
returned about the end of April without having brought
about peace.[4] On 15 April the death occurred of Robert

dates receive confirmation in P.R.O., E. 364/18, m. 66; cf. Mirot and Déprez,
in *B.E.C.*, lx, p. 207 (nos. 478-81). The envoys returned to London on 30 Apr.

1385 episcopus,[1] cui per eleccionem ac confirmacionem papalem successit magister Walterus Skyrlow clericus privati sigilli domini regis.

Captus est Barnabos. Item vj°. die Maii captus est Barnabos dominus Mediolani extra portam Vercell' prope muros civitatis predicte juxta hospitale Sancti Ambrosii cum duobus filiis suis per nepotem suum comitem Virtutum[2] filium fratris sui Galeas et missus est in quoddam castrum fortissimum[3] quod ipsemet construxit pro perpetuo*ᵃ* ibidem incarcerandis, scilicet ut si contingat quempiam illic carcerali custodia detineri sciret se ibidem sine spe exeundi vitam finire. Cecidit ipse *ᵇ*in laqueum*ᵇ* quem aliis inmitis paraverat.[4] Nichilominus tamen captus fuit dolose, quia dictus comes Virtutum simulavit se velle quendam locum in Alpibus[5] visitare ubi ymago beate Virginis in veneracione maxima colebatur, set propter predones in patria dixit se non audere *ᶜ*illuc transire,*ᶜ* unde peciit a domino Barnabos ut in manu forti per civitatem Mediolani*ᵈ* versus locum predictum posset*ᵉ* transire. Annuit Barnabos, nichil mali de suis callidis insidiis in suo corde revolvens, ordinavitque in civitate erga adventum suum hastiludia torneamenta, tripudia et alia spectacula curiosa que inspiciencium animos cum ingenti leticia jocundarent. Denique die statuto dominus Barnabos cum xl. equitibus ad duo vel tria miliaria exivit ei obviam et cum maximo gaudio eum recepit. Comes predictus jussit suos viros armatos precedere, qui celeri cursu equorum ad muros civitatis velociter pervenerunt, custodientes portas civitatis ea parte ut nullus intraret aut exiret. Appropinquantibus illis civitati predicte comes Virtutum arestavit dominum Barnabos primo, et tunc irruerunt predicti armati in homines domini Barnabos: quosdam vulneratos ceperunt, quosdam in terram non sine lesione ab equis prostrarunt. Unde dominus Barnabos

---

ᵃ perpetuo *Winterbottom;* perpetuis *MS. Cf. pp. 108, 160 etc.* *ᵇ⁻ᵇ Interlined.* *ᶜ⁻ᶜ Added in the margin after* audere, *which ends a line.* *ᵈ MS. Mediolane.* *ᵉ MS.* possit.

[1] Correctly (or more usually), Robert Stretton, bishop of Coventry and Lichfield from 1360; he died on 28 Mar. 1385. For the customary title of 'Chester', see *Handbook of British Chronology*, 2nd edn. (ed. F. M. Powicke and E. B. Fryde, London, 1961), p. 232 n. Walter Skirlaw was provided to the see on 28 June 1385. See also below, p. 156.

[2] Giangaleazzo Visconti. For the rivalry between Bernabò, lord of Milan, and

Stanton, bishop of Chester,[1] whose successor, by election and papal confirmation, was Master Walter Skirlaw, keeper of the king's privy seal.

Capture of Bernabò. On 6 May Bernabò, ruler of Milan, together with his two sons, was captured under the city wall, just outside the Vercelli gate near the hospital of St. Ambrose, by his nephew, the count of Vertus,[2] son of his brother Galeazzo. He was committed to an immensely strong castle[3] that he had himself built to accommodate prisoners for life, with the intention that anyone whose fate it was to be confined in it might be sure that he would end his days there without hope of emerging again. Bernabò thus fell himself into a snare that he had callously made ready for others.[4] None the less it was by a trick that he was captured: the count of Vertus pretended that he wanted to visit a place in the Alps[5] where there was a likeness of the Blessed Virgin, held in the utmost veneration; but because of the brigands in the countryside he said he dared not make the journey and therefore asked Bernabò for leave to pass through Milan with an armed escort on his way to his destination. Bernabò, with never a suspicion in his head about his nephew's cunning trap, consented and against his arrival arranged for jousts, tournaments, dances, and other elaborate shows calculated to amuse and gladden the heart of the onlooker. On the appointed day, with forty mounted companions, he went two or three miles out of Milan to meet the count, to whom he gave a rapturous welcome. The count now ordered his armed escort to ride on ahead; and the pace of their horses quickly brought them to the city walls, where they mounted guard over all the city gates on that side, so that nobody might enter or leave. As they neared the city, first of all the count of Vertus arrested Bernabò and then his escort set upon Bernabò's men, some of whom they wounded and took prisoner, while others were thrown from their horses to the ground, suffering some injuries in consequence. Dazed by all

Giangaleazzo, lord of Piedmont, respectively nephew and great-nephew of Giovanni Visconti, archbishop of Milan and founder of Visconti greatness, and for the particular events leading to this episode, see D. M. Bueno de Mesquita, *Giangaleazzo Visconti, duke of Milan (1351–1402)* (Cambridge, 1941), pp. 22-32.

[3] Trezzo.   [4] Cf. Ps. lvi. 7 (lvii. 6).   [5] Varese.

1385 super hoc stupefactus quesivit a nepote suo quidnam facere
vellet cum illo. Cui comes respondit: 'Hac de causa huc veni
ut te caperem, quia diucius hic non regnabis; nam quasi
tirannus hucusque regnasti et terram istam injuste, immo^a
tirannice, invasisti.' Et sic isto modo captus fuit dominus
Barnabos predictus bonaque sua omnia que poterant inveniri
fuerant confiscata. Quidam tamen volunt dominum Barnabos
sui nepotis mortem multis viis et modis longe ante excogi-
tasse, ut ipse solus in Lombardia regnaret, set de hoc erat
comes caute premunitus ⟨et⟩^{b} casum sibi machinatum prevenit.

In ista vero estate erant calores nimii, nam a principio
Maii usque ad festum Nativitatis beate Marie fere durabant;
aqua tamen non erat ita cara sicut proximo fuit anno.

Circa principium Junii rex apud Radyngum consilium
celebrare decrevit, misitque pro suis dominis tam ecclesiasticis quam laicis.[1] Dux vero Lancastr' excusavit se propter
adventum domini Johannis de Vienna, qui eo tempore
applicuit in terra Scocie cum multitudine ^{c}ij. milium^c
armatorum paratus una cum Scotis fines Anglie invadere ac
borealem plagam penitus relinquere desolatam, presertim
nisi succursus remedium sibi cicius apponatur.[2] Erat tunc
temporis dux Lanc' cum suo retenemento apud Pomfreyt.
Rex igitur super hiis sumpto consilio jussit suis ut prepararent
se erga principium mensis Julii ad eundum cum illo in
Scociam ad fugandum suos hostes inibi congregatos;[3] unde
die prefixo cum exercitu copioso ac sufficienti cariagio
versus Eboracum iter arripuit. Habuit namque currus tam de
episcopis quam de abbatibus et de prioribus opulentis, et
de quibusdam eciam sumpsit viros pugnaces. Continuatisque
diebus itiner⟨ando⟩ festinus venit Eboracum et in manerio
archiepiscopi Eboracensis vocato Bisshopisthorp' aliquamdiu
quievit, expectando illos qui nondum venerant ad transeun-
dum cum illo.

^{a} Interlined. ^{b} MS. om. $^{c-c}$ Interlined.

---

[1] The council was summoned for 12 May (P.R.O., E. 403/508, 9 May).

[2] Cf. *Fordun*, i. 383, where Vienne's arrival in Scotland is placed at the end
of May 1385. For this expedition, see also Terrier de Loray, *Jean de Vienne,
Amiral de France, 1341–1396* (Paris, 1877), pp. 179–205, and Campbell, in
Europe in the Late Middle Ages, ed. Hale, Highfield, and Smalley, pp. 209–10.

[3] Writs summoning a general feudal levy to muster at Newcastle-on-Tyne on
14 July were issued on 4 and 13 June, but the army of c.14,000 which Richard II

this, Bernabò asked his nephew what he meant to do with 1385
him. 'My purpose in coming here', replied the count, 'was to
put you under arrest. You will reign here no longer. Your
rule hitherto has been that of a tyrant; and you have made
this country the victim of injustice and sheer despotism.' In
this way, then, Bernabò was captured and all his discoverable
property confiscated. Some people, however, maintain that
long before this Bernabò had plotted various ways and means
of bringing about his nephew's death in order that he might
reign alone in Lombardy, but that the count was wary
enough to get warning of this and forestalled the fate planned
for him.

There was excessive heat during this summer, lasting
almost from the beginning of May until the Nativity of the
Virgin [8 September], but there was not such a dearth of
water as in the preceding year.

About the beginning of June the king decided to hold a
council at Reading and sent summonses to his lords, ecclesiastics and laymen alike.[1] The duke of Lancaster, however,
excused himself in view of the advent of Sire Jean de Vienne,
who had just landed in Scotland with an army 2,000 strong,
ready to join the Scots in an attack on English territory and
to leave our northern districts utterly devastated — the more
so if measures for their succour were not promptly applied.[2]
At this time the duke of Lancaster and his retinue were at
Pontefract. The king therefore took counsel upon the situation and gave orders that his men were to be ready by the
beginning of July to accompany him into Scotland to put to
flight the enemy forces assembled there.[3] On the appointed
day he set out for York with a large army and ample transport, wagons having been supplied to him by bishops and
abbots and the wealthier priors, from some of whom he
received fighting men too. By a series of daily marches he
rapidly reached York, and rested for a while at the archbishop's manor of Bishopthorpe, waiting for those who
had not yet arrived to join him in the expedition.

led into Scotland in the first week of Aug. was recruited on a contractual basis.
See N. B. Lewis, 'The last medieval summons of the English feudal levy, 13 June
1385', in *E.H.R.*, lxxiii (1958), 1-26, and esp. pp. 15-16, where the Monk's
chronology for the king's progress into Scotland is confirmed. For the Monk's
source see below, p. 126 n.

1385 Interim xvj°. die Julii apud Eboracum orta discordia inter duos armigeros domini Johannis Holand' fratris regis ex parte matris et duos valettos comitis Stafford', qui armigeros predictos occiderunt et ad ecclesiam confugerunt; populus vero nitebatur eos extrahere, quod vero fecisset nisi rex velocius occurrisset, qui eos fecit inmunitate percepta gaudere.

Filius comitis Stafford' ⟨*occi*⟩*ditur.* Dominus Johannes Holand' dolens super morte suorum interfectorum conquerendo venit ad regem, quem rex sagaciter et leniter alloquens promisit ei istud factum ad talem finem perducere quod sibi cederet ad comodum et honorem, prohibens expresse ne se super hoc ullatenus vindicaret. Qui a rege optenta licencia versus Eboracum dirigit viam suam; et itinerando accidit filio et heredi comitis Stafford'[1] obviare, quem post verba injuriosa ex utraque parte prolata protinus interfecit in ulcionem suorum interfectorum. Publicata vero morte filii comitis predicti rex diucius vacavit in lacrimis et lamentis, quia illum quasi coevum et sodalem sue juventutis in flore magis corditer diligebat: comes itaque quadam paternali affeccione quasi amens effectus eciam inconsolabiliter ipsum planxit. Postquam innotuit regi de ejus mesticia nisus est eum verbis consolatoriis confortare, protestans cum juramento non obstante fraternali proximitate aut aliqua prece sibi porrecta quin communem legem J. Holand' haberet ut publicus homicida: quare ille hoc audiens retraxit se et in comitatum Lancastr' se recepit.[2] Corpus quoque filii comitis apud Langeleye in Chylterne rege jubente fuit sepultum.[a]

Item in ista estate, ut quidam volunt, capta est insula de Rhodes a Saracenis sive a paganis.[3] Item xv. die Julii apud London' et eciam apud Dovorriam post solis occasum apparuit species ignea ad modum capitonis ab australi parte celi tendens in plagam borealem, que volando in tres partes se divisit, et transierunt in aere quasi auce silvestres

---

[a] Cave *in the margin.*

[1] Ralph de Stafford, 1st son of Hugh, 2nd earl of Stafford (d. 1386).
[2] Cf. Walsingham (*Hist. Ang.*, ii. 130), who says that Holland went into sanctuary at Beverley; so too Froissart, *Chroniques*, x. 386. The extant writ taking his lands into custody is dated 14 Sept. 1385.

During this wait a quarrel broke out at York on 16 July 1385 between two squires in the service of Sir John Holland, the king's uterine brother, and two of the earl of Stafford's grooms, who killed the squires and fled to sanctuary. The populace attempted to drag them out and would, indeed, have succeeded if the king had not swiftly intervened and seen to it that the grooms enjoyed the immunity they had won.

Son of the earl of Stafford killed. Distressed over the deaths of his men who had been killed, Sir John Holland went with a complaint to the king, who, in a wise and soothing reply, promised to bring the affair to such a conclusion that it would conduce to his interests and his honour alike, but expressly forbade him to take his own revenge at all. He then took his leave of the king and bent his steps towards York. On the way he happened to meet the son and heir of the earl of Stafford[1] and after an exchange of insulting language avenged his murdered squires by killing him outright. When the death of the earl's son was made known the king abandoned himself for some time to tears and mourning, since he had loved the lad all the more tenderly for having been a contemporary and comrade in the heyday of his own youth: and the earl too, almost distracted by his emotions as a father, grieved inconsolably for him. On becoming aware of his sorrow the king spoke consolingly to him in an effort to give comfort, and declared upon his oath that neither his kinship with his brother nor any entreaty that might be addressed to him should prevent John Holland from being subjected to the common law as a vulgar homicide. This caused the latter, when he heard of it, to retire and install himself in Lancashire.[2] On the king's orders the body of the earl's son was buried at Langley in the Chilterns.

It was in this summer, as some people maintain, that the island of Rhodes was captured by the Saracens and pagans.[3] After sunset on 15 July there appeared at London, and also at Dover, a fiery shape resembling a bull-head, travelling from the southern sky towards the northern quarter. As it flew it split into three parts, which passed through the air like wild

[3] Rhodes did not fall until 1523. Around 1385 the main thrust of the Turks, to whom the Monk refers, was in Serbia. See *Cambridge Medieval History*, IV (i) (1966), p. 764.

1385 in volatu, demum in unum, ut prius, insimul coierunt, et subito immediate disparuit.

Capcio de Damme. Item xvj. die Julii[1] Gandavenses ceperunt villam de Damme: statimque illi de Sclusa et Bruges venerunt et graves insultus eis dederunt; nichilominus illi viriliter ipsam defenderunt et invitis eorum hostibus tenuerunt. Item xvij. die Julii fuit terremotus nocte inter horam x^{mam}. et xj^{mam}.

Item xx. die Julii rex cum suo exercitu removit se de Eboraco et venit Dunolm', ubi ad instanciam domini regis concordatus est dux Lancastr' cum comitibus de Notyngham, Oxenford' et Saresbury,[2] ut unanimes et concordes ad hostes nostros accederent et eos viriliter debellarent sopitis injuriarum accionibus pro tempore universis. Ad hec rex totam gentem suam in tres acies rite divisit:[3] primam aciem,[a] que precederet, commisit duci Lancastr' senescallo Anglie, comiti de Bukyngham constabulario Anglie et comiti de Notyngham marescallo Anglie, quibus adjunxit episcopum Northwycensem cum cruciata et vexillo Sancti Cuthberti,[4] cum aliis eciam nobilibus strenuis et robustis; secundam vero aciem,[b] que et media custodia vocatur, duxit idem rex, et secum habuit comites de Cantebrig', Oxenford', Stafford', Arundell', Warwyk' et Saresbur' ac alios nobiles dominos et potentes; terciam quoque aciem[c] et ultimam posuit sub ductu et regimine comitis de Northumberlond', domini de Nevile, domini de Clifford', baronis de Graystoke et domini Ricardi de Scrop', qui habuerunt cum illis viros validos et fortes in armorum strenuitate multipliciter commendatos. / Estimacio namque hominum armatorum erat quinque milia, sagittariis, valettis ac aliis personis mediocribus minime computatis. Et circa finem mensis Julii venit rex Berewycum.

Interea rex Francorum in multa ordinacione disposuit transire in Angliam et illam suo dominatui subjugare; set audita capcione ville de Damme statuit illam primitus

p. 150

---

[a] j. *in the margin.*   [b] ij. *in the margin.*   [c] iij. *in the margin.*

[1] Some other sources give 14 or 17 July.   [2] Cf. above, p. 114.

[3] A document which seems to be an official description of Richard II's battle-order on the Scottish expedition of 1385 confirms the substantial accuracy of the following account but not the statement that Ralph, Baron Greystoke and Sir Richard Scrope were present in the rearguard (Armitage-Smith, *John*

geese on the wing and finally merged into the original single 1385
whole before suddenly disappearing without warning.

Capture of Damme. On 16 July[1] the Gantois captured
the town of Damme. The townspeople of Sluys and Bruges
very soon arrived and delivered heavy assaults on them, but
they defended the town manfully and held it in their
enemies' despite. On the night of 17 July there was an
earthquake between the hours of ten and eleven.

The king and his army moved on from York on 20 July
and proceeded to Durham, where, at the king's prompting,
the duke of Lancaster was reconciled with the earls of
Nottingham, Oxford, and Salisbury,[2] so that it might be
as one in heart and mind and with a temporary lull in all
hurtful activities that they advanced upon our enemies and
resolutely fought them into submission. The king now
systematically divided his army into three divisions:[3] the
first, which was to form the van, he entrusted to the duke
of Lancaster, the earl of Buckingham, and the earl of
Nottingham, who were respectively steward, constable, and
marshal of England, and to them he added the bishop of
Norwich, with his crozier and the banner of St. Cuthbert,[4]
together with other active and vigorous noblemen; the
second division (called also the middleward) was led by
the king himself, who had with him the earls of Cambridge,
Oxford, Stafford, Arundel, Warwick, and Salisbury, and
other noble and powerful lords; and the third, or rearmost,
division he put under the command and control of the earl
of Northumberland, Lords Nevill and Clifford, Baron
Greystoke, and Sir Richard Scrope, who had with them
stalwart men of mettle abundantly recommended by their
soldierly prowess. The number of men under arms was
estimated at 5,000, not counting bowmen, grooms, and
other humble persons. The king reached Berwick at about
the end of July.

In the meantime the king of France had made plans to
marshal a large force and to cross to England and bring it
under his sway; but on hearing of the capture of Damme

of Gaunt, pp. 437-8; Lewis, art. cit., pp. 3, 25).

[4] A detail identifying the bishop as actually Durham: he was in fact in the rear
(Lewis, art. cit., pp. 25-6; Armitage-Smith, op. cit., p. 438).

1385 oppugnare; quare de mense Augusti cum multitudine pugnatorum glomerose ad illam descendit atque obsedit, erectisque prope illam in multa ordinacione machinis bellicis duros et graves insultus in dies ville defensoribus impulit indefesse. Tandem consumptis armis defensivis quibus tam illos quam villam defendere debuerunt neque succursum aut auxilium, prout sperabant, ab Anglia habuerunt, iccirco cum aliquibus bonis circa finem mensis Augusti villam predictam latenter nocte deseruerunt et ad civitatem Gandavensem celeriter aufugerunt; Francigene vero depredati sunt omnia que in prefata villa Gandavenses propter defectum cariagii reliquerunt.[1] Demum illam cum ceteris villulis adjacentibus incendio destruxerunt et ante civitatem Gandavensem aliquamdiu causa obsidii jacuerunt; set in removendo rex Francorum plures de suis amisit.

Sexto die Augusti rex Anglie intravit Scociam cum exercitu copioso ac vexillo expanso; fecitque milites, comites et duces: videlicet comitem de Cantebrig' promovit in ducem de Canterbury et comitem de Bukyngham in ducem Daumarle, dominum Michaelem de Pool erexit in comitem de Southfolk' et dominum de Nevyle ⟨in⟩[a] comitem de Combirlond.[2] Ea vero nocte hospitatus est rex cum suo exercitu apud forestam de Edryk'; et quoscumque potuit capere de Scotis et Francigenis fecit occidi. Ceperuntque illi de exercitu tam grossa animalia ibidem quam parva, ob quorum capcionem exercitus fuit inde aliqualiter recreatus. Et ab hinc quasi per unam septimanam transeuntes versus abbaciam

[a] MS. om.

---

[1] Charles VI and the French entered Damme on 27 Aug.; the men of Ghent had left the night before (*Croniques . . . de Tournay*, ed. Hocquet, pp. 273–8; Froissart, *Chroniques*, x. 366–9). For Charles VI's manœuvres before the projected invasion of England see L. Mirot, 'Une tentative d'invasion en Angleterre pendant la Guerre de Cent Ans (1385–1386)', in *Révue des Études Historiques*, n.s., xvii (1915), 422 ff. From Damme Charles moved to Ertevelde. He left Ertevelde in the 2nd week of Sept. in order to besiege Gavere before assaulting Ghent but did not carry out his intention.

[2] On 6 Aug. 1385, at Hoselaw in Teviotdale, the king did indeed create Sir Michael de la Pole earl of Suffolk; but Edmund of Langley, earl of Cambridge, was created duke of York. John Nevill of Raby, though present in Richard's army with a contingent, was not in fact created earl. Pole and Edmund of Langley were invested with their new honours on 9 Nov., in parliament, when Thomas of Woodstock, earl of Buckingham, was also invested with the dukedom of Gloucester, and these investitures are reported by the Monk (*R.P.*, iii. 205–6;

he determined first to attack that town. In August, therefore, 1385 he descended upon it with a serried host of fighting men and invested it, setting up a powerful array of siege-engines hard against it and delivering day after day a tireless series of heavy and severe attacks upon the defenders. The latter, having exhausted all the equipment for their own and the town's defence and not having received from England the relief or assistance they had hoped for, eventually quitted the place unobserved with a certain quantity of goods one night about the end of August and quickly made their escape to Ghent; while the French made plunder of everything in the town that for lack of transport the Gantois had abandoned.[1] The town itself, together with other townships in the neighbourhood, was ultimately fired and destroyed by the French, who lay for some time before the city of Ghent for the purpose of besieging it; but the French king lost numbers of his troops in marching away.

On 6 August, accompanied by a large army and with his banner unfurled, the king of England entered Scotland and created knights, earls, and dukes: advancing the earl of Cambridge to duke of Canterbury and the earl of Buckingham to duke of Aumale; while Sir Michael de la Pole was raised to earl of Suffolk and Lord Nevill to earl of Cumberland.[2] That night the king encamped with his army in the forest of Ettrick, causing to be put to death all the Scots and Frenchmen he was able to take prisoner. Here the soldiery captured some livestock of both the larger and the smaller kinds, and through its seizure the army was in some measure reinvigorated. From this point they marched on for about a

below, p. 140). However, Thomas of Woodstock was summoned to this parliament as duke of Aumale (*Lords' Reports on the Dignity of a Peer*, iii. 718), and the occurrence of this title at this point in the narrative suggests that Thomas used it for a brief period. It is possible that Edmund of Langley was indeed created duke of Canterbury and that his title, too, was later changed, or 'duke of Canterbury' may be an egregious blunder. Both this account of the creations at Hoselaw and that of the investitures 3 months later were written several years after the event, when Edmund of Langley and Thomas of Woodstock had long been using the titles mentioned in the latter. The fact that the Monk allowed the discrepancies between the two passages to pass unremarked and uncorrected suggests that he had a written source for the Scottish campaign, perhaps a news-letter, and slavishly copied what he found in it. Cf. on the reference to Nevill, J. J. N. Palmer, 'The parliament of 1385 and the constitutional crisis of 1386', in *Speculum*, xlvi (1971), 489-90.

1385 de Mailros ad duas leucas in latitudine cedi predis et incendiis continuis indulserunt, totam patriam post se relinquentes
destructam: abbaciam Mailrocen' quia fuit quoddam re-
ceptaculum hostium nostrorum voraci incendio consumpserunt;[1] et ab hinc usque ad Scoticum mare[2] totam terram
Laudiam vastaverunt; hostes vero tam Francos quam Scotos[a]
coram eis eciam fugaverunt; omnia loca et castella eorum
exceptis regalibus in quibus hostes fuerant recreati eciam
combusserunt; abbaciam de Neubotel in pulverem redig-
erunt;[b] nam ista mala eis ingesserunt quia erant scismatici
tenentes cum antipapa Gebenensi. Et semper hostes fugerunt
coram eis, Scoti versus occidentalem plagam et Francigene
versus orientalem, et sic in duas partes divisi nullus eorundem
audebat alterum appropinquare.[3] Postea xj°. die Augusti
venit rex ad urbem Scocie capitalem vocatam Edenburgh',
quam cum quadam abbacia eidem annexa[4] jussit igne con-
sumi.

Item viij°. die Augusti apud Walyngford' obiit Johanna
comitissa Cancie et principissa Wallie mater domini regis et
apud Staunford' in ecclesia Fratrum Minorum satis honeste
est sepulta.[5] Item circa festum Sancti Laurencii venerunt
sex galee London' bene apparate misse domino regi pro
tempore autumpnali per regem Portyngalie, que victualibus
et aliis necessariis per Londonienses referte sive refocillate
in mare remigando cursu celeri pervenerunt, ubi quicquid
adquisierunt secum ad Portyngaliam deduxerunt.[6]

Existente rege cum suo exercitu super ripam Scotici
maris consuluit eum dux Lancastr' ultra illud mare cum suo
exercitu se transferre ac fines tocius Scocie pervagare.[7]
Cui rex ait: 'Nosti quomodo jam exercitus noster hic fere[c]
inedia et fame tabescit, et indubie omnia victualia ea parte

---

[a] *Interlined.*   [b] *Sic MS.; cf. above, p. 38.*   [c] *A letter has been deleted
after this word.*

[1] Cf. *Fordun*, i. 383.   [2] See above, p. 66.
[3] In fact the Scots and the French went south-westwards, into the West March,
as the English advanced north (Froissart, *Chroniques*, x. 376 ff.; cf. Walsingham,
Hist. Ang., ii. 132–3; Knighton, *Chronicon*, ii. 205).
[4] Holyrood Abbey.
[5] Not, however, until the end of Jan. 1386 (*D.N.B.*, x. 830; and for Joan of
Kent see also above, p. 101 n.).
[6] In or about Oct. 1384 João I of Portugal promised to put a squadron of

week towards Melrose Abbey, giving free and uninterrupted 1385
play to slaughter, rapine, and fire-raising all along a six-mile
front and leaving the entire countryside in ruins behind
them: and Melrose Abbey itself, since it provided harbour for
our enemies, was swallowed up in devouring flame.[1] From
there as far as the Scottish sea[2] they laid waste the whole
territory of Lothian, driving their adversaries, French and
Scots alike, before them, burning down every place and every
castle (royal property excepted) in which the enemy had re-
freshed themselves, and reducing Newbattle Abbey to dust.
These evils they inflicted upon the enemy because they were
schismatics and supported the Genevan antipope. And always
their foes fled before them, the Scots to westward and the
French to eastward; thus they were split into two groups
of which neither dared approach the other.[3] Later, on 11
August, the king reached Edinburgh, the capital city of Scotland, which he ordered to be destroyed by fire together with
an abbey adjacent to it.[4]

Joan countess of Kent and princess of Wales, the king's
mother, died at Wallingford on 8 August and was buried in
some state at the Greyfriars', Stamford.[5] About St.
Lawrence's Day [10 August] six well-found galleys reached
London, having been sent on an autumn visit to the king by
the king of Portugal. When they had been replenished and set
up again by the Londoners in food and other necessaries,
they used their oars to make a rapid passage to the open sea
and so bore off their acquisitions with them to Portugal.[6]

The king, who, with his army, was now on the shores
of the Scottish sea, was advised by the duke of Lancaster to
cross the water with his forces and overrun the whole of
Scottish territory.[7] 'You know', the king replied, 'how even
on this side the army is already wasting away from hunger
and starvation, and there can be no doubt that all the food

galleys at the disposal of the English government, in return for permission to
recruit an English force for service in Portugal (*The Diplomatic Correspondence
of Richard II*, ed. E. Perroy (Camden, 3rd ser., xlviii), no. 44 A). The Monk's
account conveys something of the ill-will created in London for the Portuguese
by the financial operations of the envoys who carried out the recruitment
(Russell, *English Intervention*, pp. 365 ff.).

[7] So too Walsingham, *Hist. Ang.*, ii. 131–2; cf. Froissart, *Chroniques*, x. 395 ff.
For the political context see Aston, in *B.I.H.R.*, xxxviii (1965), 141.

1385 inimici nostri preripuerunt et ea in locis firmis et securis intulerunt. Quod si nos jam juxta tua vota istud mare cum exercitu nostro debuerimus pertransire, sequeretur quod omnes hii pro majori parte, qui mei causa huc venerunt, ad sua cum salute vix aut numquam redirent. Licet tu et alii domini hic existentes pro se ipsis copiam victualium possent habere ceteri tamen mediocres et inferiores nostri exercitus nequaquam tantam ciborum opulenciam inibi reperirent quin fame perirent.' Consilium igitur ducis Lancastr' rex improbat et impugnat, dicens illud consilium nullatenus ex fidelitatis zelo procedere set pocius destestabilis prodicionis errore: multa quoque et alia obprobriosa verba protulit contra ducem Lancastr'. Set demum sermonibus injuriosis sedatis xx^{mo}. die Augusti rex decrevit ulterius non procedere set in Angliam quantocius repedare,[1] ex quo manifeste constabat hostes suos nolle expectare; qui jugiter tam Franci quam Scoti a facie ejus fugerunt. Igitur rex post reconciliacionem sibi ducis Lancastr' rediit de Scocia et apud Novum Castrum venit cum suis, ubi unicuique divertere^a ad propria tribuit liberam facultatem.

Item xiij.^{b} die Augusti obiit magister Willelmus Rud doctor sacre theologie episcopus Cicestren' qui in astro⟨no⟩mia sensus suos multum vexabat quia in illa facultate fuit peritus.[2] Quo sepulto canonici ejusdem ecclesie elegerunt in eorum episcopum magistrum Ricardum Scrop' decanum dicte ecclesie: rex vero misit ad illos ut postularent episcopum Landavensem confessorem suum[3] in eorum episcopum; qui eciam pro eodem scripsit pape, et sic optinuit votum suum. Item xx. die Augusti papa transtulit se de Nuceria et industria seu auxilio Januensium circa finem Septembris venit Januam eorum urbem.^{c4}

Tercio die Septembris venit rex London', et eodem die circa horam vesperorum antequam ingressus fuerit locum

---

^{a} Interlined. ^{b} Deleted. ^{c} De papa hic parum in the margin in a fifteenth-century hand.

[1] By 20 Aug. the king, if not the main body of his army, was again in England (Lewis, in E.H.R., lxxiii (1958), 16).

[2] For Reade see B.R.U.O., iii. 1556–60, s.n. Rede. He died on 18 Aug.

over there has been seized in advance by our enemies and 1385
conveyed to places of strength and safety. If we were now to
do what you want and cross this sea with our forces, the
result would be that all, or the greater part, of these people
who have come thus far on my account would have difficulty,
or never succeed at all, in getting back safely to their homes.
Though you and the other lords here might have plenty of
food for yourselves, the rest, the humbler and lowlier members of our army, would certainly not find over there such a
wealth of victuals as would prevent their dying of hunger.'
The duke's plan was accordingly censured and assailed by the
king, who declared that it emanated not from the ardour of
loyalty but from the warped notions of rank treason, and
came out with a great deal of further abusive language against
the duke of Lancaster. Finally, however, recriminations were
stilled, and on 20 August the king determined to advance
no further but to make a speedy return to England,[1] since it
had been clearly established that his enemies declined to stay
for him but, French and Scots alike, consistently fled from
his path. And so, after a reconciliation with the duke of
Lancaster, the king returned from Scotland, and upon reaching Newcastle with his forces gave all of them free leave to
disperse to their homes.

The death occurred on [13] August of Master William
Reade, D.D., bishop of Chichester, who severely taxed his
faculties in the study of astronomy, a subject in which he was
expert.[2] After his burial the canons of Chichester elected
their dean, Master Richard Scrope, as bishop: but the king
sent to them suggesting that they should ask for his confessor,
the bishop of Llandaff,[3] on whose behalf he also wrote to the
pope and thus got his wish. On 20 August the pope transferred his quarters from Nocera and aided by the efforts of
the Genoese reached their city of Genoa about the end of
September.[4]

The king got to London on 3 September and on the same
day, before going into his lodging, went about the time of

[3] Thomas Rushock, O.P. He was provided to the see of Chichester on 16 Oct.
1385; see also below, p. 144.
[4] Urban VI left Nocera on 7 July and reached Genoa on 23 Sept. (*Valois*,
ii. 115–16). See also below, p. 140.

1385 mansionis accessit ad monasterium visitare Sanctum Edwardum et alias reliquias ibi per predecessores suos repositas.

⟨V⟩illa de Damme amittitur. Item vij°. die Septembris venerunt nova de amissione ville de Damme.[1]

Bellum Portuall'. Quo in tempore venerunt certa nuncia de quodam bello commisso in Portyngalia inter reges Hispannie et Portyngalie.[2] Cessit victoria regi Portyngalie, divina gracia opitulante, qui secum habuit in exercitu suo Anglicos viros bellicosos cum sagittariis quasi septingentos. Cecidit quoque in illo bello flos nobilium tocius Hispannie, in primis comes de Mayorka,[3] comes de Carion,[4] Consalmus Valasci,[5] Johannes Gondissalvi,[6] Didacus Comecii,[7] prior Sancti Johannis de Castila,[8] magister de Calkatrava,[9] dominus Johannes Ducis,[10] Didacus Alvarus[11] et frater ejus, dominus Johannes Remiles,[12] filius marcasir de Villena comitis[a] de Deene,[13] Lupus de Rodeneye,[14] Lupus Comecii de Lile proditor.[15] Commissum fuit istud bellum in vigilia Assumpcionis beate Marie; in quo bello erant de Hisperis interfecti amplius quam septem milia quingenti. Et sic rex Portyngalie per hoc recuperavit amissa que per regem Hispannie fuerant ab eo violenter ablata.[16]

Item vij°. die Septembris Scoti cum Francigenis urbem de Caerlill' invaserunt, appositisque scalis et machinis ad muros ejusdem illam in multa ordinacione aut omnino destruere aut per insultus capere satagebant. Set Deus ob

_____
[a] MS. comes.

[1] i.e. news of the capture of Damme by the French on 27 Aug., for which see above, p. 126.

[2] The battle of Aljubarrota, in which the Portuguese under João I (John of Aviz) defeated Juan I (John of Trastamara) and the Castilians, on 14 Aug. 1385 (Russell, English Intervention, pp. 384 ff.). The substantial accuracy of the Monk's list of casualties is confirmed by that in Fernão Lopes, Crónica del Rei Dom Joham I, part ii, ed. W. J. Entwistle (Lisbon, 1968), pp. 108-9. The fact that Lopo Gomez de Lira, a Portuguese in the service of Juan I of Castile, is described as a traitor suggests that the Monk's source was Portuguese and not Castilian. For this point and for generous help in identifying names in the list I am greatly indebted to Dr. J. R. L. Highfield.   [3] Juan Alonso Tello de Meneses.

[4] Juan Sánchez Manuel, adelantado of Murcia. (Lopes omits this name.)

[5] Apparently a conflation of 3 names listed separately by Lopes: Pedro de Valassco, Joham de Valasco, and Gonçalo Vaasquez d'Azeuedo, the last of whom was one of the Portuguese in Castilian service at this time.

[6] A Portuguese in Castilian service: appointed alcalde of the Portuguese town

Vespers to the monastery to visit St. Edward and the other relics deposited there by his predecessors.

Town of Damme lost. On 7 September came news of the loss of the town of Damme.[1]

Battle in Portugal. Reliable reports arrived at this time of a battle fought in Portugal between the kings of Spain and Portugal.[2] By the help of God's grace victory went to the Portuguese king, who had with him in his army English troops numbering, with bowmen, about 700. The fallen in this battle included the flower of the whole nobility of Spain, prominent among them being the count of Mayorga,[3] the count of Carrion,[4] 'Gonçalo Valasco',[5] Joham Gonçalves,[6] Diego Gomes,[7] the prior of St. John of Castile,[8] the master of Calatrava,[9] Juan Duque,[10] Diego Alvarez[11] and his brother, Juan Ramirez,[12] the son of the marquis of Villena and count of Denia,[13] Lopo 'de Rodeneye',[14] and Lopo Gomez de Lira, the traitor.[15] The battle was fought on the Eve of the Assumption of the Virgin [14 August]; and in it the killed on the Spanish side amounted to more than 7,500. Such was the manner and the means whereby the king of Portugal recovered what he had lost through forcible seizure by the king of Spain.[16]

On 7 September the Scots, in company with the French, attacked the city of Carlisle, bringing up ladders and siege-engines to its walls and mustering powerful forces in a busy attempt either to destroy it altogether or take it by storm.

of Obidos by Juan I of Castile.

[7] Probably Diego Gomez Manrique, *adelantado mayor* of Castile; but Diego Gomez Sarmento (*adelantado* of Galicia) also appears in Lopes's list.

[8] Pedro Diaz, prior of the Order of St. John of Jerusalem in Castile (a Galician).

[9] Pedro Alvarez Pereira, a Portuguese in Castilian service.

[10] Juan Duque, a Castilian *calsallero* appointed *alcalde* of Torres Vedras by Juan I of Castile (Fernão Lopes, *Crónica de D. João I*, ed. A. Sérgio, i (1945), p. 328).

[11] Diego Alvarez Pereira, the brother of Pedro Alvarez Pereira, already mentioned among the slain; but the Monk was evidently confused on this point.

[12] Juan Ramirez de Arellano.   [13] Pedro de Aragon.

[14] Another name omitted by Lopes.

[15] A Portuguese *desnaturado* appointed *alcalde* of Ponte do Lima by Juan I of Castile; formerly a servant of Fernando I of Portugal (Fernão Lopes, *Crónica de D. João I*, ed. Sérgio, i. 329; *Crónica*, pt. ii, ed. Entwistle, p. 29). Lopes does not list him among the slain.

[16] A reference to the Castilian invasion of and partial conquest of Portugal after the death of Fernando I in 1383; see Russell, op. cit., pp. 357 ff.

1385 reverenciam sue matris, cujus festum tunc imminebat,[1]
id fieri non permisit; nam omnia eorum machinamenta erant
inepta, unde illis deservire protunc minime potuerunt. Ideo
tanquam homines devicti et confusi ab illa recedentes ipsam
indempnem reliquerunt. Quod comperiens dominus Henricus
Percy[2] filius et heres comitis Northumberlond' insecutus est
eos et nocte irruit in eos, pluresque ex eis interfecit, plures
fugavit et quosdam captivavit (cepit quoque ex eis xxvj.
p. 151 valentes personas) reversusque est postea / ad sua cum
gloria triumphali.

Item xiij°. die Septembris in portu Cales' per tempestatem
marinam due galee et novem naves alie de Francia sunt con-
fracte multis bonis et diviciis hominibusque armorum onuste.[3]
Fuerantque Francigene venientes de Sclusa cum diversis mercimoniis ibidem emptis, qui relictis inibi universis per terram
versus Gravenyng fugerunt. Hoc audiens dominus de Beauchamp capitaneus Cales' fecit gentem suam equos ascendere et
persecutus est eos, cepitque ex eis quingentos et plures, videlicet armirallum eorundem de Normannia et de Seyne cum aliis
mercatoribus diviciis plenis. Item xvj. die mensis predicti
classis Francie venit de Sclusa circa octoginta naves sulcantes
maria versus Normanniam et villam de Rochell'. Postquam
innotuit adventus earum domino Willelmo de Beauchamp',
confestim paratis navibus et balengers quas habuit cum suis
viris bellicosis irruit in classem predictam et cepit ex eis
fortissimam navem vocatam barge, que eciam fuit pulcrior
quam rex Francorum habuit in mundo, cum aliis navibus
xxj., que fuerunt cum bonis et spoliis Flandrensium plene
onuste. Item xviij. die mensis predicti in medio mari coram
Cales' demonstrarunt se due naves vocate cogges Hispannie
optime ad bellum parate: una vero erat regis Francorum
et altera domini de Clisson',[4] neque in Anglia neque in
Francia fuerant due tales. Quamobrem capitaneus predictus
disposuit se pugnare cum illis; et acceptis navibus quas

[1] The feast of the Nativity of the B.V.M. (8 Sept.).

[2] Warden of the East March and of Berwick (Storey, in E.H.R., lxxii (1957), 598, 611).

[3] For events in, around, and off Calais in Sept. and Oct. 1385 see Mirot, in Révue des Études Historiques, n.s., xvii (1915), 427–8. The detail of the Monk's account, its exact chronology and the idiom of 'nostri viri' etc. point to the use of a written source; this probably originated in the circle of Sir William

But out of regard for his mother, whose feast was at hand,[1] 1385
God did not let anything of the kind come about: all their
contrivances were futile and on this occasion powerless to
avail them; and so it was like men beaten and discomfited
that they retired from Carlisle, leaving it unscathed. On
learning of their withdrawal Sir Henry Percy,[2] son and heir
of the earl of Northumberland, followed them up and fell
upon them by night, killing many of them and putting
numbers to flight besides taking prisoners (his captures
included 26 persons of substance) before returning home
covered with triumphal glory.

Two galleys and nine other French ships, carrying, besides
men at arms, large quantities of goods and valuables were
wrecked in Calais harbour on 13 September through a storm
at sea.[3] The French, who had been on their way from Sluys
with various commodities purchased there, abandoned them
all and made off overland towards Gravelines. On hearing of
this Sir [William] Beauchamp, the captain of Calais, got his
people mounted and gave chase, taking 500 or more prisoners,
including the admiral of Normandy and the Seine as well as
merchants brimful of riches. On the 16th of the same month
a French fleet of about 80 sail came ploughing its way through
the sea from Sluys, bound for Normandy and the town of
La Rochelle. When their approach became known to Sir
William Beauchamp he hastily got ready what ships and
balingers he had and led his fighting men in a swoop upon
the French fleet, capturing an extremely powerful craft
called a barge, the finest vessel the French king had in the
world, and also 21 other ships heavily laden with Flemish
goods and plunder. Next there showed themselves in mid-
Channel opposite Calais on 18 September two of the ships
known as Spanish cogs, splendidly equipped for combat:
one of them belonged to the French king and the other to
the Sire de Clisson;[4] and neither in England nor in France
were there two to match them. The captain of Calais accordingly made plans for an engagement; and taking the ships he

Beauchamp, the hero of the events described. The use of Middle English forms for
three of the types of ship mentioned — *balenger, barge,* and *cogge* — is a clue to
the language of the original.
    [4] Olivier de Clisson, constable of France 1380-92.

1385 cepit de eis cum aliis de suis[a] cum viris bellicosis bene munitis accessit ad illas. Et inito certamine illi existentes in predictis duabus navibus egregie et nobiliter defenderunt se de illis per spacium quinque horarum; fatebantur enim nostri viri pugnaces se numquam tam strenuos bellatores experimentaliter in navibus didicisse. Nichilominus tamen in fine se necessario reddiderunt.

Item circa illa tempora[1] quidam ex nostris de Caleys, de Gynes et de Hammes exierunt et equitarunt in partes Pycardie, ceperuntque[b] xxv. captivos et quatuor ⟨milia⟩[c] ovium ac grossorum animalium et ea absque contradiccione quacumque ad nostra presidia deduxerunt. Circa finem mensis Septembris Cales' captus fuit quidam frater Minor Anglicus decens persona set proditor regni manifestus, missus a domino Johanne de Vienna cum literis credencie ad regem Francorum; qui apud Turrim London' aliquamdiu incarceratus pro nullo tormento voluit rei veritatem fateri; unde paucis supervixit diebus.

Item xiij. die Octobris Londonienses, ut moris est eo die majorem eligere, iterato dominum Nicholaum Brembre in eorum majorem satis concorditer elegerunt, rege annuente.[2] Qui confestim de consilio seniorum civitatis predicte statuit ut nullus presumeret interesse eleccioni novi majoris nisi seniores et boni ac valentes de communitate civitatis prefate; item quod nullus inferat convicium seu obloquium palam vel occulte majori seniori aut alicui bono et valenti de communitate civitatis predicte sub pena privacionis sue vite et confiscacione omnium bonorum suorum;[3] item quod nullus audeat clam vel aperte dominos in parliamento proxime congregandos novis relacionibus super gubernacione dicte civitatis aliquatenus movere; quod si quis in hoc inventus sit culpabilis, talem penam subiret quod ceteris ad committenda similia terrorem incuteret.

Parliamentum. Item xx. die Octobris tenuit rex suum

---

[a] MS. inserts at; deleted by Winterbottom.   [b] Followed by quinque, deleted.
[c] MS. om.

[1] 9 Oct. (Walsingham, *Hist. Ang.*, ii. 136).
[2] For Brembre's re-election as mayor see *Letter Book H*, p. 276. However, the ordinances attributed by the Monk in his next sentence to this year of Brembre's mayoralty were in fact made by the mayor and common council between 31

had captured from the French together with others of his 1385 own, fully manned with combat troops, he bore down upon the enemy. When battle was joined, the crews of the two ships put up an extraordinarily fine defence against the attack for the space of five hours: indeed our fighting men admitted that in all their experience afloat they had never known such lusty warriors. None the less, however, they were compelled in the end to surrender.

At about this time[1] some of our countrymen carried out a mounted foray from Calais, Guînes, and Hammes into Picardy; they captured 25 prisoners and 4,000 sheep and cattle and brought them back to our fortresses without any opposition. An English Franciscan was arrested at Calais about the end of September, a man of respectable appearance but a manifest traitor to his country, who had been sent by Jean de Vienne with letters of credence to the French king. He was imprisoned for a time in the Tower of London, but under no torture would he confess the truth of the matter, so that he survived only a few days.

On 13 October (it being the custom to elect the mayor on that day) the Londoners, with a fair measure of harmony and with the king's approval, re-elected Sir Nicholas Brembre as mayor.[2] He very soon decreed, on the advice of the aldermen, first, that nobody should venture to participate in the election of a new mayor except aldermen and respectable and substantial members of the city commons; secondly, that nobody should utter any abuse or scurrility, in public or in private, against the mayor or an alderman or any respectable and substantial member of the commons of the city, on pain of losing his life and forfeiting all his goods;[3] and thirdly, that nobody should dare either secretly or openly, by means of fresh representations about the city's administration, to influence in any degree the nobles shortly assembling in parliament: anybody found guilty of this would suffer such punishment as would strike into others a terror of doing likewise.

Parliament. The king held a parliament at Westminster on

July and 21 Sept. 1384: they belong to the 1st year of this mayoralty, not to the 3rd (ibid., pp. 241 ff.).

[3] So the Monk summarizes the proclamation against covins and conspiracies of 15 Aug. 1384 (ibid., p. 247).

1385 parliamentum apud Westmonasterium; in quo multa per
communitatem pro salvacione regni fuerunt mota et hinc
inde proposita, quorum aliqua inferius describentur.[1] Quarto
die parliamenti episcopus Northwycen' habuit restitucionem
suorum temporalium, que quidem temporalia statim postquam venit de Flandria in quodam parliamento ad nutum
dominorum amisit, sicut est supra relatum.[2]

Quo in tempore Scoti latenter Angliam intraverunt et
villam de Exham cum tota provincia adjacenti rapinis et
incendiis solitis devastabant; et profecto ista dispendia nobis
jam per illos inflicta excedunt ea que dudum noster exercitus
illis in Scocia irrogabat. Quamvis enim nostri boreales olim
multa strenuitate vigebant, nunc vero mutato velo desides
et vecordes effecti eorum patriam vigiliis sive excubiis ab
inimicorum insidiis custodire contempnunt; unde causante
illorum negligencia et desidia accidit illis patriam perdere
ac bona eorum fortuna; et pro certo multo majora medio
tempore forsitan amisissent nisi magnanimitas et nobilitas
domini Henrici de Percy[3] fuisset, qui cum Scotis post
recessum domini regis cum exercitu suo de Scocia quinquies
dimicavit et de eis semper victoriam reportavit.

Item xxiij. die Octobris mediante episcopo London'
reconciliatus est[a] domino regi archiepiscopus Cantuar'.[4]
Rex autem, glorie cupidus appetensque ab omnibus prout
regi decuit venerari, permisit archiepiscopum veniam ab eo
petentem genuflectere coram ipso. Set si tam effectualis
constancia vigoreque racionis munita in dicto archiepiscopo
protunc efficaciter claruisset quanta perseveranter in beato
Thoma Martire dinoscitur floruisse, numquam, pro veritatis
prolacione, salva[b] semper tramite recte justicie capud eo
modo alicui inclinaret aut genu, cum pocius juxta canonicas
sancciones regum colla et principum genibus pontificum
inclinari debeant et submitti.[5]

---

[a] Interlined.   [b] Recte salvo (Winterbottom).

[1] pp. 144–50.   [2] p. 52; see also Cal. Pat. R., 1385–9, p. 34.
[2] For whom see above, p. 134 n.   [4] Cf. above, p. 116.
[5] A reference to the 39th decretal letter ascribed to Pope Clement in Pseudo-
Isidore, for which see R. W. and A. J. Carlyle, History of Mediaeval Political
Theory in the West, i (2nd edn., 1927), p. 275 n. (I am indebted to Mrs. Jean
Dunbabin for this reference.)

20 October, and in it many matters affecting the preser-
vation of the realm were introduced by the commons and
made the subject of suggestions from one quarter or
another: some of them will be set out below.[1] On the
fourth day of the parliament the bishop of Norwich had
the temporalities restored to him which he had lost, just
after his return from Flanders, by a decision of the lords in
an earlier parliament, as is recounted above.[2]

About this time the Scots slipped into England and
with their usual looting and burning made havoc of the
town of Hexham and the whole of the neighbouring
district: indeed the damage they did to us on this
occasion surpassed what our army had inflicted on them
some time previously in Scotland; for whereas in the old
days our Northerners used to be very active and vigorous,
they have now changed their tack and become lazy and
spiritless, disdaining to protect their homeland against the
wiles of the enemy by keeping watch and ward, so that
as a result of their neglect and slackness they were fated
to lose their homes and possessions; and indeed they
would have lost much more during this period had it not
been for the mettlesome and generous temper of Sir
Henry Percy,[3] who, after the king's withdrawal with his
army from Scotland, fought five engagements with the
Scots and gained the day on every occasion.

Through the good offices of the bishop of London the
archbishop of Canterbury was reconciled with the king on
23 October.[4] In his lust for glory and his eagerness to
have from everybody the deference properly due to his
kingship, the king allowed the archbishop to kneel before
him to beg his pardon. But if on this occasion the
archbishop had displayed a decisive flash of the same
steadfast purpose, backed by the force of logic, as is
known to have been consistently strong in St. Thomas
the Martyr, the truth is that with due regard always to
the paths of righteousness and justice he would never
have bent head or knee in that fashion to anybody,
when according to the canonical rule it is rather the
necks of kings and princes which should be bowed in
submission at the feet of pontiffs.[5]

1385 Papa[a] vero de manu regis Karoli liberatus et apud urbem Januensem cum suis cardinalibus in prospero satis statu existens curiam suam, que diu vacavit, circa finem mensis Octobris resumpsit et omnes confluentes ad eum quantocius expedivit.[1] Nonnulli eciam habitatores circumadjacencium provinciarum antipapam relinquentes sibi ut Christi vicario adherebant.

Rex creavit duces et comites.[2] Item ix°. die Novembris apud Westmonasterium in pleno parliamento rex duos suos patruos prefecit in duces, videlicet dominum Edmundum Langelee comitem Cantebrig' promovit in ducem Eboracen' et dominum Thomam Wodestok' comitem Bukyngham in ducem Gloucestr' exaltavit; qui variis ornamentis eorum statui congruentibus insigniti ac per regem competenter dotati homagium sibi flexis genibus prestiterunt. Item eodem die in parliamento dominum Michaelem de Poole, militem et cancellarium Anglie, rex eciam terris dotatum erexit in comitem de Southfolk';[3] appropriatisque sibi eciam ornamentis ejus statum concernentibus facto regi homagio inter alios comites juxta suum gradum secessit. Item eodem die dominus Jacobus comes de Ormond'[4] cingulum milicie recepit a rege. Quibus rite peractis rex et regina una cum predictis magnatibus taliter insignitis ceterisque nobilibus tunc ibidem presentibus ad convivium ducis Lancastr' ea de causa laute ac splendide apparatum communiter adierunt.

Bis in isto mense Calesienses Flandriam intrabant, scilicet xiij. et xvij. diebus Novembris, hominesque illius patrie ultra ccc[tos]. captivos secum duxerunt, magnam eciam predam animalium secum Cales' attulerunt, in tantum quod omnes[b] existentes in ea diu postea erant opulenciores.

Dux Lancastr' audito rumore quomodo Portyngalenses p. 152 Hiberos / in dedicionem dederunt, quia circa ista tempora venerunt nova quod post primam stragem eis inflictam bis vel ter cum illis tam valide conflixerunt quod lx. milia ex eis

---

[a] Et hic de papa *in the margin, in a fifteenth-century hand. inserts* ex.   [b] MS.

[1] For Urban VI's arrival in Genoa on 23 Sept. 1385 see above, p. 130 and n., and for his escape from Charles of Durazzo at Nocera — an episode not explicitly related by the Monk — ibid., p. 111 n.   [2] Cf. above, p. 126 and n.
[3] The grant to the earl of Suffolk of lands worth £500 per annum is dated 12

After his deliverance from the clutches of King Charles the 1385 pope established himself with his cardinals in fairly favourable conditions at Genoa and about the end of October resumed his court, which had long been in abeyance, and dealt rapidly with the business of all those who thronged upon him.[1] Furthermore some of the inhabitants of the neighbouring provinces abandoned the antipope and attached themselves to him as the true vicar of Christ.

Creation of dukes and earls by the king.[2] On 9 November, in full parliament at Westminster, the king raised two of his uncles to the rank of duke, advancing Edmund of Langley, earl of Cambridge, to duke of York and elevating Thomas of Woodstock, earl of Buckingham, to the dukedom of Gloucester. After being invested with the various insignia befitting their rank and receiving appropriate endowments from the king, they knelt and did homage to him. Sir Michael de la Pole, the chancellor, was also endowed in parliament with land on the same day by the king and raised to earl of Suffolk;[3] whereupon he too assumed the insignia proper to his rank, did homage to the king, and withdrew to his place, according to his degree, among the other earls. On the same day also James earl of Ormond[4] received the belt of knighthood from the king. The ceremonies over, the king and queen joined the newly invested great ones and the other nobles present in attending a banquet arranged for the occasion with great taste and brilliance by the duke of Lancaster.

Twice during this month, on 13 and 17 November, troops from Calais entered Flanders, carrying off more than 300 of the inhabitants as prisoners besides bringing back with them to Calais considerable booty in cattle — so much so that for some time afterwards everybody there was well off.

The duke of Lancaster had heard reports of how the Portuguese had brought the Spaniards into a state of submission, for about this time news came that after administering the initial defeat the Portuguese had had two or three such vigorous clashes with the enemy that, acquitting themselves

Sept. The duke of Gloucester and the duke of York each received lands worth £1,000 per annum, or an income in lieu thereof, by letters patent dated, respectively, 12 and 15 Nov. 1385. See Rymer, *Foedera*, vii. 481–3; *R.P.*, iii. 205 ff.

[4] James le Boteler, 3rd earl of Ormond, 1382–1405.

1385 viriliter occiderunt et usque ad civitatem eorum magnam
vocatam Cuntregrant sunt eos in ore gladii persecuti;[1] et si
dux Lancastr' ibi tunc presens fuisset totam Hispanniam sibi
protinus subjugasset, quia potestas, virtus defensionis et
eorum animositas ab eis penitus sunt ablate. Quare vigili
cura plures vias attencius exquisivit dux Lancastr' qualiter
ad id optinendum posset in hoc casu consulcius agere et ad
suum votum maturius pervenire. Igitur dominum regem et
alios dominos parliamenti est interim allocutus ut suam in
hujusmodi impleant voluntatem; et si vellent condescendere
votis suis procuraret et faceret, ut speravit, quod florem
milicie Scocie secum adduceret ac eciam comitem de
Armynak' et dominum le Bryt,[2] qui Burdegalenses jugiter
infestabant, allicere et penes se in illo negocio retinere
promisit: Burdegalenses propterea cicius pace verisimiliter
fruerentur, et si contingat dictum regnum favente divina
gracia per illum forsitan adipisci pacem proculdubio inter
regnum Anglie et illud pro perpetuo stabiliret. Ista eciam
coram regni communitate sepius publicavit ac juxta promissa
perficere affirmavit, dum tamen ipsum juvarent de xl. milibus
librarum. Rex autem et alii nobiles regni auditis promissis
ducis predicti cum consensu dicte communitatis regni sui
quod petivit liberaliter concesserunt.[3]

Item xxvij°. die Novembris venerunt nova domino regi de
morte domini Johannis Bacon' clerici sui apud urbem Janue
decedentis; qui fuit missus a rege et ejus consilio ad papam
ut tolleret privilegium pro debito ab ecclesia Westmon'
(qua de causa dominus Johannes Waltham clericus regis de

---

[1] The reports came from Fernando Afonso de Albuquerque and Lourenço
Anes Fogaça, envoys of João I of Portugal. Cf. Froissart, *Chroniques*, xi. 272 ff.;
and see also Russell, *English Intervention*, pp. 401–2. Santarem, in the Ribatejo,
was the main garrison of the Castilian forces in Portugal before the battle of
Aljubarrota and their main refuge in its aftermath. There follows the Monk's
first explicit reference to Lancaster's pretendership to the throne of Castile, in
virtue of his marriage in 1371 to Constanza, daughter and heiress of Pedro I of
Castile, and to his desire to lead an English expedition which should advance both
his own claim to Castile and those of Urban VI to its obedience, Juan I of Castile
being an adherent of Clement VII.

[2] Jean III, count of Armagnac (1384–91) and his cousin, Arnand-Amaineu,
lord of Albret (1358–1401). The appeal of the latter and of the grandfather of the
former to Charles V of France against the Black Prince's decision to levy a hearth-
tax in their domains precipitated the renewal of the Anglo-French war in 1369.
Lancaster's confidence that these lords would fight on his side – and in a war

like men, they had killed 60,000 of them and chased the rest 1385
at the sword's point into a big town called Santarem;[1] and
if the duke of Lancaster had then been on the spot he would
have subjected the whole of Spain to himself forthwith, since
the strength of the Spaniards, their courage to resist, and
their fighting spirit had been wholly drained away from
them. The duke accordingly devoted all the more anxious
and lively attention to finding out the various courses of
action best calculated in the circumstances to gain his ends
and enable him to arrive soonest at his heart's desire. Meanwhile he addressed to the king and his fellow lords of parliament a speech requesting them to give effect to his purpose
in this matter; if they were willing to meet his wishes he
would, he hoped, manage to arrange to fetch away with him
the flower of Scotland's chivalry, and he further promised to
lure to his side, and keep there in this enterprise, the count
of Armagnac and the Sire d'Albret,[2] who were a source of
constant vexation to the people of Bordeaux; the latter
would in consequence probably enjoy peace the sooner, and
if by God's grace it should turn out that he won the kingdom
of Spain, he would undoubtedly establish peace in perpetuity
between it and that of England. These intentions he also
repeatedly advertised to the commons of the realm, declaring
that he would carry them out in conformity with his undertaking, provided that they would help him to the extent of
£40,000. After listening to the duke's promises, the king and
the remaining nobles of the realm, with the commons'
consent, generously granted him what he asked.[3]

News reached the king on 27 November of the death
of his clerk, John Bacon, which had taken place at Genoa:
he had been sent to the pope by the king and his council
to secure the withdrawal from the church of Westminster
of its privilege in the matter of debt (on this account John
Waltham, keeper of the rolls, in the king's name begged

---

against France's Castilian ally — was based no doubt on the calculation that they
would be glad to find this occupation for the *routiers* whom they commanded.
Mutatis mutandis, the same consideration must have informed his belief that
Scottish knights would serve on the expedition.
  [3] Parliament granted one and a half tenths and one and a half fifteenths; see
below, p. 149 n. The yield of these taxes was probably *c*.£50,000, but the grant
was not only for Lancaster's expedition. Cf. Knighton, *Chronicon*, ii. 206.

1385 rotulis nomine suo peciit veniam ab abbate et conventu Westm', rogans eos instanter ut sibi misericorditer perdonarent); et quia erat morte preventus ante adventum pape non est suum votum neque in hiis neque in aliis consecutus.[1]

Item xxvij°. die Novembris, quia placuit regi dominum Johannem Holand pro nece filii et heredis comitis Stafford' communem legem debere subire, igitur idem comes fecit eum in banco regis per breve de exigent vocari,[2] presentibus ibidem septem aliis comitibus et cum illis magno nobilium comitatu; set non comparuit neque quispiam alius loco ejus.

Quo eciam die rex fecit solempnem missam fieri in ecclesia Westmon' pro clerico suo paulo superius nominato; habuit eciam die lapso ibidem Placebo et Dirige in conventu pro anima dicti clerici: et utroque die ipsemet fuit presens in choro dum pro dicto clerico erat obsequium peragendum. Item divulgatum fuit eo die quomodo ad peticionem domini regis papa transtulit fratrem Thomam Russhok confessorem regis de ordine Predicatorum de ecclesia Landaven' ad ecclesiam Cicestr',[3] et episcopum Beethlemitanum ejusdem ordinis transtulit ad ecclesiam Landavensem.[4] Cujus contemplacione hoc factum sit nescitur.

Marchio. Primo die Decembris rex contulit dominium Hibernie de eo tenendum comiti Oxon', qui pro illa confestim fecit regi homagium, et statuit illum appellari marchionem Dublinne.[5] Marchio enim est major comite et minor duce; unde rex in parliamento supra comites fecit eum sedere.

Item quinto die Decembris reconciliatus est major London'[6] duci Lancastr' et cum eo ea nocte cenavit: fuit ibi eciam rex et regina.

Item vj°. die Decembris parliamentum sortitum est finem; in cujus principio multa pro bono communi mota fuerunt,

[1] Bacon, the king's secretary, left England with Nicholas Dagworth and others in May 1385 on an embassy the main purpose of which was the conclusion of alliances associating England more closely with the Urbanist cause. See *Perroy*, p. 289 and nn.; for Bacon, Tout, *Chapters*, iv. 334–5 and v. 214–15; and for Urban VI's arrival at Genoa on 23 Sept. 1385, above, p. 130 and n. The Monk's parochial explanation of this embassy suggests that the Abbey had not acquiesced in parliament's decision in 1378 to except fraudulent debt from the scope of its sanctuary; see below, p. 324.

[2] The first step in an appeal of felony.

[3] See above, p. 130 and n.

the pardon of the abbot and convent and earnestly requested 1385 them to be merciful and forgive him); but since Bacon was forestalled by death before the pope's arrival, he failed to achieve his object in this as well as in other respects.[1]

As the king had decided that Sir John Holland was to be subjected to the common law for the murder of the son and heir of the earl of Stafford, the earl had him summoned in the King's Bench by writ of exigent[2] on 27 November, when a considerable company of nobles, including seven other earls, attended; but he did not appear, nor did anyone else in his place.

On the same day the king caused a solemn Mass to be celebrated in the church of Westminster for his clerk, named just above; and on the following day he had a Placebo and a Dirige in the convent for the clerk's soul: on both days he was himself present in the choir while the service for the clerk was being conducted. It was revealed on this day that at the king's request the pope had translated his confessor, Thomas Rushock, of the order of Friars Preachers, from the church of Llandaff to that of Chichester:[3] he translated the bishop of Bethlehem,[4] a member of the same order, to Llandaff, but out of regard for whom this was done is not known.

The marquis. On 1 December the king conferred the lordship of Ireland, to be held of himself, on the earl of Oxford (who forthwith did homage to the king for it) and decreed that he should be styled marquis of Dublin.[5] A marquis is superior to an earl and less than a duke; so that the king caused him to be seated in parliament above the earls.

The mayor of London[6] was reconciled with the duke of Lancaster on 5 December and took supper with him that night, when the king and queen were also present.

The parliament came to an end on 6 December. At its outset there had been many proposals in furtherance of the

---

[4] William Bottlesham. He was translated to Llandaff on 16 Oct. 1385 but did not receive the temporalities until 21 Aug. 1386 (Rymer, *Foedera*, vii. 478-9; *Cal. Pat. R., 1385-9*, p. 209).

[5] A title without precedent. See *R.P.*, iii. 209-10; *Lords' Reports on the Dignity of a Peer*, v. 78-9.

[6] Nicholas Brembre. Lancaster was the patron of Brembre's imprisoned rival, John Northampton (above, p. 92 and n.; below, p. 148).

1385 set ejus finis non corespondebat sui inicio, nam inter cetera
petebat communitas ut rex ea revocaret que aliis e corona
erant indiscrete collata; quia notum est quod magis honor
foret regi, immo et suis subditis utile, de suis propriis vivere
quam illos pro victu et aliis necessariis continue expoliare.[1]
Istam peticionem dux Lancastr' evacuavit, dicens non esse
equum neque justum ut rex nunc concederet alicui per
patentem terras et tenementa pro termino sue vite at illa[a]
nunc cum sibi placuerit revocaret;[b][2] et quia tunc non surrexit
contradictor expressus, prevaluit sermo ejus. Sui ipsius tamen
inter alia non est oblitus, nam in pleno parliamento peciit
ut omnes post eum jure hereditario in ducatum Lancastr'
succedentes duces vocentur: et confestim fuit sibi concessum.[3] Item assensu omnium existencium in parliamento de
partibus transmarinis fuit stapula revocata ut pro majori
utilitate in Anglia haberetur.[4] Item in fine parliamenti
Gandavenses miserunt domino regi et ejus consilio, expresse
dicentes quod nisi cicius[c] subsidio virorum belligerorum
fulcirentur[d] oporteret eos[d] necessario reddere civitatem
eorum regi Francorum. Set quid profuit ista missio regi
Anglorum cum tunc omnes pro majori parte essent Francigene?* Revera modicum ut infra patebit.[5] Tamen rex cum
suo consilio in defensionem dicte civitatis ordinavit cum
omni celeritate ccc. lances et dcc. viros sagittarios ad illos
transmittere; set illa ordinacio postea erat quassata et illi

---

* Nota quia isti Gandavenses non coacti set sponte a rege Anglie diverterunt
in the margin.

---

[a] *Interlined.*   [b] *MS.* revocare.   [c] *An erasure, covered by a dash, follows.*
[d] *Interlined.*

---

[1] The Monk understands 'the king to live of his own' in a moderate sense: the
Crown lands should provide the income needed for the king's household. On these
important themes see B. P. Wolffe, *The Royal Demesne in English History* (London,
1971), pp. 72–5; G. L. Harriss, *King, Parliament and Public Finance in Medieval
England to 1369* (Oxford, 1975), pp. 160 ff. See also below, p. 244 and n.

[2] A reference to the grant to de Vere, who received the lordship of Ireland and
the title of marquis for life.

[3] John of Gaunt received the title of duke of Lancaster for himself and the
heirs male of his body in 1362 (*Cal. Ch. R.*, v (1341–1417), p. 174; *Lords'
Reports on the Dignity of a Peer*, v. 53).

[4] *R.P.*, iii. 204. The decision when to move the staple, and where in England to
locate it, was left to the Council, and in the event it remained at Middelburg.

common weal, but its end did not match its beginning. 1385
Among these proposals was a petition from the commons
that the king should revoke grants imprudently made to
others out of the possessions of the crown: it was well known
to be more to the king's credit, and, indeed, to his subjects'
advantage, for him to live of his own than for him to be
eternally fleecing them for the means of subsistence and
other necessities.[1] This petition was rendered nugatory by
the duke of Lancaster, who said that it was not fair or right
that the king should at one moment grant somebody lands
and tenements by patent for the term of his life and at
another, when it pleased him to do so, resume them;[2] and
since nobody thereupon rose to gainsay him explicitly, his
argument carried the day. Yet he was not unmindful of his
own case among others; in full parliament he requested that
all those who after himself should succeed to the duchy of
Lancaster should be styled dukes; and his request was
promptly granted.[3] With the consent of everybody present
in the parliament the staple was recalled from overseas, to
be established to greater advantage in England.[4] As the parliament ended the people of Ghent sent to the king and council
to say, in so many words, that unless they were very soon
supported by armed assistance they would inevitably have to
surrender their city to the French king. But of what use was
it for them to send like this to the English king when they
were all, or most of them, French at this time?* Little
indeed, as will appear below.[5] However, the king, with the
approval of the council, gave orders for the speedy dispatch
to them of 300 lances and 700 bowmen for the defence of
Ghent; these orders were later rescinded, and the troops

---

* Note that it was not under compulsion but of their own free will that these
Gantois turned away from the king of England *in the margin.*

[5] pp. 150-2. Cf. Vaughan, *Philip the Bold*, p. 37. The council which the Monk
mentions in his next sentence met in London during the king's absence in Scotland. It authorized the dispatch of a force for the relief of Ghent, smaller than
that described by the Monk, under Sir Hugh Despenser and Sir William Drayton;
the decision to divert the expedition to Berwick had been taken before the end
of the first week in Nov. (*Perroy*, p. 208 and n.; and see below, p. 154). Despenser
and Drayton were formally retained by the king for the defence of Berwick for
100 days from 15 Jan. 1386 (Rymer, *Foedera*, vii. 488-9).

1385 transmissi sunt ad villam de Berewyk causa custodie illius.
Item ordinatum est *in parliamento* quod priores Francigene
omnes de Anglia exirent, sic quod nullus eorum in hac terra
ultimo die Januarii sit inventus, cum pena adjecta, hiis tamen
exceptis qui tales prioratus habent ad terminum vite per
patentem eisdem assignatos, qui eciam jurabunt quod non
prodant consilium regis alienis intra vel extra habitantibus
colloquio scripto vel signo, sub pena que*b* incumbit. Istud
non est novum set antiquum.[1] Item volunt quod omnes
seculares laici tales prioratus jure possessorio*c* optinentes vel
ad firmam a rege eosdem tenentes ab eisdem penitus exclu-
dantur, quia non competit laicis spiritualia possidere sive
ad firmam tenere. Finis parliamenti fuit iste, nam isti de
consilio domini regis dixerunt: 'Satis constat omnibus
quomodo dominus noster rex pro defensione et tuicione
sui regni fovet bella erga terras diversas; et adhuc necessitas
ipsum cogit, velit nolit, si suos adversarios debeat resistere
ulterius, continuare, quod sibi foret impossibile sine vestro
auxilio, tale onus super se assumere cum effectu. Igitur etc.'[2]
Sic itaque talibus sermonibus inducti sunt laici unam quintamdecimam et dimidiam concedere, licet inviti: prelati vero
ecclesiarum laicos in concessione, ut tempus parliamenti
diminuerent, prevenientes non multum post ejus incepcionem
apud Sanctum Paulum London' convenerunt et domino
regi unam decimam cum una dimidia decima*d* concesserunt.[3]
Item in fine parliamenti dux Lancastr' talem graciam in-
petravit a rege quod J. Northampton' et ejus socii a carcerali
custodia liberarentur: concessit rex dumtamen civitatem
London' per decem leucas minime approximarent.
Londonienses vero eorum emuli hiis auditis insteterunt
penes regem quod per centum miliaria non appropinquarent

a–a Interlined.   *b MS. qua.*   *c MS. possessiorio.*   *d MS. decime.*

[1] The oath mentioned here was that required of alien monks on the outbreak
of the Anglo-French war in 1337 and on its renewal in 1369. The inmates of alien
priories, with exceptions which included priors with a life-title, had been expelled
from England in 1378; but the statute and ordinance giving effect to these
decisions were reaffirmed in the parliament of Oct.–Dec. 1385, in response to a
petition against the practice of farming such priories to laymen, widely adopted
in the interval. The Monk summarizes this petition in his next sentence. See *R.P.*,
iii. 213; D. Matthew, *The Norman Monasteries and their English Possessions*
(Oxford, 1962), pp. 109–12.

were sent to the town of Berwick to safeguard it. In this 1385
parliament it was decreed also that all French priors were to
leave England, so that by the last day of January none of
them must be found in this country; and a penalty was
attached: but those persons were excepted who had had such
priories assigned to them by patent for life. These were to
take an oath that upon the pains and penalties prescribed
they would not by speech, writing, or other indication,
betray the king's secrets to foreigners living in or out of
England. There was no novelty in this; it was ancient practice.[1] It was further decided that all secular persons and laymen occupying such priories by possessory right or holding
them at farm from the king should be expelled from them
completely, since it was not the province of laymen to
possess spiritualities or to hold them at farm. The end of the
parliament came with the members of the king's council
having this to say: 'It is well enough known to everybody
how, for the defence and protection of his realm, our lord
the king is maintaining a struggle against various countries;
and necessity still constrains him, willy-nilly, if he is to go
on resisting his adversaries, to continue (as he could not do
without your help) to take this burden upon himself to real
purpose. Therefore etc.'[2] By speeches like this the laity were
thus brought to grant, albeit reluctantly, one and a half
fifteenths: in this respect they had been anticipated by the
churchmen, who, in order to reduce the duration of the
parliament, had met at St. Paul's shortly after its opening and
granted the king one and a half tenths.[3] At the parliament's
close the duke of Lancaster obtained a favour from the king
— that John Northampton and his associates might be released
from their confinement in prison — which the king granted
on condition that they did not approach within thirty miles
of the city of London. On hearing of this, however, their
London enemies urged upon the king that they should not
come nearer than a hundred miles from the city; and the

[2] The concluding 'etc.' suggests that the Monk was using a written source.
[3] The lay subsidy, payable by 24 June 1386, was granted for Lancaster's
expedition to Spain, for naval defence and the defence of the Marches, and for
the relief of Ghent (*R.P.*, iii. 204; and see above, p. 142 and n.). The clerical grant
was not made until 7 Dec. and was of one tenth (*Cal. Fine R., 1383–91*, p. 128;
and for the contentious circumstances see Walsingham, *Hist. Ang.*, ii. 139–40).

1385 civitati predicte: annuit rex votis eorum, sicque cassatis hiis
que pro eorum comodo fuerant inpetrata diu postea manserunt in custodia cartis frustrati et bonis.[1]

p. 153   Gandavenses vero, quibus sepius ex parte regis Anglie
fuit auxilium pulcre promissum set, ut eis videbatur, non ita
tempestive fuit eis transmissum ut deberet, graviter sunt
conquesti super ejus longa expectacione, quia dixerunt se
fore artifices et operarios ⟨qui⟩[a] victum et vestitum operibus
manuum suarum necessario haberent adquirere, bellorum
tumultibus jugiter insistere non valentes, nec ea posse fovere
tempore diuturno: quo circa nisi tales[b] succursus virorum
belligerorum haberent quorum potencia et defensione civitas
eorum cum tota patria circumadjacente ab hostium incur-
sionibus posset tueri viriliter et defendi, et illi interim suis
artibus lucrativis intendere valerent assidue in quiete, nequaquam eos vivere posse comode asserebant. Preterea brevi
intervallo post inter eos super hujusmodi materia murmure
suscitato quidam illorum adherebant parti regis Anglie,
quidam vero regi Francie et eorum domino duci Burgundie.
Sicque illis adinvicem aliquamdiu taliter contendentibus
tandem circa festum Sancte Lucie Virginis placuit eis pro
majori parte cum rege Francie et eorum domino duce
Burgundie pro securiori via[c] componere.[2] Igitur cum illis
convenire sic finaliter decreverunt, scilicet quod libertates
et consuetudines antiquas approbatas et inter illos actenus
usitatas ac legittime prescriptas possent ita libere, quiete
et pacifice deinceps absque molestacione violenta imperpetuum optinere, sicut umquam temporibus retroactis illas
habuerunt et eciam possederunt; item quia amicicias affectabant pocius cumulare quam inimicicias aggregare, cum sint
artifices[d] et operarii, igitur de guerris motis sive in posterum

---

[a] *MS. om.*   [b] *MS. talis.*   [c] *Recte* vita, 'with a view to a less troubled
existence'?   [d] sint *repeated after this word, but deleted.*

---

[1] Cf. *Cal. Plea and Memoranda Rolls of the City of London, 1381–1412*,
ed. Thomas, pp. 109–13, attesting the substantial truth of the Monk's story.
The capital sentences against Northampton, John More, and Richard Northbury,
together with the sentences of imprisonment, were finally remitted in June 1386,
but the 3 men were then forbidden to approach within 80 miles of the City (*Cal.
Pat. R., 1385–9*, pp. 158–9, 161; *Letter Book H*, pp. 279–82, 307; and cf. above,
p. 96 and n.).

[2] There follows a summary of the Treaty of Tournai, concluded between the

king met their wishes. The concessions obtained on the 1385 prisoners' behalf were thus annulled, and for a long time after this they remained in confinement, baulked of their charters of pardon and of their property.[1]

The people of Ghent, to whom frequent and specious promises of help had been made on behalf of the king of England, but to whom such help had not, in their view, been sent with the timeliness it should have been, now made bitter complaints about the length of their wait for it. They were, they said, craftsmen and artificers, obliged to earn their food and clothing with the work of their hands and unable to give their constant attention to the turmoil of war, which, indeed, they could not maintain over a long period. Unless, therefore, they had such assistance in the shape of fighting men as would provide a powerful defence and enable their city and the whole of the surrounding countryside to be resolutely protected and safeguarded against hostile invasion, and they themselves could meanwhile concentrate in peace on the active pursuit of their remunerative crafts, they declared that they could not well support life. When, shortly afterwards, murmurs were raised among them on the subject, some of them sided with the king of England and some with the king of France and their own overlord, the duke of Burgundy. For some time there was thus dispute among them along these lines, until at last, about the feast of St. Lucy the Virgin [13 December] a majority of them favoured a settlement with the king of France and their overlord, the duke of Burgundy, as the safer course to take. They finally decided, therefore, to conclude an agreement with them on the following terms.[2] They were to be allowed to enjoy henceforward in perpetuity and without forcible interference the time-honoured liberties and customs hitherto practised among them, and lawfully prescribed, as freely, quietly, and peaceably as they had ever in times past had and possessed them. Next, since it was their aim, as craftsmen and artificers, to accumulate friendships rather than to lay up a store of enmities, they did not wish to

city of Ghent and Philip the Bold, duke of Burgundy, on 18 Dec. 1385, for which see Froissart, *Chroniques*, x. 427 ff.; Vaughan, *Philip the Bold*, pp. 37–8. Among the liberties tacitly guaranteed to the citizens of Ghent by the Treaty was that of continued allegiance to Urban VI.

1385 movendis inter regem Anglorum et regem Francorum
noluerunt intromittere nec alicui eorum opem ferre seu
^acum altero illorum^a tenere, set vellent omnino ad utramque
partem se indifferenter habere durante inter eos turbine
preliorum. Demum istis concessis et in debitam formam
redactis atque cum sufficienti securitate firmatis ducem
Burgundie in eorum dominum placide admiserunt. Quorum
exemplo illi de Ipres et Bruges quantocius provocati ducem
Burgundie in eorum dominum consimili modo quo Gandavenses fecerunt eciam receperunt.[1]

Quo in tempore Parisius rex Francorum suum tenuit
parliamentum ac pro suis dominis et terre magnatibus
specialiter misit quos protunc voluit ibi habere; et inter
alios misit pro duce Britannie, ut ipse cum ceteris dominis
ad suum parliamentum veniret. Dux vero super hujusmodi
legacione aliqualiter stupefactus nichilominus super hac
re sumpto sano consilio noluit illuc transire nisi prius datis
obsidibus de^b plena securitate eundi^c et redeundi ^dcum
salute^d ad sua; et pro certo secundum fidedignos nisi sic
fecisset proculdubio numquam corpore vitali ad propria
remeasset.[2]

Item de mense Decembris dominus Johannes Harpedene
strenuus miles factus jam seneschallus Vascon'[3] in eundo
versus Burdegaliam cepit septem naves vino et aliis mercimoniis plene onustas, quas circa festum Natalis Domini
misit domino nostro regi. Erat namque iste J. Harpedene
tempore Edwardi principis Wallie ^eet domini Aquitannie^e
capitaneus ville de Rochell' et ibi viriliter cum comite de
Penbrok' fuit captus ab Hispanis et mansit apud illos in
custodia carcerali usque ad proximum annum elapsum, quo
inde fuit liberatus.[4]

---

^{a-a} *Added in the margin after* seu, *which ends a line.*   ^b *In the margin but*
marked for insertion at this point.   ^c *Interlined.*   ^{d-d} *In the margin but*
marked for insertion at this point.   ^{e-e} *Interlined.*

[1] Ypres and Bruges submitted to Philip the Bold on 10 May 1384.
[2] Or did Duke John IV refuse to attend the *parlement* of Paris for the hearing
of an appeal from one of his subjects that had not gone through the *parlement*
of Brittany? For such a case in 1383–4 see B.-A. Pocquet, 'Les Fauxétats de
Bretagne de 1315 et les premiers états de Bretagne', in *B.E.C.*, lxxxvi (1925),
402–3, and for the background, M. Jones, *Ducal Brittany, 1364–1399* (Oxford,
1970), pp. 95-6.

intervene in any wars initiated, or to be in future initiated, 1385
between the English and the French kings, or to give help
to, or side with, either of them, but altogether preferred
to behave impartially towards both sides so long as the
whirl of war persisted between them. At length, when
these terms had been conceded, drawn up in the proper
form, and secured with adequate guarantees, the people
of Ghent accepted the duke of Burgundy as their overlord
without demur. Their example very soon prompted the
people of Ypres and Bruges also to embrace the duke of
Burgundy as their lord in the same way as the Gantois had
done.[1]

At about this time the French king held his parliament at
Paris and sent special summonses to those nobles and leading
men of the country whom he wished to have present on this
occasion; among others he summoned the duke of Brittany
to attend the parliament in company with the rest. The duke
was somewhat surprised to receive a message of this sort, but
adopting the counsel of prudence in this matter he nevertheless declined to make the journey to Paris unless hostages
were given beforehand to provide full assurance of his going
and returning home in safety; and it is a fact, according to
trustworthy sources, that if he had not done this he would
undoubtedly never have come back alive.[2]

During December Sir John Harpeden, a vigorous knight
who had just been made seneschal of Gascony,[3] captured on
his way to Bordeaux seven ships with full cargoes of wine
and other merchandise, which he sent about Christmas to
the king. In the time of Edward, prince of Wales and lord of
Aquitaine, this John Harpeden was captain of La Rochelle,
and there, in company with the earl of Pembroke, he was
captured after a valiant struggle by the Spaniards, in whose
country he had remained in prison until the year just past,
when he had been released.[4]

[3] On 1 Mar. 1385 (*Carte*, i. 173; see also Rymer, *Foedera*, vii. 470-1).
[4] For the capture of John Hastings, 2nd earl of Pembroke (1348-75), by a
Castilian fleet off La Rochelle in 1372, when he was the king's lieutenant in
Aquitaine, see R. Delachenal, *Histoire de Charles V* (Paris, 1909-31), iv. 408-18;
J. W. Sherborne, 'The Battle of La Rochelle and the War at Sea, 1372-5', in
B.I.H.R., xlii (1969), 17 ff. See also, on Harpeden's capture, *Cal. Cl. R., 1381-5*,
pp. 543-4.

1385   Item non multum ante festum Natalis Domini in Cancia applicuit rex Armenie;[1] qui in principio festi predicti apud Eltham veniens, ubi rex Anglie tenuit suum Natale, ab eo honorifice est receptus et tam ab ipso quam a regina ac aliis dominis ibidem existentibus multis donis et muneribus revera magnificis est ditatus.

Porro dominus Hugo Despenser dominus Willelmus Drayton' et alii jamdudum ordinati transire ad civitatem de Gaunt in fine mensis Decembris iter arripuerunt versus Berewycum et ibidem se contra Scotos viriliter habuerunt vicibus iteratis.[2]

Quadam vero die infra Natale rex Anglie apud Eltham cum suorum nobilium comitiva circa diversa tractabat; accessit ad eum rex Armenie et ei causam sui adventus reverenter, ut decuit, explicavit, asserens se venisse ea de causa ut quietem et tranquillitatem utriusque regni efficaciter procuraret, quia[a] si illa antiqua discordia posset sedari et vera pax atque finalis inter duo regna poterat adipisci, profecto foret maxima leticia que toti Christianitati potuit evenire et indubie Saracenis paganis et aliis inimicis crucis Christi quibuslibet esset confusio manifesta. Cumque hec et hiis similia pro pace habenda dictus rex in presencia regis et regni nobilium in multa verborum facundia protulisset, placuit regi ejus suasione aliquos de suis ad tractandum de pace cum Francigenis Calesiis destinare.[3]

1386   Denique rex Armenie a duce Gloucestr' invitatus ut die Epiphanie apud Pleyssh' secum existeret igitur primo die Januarii peciit licenciam recedendi a rege, et optinuit. Tandem [b]mane facto[b] innotuit regi Anglie predictum regem velle transitum facere per London'; accinxit se apparatu nobiliori et eundem regem[c] usque

[a] MS. inserts et.   [b-b] Interlined.   [c] Interlined.

---

[1] Leo VI (1373-93). The purpose of his visit was mediation between England and France, as part of the pacification of Europe which was the necessary preliminary to a crusade; Armenia had been in Muslim hands since 1375, 2 years after Leo VI's accession. Cf. *Chronique du religieux de Saint Denys*, ed. M. L. Bellaguet (Collection de Documents inédits sur l'histoire de France, 1st ser., 1839-52), i. 418 ff. See also Mirot, in *Révue des Études Historiques*, n.s. xvii (1915), 436 ff.

The king of Armenia[1] landed in Kent shortly before 1385 Christmas. On his arrival at Eltham at the beginning of that feast, which the king of England was celebrating there, he received a courteous welcome from him and was enriched by a quantity of truly splendid gifts and presents not only from the king but from the queen and the nobles who were there.

Sir Hugh Despenser, Sir William Drayton, and others who had some time before been under orders to cross to Ghent set out at the end of December for Berwick, where on repeated occasions they acquitted themselves valiantly against the Scots.[2]

One day during the Christmas season the king of England was discussing various matters with his attendant nobles at Eltham, when the king of Armenia called upon him and with proper deference explained to him the reason for his visit, announcing that the purpose for which he had come was that he might effectively procure the quiet and tranquillity of both kingdoms: if that ancient quarrel could be composed and a real and final peace attained between the two kingdoms, it would represent the greatest joy that could come about for the whole of Christendom and overt discomfiture for the pagan Saracens and all other enemies whatsoever of the Cross of Christ. After this and similar arguments for embracing peace had been advanced with great eloquence by the Armenian king in his presence and that of the nobles of the realm, the king decided, as a result of the other's persuasion, to dispatch some of those in his service to Calais to discuss peace with the French.[3]

Eventually the king of Armenia, who had been invited 1386 by the duke of Gloucester to join him at Pleshey on the feast of the Epiphany [6 January], sought and obtained the king's leave to withdraw on 1 January. On the following morning the English king learned that the other was minded to pass through London: and donning some of his more impressive finery he escorted the Armenian

[2] Cf. above, p. 146 and n.
[3] Ambassadors were appointed on 22 Jan. 1386 and crossed to Calais in the 2nd week of Feb. (Rymer, *Foedera*, vii. 491–4; below, p. 160 and n.).

1386 Westmonasterium commeavit, supervenienteque noctis umbraculo nichilominus accensis cereis adduxit illum ad monasterium, factisque oblacionibus et visis reliquiis ibidem repositis ostendebat ei eciam insignia regalia quibus olim fuerat coronatus.

Inundaciones. Item circa principium mensis Januarii, immo parum post, erat magna inundacio aquarum in Devonia juxta civitatem Exon', que violenter a stacione sua asportavit pontes et domos in ejus cursu constructas ac eciam plures submersit. Similis inundacio erat isto anno in urbe Veneciarum mense Julii, que omnes pauperes debiles et impotentes qui ad alciora loca ascendere minime valuerunt submersit.

Tercio decimo die Januarii[1] apud monasterium de Westmon' facta est solempnis consecracio episcopi Cestren' de magistro Waltero Skyrlowe clerico privati sigilli domini regis per Willelmum Courteneye archiepiscopum Cantuar' presentibus regibus Anglie et Armenie, Eboracen' archiepiscopo et quinque aliis episcopis, ducibus Lancastr' et Gloucestr' cum aliis Anglie nobilibus profecto non paucis. Item xvij. die Januarii factus est episcopus Dunolm'[2] thesaurarius Anglie.

Circa principium vero istius mensis venit ad curiam domini regis *quidam armiger,* qui aliquamdiu in Lombardia stetit in comitiva domini Johannis Haukewode,[3] et narravit de quodam religioso in illis partibus demorante, quomodo predicebat gentem Anglorum infra tres annos proxime secuturos propter eorum malam vitam fore attrociter castigandam, et hoc potissime per famem et pestilenciam, ut asseruit, set post hec omnium regnorum erit patria illa felicissima, quia homines illius terre erunt ita fideles et stabiles quod eorum simplici assercioni unusquisque poterit

---

a–a Interlined.

[1] Correctly, 14 Jan.; and see above, p. 118 and n.
[2] John Fordham.
[3] For this soldier of fortune see *D.N.B.*, ix. 236 ff., and R. A. Pratt, 'Geoffrey

to Westminster, where, although the dusk of evening was 1386
coming on, he none the less took him to the monastery by
candle-light and, after they had made their offerings and
viewed the relics deposited there, went on to show him the
royal insignia with which he had been invested at his coronation some years before.

Floods. About the beginning of January, or rather a
little later, there was a great flood in Devon in the neighbourhood of Exeter, which in its violence carried away
from their sites bridges and buildings standing in its path
and drowned a number of people. There was a similar
flood in July of this year at Venice, where all the poor,
weak, and helpless who were unable to climb to higher
levels were drowned.

The ceremonial consecration of Master Walter Skirlaw,
keeper of the king's privy seal, as bishop of Chester
was performed by William Courtenay, archbishop of
Canterbury, at the monastery of Westminster on 13
January[1] in the presence of the kings of England and
Armenia, the archbishop of York, and five other bishops,
and the dukes of Lancaster and Gloucester as well
as other English nobles in no small numbers. On 17
January the bishop of Durham[2] became treasurer of
England.

About the beginning of this month a squire who
had for some time been in the company of Sir John
Hawkwood in Lombardy[3] arrived at the king's court
with a story about a man of religion living in those
parts, who predicted that within the ensuing three years
the English nation, because of its evil life, would be
mercilessly punished, chiefly, so he said, by famine and
pestilence, but that after this the country would be the
happiest of all kingdoms, since its people would be so
trustworthy and reliable that every man would be able

Chaucer Esq. and Sir John Hawkwood', in *Journal of English Literary History*,
xvi (1949), 188-93. The mention of him precipitates the marginal reference to
Bernabò Visconti: Hawkwood married a natural daughter of Bernabò.

1386 sine hesitacione et fallacia fidem dare. Hec ille.*

In festo Purificacionis beate Marie tenuit rex curiam suam
p. 154 apud Wyndeshoram, habuitque / secum ibidem regem
Armenie, quem vultu jocundo et facie leta studuit in omnibus honorare; nam contulit sibi quoddam jocale argenteum et
deauratum formatum ad modum navis, vocatum discum
elemosinarum, longitudinis trium pedum, eratque magni
precii, et implevit illud auro usque ad summum. Hec et alia
hic accepit ante suum recessum rex predictus; que omnia
pro majori parte juxta Cales' per predones amisit.

Item eodem die dominus J. Holand' veste lugubri indutus
inter manus archiepiscopi Cantuar' et episcopi London'
intravit ad regem et ter corruit in terram super genua sua et
brachia antequam pervenit ad eum; demum super genua sua
erigens se manusque suas sursum extendens, flens et ejulans,
petens a rege humiliter misericordiam ac obnixe eum ob-
secrans ut sibi indulgeret quod contra eum et ejus prohibicionem improvide et indiscrete deliquid tantum facinus
committendo.[1] Flebant nonnulli de circumstantibus hoc
videntes. Tercia vero vice prefati episcopi ante regem genu-
flexerunt cum illo. Tunc rex aliquantisper pietate motus

* In the right-hand margin, with no indication of the place for insertion:
1385 Quo in tempore dominus Barnabos moriebatur in carcere, qua morte, an gladio
aut fame seu veneno, ignoratur.[2]

And in the lower margin: Item anno domini millesimo ccclxxxv[to]. rex Anglie
misit speciales literas domino pape pro canonizacione regis Edwardi secundi post
conquestum, qui jacet Glovernie; nec tamen optinuit quod optavit.[3] Eodemque
anno Hibernienses satis solliciti fuerunt in curia pape pro canonizacione magistri
Ricardi filii Radulfi archiepiscopi ecclesie Armachane; contra quos viriliter
steterunt fratres Mendicantes et inpediverunt in quantum potuerunt.[4] Item eodem
1386 anno circa festum Natalis Domini Greci submiserunt se domino pape; qui antea
obstinati sedi apostolice parere minime curaverunt.[5]

[1] Viz. the slaying of Ralph de Stafford, for which see above, p. 122.

[2] Bernabò Visconti, lord of Milan, died at Trezzo in Dec. 1385, 7 months after
his fall from power. The reports, echoed by the Monk, that his death was un-
natural, lack proof. See Bueno de Mesquita, Giangaleazzo Visconti, Duke of Milan
(1351-1402), p. 34; and above, pp. 118-20.

[3] See Diplomatic Correspondence of Richard II, ed. Perroy, p. 210, and below,
pp. 436-8; and on the resting-place of Edward II, G. P. Cuttino and T. W. Lyman,
'Where is Edward II?', in Speculum, liii (1978), 522 ff.

[4] On this or a later occasion Urban VI appointed a commission of cardinals to
inquire into the life and miracles of Richard FitzRalph, but the matter came to
nothing. See Cal. Papal Letters, v (1396-1404), p. 245; for the miracles, D.N.B.,

without hesitation or the risk of deceit to believe their bare 1386
word. Such was the story.*

On the feast of the Purification of the Virgin [2 February] the king held court at Windsor. With him he had the king of Armenia, whom, with an expression of pleasure on his smiling face, he laid himself out to honour in every particular, presenting him with a piece of plate of silver and gilt shaped to resemble a ship and styled an alms-dish; it was three feet long and very valuable; and this he filled to the brim with gold. Such, among others, were the gifts the king of Armenia received here before his departure, but owing to thieves he lost all or most of them near Calais.

On the same day Sir John Holland, attired in mourning and supported on the arms of the archbishop of Canterbury and the bishop of London, entered the king's presence. Three times, before reaching him, he flung himself to the ground on his knees and arms; finally he rose to his knees and stretched his hands upwards and with tears and wails humbly begged the king for mercy, earnestly entreating him to overlook his rash and thoughtless offence against the king himself and his prohibition, by committing so grave a crime.[1] Some of the bystanders were in tears as they watched. At the third obeisance the two bishops knelt by his side before the king. The latter, who had for some time been

* In the right-hand margin, with no indication of the place for insertion: During this period Bernabò died in prison, but the manner of his death, whether 1385 by cold steel, by starvation, or by poison, is not known.[2]

And in the lower margin: In the course of the year 1385 the king of England sent a special letter to the pope in favour of the canonization of King Edward II, who lies at Gloucester; but he did not get his wish.[3] During the same year the Irish went to some pains in the papal court to secure the canonization of Richard FitzRalph, archbishop of Armagh; the Mendicant friars came out in strong opposition and obstructed them as far as they could.[4] About Christmas-time in the same year the Greeks submitted to the pope; they had hitherto been stubborn in their 1386 disregard of obedience to the apostolic see.[5]

vii. 197; and for the Franciscan attitude to FitzRalph, A. Gwynn, 'Archbishop FitzRalph and the Friars', in Studies, xxvi (1937), 50-67.

[5] A reference to the submission of Manuel II of Thessalonica to Urban VI in 1386, in return for the promise of military aid against the Turks (G. T. Dennis, The Reign of Manuel II Palaeologus in Thessalonica, 1382-1387 (Rome, 1960), pp. 146 ff). (For this reference I am indebted to the Revd. J. Gill, S.J.)

1386 ad preces nobilium qui aderant, et precipue*a* comitum Stafford' et Warwyk' quos pre ceteris dominis J. H. offenderat, eidem perdonavit id quod contra eum inique peregit. Erat autem dictus J. Holand*b* perante cum predictis comitibus finaliter concordatus*c* quid pro anima occisi faceret annuatim;[1] alias nequaquam rogarent pro eo. Desponsavit itaque comes Stafford' antedictus sororem comitis Warwyk', de qua suscepit unum clitonem, quem sepedictus dominus J. Holand', ut est*d* supra relatum, sic nepharie peremit.[2] Non multum vero post rex concessit prefato domino J. Holand' fratri suo omnia que racione dicte transgressionis erant fisco regio forisfacta;[3] et acceptis cartis perdonacionis preparavit se transire cum duce Lancastr' in Hispanniam.

Tractatus. Item decimo die Februarii transierunt Cales' causa tractatus episcopus Cestren', comes Southfolk', dominus Hugo Segrave, et alii ad tractandum cum Francigenis deputati.[4] Et incontinenti post secutus est eos rex Armenie, quem dominus Symon Burle et alii valentes rege volente et expensas ministrante usque Dovorriam honorifice commearunt. Et profecto circumspectus fuit iste rex*e* Armenie et valde astutus, quia talem patentem a rege *f*ante recessum suum*f* optinuit sigillatam quod si pax inter duo regna posset procurari pro perpetuo et firmari mille libras ab eo reciperet annuatim, sin autem mille marcas tantummodo ab eo perciperet annuatim.[5]

Quo in tempore rex quasdam mulieres domine regine compatriotas viris nobilibus suis sumptibus nuptui tradidit. Erat namque rex iste in sui primordio tam liberalis ut si quis

---

a An erasure, covered by a dash, follows.   *b MS. inserts* cum.   *c MS. inserts* et.   *d Interlined.*   *e Interlined.*   *f-f Added in the margin after* rege, *which ends a line.*

---

[1] He had undertaken to found a chantry of 3 chaplains (*Cal. Pat. R., 1385–9*, p. 114; cf. ibid., p. 368).

[2] Hugh de Stafford, 2nd earl of Stafford (1372–86), married Philippa, daughter of Thomas de Beauchamp, 11th earl of Warwick (1315–69). Ralph de Stafford was not the only son of this marriage, but the first-born.

[3] i.e. the lands taken into custody in the aftermath of the slaying, and the goods and chattels forfeited when Holland failed to appear to answer the appeal of felony against him in Nov. 1385. Holland was pardoned on 8 Feb. 1386 and his goods and chattels restored on 17 Mar.; his lands, to the value of 500 marks per annum, were restored on 6 Apr. (*Cal. Pat. R., 1385–9*, pp. 99, 122, 130; and see above, pp. 122 n., 144).

stirred by compassion, at the supplication of the nobles 1386
present, and especially of the earls of Stafford and Warwick,
whom John Holland had offended above all the other lords,
then pardoned the wrong done to himself. Holland had come
to an agreement with the two earls beforehand about what he
would do every year for the soul of the murdered youth;[1]
otherwise they would certainly have made no requests on his
behalf. The earl of Stafford had married the sister of the earl
of Warwick and by her had fathered a single scion, who was
cut off by Sir John Holland in the wicked way described
above.[2] It was not long after this that the king restored to his
brother John Holland everything that his misdeed had
rendered forfeit to the royal exchequer;[3] after receiving his
charters of pardon he prepared to join the duke of Lancaster
in his journey to Spain.

Negotiations. The bishop of Chester, the earl of Suffolk,
Sir Hugh Segrave, and others who had been commissioned to
treat with the French crossed to Calais on 10 February.[4]
After a very brief interval they were followed by the king of
Armenia, who at the desire (and at the expense) of our own
king enjoyed as far as Dover an escort of honour consisting
of Sir Simon Burley and other doughty warriors. This king of
Armenia was unquestionably a very prudent and crafty person: before leaving England he obtained a sealed royal patent
under which if a permanent peace between the two kingdoms
could be achieved and consolidated he was to receive £1,000
a year from King Richard; but if not the yearly payment was
to be 1,000 marks only.[5]

During this period the king at his own expense married
some of the queen's countrywomen to men of rank: in his
early years this king of ours was so open-handed that to make

[4] There also served on this embassy Sir John Devereux, Sir John Clanvow,
Mr. Richard Ronhale, and Roger Elmham, a privy seal clerk. Walter Skirlaw,
bishop of Coventry and Lichfield (*alias* of Chester) and Ronhale set out on the
date given above; the other envoys, a little earlier or a little later. See P.R.O.,
E. 364/19, mm. 68, 68^V, 69^V; ibid., E. 403/511, 8 Feb.; Mirot and Déprez, in
B.E.C., lx, pp. 207-8 (nos. 483-5). For the ensuing, fruitless, negotiations with
the French see below, pp. 164-6, and *Palmer*, pp. 68 ff.

[5] In fact the only stated proviso to Richard II's grant of an annuity of £1,000
per annum to Leo VI of Armenia on 3 Feb. 1386 was that it should cease were
Leo to recover his own kingdom (Rymer, *Foedera*, vii. 494; and see above,
p. 154 n.).

1386 ab eo quicquam rite peciisset ilico sibi concederet, immo quandoque petencium voluntates ipse prevenit et ultra petita sepe conferre solebat; verumptamen tam profuse est sua largitus quod omnia que sue corone pertinuerunt[a] diversis personis hec et illa postulantibus particulatim cum aliis emolumentis fisco regio pertinentibus fere distribuit. Sic enim suis aliis erogatis communitatem de necessitate opprimere est compulsus; unde pauperes super hoc graviter conqueruntur, asserentes se tale onus diu sustinere non posse. Utinam rex disponeret eosdem in aliquo alleviare; et profecto comodum inde non modicum, ut estimo, reportaret.

Denunciata vero morte regis Hungarie heredes masculos non habentis Carolus de Pace, qui filium suum filie regis predicti cogitaverat matrimonialiter copulare, Hungariam celeriter adiit et circa principium mensis Februarii ibi sanus[b] applicuit. Hungari namque filiam dicti regis in eorum reginam solempniter coronabant quinto die mensis predicti; mox Carolus predictus affuit et coronam de capite regine vi abstulit et capiti suo imposuit ac in decretam sibi cameram est confestim ingressus. Hungari vero ipsum a tergo insequentes vulnera gravia ibidem sibi imprimebant, sic quod infra decem dies sequentes diem clausit extremum.[1] Commisit quoque Carolus prelibatus regnum suum Neapolitanum[c] interim cuidam armigero custodiendum, quem Neapolitani eodem die eciam occiderunt. Qui dudum a prefato Carolo fuit missus ad arestandum dominum nostrum papam Urbanum,[d] set ilico manus ejus que summum pontificem tetigit usque ad ejus cubitum aruit, et ita usque ad ejus obitum perduravit.[2] Miro modo egit divina clemencia pro domino nostro papa Urbano, ut cunctis claresceret manifeste quod ipse verus Christi vicarius in terris fuisset: et profecto constat istos a domino papa fore excommunicatos, ideoque credendum est eos turpiori et acerbiori morte tanquam sacrilegos et maleficos interire.

[a] MS. pertinuit.   [b] *Interlined.*   [c] *Added in the margin.*   [d] Hic de papa parum *in the margin in a fifteenth-century hand.*

---

[1] Charles III of Sicily (Charles of Durazzo) died on 27 Feb. 1386, at Vissegrad, in Hungary, 2 months after his usurpation of the throne of Hungary from Mary, daughter and heir of Lewis the Great of Hungary; Lewis died in 1382. For the circumstances of his death, which were not exactly those recounted by the Monk,

any legitimate request of him was to have it immediately 1386
granted; indeed at times he anticipated the wishes of peti-
tioners and he used often to give more than had been asked
for. So lavish was his bounty, however, that all the property
attaching to the Crown, in common with the revenues
belonging to the royal exchequer, was virtually dealt out
piecemeal to various people who presented demands for this
or that. Having thus handed out his own substance to others,
he had perforce to come down on the commons, with the
result that the poor are loud in their complaints and declare
that they cannot go on supporting the burden. If only the
king would arrange matters so as to give them some relief!
He would, I think, reap no small benefit by doing so.

When the death of the king of Hungary without male heirs
was made known, Charles the Peacemaker, who had had
visions of uniting his son in marriage to the king's daughter,
set off in haste for Hungary, where he arrived without mishap about the beginning of February. On 5 February the
Hungarians were in the solemn act of crowning the king's
daughter as their queen when Charles appeared and snatched
the crown from her head and set it on his own, before
making a hurried withdrawal to the room allotted to him.
Here the Hungarians, who had followed hard on his heels,
dealt him wounds so serious that within ten days his life was
over.[1] For the period of his absence Charles had entrusted
his kingdom of Naples to the keeping of a squire who was
killed by the Neapolitans on the very same day. This was the
man who long ago had been sent by Charles to effect the
arrest of our lord Pope Urban, but the hand laid on the
supreme pontiff had instantly withered up to the elbow and
so remained until the owner's dying day.[2] Wonderful indeed
were the workings of God's mercy in favour of our lord Pope
Urban to make it plainly apparent to everybody that he was
Christ's true vicar on earth! Since these two are well known
to have been excommunicated by the pope, it may be
assumed that the death they died, as sacrilegious evildoers,
was all the more ignominious and bitter.

see *Valois*, ii. 118; and Léonard, *Les Angevins de Naples*, p. 476.
    [2] A reference to the arrest of Urban VI by Charles III at Aversa in 1383, for
which see *Valois*, ii. 65–6; see also above, pp. 108–10 and n.

1386   Item decimo die Februarii villa de Calays fere a Francigenis
fuit capta in dolo, set postquam innotuit stipendiariis et aliis
viris existentibus in villa exierunt armati ad hostes, qui in
fugam continuo sunt conversi.

Item xviij°. die Februarii apud Sanctum Paulum London'
publicata fuit quedam cruciata domino duci Lancastr' per
papam con⟨cess⟩a:[a][1] fuit tamen auctoritas hujus cruciate ad
instanciam dicti ducis certis personis sub isto tenore commissa, scilicet dominis episcopis Landavensi,[2] Herefordensi,[3]
et Aquensi,[4] et fratri Waltero Dysse sacre pagine professori
ordinis Carmelitarum,[5] conjunctim et divisim in regnis Anglie,
Castelle et Legionis, Navarr' et Portualie et Arragonie ac in
partibus Vasconie apostolice[b] sedis nunciis ac eorum com-
missariis delegata, et exnunc usque post annum qui in primo[c]
die Junii proximo futuro inchoabitur duratura. Cetera
⟨pap⟩e[d] supra in principio papiri.[6]

Item v°. et vj°. die Marcii erant hastiludia apud Smethefeld'. Item octavo die Marcii dominus noster rex in pleno
consilio in quantum potuit confirmavit et declaravit
dominum ducem Lancastr' verum fore heredem Hispannie,
ac in signum regii honoris illum in consilio supra archi-
episcopos fecit juxta se sedere. Quo in tempore quidam ex
nostris ceperunt naves de nostris inimicis numero xxj. Hoc
anno xxv. die Marcii dux Lancastr' factis suis peregrinacioni-
bus in orientalibus et australibus ac borealibus partibus
Anglie cepit suum iter versus partes occidentales, visitatis-
que inibi locis sacris, divertebat se ad villam de Plummouthe,
ubi ea que sibi fuerant oportuna usque ad ix. diem Julii[7]
expectabat.

Item xxvij°. die Marcii redierunt sine pacis effectu illi
qui dudum Cales' ad tractandum de pace cum Francigenis

---

[a] Part of this word is obliterated.   [b] MS. apostolicis.   [c] MS. prima.
[d] The reading of this word is uncertain.

[1] Urban VI's bulls authorizing an English crusade against the Trastamaran
rulers of Castile were issued in 1382, possibly on the same day, 15 May, as
Dignum censemus (for which see above, p. 30 n.), in favour of the bishop of
Norwich; they do not survive but are mentioned in the chancellor's speech at the
parliament of Oct. 1382 (R.P., iii. 134; Perroy, p. 223 and n.). The bull referred
to by the Monk was one of those issued on 21 Mar. and 8 Apr. 1383, appointing
Lancaster captain of the crusade against Castile and granting the full crusading
indulgences and privileges of Innocent III's decretal Ad liberandam to those

On 10 February Calais nearly fell to a French ruse, but as 1386 soon as the news reached the mercenaries and the others in the town they made an armed sortie against the enemy, who at once turned tail.

On 18 February the crusade granted to the duke of Lancaster by the pope was made public at St. Paul's, London.[1] Power to grant indulgences in respect of this crusade was at the duke's instance conferred on named persons in these terms: it was 'delegated to the bishops of Llandaff,[2] Hereford,[3] and Dax,[4] and to Brother Walter Diss, D.D., of the Carmelite Order,[5] jointly and severally nuncios of the apostolic see in the kingdoms of England, of Castile and León, of Navarre, of Portugal, and of Aragon, and in the parts of Gascony, or to their commissaries, to endure from now until the end of the year beginning on the first day of June next' [1 June 1386]. Other references to the pope appear above on the recto.[6]

On 5 and 6 March there was jousting at Smithfield. At a full council on 8 March the king made a declaration confirming, so far as it lay with him to do so, that the duke of Lancaster was the true heir of Spain, and in token of the duke's royal dignity caused him to be seated at the council table above the archbishops and next to himself. During this period some of our countrymen captured enemy ships to a total of twenty-one. On 25 March this year the duke of Lancaster, after pilgrimages in the east, south, and north of England, set out for the west and after visits to holy places in the area fetched up at Plymouth, where he waited until 9 July[7] for conditions favourable to his success.

The envoys who had been sent some time earlier to Calais for peace talks with the French returned on 27 March with

accompanying him (*Cal. Papal Letters*, iv (1362-1404), pp. 264-5; Rymer, *Foedera*, vii. 507-8). For the preaching of the crusade, see *Perroy*, p. 235. Evidently the Monk had a copy of Urban VI's bull empowering nuncios to grant the indulgences and privileges of the crusade; cf. *Registrum Johannis Gilbert, Episcopi Herefordensis, A.D., 1375–1389*, ed. J. H. Parry (Canterbury and York Soc., 1915), pp. 99–101.

[2] William de Bottlesham, bishop of Llandaff, 1385-9.

[3] John Gilbert, bishop of Hereford, 1375-89.

[4] Juan Gutiérrez, Lancaster's Castilian secretary.   [5] Lancaster's confessor.

[6] See above, p. 158 (= MS., p. 153).   [7] So too Knighton, *Chronicon*, ii. 207.

1386 erant transmissi.[1] Et quia vulgaris fama se protunc habebat quod rex Francorum disposuit Calesiam obsidere, igitur rex Anglorum illam munivit tam victualium copia quam proborum milicia in ista estate,[2] sic quod rex Francorum illam aggredi non presumpsit. Ordinatum est hoc anno per consilium regis et ejus expensis ut per totam estatem quidam de familia regis, scilicet superhabundantes in suo hospicio, transirent Sandycum et custodirent loca maritima ibidem ab inimicorum invasione, quorum aggressione incole et patria dampnum incurrerent forsitan et jacturam nisi defensio hujusmodi apponeretur.[3]

[a]"Richard[4] par la grace de Dieu roy Dengleterre et de Fraunce et seignur Dirland a touz ceux qe cestes lettres verront ou orrount saluz. Nous avons certeinement conceux de la grevouse compleinte dez[b] seignurs et comunes de nostre roialme en ceste present parlement assemblez qe noz profites, rentes, et[c] revenuz de nostre dit[d] roialme par singuler et noun suffisaunte conseille et mal governaille sibien dascuns nadgeirs noz grandes officeres come de diverses autres persones esteantz entour nostre persone sont en tant destruitz[e] et[d] degastez et[d] esloignez, donez, grantez, alienez, destruitz et malment despenduz qe nous sumes tant empoverez, voides et nuez de tresor et davoir et la substance de nostre corone entant amenuz et destruit[f] qe lestat de nous et de nostre hostelle ne poet honorablement estre sustenuz come affiert ne lez guerres qe se abundent tout environs nostre roialme de jour en autre meintenuz ne governez sanz tresgrandes et outragiouses oppressions et importables charges de nostre dit roialme[g] et auxint qe les bons leys, estatutz et custumes de nostre dit roialme as queux nous sumes estreintz[h] et obligez de tenir et garder ne sont nent estee duement tenuz ne execut⟨e⟩z ne plein[a] / justice ne droitz[i] faitz a nostre dit poeple, paront plusours desheretesons et autres tresgrandez meschiefs et damages sont avenuz, si bien a nous come a nostre dit poeple et a tout nostre[j] roialme; et nous a lonour de Deu et pur le[k] bien de nous et [de nostre[l] dit roialme et pur le[m] quiete et relevacion de nostre dit poeple, qont este grandement chargez en plusours maneres devant ces hoeures, veullantz ove la grace de Dieu contre tielx meschiefs

p. 155

[a–a] W; in MS. on the lost leaf.   [b] S.R. de.   [c] S.R.; W om.   [d] S.R. om.
[e] W destruitz; recte sustretz, as in S.R., giving the sense 'withdrawn'.   [f] W destrut; S.R. descreuz.   [g] S.R. poeple.   [h] S.R. astrictz.   [i] W and S.R. droit.   [j] W inserts dit.   [k] S.R. la.   [l–l] W and S.R.; MS. om.   [m] W la.

[1] For this embassy see above, p. 160 and n.
[2] For some of the details see P.R.O., E. 403/511, 3 Apr.; ibid., 512/5 May; see also Walsingham, *Hist. Ang.*, ii. 144.
[3] A long hiatus, occasioned by the loss of a leaf of the MS., occurs here; see above, p. xvii n.

peace unachieved.[1] In consequence of popular rumours at 13
this time that the French king had plans to besiege Calais,
the king of England during this summer increased the town's
strength by providing stocks of food as well as sound fighting
men;[2] with the result that the French king did not venture
on an attack. Orders were given this year by the king's
council that certain members of his establishment, that is
those who were superfluous to the needs of the household,
should go to Sandwich and, at the king's expense, devote the
whole summer to guarding the neighbouring coastal districts
against assault by the enemy, whose attacks might possibly
inflict loss and damage on the area and its inhabitants unless
some such protection were afforded.[3]

Richard[4] by the grace of God king of England and of France and
lord of Ireland, to all those who shall see or hear these letters, greeting.
We have been apprised by the grievous complaint of the lords and commons of our realm assembled in this present parliament that our profits,
rents, and revenues of our said realm, by singular and insufficient
counsel and evil governance as well as of some of our late great officers
as of diverse other persons being about our person, are so much brought
low and wasted and eloigned, given, granted, alienated, brought low,
and evilly expended that we are so much impoverished, voided, and
denuded of treasure and goods and the substance of our crown so much
diminished and brought low that the estate of ourselves and of our
household cannot be honourably sustained as befits nor the wars which
daily abound on every side of our realm be maintained nor governed
without very great and outrageous oppressions and insupportable
charges of our said realm and also that the good laws, statutes, and
customs of our said realm which we are constrained and bound to hold
and keep are not and have not been duly kept or executed, nor has
full justice nor right been done to our said people, whereby many
disherisons and other very great mischiefs and damages have befallen
both us and our said people and all our realm; and we, to the honour of
God and for the weal of ourselves and our said realm and for the quiet
and relief of our said people, who have heretofore been greatly burdened in several ways, wishing with God's grace to provide a good and

[4] There follow the letters patent of 19 Nov. 1386 containing the commission
of appointment of the continual council forced upon Richard II in the parliament
which met at Westminster on 1 Oct. 1386. The Monk's text is that recited in the
pardons granted at the end of the Merciless Parliament. See *S.R.*, ii. 44-6, and
Cal. Pat. R., *1385-9*, p. 244; and for this, the so-called 'Wonderful Parliament',
R.P., iii. 215-24, and Knighton, *Chronicon*, ii. 215-33. The text has been collated with that in *S.R.* and with W.A.M., 12227 (= *W*), for which see above,
pp. xlviii-li.

1386 mettre bone et due remedie, si avons de nostre franche volunte et
^aal requeste^a des seignurs et comunes suisditz ordeignez^b et assignez^c
noz grandez officeres, cest assavoir noz chaunceller, tresorer et gardein
de nostre prive seal, tielx come nous tenons bones, foialx^d et sufficiantz
pur honour et profit de nous et de nostre dit roialme,[1] et outre ceo de
nostre auctorite roiale, certeine science, bone gre et franche volunte et
par avys et^e assent de^f prelatz, seignurs et comunes suisditz^c en plein
parlement en ayde de^g bone governance de nostre roialme et bone
et due execucion de noz ditz leies^h et en relevement del estat de nous
et de nostre poeple en temps avenir, confiantz pleinement del bone
avisement, sen et discrecion de les honurables pieres en Dieu William
ercevesqe de Cantebires,[2] Alisandre ercevesqe Deverwyk',[3] noz tres-
chers uncles Esmon duc Deverwyk', Thomas duc de Gloucestre, les
honurables pieres en Dieu William evesqe de Wyncestre,[4] Thomas
evesqe Dexcestre[5] et Nichol abbe de Waltham,[6] noz chers et foialx
Richard count Darundell', Johan seignurⁱ de Coboham,[7] Richard
Lescrop'[8] et Johan Deverouse,[9] yceux avons ordeignez, assignez et
deputez, ordeignons, assignons et^j deputons, destre de nostre grande^k
conseil par un an entier proschein apres la date de cestes, a surveier
et examiner ovesqe noz ditz grandez officeres si bien lestat et governale
de nostre hostell' et de touz noz courtz, lieux et places come lestat
et governaille de tuit nostre roialme et de touz noz officeres et ministres
de qeconqe estat, degree ou condicion qils soient, si bien deinz nostre
houstell' come dehors, et denquerrer et^j de prendre^l enformacion par
touz les voies qe mielx lour semblera de toutes les rentes, revenuz et^j
profitz qe^m nous appartient et sont duez et duissent appartiner et estre
duez,ⁿ si bien deinz nostre roialme come dehors en qeconqe manere
ou condicion,^o et de touz ^pmaneres des^p douns, grantez, alienacions et
confirmacions par nous faitz de terrez, tenementz, rentes, annuites,
profitz, revenuz, gardez, mariagez, eschetez, forfaitures, franchises,
libertes, voidanz des ^qerchevescies, eveschies,^q abbeyes^r priories, fermes
des^s maisons et possessions des alieinz et de^t touz autres possessions,
sommes^u de deniers, bienz et chateulx et de^v autres choses qeconqes
et as queux personez et par quele cause et coment et en quele manere
et nomement^w de ceux personez qe lont prise sanz desert et auxint de^t
revenuz et profitz qeconqes si bien de nostre dit roialme come de^v

^{a-a} W. as requestes.   ^b S.R. inserts faitz.   ^c MS. inserts et.   ^d W
and S.R. loialx.   ^e W inserts par.   ^f W dez.   ^g W e.   ^h S.R.;
MS. and W lieges.   ⁱ W and S.R. sire.   ^j W and S.R.; MS. om.   ^k W
and S.R. insert et continuel.   ^l W (for de prendre) denprendre.   ^m S.R.
qa.   ⁿ W om.   ^o S.R. inserts qil soit.   ^{p-p} W autres de; S.R. maneres
de.   ^{q-q} W ercevesqeez evesqez; S.R. ercevesches, evesches.   ^r W and S.R.
insert et.   ^s S.R. de.   ^t W dez; S.R. des.   ^u W and S.R.; MS. commes.
^v W om.   ^w W; MS. and S.R. mesment.

---

[1] On 24 Oct. Thomas Arundel had been appointed chancellor; John Gilbert,
treasurer; and John Waltham, keeper of the privy seal.

[2] William Courtenay.   [3] Alexander Nevill.   [4] William of Wykeham.

due remedy against such mischiefs, have of our free will and at the 1386
request of the lord and commons abovesaid ordained, and assigned such
persons for our great officers (that is to say our chancellor, our
treasurer, and the keeper of our privy seal) as we hold good, faithful,
and sufficient for the honour and profit of us and of our said realm.[1]
And moreover of our royal authority and sure knowledge and of our
own accord and free will, and with the advice and consent of the prelates, lords, and commons abovesaid in full parliament, in furtherance
of the good government of our realm and the proper and due execution
of our said laws and in relief of the estate of ourselves and our people
in time to come, having full confidence in the good judgement, knowledge, and discretion of the honourable fathers in God William archbishop of Canterbury,[2] Alexander archbishop of York;[3] our most dear
uncles Edmund duke of York and Thomas duke of Gloucester; the
honourable fathers in God William bishop of Winchester,[4] Thomas
bishop of Exeter[5] and Nicholas abbot of Waltham;[6] our trusty and
beloved Richard earl of Arundel, John, Lord Cobham,[7] Richard
Scrope[8] and John Devereux,[9] have ordained, assigned, and deputed
and do ordain, assign, and depute them to be of our great council
for one whole year next after the date hereof, to survey and examine
with our said great officers both the estate and government of our
household, with all our courts, places, and offices, and the estate and
government of all our realm and of all our officers and ministers, of
whatsoever estate, degree, or condition they may be, as well within our
household as without; and to inquire and take information by all such
ways as they shall deem best concerning all the rents, revenues, and
profits which belong and are due and ought to belong and be due
to us as well within our realm as without in whatsoever manner or
condition; and concerning all manner of gifts, grants, alienations
and confirmations made by us of lands, tenements, rents, annuities,
profits, revenues, wardships, marriages, escheats, forfeitures, franchises,
liberties, voidances of archbishoprics, bishoprics, abbeys, priories,
farms of houses, and possessions of alien religious; and of all other
possessions, sums of money, goods and chattels, and other things
whatsoever; and to what persons and for what reason and how and
in what way; and particularly concerning those persons that have
received them without desert; and also concerning all revenues and
profits whatsoever both of our said realm and of our lands, lordships,

[5] Thomas Brantingham.

[6] Nicholas Morice. The king was patron of Waltham Abbey.

[7] John de Cobham, 3rd Baron Cobham (d. 1408), for whom see *D.N.B.*, iv.
611-12.

[8] Sir Richard Scrope, 1st baron Scrope of Bolton (d. 1403). This experienced
soldier, councillor, and minister was included in the commission despite his
spirited defence of Michael de la Pole, his brother-in-law, in this parliament (*R.P.*,
iii. 217; G. Holmes, *The Good Parliament* (Oxford, 1975), pp. 64-5).

[9] For whom see above, p. 116 and n.

1386 terres, seignuries, citees, villes, chastelx, forteresces et qeconqes noz autres possessions si bien de cea la mere come de la et de^a profitz et^b emolumentz de noz ^{c}monoiez et billions^c et de la prise de prisoneres, villez et lieux, niefs, carrekes, biens, et ranseons de guerre par^d terre et par mere et de benefices et autres possessions de cardinalx rebealx et touz autres alieinz et auxint des aportes de monoie^e hors de nostre roialme par lez collectours du^f pape, procuratours des^g cardinalx, Lombardes et autres persones qeconqes, si bien alieinz come denseins, et de^h emolumentz et^b profitz provenantz et surdantz des^f custumes et subsides des leyns, quirs et pealx lanutz et de les petit^i custumez et autres subsidez de draps, vyns et touz autres merchandises ^{j}et dismes, quinsimes et touz^j autres subsides et charges grantez par la^k clergie et la comune et auxint de lez resceutes, profitz et paiement del hamper^l de nostre chauncellarie et de qeconqes noz autres resceutez du^m temps de nostre corounement tancqencea et des^n fees, gages et re-wardez des officeres et ministres greindres et meindres et auxint dez annuitez et autres ^{o}rewardez, grantes et douns faitz^o a ascunes per-sones^p par nous et^q noz piere et aiel en fee ou a terme de vie ou en ascune autre manere et si gre ou paiement lour ent soit fait et par queux et en quele manere et come bien ils ont relessez ou donez as officeres et autres pur avoir lour paiement^r et as queux persones, coment et en quele manere et des^n terres et^s tenementz, rentes,^{t} revenuz et^u for-faitures, bargeinez et^t venduz a prejudice et damage de nous et de nostre coroune et par queux et as queux et coment et en quele manere et de vent et^v bargaine de tailles et patentz pur singuler profit si bien en temps de^w nostre dit aiel comme en nostre temps et coment et par queux^x persones et ensement de toutz les joyalx et^y biens qe fuerent^z nostre dit aiel a^{aa} temps de son moriant et queux et de quele pris ou value et ou ils sont devenuz et^w coment et en quele manere et de^{bb} chevesances^1 ascunement faitz a nostre oeps et^w par qeconqes persones et de toutz les perdez et damages qe nous avons eu et sustenez^{cc} par ycelles et par queux persones et coment et en quele manere et de chartres de pardones^{dd} generalx et especialx et auxint de les sommes,^{ee} paiementz et manere de^{ff} despensez si bien de nostre dit houstell' come pur la salvacion et defense de noz roialme,^{gg} terrez, seignuriez, villes, chastelx, forteresces et autres lieux de cea la mere et de la ^{hh}faitz et resceuz^{hh} par qeconqes persones si bien soldiours come autres et par qeconqe voie et coment et en quele manere, et come bien ils ont donez pur avoir lour paiementz et des^{ii} concellementz de noz

---

^{a} W inserts lez. ^{b} W and S.R.; MS. om. $^{c-c}$ W moines. ^{d} W de. ^{e} W mones; S.R. for the last two words, du monoie. ^{f} S.R. de. ^{g} W and S.R. de. ^{h} S.R. des. ^{i} W and S.R. petites. $^{j-j}$ W et de dismes et quinzismes et de touz; S.R. et des dismes et quinzismes et touz. ^{k} S.R. le. ^{l} W and S.R. hanaper. ^{m} W and S.R. de. ^{n} S.R. de. $^{o-o}$ MS. and W (W regardes for rewardez); S.R. rewardes et douns grauntez et faitz. ^{p} W (for the last three words) as ascuns; S.R. as ascunes persones. ^{q} S.R. inserts par. ^{r} S.R. paiementz. ^{s} W and S.R. om. ^{t} W om. ^{u} W and S.R.; MS. om. ^{v} W om; S.R. ou. ^{w} S.R. om. ^{x} S.R. quelles. ^{y} W

cities, towns, castles, fortresses, and our other possessions whatsoever, 1386
both on this side of the sea and beyond it, and concerning the profits
and emoluments of our coinage and bullion; and concerning the taking
of prisoners, towns, and places, ships, carracks, goods, and ransoms of
war by land and sea; and concerning benefices and other possessions of
rebel cardinals and all other aliens; and also concerning the carrying of
moneys out of our realm by the collectors of the pope, the proctors of
cardinals, Lombards, and all other persons whatsoever, aliens as well as
denizens; and concerning the emoluments and profits proceeding and
arising from the customs and subsidies upon wool, hides, and woolfells,
and from the petty customs and other subsidies on cloths, wines, and
all other merchandise; and concerning tenths, fifteenths, and all other
subsidies and charges granted by the clergy and the commons; and also
concerning the receipts, profits, and payment[s] of the hanaper of our
chancery; and concerning all our other receipts whatsoever from the
time of our coronation until now; and concerning the fees, wages, and
rewards of officers and ministers, greater and lesser; and also concerning
the annuities and other rewards, grants, and gifts made to any persons
by us, our father, and grandfather, in fee or for term of life or in any
other manner, and whether satisfaction or payment thereof has been
made to them and by whom and in what manner, and how much they
have conceded or given to officers and others to have their payments,
and to what persons, how, and in what manner; and concerning lands
and tenements, rents, revenues, and forfeitures bargained and sold to
the prejudice and damage of ourselves and of our crown, and by whom
and to whom and how and in what manner; and concerning the sale
and bargain of tallies and patents for personal profit both in our said
grandfather's time and our own, and how and by what persons; and likewise concerning all the jewels and goods which were of our said grandfather at the time of his death, what these were and of what price or
value and what has become of them and how and in what manner; and
concerning chevisances[1] in any way made for our use by any persons
whatsoever, and concerning all the losses and damage which we have
had and sustained in consequence, and through what persons and how
and in what manner; and concerning charters of pardon, general and
special; and also concerning the totals, the payments, and the manner
of the expenses (both of our said household and for the safety and
defence of our realm, lands, lordships, towns, castles, fortresses, and
other places on this side of the sea and beyond it) which have been
incurred and received by any persons, soldiers as well as others, and by
any kind of way, and how and in what manner, and how much they have
given to obtain their payments; and concerning concealments of our

and S.R.; MS. om.   [z] *W and S.R. insert* a,   [aa] *W* en.   [bb] *W and S.R.*
insert toutes.   [cc] *S.R.* sustenu.   [dd] *S.R.* pardon.   [ee] *W and S.R.*
insert et.   [ff] *W* dez.   [gg] *W om.*   [hh–hh] *W and S.R. (S.R.* receux*); MS.*
fait resceutes.   [ii] *S.R.* de.

[1] Here in the sense of loans at interest.

1386 [a]droitz et[a] profitz et par queux et[b] coment et en quele manere et des[c] mayntenours et empernours des querelles et dustres[d1] denquestes et de officeres et[e] ministres faitz par brocage [f]et de lour brocours et[g] de ceux qont prise la[h] brocage[f] et[g] coment et en quele manere, et de touz les defautez et mesprisones faitz sibien en nostre dit[g] houstel et en[i] noz autres courtes places et lieux suisditz come en touz autres lieux deinz nostre[j] roialme par qeconqes persones[g] paront les profitz de nous et de nostre coroune ont estee empires et amenusez ou la comune leye est[i] destourbe et[k] delaye ou [l]autrement damagez[l] a nous[g] avenuz, donantz et comettans par ycestes de nostre auctorite[m] par avys et

p. 156 assent de / suisditz a noz ditz conseillers et sys de eux et a noz grandez officeres avantditz plein poair et auctorite generale et especial dentrer nostre dit hostell' et touz les [n]offices dycell[n] et touz noz autres courtez, places [o]et lieux[o] tant dez[p] foitz come lour plerra et de fair venir devant eux ou et qant lour plerra [q]rolles et recordes[q] et autres munimentz et evidencez tielx come lour semblera et touz les defautez, gastes et excesses trovez [r]en dit[r] hostell' et auxint [s]touz defautes[s] et mesprisones trovez en lez autres courtz et[t] places, lieux, officeres et ministres suisditz et en touz lez autres articles et pointz desuis nomez et chescun dycelles [u]et auxint[u] touz autres defautes, mesprisones et[t] excesses, fauximes, desceites,[v] extorsions, oppressions, damages et grevances faitez en prejudice, damage et descresce de nous et[w] nostre coroune et[x] lestat de nostre dit[y] roialme en general ou en special nient expressez ne[z] specefiez paramont amendre et[aa] corriger, reparer,[bb] redresser, reformer et mettre en bone et due estat et establissement[cc] et auxint doier et resceiver touz manerez de[dd] pleintz et querellez de touz noz lieges qi vorront[ee] suir et se pleindre sibien pur nous come pur lour mesme[ff] devant [gg]noz ditz officeres et conseillers[gg] de touz manerez de[hh] duressez, oppressions, injurez, tortz et mesprisones queux ne purront bonement estre[y] amendez ne terminez par la cours[ii] de[jj] comune ley de la terre avant use et de ent doner[kk] et faire [ll]due et bone[ll] remede et recoverer[mm] si bien pur nous come pur[nn] noz liegez suisditz; et[oo] a [pp]touz les chosez avantditz et[pp] chescun deux pleinement descuter et finalment[qq] terminer et de ent faire plein execucion solonc ceo qe lour semblera mielx pur lonour et profitz de nous et de nostre estat et reintegracion dez[rr] droitz et profitz de nostre dit coroune et meillour governance [ss]del pais et leys[ss] de nostre terre

---

[a-a] W om.; S.R. droitures et.   [b] W and S.R. om.   [c] S.R. de.
[d] W du restes.   [e] W and S.R.; MS. om.   [f-f] Written in the lower margin but marked for insertion at this point.   [g] W om.   [h] W le; S.R. om.
[i] S.R. om.   [j] W inserts dit.   [k] S.R. ou.   [l-l] S.R. autre damage.   [m] W and S.R. insert et.   [n-n] S.R.; W offices dycell'; MS. officeres dycellez.   [o-o] MS. lieux et; W and S.R. et lieux a.   [p] W and S.R. de.   [q-q] W; MS. rolles et cordes; S.R. rolles, recordes.   [r-r] W en le dit; S.R. el dit.   [s-s] W touz lez defautes; S.R. toutes autres defautes.   [t] S.R. om.   [u-u] W and S.R.; MS. auxint et.   [v] W and S.R.; MS. desertes.   [w] W and S.R. insert de.
[x] W and S.R.; MS. om.   [y] W om.   [z] W ou.   [aa] W and S.R. om.   [bb] S.R.; MS. repaier; W repaier.   [cc] W and S.R.; MS. establement.   [dd] W dez;

rights and profits, and by whom, how, and in what manner; and con- 1386
cerning maintainers and undertakers of quarrels and ousters[1] of
inquests; and concerning officers and ministers made by bribery and
those who have given and those who have accepted bribes, and how and
in what manner; and concerning all defaults and misprisions committed
both in our said household, our other courts, offices, and places abovesaid, and in all other places within our realm by any persons whatsoever,
whereby the profits of ourselves and of our crown have been impaired
and diminished or the common law has been disturbed and delayed or
damage has otherwise befallen us; giving and committing by these
presents, of our authority by the advice and assent abovesaid, to our
said councillors and six of them and to our great officers aforesaid full
power and authority general and special, to enter our said household
and all the offices thereof and all our other courts, offices, and places
as often as they please; and to cause to be brought before them where
and when they please, such rolls, records, and other muniments and
evidences as they think fit; and to amend, and correct, repair, redress,
reform, and put into good and due order and settled condition all the
defaults, waste, and excesses found in the said household and also all
the defaults and misprisions found in the other courts, offices and
places, officers, and ministers abovesaid and in all the other articles and
points above named and each of them, and also all other defaults,
misprisions, and excesses, falsities, deceits, extortions, oppressions,
damages, and grievances committed to the prejudice, damage, and
diminution of ourselves and our Crown and the estate of our said realm
in general or in particular (though not above expressed or specified);
and also to hear and receive all manner of complaints and quarrels of
all our lieges who wish to sue and complain, both for us and for themselves, before our said officers and councillors about all manner of acts
of duress and oppression, injuries, wrongs, and misprisions which
cannot well be amended or determined by the course of the common
law of the land heretofore in use, and to provide and make for them
good and due remedy and recovery both for us and for our lieges
abovesaid; and fully to discuss and finally to determine all the matters
aforesaid and each of them, and to do full execution thereof according
to what seems best to them for the honour and profit of ourselves and
of our estate and the re-establishment of the rights and profits of our
said crown, the better governance of the peace and laws of our land,

---

S.R. des. [ee] W verront. [ff] S.R. mesmes. [gg-gg] W noz conseillers
et officeres; S.R. noz ditz conseillers et officers. MS. and W insert et after this
phrase. [hh] Interlined. [ii] MS. and W court. [jj] W and S.R. insert la.
[kk] MS. donerez; S.R. donir; W don'. [ll-ll] W and S.R. bone et due. [mm] W recorder; S.R. recoverir. [nn] MS. and W par. [oo] MS. om. [pp] W om.
[qq] W finablement. [rr] S.R. de. [ss-ss] W de la pais leys; S.R. de la paix
et leis.

---

[1] On 'oust' see M. D. Legge, 'Ouster-le-Mer', in Studies in Romance Philology
and French Literature presented to John Orr (Manchester, 1953), pp. 164–5.

1386 et relevement de nostre dit poeple, veullantz auxint qe si diversite ou variance doppinion*a* surde ou aviegne entre noz ditz conseillers et officeres qe le*b* juggement et opinion de la greindre partie *c*eit force*c* et tiegne lieux, comandantz et chargeantz a touz*d* prelates, duks, countz, barons, seneschalles,*e* tresorer*f*, conterollour et touz autres officeres de nostre hostell', justicez de lun banc et de lautre et autres noz justicez qeconqes, barons et chamberleins de lescheqer,*f* viscontz et*g* eschetours, mairs,*h* baillifs et *i*touz noz autres*i* officeres, ministres et lieges qeconqes qe*j* a noz ditz conseillers et officeres en le*k* manere avantdit soient entendantz; obeiantz, conseilantz*l* et eidantz si sovent et par manere come noz ditz conseillers et officeres lour ferront assavoir *m*de par nous.*m* En tesmoignance de quele chose etc.*n* Donez souz nostre grant seal a Wymoustre*o* le xix. jour de Novembre 1an de nostre reigne disme.*p*

Et pro majoris firmitatis gracia in pleno parliamento super hoc editum est statutum cujus tenor sequitur.[1]

Sur quoi nostre*q* seignur le roi voillant qe les correccions et redressez des*r* defautez et mesprisones desuisditz puissent estre pur son profit et pur le profit de son*s* roialme avantdit*t* en la fourme desuisdit mys en due execucion sanz estre enfreint*u* ou destourbez par ascuny de lassent de*v* seignurs et de*w* cominalte*x* de son dit roialme en cest present parlement ad ordeigne et establie qe chescun de ses lieges greindre et meindre, de quel estat ou condicion qil*y* soit soit*r* entendant et obeisant en qant qe toche les articles suisditz et chescun dependance dycelle a*z* les avantditz conseillers et officeres en la fourme suisditz et qe chescun qe serra ajugge*aa* devant eux*bb* come convict dascun des defautes ou mesprisones suisditz pregne et resceive*cc* sanz debate faire tiel correccion come luy serra*dd* par les conseillers et officeres avantditz en la fourme desuisditz ajugge et qe nulle persone de quele estat*ee* ou condicion qil soit, greindre ou meindre, ne donne a nostre dit*ff* seignur le roi en*gg* prive ne en apert conseill' excitacion ou mocion paront qe*hh* nostre seignur le roi repelle lour poair deinz le temps suisditz en ascun point ou face riens contrarie*ii* de son dit grant ou dascunez*jj* des articles suisditz, et si ascun persone, greindre ou meindre, de quel

---

a W dez opinions.   *b* W la.   *c-c* MS. ert forte.   *d* W inserts lez.   *e* S.R. seneschall.   *f* W inserts et.   *g* W and S.R. om.   *h* S.R. maire.   *i-i* S.R. toutz autres noz.   *j* W om.   *k* W and S.R. la.   *l* W om.   *m-m* W deparavant.   *n* S.R. om. but inserts Nous avons fait faire cestes noz lettres patentz.   *o* W and S.R. Westm'.   *p* W inserts etc.   *q* W and S.R. insert dit.   *r* W and S.R.; MS. om.   *s* S.R. inserts dit.   *t* S.R. om.   *u* S.R. enfreintz.   *v* W dez; S.R. des.   *w* W and S.R. insert la.   *x* W also cominalte.   *y* W and S.R.; MS. qils.   *z* S.R. as.   *aa* MS. a jugge.   *bb* W om.   *cc* W and S.R.; MS. resteure.   *dd* W and S.R.; MS. om.   *ee* W and S.R. insert nacion.   *ff* W om.   *gg* W nen.   *hh* W om.   *ii* W acontraire; S.R. a contraire.   *jj* W and S.R. dascun.

and the relief of our said people. Our will, moreover, is that if differ- 1386
ence or variance of opinion arise or occur amongst our said councillors
and officers, the judgement and opinion of the majority shall have force
and hold place. And we command and charge all prelates, dukes, earls,
barons, and stewards, the treasurer, comptroller, and all the other
officers of our household, the justices of both benches and all our other
justices whatsoever, the barons and chamberlains of the exchequer,
sheriffs and escheators, mayors, bailiffs, and all our other officers,
ministers, and lieges whatsoever to be to our said councillors and
officers in the manner aforesaid attentive, obedient, counselling, and
assisting, so often and in such manner as our said councillors and
officers shall give them warning on our behalf. In witness whereof etc.
Given under our great seal at Westminster the 19th. day of November
in the tenth year of our reign.

In order to give greater strength to these provisions, there
was now enacted in full parliament the statute of which the
following is the tenor:[1]

Whereupon our lord the king, wishing the amendment and redress
of the defaults and misprisions abovesaid to be, for his profit and for
the profit of his realm aforesaid in the form aforesaid, put in due execution without being infringed or disturbed by anyone, with the assent
of the lords and of the commons of his said realm in this present parliament has ordained and established that every one of his lieges, greater
or less, of whatsoever estate or condition he may be, shall be attentive
and obedient in whatever touches the articles abovesaid and every
appurtenance of the same to the aforesaid councillors and officers in
the form abovesaid; and that every person that shall be adjudged before
them to be convicted of any of the defaults or misprisions abovesaid
shall take and receive, without dispute, such correction as shall be
awarded to him by the councillors and officers aforesaid in the form
abovesaid; and that no person, of whatsoever estate or condition he
may be, greater or less, shall give to our said lord the king, in private
or openly, counsel, exhortation, or impulse whereby our lord the king
should revoke their power within the time abovesaid in any particular
or should do anything contrary to his said grant or to any of the articles
abovesaid; and if any person, greater or less, of whatsoever estate or

[1] There follows the 2nd part of the statute in which the commission of
appointment of the continual council first announced in the letters patent of 19
Nov. 1386 was enacted before the termination of parliament; the letters patent
had the status of an ordinance. (The 1st part, omitted by the Monk, rehearsed
the letters patent.) See *S.R.*, ii. 42-3, and, on the significance of the re-enactment
of the ordinance as a statute, D. Clementi, 'Richard II's ninth question to the
judges', in *E.H.R.*, lxxxvi (1971), 101-2.

1386 ^{a}estat qil soit ou condicion^a face encontre^b la ordinance et establis-
mentz suisditz ou procure ou face chose qeconqe en ascune manere
paront les ditz conseillers ^{c}et officeres^c soient destourbez en ascun
point sur lexcercice de lour poair avantdit ou qe excite ou procure
nostre dit seignur le roi ^{d}a faire^d ou^e comander chose qeconqe paront
le poair des ditz conseillers et^f officeres ou lexecucion de lour jugge-
mentz^g et agardez ^{h}a faire^h en ycelles soit defait en ascun point et ceo
soit duement provee par bonez et verraies tesmoignes qe soient notoire-
ment de bone fame et condicion, nient suspectz, covenablement
examinez devant le roi et les^i conseillers et officeres desuisditz, prisez
as^j eux ascuns des justices de lun banc ou de lautre ou autres sagez
apris de la ley tielx come plerra as ditz conseillers et officeres, eit
tiel penance cest assavoir al primere foitz qil serra issint convict forfaite
touz ses biens et chateux au roi et ^{k}nient moins^k soit emprisone al
volunte le roi et si ascune tiel persone soit duement atteint en la fourme
suisdit de conseill', excitacion ou mocion done au roi defaire la^l
contraire de son dit^i grant come desuis est dit ^{m}tout ne face le roy
riens par tiel conseill,' excitacion ou mocion unquore il avera tiel
penance come desuis est dit^m et sil aviengne (qe Dieux defende) qil se
porte en apres qil soit autre foithe atteint come desus dascuns des
defautez ou mesprisones avantditz, adonqes eit le^n dit persone al
seconde foitz issint convict ou atteint la penance de vie et de membre,[1]
sauvez touz foitz^o dignite pontifical et privilege de seinte esglise et
clerical en touz les choses avantditz et qe cest estatut tiegne force et
effect durant la dit commission tantsoulement.

Istis rite peractis et soluto parliamento[2] unusquisque ad
propria repedavit.

Item^p xxix. die Novembris obiit frater Nicholaus Litlyng-
ton' abbas Westmon', et xvij. die Decembris fuit sepultus.
Interim dominus rex misit ter priori et conventui pro fratre
Johanne Lakyngheth' ut ejus personam sui contemplacione
haberent merito commendatam. Igitur xxj. die Decembris
celebrata eleccione electus est per viam compromissi^q frater
Willelmus Colchestre archidiaconus dicti monasterii in
p. 157 abbatem. Quo audito rex / indignatus quasi per aliquot
tempus distulit illum admittere, set mediantibus amicis

$^{a-a}$ W and S.R. estat ou condicion qil soit. ^{b} MS. econtre. $^{c-c}$ S.R. om.
$^{d-d}$ W and S.R.; MS. affaire. ^{e} W inserts a. ^{f} W ou. ^{g} W and S.R.;
MS. juggement. $^{h-h}$ From S.R.; MS. affaire; W faire. ^{i} W om.
^{j} W and S.R. a. $^{k-k}$ W nientmeyns; S.R. nientmeins. ^{l} W and S.R. le.
$^{m-m}$ From W and (omitting the last two words) S.R.; MS. om. ^{n} S.R. la.
^{o} W inserts la. ^{p} Abbas Westm' in the margin opposite this passage, in a
fifteenth-century hand. ^{q} electus est repeated but deleted the second time.

condition he may be, acts against the ordinance and establishments 1386
abovesaid or procures or does anything in any manner whereby the said
councillors and officers are disturbed in any particular concerning the
exercise of their power aforesaid or which excites or procures our said
lord the king to do or to command anything whereby the power of the
said councillors and officers, or the execution of their judgements and
awards to be made in the same, is defeated in any particular, and this is
duly proved by good and true witnesses who are notoriously of good
repute and condition, not suspect, properly examined before the king
and the councillors and officers abovesaid (they taking unto themselves
any of the justices of the one bench or of the other or such other discreet persons learned in the law as the said councillors and officers
please) he shall have such punishment, that is to say, at the first time
that he shall be so convicted he shall forfeit all his goods and chattels
to the king and nevertheless shall be imprisoned at the king's will;
and if any such person is duly attainted in the form abovesaid of
counsel, exhortation, or impulse given to the king to do the contrary of
his said grant, as is said above, even if the king has never done anything
on such counsel, exhortation, or impulse, he shall have such punishment as is said above; and if it happens (which God forbid) that he so
bears himself thereafter that he is another time attainted as above of
any of the defaults or misprisions aforesaid, then shall the said person
at the second time so convicted or attainted have judgement of life and
limb,[1] saving always the dignity of pontiffs and the privilege of Holy
Church and of clergy in all the things aforesaid; and that this statute
shall retain force and effect during the said commission only.

This business duly completed, the parliament broke up[2]
and everybody returned home.

Brother Nicholas Litlington, abbot of Westminster, died on
29 November and was buried on 17 December. Meanwhile
the king sent to the prior and convent three messages in
support of Brother John Lakingheath, urging that out of
respect for himself they should look on him as having a
recommendation he deserved. At the election held on 21
December, the choice of an abbot by way of compromise
fell on Brother William Colchester, archdeacon of the house;
when word of this reached the king, he was indignant and for
some little time put off admitting the new abbot. Eventually,
however, he was reconciled to him through the good offices

---

[1] i.e. misprision was to be punished with the penalty for treason; cf. Bellamy,
Law of Treason, p. 220.
[2] On 28 Nov.

1386 fuit sibi postea reconsiliatus et satis graciose scripsit pro eo
curie Romane.[1]

Quo in tempore obiit dominus[a] Hugo comes Stafford' in
partibus transmarinis ab Anglia longe distantibus peregrinus.[2]
Stapula vero lanarum mansit apud Middelborgh isto anno ac
anno sequenti.

Rex[b] autem tenuit suum Natale apud Wyndesore, ubi
permisit dominum Michaelem[c] de Poole comitem South-
folchie libertate gaudere et penes eum retinuit, et[d] ad quem-
cumque locum se divertere contingebat deinceps fuit ipse
cum eo.[3]

1387   Item de mense Januarii rex Francorum retraxit suas naves
que apud Slusam[e] et illas in ostio Sequane fluminis collocavit; de quibus tamen Calesienses ceperunt quatuor diversis
rebus onustas.[4] Quo in tempore dominus papa transtulit se
de civitate Januensi ad Lucam.[5] Quo eciam mense dominus
rex mutavit quosdam de suis officiariis: dominum Johannem
de Monte Acuto militem de officio senescalli amovit et
dominum Johannem de Bello Campo militem in ejus loco
substituit, qui bene se habuit in officio antedicto; rex vero
eum postea fecit baronem.[6] Item iiij.[f] die Februarii obiit
dominus Hugo de Segrave miles quondam thesaurarius
Anglie.[7]

Item ix. die Februarii venit rex Westmon' audivitque
missam ad altare sancti Edwardi. Et ab hinc arripuit iter
versus partes boreales; venitque Eboracum causa archiepiscopi Eboracen' discordantis cum clero et populo sue
diocesis; ubi rex quosdam pacificavit et quosdam implacatos
reliquit. Collegium vero Sancti Johannis Beverlacensi[g]

[a] comes *deleted*.   [b] Cave *in the margin*.   [c] *MS.* Michalem.
[d] *Interlined*.   [e] *Supply* fuerant, *or some such word*.   [f] *Corrected from* ix⁰.
[g] *Sic MS.*

[1] The king notified Urban VI of his assent to the election on 21 Jan. 1387.
Urban confirmed the election on 8 July 1387; his bulls were received in England
on or about 1 Sept., and the temporalities were restored on 10 Sept. (*Cal. Pat. R.,
1385-9*, pp. 270, 347; cf. p. 245; *Cal. Cl. R., 1385-9*, p. 450; below, p. 196 and n.).

[2] At Rhodes, in Sept. or Oct. 1386 (*Cal. Inq. p.m.*, xvi. 432-54; *G.E.C.*, xii
(i). 179).

[3] A passage suggesting that the lost leaf of the MS (for which see p. xvii n.)
included an account of Pole's impeachment and condemnation in the parliament
of 1386. Pole was sentenced to imprisonment at the king's will, and pending a
fine, and to the forfeiture of the king's irregular grants to him; he was sent to

of friends and wrote graciously enough on his behalf to the 1386
Roman curia.[1]

During this period the death occurred of Hugh earl of
Stafford on a pilgrimage far over the sea from England.[2] The
wool-staple continued this year and the next to be at Middelburg.

The king celebrated Christmas at Windsor, where he not
only allowed Michael de la Pole, earl of Suffolk, to enjoy his
freedom but kept him in his own society, so that wherever
circumstances took the king he was henceforward joined by
the earl.[3]

During January the French king withdrew the ships he had 1387
held at Sluys and stationed them in the Seine estuary; but
four of them, with mixed cargoes, were captured by the men
of Calais.[4] The pope removed himself at this time from
Genoa to Lucca.[5]

In the same month the king made changes among his
officers, dismissing Sir John Montague from the steward-
ship and replacing him by Sir John Beauchamp, who acquitted
himself well in the post: the king subsequently made him a
baron.[6] Sir Hugh Segrave, sometime treasurer of England,
died on 4 February.[7]

On 9 February the king visited Westminster and heard
Mass at the altar of St. Edward. He now set out for the north,
and visited York in consequence of a dispute that the archbishop of York was conducting with the clergy and people
of his diocese: here the king appeased some elements but left
behind him others still unreconciled. In deference to the
king the college of St. John at Beverley volunteered their

Windsor castle. See *R.P.*, iii. 216-20; Plucknett, in *T.R.H.S.*, 5th ser., ii (1952),
165-6; and below, p. 272.

[4] Cf. *Chronique du religieux de Saint Denys*, ed. Bellaguet, i. 460. Charles VI
himself had left Sluys in mid-Nov. (Mirot, in *Révue des Études Historiques*,
n.s., xvii (1915), 465).

[5] Urban VI left Genoa for Lucca on 16 Dec. 1386 (Ranieri Sardo, *Cronaca
Pisana*, in *Archivio Storico Italiano*, ser. i, vol. vi (2) (1845), p. 206). See also
below, p. 344 n.

[6] Beauchamp was created baron of Kidderminster in tail male by letters patent
on 10 Oct. 1387, the first such creation (*Cal. Pat. R., 1385-9*, p. 363; see also
ibid., p. 348). He had replaced Montague as steward of the household by 5 Feb.
1387.

[7] Segrave was treasurer from 10 Aug. 1381 to 17 Jan. 1386.

1387 contemplacione domini regis se dicto archiepiscopo sponte submisit: nichilominus aculeus latebat in cauda, quia pocius regis timore quam favore archiepiscopi se subegit.[1] Quibus peractis ad villam de Notyngham se divertit, ubi in festo Paschatis perhendinavit, quod erat septimo die Aprilis; et ab hinc gracia festivitatis sancti Georgii ad castrum suum de Wyndeshore accessit. Item xj. die Februarii obiit frater Michael abbas Sancti Augustini; quo tradito sepulture celebrataque eleccione ex more electus est in abbatem dicti monasterii frater Willelmus Welde doctor decretorum.[2] Item isti de consilio jam de novo creati suscepto onere tocius regiminis affectantes eorum gubernacione bona multimodaque prospera regi et regno succedere cum honore ordinarunt unum navigium, cui prefecerunt in ducem dominum Ricardum comitem Arundell'.[3] Item circa principium mensis Marcii quidam mercatores Anglie satis locupletes intrabant quandam navem vocatam passajour de Cales' cum bonis eorum et mercimoniis: veneruntque inimici eis obviam, set nostri mercatores noluerunt viriliter se defendere set veluti vecordes elegerunt pocius cum eis tractare; propterea erant capti et cum seipsis omnia amiserunt. Hoc audientes quidam ex nostris ix. die Marcii exierunt et quatuor naves vino de la Rochell' onustas de inimicis ceperunt.

Item xij. die Marcii comes Arundell' venit ad mare;[4] paratisque omnibus pro tanto expedicionis negocio oportunis xvj. die Marcii unum mirabile nostro pro voto casualiter occurrebat, nam Franci et Hispani in uno balynger et una lyna[5] sulcantes maria circa *oras maritimas* Anglie explorando quonam nostrum navigium divertere voluerit repente in eos illi de portubus irruerunt ceperuntque omnes. A quibus pro eorum redempcione didicerunt quomodo et quando classis Francorum et Flandrensium transiret per maria ad eorum

a-a MS. ora maritima.

[1] In fact the dispute between the canons and vicars choral of St. John's College, Beverley, of the one part and Archbishop Nevill of the other, which began with Nevill's claim to visitation rights in 1381, ended only with his fall in 1388 (*Cal. Pat. R., 1385-9*, p. 465; *V.C.H. Yorks.*, iii. 358; *R.P.*, iii. 182; and below, p. 245 n.).

[2] On 28 Feb. 1387. For Welde see *B.R.U.O.*, iii. 2007. His predecessor was Michael Pecham.

[3] Since 10 Dec. 1386, admiral of the north and west fleets. On 16 Dec.

submission to the archbishop; all the same there was a sting 1387
concealed in the tail here inasmuch as it was out of fear of
the king rather than goodwill for the archbishop that they
humbled themselves.[1] This business disposed of, the king
went to Nottingham, staying there for Easter, which fell on
7 April, and from there he made his way to Windsor castle
to honour St. George's Day [23 April]. Brother Michael,
abbot of St. Augustine's, died on 11 February; after his
burial the usual election was held and Brother William Welde,
D.Cn.L., was chosen abbot of the monastery.[2] The persons
who had just been appointed to the council and had taken
upon themselves the whole burden of government were
anxious that their administration should be attended by
striking all-round success and prestige for king and kingdom,
and gave orders for a fleet to the command of which they
appointed Richard earl of Arundel.[3] About the beginning of
March a number of well-to-do English merchants took ship
with their property and merchandise in a Calais 'passage-boat'.
When the enemy fell in with them, these merchants of ours
declined to defend themselves like men and cravenly preferred
to parley, with the consequence that they were made
prisoners and lost their liberty as well as everything else.
Hearing of this, some of our people sallied out on 9 March
and captured four enemy ships carrying cargoes of La
Rochelle wine.

The earl of Arundel arrived at the coast on 12 March,[4] and
all the preparations occasioned by an enterprise on the scale
of this expedition had been made, when on 16 March a wonderful stroke of luck came like an answer to our prayers.
Some Frenchmen and Spaniards in a balinger and a 'line'[5]
were patrolling the waters off the English coast to learn the
objective for which our fleet would decide to make, when
they were suddenly pounced on and captured to a man by
forces issuing from the harbours, who by way of ransom
obtained from them information as to how and when the

Arundel was retained to serve the king with 2,500 men for 3 months from 1 Mar.
1387. See *Palmer*, p. 91. The detail of the following account, its command of
the vocabulary of shipping, and the idiom of 'nostri' betray the use of a written
source originating in Arundel's fleet.
    [4] Arundel embarked at Sandwich.   [5] A small, swift rowing galley.

1387 partes optatas;[1] quo facto nostri naute permiserunt illos ad propria libere remeare. Comes vero Arundell' super hiis non modicum confortatus xxiij. die Marcii animose cum suis mare intravit. Sequenti vero die venit predicta classis Francorum et Flandrensium vino de la Rochell' onusta: nec mora, irruunt nostri in eos impetu odioso et durum prelium committitur inter eos eratque longa concertacio inter nostros et illos que pars victoriam reportaret. Set demum Deo favente vicerunt nostri captisque navibus quinquaginta magnis et parvis, quas misit dictus comes sub salvo conductu ad portum de Orewell'. Durante vero prelio alia pars dicte classis evasit, quam a tergo dictus comes insequens plures *ex eis* cepit viriliter, sex vero submersit et quinque igne consumpsit. Venit quoque ad Slusam, ubi in le cogrode aliquamdiu cum suis pausavit:[2] omnes itaque naves accedentes ad portum predictum dum ipse ibidem jacuit arestavit; sicque cepit illic tres carrekes mercimoniis diversis onustas,*b* duas barget' *de Normannia,* unam navem bonam de Hispannia et quasdam naves de Scocia lana onustas. Interim, dum inibi quiescebat comes predictus, quidam de suis descendentes in terram molendina et viculos succenderunt, patriam circumquaque vastabant, captas predas asportabant et ad naves redibant. Plura vero idem comes ibidem fecisset,[3] set aque dicte patrie circumjacentis tante amaritudinis erant et tante insalubritatis quod gravis tuscis eos universaliter fatigaret aliasque infirmitates incurrebant; propter quod si ibidem diucius moram traxisset proculdubio plures de suis finaliter amisisset. Igitur xiiij. die Aprilis, subductis anchoris solutisque navibus, salvus cum suis et omnibus que ceperat ad portum de Arewelle pervenit.[4] Summa vero navium captarum lxviij., exceptis carrekes, bargez, aliisque navibus mediocribus; in quibus habebantur*d* plus quam octo milia dolia vini de la Rochell', de quo

*a–a*Interlined.   *b* MS. onustis.   *c–c* Interlined.   *d* de vino deleted after this word.

---

[1] A reference to the fleet gathered in 1386 for the invasion of England; this had wintered at La Rochelle and was now in fact making for Sluys, loaded with the wine harvest from La Rochelle.

[2] Cf. Croniques . . . de Tournay, ed. Hocquet, p. 313, where Arundel is said to

French and Flemish fleet would be making the voyage to its 1387
chosen destination;[1] after which they were allowed by our
seamen to return without hindrance to their homes. Much
encouraged by this turn of events, the earl of Arundel put to
sea in good heart with his forces on 23 March. On the following day there came up the French and Flemish fleet laden
with wine from La Rochelle; our men at once swooped upon
it in a hate-inspired onslaught, and a grim battle began. The
struggle between our forces and the enemy to decide which
way victory should go was a long one, but in the end, by the
favour of God, it was our men who prevailed, capturing
fifty ships, large and small, which the earl sent under safe-
conduct to Orwell Haven. In the course of the engagement
a part of the enemy fleet made off, but after a stern chase the
earl by resolute action captured several ships, sank six, and
destroyed five by fire. He went on to Sluys, where he
anchored with his fleet for a time in the roadstead used by
cogs;[2] and arrested all the ships that approached the port
while he lay there. As a result he took three carracks with
miscellaneous cargoes, two Norman 'bargettes', a fine Spanish
vessel, and some Scottish ships carrying wool. During the
period that the earl lay at anchor, some of his men landed
and set fire to mills and villages, and played havoc in the surrounding countryside before returning to the fleet with the
booty they had seized. Indeed the earl would have accomplished more in those parts,[3] but the water of the district
round about was so bitter and unwholesome that every man
he had was exhausted by a severe cough, and other maladies
were attacking them; so that if he had prolonged his stay
there he would undoubtedly have lost many of them for
good. On 14 April, therefore, he weighed anchor and set sail,
reaching Orwell Haven in safety with his forces and all his
prizes.[4] The captured ships, not counting carracks, barges,
and other humble craft, totalled 68 and had aboard them
more than 8,000 tuns of wine of La Rochelle, which was

have been anchored off Sluys from Mon., 25 Mar. to Thurs., 11 Apr.
    [3] A hint of the possibility of the capture of Sluys itself and of other English
gains on the Flemish mainland.
    [4] In fact Arundel probably reached Orwell by 13 Apr. (*Cal. Pat. R., 1385-9*,
p. 323).

1387 statim postea factis distribucionibus fere per totam Angliam
vendebatur lagena pro quatuor denariis.

Item existente rege apud Wyndeshoram in festo sancti
Georgii quidam iniqui et pessimi excitarunt regem contra
dominum Thomam ducem Gloucestr' avunculum suum in
tantum ⟨quod⟩[a] si ibidem diem crastinum expectasset indubie
mortis laqueum[1] minime evasisset. Quo comperto ac prandio
celebrato petita a rege licencia confestim recessit. Item
xxiiij. die Aprilis capti sunt per Calesienses de Normannia
quindecim piscatores. Item xxvij. die Aprilis ad instanciam
ducis Hibernie rex concessit Johanni Northampton' unam
cartam plenariam super omnibus forisfactis suis et quod
rehaberet omnia bona sua mobilia et immobilia; quod[b]
modicum sibi profecit.[2]

p. 158   Comes[3] vero / Arundell' existens apud Orewelle cum suis
inter alios quasdam egritudinum sustinuit passiones. Tandem
redditus sanitati primo die Maii mare intravit, venitque ad
villam de Brest, quam victualibus vacuam inveniens opulenter
refecit; obsidionem vero circa eam[c] positam[d] non removit,
set promisit illis existentibus in bastilis quod cum tali
apparatu in proximo reveniret quod eos finaliter optineret
aut eos turpiter omnino fugaret.[4] Deinde cum suis ad x.
miliaria armatus processit in terram, ubi combussit unam
villam et unum fortissimum bastilum[5] preparatum pro
obsidione predicta. Istis et aliis in isto termino per illum
gloriose[e] peractis modicum ante festum Nativitatis Sancti
Johannis cum suis in Angliam est reversus.

Rex autem postquam dictis prelatis et dominis concesserat
omnem potestatem regendi sive gubernandi, corrigendi

[a] MS. om.   [b] MS. cui.   [c] MS. ea.   [d] Interlined.   [e] MS. graciose.

---

[1] Cf. 'laquei mortis' in 2 Kgs. (2 Sam.) xxii. 6; Ps. xvii. 6 (xviii. 5); Prov. xxi. 6.

[2] A garbled report. John Northampton had been released from prison in June
1386 but forbidden to approach within 80 miles of the City; a general pardon and
the consequential restitution of forfeited property were delayed until 1390
(above, p. 150 n.; below, p. 454 n.). In 1387, however, it was rumoured that
William, Lord Zouche of Harringworth was attempting to get a full pardon for
Northampton, and on 27 Apr. the mayor and aldermen wrote asking him to desist
(*Letter Book H*, pp. 305–6; Bird, *Turbulent London of Richard II*, p. 141).

The episode occasions the Monk's first extant reference to Robert de Vere as
duke of Ireland. The king's grant to de Vere of this dignity on 13 Oct. 1386, in
the course of the Wonderful Parliament, was perhaps another of the items recorded on the now missing leaf of the MS. (cf. above, p. 178 n.).

shortly afterwards distributed and sold over almost the whole 1387 of England at 4*d*. a gallon.

While the king was at Windsor for St. George's Day [23 April] certain wicked and evilly-disposed persons stirred him up against his uncle, Thomas duke of Gloucester, and were so far successful that, if the duke had waited a day longer, he would unquestionably not have escaped the 'snare of death'.[1] When he became aware of this, he stayed only until dinner was over before taking his leave of the king and making a hasty departure. On 24 April fifteen Norman fishermen were captured by the men of Calais. At the instance of the duke of Ireland, the king on 27 April granted to John Northampton a plenary charter in respect of everything he had forfeited, entitling him to resume possession of all his goods, movable and immovable; but little good it did him.[2]

While[3] he was at Orwell with his forces, the earl of Arundel was among those who suffered some bouts of sickness. Eventually, restored to health, he put to sea on 1 May and sailed to Brest, which, finding it emptied of foodstuffs, he lavishly revictualled. He did not, however, raise the siege the enemy had laid to it, though he promised the occupants of the siege-towers that when he came again soon it would be in such array that he would get his hands on them once for all or put them to utter and ignominious rout.[4] He then made an armed advance ten miles inland with his forces, burning down a town and an exceptionally strong siege-tower,[5] which had been made ready for use in the siege. At the triumphant conclusion of these and other exploits during this season, the earl and his men returned to England shortly before Midsummer Day.

After the king had committed to the prelates and lords named above complete power to exercise authority and

[3] An error in transcription ('graciose' for 'gloriose') toward the end of the ensuing passage suggests that the Monk was again using a written source. In their abbreviated forms the two words are readily confused.

[4] Brest had been in English hands since 1372, originally by agreement with John de Montfort IV, duke of Brittany. Since 1381, however, de Montfort had been trying to bring this arrangement to an end, and he was currently besieging the English garrison there (Jones, *Ducal Brittany, 1364–1399*, pp. 103–4, 147 ff.; A. De la Borderie, 'Le Siège de Brest en 1387', in *Révue de Bretagne, de Vendée et d'Anjou*, ii (1889), 198–203.

[5] One of two on the coast by Brest built of stone (Jones, op. cit., pp. 158–9).

1387 [a]et puniendi[a] ubicunque in regno et extra[1] ad informacionem archiepiscopi Ebor', ducis Hybernie, Michaelis de la Pole et aliorum sibi in hac parte favencium 'tactus dolore cordis intrinsecus'[2] penituit se fecisse hoc factum, asserens se ad hoc coactum fuisse, nec fuit intencionis sue, ut dixit, omnem potestatem suam regalem aliis delegare et sibi quasi nullam penitus reservare. Indignanter igitur[b] retraxit se ab eis et ad partes remociores divertit; consilia vero in ista estate diversis locis interim celebravit, videlicet unum apud Redyng', in quo dictus Michael de la Pole peciit reversionem illius judicii quo fuerat perpetuo carceri condempnatus, set propter absenciam ducis Glouc' et aliorum dominorum ejus peticio nullius erat momenti.[3] Secundum consilium erat apud Wodestoke et tercium apud Notyngham;[4] que dominos magis fatigabant quam illis sive regno proficiebant. Post hec autem rex lustravit partes Cestrie et borealem plagam Wallie, venitque Salopiam;[5] et in eundo et in redeundo semper retinuit penes se homines ejusdem patrie pervagate. Insuper misit quendam clavigerum in Estsex' et comitatum Cantebrig' ac in Northfolk' et Southfolk', qui faceret virtute commissionis sue valenciores et potenciores cujuslibet patrie predicte sibi jurare quod postpositis ceteris dominis quibuscumque cum ipso utpote eorum vero rege tenerent, datisque eisdem signis, scilicet coronis argenteis ac[b] deauratis, ut ad dominum regem cum eorum armis parati venirent quandocumque inde[b] fuerant requisiti.[6] Demum iste claviger fuit captus ibidem juxta Cantebrig' et carcerali custodie demandatus.

Item rex in ista estate prefecit ducem Hybernie in

[a-a] *Added in the margin, after* corrigendi, *which ends a line.*   [b] *Interlined.*

---

[1] Above, p. 168.   [2] Gen. vi. 6.

[3] For the king's itinerary in the summer of 1387 see Tout, *Chapters*, iii. 419 ff., and nn.; and A. Tuck, *Richard II and the English Nobility* (London, 1973), pp. 227-8. He was at Reading from 8 to 13 May. Pole had been sentenced to imprisonment at the king's will, pending a fine, and had already been allowed his liberty (above, p. 178 and n.).

[4] The king was at Woodstock on 22 May and from 20 Sept. to 15 Oct. 1387. The council at Woodstock probably occurred in the latter period and, if so, it did not precede but follow the council at Nottingham; this was held on 25 Aug.

[5] The Monk does not explicitly mention the *council* at Shrewsbury, the

control and to administer correction and punishment every- 1387
where within the kingdom and outside it,[1] the prompting of
the archbishop of York, the duke of Ireland, Michael de la
Pole, and other sympathizers with his predicament brought it
about that 'it grieved him at his heart'[2] and he regretted
having taken this step. He declared that he had been coerced
into it; and it had been no part of his intention, he said, to
delegate the whole of his royal power to others and to retain
virtually none at all for himself. He therefore withdrew in a
huff from contact with the commissioners and travelled far
afield; though from time to time during this summer he did
hold councils at various places, one of them at Reading, in
which Michael de la Pole petitioned for the reversal of the
judgement condemning him to life-imprisonment, but owing
to the absence of the duke of Gloucester and other nobles
the petition was nugatory.[3] The second council was at Woodstock, and the third at Nottingham;[4] but they served rather
to exhaust the nobles than to benefit them or the kingdom.
The king afterwards made the round of Cheshire and the
northern districts of Wales and visited Shrewsbury;[5] on both
the outward and the return journeys he continually took into
his personal service men of the country through which he
travelled. Besides this he sent into Essex, Cambridgeshire,
Norfolk, and Suffolk a serjeant at mace, who was commissioned to cause the more substantial and influential
inhabitants of those counties to swear that to the exclusion
of all other lords whatsoever they would hold with him
as their true king, and they were to be given badges, consisting of silver and gilt crowns, with the intention that
whenever they were called upon to do so they should join
the king, armed and ready.[6] This serjeant was eventually
arrested in those parts, not far from Cambridge, and committed to prison.

In the course of this summer the king appointed the duke

occasion of Richard II's first consultation with his judges. This probably occurred
between 1 and 5 Aug.; but cf. Knighton, *Chronicon*, ii. 236, and Tout, *Chapters*,
iii., 422 n. The king was at Chester from 12 to 16 July. Thus, contrary to the
Monk's belief, the expedition to these remoter parts preceded the councils at
Woodstock and Nottingham.

[6] Cf. *Favent*, p. 4; and J. L. Gillespie, 'Richard II's Archers of the Crown',
in *Journal of British Studies*, xviii (1979), pp. 17-18.

1387 justiciarium Cestrie,*a* contulitque sibi castrum de Flynt in
Wallia;[1] dedit eciam sibi quasdam terras ad valorem mille
marcarum per annum de dominio domini de Audeleye;
contulitque sibi Johannem filium et heredem Caroli de
Bloys, qui olim contra ducem Britannie est congressus
pro illius ducatu, quem sibi vendicavit: occubuit in plano
campo juxta Orreye.[2] Cujus filii duo*a* inter ceteros erant
capti et in Angliam missi ac inibi longo tempore custoditi
ne aliquando contra ducem predictum insurgerent, illum
infestando pro ducatu predicto. Altero quidem nunc
sublato de medio, iste vero jam ad peticionem ducis
Hybernie pro viginti milibus librarum sibi solvendis est a
vinculis relaxatus et ad Francos transmissus. Majora tamen
et ampliora pro ipso optulit dux Britannie predictus, set
non optinuit quod petebat.

Duxerat namque iste Robertus de Veer dux Hibernie
filiam domini Ingelrami de Coucy et domine Isabelle filie
regis Edwardi iij. in uxorem;[3] quam habens exosam misit
Johannem Ripon' clericum ad curiam Romanam ad divor-
ciandum matrimonium inter eos; qui ad hoc in tantum
laboravit ibidem quod per falsos testes ea de causa con-
ductos sentenciam divorcii prolatam recepit; quod quidem
factum multum displicuit ducibus Lancastr', Everwyk'
et Glouc', avunculis mulieris predicte. Qua tandem*a*
sic repudiata dictus Robertus de Veer dux Hybernie
quandam mulierem Boemicam de camera domine regine,

---

a Interlined.

[1] De Vere received life-grants of the offices of chief justice of Chester and
justice in North Wales on, respectively, 8 Sept. 1387 and 10 Oct. 1387 (*31st.
Report of the Deputy Keeper of the Public Records* (1870), Appendix, p. 254;
ibid., *36th Report* (1875), Appendix, ii. 494; *Cal. Pat. R., 1385–9*, p. 357).

[2] Both grants were made earlier than the Monk implies. By letters patent dated
12 Oct. 1385, Robert de Vere was granted the reversion of the lands of Sir James
de Audley in Devon, Cornwall, and Somerset, to hold free of rent until the grant
to him of the lordship of Ireland (for which see above, p. 144 and n.) should
become effective by conquest, and the reversion took effect on Audley's death in
1386 (*Cal. Pat. R., 1385–9*, pp. 112–13, 115; *Lords' Reports on the Dignity of
a Peer*, v. 426). For the grant to de Vere on 23 Mar. 1386 of the ransom of Jean
de Bretagne, son of Charles de Blois, count of Penthièvre, to meet the costs of
maintaining 500 men-at-arms and 1,000 archers in Ireland for two years, see
Cal. Pat. R., 1385–9, p. 123 (cf. ibid., pp. 132, 136); M. Jones, 'The ransom of
Jean de Bretagne, count of Penthièvre: an aspect of English Foreign Policy,
1386–8', in *B.I.H.R.*, xlv (1972), 14 ff.; and Jones, *Ducal Brittany, 1364–99*,

of Ireland to the office of justice of Chester and conferred 1387
on him the castle of Flint in Wales.[1] He also granted him
lands worth 1,000 marks a year out of the lordship of Lord
Audley, and made over to him Jean, the son and heir of that
Charles de Blois who had once come to grips with the duke
of Brittany over his dukedom, which he claimed for himself,
and had fallen on the field of battle outside Auray.[2] In
company with others, his two sons were seized and sent to
England where they were long kept under guard to prevent
them from one day rising against the duke and taking aggressive action to win the dukedom. One of them had now been
removed from the scene, and the other, on the petition of the
duke of Ireland (to whom £20,000 was to be paid by way of
consideration) was released from confinement and handed
over to the French. The duke of Brittany made a bigger and
more handsome offer for him, but failed to obtain his request.

This Robert de Vere, duke of Ireland, had married the
daughter of Enguerrand, sire de Coucy, by the lady Isabel
daughter of King Edward III;[3] but he grew to detest her,
and sent the clerk John Ripon to the Roman curia to secure
a divorce terminating the marriage — a task at which he
worked to such effect that through perjured witnesses,
hired for the purpose, he came away with the pronouncement of a sentence of divorce. These proceedings greatly
displeased the lady's uncles, the dukes of Lancaster, York,
and Gloucester. When she had eventually been thus repudiated, this Robert de Vere, duke of Ireland, to his everlasting disgrace and reproach committed the iniquity of
taking to wife a Bohemian chamber-woman of the queen's,

p. 102 and n. Jean and his brother, Guy, were made hostages for the payment of
the ransom of their father on his liberation after capture by the English in 1345
and lived in England from 1356. Guy died in Jan. 1385. Jean was ransomed to
the French for 120,000 francs (c.£20,000) at Calais on 20 Nov. 1387, the day
after the expiry of the commission of the continual council of 1386.

For the long-standing rivalry of the house of Blois with that of de Montfort
for the duchy of Brittany referred to in the above passage, see Jones, op. cit.,
pp. 1 ff. The victor at Auray on 29 Sept. 1364 was John de Montfort IV. His
tenure of the duchy, though interrupted by exile from 1373 to 1379, lasted
until his death in 1399, and he is the duke of Brittany referred to later in this
paragraph.

[3] She was Philippa de Coucy; de Vere married her in 1378. For John Ripon
see below, p. 202 and n.

1387 Lancecronam vocatam,[1] regina semper reclamante sibi in conjugem nepharie copulavit in sui ipsius scandalum et obprobrium sempiternum. Mater vero dicti Roberti de Veer in tantum dilexit istam nobilem mulierem sic repudiatam quod cariorem eam habuit quam si fuisset filia propria; cui revera tota animi virtute studuit perplacere, sic quod[a] proprio filio propter ejus repudium maledicere non pepercit.

Contulit quoque rex predicto Roberto de Veer plura alia, quorum quedam ab antiquo pertinuerunt ad coronam, prout in sequentibus manifeste liquebit.[2]

De duce Lancastr'. Item circa festum Nativitatis sancti Johannis Baptiste innotuit fama loquaci[3] qualiter duci Lancastr' successerat in Hispannia isto anno: nam sine hostium insultu majorem partem Galicie cum suo exercitu strenue pervagavit, set adveniente estate quosdam inclitos dominos ac quamplures strenuos milites, armigeros quoque et valettos, viros utique nominatos, dux ipse amisit; et hoc, ut quidam volunt, propter aeris intemperiem — talis pestis mortifera illos sic invasit.[4] Decesserunt namque ibidem in ista clade nociva dominus de Ponyngg',[5] dominus Filius Walteri,[6] dominus de Scales,[7] dominus Ricardus de Burle,[8] dominus Johannes Marmeon,[9] dominus [b]Hugo de Hastyngg'[10] et dominus[b] Thomas Morreus,[11] aliique milites istis inferiores, scilicet Thomas Symound et Thomas Fychet,[12] pluresque alii quorum nomina hic propter prolixitatem omitto. Igitur dux Lancastr' rediens de Hispannia venit ad regnum Portualie,

---

[a] *Interlined.*   [b-b] *Added in the margin after* dominus, *which ends a line.*

[1] Agnes Lancecron, whom two of de Vere's dependants abducted; she was reputedly the daughter of a saddler (*Cal. Pat. R., 1388–92*, p. 20; Walsingham, *Hist. Ang.*, ii. 160; see also M. V. Clarke and V. H. Galbraith, 'The Deposition of Richard II', in *Bulletin of the John Rylands Library*, xiv (1930), 167).

[2] Below, p. 244 and n.

[3] Perhaps suggested by Ovid, *Ep. ex Pont.* II.·ix. 3: 'Fama loquax vestras si iam pervenit ad aures'.

[4] The epidemic afflicted Lancaster's army most severely, not in the summer of 1387 (when the army was in León), but in the winter of 1386–7; for the campaign in Galicia between July 1386 and Mar. 1387, and the limits of its success, see Russell, *English Intervention*, pp. 422 ff., 452–3.

[5] Richard, Lord Poynings; he died on 25 May 1387, at Villalpando (*Cal. Inq. p.m.*, xvi. 610–23; *G.E.C.*, x. 663).

[6] Walter, Lord Fitz Walter; he died on 26 Sept. 1386, at or near Orense (*Cal.*

named Lancecron,[1] and this in face of the queen's unremitting 1387
protests. But Robert de Vere's mother had such love for the
noble lady he had repudiated as to hold her more dear than
if she had been her own daughter, and, devoting herself heart
and soul to endeavours to give her pleasure, did not hesitate
to curse her own son for bringing about the divorce.

There were several other things which the king conferred
on Robert de Vere, of which some had belonged to the
Crown from ancient times, as will be made abundantly clear
in what follows.[2]

The duke of Lancaster. About Midsummer Day [24 June]
the wagging tongue of rumour[3] brought intelligence of the
fortune attending the duke of Lancaster in Spain this year.
Unmolested by the enemy, he and his army overran most of
Galicia in the course of vigorous operations; but with the
coming of summer he suffered losses which included some
well-known nobles and a large number of stalwart knights,
besides squires and valets, all unquestionably men of reputation. This, so some say, was owing to the unfavourable
weather, in consequence of which they were attacked by a
deadly plague.[4] Among those who died in this grievous
calamity were Lords Poynings,[5] Fitz Walter[6] and Scales,[7]
Sir Richard Burley,[8] Sir John Marmion,[9] Sir Hugh Hastings,[10]
and Sir Thomas Morieux;[11] and, knights ranking below them,
Thomas Symond and Thomas Fitchet,[12] and many more
whose names, to avoid prolixity, I omit here. Withdrawing
now from Spain, the duke of Lancaster reached Portugal,

Inq. p.m., xvi. 377-93; *G.E.C.*, v. 479).

[7] Roger, Lord Scales; he died on 25 Dec. 1386 (*Cal. Inq. p.m.*, xvi. 482-7; *G.E.C.*, xi. 503).

[8] A marshal of Lancaster's army, for whom see Knighton, *Chronicon*, ii. 207; *John of Gaunt's Register, 1379-1383*, ed. Lodge and Somerville, i, pp. xxxi n., xxxii. He died at Villalpando, on 23 May 1387 (*Cal. Inq. p.m.*, xvi. 514-15; Froissart, *Chroniques*, xii. 324).

[9] Lancaster's chamberlain; he died on 25 Feb. or 24 Mar. 1387 (Knighton, loc. cit.; *Cal. Inq. p.m.*, xvi. 414-15; and see also *John of Gaunt's Register, 1379-1383*, i, p. xxxi n.).

[10] Died on 6 Nov. 1386 (*Cal. Inq. p.m.*, xvi. 406-7; *G.E.C.*, vi. 356).

[11] A marshal of Lancaster's army (Froissart, *Chroniques*, xii. 212); and see above, p. 72 n.

[12] Symond and Fitchet were both feed retainers of Lancaster (*John of Gaunt's Register, 1379-1383*, i, p. 8; ibid., nos. 499, 709; and for Symond see also ibid., ii. no. 822).

1387 ubi regi ejusdem regni Philippam suam filiam copulavit.¹
Erat autem rex iste quondam frater et miles cum ceteris
militibus cuidam ordini professus cui castitas est annexa;
unde super hujusmodi pro dispensacione habenda misit dux
predictus ad papam quatinus ut isti taliter copulati sua gracia
mediante valeant deinceps ita stare conjuncti.²

Notandum*a* est hic solerter, ne lector deviet*b* a tramite
veritatis, quod primo dux Lanc' desponsavit Blancham filiam
et heredem Henrici ducis Lanc', de qua suscepit filios et filias
procreatos utique generosos; de quibus supersunt adhuc
Henricus filius suus et heres, comes Derbeye, et due filie
Philippa et Elizabeth nuncupate.³ Prima, ut predictum est,
regi Portualie copulatur; altera vero fuit desponsata comiti
Pembrok', puero immature etatis,⁴ set illa viripotens tunc
effecta in regalem curiam est delata ad*c* conspicandum gestus
aulicos et mores eorum. Quam ut aspexit dominus Johannes
Holand, frater domini regis nunc ex parte materna, vehementer captus est ejus amore, propter quod die noctuque
eam sollicitavit; tamen*c* per temporum intervalla tandem tam
fatue illam allexit sic quod tempore transitus domini ducis
p. 159 patris sui ad mare per eum extitit / impregnata; unde illam
incontinenti postea duce acceptante duxit in uxorem ante
prolis exortum, transivitque in Hispanniam cum illo.⁵ Aliam-
que filiam suscepit idem dux de filia Petri quondam regis
Hispannie, nomine Katerinam.⁶ Item*d* Umfredus de Bohoun
comes Herefordie duas filias reliquit heredes, cujus primo-
genitam Alienoram*e* dux Glouc' in uxorem accepit, altera
vero copulata est comiti Derbeye predicto.⁷ Item est atten-
dendum quod dominus Leonellus secundus filius regis

---

a In the margin opposite this passage Hic, *followed by a diagrammatic repre-
sentation of a flight of steps.*   *b* MS. deviat.   *c Interlined.*   *d* Nota *in
the margin opposite this passage.*   *e Written above the word it here follows.*

---

¹ The marriage of João I of Portugal and Philippa, elder daughter of John of
Gaunt and Blanche of Lancaster, in accordance with the treaty of Ponte do
Mouro, of Nov. 1386, took place in Oporto Cathedral on 14 Feb. 1387. The
Monk is mistaken in his belief that Gaunt's campaign in 'Spain' was at an end:
the fighting in León was not yet begun. See Russell, op. cit., pp. 439–40, 449–51;
and see also below, p. 194 and n.

² Cf. Russell, *English Intervention*, p. 449, n. 2. João I had been a member of
the Order of Calatrava and master of its house in Aviz. The papal dispensation for
his marriage was delayed until 1391. See *Cal. Papal Letters*, iv (1362–1404),
p. 367.

where he made a match between the king of that country and 1387
his daughter Philippa.[1] This king had formerly made his profession as a brother and knight in a military order of which
chastity was a condition; and in consequence of this the duke
sent to the pope for a dispensation, requesting his gracious
intervention to enable the couple to remain joined in
wedlock.[2]

Here, to prevent the reader from straying from the path of
truth, it should be carefully noted that the duke of Lancaster's first marriage was to Blanche, the daughter and heiress of Henry duke of Lancaster, by whom he became the
father of sons and daughters of undeniably noble blood:
those who still survive are his son and heir, Henry earl of
Derby, and two daughters, Philippa and Elizabeth.[3] The first,
as was said above, is married to the king of Portugal; the
other had been betrothed to the earl of Pembroke a child of
tender age,[4] before, having herself come to womanhood, she
was introduced into the royal court to study the behaviour
and customs of courtly society. Here Sir John Holland, the
present king's uterine brother, fell violently in love with her
at first sight and pursued his wooing night and day until at
last his constantly renewed campaign of enticement led to
such folly that by the time her father the duke left for the
coast she was with child. With the duke's approval Holland
made haste to marry her before the baby should be born,
and then accompanied his father-in-law to Spain.[5] By the
daughter of Pedro, formerly king of Spain, the duke was the
father of another daughter, named Katherine.[6] Humphrey de
Bohun, earl of Hereford, left as his heirs two daughters: the
elder, Eleanor, became the wife of the duke of Gloucester
and the other was married to the earl of Derby.[7] It is further
to be observed that Lionel, the second in order of birth of

[3] Gaunt married Blanche of Lancaster (d. 1369) in 1359. Two sons of the
marriage died in infancy.

[4] John Hastings, 3rd earl of Pembroke of the Hastings line (1375–89). He was
born in 1372 and the betrothal took place in 1380.

[5] Holland was appointed constable in Lancaster's army (Knighton, *Chronicon*,
ii. 207); and see above, p. 164.

[6] Known as Catalina, the Castilian form of the name; for her see below, p. 370.

[7] For the marriages of Eleanor and Mary de Bohun, daughters and co-heiresses
of Humphrey de Bohun, earl of Hereford, Essex, and Northampton (d. 1373),
see below, p. 520 and nn.

1387 Edwardi iij. in ordine geniture duxit in uxorem heredem comitatus Ultonie et dominii de Clare genuitque ex ea unam filiam, que fuit copulata comiti de la Marche; de qua idem comes sustulit duos filios, quorum senior duxit filiam comitis Cancie fratris regis nunc in conjugem. Ad unum istorum fratrum profecto jure hereditario deveniret regnum Anglorum si (quod absit) rex sine liberis decessisset.[1]

Copulata itaque filia ducis Lanc' regi Portualie dux ipse venit Bayonem, ubi per certos nuncios iniit tractatum cum rege Hispannie sub ista forma:[2] scilicet quod filius *et heres* regis predicti desponsaret filiam prefati ducis nomine Katerinam, et quod ipse dux annuatim perciperet a rege predicto durante vita *ipsius ducis* xx. milia librarum auri, et quod pax inter duo regna, scilicet Anglorum et Hispannorum, pro perpetuo firmaretur, non obstante federe inito inter Francos et ipsos. Quod si istis rex predictus noluerit consentire, nimirum*c* dux ipse contra eum procedat manu valida et robusta ad delendum ipsum et suos utpote crucis Christi verissimos inimicos. Super istis vero articulis et aliis incidentibus et emergentibus duravit tractatus inter ipsos usque in finem mensis Maii anni sequentis. Interim tamen misit dux Lancastr' ad dominum nostrum regem et ejus consilium exquirendo voluntatem eorum, scilicet an placeat illis talem concordiam acceptare et ratam*d* habere. Ad hec fuit sibi responsum ex parte regis et ejus consilii quod si prefata concordia valeat ad finem effectualem perduci, prout supra premittitur, libenter illam admitterent et pro rato haberent.[3]

a-a In the margin but marked for insertion at this point.   *b-b* Interlined.
c licet added later after this word, which ends a line.   *d* MS. ratum.

[1] And in that eventuality, if both brothers were to be alive, the crown would devolve on the elder brother. The Monk, of course, knew this. The point of his remark is that the heir presumptive to Richard II was to be sought in the Mortimer family and not in the family of John of Gaunt. Lionel — the 3rd son of Edward III, but the 2nd to survive infancy — married, as his 1st wife, Elizabeth de Burgh (1332–63), daughter and heir of William de Burgh, earl of Ulster (1312–33), through which marriage he acquired the lordship of Clare. Philippa, their daughter (1355–*c*.1382), who was her father's heir, married, in 1368, Edmund Mortimer, earl of March (1352–81). Roger (1374–98), the elder of their two sons, married, in *c*.1388, Eleanor, daughter of Thomas Holland, earl of Kent (*c*.1350–97), the king's half-brother; Edmund, the younger (1376–1409) married, in 1402, a daughter of Owen Glendower. Cf. *Eulogium Historiarum*, ed. F. S. Haydon (3 vols., R.S., 1858–63), iii. 369–70.

[2] Preliminary negotiations between Lancaster and Juan I of Castile began in

the sons of King Edward III, married the heiress of the earl- 1387
dom of Ulster and the lordship of Clare and by her had an
only daughter, who became the wife of the earl of March and
bore him two sons, of whom the elder married the daughter
of the earl of Kent, the present king's brother. If (as God
forbid) the king were to die childless it would be upon one
of these brothers that the crown of England would devolve
by hereditary right.[1]

After his daughter's wedding to the king of Portugal the
duke of Lancaster went to Bayonne, where through his
envoys he opened negotiations with the king of Spain on the
following proposals.[2] The king's son and heir was to marry
the duke's daughter Katherine; the duke himself was to be
paid by the king £10,000 a year in gold for life; and perpetual
peace was to be established between the two kingdoms of
England and Spain, notwithstanding the alliance entered
into between the French and the Spaniards. If the king of
Spain refused to agree to these terms, the duke was of course
free to take vigorous military action against him to destroy
him and his people, as being in the truest sense enemies of
Christ's cross. Negotiations between the parties about these
articles and riders and corollaries to them lasted until the end
of May in the following year. During this period the duke of
Lancaster sent to our king and his council to ascertain their
wishes — would they be willing to accept and endorse an
agreement on these conditions? The answer returned to this
inquiry by the king and council was that if the agreement
could be brought to a successful conclusion in the terms set
out above they would gladly recognize and ratify it.[3]

June 1387, as soon as the Anglo-Portuguese invasion of León was over. Negotiations opened at Bayonne early in 1388 and continued until the following July.
The Monk, having misdated the marriage between João I of Portugal and Philippa
of Lancaster, shortens the interval between that event and the negotiations. See
above, p. 192 and n.; Russell, *English Intervention*, pp. 490 ff.

[3] A hint at the conflict of interest between Lancaster and the English government laid bare in the negotiations at Bayonne. In Feb. 1386, as a condition of
official support for his expedition, Lancaster undertook to make no settlement
leaving the crown of Castile to Juan I that did not include a treaty of perpetual
alliance between the two countries of England and Castile. Lancaster, however,
was tempted by the lucrative terms on which he was offered a settlement of his
claims to the throne of Castile and, in the end, disregarded his undertaking of
1386. See Rymer, *Foedera*, vii. 495, 587–8; *Perroy*, pp. 254–6; and below, pp.
344, 370 and n.

1387   Papa*a* vero quamvis plurimum requisitus electum Westm'
confirmare aliquantulum distulit, volens, sicut alias,[1] cassare
eleccionem et electo postea providere; set ad peticionem
magistri Ricardi Rounhale domini regis ambassiatoris
concessit ut illi in rota ibidem in causa cognoscerent ac
eleccionem examinarent et fine debito terminarent. Sicque
primo die Septembris electus predictus omnes suas bullas
suam*b* eleccionem concernentes recepit.

Item in isto autumpno illi de consilio statuerunt aliud
navigium redire ad mare, cui prefuit dominus Henricus de
Percy. Qui *c*circa principium mensis Septembris*c* sulcans
maria cum suis navibus et aliis diversis mercimoniis onustis
directis ad urbem Burdegalensem pro vino, circa crepusculum
venit prope villam de Brest. Accensis lucernis in castellis
erectis in summitate malorum feliciter et gloriose portum
illius ville intravit; cujus adventus terruit eos existentes in
eorum bastilis juxta villam predictam firmatis, putantes
secundum promissa eis dudum comitem Arundell' in eorum
confusionem cum tam ingenti classe et cum tam glomerosa
multitudine advenisse;[2] combustisque bastilis furtive inter
noctis tenebras recesserunt. Et sic ab obsidione liberata
fuit dicta villa protunc miraculose virtute divina.

Item memorandum[3] quod xxv*to*. die mensis Augusti anno regni
regis Ricardi secundi xj*mo*. apud castrum de*d* Notyngham coram dicto
domino nostro rege Robertus Tresylian capitalis justiciarius et Robertus
Beleknapp' capitalis justiciarius de communi banco domini nostri regis
predicti et Johannes Holte, Rogerus Fulthorp'[4] et Willelmus Borgh'
milites justiciarii*e* socii predicti Roberti Beleknapp' ac Johannes
Lokton' serviens dicti domini regis ad legem, in presencia dominorum

----

a Westm' abbas *in the margin opposite this passage, in a fifteenth-century
hand.*   *b* *Interlined.*   *c-c* *In the margin but marked for insertion at this
point.*   *d* *R.P. and S.R. om.*   *e* *S.R. om.*

----

[1] Not, however, at Westminster, where the pope had never quashed an election
or provided.
[2] See above, p. 184. One of the siege-towers attacked by Percy was refortified
by him and incorporated into the English defences at Brest. See *Cal. Pat. R.,
1385–9*, pp. 358–9; Jones, *Ducal Brittany, 1364–99*, pp. 158–9; and for Percy's
expedition see also *Palmer*, pp. 100–1.
[3] The following text is extracted from the Appeal in the Merciless Parliament,
1388, but placed here by the Monk in order to achieve a strictly chronological
account of events. See below, p. 258; and for comment, S. B. Chrimes, 'Richard

In spite of repeated requests to confirm the abbot-elect 1387 of Westminster, the pope for some time put off doing so because, as on other occasions,[1] he wanted to quash the election and make provision later for the abbot-elect; but upon the petition of the king's ambassador, Master Richard Ronhale, he agreed to allow jurisdiction in the matter to the members of the rota, who were to examine the election and make the appropriate final decision. The abbot-elect consequently received on 1 September all the bulls affecting his election.

In the course of this autumn the members of the council decided that another naval expedition should put to sea, with Sir Henry Percy in command. About the beginning of September he and his fleet were sailing in company with some other vessels which, with mixed cargoes aboard, were bound for Bordeaux to fetch wine; as twilight was falling he arrived off Brest. With lanterns ablaze in the masthead top-castles he made a triumphantly successful entrance into the town harbour, striking terror, by his coming, into the occupants of the siege-towers planted close by, who thought that the earl of Arundel was making good his recent promise, and had arrived with this huge fleet and a host of men to discomfit them.[2] Setting fire to the siege-towers, they slunk away under cover of darkness. Thus it was that by a heaven-sent miracle the town was delivered from investment.

Be it remembered[3] that on the 25th day of the month of August in the eleventh year of the reign of King Richard II at the castle of Nottingham before our said lord the king Robert Tresilian chief justice [of the King's Bench] and Robert Bealknap chief justice of the Common Bench of our lord the king aforesaid, John Holt, Roger Fulthorpe,[4] and William Burgh, knights, justices, fellows of the aforesaid Robert Bealknap, and John Lockton serjeant at law of the said lord the king, being in person in the presence of the lords and the

II's Questions to the Judges, 1387', in *Law Quarterly Rev.*, lxxii (1956), 365–90; Clementi, in *E.H.R.*, lxxxvi (1971), 96–113; and for the difficult legal points at issue, Bellamy, *Law of Treason*, pp. 87 ff., 111–12. The text has been collated with *R.P.*, iii. 233–4 and *S.R.*, ii. 102–4.

[4] The only justice in the list who was not present earlier at Shrewsbury when the same questions were put; on that occasion Sir John Cary, chief baron, was present.

1387 et aliorum testium subscriptorum personaliter existentes, per dictum dominum nostrum regem requisiti in fide et ligencia quibus eidem domino nostro regi firmiter sunt astricti quod ad certas questiones inferius designatas et coram eis recitatas fideliter responderent et super eis secundum^a discrecionem suam legem dicerent.

j.^{b} In primis[1] querebatur ab eis an illa nova statutum et ordinacio atque commissio facta ^{c}et edita^c in ultimo parliamento apud Westmonasterium celebrato derogant regalie et prerogative dicti domini nostri regis. Ad quam quidem questionem unanimiter responderunt quod derogant, presertim eo quod fuerant contra voluntatem^d regis.

ij. Item querebatur ab eis qualiter illi qui statutum, ordinacionem et commissionem predicta fieri procurarunt sunt puniendi. Ad istam questionem unanimiter responderunt quod pena capitali, scilicet^e mortis, puniri merentur nisi rex in ea parte voluerit eis graciam indulgere.

iij. Item querebatur ab eis qualiter sunt illi puniendi qui regem prefatum^f excitarunt^g ad consenciendum statuti ordinacionis et commissionis hujusmodi^h faccioni. Ad quam quidem questionem unanimiter responderunt ^{i}quod nisi rex eis graciam fecerit sunt^i pena capitali merito puniendi.

iiij. Item querebatur ab eis qualem penam merentur illi qui compulerunt sive artarunt regem ad consenciendum confeccioni dictorum statuti, ordinacionis et commissionis. Ad quam quidem questionem unanimiter responderunt quod sunt ut proditores merito puniendi.

v. Item querebatur ab eis quomodo sunt illi eciam puniendi qui impediverunt regem quominus poterat exercere que ad regaliam et prerogativam suam pertinuerunt. Ad istam questionem unanimiter responderunt quod sunt ut proditores eciam puniendi.

vj. Item quesitum erat ab eis an postquam in^j parliamento congregato negocia regni et causa congregacionis parliamenti de mandato regis fuerint^k exposita et declarata et certi articuli limitati^l per regem super quibus domini et communes regni^m in eodem parliamento procedere debeant, si domini et communes super aliis^m / articulis velint omnino procedere et nullatenus super articulis limitatis^n per regem donec super articulis per eosdem expressatis fuerit per ipsum regem primo responsum, non obstante quod fuerit ^{o}eis per regem injunctum^o in contrarium,[2] numquid rex debeat habere in ea parte regimen parliamenti et de facto regere ad effectum quod super limitatis^n articulis per regem primo debeant procedere, vel an domini et communes primo debeant habere responsum a rege super articulis per

p. 160

---

^{a} MS. super. ^{b} The numerals here printed at the beginning of each paragraph are in the margin of the MS. $^{c-c}$ R.P. and S.R.; MS. om. ^{d} R.P. voluntates. ^{e} MS. inserts quod. ^{f} S.R. predictum. ^{g} Corrected in MS. from excitaverunt, ^{h} MS. hujus. $^{i-i}$ R.P. and S.R.; MS. nisi eis graciam fecerit. ^{j} R.P. and S.R.; MS. om. ^{k} R.P. and S.R.; MS. fuerunt. ^{l} R.P. and S.R.; MS. liniati. ^{m} R.P. and S.R.; MS. om. ^{n} R.P. and S.R.; MS. liniatis. $^{o-o}$ R.P. and S.R. eis injunctum per regem.

other witnesses underwritten were requested by our said lord the king 1387
in the faith and allegiance whereby they were firmly bound to our same
lord the king that to certain questions specified below and rehearsed
before them they should make faithful answer and thereupon pronounce the law according to their discretion.

1. First,[1] they were asked: Whether that new statute and ordinance
and commission made and published in the last parliament held at Westminster derogate from the regality and prerogative of our said lord the
king? To which question they answered unanimously that they do so
derogate, especially as they had been against the king's will.

2. Next, they were asked: How those should be punished who procured the making of the statute, ordinance, and commission aforesaid?
To this question they answered unanimously that they deserve to be
punished capitally, that is to say by death, unless the king should be
disposed to grant them grace in that regard.

3. Next, they were asked: How those should be punished who
prompted the king aforesaid to consent to the making of a statute,
ordinance, and commission of this kind? To which question they
answered unanimously that unless the king should do them grace they
deserve to be punished capitally.

4. Next, they were asked: What punishment do those deserve who
compelled or constrained the king to consent to the making of the said
statute, ordinance, and commission? To which question they answered
unanimously that they deserve to be punished as traitors.

5. Next, they were asked: How those also should be punished who
prevented the king from exercising what belonged to his regality and
prerogative? To that question they answered unanimously that they too
should be punished as traitors.

6. Next, they were asked: Whether (after a parliament has assembled
and the business of the realm and the cause of the parliament's assembling have by the king's command been expounded and declared, and
certain articles have been defined by the king upon which the lords and
commons of the realm are to proceed in the same parliament), if the
lords and commons wish to proceed entirely upon other articles, and
not at all upon the articles defined by the king until there has first been
an answer by the king upon the articles specified by themselves (notwithstanding that the contrary has been enjoined upon them by the
king)[2] — whether the king ought in this regard to have control of the
parliament and in fact to exercise control so that they must first proceed
upon the articles defined by the king, or whether the lords and commons ought first to receive an answer from the king upon the articles

---

[1] In this question and subsequently the 'commission' is the commission of
appointment of the continual council established in the parliament of 1 Oct.-
28 Nov. 1386, or the letters patent of 19 Nov. 1386 — also called the 'ordinance'
— in which this was first announced and which preceded the enactment of the
commission as a statute. See above, pp. 166–76.

[2] As in 1386 (Knighton, *Chronicon*, ii. 215).

1387 eosdem expressis antequam ulterius procedatur. Ad quam quidem questionem unanimiter responderunt quod rex in ea parte haberet regimen et sic seriatim in omnibus aliis articulis tangentibus parliamentum usque ad finem ejusdem parliamenti; et si quis contra hujusmodi regimen regis fecerit^a tanquam proditor est puniendus.

vij. Item querebatur ab eis numquid rex quandocumque sibi placuerit poterit dissolvere parliamentum et suis dominis et communibus precipere quod abinde recedant an non. Ad quam quidem questionem unanimiter responderunt quod potest; et si quis extunc contra voluntatem regis procedat ut in parliamento tanquam proditor puniendus existit.

viij. Item quesitum erat ab eis ex quo rex potest quandocumque sibi placuerit removere^b quoscumque officiarios et justiciarios suos et ipsos pro delictis eorum justiciare^c et punire, numquid domini et communes possent^d absque voluntate regis officiarios et^e justiciarios ipsos^e impetere super delictis ipsorum^f in parliamento an non. Ad ^{g}quam quidem^g questionem unanimiter responderunt quod non possunt; et si quis in^e contrarium fecerit est ut proditor puniendus.[1]

ix. Item querebatur ab eis qualiter est ille puniendus qui ^{h} in parliamento movebat^h quod mitteretur pro statuto per quod rex Edwardus filius ^{i}regis Edwardi^i proavus regis nunc erat alias adjudicatus in parliamento,^{j}[2] per cujus statuti inspeccionem nova statutum et ordinacio atque^k commissio supradicta fuerunt in parliamento concepta. Ad quam quidem questionem unanimiter responderunt quod tam ille qui sic movebat quam alius qui pretextu hujusmodi mocionis statutum illud portavit ad parliamentum sunt ut proditores et criminosi merito puniendi.

x. Item quesitum erat ab eis an judicium in ultimo parliamento apud Westmonasterium celebrato redditum contra comitem Suff' fuit erroneum et revocabile an non. Ad quam quidem questionem unanimiter responderunt quod si illud judicium esset modo reddendum illi justiciarii et serviens predicti illud reddere nollent, quia videtur illis^l quod judicium illud revocabile est^m tanquam erroneum in omni sui parte.[3]

In quorum omnium testimonium justiciarii et serviens predicti sigilla sua presentibus apposuerunt. Hiis testibus, reverendis patribus^n Alexandro archiepiscopo Eboracen', Roberto archiepiscopo Dublinnens',[4] Johanne episcopo Dunelmen',[5] Thoma Cicestr' episcopo,[6] Johanne

---

^{a} *R.P. and S.R.; MS.* faceret. ^{b} *R.P. and S.R.; MS.* revocare. ^{c} *R.P. and S.R.* justificare. ^{d} *R.P. and S.R.* possint. ^{e} *R.P. and S.R.; MS. om.* ^{f} *R.P. and S.R.* eorum. $^{g-g}$ *R.P. and S.R.* istam. $^{h-h}$ *R.P. and S.R.* movebat in parliamento. $^{i-i}$ *R.P. and S.R.* Edwardi regis. ^{j} *MS. inserts* qui. ^{k} *R.P. and S.R.* et. ^{l} *R.P. and S.R.* eis. ^{m} *MS. inserts* et. ^{n} *R.P. and S.R. insert* dominis.

---

[1] Question and answer refer to the impeachment of Michael de la Pole in 1386 but also express the belief, long upheld by the king and his advisers, that the

specified by themselves before further proceedings? To which question 1387
they answered unanimously that the king would in this regard have
control and so successively in all other articles touching the parliament
until the end of the same parliament; and if any one should act contrary to such control by the king, he ought to be punished as a traitor.

7. Next, they were asked: Whether or not the king can whenever he
pleases dissolve parliament and bid his lords and commons depart
thence? To which question they answered unanimously that he can;
and, if anyone thereafter proceeds, contrary to the king's will, as if he
were in parliament, he ought to be punished as a traitor.

8. Next, they were asked: Whether or not — inasmuch as the king
can at pleasure remove any of his officers and justices and bring them
to justice for their misdeeds and punish them — whether or not the
lords and Commons could, without the king's will, impeach in parliament those officers and justices for their misdeeds? To which question
they answered unanimously that they cannot; and if anyone acts to the
contrary, he ought to be punished as a traitor.[1]

9. Next, they were asked: How ought he to be punished who in
parliament moved that that statute be sent for whereby King Edward
[II], son of King Edward and great-grandfather of the present king, was
in time past adjudged in parliament,[2] by examination of which statute
the new statute, ordinance, and commission abovesaid were conceived
in parliament? To which question they answered unanimously that
both he who moved to this effect and any other who by colour of such
a motion carried that statute to parliament deserve to be punished as
traitors and criminals.

10. Next, they were asked: Whether or not the judgement delivered
in the last parliament held at Westminster against the earl of Suffolk
was erroneous and revocable? To which question they answered unanimously that if that judgement had now to be delivered, they, the aforesaid justices and the serjeant, would not be willing to deliver it, because it
seems to them to be revocable on the ground of error in every part of it.[3]

In witness of all whereof the justices and serjeant aforesaid
have hereunto set their seals. Witnesses: the reverend fathers Alexander archbishop of York, Robert archbishop of Dublin,[4] John
bishop of Durham,[5] Thomas bishop of Chichester,[6] John bishop

Crown should control the procedure of impeachment (Plucknett, in *T.R.H.S.*,
5th ser., ii (1952), 159 ff.).

[2] A reference to a statute, now lost, announcing Edward II's acceptance of the
election of the Ordainers in the parliament of 1310 (Clementi, in *E.H.R.*, lxxxvi
(1971), 104-6).

[3] Cf. M. V. Clarke, *Fourteenth Century Studies* (1937), pp. 48 ff.; N. B. Lewis,
'Article VII of the Impeachment of Michael de la Pole in 1386', in *E.H.R.*, xlii
(1927), 402-7; J. J. N. Palmer, 'The Impeachment of Michael de la Pole in 1386',
in *B.I.H.R.*, xlii (1969), pp. 96 ff.

[4] Robert Wikeford, for whom see *B.R.U.O.*, iii. 2045-6 and below, p. 206
and n.   [5] John Fordham.

[6] Thomas Rushock, O.P., the king's confessor. See also below, p. 316.

1387 Bangorensi episcopo,[1] Roberto duce Hibern' et Michaele comite Suff'
et Johanne Ripon' clerico[2] et[a] Johanne Blake scutifero.[3] Datum loco,
die, mense, et anno predictis.[4]

Ista et alia per illos qui regi jugiter adherebant contra
mentem littere patentis peracta et a noticia dominorum
predictorum[5] protunc undecumque celata causabant aliis
postea gravia detrimenta, nam plures propterea in proximo
parliamento sequenti eorum vitas cum eorum bonis temporalibus perdiderunt.

Quo eciam anno Urbanus papa Luca relicta venit
Perusium, ubi deposuit cardinalem Pileum archiepiscopum[b]
Ravenn' quia reliquerat eum et antipape Roberto Gebenen'
adhesit, privavitque eum propterea omnibus beneficiis suis
et inter cetera contulit archiepiscopatum Ravenn' Cosmati
Gentili alienigene collectori suo in Anglia, viro utique
reverendo et multe litterature perito.[6] Nec mora: confirmata eleccione Westmon' electi[7] intravit curiam dictus
Cosmas Gentilis, confestim papam consuluit ne elecciones
abbatum exemptorum ipsis absentibus deinceps in curia
confirmaret, set absque ulla spe misericordie hujusmodi
electi se personaliter apostolico conspectui presentarent,
recepturi ibidem post congruam examinacionem, prout
moris est, munus sacrum benediccionis ab episcopo ad
hoc specialiter deputato. Et quamvis monachi Sancti
Augustini Cantuar' profusis expensis amplius quam per
unum annum in curia pro confirmacione sui electi
stetissent, non obstantibus litteris regis aut aliorum
magnorum dominorum aliud responsum habere nequirent[c]

[a] R.P. and S.R. ac.   [b] The first letters of this word are interlined.
[c] Recte nequibant aut nequierunt (Winterbottom).

---

[1] John Swaffham, a Carmelite, for whom see Tout, Chapters, iii. 424, n. 1.
[2] A royal clerk with experience as a justice; in 1385 he accompanied de Vere
to Scotland (Cal. Pat. R., 1385–9, p. 51; Cal. Cl. R., 1385–9, p. 106; and above,
p. 188).
[3] Described in 1388 as a referendary and said to have drafted the questions to
the judges (below, p. 258; R.P., iii. 240). See also Walsingham, Hist. Ang., ii. 162.
[4] Above, p. 196.
[5] Probably a reference to a passage on the now lost leaf (for which see p. xvii
n.) naming the lords who took the initiative in the parliament of Oct.–Nov.
1386. The phrase 'domini predicti' is of interest, since this becomes the Monk's
usual way of referring to the Lords Appellant of 1387–8.

of Bangor;[1] Robert duke of Ireland, Michael earl of Suffolk, John 1387
Ripon clerk,[2] and John Blake esquire.[3] Dated the place, day, month,
and year aforesaid.[4]

These proceedings, and other breaches, by the king's
persistent supporters, of the intention of the letters
patent, were at the time completely concealed from the
knowledge of the lords above-mentioned,[5] but they were
later the cause of grave harm to others, since because of
them a number of people lost their lives and their worldly
goods in the parliament next following.

Pope Urban left Lucca this year for Perugia, where he
deposed Cardinal Pileus, the archbishop of Ravenna,
who had deserted him and given his support to the
antipope, Robert of Geneva. The pope consequently
deprived him of all his benefices and among other things
conferred the archbishopric of Ravenna on Cosmas
Gentilis, an alien who had been papal collector in England, a truly reverend character and a highly accomplished
man of letters.[6] The consequences were swift: scarcely
had the election of the abbot-elect of Westminster been
confirmed[7] when this Cosmas Gentilis appeared in the
curia and recommended to the pope that the elections
of exempt abbots should not henceforward be confirmed
in the curia in their absence, but that abbots-elect,
without any expectation of being excused, should present
themselves in person to the pope's view, and only after
the appropriate investigation which custom requires should
there receive the sacred gift of benediction from the
bishop especially appointed for this purpose. And although
the monks of St. Augustine's Canterbury stayed at great
expense for over a year in the curia seeking confirmation
for their abbot-elect, the only answer they could get,
despite letters from the king and other great nobles,

---

[6] Urban VI left Lucca on 23 Sept. 1387 and arrived at Perugia on 2 Oct.
(*Theoderici de Nyem De Scismate Libri Tres*, ed. G. Erler (Leipzig, 1890), p. 117).
He promoted Cosmas Gentilis Megliorato to the see of Ravenna on 4 Nov. 1387
(Eubel and Van Gulik, *Hierarchia Catholica Medii Aevi*, i. 436 and n.). Pileus de
Prata, who had been archbishop of Ravenna since 1370, adhered to Clement VII
in 1386. In 1379 Urban had appointed Cosmas Gentilis papal collector in
England.   [7] On 8 July 1387 (above, p. 178 n.).

1387 quam ut eorum electum sub forma predicta domino pape personaliter presentarent.[1]

Transiit annus iste satis frugifer, habens in estate calores multum ferventes; unde in mense Septembris secuta est magna mortalitas hominum, precipue juvenum utriusque sexus; tamen (benedictus Deus) diu non duravit.

Igitur[a] electus Westmon' primo die Septembris receptis bullis sue confirmacionis xij[mo]. die Octobris rite fuerat installatus et sequenti die, scilicet in festo Translacionis Sancti regis Edwardi, magna missa ab eo peracta fecit suum introitum, [b]omnesque confluentes[b] ad suam aulam in multa rerum vescibilium ubertate eo die refecit.

Quo in tempore dicebatur quod rex Anglie ad instanciam quorumdam consiliariorum eidem assistencium proposuit remittere regi Francorum castella et villas ceteraque omnia que in transmarinis partibus possidebat pro certa summa pecunie, prout inde poterint[c] adinvicem melius concordare, excepta Aquitannia, pro qua libenter regi Francorum homagium faceret sic quod libere poterit eam in sua manu tenere sicut eam[d] sui predecessores actenus tenuerunt pacifice et quiete. Consideravit namque rex cum suo consilio quia[e] si oporteret ipsum contra regem Francorum continua bella fovere, necessario haberet suum populum novis imposicionibus semper gravare, quod esset sibi dampnosum; igitur melius sibi videbatur a bellorum tumultu ea parte aliquantulum respirare et in pace quiescere quam continuis guerrarum vexacionibus anxiari.[2] Et quamvis ista non sortiebantur effectum, nichilominus tamen pro hiis et aliis premissis et inferius specificandis exorta est causa quare domini surrexerunt; alia causa fuit propter imminens periculum

---

[a] Abbas Westm' *in the margin opposite this passage, in a fifteenth-century hand.* [b-b] MS. omnes confluentesque. [c] *Sic MS.; cf. p. 410.* [d] *Interlined.* [e] *MS. inserts* et.

---

[1] The election of William Welde in Feb. 1387 (for which see above, p. 180) was confirmed by Urban VI in consistory on 21 Nov. 1388; his proctor had been active at the curia since June 1387. For this episode see *William Thorne's Chronicle of Saint Augustine's Abbey, Canterbury*, trans. A. H. Davis (Oxford, 1934), pp. 654 ff. For the requirement that prelates-elect of exempt houses attend at the curia in person for confirmation, see W. E. Lunt, *Papal Revenues in the Middle Ages* (2 vols., Columbia University Records of Civilisation, xix, 1934),

was that they must present their abbot-elect in person to
the pope in accordance with the above procedure.[1]

This year ran its course with a fair harvest, and spells of
intense heat during the summer; so that there followed in
September a pestilence which caused a heavy loss of life,
especially among the young of both sexes; but — blessed be
God — it did not last long.

The abbot-elect of Westminster, then, received the bulls
confirming him on 1 September; and on 12 October, with
due ceremony, he was installed. On the following day, which
was the feast of the Translation of St. Edward the King, after
celebrating High Mass, he made his entry and on the same
day provided eatables in lavish quantities for all those who
came flocking to his hall.

There were reports at this time that, prompted by some of
the counsellors who surrounded him, the king of England
proposed to relinquish to the king of the French, for a lump
sum to be mutually agreed, all his overseas castles, towns,
and other possessions, except Aquitaine, for which he would
willingly do homage to the French king provided that he was
freely allowed to hold it in his own hand as peaceably and
quietly as his predecessors had done in the past. In common
with his council the king had concluded that if he was going
to have to maintain a ceaseless state of war against the king
of the French, he would inevitably be compelled to be for
ever burdening his people with new imposts, with damaging
results for himself; he therefore thought it better to secure
a short breathing-space from the tumult of strife in that
quarter than to be harassed by the unending troubles of
war.[2] Although it came to nothing, it was nevertheless this
project (with other matters already mentioned or to be
particularized below) that formed a reason for the lords'
rising. A second reason lay in the danger that impended of

i. 84. It had not been strictly enforced in the case of England since the beginning
of the Hundred Years War, and even before that time by no means all such
prelates had been blessed at the curia. See also below, p. 384.

[2] A passage conflating proposals for a truce and the concessions which were
likely to be the cost to England of a final peace. Both truce and peace were
discussed in the course of the negotiations of 1387. For Simon Shiryngham, the
king's agent in the early stages, see below, p. 302; for comment see above, pp.
lxi–lxii and *Palmer*, pp. 105 ff.

1387 destruccionis tocius regni; tercia causa[a] fuit propter malam gubernacionem regis et regni,[b] quia per minus sufficientes

p. 161 homines fuit rex / actenus gubernatus; item quia dicti consiliarii domini regis predictorum dominorum conspirarunt in mortem.[c][1] Robertus vero archiepiscopus Dublinnens' suo consideravit in animo quod nisi ista cicius frustrarentur in confusionem tocius regni Anglie profecto, immo in subversionem illius, tenderent manifeste. Igitur quadam die idem archiepiscopus casualiter duci Glouc' obviavit, et ab eo primo peciit veniam, deinde cuncta que coram rege sunt gesta sibi per ordinem propalavit:[2] et ideo quia alii ⟨qui⟩[d] ea celarunt turpiter perierunt, iste namque ab omni impeticione immunis evasit. Major itaque London' Nicholaus Exton' in suo officio permansit rege volente per totum annum sequentem.[3]

Item xxviij. die Octobris misit rex archiepiscopum Eboracen' et Michaelem de la Pole comitem Suff' ad majorem et cives London' ad inquirendum ab eis an essent inter se unanimes in civitate London' et an ipsi vellent stare cum rege, si opus[e] exposceret, aut non.[4] Ad ista fuit eis responsum quod illi forent unanimes et suo regi vellent obedire in omnibus, prout sua regia majestas exigit et requirit, ac secum tenere aliis postpositis quibuscumque. Accepto vero responso ad regem cum gaudio redierunt. Rex autem super hujusmodi responso exhillaratus x^mo. die Novembris civitatem London' intravit, contra quem major et ceteri cives dicte civitatis in una secta, alba scilicet et rubea, honorifice exierunt et ante eum per medium civitatis usque le Muwes apud Charryngg' processionaliter equitarunt,[5] ubi rex discalciavit se et archiepiscopus Ebor', Robertus de[f] Veer dux Hibernie, et Michael de la Pole comes Suff' cum eo pariter nudipedes ad ecclesiam

---

[a] iij. *in the margin. (The numerals* j. *and* ij. *have probably been lost at the edge of the page.)* [b] *A short erasure, covered by a dash, follows.* [c] iiij. *in the margin.* [d] MS. om. [e] inst *deleted after this word.* [f] MS. le.

[1] Cf. below, pp. 258-60, 274.

[2] And principally, no doubt, the king's consultation with the judges in Aug. 1387; see above, p. 200.

[3] Exton was elected, for a 2nd term, on 13 Oct. 1387 (*Letter Book H*, p. 320; see also ibid., pp. 289-90).

[4] Cf. the oath of allegiance taken by Londoners at the beginning of Oct. 1387

the destruction of the entire realm; a third in the misgovern- 1387
ment affecting the king and his kingdom (for the king had
hitherto been under the influence of incompetent advisers);
and yet another in that these counsellors of the lord king
conspired to bring about the deaths of the above-mentioned
lords.[1] But Robert archbishop of Dublin privately decided
that unless swift action was taken to counteract these
courses, they would obviously lead to nation-wide chaos in
England — indeed to the overthrow of the kingdom. Happening therefore one day to meet the duke of Gloucester, he
opened by asking for pardon for himself and went on to
reveal to him in full detail what had been going on in the
king's immediate circle.[2] It was because of this revelation that
whereas others, who kept their knowledge of these matters
to themselves, met ignominious deaths, this archbishop came
off without having to meet any kind of impeachment. With
the king's approval the mayor of London, Nicholas Exton,
remained in office throughout the succeeding year.[3]

On 28 October the king sent the archbishop of York and
Michael de la Pole, earl of Suffolk, to the mayor and citizens
of London to ask whether people were united in the city
and whether or not they were willing, if the need arose, to
take their stand with the king.[4] To this the answer given was
that the Londoners were indeed united, and that they were
willing to give to their king such obedience in everything as
his royal majesty required and demanded of them, and to
support him without regard to anybody else whatever. The
envoys returned jubilant with this reply to the king, who,
greatly cheered by its nature, made an entry into the city of
London on 10 November. The mayor and the other citizens
did him the honour of coming out to meet him uniformly
dressed in white and red and rode ahead of him in procession through the city as far as the Mews at Charing.[5] Here
the king removed his shoes, and the procession, in which the
king was accompanied by the archbishop of York, Robert
de Vere duke of Ireland, and Michael de la Pole earl of
Suffolk, all barefooted like himself, moved on to the church

(below, p. 232 and n.).
    [5] The king went from Sheen via London to Westminster; Charing lay on his
way out of the City. See *Favent*, p. 9.

1387 Sancti Petri Westmon' processerunt; contra quem eciam
abbas et conventus dicti monasterii in capis usque portam
regiam[1] ei obviam modo solempni venerunt et illum super
tapetis ab illo loco stratis usque in ecclesiam deduxerunt;
factisque suis devocionibus ex more ad suum palacium
remeavit.

Sequenti vero die[2] misit rex pro duce Gloucestr' et
comite Arundell' ut venirent ad illum. Illi autem excusa-
bant se, asserentes eos inimicos capitales juxta latus suum
habere, et ideo non audebant sibi appropinquare. Igitur
precepto regis xij°. die Novembris fuit proclamatum
London' sub forisfactura omnium bonorum quod nullus de
civitate comiti Arundell' aliquid venderet seu illi in aliquo
necessaria ministraret;[3] quodque factum multis displicuit eo
quod erat unus de valencioribus optimatibus tocius terre.
Item Michael de la Pole comes Suff' nequiter *et sepius*
semper suasit regi quatinus ut ceteris pretermissis ante
omnia comes Warwyk' occideretur ista racione quia per
eum stetit quominus illi domini jussi venire ad regem ejus
suasu nephario nequaquam venerunt set ei resistere
tanquam rebelles nequiter paraverunt, sicque patet magis
illum dictis dominis ita rebellantibus adherere quam suo
regi, cui juvamen inpenderet et illum pro viribus sustineret
ceteris postpositis quibuscumque: item comes iste cum aliis
dominis, scilicet duce Glouc', comite Arundell', comite
Derbeye, et comite Notyngham, in mortem regis sive in ejus
deposicionem proditorie conspiravit, igitur dignus morte
manifeste probatur; et profecto eo extincto ceteri domini
contra regem erigere cornua[4] non audebunt, quia ejus
sensu et industria atque consilio hucusque sunt ducti
pariterque fortificati. Ad quem rex ait quod penes se

---

a-a Added above the line in a different (and perhaps slightly later) hand.

---

[1] North of the church.

[2] From this point in his narrative until the narrative for 18 Jan. 1388 the Monk
was probably using a written source originating in the circle of the Appellants,
for which see above, pp. lii–iv.

[3] The earl himself was at a distance from London (below, p. 210), but some of
his followers were secreted in the environs. See *Favent*, p. 8; Knighton, *Chronicon*, ii. 246–7; and below, p. 264.

[4] Perhaps an echo of Zech. i. 21, where the Vulgate has 'levaverunt cornu'.

of St. Peter, Westminster. The abbot and convent of the 1387 monastery, in their turn, came, wearing copes, as far as the King's Gate[1] to give him a ceremonial welcome and to escort him over the carpets laid from that spot to the church; and when he had completed his devotions he returned in the usual way to his palace.

On the following day [11 November][2] the king sent to the duke of Gloucester and the earl of Arundel commanding their attendance. But they excused themselves on the ground that they had arch-enemies at the king's elbow and that therefore they dared not come near him. Proclamation was consequently made in London by the king's orders on 12 November that on pain of forfeiture of all his goods nobody in the city should sell anything to the earl of Arundel or provide in any respect for his needs;[3] this move caused widespread displeasure, for the earl was one of the most heroic figures among the great men of the entire country. At the same time Michael de la Pole earl of Suffolk never stopped urging upon the king the iniquitous suggestion that he should neglect everything else and make it his very first task to bring about the death of the earl of Warwick, on the ground that it was through him and his mischievous persuasion that the lords, when they were summoned to the king's presence, had failed to appear and were now wickedly preparing a rebellious opposition to him: it was thus obvious that he sided with those disaffected lords in preference to his king, whom before anybody else whatever he should have succoured and supported to the utmost of his power. Besides, the earl, with other nobles, that is to say the duke of Gloucester and the earls of Arundel and Derby and Nottingham, was in a traitorous conspiracy to compass the king's death or dethronement, which is clear proof that he deserved to lose his life; and, of course, once he was removed the remaining lords would not dare to 'lift up their horns'[4] against the king since it was by his intelligence, his activity, and his counsel that they had thus far been at the same time guided and encouraged. In reply to this the king said that before

The preceding passage contains an anachronism: Derby and Nottingham had not yet joined the three original Appellants.

1387 vellet consulcius deliberare antequam per eum tantus et talis nobilis moreretur.

Ad consilium autem archiepiscopi Eboracen', Roberti de Veer ducis Hibernie, et Michaelis de la Pole proposuit rex mittere pro suo retenemento contra istos dominos jam contra illum, ut sibi videbatur, protunc levatos; set illi per eorum amicos de hoc[a] certificati confestim ad arma prosiliunt, videlicet dux Glouc' in Estsex', comes Arundell' in Southsex',[1] et comes Warrewyk' tunc cum suis existens in Middelsex', et apud parcum de Haryngge in aquilonali parte London'[2] cum eorum cuneis armatorum xiij°. die Novembris insimul convenerunt: quo in partibus divulgato ex omni parte confluebat ad eos generosorum maxima multitudo. Sequenti vero die moverunt se de illo loco et secesserunt apud Waltham Cross. Rex vero stupefactus ad tam subitam tantorum coadunacionem; unde super hoc habito consilio xiiij^mo. die Novembris misit ad eos Cantuar' archiepiscopum et ducem Eboracen', episcopos eciam Wynton' et Elyen', dominum Johannem de Waltham portitorem privati sigilli clericum, dominum Johannem de Coboham nobilem, et dominos Ricardum Scrop' et Johannem Deverose milites providos et discretos,[3] ad tractandum cum prefatis dominis qua de causa cum tanta multitudine surrexerunt. Ad quod responderunt domini predicti quia clare prospiciebant quod per proditores juxta latus regis jugiter assistentes regnum Anglie in brevi subverteretur nisi remedium super hoc celerius apponatur: 'igitur nos fideles regi et regno contra tales procedere quantocius hanelamus, ut nos, immo totum regnum, a cecis insidiis et a laqueis mortiferis salvare possimus'.[4] Sicque tunc constanter appellabant de prodicione Alexandrum archiepiscopum Eboracen', Robertum de Veer ducem Hibernie, Michaelem de la Pole comitem Southfolch', Robertum Tresilian justiciarium et Nicholaum Brembre militem

---

[a] cerf' *deleted after this word.*

---

[1] Cf. Walsingham (*Hist. Ang.*, ii. 163), who says that Arundel was in Reigate castle.

[2] i.e. Hornsey: 'Haringay' is an early form of this name (Gover, Mawer, and Stenton, *Place-Names of Middlesex* (E.P.N.S. xviii), 121).

[3] All members of the continual council of 1386, now entering the last week of

becoming responsible for the death of a noble of this stature 1387
and quality he would want to give the matter more mature
personal thought.

On the advice of the archbishop of York, Robert de
Vere duke of Ireland, and Michael de la Pole, the king now
proposed to summon his followers to deal with the lords who
in his view were already in a state of insurrection against him,
but they, informed by friends of what was afoot, sprang
immediately to arms, the duke of Gloucester in Essex, the
earl of Arundel in Sussex,[1] and the earl of Warwick with
his personal following in Middlesex. On 13 November they
met each with his own armed contingent at Haringay Park
to the north of London,[2] where, when the news spread
through the country, huge numbers of gentry came flocking from all directions to join them. Next day they left
Haringay and retired to Waltham Cross. The king was
stunned by this sudden combination of powerful adversaries;
and after holding a council on 14 November dispatched to
them the archbishop of Canterbury and the duke of York,
accompanied by two bishops, of Winchester and of Ely;
one cleric, Sir John Waltham, keeper of the privy seal; one
nobleman, Sir John Cobham; and two discerning and saga-
cious knights, Sir Richard Scrope and Sir John Devereux;[3]
who were to discuss with the lords above-mentioned their
reason for rising in such force. It was, said the lords in reply,
that unless counter-measures were promptly taken, they
clearly foresaw the speedy overthrow of the kingdom of
England by the traitors who haunted the king's presence:
'and therefore our own loyalty to the king and the realm
makes us eager to move as quickly as possible against these
creatures so that we can save ourselves — indeed, the entire
kingdom — from treachery lurking unseen and the snares that
spell death.'[4] And so they proceeded without wavering to
appeal of treason Alexander archbishop of York, Robert de
Vere duke of Ireland, Michael de la Pole earl of Suffolk,
Robert Tresilian justice, and Nicholas Brembre of London,

its appointed life. The choice of negotiators was probably imposed by Gloucester,
Arundel, and Warwick in less formal discussions before 14 Nov.; cf. the initiative
on the part of the three described in Knighton, *Chronicon*, ii. 242-3. For the
meeting on 14 Nov. see *R.P.*, iii. 229.

[4] For 'laquei mortis' in the Vulgate see above, p. 184 n.

1387 London': et quod isti sunt nequissimi proditores vellent
probare contra quemlibet opponentem nulli parcendo in
hoc casu, rege semper excepto. Nec ab incepto desistere
eos velle*a* dixerunt quousque habuerint prefatos proditores
in tuta custodia ad respondendum objectis sibi imponendis
in proximo parliamento sequenti.[1] Verumptamen isti domini
a rege missi multum laboriose steterunt erga prefatos
dominos ut relicta sequela suorum armatorum eorum regi

p. 162 se*a* utpote homines ligii conformarent. / Quibus responderunt
se velle eorum regem in omnibus honorare tanquam eorum
dominum ligium et ad eum cum omni subjeccione venire
dummodo dicti proditores sub fida custodia usque in proximum parliamentum interim fuerint custoditi atque habita
securitate sufficienti libere revertendi ad suos quandocumque eis placuerit absque dolo et fraude procurata sive
ymaginata: que eis omnia *b*servare bona fide*b* predicti nuncii
promiserunt.

Interim innotuit istis dominis quomodo dominus Thomas
Tryvet consuluit regem exire in latum campum et suum
vexillum expandere contra istos dominos sic levatos:
quodque consilium valde eis displicuit.[2] Nichilominus tamen
ad instanciam reverendorum virorum*c* xvij. die Novembris*d*
cum ccc. equis venerunt ad regem in Magna Aula apud
Westmon' in sede*e* regia collocatum, et intrantes aulam hii
tres, scilicet dux Glouc', comes Arundell', et comes Warwyk',
videntesque regem protinus corruerunt proni*e* in terram,
sicque tribus vicibus fecerunt antequam pervenerunt ad eum.
Demum jussu regis erexerunt se stantes dixeruntque ei quod
non miraretur quamvis tarde venerunt ad eum nec jam
propter eorum adventum sub tali apparatu obstupesceret,
quia, prout didicerant ab aliis, eorum capitales inimici juxta
latus suum continue residebant; unde mirum non esset, licet
fuissent morosi in veniendo ad eum, quia vitam eorum

---

a Interlined.   *b–b* In the margin but marked for insertion at this point.
c Interlined.   *d* MS. inserts et.   *e* Interlined.

[1] Cf. below, p. 238, where it is implied that the first suggestion of a hearing in
parliament was made by the king; and for comment, Clarke, *Fourteenth Century
Studies*, pp. 134–5.

[2] A reference to ambushes prepared by Trivet for the Appellants at the Mews
in Charing and in the archbishop of York's house in Westminster. On account of
these the Appellants were 2 hours late for their meeting with the king on 17 Nov.,

knight; that these were the wickedest of traitors they were 1387
willing to prove against any adversary, none being spared this
challenge save always the king himself. They would not cease
from the task they had begun, they said, until they had those
traitors safely in custody ready to answer, in the parliament
next following, the charges to be laid against them.[1] The
king's emissaries, for their part, strongly pressed the lords to
leave their armed followers behind and to show compliance
to their king whose liege subjects they were. To this they
replied that they were willing to honour their king, as their
liege lord, in everything, and to wait upon him with all sub-
missiveness, provided that throughout the period until the
next parliament the above-mentioned traitors were kept in
the custody of trustworthy persons and that the lords themselves received adequate assurances of their freedom to return
whenever they pleased to their followers without the fear
that any trickery or deception would be contrived or planned
against them. All these conditions the king's envoys undertook faithfully to observe.

Meanwhile it came to the knowledge of the lords that Sir
Thomas Trivet had advised the king to take the field and
unfurl his standard against the insurgents, a piece of advice
which caused them intense displeasure.[2] Nevertheless, at
the request of the ecclesiastics in the deputation, on 17
November they arrived with 300 horse to visit the king, who
had seated himself on the royal throne in the Great Hall at
Westminster. When they entered the hall, the three of them,
the duke of Gloucester and the earls of Arundel and Warwick,
at sight of the king immediately prostrated themselves and
did so three times before they reached him. Eventually,
bidden by the king, they rose to their feet and told him not
to be surprised that their coming had been so long delayed
nor, now that they had come, to feel any astonishment that
they were thus panoplied, seeing that, as they had learned
from other sources, their arch-enemies never left the king's
side; it was therefore not to be wondered at that they had
been slow in coming, since their paramount desire was to

and this explains their opening words to the king on that occasion. See Knighton,
Chronicon, ii. 248; and Walsingham, *Hist. Ang.*, ii. 165. (Walsingham associates
Nicholas Brembre with Trivet in the plot.)

1387 quamdiu possent salvis semper eorum ligeanciis vellent ceteris postpositis conservare. Responsis hinc inde habitis inter regem et ipsos tandem finitis rogabant regem predicti domini prebere auditum ad ea que dominus Ricardus Scrop' miles eorum ex parte in communi audiencia foret dicturus; annuit rex.

Qui constanter dixit quod ista mocio dominorum habuit exordium principaliter propter quinque personas domino nostro regi jugiter adherentes parum superius nominatas, quas isti domini appellarunt de prodicione facta per eos tam regi quam regno et cum eorum appellacione non obstantibus contradicentibus volunt stare. 'Quare supplicant celsitudini vestre quod iste persone in tuto loco usque in proximum parliamentum custodirentur et communi lege pro eorum maleficiis favore postposito plecterentur,^{a} si contingat taliter inveniri.'[1] Rex autem adquievit peticioni eorum et accepit causam in manu sua prefixitque terminum parliamenti fore tercio die Februarii.

Quo facto latuerunt omnes isti taliter diffamati excepto domino Nicholao Brembre:[2] archiepiscopus vero Eboracen' quo divertit se nescitur, set iste et Robertus Tresilyan constabat se veraciter abscondisse;[3] dux vero Hibernie acceleravit gressus suos cum litteris regiis versus Cestr', ubi virtute dictarum litterarum congregavit magnam potenciam hominum armatorum;[4] comes itaque Southfolch' in apparatu negociatoris venit Calesiam et custodem castri ville predicte dominum Edmundum de la Pole fratrem suum adivit ut ipsum ibidem foveret; qui timens fortuitos casus tradidit illum capitaneo ville predicte,[5] qui infra breve post in Angliam illum reduxit, qui aliquantulum ibi commorans in hospicium suum in Hull' furtive accessit. Item parum ante finem mensis Novembris jussu regis fuit proclamatum London' quod nullus omnino loqueretur malum de hiis

---

^{a} *Interlined.*

[1] i.e. the accused should suffer drawing, hanging — and possibly disembowelling — and forfeiture of lands and chattels.

[2] In mid-Dec., Brembre was committed to Gloucester castle (below, p. 230 n.).

[3] Nevill fled north (Knighton, *Chronicon*, ii. 250). Tresilian lay in hiding in Westminster until his discovery on 19 Feb. 1388, for which see below, pp. 282 and n., 310.

preserve their own lives as long as they could do so without 1387 prejudice to their allegiance. There was an exchange of conversation between the king and the lords, at the end of which they asked him to listen to what Sir Richard Scrope had to say on their behalf in the hearing of everybody present; and the king agreed.

Their spokesman steadfastly maintained that the unrest among the lords had its origin primarily in the conduct of the five persons (named just above) continually in the king's company whom the lords had appealed of treason committed against both king and kingdom; and by their appeal, regardless of opposition, they intended to stand. 'They therefore beg your Highness that these persons may be kept in a place of safety until the next parliament and that no favour shall spare them the common-law punishment for their misdeeds, if misdeeds they are in the event found to be.'[1] The king assented to this petition, and, taking the matter into his own cognizance, fixed a date for the parliament on 3 February.

Following this, all the persons who had been thus denounced, with the exception of Sir Nicholas Brembre, kept out of sight.[2] Where the archbishop of York went is not known, but it is generally accepted that he and Robert Tresilian did in fact go into hiding.[3] The duke of Ireland, armed with letters from the king, hastily bent his steps towards Chester, where the letters enabled him to assemble a considerable armed force.[4] The earl of Suffolk, disguised as a trader, got as far as Calais and approached his brother, Sir Edmund de la Pole, keeper of the castle there, with a request for harbour. Sir Edmund, however, was afraid to take chances, and handed him over to the captain of Calais,[5] by whom he was shortly afterwards brought back to England, but very early in his stay here he slipped away to his house in Hull. Just before the end of November, royal proclamation was made in London that nobody whatever was to speak ill of the members of the king's entourage or

[4] Cf. Knighton, *Chronicon*, ii. 251, and below, pp. 256 and n., 266.
[5] Sir William Beauchamp, brother of the earl of Warwick, for whom see also Knighton, op. cit., pp. 244, 251.

1387 qui circa regem steterunt neque de hiis qui erant per dominos temporales jam noviter impetiti seu forsitan diffamati.[1]

Item ultimo die Novembris[2] misit rex pro majore London' cum senioribus ejusdem civitatis ad investigandum ab eis quot homines armorum possent ei si opus fuerit subvenire. Ad quod responderunt quod omnes in dicta civitate pro majori parte erant *artifices et* mercatores nec in bellis multum experti, nec licuit eis bellis vacare nisi pro defensione tantummodo civitatis predicte. Major vero instetit penes regem quod posset ab officio suo exonerari; tamen non optinuit quod petebat. Secundo die illis reversis misit rex pro quibusdam de qualibet arte dicte civitatis causa predicta, set non est votum suum in omnibus assecutus.

Igitur dominus rex suo sigillo privato misit dominis universis ut eo die apud Westmonasterium convenirent super diversis regni negociis tractaturi.[3] Nec mora: statuto die*b* venerunt domini, set rex dedignans venire usus insano consilio contra prefatos dominos animum odiosum concepit, protestando eos velle in tam arto loco includere sicut ipse jam tarde apud Westmonasterium per illos erat conclusus. Ad hec illi de consilio super hoc multum laborabant cum aliis episcopis et dominis ut ferocitatem*c* ejus animi contra dominos prefatos conceptam in aliquo mitigarent, set nil proficiebat eorum sollicitudo, quia voluntati eorum semper se contrarium exhibebat nec servare voluit promissiones quas dictis dominis nuper spoponderat conservare, scilicet quod omnes cause sive acciones injuriarum jam mote quiescerent usque in proximum parliamentum, immo fortiter stetit cum duce Hibernie, affirmans cum juramento quod nullo modo videret eum confusum neque detrimentum sue persone, prohibensque cancellario ne transmitteret brevia

---

a–a Interlined.   *b* Interlined.   *c* illius *is underlined for deletion after* this word.

---

[1] A conflation of two proclamations, both issued in London at this time: one addressed generally, announcing the grant of royal protection to the Appellants and the accused until parliament should meet; the other forbidding Londoners to speak ill of the king, the queen, or of those about the king's person. For the

of the persons who had lately been impeached or, as some 1387
might perhaps say, slandered, by the lords temporal.[1]

On the last day of November[2] the king sent for the mayor
and aldermen of London to ask them how many men-at-
arms could, at need, come to his help. They replied that the
inhabitants of the city were in the main craftsmen and
merchants, with no great military experience, and it was
not permissible for them to devote themselves to warfare
save for the defence of the city alone. The mayor, indeed,
pressed the king to make it possible for him to be relieved
of his office; but he failed to obtain his request. On the
day after the departure of the mayor and aldermen the king,
with the same object in view, summoned representatives
of each of the city's crafts, but he did not entirely achieve
his desire.

The king now sent letters under the privy seal to all lords
fixing a day for them to meet at Westminster to discuss
various items of public business.[3] On the appointed day,
which came soon afterwards, the lords attended, but the
king refused to appear: accepting unsound advice, he had
conceived a strong dislike for the lords, whom, he declared,
he would like to confine in the same constricting conditions
as those in which he himself had recently been cornered
by them at Westminster. At this the members of the council,
assisted by other lords and prelates, worked very hard to
moderate to some extent the animosity he entertained
towards the lords, but their concern had no effect: he
displayed persistent opposition to their purpose and was
unwilling to stand by the undertaking he had lately promised the lords he would honour, that all proceedings and
actions for tort already instituted should remain in abeyance until the next parliament, on the contrary, he sided
emphatically with the duke of Ireland, whom he swore he
would in no circumstances see discomfited or personally
harmed, and he forbade the chancellor to pass the writs

former see below, p. 238 and n.; for the latter, ibid., p. 266 and n.
    [2] Correctly, on 28 Nov.; on that day the mayor, Nicholas Exton, and aldermen
were summoned to attend the king at Windsor castle on 1 Dec. (Riley, *Memorials*,
p. 499; *Letter Book H*, p. 321).
    [3] And principally the arrangements for the promised parliament; see Knighton,
Chronicon, ii. 250.

1387 pro parliamento ante festum Sancti Thome Apostoli.[1]
Mutata postea voluntate misit ad illos de consilio ut omnia
rite fierent secundum quod eis videbatur melius[a] pro suo
comodo et honore.

Audientes domini predicti quomodo rex intentabat eis
minas proposuerunt ipsum deponere, tum quia non servabat
convencionem eis promissam tum quia, ut apparet, magis
sibi placet gubernari per falsissimos proditores quam per
suos nobiles et dominos regni sui fidelissimos amatores;
quibus restitit comes Warwyk' et illos ab hac sentencia
protinus revocavit:

'Absit', dixit ipse, 'quod hoc viderem, ut tam gloriosus
princeps de tam generosa stirpe progenitus et de tam nobili
prosapia oriundus, cui ego cum aliis hujus[b] regni dominis
in coronacione sua homagium et sacramentum fidelitatis
corporaliter prestiti, foret nunc depositus et dejectus. Revera
nobis hujusmodi facto modicum honoris et glorie possit
adquiri, immo pocius dedecus nobis et posteris nostris
obprobrium sempiternum. Igitur ab hac intencione vestrum
animum retrahatis et detis operam virtuose duci Hibernie
perfido proditori resistere,[c] qui cum manu valida et robusta
de comitatu Cestr' veniens per medium Anglie ad regem
transire contendit, forte nobis dampna et incomoda illa-
p. 163 turus. / Quod si ita fieri contingat, profecto supervacuus[d]
tunc videbitur labor noster: propter quod, ut omnia sub
racionis tramite consulte agantur, primo subtrahamus ei
copiam transeundi, vias pontesque sibi undique precludendo
in tantum quod manus nostras non evadat.'

Cujus dicta placuerunt dominis universis; et sic fieri
contrariis penitus annullatis universaliter decreverunt.
Quamobrem redintegratis iterato cuneis armatorum una
cum comite Derbeye et comite Notyngham[2] parum post

---

[a] *Interlined;* melius *is also in the margin.*   [b] *Interlined.*   [c] *Interlined;*
resistere *is also in the margin.*   [d] *MS.* supervacue.

---

[1] The writs are dated 17 Dec., but expenses in connection with the dispatch
of some of them are entered on the Issue Roll a week earlier (P.R.O., E. 403/518,
10 Dec.; *Cal. Cl. R., 1385–9*, pp. 456–7; *Lords' Reports on the Dignity of a Peer*,
iii. 725). Sheriffs were ordered to secure the return of knights 'in debatis modernis
magis indifferentes', but this clause was withdrawn when the writs were reissued
on 1 Jan. 1388 (ibid., iii. 726–7).

for the parliament before St. Thomas the Apostle's Day 1387 [21 December].[1] He later changed his mind and sent word to the members of the council that everything should proceed according to rule and to what they thought best for his advantage and dignity.

When they heard that the king was aiming threats in their direction the lords proposed to dethrone him on the double ground that he was failing to keep the agreement to which he was pledged and that he was apparently better pleased to be guided by the falsest of traitors than by those of his nobles and lords who were his most loyal supporters. The suggestion was opposed by the earl of Warwick, who hastened to recall the lords from this way of thinking:

'Heaven forfend', he said, 'that I should see a prince so glorious, born of a line so noble and sprung from a stock so illustrious, a prince to whom at his coronation in common with the other lords of this realm I did homage and swore my corporal oath of fealty, now deposed and brought low! For ourselves, indeed, such a proceeding could win little honour or glory — on the contrary it would be discredit for us and undying reproach for our descendants. Instead, then, of letting your minds run on this project, apply yourselves purposefully to resisting that faithless traitor the duke of Ireland, who, with a powerful and effective force is on his way from Cheshire across England in an attempt to reach the king, and may yet inflict on us losses and setbacks. If that should come about, our efforts will quite obviously have been wasted. In order, therefore, that all our actions shall be in accordance with a deliberate rational plan, let us begin by denying him any opportunity of getting through, by barring to him roads and bridges in every direction so that he does not slip through our fingers.'

These words won the approval of all the lords, who, setting aside entirely any proposals to the contrary, unanimously decided that so it should be. The armed units were accordingly once more re-formed, and, reinforced by the earls of Derby and Nottingham,[2] took the field shortly after the

[2] Henry Bolingbroke, earl of Derby, later duke of Lancaster and king of England (1366-1413), and Thomas Mowbray, earl of Nottingham, later duke of Norfolk (1366-99). Cf. *Favent*, p. 11.

1387 principium Decembris*a* equitare ceperunt. Transeuntes autem per Newmarketheth, ubi in quadam cessione tenta protunc ceperunt dominum Johannem Holte justiciarium,[1] Robertum Pynchebek' serjant, et Ricardum Skelton' servientem ad leges, detinentes eos per aliquod tempus cum illis dixerunt illos in tam arduo negocio jam incepto tales peritos utile habere semper presentes. Transieruntque per plura loca usque Northampton'; in quibusdam saltem proclamari fecerunt omnino se velle tenere cum rege et cum omnibus fidelibus regni sui usque ad mortem, proditores vero regni affectant de terra penitus extirpare et sine intermissione vellent ad hoc sinceriter laborare.

Item xvj. die Decembris illi de consilio transierunt ad regem existentem apud Wyndeshore, ubi disponebat tenuisse suum Natale; set quia tempore turbacionis necessarium videbatur habere suum consilium prope ipsum verum quia non potuit comode ibi esse, igitur ordinatum est inter illos quod suum Natale teneret in Turri London': et factum est ita.[2]

Predicti vero domini in eorum propositis estuantes miserunt eorum exploratores ad investigandum sollerter per quam viam dictus dux Hibern' vellet transire; quod ipse persenciens declinavit ab eis venitque per quoddam manerium abbatis de Evesham *b*juxta Chepyngstowe.*b*[3] Erat enim aer tenebrosus valde et densus. Domini vero occupaverunt totam patriam in circuitu, scilicet Bannebury, Braylles, Chepyngnorton', Campedene,[4] Blokkeleye et Bourton' sub Coteswold'.[5] Igitur xx^{mo}. die Decembris dux predictus iter faciens cum suis Cestren' et Walensibus, numero quinque milibus, versus Wytteneyam, ubi in lato campo primo cum suis comes Arundell' occurrebat. Quos videns dux predictus animavit suos ad bellum distinctis aciebus ad pugnam,

---

a The first three letters of this word are written over an erasure.   *b–b* Added in the margin after **Evesham**, which ends a line.

---

[1] For whom see above, p. 196.

[2] The king withdrew to the Tower of London for safety after the battle of Radcot Bridge (Walsingham, *Hist. Ang.*, ii. 170; and see below, p. 224). The council at Windsor was summoned by privy seal letters in mid-Nov. (P.R.O., E. 403/518, 15 Nov.).

[3] Probably Broadwell and Donnington, north of Stow. For this and other

beginning of December. They went by way of Newmarket 1387
Heath, where, at sessions then being held, they laid hold of
Sir John Holt, justice,[1] Serjeant Robert Pinchbeck and
Richard Skelton, serjeant at law, and kept them for some
time in their company, remarking that in the difficult enterprise on which they had now embarked it would be useful
to have such experts constantly within call. On their way to
Northampton they passed through a number of places, in
some at least of which they caused proclamation to be made
that their whole desire was to support to the death the king
himself and all the loyal elements in the kingdom, but its
traitors they meant to root out completely from the country
and they would work unceasingly and single-heartedly to
that end.

On 16 December the members of the council joined the
king at Windsor, where he was planning to celebrate Christmas; but since in such troubled times it seemed necessary
for him to have his council near at hand, and that was not
conveniently possible at Windsor, it was arranged between
them that he should keep Christmas in the Tower of London;
and this he did.[2]

All zeal to carry out their plans, the lords sent out scouts
to use their skill to discover what route the duke of Ireland
intended to take; becoming aware of this he bore away from
them and passed through a manor belonging to the abbot of
Evesham near Stow-on-the-Wold.[3] The weather was now
extremely dark and foggy. The lords were in possession of
all the country round — Banbury, Brailes, Chipping Norton,
Campden,[4] Blockley, and Bourton under Cotswold.[5] On
20 December, then, the duke, with his Cheshire and Welsh
forces, numbering about 5,000, was on his way towards
Witney when contact was first made with him in open
country by the earl of Arundel and his men. At sight of
them the duke roused the fighting spirit of his troops and,

details of the rout of de Vere and his forces by the Appellants see Myres, in
E.H.R., xlii (1927), 20-33, and Davies, ibid., lxxxvi (1971), 556-7. The engagement on the road from Stow 'towards Witney' described in the following passage
probably took place at or near Burford. The main encounter took place at Radcot
Bridge, and it is to that site that we should transfer the slaying of Molyneux
narrated below. For comment see above, pp. lxiv-lxv.
    [4] Chipping Campden.   [5] Bourton-on-the-Hill.

1387 erexitque vexilla regis et Sancti Georgii.[1] Quod comperiens
comes Arundell' et ceteri domini qui tunc aderant miserunt
ad illos dicentes se tenere cum rege sicuti suos ligios homines,
nec velle contra illos ullatenus dimicare nisi voluerint omnino
stare cum regis et regni proditoribus qui sunt super certis prodicionibus legittime appellati. At illi respondentes dixerunt se
nullatenus causa pugne venisse, 'set jussu regis gracia tuicionis
persone ducis Hibernie noverint nos secum pariter equitasse,
proditoribus vero regis seu regni opem impendere nolle nec[a]
in aliquo juvamen prestare'.[2] Unde protinus ostenderunt
signa pacis, erectis arcubus et eorum ceteris armamentis.
Quos tunc jusserunt domini ad eorum lares redire nec cum
duce predicto debere ulterius procedere ullo modo si voluerint eorum vitam salvare. Dominus vero Thomas de Mortuo
Mari non obstante tractatu irruit in quendam vocatum
Molineres,[3] precipuum consiliarium ducis predicti, et ipsum
protinus interfecit. Tunc vero venerunt ad dictum locum
ceteri domini cum eorum cuneis armatorum qui ab eo loco
ceteris remociores fuerunt, disponendo se tanquam inirent
certamen mortale. Dux itaque ad hujusmodi spectaculum
stupefactus perpendensque suos fore devictos fugam arripuit,
venitque ad pontem vocatum Rodecotebrigg', quem fractum
invenit; igitur eques flumen Thamysie intravit transnatatoque
alveo ab oculis eorum evanuit.[4] In illo enim gurgite quidam
de suis erant submersi; et quamplures ibi prope alveum in
paludibus ab insequentibus ducem predictum fuerant eciam
conculcati; ceteri vero armis amissis atque eorum equis
dolentes ad propria redierunt; supellectilia itaque omnia
prefati ducis ad dominos sunt adducta. Dux itaque Hiberni-
cus taliter a manibus dominorum evasus in habitu garcionis
ad regem accessit, habitoque colloquio aliquali[b] cum eo

---

[a] *Written above* aut, *which has not been deleted.*   [b] aliquali *Winterbottom;*
tali quali *MS. Cf. p. 226.*

---

[1] Cf. below, p. 268, where this act, signifying a state of war, is said to have
occurred at Radcot Bridge.

[2] A reference to the royal letters to de Vere which formed one of the gravamina of the appeal in the Merciless Parliament (below, pp. 266–8).

[3] Sir Thomas Molyneux, constable of Chester castle, for whom see J. L.
Gillespie, 'Thomas Mortimer and Thomas Molineux: Radcot Bridge and the
Appeal of 1397', in *Albion*, vii (1975), 164 ff. Molyneux had recruited men in
Lancs. and Cheshire on behalf of the king and de Vere. Mortimer, his slayer, was

raising the royal standard and that of St. George,[1] disposed 1387
his lines in battle-order. When the earl of Arundel became
aware of this, he and the other lords with him at the time
sent to the forces opposite to say that they themselves held
with the king as his liege subjects, and that they did not in
the least wish to try conclusions with them unless they were
determined to support those traitors to the king and to the
kingdom who had been lawfully appealed of certain treasons.
In their reply the duke's men said that they had certainly not
come to do battle, but they wished the lords 'to understand
that it is by the king's orders that we have been riding in
company with the duke of Ireland to provide protection for
his person, but that we do not want to give any help or in
any way to render assistance to traitors to the king or the
kingdom'.[2] Thereupon they demonstrated their peaceful
intentions forthwith by holding up their bows and their
other weapons. They were then ordered by the lords to
return to their homes and forbidden to go any further in
any capacity with the duke if they wanted to preserve their
lives. Despite the parley, however, one Molyneux,[3] a leading
henchman of the duke, was attacked by Sir Thomas Mortimer,
who killed him on the spot. At this point came the arrival on
the scene with their armed units of the remaining lords, who
had been further afield than their fellows and who now took
up positions presaging a battle to the death. Astonished at
the sight thus presented, and reckoning on the rout of the
forces under him, the duke fled, eventually reaching Radcot
Bridge, which he found broken. He therefore took to the
water and swam his horse across the Thames before disappearing from view.[4] Some of his men were drowned in the
stream; and in the marshes flanking its course large numbers
were ridden down by the duke's pursuers; the rest made their
rueful way homeward with the loss of their weapons and
horses; and all the gear which had belonged to the duke was
brought to the lords. Having eluded their grasp in the way
described, the duke of Ireland himself reached the king
dressed as a groom and after having had with him a discussion

an illegitimate son of the 2nd earl of March, and it is implied in his arraignment in
1397 that he took part in the muster at Haringay (R.P., iii. 380–1).
    [4] De Vere probably crossed the Thames at Bablock hythe.

1387 celeriter adiit castrum de Queneborgh', ubi confestim navigio perquisito in partes transmarinas secessit.

Denique in auxilium dominorum supervenerunt ex omni parte viri cordati, promittentes[a] eos velle cum illis pro viribus stare usque ad unguem; quibus ex parte dominorum suaviter fuit locutum quod redirent ad propria, et, si necessitas id exposceret quandocumque et videbatur eis eciam oportunum eorum auxilium et juvamen habere, pro illis tanquam pro fidis amicis vellent libencius destinare. Istis namque transactis transierunt domini predicti Oxon', ubi per eos consilio celebrato quid foret super incepto negocio consulcius faciendum omnes in unam sentenciam convenerunt, scilicet quod transirent London' locuturi cum rege et quomodo staret cum illo eciam vellent scire et cum ceteris convicinis ibidem.

Rex vero tunc[b] temporis transtulit se de Wyndesora in Turrim London',[1] disponensque pro suis hospicia capere tam infra muros quam extra, sicut alibi, ad sue libitum voluntatis. Ad hec major et seniores dicte civitatis regi dixerunt tales assignaciones hospiciorum nullatenus fieri posse in civitate, quia numquam ante ista tempora fuit visum quod quisquam regum precedencium de suis domibus expulit quempiam mercatorem causa multitudinis sibi aliquando London' occurrentis, cum et ipsi sine eorum mercimoniis ibidem vivere nequeant nec sine domibus poterunt ea emptoribus exhibere, quia non habent unde ea valeant custodire; item quando ad civitatem eandem in regum[b] coronacionibus sive in aliis diversis spectaculis raro visis confluxerat multitudo, adhuc tamen in illa omnes satis comode fuerant hospitati absque assignacione quacumque. Auditis hiis sermonibus rex[b] ab inceptis destitit mitigatus.

Nec mora: dicti domini die Sancti Johannis Evangeliste[2] venerunt London' in bellico apparatu et monstraverunt se in campo juxta Skynneriswelle in aquilonali parte London'[3]
p. 164 eo modo ac si incontinenti / mortale certamen inirent,

---

[a] *An erasure, covered by a dash, follows.*   [b] *Interlined.*

[1] Cf. above, p. 220.
[2] So also *Favent*, p. 12; cf. Knighton, *Chronicon*, ii. 254.
[3] Skinners Well was near Clerkenwell (Gover, Mawer, and Stenton, *Place-Names of Middlesex* (E.P.N.S. xviii), 95).

of a sort hurried on to Queenborough castle, where he 1387
quickly obtained a ship and retired overseas.

In the end men with stout hearts came from every quarter
to the help of the lords, with promises of willing support to
the limit of their strength and with every fibre of their being.
On behalf of the lords it was tactfully suggested to them that
they should return to their homes, and that if circumstances
ever made it necessary and the time appeared to have come
for the lords to have their aid and assistance, they would
gladly send for them as for their true friends. This business
over, the lords proceeded to Oxford, where, at a council
held to discuss what they would be best advised to do next
in the enterprise on which they had embarked, they unanimously agreed to go to London to speak with the king and
also to find out how matters stood with him and with his
neighbours in those parts.

It was at this time that the king transferred himself from
Windsor to the Tower of London:[1] he proposed to com-
mandeer lodgings for his followers whether inside or outside
the city walls, in the way he had done elsewhere, as the fancy
took him. At this, the mayor and aldermen told the king
that the allotment of accommodation in this way was quite
out of the question in London, where it was unheard of for
any of his royal predecessors to turn any merchant out of
his own premises because at any given time the king's
presence brought large numbers of people to London:
without their wares the merchants could not make their
living there, and without their houses they would be unable
to show them to purchasers, since they had no means of
keeping them [elsewhere]: moreover, when in the past, on
the occasion of a royal coronation or some other rarely seen
spectacle, great crowds had flocked to London, everybody
had hitherto been quite comfortably accommodated without
any sort of billeting. After listening to these arguments the
king relented and abandoned his intentions.

Immediately after this, on St. John the Evangelist's Day
[27 December],[2] the lords arrived in London accoutred
for war, and in the open country near Skinners Well to
the north of London[3] presented themselves to view as
if they were about to engage in a struggle to the death,

1387 aciebus distinctis et in modum alarum expansis. Quod audientes major et seniores civitatis predicte continuo exierunt ad illos suscipientes eos pacifice: mox illi depositis armis versus civitatem equitarunt cum eis et in suburbiis dicte civitatis omnes fuerunt satis congrue pro tempore hospitati. Die vero crastina domini miserunt ad regem rogantes eum illas personas de prodicione notatas sibi transmittere aut securitatem eis dare cum warento ad inquirendum tales personas ubicumque possent in Anglia inveniri.*a* Quibus respondit rex et dixit se tales personas nescire neque warentum ad inquirendum eis velle concedere, quia majora et plura hiis fecerunt sine warento. Illi namque talibus responsis non contenti immo dixerunt quod super hiis finem expediciorem vellent habere. Referendarii et pacificatores inter regem et prefatos dominos fuerunt episcopi tocius Anglie famosiores,[1] dux Eboracen', comes Northumberland', et ceteri domini temporales, qui mane et sero quolibet die satis sollicite inter eos de pace et concordia tractaverunt. Demum induxerunt eos venire ad regem ad colloquendum cum eo.

Igitur sexto die Natalis Domini accesserunt domini predicti ad Gildam Aulam London', ubi in presencia majoris et communitatis civitatis predicte declarabant se quomodo et sub qua forma et quare premissa agebant ac cum tanta multitudine equitarunt. Quo facto ad Turrim London' cum quingentis viris bene armatis illico pervenerunt, videntesque regem juxta capellam in suo solio sub divo sedentem factaque sibi debita veneracione, scilicet cum trina prostracione in terram, tandem rege annuente cum modestia surrexerunt, habitoque cum illo ibidem aliquali colloquio set propter tumultum populi[2] non ad plenum, ideo rege volente prefatam capellam intrabant, ubi sunt regem super factis suis satis rigide allocuti: primo*b* in

---

a MS. invenire.   *b* j., ij., iij. *in the margin opposite this passage, at the* appropriate points.

---

[1] Viz. William Courtenay, archbishop of Canterbury, Thomas Arundel, bishop of Ely and chancellor, William of Wykeham, bishop of Winchester, and John Gilbert, bishop of Hereford and treasurer (Walsingham, *Hist. Ang.*, ii. 171; *E.H.R.*, lxxxvi (1971), 557). All had been members of the continual council of 1386; so too the duke of York.

their lines drawn in battle-array and deployed so as to form 1387 wings. At news of this, the mayor and aldermen promptly went out to give them a peaceable reception; and shortly afterwards the lords, their weapons laid aside, rode back with them towards the city, in the suburbs of which they were all suitably lodged for the time being. On the following day [28 December] the lords sent to the king requesting him to hand over to them those persons who had been stigmatized as traitors or to provide them with assurances, together with a warrant to search for such persons wherever they might be found in England. The king replied to this that he knew of no such persons and that he refused to grant them any search-warrant, seeing that without any warrant at all they had done more and gone further than this. Dissatisfied with this answer, the lords declared that they wanted this business more speedily disposed of. Those who acted as delegates and mediators between the king and the lords included the most prominent of all the English bishops,[1] the duke of York, the earl of Northumberland, and others of the lords temporal: day in and day out they painstakingly conducted negotiations between the parties to secure peace and harmony. At length the lords were persuaded to visit the king for conversations with him.

Accordingly on the sixth day of Christmas [30 December] they attended at the London Guildhall, where, in the presence of the mayor and the commonalty of the city they explained how, under what legal forms, and why they had done what they had and had made their foray at the head of so numerous a following. This done, they at once made their way with an escort of 500 well-armed men to the Tower; and on seeing the king, who was enthroned in the open near the chapel, did him due reverence by three times prostrating themselves before, with the king's permission, they rose with diffidence to their feet and then and there had with him a discussion of a sort. But owing to the uproar from the people[2] it could not be exhaustive, and so with the king's approval they withdrew into the chapel, where they spoke to the king with some asperity about his conduct, first in

[2] Cf. Knighton, *Chronicon*, ii. 255. (Knighton mistakenly assigns the whole episode to 27 Dec.)

1387 contraveniendo suum proprium juramentum non servando illis ea que promisit,[1] secundo immerenter mortem eis intentans contra suam nobilitatem et statum, tercio in defendendo falsissimos proditores in sui ipsius destruccionem et tocius regni enervacionem.[a] Plura alia inibi sibi dixerunt que in publicum non venerunt; set finaliter protestando asseruerunt ipsum necessario oportere errata corrigere et deinceps subicere se regimini dominorum: quod si renuerit ita facere, sciret utique suum heredem fore indubie perfecte etatis, qui libenter propter comodum regni ejusque salvacionem effectualiter eis vellet parere ac sub eorum regimine gubernari.[2]

Ad hec stupefactus rex ait se velle ipsis prout decuit in licitis obtemperare et eorum salubri consilio gubernari, salva corona sua ac eciam regia dignitate; et hoc juramento proprio affirmavit. Quo facto dixerunt domini quod nullo modo ipsos in istis promissionibus falleret neque de cetero suam voluntatem vi aut arte circa premissa mutaret prout in posterum sua regalitate et corona vellet gaudere. Igitur[b] ultimo die Decembris venerunt Westmonasterium, ubi tractarunt de illis qui steterunt circa regem, an digni forent stare ulterius cum rege vel non; et de multitudine officiariorum in unoquoque officio existencium sunt scrutati. Et inventi sunt in officio bottelarie c. officiarii, sicque in officio coquine ac in omnibus aliis officiis superfluos invenerunt; unde defalcata illorum numerositate satis competentes adhuc in dictis officiis reliquerunt. Item dominum Simonem de Burlee custodia castri de Dovorr' privarunt, ac dominum Johannem Beauchamp' tunc seneschallum hospicii domini regis ab illo officio amoverunt.

1388 Primo namque die Januarii celebrato apud Westmonasterium consilio plures arestari fecerunt, videlicet dominum Thomam Tryvet, dominum Simonem Burle, dominum Johannem Beauchamp', dominum Nicholaum Daggeworthe, dominum Willelmum Elmham, dominum Jacobum Berneres, dominum Johannem Salesbury, et dominum Nicholaum Brembre, milites, item dominum Ricardum

[a] *Written above* suppeditacionem, *which has not been deleted.*   [b] *Interlined.*

[1] Specifically, promises made by the king on 17 Nov. and by his representatives in the preliminaries to the meeting on that day (above, pp. 212–14; and see also below, p. 238 and n.).

violating his personal oath by failing to keep his promises to them,[1] secondly, in threatening to procure for themselves, in defiance of their noble condition, a death they did not deserve, and, thirdly, in defending to his own undoing and the enfeeblement of the entire kingdom the falsest traitors. There was much else in what they said to him that did not come to public knowledge; but they ended with a solemn declaration that he must of necessity correct his mistakes and henceforward submit himself to the control of the lords: if he refused to do so, he must understand that his heir was unquestionably of full age and for the profit and salvation of the kingdom would gladly consent to give them real obedience and to accept guidance under their control.[2]

Taken aback at this, the king said that he was prepared, as was proper, to defer to them in all permissible respects and to be guided by wholesome advice from them, without prejudice to his crown and royal dignity; and supported this by his personal oath. Thereupon the lords warned him that, as he valued his continued enjoyment of his crown and king-ship, he must in no way disappoint them over his undertaking or in future allow force or cunning to change his mind about the subjects mentioned above. And so on the last day of December they came to Westminster, where they discussed the persons who stood about the king, considering whether or not they deserved to remain in attendance on him; and inquired into the horde of officials ensconced in every department. The buttery was found to contain a hundred office-holders; and in the kitchen and all the other depart-ments they likewise discovered superfluous numbers, whose excess they pruned, while still leaving those departments adequately staffed. They deprived Sir Simon Burley of the wardenship of Dover castle, and removed Sir John Beauchamp from his post as steward of the king's household.

On 1 January, after a council held at Westminster, the lords caused a number of people to be arrested: Sir Thomas Trivet, Sir Simon Burley, Sir John Beauchamp, Sir Nicholas Dagworth, Sir William Elmham, Sir James Berners, Sir John Salisbury, and Sir Nicholas Brembre, knights, and Sir Richard

---

[2] A reference to the duke of Gloucester: Roger Mortimer, heir presumptive to the throne, was still a minor.

1388 Medford', dominum Ricardum Clifford', et*a* dominum Johannem Lincoln' clericos; qui omnes causa custodie ad diversa fortalicia erant per dominos predictos transmissi usque ad proximum parliamentum.[1] Item isti domini coegerunt curiam abjurare inter alios specialiter infrascriptos:*b*

Episcopum Dunolm';[2] episcopum Cicestren';[3] dominum Baldewinum de Bereford'.[4]

Dominum Ricardum de Abberisbury;[5] dominum Johannem Worthe;[6] filium domini de Clyfford';[7] dominum Johannem Lovell'.[8]

Dominum de la Souche;[9] dominum de Beaumond';[10] dominum de Burnell';[11] dominum Aubrey de Veer.[12]

Dominum Thomam Caymos;[13] et dominum Thomam Blount.[14] Omnes isti fuerunt jurati ne omnino in curiam regis intrarent.

Qui illo in tempore erant milites nominati et viri famosi multisque virtutibus insigniti. Abjurarunt eciam curiam domini regis tunc temporis tres domine, scilicet domina de Ponyngg',[15] domina de Mohon,[16] et domina de Molyns.[17] Johannes vero Blake remansit in custodia dominorum.[18]

---

a Interlined.   *b* The names which follow are arranged in the MS. in four columns.

---

[1] To this list add Nicholas Slake, dean of the king's chapel (Walsingham, *Hist. Ang.*, ii. 173; Knighton, *Chronicon*, ii. 256); and Walsingham makes this the occasion of John Blake's arrest. Trivet, Dagworth, Elmham, and Berners were chamber knights; Salisbury, an usher of the chamber; Medford, the king's secretary; Clifford, a clerk of his chapel; Lincoln, a chamberlain of the Exchequer. For Burley see below, p. 274 n.; for Trivet see above, pp. 116 n., 212. Beauchamp, too, was a chamber knight. Brembre was sent to Gloucester castle; Burley, Elmham, and Slake to Nottingham castle; Beauchamp, Trivet, Salisbury, and Lincoln to Dover castle; Berners and Medford to Bristol castle; and Dagworth and Clifford to Rochester castle (*Cal. Cl. R.*, *1385-9*, pp. 393-5). Some of these arrests may have taken place earlier than the date implied above. The order for Brembre's arrest is dated 21 Dec. 1387, and expenses in connection with his committal to Gloucester castle are entered on the Issue Roll under 16 Dec.; expenses in connection with the arrest of Burley and Elmham are entered in the roll under 20 Dec. (P.R.O., E. 403/518; *Cal. Cl. R.*, *1385-9*, p. 461).

[2] John Fordham, for whom see above, p. 200 and n.

[3] Thomas Rushock (above, p. 130 n.).

[4] A knight retained by the king (*Cal. Cl. R.*, *1385-9*, pp. 584-5).

[5] A chamber knight, formerly in the retinue of John of Gaunt; also knight of the shire for Oxon. in the parliament of 1386 (ibid., p. 299; *John of Gaunt's Register, 1379-1383*, ed. Lodge and Somerville, i, p. 7; McFarlane, *Lancastrian*

Medford, Sir Richard Clifford, and Sir John Lincoln, clerks; 1388
all of whom were dispatched to various fortresses for safe
custody to await the next parliament.[1] Among those whom
the lords compelled to abjure the court special attention was
given to the following:

The bishops of Durham[2] and Chichester;[3] Sir Baldwin
Bereford.[4]

Sir Richard Abberbury;[5] Sir John Worth;[6] the son of
lord Clifford;[7] Sir John Lovell.[8]

Lord la Zouche;[9] Lord Beaumont;[10] Lord Burnell;[11]
Sir Aubrey de Vere.[12]

Sir Thomas Camois;[13] and Sir Thomas Blount.[14] All of
them were sworn not to set foot in the king's court.

These were illustrious names in the chivalry of the day, men
of repute who were distinguished by many virtues. There
were also three ladies who abjured the royal court at this
time: Lady Poynings,[15] Lady Mohun[16] and Lady Moleyns.[17]
John Blake continued to be kept in custody by the lords.[18]

Kings and Lollard Knights, p. 25).

[6] Formerly steward of the lands of Joan of Kent, and an executor of her will
(Tout, *Chapters*, iii. 332 n.; see also *Cal. Cl. R., 1385-9*, p. 398).

[7] Thomas Clifford, son of Roger, Lord Clifford, for whom see *G.E.C.*, iii. 292.
He, too, was a chamber knight, and he is described in 1385 as a kinsman of the
king (*Cal. Pat. R., 1385-9*, pp. 42, 65, 267).

[8] For whom see *G.E.C.*, viii. 219-21.

[9] William, Lord Zouche, of Harringworth, for whom see above, p. 70 and n.

[10] John, Lord Beaumont (d. 1396), for whom see *G.E.C.*, ii. 61. See also
Knighton, *Chronicon*, ii. 233.

[11] Hugh, Lord Burnell (d. 1420). His first wife was the daughter of Michael
de la Pole, 2nd earl of Suffolk. See *G.E.C.*, ii. 435.

[12] Uncle and heir of Robert de Vere, earl of Oxford; see below, p. 510 and
G.E.C., x. 233-4. For a time early in the reign he deputized for his nephew as
chamberlain (Tout, *Chapters*, iii. 356-7, 406).

[13] For whom see *G.E.C.*, ii. 507-8.

[14] By Oct. 1389, a chamber knight (Tout, *Chapters*, iv. 345). See also *G.E.C.*,
ii. 195.

[15] The wife of Sir John Worth, for whom see above, n. 6. She was Blanche,
daughter of John, Lord Mowbray, and formerly wife of Thomas, Lord Poynings,
who died in 1375. See Walsingham, *Hist. Ang.*, ii. 173; *G.E.C.*, x. 662.

[16] Joan, widow of John, Lord Mohun (d. 1375); she was the daughter of
Bartholomew de Burghersh (d. 1355), chamberlain to Edward III (*G.E.C.*, ii.
426; ix. 24).

[17] Margery, widow of Sir William de Moleyns (d. 1381) (ibid., ix. 40).

[18] The first intimation of the arrest of Blake, for whom see above, p. 202 n.;
at the time of his trial, on 3 Mar. 1388, he was in the custody of the duke of
Gloucester (*R.P.*, iii. 240).

1388 Item pro gubernacione regis continua ordinarunt episcopum Wyntonien', episcopum Bathonien', dominum Johannem Coboham, dominum Ricardum Scrop', et dominum Johannem Deverose, quem statuerunt eciam seneschallum hospicii domini regis et constabularium castri de Dovere.[1] Item secundo die Januarii omnes familiares precipue domino regi proximiores dicti domini a curia removerunt et loco eorum ad libitum alios subrogarunt. Hoc quidem factum cor regis merore implevit, quamvis aliter protunc fieri non potuit: iccirco hec et alia pacientissime tolleravit.

Item ix°. die Januarii erat grandis tempestas nivis et grandinis cum magno impetu venti variis coruscacionibus[a] fulguris et tonitrui interpolatis, duravitque jugiter per tres dies sequentes.

Item xvij. die Januarii erant predicti domini apud Westmonasterium, volentes London' artes artibus concordare, quia longe ante[b] adinvicem discordabant. De qualibet arte pro certis miserunt ut si eis aliqua gravamina fuerint a quoquam illata crastina die venirent apud Gyldam Aulam, ubi ipsi domini cum aliis sibi adjunctis disposuerunt audire ac terminare querimonias singulorum. Igitur xviij. die Januarii apud Gyldam Aulam London' occurrerunt archiepiscopus Cant', Wynton', Bathonien', Elien', Hereford', et Exonien' episcopi, ac predicti domini cum clerico de privato sigillo domini regis[2] et aliis nobilibus providis et discretis. Primo quidem ante omnia, quia Londonienses erant illicitis juramentis astricti,[3] dictus archiepiscopus ab hujusmodi p. 165 eosdem absolvit. Tunc dixit eis episcopus Elyen' / thesaurarius Anglie[4] quod nullus obloqueretur aliquod sinistrum de predictis dominis propter malam gubernacionem regis et regni jam motis, 'cum ipsi eciam et nos omnes pro majori parte simus nequiter et falsissime indictati, ac inter vos sunt

---

[a] interpolatis *deleted after this word.* [b] *Interlined.*

[1] Devereux became steward of the household on 1 Jan. 1388 and constable of Dover castle not later than 4 Jan.; on the latter point see Rymer, *Foedera*, vii. 566. Of the 5 persons named here by the Monk, only Walter Skirlaw, bishop of Bath and Wells, was not a member of the continual council appointed in 1386.

[2] John Waltham, keeper since Oct. 1386.

[3] A reference to the oath of allegiance to the king 'against all those who are or shall become rebels or opposed to his person or royalty' taken by the mayor, aldermen, and commonalty of London on or just before 5 Oct. 1387 (*Letter*

For the day-to-day guidance of the king they appointed the 1388
bishops of Winchester and Bath, Sir John Cobham, Sir
Richard Scrope, and Sir John Devereux, the last of whom
they also established as steward of the king's household and
constable of Dover castle.[1] On 2 January they removed from
the court all the members of the household and especially
those who had been closest to the king, and replaced them
by others of their own choice, a proceeding which filled the
king's heart with unhappiness, though at the time there was
no altering it, and so he put up with it and other things with
the utmost patience.

On 9 January there was a great storm of snow and hail,
accompanied by a gale-force wind and interspersed with
sundry flashes of lightning and thunder, which lasted without
stopping for three days on end.

Out of a desire to restore harmony between the London
gilds which had for some time previously been at odds
with one another, the lords attended at Westminster on
17 January. Representatives of each gild were summoned,
if an injury had been done them by anybody, to come
on the following day to the Guildhall, where the lords
proposed in association with others to hear and determine
all complaints. And so on 18 January there foregathered
at the London Guildhall the archbishop of Canterbury,
the bishops of Winchester, Bath, Ely, Hereford, and Exeter,
and the lords themselves, together with the clerk of the
king's privy seal[2] and other prudent and discerning noblemen. Since the Londoners were bound by unlawful oaths,[3]
the very first step was for the archbishop to absolve them
from any resultant obligations. Next the bishop of Ely,
treasurer of England,[4] told them that nobody was to speak
any evil in detraction of those lords who had lately been
moved to action on account of the misgovernment to
which the king and the kingdom had been subjected, 'since
they, and we too, or most of us, have been most wickedly
and falsely indicted, and there are among you also some

Book H, pp. 314–15; see also Bird, *Turbulent London of Richard II*, p. 92 and n.).
    [4] Thomas Arundel, bishop of Ely, was chancellor; John Gilbert, bishop of
Hereford, treasurer. The former was probably the speaker; his audience will not
have forgotten that he was the earl of Arundel's brother.

1388 quidam eciam indictati, si vero juste sive injuste penitus ignoramus; apparebit quoque in fine cum per^a parliamentum fuerit declaratum.[1] Nunc autem si que gravamina sive querimonie inter vos versantur producite in medium coram nobis: jam est tempus audiendi. Nam constat omnibus nobis vos nullatenus esse unanimes utrobique quia, ut apparet, una ars istius civitatis aliam delere affectat; quod est absurdum, presertim inter cives tales inter illos discordias sustinere; immo si pacem et concordiam inter vos fovere volueritis nullam adversitatem vobis dominari sperare poteritis.' Pauca vero ad ista erant prolata, quia videbatur eis non equaliter eos stare cum omnibus prout decet: ideo forte noluerunt eos tanquam judices acceptare nec coram illis aliquid allegare.

Item primo die Februarii fluvius Thamis' juxta Abendon' fuit vacuus in suo alveo per tractum^b unius arcus absque aqua; et duravit sic per unam horam, magnum omen significans ⟨de⟩^{c} post futuris.

Parliamentum.[2] Tercio die Februarii tenuit rex parliamentum apud Westmonasterium, in quo T.^{d} dux Gloucestr', Henricus comes Derbeye, Ricardus comes Arundell', Thomas comes Warwyk', et Thomas comes Notyngham excusarunt se publice coram toto parliamento quod numquam consenserunt, cogitarunt aut ymaginarunt mortem regis neque occulte neque aperte; et hoc cuilibet contradicenti manu propria vellent probare et se de hiis defendere contra quemlibet opponentem^d capud habentem, rege solo excepto.[3] Cumque ad hec nullus apparuit contradictor, pro excusatis ab omnibus habebantur.

---

^{a} *Interlined.* ^{b} MS. tractus. ^{c} MS. *om.* ^{d} *Interlined.*

---

[1] A reference to Nicholas Brembre and Thomas Usk, the two Londoners among those to be tried in the forthcoming parliament; but some in the audience may have recalled the returns of disloyal persons which Richard II required of the mayor and aldermen on 3 Dec. 1387 (*Letter Book H*, p. 321).

[2] The Monk now begins the first of his two narratives of the Merciless Parliament of 1388, and this, his own work, fills pp. 234–6 and pp. 308–42 of the present edition. His second narrative (below, pp. 280–96) and the ancillary documents which follow it (ibid., pp. 296–306) were copied from a roll of the parliament which was probably made by or for John Burton, clerk of the Chancery rolls. This roll was also the source of the text of the articles of the impeachment of Burley, Berners, Beauchamp, and Salisbury inserted in the first narrative (below, pp. 268–78) and probably the source of that of the articles of the

who have been indicted, whether with justice or not is quite 1388
outside our knowledge and will ultimately appear when a
pronouncement upon it is made by the parliament.[1] But
today, if there are any grievances or complaints which are
being bandied about between yourselves, bring them out
into the open before us; now is the time for them to be
heard. It is evident to us all that the different elements
among you are by no means of one mind when, as it seems,
one city craft is seeking to destroy another; which is sense-
less, especially when it is between fellow citizens that
quarrels of this sort are kept alive. If, on the contrary, you
are prepared to foster peace and harmony among you, you
can count on never having to bow to misfortune.' Few
matters, however, were raised in response to this invitation,
because it seemed to the citizens that the members of the
tribunal were not as impartial in their sympathy for all
parties as they should have been: it was therefore perhaps
for this reason that they declined to accept them as judges
and to make any allegations before them.

On 1 February near Abingdon the bed of the river Thames
was empty of water for the length of a bowshot; and remained so for an hour, conveying a striking omen of events
that were to follow.

Parliament.[2] On 3 February the king held a parliament at
Westminster, when Thomas duke of Gloucester, Henry earl
of Derby, Richard earl of Arundel, Thomas earl of Warwick,
and Thomas earl of Nottingham, publicly justifying themselves before the whole parliament, declared that they had
never countenanced, devised, or meditated the death of the
king by any means, secret or open; they were willing to
prove this by their own right hand to any that would gainsay it, and on this issue to defend themselves against any
adversary with a head on his shoulders, the king alone
excepted.[3] As nobody came forward to dispute their statements, they were universally held to have cleared themselves.

Appeal against the five principal defendants which was also inserted in that narrative (below, pp. 236–68). For these points see above, pp. xlviii–li.

[3] A reference to a disclaimer made in fact by the duke of Gloucester alone, of
an intention to depose the king and usurp the throne; it is this that reveals
Gloucester as the 'heir full of age' referred to in the course of the interview in the
Tower on 30 Dec. (above, p. 228; *R.P.*, iii. 229).

1388 Unde illi constanter pecierunt Alexandrum archiepiscopum Eboracen', Robertum de Veer ducem Hibernie, Michaelem de la Poole comitem Suff', Robertum Tresilyan justiciarium, et Nicholaum Brembre militem London' coram toto parliamento adduci et ad articulos in eorum appellacione positos vivaciter respondere. Verum quia tempus Carniprivii jam instabat, rex negocium prorogabat usque diem Jovis proximum post Diem Cinerum.[1]

Veniente igitur die statuto predicti domini cum aliis regni proceribus ac dominis spiritualibus et temporalibus coram rege in pleno parliamento assistentibus suas appellaciones protulerunt in scriptis contra prefatas personas superius nominatas, protestando eas velle prosequi manutenere et declarare ad profectum et comodum regis et regni prout fideles ligii facere astringuntur usque mors eos absolvat de vita presenti: unde instancius rogabant quod jus cum justicia super hujusmodi appellacionibus posset procedere in isto parliamento, non habendo respectum ad qualemcumque personam nisi solummodo ad justiciam et veritatem coram eis prolatas. Tunc rex volens audire hos articulos sive punctus de quibus dicti domini quinque personas principaliter appellarunt fecit legi coram se:[2] Gallico enim sermone fuerant conscripti numero xxxix. in toto; fuerunt eciam alii articuli contra dominum Simonem Burle, dominum Johannem Beauchamp', dominum Jacobum Berneres et dominum Johannem Salesbury propositi numero xvj., qui omnes eciam Gallico ydiomate fuerant exarati. Nunc vero ceteris omissis ad presens de quinque personis principalibus primitus est loquendum quomodo contra eos predicti domini processerunt.

A[a]3 tresexcellent et tresredoute seignour [b]nostre seignur[b] le roi et son conseill' de ceste[c] parlement moustrent Thomas duc de Gloucestre conestable Dengleterre, Henry conte de Derby, Richard conte Darundell'

---

[a] R.P. inserts nostre. Nota is in the margin of MS. at this point, in a slightly later hand.   [b-b] R.P. om.   [c] R.P. inserts present.

---

[1] There were open sessions of parliament on 4 and 5 Feb., and from 5 to 13 Feb. the lords temporal considered the articles of the Appeal.

[2] The articles were in fact read on 3 Feb. (R.P., iii. 236; and see below, p. 280 and n.).

They went on to demand steadfastly that Alexander arch- 1388
bishop of York, Robert de Vere duke of Ireland, Michael
de la Pole earl of Suffolk, Robert Tresilian justice, and
Nicholas Brembre knight of London should be brought
before the whole parliament and should answer orally the
articles comprised in their appeal. Since, however, the Lenten
season was now almost upon them, the king adjourned the
business until the Thursday following Ash Wednesday [13
February].[1]

And so, when the appointed day arrived, and the lords
spiritual and temporal were in attendance before the king in
full parliament, the lords above mentioned, with others of
the great ones of the kingdom, produced in writing against
the persons named above the appeals which they declared
themselves ready to prosecute, maintain, and expound, to
the profit and advantage of the king and the realm, as the
actions of loyal subjects are bound to be until death releases
them from this life's obligations. They therefore earnestly
requested that in the consideration of these appeals in the
present parliament right should go hand in hand with justice
and that regard should be had not to persons of any condition but only to the righteousness and truth brought into
view. Thereupon the king, wishing to hear the articles or
points of which the five accused were appealed as principals
by the lords, had them read before him:[2] they were written
out in French and numbered thirty-nine in all. Other articles,
put forward against Sir Simon Burley, Sir John Beauchamp,
Sir James Berners, and Sir John Salisbury also all drawn up in
French, totalled sixteen. But, to leave other topics aside for
the moment, an account must first be given of the way in
which the lords proceeded against the five principals.

To[3] the most excellent and dread lord, our lord the king and his
council of this parliament, Thomas duke of Gloucester constable
of England, Henry earl of Derby, Richard earl of Arundel and of

[3] The text of the ensuing Appeal has been collated with that in *R.P.*, iii. 229 ff.
Gloucester's style of constable and Nottingham's of marshal may mean that the
Appellants at one time hoped for a hearing in the court of chivalry; see Clarke,
Fourteenth Century Studies, pp. 134–5; M. H. Keen, 'Treason Trials under the
Law of Arms', in *T.R.H.S.*, 5th ser., xii (1962), 102 n.

1388 et de Surr', Thomas conte de Warrewyk, et Thomas conte mareschall'
qe come les avantditz Thomas duc de Gloucestre conestable Dengleterre, Richard conte Darundell' et de^a Surr', et Thomas conte de
Warrewyk' come loialx lieges nostre seignur le roi, pur profit du roy
et du roialme, le xiiij. jour de Novembre darrein passee a Walthamcross'
en^b countee de Hertf' devant le tresreverent pier en Dieux William
lercevesqe de Canterbirs, Esmon duc Deverwyk', les reverentz pieres
en Dieux William evesqe de Wyncestre, Thomas evesqe de Ely alors
chaunceller Dengl', Johan de Waltham alors gardeyn de^c prive seal
nostre seignur le roy, Johan sire de Coboham, mes seignurs Richard
Lescrop' et Johan Devereux, adonqes commissairs^d nostre seignur
le roy ordenez et faitz en le darrein parlement, appellerent Alexandre
ercevesqe^e Deverwyk', Robert de Veer duc Dirland, Michel de la Pole
counte de Suff', Robert Tresilyan faux justice, et Nichol Brembre
faux chivaler du Loundres de hautes tresons par eux faitz encountre
le roy et son roiaume et ^{f}se offreront^f de ceo pursuier et meintenir
et suffisante seurte trover et prierent as ditz seignurs de ceo certifier
a lour dit seignur liege, quele chose estoit certifie mesme le jour a
nostre dit seignur le roy par les ditz seignurs commissairs^d a Westm',
ou plusours des ditz appelles estoient presentez pleinement enfourmez
et certifiez ^{g}du dit appellez.^{g} Et puis par assent du roy et son counseill'
les avantditz Thomas duc de Glouc' conestable Dengl', Richard conte
Darundell' et de Surr', et Thomas conte de Warrewyk' le dymenge^h
proschein ensuiant viendrent a Westm' en la^i presence du roy et de
soun conseill' et illoeqes pur profit du roy et du roiaume appellerent
les avantditz Alexandre ercevesqe^j Deverwyk' ^{k}et autres trestoutz
ces compaignons^k de ^{l}hautes tresons par eux faitz^l encountre le roy
et son roiaume come traitours et enemys du roy et du^m roiaume
en affermantz lour appell' avantdit et soi offreront de le pursuir et
meintenir come avant^n est dit. Le^o quele appell' nostre seignur le roy
accepta et sur ceo assigna jour as dictes parties a son primere parlement
qe serroit tenuz a Westm' lendemayn de la Chaundelheure alors
proschein ensuiant, de prendre et resceiver adonqes sur le^o dit appelle
plein justice, et en ^{p}le moien^p temps prist en ces^q sauf et especial'
proteccion les dictes parties ove toutes lour gentz, biens et chateux,
et ceo fist proclamer et publier en sa presence a mesme le temps.^{1}
Et puis le^r Lunedy proschein apres le jour de la Nativite nostre
seignur Jesu Crist proschein ensuiant les avantditz Thomas duc de
Glouc' conestable Dengl', Richard conte Darundell' et de Surr',^{s}
Thomas conte de Warr', ensemblement ove les avantditz Henry

---

^{a} *Interlined.* ^{b} *R.P. inserts* la. ^{c} *R.P.* du. ^{d} *R.P.* commissioners.
^{e} *R.P.* l'ercevesqe. $^{f-f}$ *R.P.* soi offrerunt. $^{g-g}$ *R.P.* de dit appell.
^{h} *R.P. inserts* lors. ^{i} *R.P. om.* ^{j} *R.P.* l'ercevesqe. $^{k-k}$ *R.P.* Robert
de Veer duc d'Irland, Michel de la Poule count de Suff', Robert Tresilian faux
justice et Nichol Brembre faulx chivaler de Loundres; *so too (unless otherwise
noted) with only minor variations of spelling, in subsequent articles where the
names and titles of the appellees, either as a group or one or more of them*

Surrey, Thomas earl of Warwick, and Thomas earl marshal show that 1388
whereas the aforesaid Thomas duke of Gloucester constable of England,
Richard earl of Arundel and of Surrey, and Thomas earl of Warwick,
as loyal lieges of our lord the king, for profit of the king and of the
realm, on 14 November last past at Waltham Cross in the county of
Hertford before the most reverend father in God William archbishop of
Canterbury, Edmund duke of York, the reverend fathers in God
William bishop of Winchester and Thomas bishop of Ely then chancel-
lor of England, John Waltham then keeper of the privy seal of our lord
the king, John lord Cobham, and my lords Richard Scrope and John
Devereux, then commissioners of our lord the king ordained and
created in the last parliament, appealed Alexander archbishop of York,
Robert de Vere duke of Ireland, Michael de la Pole earl of Suffolk,
Robert Tresilian false justice and Nicholas Brembre false knight of
London of high treasons by them committed against the king and his
realm and offered themselves to prosecute and maintain this and to
find sufficient surety and prayed the said lords to certify this to their
said liege lord, which matter was that same day certified to our said
lord the king by the said lords commissioners at Westminster, where
several of the said appellees were present, fully informed, and certified
concerning the said appeals. And afterwards, by assent of the king and
his council the aforesaid Thomas duke of Gloucester constable of
England, Richard earl of Arundel and of Surrey, and Thomas earl of
Warwick on the Sunday next following [17 November 1387] came to
Westminster in the presence of the king and of his council and there
for profit of the king and of the realm appealed the aforesaid Alexander
archbishop of York and all the others his companions of high treasons
by them committed against the king and his realm as traitors and
enemies of the king and of the realm, affirming their appeal aforesaid,
and offered themselves to prosecute and maintain it, as is before said.
Which appeal our lord the king accepted and thereupon assigned a day
to the said parties at his first parliament that should be held at Westminster on the morrow of Candlemas then next following [3 February
1388], to take and receive then upon the said appeal full justice, and in
the meantime took into his safe and especial protection the said parties
with all their people, goods, and chattels and caused this to be proclaimed
and published in his presence at that same time.[1] And afterwards on
Monday next after the day of the Nativity of our Lord Jesus Christ
next following [27 December 1387] the aforesaid Thomas duke of
Gloucester constable of England, Richard earl of Arundel and of
Surrey, Thomas earl of Warwick, together with the aforesaid Henry

severally, are omitted or abbreviated in the MS.   *l–l* R.P. haut traison . . .
fait.   *m* R.P. de.   *n* R.P. devant.   *o* R.P. la.   *p–p* R.P. mesme le.
q R.P. sa.   *r* R.P. om.   *s* R.P. *inserts* et.

[1] For this proclamation see Knighton, *Chronicon*, ii. 249; *Letter Book H*,
pp. 320–1. Knighton assigns it to 19 Nov. 1387.

1388 conte de Derby et Thomas conte mareschall', en presence du roy en
la[a] Tour de Loundres come loialx lieges nostre dit seignur le roy, pur
profit du roy et du[b] roiaume, appellerent [c]les ditz[c] Alexandre ercevesqe
Deverwyk', Robert de Veer etc., Michel de la Pole etc., Robert Tresilyan
etc., Nichol Brembre etc. de hautes tresons par eux faitz encountre le
roy et son roiaume come traitours et enemys du roy et soi offrerent de
p. 166 le[d] / pursuir et meintenir et suffisant seurte trover come desus. Et sur
ceo le roy[e] assigna jour a son dit proschein parlement a pursuir et
declarer lour dit appelle, sur qoy le roy par avys de son consaill' fist
proclamer en toutes les citees[f] Dengl' par brief de son grand seal qe
toutes les[g] appellez serroient a dite parlement a dit jour de parlement
a y[d] respoundre sur lapell' suisdit.[1] Et quele appell' les avantditz
Thomas duc de Glouc' conestable Dengl', Henry conte de Derby,
Richard conte Darundell' et de Surr', Thomas conte de Warr', et
Thomas counte mareschall', appellantz, sont prestez de pursuir, meintenir et declarer et come loialx lieges nostre seignur le roy pur profit
du roy et du[h] roiaume appellont les avantditz Alexandre ercevesqe etc.
des[i] hautes tresons par eux faitz encountre nostre seignur le roy et son
roiaume come traitours et enemys du[i] roy et du[i] roiaume queles
[j]appelles et tresons[j] sont declarez, appointez et specifiez plenerement
si come est contenuz en diverses [k]cedules annexes a ycestes.[k] Et priont
qe les ditz appellez soient demaundez et qe droit et justice ent soit
faite en cest present parlement avandit.

　　　j.[l] Primerement Thomas duc de Glouc' conestable Dengl', Henry
counte de Derby, Richard conte Darundell' et de Surr', Thomas conte
de Warr', et Thomas conte mareschall' appellont et diont qe Alexandre
ercevesqe Deverwyk', Robert de Veer duc Dirl',[m] Michel de la Pole
conte de Suff', faux traitours[n] du roy et du roiaume veiantz le[o] ten-
dresce del age nostre[p] seignur le roi et la innocence de sa roial persone
luy firent entendre[q] com pur verite tantz de[r] faux choses par eux
countre loialte et bone foy ymaginez et controvez qe entierement eux
luy firent de tout a eux doner son amour et ferme foy et credence et[s]
haier ses loialx seignurs et[t] lieges par queux il duist de droit pluis avoir
este governe. Et auxint accrochantz[u] a eux roial poair en defranchisantz
nostre dit seignur[v] le roy de soveraignete,[w] emblemissantz et amenus-
santz sa roial prerogative et regalie, luy firent si avant obeiser qil fuist
jurre destre governe, conseille et demesne par eux. Par vertue de quele
serement eux luy ont si longement tenuz en obeisance de [x]lour faux[x]
appensementz et[y] ymaginacions et[z] faitz qe les meschiefs, enconvenientz,

---

[a] R.P. le.　　　[b] R.P. de.　　　[c-c] R.P. om.　　　[d] R.P. om.　　　[e] R.P.
inserts lour.　　　[f] R.P. counteez.　　　[g] R.P. inserts ditz.　　　[h] R.P. de.
[i] R.P. de.　　　[j-j] R.P. appell et traison.　　　[k-k] R.P. articles desouz escritz.
[l] (Tr)eson'. Notes tous les (a)rticles de traison in the margin opposite this paragraph, in a contemporary hand. The numerals here printed at the beginning of the
articles of the appeal are in the margins of the MS. Many of them are wholly or
in part bled off.　　　[m] R.P. inserts et.　　　[n] R.P. inserts et enemys.　　　[o] R.P.
la.　　　[p] R.P. inserts dit.　　　[q] R.P.; MS. attendre.　　　[r] R.P. des.　　　[s] R.P.;

earl of Derby and Thomas earl marshal, in the presence of the king in 1388 the Tower of London as loyal lieges of our said lord the king for profit of the king and of the realm appealed the said Alexander archbishop of York, Robert de Vere etc., Michael de la Pole etc., Robert Tresilian etc., Nicholas Brembre etc. of high treasons by them committed against the king and his realm as traitors and enemies of the king, and offered themselves to prosecute and maintain it and to find sufficient surety, as above. And thereupon the king assigned a day at his said next parliament to prosecute and declare their said appeal, whereupon the king by the advice of his council caused to be proclaimed in all the cities of England by writ under his Great Seal that all the appealed should be at the said parliament on the said day of parliament, there to answer upon the appeal abovesaid.[1] And which appeal the aforesaid Thomas duke of Gloucester constable of England, Henry earl of Derby, Richard earl of Arundel and of Surrey, Thomas earl of Warwick, and Thomas earl marshal, appellants, are ready to prosecute, maintain, and declare; and as loyal lieges of our lord the king and for profit of the king and of the realm they appeal the aforesaid Alexander archbishop of York etc. of the high treasons by them committed against our lord the king and his realm as traitors and enemies of the king and of the realm, which appeals and treasons are declared, appointed, and fully specified as is contained in sundry schedules hereto annexed. And they pray that the said appellees may be called and that right and justice may be done upon them in this present parliament aforesaid.

1. In the first place, Thomas duke of Gloucester constable of England, Henry earl of Derby, Richard earl of Arundel and of Surrey, Thomas earl of Warwick, and Thomas earl marshal appeal and say that Alexander archbishop of York, Robert de Vere duke of Ireland, Michael de la Pole earl of Suffolk, false traitors of the king and of the realm, seeing the tenderness of the age of our lord the king and the innocence of his royal person, caused him to apprehend as truth so many false things by them against loyalty and good faith imagined and contrived that they entirely engrossed in all things his love and firm faith and belief and caused him to hate his loyal lords and subjects by whom of right he ought rather to have been governed. And moreover, accroaching to themselves royal power, by disfranchising our said lord the king of his sovereignty and impairing and diminishing his royal prerogative and regality they made him so far obey them that he was sworn to be governed, counselled, and guided by them. By virtue of which oath they kept him so long in obedience to their false thoughts and imaginations and actions that the mischiefs, inconveniences,

---

MS. de.   [t] *R.P.; MS. om.*   [u] *R.P.* enchrochantz.   [v] *An erasure follows.*
[w] embless' *deleted after this word.*   [x-x] *R.P.* lours fauxes.   [y] *R.P. om.*
[z] *R.P.; MS.* ont.

---

[1] Writs to this effect were sent to the sheriffs on 4 Jan. 1388 (*Cal. Cl. R., 1385-9*, p. 463).

1388 deseases et destruccions contenuz es articles si apres ensuantz sont avenuz, come sont overtement*a* a moustrer et declarer pur profit *b*du roy et du roiaume.*b*1

ij. *c* Item la ou le roy nest*d* tenuz de faire nul serement envers nully *e*de ces lieges*e* si noun le jour de son coronement ou pur comune profit de luy et de son roiaume, les avantditz Alexandre ercevesqe Deverwyk', Robert de Veer duc Dirl',*f* Michel de la Pole conte de Suff', faux traitours et enemys du*g* roy et du*g* roiaume, ont fait luy jurrer et asseurer envers eux *h*qil les*h* meintiendra et sustiendra a viver et a*i* morir ove eux. Et issint la ou le roy doit estre de franc condicion pluis qe null' autre de son roiaume, ils luy ont mys pluis en servage encountre son honour, estat et regalie et encountre lour ligeance come traitours.*j*

iij. Item les avantditz Robert de Veer duc Dirl', Michel de la Pole conte de Suff', Alexandre ercevesqe Deverwyk', par assent et conseill' Robert Tresilyan faux justice et Nichol*k* Brembre faux chivaler de Loundres par lour faux covyn ne suffrerent pas les grands du*g* roiaume ne les bones conseillers le roy parler ne aprocher a*l* roy pur luy bien conseiller ne le roy parler as*m* eux forsqe en la*n* presence et loier des ditz Robert de Veer duc Dirl', Michel de la Pole conte de Suff', Alexandre ercevesqe Deverwyk', par assent et conseill'*o* Robert Tresilyan faux justice et Nichol Brembre faux chivaler du*p* Loundres, ou*q* en la*r* presence daucun deux ameins a lour volunte et solonc lour taille et chose qils voillent en rebottant les grandes et les bones conseillers le roy de lour bone volunte vers lour seignur liege et accrochantz a eux roial poair, seignurie et soveraignete sur la persone le roy a grant deshonour et perill' du*p* roy del corone et del*s* roiaume.

iiij. Item les avantditz Alexandre ercevesqe Deverwyk', Robert de Veer duc Dirl', Michel de la Pole conte de Suff', Robert*o* Tresilian faux justice, et Nichol Brembre faux chivaler du*p* Loundres, par lour faux covyn et accrochement de lour faux malveistes mesnerunt*t* et mal conseillerent nostre seignur le roy si qe sa presence quell' il doit de soun devoir moustrer a les grandes seignurs et*u* soun poeple*v* et a les graces*w* et droit queux requerroient respoundre ne le*x* fist point forsqe a la volunte et a la taille des*y* ditz Alexandre ercevesqe Deverwyk', Robert de Veer etc., Michel de la Pole etc., Robert Tresilian etc., Nichol Brembre etc., en oustantz le roy de son devoir countre soun serement et les coers des grandes seignurs et du*p* poeple de soun*z* seignur*aa* liege,

---

a *R.P. inserts* en partie.　　　　　*b-b* *R.P.* nostre seignur le roi et de tout son roialme.　　　*c* *Part of the word* Treson *can be read in the margin,*　　　*d* *R.P.;* MS. est.　　　*e-e* *Interlined.*　　　*f* *R.P. inserts* et.　　　*g* *R.P.* de.　　　*h-h* *R.P.;* MS. qils.　　　*i* *R.P. om.*　　　*j* *R.P. adds* a lui.　　　*k* *R.P. inserts* de.　　　*l* *R.P.* au.　　　*m* *R.P.* a.　　　*n* *R.P.* le.　　　*o* *R.P. inserts* de.　　　*p* *R.P.* de.　　　*q* el *deleted after this word.*　　　*r* *R.P. om.*　　　*s* *R.P.* de son.　　　*t* *R.P.;* MS. om.　　　*u* *R.P. inserts* a.　　　*v* *R.P. inserts* liege.　　　*w* *R.P.;* MS. grace.　　　*x* *R.P.;* MS. les.　　　*y* *R.P.* les.　　　*z* *R.P.* lour.　　　*aa* *R.P.;* MS. seignurie.

---

1 In this and subsequent articles the Appellants tried to designate the offence of accroaching the royal power, under the several forms enumerated, as treason.

diseases and destructions contained in the following articles have come 1388
about, as [the appellants] are openly to show and declare for profit
of the king and of the realm.[1]

2. Also whereas the king is not bound to make any oath to any of
his subjects except on the day of his coronation or for the common
profit of himself and of his kingdom, the aforesaid Alexander archbishop
of York, Robert de Vere duke of Ireland, Michael de la Pole earl of
Suffolk, false traitors and enemies of the king and of the realm, have
made him swear and assure them that he will maintain and support
them, to live and die with them. And so whereas the king ought to be
of a free condition above any other in his realm, they have put him
more in servitude against his honour, estate, and regality, contrary to
their allegiance and as traitors.

3. Also the aforesaid Robert de Vere duke of Ireland, Michael de
la Pole earl of Suffolk, Alexander archbishop of York, by the assent
and counsel of Robert Tresilian false justice and Nicholas Brembre
false knight of London by their false covin would not suffer the great
men of the realm or the good counsellors of the king to speak to or
approach the king to give him wholesome advice nor the king to speak
to them except in the presence and hearing of the said Robert de Vere
duke of Ireland, Michael de la Pole earl of Suffolk, Alexander archbishop of York, by assent and counsel of Robert Tresilian false justice
and Nicholas Brembre false knight of London, or in the presence of
some one of them at least, at their will and pleasure and about such
things as they thought fit, barring the great lords and good counsellors
of the king from their goodwill towards their liege lord and accroaching
to themselves royal power, lordship, and sovereignty over the person
of the king to the great dishonour and peril of the king, of the crown,
and of the realm.

4. Also the aforesaid Alexander archbishop of York, Robert de Vere
duke of Ireland, Michael de la Pole earl of Suffolk, Robert Tresilian
false justice, and Nicholas Brembre, false knight of London, by their
false covin and accroachment of their false wickedness, led and evilly
advised our lord the king so that his personal presence which he ought
of his duty to show to the great lords and to his people, and to make
his answer to the favours and right which they requested, was not so
shown save at the pleasure and allowance of the said Alexander archbishop of York, Robert de Vere etc., Michael de la Pole etc., Robert
Tresilian etc., Nicholas Brembre etc., thereby staying the king from his
duty against his oath and turning the hearts of the great lords and of
the people from their liege lord, with design to estrange the heart of

The lords temporal, deliberating on the matter from Tues., 4 Feb. to Thurs.,
13 Feb., adjudged the offences complained of in Articles 1 and 2, 11, 15, 17,
28-32, and 37-9, and one of the offences alleged in Article 22, to be in fact
treasons (*R.P.*, iii. 237; and for the legal issues involved, Bellamy, *Law of Treason*,
pp. 95-6). The reference in this article and the next to an oath on the part of the
king, binding him to the accused, is without corroboration.

1388 encompassantz daloigner le coer nostre seignur le roy des piers de la terre pur aver entre eux soul le governement du roiaume.

v. Item par le dit accrochement*a* les avantditz Robert de Veer duc Dirl',*b* Michel de la Pole etc., par assent et counseill' du*c* dit Alexandre ercevesqe etc.*d* ont faitz qe nostre seignur le roy sanz assent du*c* roiaume ou*e* desert deux lour ad done par *f*lours abettementz*f* diverses seignuries, chastell', villes et*g* manoirs si bien annexes a sa corone come autres si come la terre Dirl' et*h* Okeham ove la*i* forest dycell' et grantz*j* terres qi feurent al seignur Daudeley et autres grandes terres*k* a duc Dirl' et as autres diversement, paront ils sont grandement enrichez et le roy est devenuz povre et nad dont il soy purra susteigner *l*et porter*l* les*m* charges du*c* roiaume si noun par imposicions, taxes ou tributz mettre et prendre sur soun poeple en desheretison de sa corone et en defeisance du roiaume.[1]

vj. Item par le dit accrochement*n* les avantditz Alexandre ercevesqe etc., Robert de Veer etc., Michel etc., par assent et counseill' des ditz Robert Tresilian etc., Nichol Brembre etc., ont fait qe nostre seignur le roy ad done diverses manoirs, terres,*o* rentes, offices et ballies*p* as diverses autres persones de lour affinite et as autres*q* persones des queux ils ont pris grantz dons *r*et broggages pur ycelles causes*r* et auxi par cause a tenir ovesqe eux en lour *s*querelles et purpos*s* en defeisance du roy et du*t* roiaume, si com est de *u*Robert Manfeld'*u* clerc, Johan Blake, et*v* Thomas Usk', et autres diversement.[2]

p. 167   *vij.* Item Robert de Veer etc., Michel de la Pole etc., Alexandre ercevesqe etc., par assent et *w*counseill' Robert Tresilian etc., Nichol*w* Brembre etc., accrochantz*x* a eux roial poair ont fait qe nostre seignur le roy lour ad done*y* grantz dons*z* dor et dargent si bien de ces biens et*aa* joialx propries come des biens et tresor du*bb* roiaume, si come des dismes,*cc* quinzismes et autres *dd*taxes as diverses parlementz grantez*dd* pur estre esploites en defence et save garde du*bb* roiaume et autrement, quele some amont a c. mil marcz et pluis, si come *ee*a duc Dirl'*ee* et autres diversement. Et outre ceo plusours bones ordenances et purposes*ff* faitz et ordenez as*gg* parlementz si bien pur les guerres come en

---

a R.P. encrochement.   *b R.P. inserts* et.   *c R.P.* de.   *d R.P.* d'Everwyk.   *e R.P.; MS.* en.   *f–f R.P.; MS.* lour abette moultz.   *g R.P.; MS. om.*   *h R.P. inserts* de.   *i R.P.* le.   *j R.P.* aultres.   *k R.P.; MS. om. In R.P. there follows* au dit Robert Veer duc d'Irland . . .   *l–l R.P.; MS. om.*   *m R.P.* le.   *n R.P.* encroch'.   *o R.P. inserts* tenementz.   *p R.P.* baillifs.   *q R.P. inserts* diverses.   *r–r R.P.* pur brogage pur ycelle cause.   *s–s R.P.* faulx querelx et purposes.   *t R.P.* de son.   *u–u R.P.* sire Robert de Manfeld.   *v R.P. om.*   *w–w R.P.* counseil de dit Nichol'.   *x R.P.* encrochantz.   *y R.P. inserts* tres.   *z R.P.* somes.   *aa MS. om.*   *bb R.P.* de.   *cc R.P. inserts* et.   *dd–dd R.P.* taxes grantez asz diverses parlementz.   *ee–ee R.P.* au dit Robert Veer duc d'Irland.   *ff R.P.; MS.* purpos.   *gg R.P.* en.

---

[1] The Appellants argue that not only lordships annexed to the Crown (Ireland) but also escheats (the lordship of Oakham and the lands of Sir James de Audley)

our lord the king from the peers of the land in order to have the government of the realm amongst themselves alone.

5. Also by the said accroachment the aforesaid Robert de Vere
duke of Ireland, Michael de la Pole etc., by assent and counsel of the
said Alexander archbishop etc., have caused our lord the king without
assent of the realm or any desert in themselves to give to them by their
abetments sundry lordships, castles, towns, and manors as well annexed
to his crown as others, as the land of Ireland, and Oakham with the
forest of the same, and great lands which were Lord Audley's and other
great estates, to the duke of Ireland and to others variously, whereby
they are greatly enriched and the king is impoverished and has not
wherewith he may maintain himself and support the charges of the
realm except by impositions, taxes, or tributes put and levied upon his
people, in disherison of his crown and to the undoing of the realm.[1]

6. Also by the said accroachment the aforesaid Alexander archbishop etc., Robert de Vere etc., Michael etc., by assent and counsel
of the said Robert Tresilian etc., Nicholas Brembre etc. have caused our
lord the king to give sundry manors, lands, rents, offices, and bailiwicks
to sundry other persons of their affinity and to other persons from
whom they have taken great gifts and bribes on that account and also
to hold with them in their quarrels and purpose, to the undoing of
the king and of the realm, as in the case of Robert Manfield clerk, John
Blake, and Thomas Usk, and others variously.[2]

7. Also Robert de Vere etc., Michael de la Pole etc., Alexander
archbishop etc., by assent and counsel of Robert Tresilian etc., Nicholas
Brembre etc., accroaching to themselves royal power have caused our
lord the king to give, as, for example, to the duke of Ireland and to
others variously, great gifts of gold and silver as well of his own goods
and jewels, as of the goods and treasure of the realm, as tenths,
fifteenths, and other taxes granted in sundry parliaments to be laid out
in defence and safeguarding of the realm and otherwise, which amount
to the sum of 100,000 marks and more. And moreover they have
disturbed, to the great detriment of the king and of the realm, many

should be applied to the maintenance of the king and the kingdom. For the principles involved see Harriss, *King, Parliament and Public Finance in Medieval
England to 1369*, pp. 128 ff. For the grants to de Vere of, respectively, the lordship of Ireland, the lordship of Oakham with the forest of Rutland, and the reversion of the Audley lands, in 1385–6, see *Cal. Pat. R., 1385–9*, pp. 69–70, and
above, pp. 146 and 190.

[2] Cf. above, p. 90, reporting collusion between Usk and Brembre in the
former's appeal against John Northampton in 1384. For Blake see above, p. 202
and n. Manfield, provost of St. John's College, Beverley, must have been one of
Nevill's *opponents* in the latter's dispute with the college over visitation rights
(above, pp. 178–80). In June 1386, however, Nevill mainprized Manfield and a
number of other persons from custody in York in the sum of £1,000, and the case
then pending may have occasioned the reference to Manfield in this article (*Cal.
Cl. R., 1385–9*, p. 150). In 1384, Walter Sibill, the London alderman, accused
Robert de Vere of maintenance and incurred damages of 500 marks and a fine
and ransom to the king for his pains (*R.P.*, iii. 186; see also below, p. 248).

1388 defence du^a roiaume ont ils destourbez a^b grant arrerissement du^a roy et du^a roiaume.[1]

viij. Item par le dit accrochement^c et pur^d grantz dons et broggages qils ont pris les avantditz Robert de Veer etc., Michel de la Pole etc., Alexandre ercevesqe etc., ont faitz qe diverses persones nient suffisantz et noun covenables ont le garde et ^{e}soveraignete des^e diverses seignuries, chastell' et paiis de guerre, come en Guyen et aillours, si bien de cea le mere come de la, paront le poeple et paiis dycelles parties lieges et loialx ^{f}au roy^f pur la grant^g partie sont destruitz et grandes seignuries de novel renduz es^h mayns ^{i}et possessions^i des enemys santz assent du^j roiaume quelles ne feurent unqes es mayns ^{k}des enemys^k puis le conquest dycell', sicome il est ^{l}en marche^l Descoce et aillours, en desheritison' del corone de^m roy et en^n grant arrerissement du roiaume, come^o de Harpedene et^n Cradok' et autres diversement.[2]

ix. Item par le dit accrochement^p les avantditz Alexandre ercevesqe etc. ^{q}et ces compaignons suisditz traitours^q ont faitz qe diverses gentz ont estee destourbez de la comune ley Dengl' et mys a grantz delaies, perdes et costagez, et estatutz et juggementz droitturelement sur causes necessairs faitz et renduz en parlement^r reversez et adnullez par procurement des ditz mesfesours et traitours, et ceo par cause des grantz dons et broggages par eux resceivez en^s celle part, en^t grant arrerissement du roy et du roiaume.[3]

x. Item les avantditz Alexandre etc. ^{q}et autres traytours suisditz,^{q} accrochantz^u a eux ^{v}roial poair^v come faux traitours a roy et a roiaume, ont fait et counseille nostre dit seignur le roy de grantier chartres de pardoun des horribles felonies et tresons sibien countre^w lestat du roy come de partie, la quell' chose fuist^x encountre la ley et le serement du roy.[4]

xj. Item^y la ou ^{z}la graunt seignurie et^z la terre Dirl' sont et ont estez de temps dont memorie ne court parcell' del corone Dengl' et les gentz de celle terre Dirl' ^{aa}par tout le temps avaunt dit^{aa} ont este lieges sanz mesne a^{bb} roy ^{cc}nostre seignur^{cc} et^{dd} ces roialx^{ee} progenitours roys Dengl', et nostre seignur et ces nobles progenitours roys Dengl' en^{ff} toutz lour chartres, briefs, lettres et^{gg} patentes et auxi en lour sealx en augmentacion de lour nouns et de lour regalte les ont fait nomer seignur^{hh} Dirl', les avantditz ^{ii}Alexandre etc., Robert de Veer etc.,^{ii}

---

^{a} R.P. de. ^{b} R.P. en. ^{c} R.P. encroch'. ^{d} R.P.; MS. par. $^{e-e}$ R.P. governance de. $^{f-f}$ R.P. a nostre dit seignur le roi. ^{g} R.P. greindre. ^{h} R.P. as. $^{i-i}$ R.P. et en possession. ^{j} R.P. de. $^{k-k}$ R.P.; MS. om. $^{l-l}$ R.P. es marches. ^{m} R.P. du. ^{n} R.P. om. ^{o} R.P. sicome. ^{p} R.P. encroch'. $^{q-q}$ R.P. om. but gives names and titles in full; see above, p. 238 n. ^{r} R.P. parlementz. ^{s} R.P.; MS. de. ^{t} R.P. inserts tres. ^{u} R.P. encrochantz. $^{v-v}$ R.P. poar roial; MS. inserts si after poair. ^{w} R.P. encontre. ^{x} R.P. est. ^{y} Treson' in the margin. $^{z-z}$ R.P.; MS. les grantz seignuries de. $^{aa-aa}$ R.P.; MS. paront les avantditz gentz. ^{bb} R.P. au. $^{cc-cc}$ R.P.; MS. seignurs. ^{dd} R.P. inserts a. ^{ee} MS. loialx; R.P. reaux. ^{ff} MS. inserts lour. ^{gg} MS. om. ^{hh} R.P. seignurs. $^{ii-ii}$ R.P. Robert duc d'Irland, Alexandre ercevesqe d'Everwyk.

good ordinances and purposes made and ordained in the parliaments 1388 as well for the wars as in defence of the realm.[1]

8. Also by the said accroachment and for great gifts and bribes which they have taken, the aforesaid Robert de Vere etc., Michael de la Pole etc., Alexander archbishop etc. have caused sundry insufficient and unsuitable persons to have the guard and sovereignty of sundry lordships, castles, and theatres of war, as Guyenne and elsewhere as well on this side the sea as beyond, whereby the people and countries of those territories, being loyal lieges of the king, have been for most part destroyed and great lordships newly surrendered without assent of the realm into the hands and possession of the enemy which had never since their conquest been in the enemy's hands, as in the march of Scotland and elsewhere, in disherison of the king's crown and to the great detriment of the realm, as in the case of Harpeden and Craddock and others variously.[2]

9. Also by the said accroachment the aforesaid Alexander archbishop etc. and his fellow traitors abovesaid have caused sundry people to be hindered of the benefit of the common law of England and put to great delays, losses, and expense; while statutes and judgements rightfully made and rendered upon necessary causes in parliament have been reversed and annulled by the procurement of the said misfeasors and traitors, and this by reason of the great gifts and bribes by them received in this behalf, to the great detriment of the king and of the realm.[3]

10. Also the aforesaid Alexander etc. and the other traitors abovesaid accroaching to themselves royal power, as false traitors to the king and to the realm have caused and advised our said lord the king to grant charters of pardon of horrible felonies and treasons, as well against the estate of the king as against that of the party, which thing was against the law and the king's oath.[4]

11. Also whereas the great lordship and land of Ireland are and have been from time immemorial parcel of the crown of England and the people of that land of Ireland for all the time aforesaid have been lieges immediate to our lord the king and his royal progenitors kings of England, and our lord and his noble progenitors kings of England in all their charters, writs, letters, and patents and also on their seals in augmentation of their styles and regality have caused themselves to be styled 'Lords of Ireland', the aforesaid Alexander etc., Robert de Vere

---

[1] An indictment of the foreign relations of the English government during the chancellorship of Pole, 1383–6, for which see *Perroy*, pp. 166 ff., and *Palmer*, pp. 44 ff.

[2] For Sir John Harpeden's appointment as seneschal of Gascony during the chancellorship of Pole in 1385, see above, p. 152 and n.; he was also, for a time, keeper of Fronsac castle (*Carte*, i. 174). 'Craddock' is probably Sir Richard Craddock, said in 1389 to be keeper of Fronsac castle (ibid., p. 176, s.a. 1389).

[3] Cf. *R.P.*, iii. 168–70, a circumstantial imputation of bribery to Pole and his clerk during Pole's chancellorship in 1384, by a litigant who was nevertheless disappointed in his suit.   [4] i.e. his coronation oath.

1388 Michel de la Pole etc., come faux traitours a roy par le dit accroche-
ment^a ont fait et conseille qe nostre^b seignur le roy en quanqe^c en luy
est ad grante ^{d}et assentu^d pleinement et soy acorde qe Robert de Veer
duc Dirl' soit fait roy del^e dite terre Dirl'. Et pur acomplier cest malveys
purpos les avantditz traitours ont conseille et excite qe nostre seignur
le roy ad envoiez ces lettres a nostre seint piere le pape de grantier,
ratefier et confermer lour traiturose purpos' sanz^f assent de son
roiaume Dengl' ou^g de la dite terre Dirl' en desceverance de la ligiance
du roy parentre le^h dit roiaume Dengl' et la dite terre Dirl' et en
descresce del honurable noun du roy nostre seignur avantdit et en
overte desheretison' de sa corone du roiaume Dengl' et pleyn destruccion des loialx lieges du roy nostre^i seignur et la^j dite terre Dyrland'.^{1}

    xij. Item la ou par la grant chartre et autres bones leyes et usages
du^k roiaume Dengl' null' homme^l serra pris nenprisone^m ne mys a mort
sanz due process' du^k ley,^{2} lavantdit Nichol Brembre etc. par le dit
accrochement^n prist par noet certeins persones hors de la prisone de
Neugate, chapelleyns et autres jesqes ^{o}a nombre^o xxij., aucuns enditez
et^p aucuns appelles de felonie et^q aucuns provours en cas ^{r}de felonie^r
et acuns pris et enprisonez illoeqes par cause de suspeccion de felonie,
et les amesnoit hors de Loundres en le countee de Kent a un lieu qest
appelle Foulhoke^s et illoeqes accrochant^t a luy roial poair come traitour
a roy sanz garrant ou process' de ley les fist decoller,^{u} toutz save un
qestoit appelle de felonie par un provour, le quele il lessoit voluntiere-
ment aler a large en^v mesme le temps.^{3}

    xiij. Item les avantdit Alexandre etc., Robert de Veer etc., Michel
etc., Robert Tresilyan etc., Nichol Brembre etc., traitours du^k roy et
du^k roiaume, ont pris en ^{w}moultz causes^w grandes dons en noun du^x
roy des^x diverses parties pur meyntenance des^x querelles et aucuns
foitz dambedeux^y parties, come^z a plein serra moustre quant mestier
serra.^{aa}^{4}

    xiiij. Item par le dit accrochement^{bb} les avantditz Alexandre
^{cc}etc. et toutz les autres ces compaignons^{cc} ont fait qe,^{dd} la ou ascuns
des seignurs et autres loialx lieges nostre seignur le roy as^{ee} diverses

---

^{a} *R.P.* encroch'. ^{b} *R.P. inserts* dit. ^{c} *MS. inserts* qe. $^{d-d}$ *R.P.*
assentu et. ^{e} terre *deleted after this word.* ^{f} *R.P. inserts* scien ou. ^{g} *R.P.*
et. ^{h} *R.P.* la. ^{i} *R.P. inserts* dit. ^{j} *R.P.* de sa. ^{k} *R.P.* de. ^{l} *R.P.*
inserts ne. ^{m} *R.P.* enprisone. ^{n} *R.P.* encrochement. $^{o-o}$ *R.P.* al noumbre
de. ^{p} *R.P. om.* ^{q} aus *deleted after this word.* $^{r-r}$ *R.P.; MS. om.* ^{s} *R.P.*
le Foul Oke. ^{t} *R.P.* encrochant. ^{u} *R.P.* estre decollez. ^{v} *R.P.* a.
$^{w-w}$ *R.P.* meintes cases. ^{x} *R.P.* de. ^{y} *R.P.* en ambes-deux. ^{z} *R.P.*
sicom plus. ^{aa} *R.P.* soit. ^{bb} *R.P.* encroch'. $^{cc-cc}$ *R.P. om. but gives
names and titles in full; see above,* p. 238 n. ^{dd} *R.P. inserts* par. ^{ee} *R.P.* es.

---

^{1}John, who was lord of Ireland before his accession, added that title to the
royal style. In his grant of the lordship of Ireland to de Vere in 1385 (for which
see above, p. 144), Richard II reserved suzerainty and the allegiance of his
subjects in Ireland. The intention here imputed to Richard, of making over these
rights to de Vere, and with them the royal title itself in respect of Ireland, could
not have been carried through without the acquiescence of the papacy, which had

etc., Michael de la Pole etc., false traitors to the king, by the said 1388
accroachment have caused and advised our lord the king so far as in him
lies to grant and fully to assent and agree that Robert de Vere duke of
Ireland should be made king of the said land of Ireland. And to accomplish this wicked purpose the aforesaid traitors have advised and excited
our lord the king to send his letters to our Holy Father the pope to
grant, ratify, and confirm their traitorous design without assent of his
realm of England or of the said land of Ireland to the division of the
allegiance due to the king between the said realm of England and the
said land of Ireland and to the diminution of the honourable style of the
king our lord aforesaid and in open disherison of his crown of the realm
of England and full destruction of the loyal lieges of the king our lord
and the said land of Ireland.[1]

12. Also whereas by the great charter and other good laws and
usages of the realm of England no man shall be taken or imprisoned or
put to death without due process of law[2] the aforesaid Nicholas
Brembre etc. by the said accroachment took by night certain persons
out of the prison of Newgate, chaplains and others to the number of
twenty-two, some indicted and some appealed of felony and some
approvers in cases of felony and some taken and imprisoned there by
reason of suspicion of felony, and carried them out of London into the
county of Kent to a place called Foul Oak and there accroaching to
himself royal power, as a traitor to the king, without warrant or process
of law caused them all to be beheaded save one who was appealed of
felony by an approver [and] whom he freely suffered to go at large at
the same time.[3]

13. Also the aforesaid Alexander etc., Robert de Vere etc., Michael
etc., Robert Tresilian etc., Nicholas Brembre etc., traitors of the king
and of the realm have taken in many causes great gifts in the king's
name from sundry parties for maintenance of quarrels and sometimes
from both parties, as will be fully shown when occasion arises.[4]

14. Also by the said accroachment the aforesaid Alexander etc.
and all the others his fellows have brought it about that whereas some
of the lords and other loyal subjects of our lord the king at sundry

confirmed Henry II's lordship in Ireland and received John's surrender of his
lordship there, together with that of the kingdom of England, in 1213. The
Appellants may have been drawing conclusions from the dispatch of William
Cheyne to the curia on royal business in the summer of 1385 (P.R.O., E. 403/
508, 12 June).
   [2] A rendering of 'per legem terre' in Magna Carta (1215), *cap*. 29. For the
14th-century understanding of these words see F. Thompson, *Magna Carta: Its
Role in the Making of the English Constitution, 1300–1629* (Minneapolis, 1948),
pp. 86 ff.
   [3] Cf. above, p. 98. The charge against Brembre owed its plausibility to the fact
that he was mayor at the time and the mayor a necessary member of commissions
to deliver the gaol at Newgate (*Letter Book H*, pp. 204, 229 etc.).
   [4] For an explicit charge of maintenance against Robert de Vere see above, p.
245 n.

1388 parlementz eiantz grant poure et doute de perde du^a roy et du^a roiaume
par causes des ditz meschiefs moverent davoir bone governance entour
le roy pur eschuer les perils avantditz, qe nostre^b seignur le roy se
moeva tant et si durement encountre eux qil^c commanda^d aucuns
qils departiroient de son counseill' et de parlement ensy qils noserent
pluis^e parler de cest matere ne toucher bone governance ^{f}du roy et du^f
roiaume pur paour de mort, en grand arrerissement du^a roy et du^a
roiaume.

xv. Item^g par le dit accrochement^h les avantditz Alexandre ^{i}etc.
et toutz ces compaignons traitours^i ount fait^j qe la ou ^{k}en le^k darrein
parlement^l toutz les seignurs et autres sages et comunes illoeqes assemblez veiantz le^l perde du roy et du^m roiaume ^{n}emynentz, tant^n pur les
perilles et meschiefs suisditz et qe le roy estoit departie^o de^p conseill'
du^a roiaume et se tenoit tout a counseill' des^q ditz mesfesours et
traitours, come par cause qe le roy Franceys ^{r}ove tout son poair roial^r
estoit eskippes en le mere prest pur avoir arrive en Engleterre ^{s}et
destruitz^s tout le^t roiaume et la langage Dengl', / et null' ordenance
ne governance estoit alors fait pur sauvete du roy ne du^u roiaume, ne
saveroient de ceo autre remede mes moustrerent^v a^w roy tout pleinement coment il estoit^x governe, counseille et demesne par les avantditz
traitours et mesfesours en declarantz a luy lour malveis condicions, et
luy requiroient^y moult humblement come ces loialx lieges pur sauvete
de luy et de tout son roiaume et pur eschuer^z les perills avantditz de^{aa}
lesser et voider^{bb} les ditz mesfesours et traitours hors de sa presence,
court^{cc} et compaignie et qe il^{dd} ne ferroit en apres apres^{ee} lour malveis
counseill' mes apres les sages loialx et discretes lieges^{cc} du^u roiaume.
Et sur ceo les ditz traitours et mesfesours, veiant ceste bone et honurable oppinioun du^u parlement et pur destourber cell' bone purpos,
par lour faux counseill' firent qe^{ff} le roy comanda al^{gg} mair de
Loundres de faire sodaignement lever un grant poair des^u gentz du^u
Loundres doccire et mettre a^{hh} mort toutz les ditz seignurs et comunes,
horspris ceux qi feurent de lour covyn, al^{gg} fesance de quele mal fait
les greindres mesfesours et traitours desuisditz serroient parties et
presentz, en defesance du^{ii} roy et de tout son roiaume.^{2}

xvj. Item quant^{jj} les avantditz^{kk} Alexandre ercevesqe ^{ll}etc. et toutz
les autres^{ll} mesfesours et traitours a roy et a^{mm} roiaume perceverent

p. 168 (margin, beside "destruitz tout le")

^{a} R.P. de.　　^{b} R.P. inserts dit.　　^{c} MS. qils; R.P. q̄.　　^{d} R.P. inserts a.
^{e} R.P. om.　　$^{f-f}$ R.P. de roi ne de.　　^{g} Treson' in the margin.　　^{h} R.P.
encroch'.　　$^{i-i}$ R.P. om. but gives names and titles in full; see above, p. 238 n.
^{j} MS. om. preceding two words, which are in R.P.　　$^{k-k}$ R.P. a.　　^{l} R.P. la.
^{m} R.P. de son.　　$^{n-n}$ R.P.; MS. en muantz tantz.　　^{o} R.P.; MS. depart.
^{p} R.P. du.　　^{q} R.P. de les.　　$^{r-r}$ R.P. ove son roial poare.　　$^{s-s}$ R.P.
a destruer.　　^{t} R.P. la.　　^{u} R.P. de.　　^{v} MS. moustrent; R.P. monstrerent.
^{w} R.P. au.　　^{x} R.P. inserts malement.　　^{y} R.P. requirerant.　　^{z} R.P. inserts
touz.　　^{aa} R.P.; MS. et.　　^{bb} R.P. ouster.　　^{cc} R.P. om.　　^{dd} Interlined;
R.P. om.　　^{ee} MS. om.　　^{ff} R.P. inserts nostre seignur.　　^{gg} R.P. a.
^{hh} R.P. au.　　^{ii} R.P. de.　　^{jj} Interlined.　　^{kk} R.P. ditz.　　$^{ll-ll}$ R.P.
d'Everwik, Robert de Veer duc d'Irland, Michel de la Pole counte de Suff',
Robert Tresilian et Nicholas Brembre.　　^{mm}R.P. om.

parliaments, having great fear and doubt about the ruin of the king and 1388
of the realm by reason of the said mischiefs, moved to have good
government about the king to avoid the perils aforesaid, our lord the
king was so moved and so hardened against them that he commanded
some of them to depart from his council and from parliament so that
they dared not speak further of this matter nor touch upon the good
government of the king and of the realm for fear of death, to the great
detriment of the king and of the realm.

15. Also by the said accroachment the aforesaid Alexander etc.
and all his fellow traitors have brought it about that whereas in the
last parliament[1] all the lords and other sages and commons there
assembled (seeing the imminent ruin of the king and of the realm by
the perils and mischiefs abovesaid and that the king had forsaken the
council of the realm and applied himself entirely to the counsel of the
said misfeasors and traitors, and also for that the French king with all
his royal power was embarked on the sea ready to have landed in
England and to have destroyed all the realm and nation of England, and
there was no ordinance nor governance then made for the safety of
the king nor of the realm) knew of no other remedy for this but to
show fully to the king how he was governed, counselled, and led by the
aforesaid traitors and misfeasors and to declare to him their wicked
dispositions, requiring him most humbly as his loyal subjects for the
safety of himself and of all his realm and to avoid the perils aforesaid,
to abandon the said misfeasors and traitors, and expel them from his
presence, court, and company and not to act thereafter according to
their evil counsel but according to the sage, loyal, and discreet subjects
of the realm. And thereupon the said traitors and misfeasors, seeing this
good and honourable opinion of the parliament, to undo this good
purpose by their false counsel brought it about that the king commanded the mayor of London to cause to be instantly levied a great
power of the people of London to kill and put to death all the said
lords and commons except those who were of their covin, to the per-
formance of which evil deed the great misfeasors and traitors abovesaid
would be parties and present, to the undoing of the king and of all his
realm.[2]

16. Also when the aforesaid Alexander archbishop etc. and all the
other misfeasors and traitors to the king and to the realm observed that

[1] The parliament of 1 Oct.-28 Nov. 1386. There follows a reference to the
threat of invasion at this time from French forces gathered at Sluys (but not in
fact embarked) for which see Vaughan, *Philip the Bold*, pp. 49-50; *Palmer*, pp. 77
ff., and above, p. 182 and n.

[2] From this article and the next it appears that the Appellants mistakenly
placed in Oct. 1386 the request for armed assistance which Richard II addressed
to the mayor and aldermen of London at the end of Nov. 1387 (above, p. 216).
They were perhaps confused by measures taken for the defence of London against
the French in Sept. 1386 (*Letter Book H*, pp. 285-6). See also Knighton, *Chronicon*, ii. 216.

1388 qe ^ale dit^a mair et les bones gentz de Loundres avoient outrement refuses en presence du roy daccomplir les^b malveis purpos et ^cprodicions touchantz^c le murdre des ditz seignurs et comunes, par lour^d traitouruse accrochement fauxement conseillerent le roy et tant firent qe nostre seignur le roy se esloignast hors du dit parlement par plusours jours et fist certifier qil ne voilloit unqes approcher le dit parlement ne comunier ove les ditz seignurs et comune ^edu busoigne^e du roiaume pur null' perill', perde ne meschief qe ^fpurroient aucun manere^f avenir a luy et^g son roiaume si ne fuisse primerement asseurez par les avantditz seignurs et comunes qils ne duissent riens dire ne faire en le dit parlement encountre aucuns des^h mesfesours avantditz,ⁱ sauvant qils duissent aler et proceder avant touchant le proces qe fuist lors comence envers ^jMichel de la Pole conte de Suff',^j a grant arrerissement de^k roy et du roiaume et encountre les aunciens ordenances et ^lcustumez et^l libertes du parlement.[1]

xvij.^m Item les avantditzⁿ seignurs et comunes^o apres qils avoient entenduz qe la volunte le^p roy par^q malveis excitacion et conseill' des ditz Alexandre etc., Robert de Veer, ^ret toutz les autres traitours^r estoit tiel qil ne voillet suffrer aucun chose estre ^scomence ou pursuie^s encountre les ditz mesfesours ^tet traitours,^t come desuis, noserent ent pluis parler ne proceder encountre la volunte le^p roy. Et puis en le dit parlement, ewes les counseilles et avisamentz de^u toutz les seignurs, justices et autres sages et comunes du dit parlement coment lestate du roy ^vet soun regalte^v purroient ^wmieultz estre^w sauvez encountre les ^xmeschiefs et perils^x desuisditz et ne saveront trover ne troverent autre remedie mes dordeigner qe xij. des loialx et sages seignurs de la terre serroient du^y counseill' du roy par^z un an entier alors prochein ensuant[2] et qe lour serroit fait tiel^{aa} estatut et commission' par mesme le temps par queux ils averoient^{bb} plein et suffisant poair dordeigner pur la ^{cc}governance de^{cc} roy et du roiaume et quanqe apportenoit ^{dd}a roi^{dd} de cea la mere et de la et de repeller, repairer et redresser quantqe estoit malement fait encountre lestat, honour et profit du roy et^{ee} du roiaume et de^{ff} faire autres choses diverses et necessairs pur profit de^p roy et du roiaume, come^{gg} est contenuz en la dite^{hh} commission' ent fait, quele est de record en la chauncellerie, et qe null' persone ⁱⁱdevoit conseiller a roy ne luy mesneroitⁱⁱ encountre la dite ordeignance et estatut, et si le ferroit a primere foithe perdroit toutz ces biens et chateux et al seconde defaute^{jj} porteroit penance de vie et de membre;

---

^{a–a} *R.P.; MS.* les ditz.   ^b *R.P. inserts* ditz.   ^{c–c} *R.P.* prodition touchant. ^d traiterouse *deleted; R.P. inserts* dit.   ^{e–e} *R.P.* des busoignes.   ^{f–f} *R.P.* purroit ascunement.   ^g *R.P.* ou a.   ^h *R.P. inserts* ditz.   ⁱ *R.P. om.* ^{j–j} *R.P.* sire Michel de la Pole.   ^k *R.P.* du.   ^{l–l} *R.P. om.*   ^m *Part of the word* Treson' *can be read in the margin.*   ⁿ *R.P.* ditz.   ^o *R.P. inserts* de roialme.   ^p *R.P.* du.   ^q *R.P. inserts* la.   ^{r–r} *R.P. om. but gives names and titles as in art.* xvi.   ^{s–s} *R.P.* commence, pursue, ou fait.   ^{t–t} *R.P. om.* ^u *R.P.* des.   ^{v–v} *R.P.* de sa regalie et du roialme.   ^{w–w} *R.P.* estre mieulx. ^{x–x} *R.P.* perils et meschiefs.   ^y *R.P.* de.   ^z *R.P.* pur.   ^{aa} *R.P.* tielx.

the said mayor and the good people of London had utterly refused in 1388 the king's presence to accomplish their evil purposes and treachery touching the murder of the said lords and commons, by their traitorous accroachment they falsely counselled the king and so far prevailed that our lord the king absented himself from the said parliament for several days and made it known that he would never approach the said parliament nor treat with the said lords and commons of the business of the realm for any peril, loss, or mischief that might in any way happen to him and his realm unless he were first assured by the aforesaid lords and commons that they would say or do in the said parliament nothing against any of the misfeasors aforesaid, except that they were to proceed and go forward with the process then begun against Michael de la Pole earl of Suffolk; to the great detriment of the king and of the realm and against the ancient ordinances, customs, and liberties of parliament.[1]

17. Also the aforesaid lords and commons, after they understood that the king's mind through the wicked instigation and counsel of the said Alexander etc., Robert de Vere, and all the other traitors was such that he would not suffer anything to be commenced or prosecuted against the said misfeasors and traitors, as above, dared not speak further thereof or proceed against the king's will. And afterwards in the said parliament, upon consideration of the counsel and advice of all the lords, justices, and other sages and commons of the said parliament how the estate of the king and his regality might best be safeguarded against the mischiefs and perils abovesaid, they could not and did not find any other remedy than to ordain that twelve of the loyal and sage lords of the land should be of the king's council for one whole year then next ensuing[2] and that there should be made for them during that time a statute and commission whereby they should have full and sufficient power to ordain for the government of the king and of the realm and whatsoever appertained to the king, as well on this side the sea as beyond, and to repeal, repair, and redress whatsoever was done amiss against the estate, honour, and profit of the king and of the kingdom and to do sundry other things necessary for the profit of the king and of the kingdom, as is contained in the said commission thereupon made and remaining of record in the chancery, and that no person was to counsel the king or move him against the said ordinance and statute, and if any did so he was to forfeit on the first occasion all his goods and chattels and on the second offence sustain penalty of life and limb;

[bb] *R.P.* avoient. [cc–cc] *R.P.* governement du. [dd–dd] *R.P.; MS.* om.
[ee] *R.P.* ou. [ff] *R.P.; MS.* du. [gg] *R.P.* sicome. [hh] *R.P.* om. [ii–ii] *R.P.*
ne dorroit conseil au roi ne luy moevereit ascunement. [jj] *R.P. inserts* il.

---

[1] For Richard II's residence at Eltham in the early weeks of the parliament of 1386, see Knighton, op. cit., ii. 215 ff.

[2] The continual council of 1386-7, as finally constituted, had 11 members in addition to the chancellor, treasurer, and keeper of the privy seal (above, p. 168).

1388 et celles ^{a}ordeinances et estatut^a serroient faitz sil plerroit au^b roy et nient autrement; a quele ordenance toutz les justices ^{c}le roy^c estoient acordez et lour counseill' a ceo doneront^d sibien en presence du roy come des ditz seignurs, ^{e}justices et autres,^{e} et auxi nostre seignur le roy soy assenta pleinement a ycelles ordenances.[1] Et sur ceo les ditz ^{f}commissiouns et estatut^f feurent faitz accordantz al assent du roy des ditz seignurs,^{g} justices et^h autres sages et comunes assemblez a dit parlement pur sauver le roy, sa regalte et son roiaume. Et apres^i finissement du dit parlement les ditz traitours et mesfesours par lour ^{j}dit malveys accrochement enfourmeront le roy fauxement^j qe les ditz ordeinances^k estoient faitz en defesance de sa regalie et qe toutz ceux qi procurerent^l les ditz ordeinance, estatut et commission' destre faitz et^m exciteront le roy dassentier a ceo sont dignes destre mortz come traitours a roy.

    xviij. Item apres ceo^n les ditz mesfesours et traitours^o ont fait le roy assembler counseill' des certeins seignurs, justices et autres plusours foitz^p saunz ^{q}assent de seignurs de^q grant counseill'[2] et les ont ^{r}demaundez diverses et moltz suspeciouses choses^r des diverses matieres, par quey le roy, les seignurs et le comune poeple ont estee en le pluis grant trouble et tout le roiaume auxi et les coers des plusours retraictz du roy, sauvant lour ligiaunce.

    xix. Item pur accomplier le dit haut treson' les ditz mesfesours et traitours^s firent le roy aler ove aucuns^t deux par mye soun roiaume pur la greindre partie et es parties du^u Gales et firent le roy faire venir avant^v luy les seignurs, chivalers, esquiers et autres bones gentz des ditz parties, sibien de^w citees et^x burghes come des autres^x lieux, et les firent estre liez, aucuns par lour obligaciouns et aucuns par lour serementz, a nostre seignur le roy destre ovesqe luy encountre toutz gentz et daccomplier le purpos le^y roy, quele purpos du roy estoit a cell' temps daccomplier ^{z}la volunte et le purpos^z de les avantditz mesfesours et traitours par^{aa} faux ymaginacions, covynes et accrochementz suisditz, ^{bb}queux seurtees et serementz^{bb} estoient faitz encountre les bones leyes et usages de la terre et encountre le serement du roy, a grant arrerissement et deshonour du roy et du roiaume.[3]

p. 169   *xx.* Item par force de tielx^{cc} lienx et serementz tout le roiaume estoit move en grant murmur et trouble par les ditz mesfesours et

$^{a-a}$ *R.P.* ordenance et remedie. ^{b} *R.P.* a. $^{c-c}$ *R.P.* du roialme. ^{d} *R.P.; MS.* deveront. $^{e-e}$ *R.P. om.* $^{f-f}$ *R.P.* ordenances estatut et commission. ^{g} *R.P. inserts* des ditz. ^{h} *R.P. inserts* des. ^{i} *R.P. inserts* le. $^{j-j}$ *R.P.* ditz malveis encrochementz fauxement et traiterousement enfourmeront le roi. ^{k} *R.P.* ordenance estatut et commission. ^{l} *R.P. inserts* ou counseillerount. ^{m} *R.P. inserts* qe touz yceux q'. ^{n} *MS. inserts* qe. ^{o} *R.P. inserts* Alisaundre erchevesqe d'Everwik, Robert de Veer duc d'Irland, Michel de la Pole comte de Suff', Robert Tresilian et Nicholas Brembre. ^{p} *MS.* faitz. $^{q-q}$ *R.P.* assent ou presence des seigneurs du. $^{r-r}$ *R.P.* faitz diverses demandes et moultz suspectuouses. ^{s} *R.P. inserts* Alisaundre erchevesqe d'Everwyk, Robert de Veer duc d'Irland, Michel de la Pole comte de Suff', par which ordinances and statute should be made if it so pleased the king 1388 and not otherwise; to which ordinance all the king's justices agreed and gave their counsel in favour thereof as well in the presence of the king as of the said lords, justices, and others, and further our lord the king gave his full assent to these ordinances.[1] And thereupon the said commissions and statute were made, according to the assent of the king and of the said lords, justices, and other sages and commons assembled in the said parliament, for the safety of the king, his regality, and his realm. And after the end of the said parliament the said traitors and misfeasors by their said wicked accroachment falsely informed the king that the said ordinances were made in derogation of his regality and that all those who procured the making of the said ordinance, statute, and commission and prompted the king to agree thereto were worthy of death as traitors to the king.

18. Also, afterwards the said misfeasors and traitors caused the king to assemble a council of certain lords, justices, and others on several occasions without the assent of the lords of the great council[2] and addressed to them diverse highly suspicious questions concerning sundry matters whereby the king, the lords, and the common people have been involved in most grievous trouble and the whole realm moreover [disquieted] and the hearts of many withdrawn from the king, saving their allegiance.

19. Also, to accomplish the said high treason the said misfeasors and traitors caused the king to go with some of them through the greater part of his realm and into the parts of Wales and caused the king to summon to him the lords, knights, esquires, and other good people of the said parts, as well of cities and boroughs as of other places, and caused them to engage, some by their bonds and others by their oaths, to our lord the king to stand with him against all people and to effect the king's purpose, which purpose was at that time to accomplish the will and purpose of the aforesaid misfeasors and traitors by their false contrivances, conspiracies, and accroachments aboveaid, which securities and oaths were contrary to the good laws and usages of the land and to the king's oath; to the great detriment and dishonour of the king and of the realm.[3]

20. Also, by force of such bonds and oaths all the realm was set astir in great murmur and trouble by the said misfeasors and traitors

assent et counseil des ditz Robert Tresilian et Nichol' Brembre.   [t] *R.P.* ascuns; MS. aucun.   [u] *R.P.* de.   [v] *R.P.* devant.   [w] *R.P.* des.   [x] *R.P.; MS. om.* [y] *R.P.* du.   [z-z] *R.P.* les voluntees et purposes.   [aa] *R.P. inserts* lour. [bb-bb] *R.P.; MS. om.*   [cc] *MS.* tiele.

---

[1] On this reference to the participation of the king's judges in the making of the ordinance and statute on the continual council in 1386, see Clementi, in *E.H.R.*, lxxxvi (1971), 112.

[2] In the Appeal, 'great council' denotes the continual council appointed in 1386. For the other councils referred to in this article, see above, p. 186 and nn.

[3] Cf. above, p. 186, where oaths but not bonds are mentioned.

1388 traitours[a] par perill' daver suffre[b] diverses meschiefs importables.

xxj. Item[c] pur afforcier lour ditz [d]traiturose purpos[d] sovent firent le roy[e] esloigner en les pluis longetismes parties du roiaume a cause qe les seignurs assignez par les ditz ordenaunce, estatut et commission' ne purroient counseiller ovesqe luy des busoignes du roiaume, en destourbance [f]des purposes et effectes[f] des ordenance, estatut et commission' avantditz, a grant arrerissement du roy et du roiaume.

xxij. Item le dit[g] Robert de Veer etc. par counseill' et abette des ditz mesfesours et traitours Alexandre [h]etc. et autres etc.[h] accrochantz a eux[i] roial poair, sanz commission' usuele[j] du roy ou autre garrant suffisant[k] se fist justice de Cestre et par luy et ces deputes tenoit illoeqes toutz maneres des plees, si bien [l]plees de la corone com autres,[l] et sur ceo renderont juggementz et firent ent execucion, et auxi fist faire diverses briefs originall' et judiciall' estre enseales de[m] grant seal le roy en ycell' parties usee.[1] Et issint par tiel accrochement de [n]roial poair[n] il fist sourdre et lever ovesqe luy grant [o]nombre de[o] gentz de tout le[p] paiis, aucuns par tiels briefs moult hydouses et manassables et[q] aucuns par enprisonement[r] de lour corps, aucuns par seysyn de lour terres, et autrement en moultz maneres deshonestes par colour du[s] dit office,[t] tout pur guerrer et destruer les ditz seignurs et autres loialx lieges nostre seignur le roy, en defesance du roy et de tout le[u] roiaume.[2]

xxiij. Item les ditz traitours Robert de Veer [v]etc. et ces autres compaignons accrochant[v] a eux roial poair firent deliverer Johan de Bloys heir de Bretaigne, qestoit prisoner et tresor a nostre[w] seignur le roy et a soun roiaume, sanz assent du[x] parlement ou[y] de grant conseill' le[z] roy et sanz garrant, en grant afforcement del adversair de France et en grant arrerissement du roy et du roiaume et encountre lestatut[aa] et ordenances avantditz [bb]en parlement faitz.[bb][3]

xxiiij. Item les ditz traitours, Robert de Veer duc Dirl' [cc]et autres ces compaignons,[cc] firent le roy de faire grant retenue[dd] de novell' des diverses gentz et a[ee] doner a eux diverses signes autrement qe il[ff] ne soloit estre dancien temps par aucuns[gg] roys ces progenitours, al effect pur avoir poair a[hh] parfourner[ii] les faux tresouns avantditz.[ii][4]

---

[a] *R.P. inserts names of five appellees as in art. xvi. (above, p. 250 n.).*   [b] *R.P., for the last four words,* et en peril d'avoir suffert.   [c] Treson' *in the margin.* [d-d] *R.P.* traiterouses purposes les ditz, *followed by the names of the five appellees as in art. xvi.*   [e] *R.P. inserts* soi.   [f-f] *R.P.* et defesance del purport et effect. [g] *Interlined.*   [h-h] *R.P.* erchevesqe d'Everwik, *followed by the names of Pole, Tresilian, and Brembre, as in art xvi, and* suis dites.   [i] *R.P., for the last three words,* acrochant a luy.   [j] *R.P. om.*   [k] *R.P. inserts* usuele.   [l-l] *R.P.* communes plees come plees de la corone.   [m] *R.P.* du.   [n-n] *R.P.* poair real.   [o-o] *R.P.* partie des.   [p] *R.P.* la.   [q] *R.P. om.*   [r] *R.P.* emprisonementz.   [s] *R.P. del.*   [t] *R.P. inserts* et ceo.   [u] *R.P.* son.   [v-v] *R.P.* duc d'Irland, Alisaundre erchevesqe d'Everwik, et Michel·de la Pole comte de Suff', par counseil et abette de Robert Tresilian et Nichol' Brembre sus dites, encrochantz.   [w] *R.P. inserts* dit.   [x] *R.P.* de.   [y] *R.P.* et.   [z] *R.P.* du.   [aa] *R.P.* l'estatutz.   [bb-bb] *R.P.* faitz en le darrein parlement.   [cc-cc] *R.P. om. but names the other appellees, as in art xvi (above, p. 250 n.).*   [dd] *R.P.* retenance.   [ee] *R.P.* de.   [ff] *R.P. om.* [gg] *R.P. inserts* des.   [hh] *R.P.* pur.   [ii-ii] *R.P.* lour faux treson avaunt dite.

because of the danger of suffering sundry intolerable mischiefs.

21. Also, to give force to their said traitorous purpose they often caused the king to absent himself in the furthest parts of the realm to the intent that the lords assigned by the said ordinance, statute, and commission could not confer with him about the business of the realm; to the disturbance of the purposes and effects of the ordinance, statute, and commission aforesaid, and to the great detriment of the king and of the realm.

22. Also the said Robert de Vere etc. by the counsel and abetment of the said misfeasors and traitors Alexander etc. and the others etc., accroaching to themselves royal power, without the usual commission from the king or other sufficient warrant, made himself justice of Chester and by himself and his deputies held there all manner of pleas, as well pleas of the crown as others, and gave judgement thereon and caused execution thereof, and further caused diverse writs, original and judicial, to be sealed with the king's great seal used in those parts.[1] And thus by such accroachment of royal power he caused to rise up with him great numbers of the people of all that country, some by means of writs of this kind in frightful and threatening terms, some by the imprisonment of their bodies, some by the seizure of their lands, and otherwise in many disgraceful ways by colour of the said office, and all this to bring war and destruction upon the said lords and other loyal subjects of our lord the king, to the undoing of the king and of all the realm.[2]

23. Also the said traitors Robert de Vere etc. and others his fellows, accroaching to themselves royal power, caused to be delivered Jean de Blois, heir of Brittany, who was a valuable prisoner belonging to the king and to his realm, without the consent of the parliament or of the king's great council and without warrant, to the great strengthening of the French adversary and to the great detriment of the king and of the realm and contrary to the statute and ordinances aforesaid in parliament made.[3]

24. Also the said traitors Robert de Vere duke of Ireland and others his fellows caused the king to have of late a great retinue of sundry people and to give them sundry badges otherwise than was wont to be done of ancient time by any kings his progenitors, to the end that they might have power to perform the false treasons aforesaid.[4]

[1] i.e. the seal of Chester. In fact the normal powers of the justice of Chester traditionally included the issue of original and judicial writs under the Chester seal, without warrant (Tout, *Chapters*, v. 296-7, 367-8). The lords in parliament discriminated between this part of Article 22 and what follows and judged only the offences complained of in the latter part to be treason. For de Vere's appointment as justice see above, pp. 186-8 and n.

[2] A reference to de Vere's raising of a force for the king in Nov.-Dec., 1387, for which see more particularly Articles 38-9. See also above, p. 214.

[3] For the ransom of Jean de Blois (Jean de Bretagne) on 20 Nov. 1387, one day after the expiry of the continual council's commission, see above, p. 188 and n.   [4] Above, p. 186.

1388   *xxv.* Item les avantditz*a* traitours Alexandre *b*etc. et ces autres compaignons*b* en plein accomplissement de toutz lour tresouns avantditz et auxi*c* pur faire le roy *d*en eux et en lour*e* counseill' croier*d* et les tenir pluis loialx a luy et pluis sages qe null' autres de soun roiaume, et sur*f* ceo pluis colurer lour faux tresouns et fauxetees suisditz firent le roy faire venir devant luy es*g* diverses lieux deins le roiaume diverses justices et gentz de*h* ley, cest assavoir Robert Tresilian, *i*Robert Bealknap,*i* Johan Cary, *j*John Holt,*j* Roger Foulthorp', William Bourgh', ces justices, Johan*k* Lokton' serjeant,*l* et ovesqe*m* eux Johan Blake referendarye,*n* les queles justices, sergeant et Johan Blake apposez et demandez*o* par les avantditz mesfesours *p*et traitours*p* si les*q* ordenance, estatut et commission' feurent faitz en derogacion de sa regalie et prerogative ou nient et des autres diverses questions, as quelles les ditz justices, sergeant et Johan Blake*r* responderont

*s*come desuis est escript en le cynk' foyll': et comence*s* 'Memorandum quod vicesimo quinto die*t* Augusti etc.'[1]

   xxvj. Item[2] les avantditz*u* traitours*v* apres qils estoient seures qils avoient sustraitz le coer et la bone volunte le*w* roy des*x* ditz seignurs et autres qi sassentirent de faire les avantditz *y*estatut et commission'*y* en darrein parlement et qe le roy les tenoit ces enemys et ces traitours, et*z* ovesqe ceo qils estoient seures qe les oppiniouns des justices estoient accordantz a lour malveis purpos suisditz*aa* et qe aucuns des *bb*ditz justices*bb* estoient de lour assent et covyne, alors par faux ymaginacions*cc* et pur attendre lour faux et traiterouse purpos*dd* entre eux *ee*ordene estoit qaucuns*ee* des ditz seignurs*ff* serroient primerement arrestuz et puis par faux enquestes enditez et atteintz dez*gg* certeins tresons par eux fauxement ymaginez sur mesmes les seignurs et comunes et issint estre mys a*hh* malveys et honteouse mort et eux et lour sanc perpetuelment desherites et qe ceux fauxes arestes, enditementz et atteindres serroient faitz en Loundres et*ii* en Midd', et par cell' cause firent un faux malveis*jj* de lour covyne, Thomas Usk',*kk* suthvic' de Midd',[3] qi par lour assent, procurement et comandement entreprist*ll* qe les ditz faux enditementz et atteindres

---

a R.P. inserts mesfesours et.   *b-b R.P.* erchevesqe d'Everwik, Robert de Veer duc d'Irland, Michel de la Pole comte de Suff', et Robert Tresilian par assent et counseil du Nicholas Brembre sus dit.   *c MS.* aux; *R.P.* autres et.   *d-d R.P.* creier en eux et en lour counseil.   *e MS.* le.   *f R.P.* desouz.   *g R.P.* as. *h R.P.* du.   *i-i R.P.; MS. om.   j-j R.P.; MS. om.   k R.P.* et John de.   *l R.P. inserts* du loy.   *m* ces *deleted after this word.   n R.P. inserts* et autres. *o R.P. inserts* en presence du roi.   *p-p R.P. om.   q R.P. inserts* avant ditz. *r R.P. om.   s-s R.P.* en manere come ensuit.   *t R.P. inserts* mensis.   *u R.P. inserts* mesfesours et.   *v R.P. inserts* names *of* appellees *with titles, as above,* p. 238 n.   *w R.P.* de.   *x R.P.* de les.   *y-y R.P.* commission et ordeignance. *z R.P.; MS. om.   aa R.P.* avant ditz.   *bb-bb R.P.* justices avant ditz. *cc R.P.* ymagynation.   *dd R.P. inserts* avaunt ditz, par faux compassement.

25. Also the aforesaid traitors Alexander etc. and others his fellows 1388
in full accomplishment of all their treasons aforesaid and also to make
the king believe in them and in their counsel and hold them to be more
loyal to himself and wiser than any others in his realm, and in addition
the more to colour their false treasons and deceits abovesaid, caused
the king to summon before him at sundry places in the realm sundry
justices and men of law, that is to say Robert Tresilian, Robert Bealknap, John Cary, John Holt, Roger Fulthorpe, William Burgh, his
justices, John Lockton, serjeant, and with them John Blake, referendary, which justices, serjeant, and John Blake, being apposed and
asked by the aforesaid misfeasors and traitors whether the ordinance,
statute, and commission were made in derogation of his regality and
prerogative or not and sundry other questions, to which the said
justices, serjeant, and John Blake answered

as is written above, five folios back, beginning 'Be it remembered that on 25 August etc.'[1]

26. Also[2] after the aforesaid traitors were assured that they had
drawn away the heart and goodwill of the king from the said lords and
others who had agreed to the making of the aforesaid statute and commission in the last parliament and that the king looked upon them as
his enemies and traitors and were further assured that the justices'
opinions were agreeable to their wicked purpose abovesaid and that
some of the said justices were in full accord and collusion with them,
by their false contrivances and to achieve their false and traitorous
purpose it was then ordained amongst them that some of the said lords
should be first arrested and afterwards, by means of false inquests,
indicted and attainted of certain treasons falsely contrived by them
against the same lords and commons and then put to an evil and shameful death and they and their blood perpetually disinherited, and that
these false arrests, indictments and attainders were to be carried out in
London and Middlesex, and for that purpose they created a false and
wicked person of their conspiracy, Thomas Usk, under-sheriff of
Middlesex,[3] and he by their assent, procurement, and command undertook that the said false indictments and attainders should be made and

ee-ee R.P. ordeigneront, qe ascuns.   *ff* R.P. *inserts* et communes.   *gg* R.P. de.
hh R.P. al.   *ii* R.P. ou.   *jj* R.P. et malveise persone.   *kk* R.P. Huske,
followed by d'estre.   *ll* R.P. emprist.

---

[1] Above, pp. 196 ff.

[2] Here and in Articles 27–34, the Appellants give their version of events in and
about the court between Richard II's consultation with his judges on 25 Aug.
1387 and the end of the official life of the continual council, on 19 Nov. 1387.
Cf. above, pp. 204 ff.; and see below, p. 274 and n.

[3] Usk, a royal serjeant-at-arms, was appointed under-sheriff of Middlesex at
the king's request between 2 Sept. and 7 Oct. 1387 (*Letter Book H*, pp. 316–17).

1388 serroient faitz et accompliz par la manere suisdite. Et a plener accomplissement[a] de mesme le[b] tresoun les ditz traitours firent nostre
seignur le roy envoier ces lettres du[c] credence par un Johan Rypon'
faux clerk'[d] directe al mair du[c] Loundres,[1] quele credence estoit qe
[e]le mair[e] duist arester le duc de Glouc' et autres[f] persones queux il
noma a cell' temps', et apres ceo[g] qe le dit duc et les autres fuissent
ensi arestuz ils duissent estre enditez [h]et atteintz[h] des[i] certeins tresons
en manere come [j]devant. Et apres ceo[j] Nichol Brembre et Johan Blake
par force du[k] dite lettre de credence porteront a[l] dit mair un bill',
qestoit en[m] enformacion de le dite faux enditement, comaundant et
chargeant[n] a[l] dit mair qil a son poair duist faire les avantditz arestez,
enditementz et atteindres estre faitz par[o] manere suisdit: leffect' de
quelle bille ensuit:[p] 'Ysemble[q] pur le mieltz qe certeins [r]etc.', ut in
confessione Blake, etc.[r2] Et outre ceo les ditz mesfesours et traitours
ordeneront qe bone espie serroit fait sur le[s] arrivall' [t]del duc du[t] Lancastre et qil serroit arrestuz meintenant sur sa arrivall'.

xxvij. Item apres qe les avantditz Alexandre ercevesqe [u]etc. et ces
autres compaignons,[u] traitours a[v] roy et a[w] roiaume avoient ensi
traiterousement enfourmez nostre seignur le roy qil creira[x] surement[y]
qe les ditz ordenance, estatut et commission[z] feurent[aa] faitz en derogacion de [bb]sa regalie et de sa[bb] prerogative[cc] luy enformeront de creyer
auxi fortement qe toutz ceux qi ordenerent les ditz ordenance, estatut
et commission' destre faitz[dd] feurent en final purpos a degrader luy[ee]
et deposer nostre[ff] seignur le roy et qils ne voilloient en null' manere
cesser [gg]dycell' et de lour[gg] purpos tanqe ils averoient ceo fait,[hh]
paront le roy les tient come ces enemys et traytours.

p. 170 / *xxviij.* Item[ii3] apres cell' faux et traiterouse [jj]purpos et[jj] enformacion
quant les avantditz Alexandre [kk]et ces compaignons traitours[kk] per-
ceveront[ll] qe nostre seignur' le roy les loialx seignurs tient com ces
enemys et traitours, les ditz mesfesours et traitours luy conseillerent
qe par chescun voie possible luy ferroit fort sibien par poair de ces
gentz lieges come par poair de ces enemys Franceys et autres a destruer
et mettre a mort les avantditz seignurs et toutz autres assentantz al
feisance des[mm] ditz ordenance, estatut et commission', et qe ceo serroit
fait si privement qe nul ent saveroit tanqe y fuist mys en fait.

---

[a] *R.P.* complicement.   [b] *R.P.* la.   [c] *R.P.* de.   [d] *R.P. inserts* qy estoit
de lour dit faux covyne.   [e-e] *R.P.* le dit maire de Loundres.   [f] *R.P. inserts*
certeins.   [g] *R.P. om.*   [h-h] *R.P. om.*   [i] *R.P.* de.   [j-j] *R.P.* le dit sire
Nichol' Brembre chivaler et John Blake, qe estoient de ceo pleinement enformes,
dussent enformer le dit mair. Et puis le dit monseignur.   [k] *R.P.* de.   [l] *R.P.*
al.   [m] *Interlined; R.P. om.*   [n] *R.P. inserts* de part le roi.   [o] *R.P. inserts* la.
[p] *MS. inserts* et.   [q] *MS.* Ysembe; *R.P.* Semble.   [r-r] *Not in R.P., which gives
in full the passage here omitted (iii. 234).*   [s] *R.P.* la.   [t-t] *R.P.* monseignur de.
[u-u] *R.P. names the five appellees as above (p. 238 n.); there follows* mesfesours et.
[v] *R.P.* au.   [w] *R.P. inserts* son.   [x] serra *deleted before this word.*   [y] *R.P.;
MS.* sovereignement.   [z] *MS.* omission'.   [aa] *R.P.* estoient.   [bb-bb] *R.P.*
le regalie et.   [cc] *MS. inserts* et; *R.P. inserts* de roi.   [dd] *R.P.; MS.* qils.
[ee] *R.P. om.*   [ff] *R.P. inserts* dit.   [gg-gg] dycell' *in the margin but marked for*

accomplished in the manner abovesaid. And for the more complete 1388
effecting of their treason the said traitors caused our lord the king to
send his letters of credence by one John Ripon, a false clerk, addressed
to the mayor of London,[1] to the effect that the mayor was to arrest
the duke of Gloucester and other persons at that time named, and after
the said duke and the others had been so arrested they were to be
indicted and attainted of certain treasons in the manner before
mentioned. And afterwards Nicholas Brembre and John Blake by virtue
of the said letter of credence carried to the said mayor a bill of information in support of the said false indictment, commanding and charging
the said mayor to do his utmost to cause the aforesaid arrests, indictments and attainders to be made in the manner abovesaid: the effect
of which bill was as follows: 'It seems best that certain' etc., as in Blake's
confession.[2] And furthermore the said misfeasors and traitors ordained
that a good watch should be kept for the coming of the duke of
Lancaster and that he should be arrested immediately upon his arrival.

27. Also, after the aforesaid Alexander archbishop etc. and others
his fellows, traitors to the king and to the realm, had thus traitorously
inspired in our lord the king the firm belief that the said ordinance,
statute, and commission were made in derogation of his regality and
prerogative, they inspired in him the equally strong belief that all those
who ordained the making of the said ordinance, statute, and commission had made it their final purpose to degrade and depose our lord the
king and that they would not in any way cease from that purpose of
theirs until they had achieved it, for which cause the king looked upon
them as his enemies and traitors.

28. Also[3] after this false and traitorous purpose and information,
when the aforesaid Alexander and his fellow traitors perceived that our
lord the king looked upon the loyal lords as his enemies and traitors,
the said misfeasors and traitors advised him that by every way possible
as well by the power of his own subjects as by the power of his enemies
of France and others, he should make himself strong to destroy and put
to death the aforesaid lords and all others who agreed to the making of
the said ordinance, statute and commission and that this should be
done so privily that none should know of it till it was done.

insertion: R.P. om. et de lour.   [hh] *R.P.* perfete.   [ii] Treson' *in the margin.*
[jj-jj] *R.M. om.*   [kk-kk] *R.P. om. but names appellees as above, p. 238 n.*   [ll] *MS.*
pursueront; *R.P.* perceuront.   [mm] *R.P.* de.

---

[1] Nicholas Exton, mayor of London 1386–8. For Ripon see above, p. 202, and
below, p. 300.

[2] In cutting short the quotation from Blake's confession the Monk was no
doubt imitating his source, for which see above, p. 234 n. For the omitted passage
see *R.P.*, iii. 234.

[3] This article and nos. 29–32 relate to negotiations between Richard II and
Charles VI of France which were under way by the autumn of 1387 but interrupted by the rise to power of the Appellants in Dec. of that year (above, p. 204
and n.; cf. *Palmer*, pp. 116–17).

1388 *xxix*. Item^a pur accomplir cest haut treson' ^{b}les avantditz Alexandre etc. et ces compaignons par lour counseill'^{b} firent le roy mander^c ces lettres du^d credence a soun adversair ^{e}du France,^{e} aucuns par^f Nichol Southwelle vadlet de sa^g chambre^1 et aucuns par autres persones de petit estat, sibien aliens come denizeins, requiront et empriant le^h dit roy Franceis qil vorroit estre ove tout sa poair et counseill' eidant^i a ^{j}nostre dit seignur le roy^j a destruer et a mort mettre les ditz seignurs et autres Engleys les queux le roy lors tenoit ces enemys et traitours, come de suis, a tresgrant^k trouble de tout le roiaume ^{l}et grant deshonour du roy et du roiaume.^{l}

xxx. Item^m lavantditz Alexandre etc. et ces autres compaignons,^{n} acrochantz^o a eux ^{p}roial poair,^{p} firent le roy promettre al roy Franceis par les^q ditz lettres et messages pur eide et afforcement avoir ^{r}du dit^r roy Franceis et^s de sa poair pur accomplir ^{t}cestez hautez tresouns^t de prodicion et murdre de doner et a^u suisrendre a dit roy Franceis la^v ville et le chastell' de Caleys et toutz ces^u autres chastell' et forcelettes en la^v marche de Pycardie et Artoys, les chastelx et villez de Chirebourgh' et de Brest, a tresgrant deshonour, trouble et arrerissement du roy et ^{w}de son'^{w} roiaume.

xxxj. Item^x les avantditz Alexandre etc. et ces compaignons apres qils^y estoient seurs davoir eide et afforcement du roy Franceys par manere come desuis, alors^z estoit accorde parentre nostre dit seignur le roy et le roy Franceis par excitacion et fesance des^{aa} ditz traitours qe parlance serroit fait en les marchez du^{bb} Caleys dun treewe de cynk' ans parentre les^{cc} ditz^{dd} deux roiaumes Dengl' et de France, a quele parlance serroient^{ee} les ditz deux roys et auxint les^{ff} seignurs Engleys queux le roy lors ^{gg}tenoit ces enemys et traitours,^{gg} et la par tresoun mesmes les seignurs Thomas duc de Glouc' ^{hh}etc. et ces autres ij. countes avantditz^{hh} serroient mys a mort.^{2}

xxxij. Item^{ii} pur accomplissement du^{jj} cest haute treson' les avantditz Alexandre ^{kk}etc. et ces compaignons^{kk} firent le roy envoier pur^{ll} certeinz saufcondites du^{jj} roy Franceys, aucuns pur le roy mesmes, aucuns pur le dit duc Dirl' et aucuns pur Johan Salesbury et Johan Lancastre chivalers ove ^{mm}certein nombre des^{mm} gentz ove eux, pur aler en France en accomplissement de lour dit malveis purpos et treson', les queux saufcondites sont prestes a moustrer.^{3}

^{a} Treson' *in the margin.* $^{b-b}$ *R.P.* avantdit, par lour consail les avant ditz Alexandre erchevesqe d'Everwik, Roberd de Veer duc d'Irland, et Michel de la Pole count de Suff'. ^{c} *R.P.* envoier. ^{d} *R.P.* de. $^{e-e}$ *R.P.* le roi Fraunceis. ^{f} *R.P. inserts* une. ^{g} *R.P.* son. ^{h} *MS.* les. ^{i} *R.P. inserts* et enforceant. $^{j-j}$ *R.P.* roi nostre seignur. ^{k} *R.P. inserts* disease et. $^{l-l}$ *R.P. om.* ^{m} ⟨Tre⟩son' *in the margin.* ^{n} *R.P., for the last seven words* les avant ditz Alexandre erchevesqe d'Everwik, Roberd de Veer duc d'Irland et Michel del Pole count de Suff'. ^{o} *MS.* acrohantz; *R.P.* encrochantz. $^{p-p}$ *R.P.* poair roial. ^{q} *R.P.* ses. $^{r-r}$ *R.P.* de. ^{s} *R.P.; MS. om.* $^{t-t}$ *R.P.* cest haut treson. ^{u} *R.P. om.* ^{v} *R.P.* le. $^{w-w}$ *R.P.* du. ^{x} ⟨Tre⟩son' *in the margin.* ^{y} *R.P., for the last nine words* apresqe les avaunt ditz Alexandre erchevesqe d'Everwik, Roberd de Veer duc d'Irland et Michel de la Pole count de Suff'. ^{z} *R.P.* lors. ^{aa} *R.P.* de. ^{bb} *R.P.* de. ^{cc} *MS.* des. ^{dd} *R.P. om.* ^{ee} *R.P.* serroit.

29. Also, to accomplish this high treason the aforesaid Alexander 1388 etc. and his fellows by their counsel caused the king to send his letters of credence to his adversary of France, some by Nicholas Southwell, groom of his chamber,[1] and some by other persons of lowly condition, as well aliens as denizens, requiring and requesting the said French king that with all his power and counsel he would help our said lord the king to destroy and to put to death the said lords and other Englishmen upon whom the king then looked as his enemies and traitors, as above; to the great disturbance of the whole realm and the great dishonour of the king and of the realm.

30. Also, the aforesaid Alexander etc. and others his fellows, accroaching to themselves royal power, caused the king to promise to the French king by the said letters and messages, in order to gain the aid and support of the said French king and his power for the accomplishing of these high treasons of betrayal and murder, that he would give up and surrender to the said French king the town and castle of Calais and all his other castles and fortresses in the march of Picardy and Artois, the castles and towns of Cherbourg and of Brest, to the very great dishonour, disturbance, and detriment of the king and of his realm.

31. Also, after the aforesaid Alexander etc. and his fellows were assured of the aid and support of the French king in manner as above, by the instigation and contrivance of the said traitors it was then agreed between our said lord the king and the French king that a parley should be held in the marches of Calais about a five-year truce between the two realms of England and of France, at which parley would be present the said two kings and also the English lords upon whom the king then looked as his enemies and traitors; and there by treachery the same lords, Thomas duke of Gloucester etc. and the other two earls aforesaid, would be put to death.[2]

32. Also, for the accomplishment of this high treason the aforesaid Alexander etc. and his fellows caused the king to send for certain safe-conducts from the French king, some for the king himself, some for the said duke of Ireland, and some for John Salisbury and John Lancaster knights, with a certain number of people accompanying them, who were to go into France to put into execution their said wicked purpose and treason, which safe-conducts are ready to be exhibited.[3]

ff R.P. inserts ditz. *gg–gg R.P.* tenoit alors ses traytours. *hh–hh R.P.* constable d'Engleterre, Richard count d'Arrondell et Surr', et Thomas count de Warr', et autres. *ii* Treson' *in the margin.* *jj R.P. de.* *kk–kk R.P.* erchevesqe d'Everwik, Roberd de Veer duc d'Irland, et Michel de la Pole count de Suff'. *ll R.P. inserts* avoir. *mm–mm R.P.* certains nombres de.

[1] For whom see also below, p. 300.
[2] The proposal was probably for a meeting between the two kings in late Nov. 1387 (*Palmer*, p. 108). Of the Appellants, only Gloucester, Arundel, and Warwick were then openly opposing the king, and the last two named are the earls referred to in this article.
[3] Cf. below, p. 278; and for Lancaster, ibid., p. 300.

1388 *xxxiij.* Item lavantdit Nichol Brembre etc,[a] par assent et conseill' des ditz Alexandre [b]etc. et ces autres compaignons[b] accrochantz[c] a eux roial poair, come devant, fist qe aucuns deux viendrent a Loundres en propres persones[d] sanz assent[e] ou savoir du[f] roy[g] et[h] fist toutz les craftes [i]du Loundres[i] estre jurrez a tenir et parfournir diverses materes nient honestes, si com est contenu en le dit serement qe est de recorde en la chauncellerie, et entre autres qe [j]les ditz craftes[j] la volunte et le[k] purpos du roy [l]tiendront et susteindront[l] a lour poair encountre toutz ceux qi sont ou serront rebelles ou contrariantz en countre sa persone ou sa regalie et prestez serront a viver et a[m] morir ove nostre dit seignur le roy pur destruer toutz ceux qi[n] purposent ou purposeront treson' encountre nostre dit seignur le roy en aucun manere, et qils[o] prestes serront et prestement viendront a lour mair qe lors estoit ou qe apres cell' temps serroit quant[p] et a quele heure qils serroient requis, pur resistier tant[q] come la vie lour dure a toutz yceux qi purposent ou purposeront encountre nostre[r] seignur liege en aucuns des pointz suisditz.[1] A quele temps le roy par malveis enfourmacion des[s] ditz mesfesours et traitours et par[t] faux respons' des ditz justices fermement tenoit les ditz seignurs et autres qestoient dassent[u] de faire les avantditz ordenance, estatut et commission' estoient rebelles a luy [v]et ces enemys et[v] traitours, la[w] quele enformacion alors estoit disconuz as gentz du[s] Loundres; et[x] par tielx parolles obscures en le dit serement contenuz lentent des ditz mesfesours et traitours estoit dexciter les avantditz gentz du[y] Loundres destier et faire lour poair a destruer les loialx seignurs suisditz.

xxxiiij. Item les avantditz Nichol Brembre faux etc., Alexandre etc. [z]et les autres[z] traitours du[y] roy et du[y] roiaume, accrochantz[aa] a eux roial poair de lour auctorite demesne sanz garrant du roy ou de soun grant counseill', firent[bb] crier et proclamer par mye la citee du[y] Loundres qe nul des lieges nostre seignur le roy ne duist[cc] susteigner, confortier ne eider Richard counte Darundell' et de Surr', piere de la terre et un des seignurs du[dd] grant counseill' nostre seignur le roy, durant la dite commission' ne armure ne[ee] vitailles ne autres choses necessairs luy vendre ne en[ee] nul autre manere luy desporter, et qe toutz[ff] ceux qestoient entour luy ly[gg] duissent voider come rebell[hh] du roy sur [ii]peine de[ii] forfaiture de qanqe ils purroient forfaire vers[jj] nostre dit[kk] seignur le roy, moustrantz et portantz un patent nostre dit[kk] seignur le roy dautri tenure en acomplisment[ll] du dit faux proclamacion et en [mm]grant arrerissement[mm] des loialx lieges nostre dit[kk] seignur le roy.[2]

---

[a] *R.P.* faux chivaler de Loundres. [b-b] *R.P.* erchevesqe d'Everwik, *followed by the names of de Vere, Pole and Tresilian as above, p.* 238 n. [c] *R.P.* encrochant. [d] *R.P. inserts* et. [e] *R.P.* l'assent. [f] *R.P.* de. [g] *R.P. inserts* illoeqes overtment en noune de roi. [h] *R.P. om.* [i-i] *R.P.* de dit cite de Loundres. [j-j] *R.P. om.* [k] *R.P. om.* [l-l] *R.P.* tiendrent et sustiendrent. [m] *R.P. om.* [n] *R.P. inserts* ount purposes. [o] *R.P.* q̄. [p] *R.P.; MS.* quantqe. [q] *R.P.; MS.* tanqe. [r] *R.P. inserts* dit. [s] *R.P.* de. [t] *R.P. inserts* la. [u] *R.P.* de l'assent. [v-v] *R.P.* ses enmys et ses. [w] *R.P.* et. [x] *R.P. inserts*

33. Also, the aforesaid Nicholas Brembre etc. by assent and counsel **1388** of the said Alexander etc. and others his fellows, accroaching to themselves royal power, as before, caused certain of them to come to London in person without the consent or knowledge of the king and caused all the London crafts to be sworn to hold and perform sundry discreditable matters, as is contained in the said oath which is of record in the chancery, and among other things that the said crafts would hold with and do their utmost to maintain the will and purpose of the king against all who are or shall be rebels or contrariants against his person or his regality, and that they would be ready to live and die with our said lord the king to the destruction of all those who did or should purpose treason against our said lord the king in any way and that they would be ready and come speedily to their mayor that then was or that afterwards would be, when and at what hour soever they should be required, to resist while their lives endured all those who did or should purpose anything against our liege lord in any of the points abovesaid.[1] At which time the king, through the wicked information of the said misfeasors and traitors and through the false answers of the said justices, firmly held the said lords and others who had agreed to the making of the aforesaid ordinance, statute, and commission to be rebels against himself and his enemies and traitors, which information was at that time unknown to the people of London, and by the use of such obscure words contained in the said oath the intention of the said misfeasors and traitors was to stir up the aforesaid people of London to stand and do their utmost to destroy the loyal lords abovesaid.

34. Also, the aforesaid Nicholas Brembre false etc., Alexander etc. and the others, traitors of the king and of the realm, accroaching to themselves royal power of their own authority and without warrant from the king or from his great council, caused it to be cried and proclaimed throughout the city of London that no subject of our lord the king was to sustain, comfort, or aid Richard earl of Arundel and Surrey, a peer of the realm and one of the lords of the great council of our lord the king, during the said commission or to sell him armour, victuals, or other necessaries or in any other way entertain him and that all those about him were to avoid him as a rebel against the king, upon pain of forfeiture of whatever might be forfeited to our lord the king, displaying and carrying about a patent of our said lord the king, but of another tenor, to effect the said false proclamation, to the great detriment of the loyal subjects of our said lord the king.[2]

ency semble qe. [y] *R.P. de.* [z-z] *R.P., de Vere and de la Pole named.* [aa] *R.P. encrochantz.* [bb] *R.P. inserts faire.* [cc] *R.P. deussent.* [dd] *R.P. del.* [ee] *R.P. om.* [ff] *Interlined.* [gg] *R.P.; MS. om.* [hh] *R.P.; MS. rebelles.* [ii-ii] *R.P. om.* [jj] *R.P. envers.* [kk] *R.P. om.* [ll] *R.P.; MS. accompassament.* [mm-mm] *R.P. evoglisment.*

[1] A reference to the oath of allegiance exacted at the beginning of Oct. 1387 (above, p. 232 and n.).

[2] Cf. above, p. 208; and *Favent*, pp. 8-9.

1388   *xxxv.* Item lavantdit Nichol Brembre etc.[a] par assent et counseill'
de [b]les avantditz Alexandre etc. et ces autres compaignouns[b] fist [c]crier
et[c] proclamer en la dite[d] cite de Loundres qe nul persone serroit si
hardy de parler ne de[d] sonner parole ne mote de male des ditz mesfesours et traitours [e]ne daucun deux[e] sur peine de forfaiture de quantqe
qils purroient forfaire envers nostre dit[d] seignur le roy, acrochantz[f]
a eux roial poair.[1]

   xxxvj. Item les avantditz Alexandre etc. Robert de Veer etc. [g]et les
autres,[g] traitours au roy et a roiaume, ont fait le roy mander a soun
counseill' de faire certeins persones par my Engl' viscontz queux
estoient a luy nomes par les ditz mesfesours et traitours alentent de
faire tiels chivalers des[h] countees venir al[i] parlement com ils voloient
nomer, en defesance des [j]bones et loialx seignurs[j] et bones comunes du[h]
roiaume et auxi des[h] bones leys et custumes de la terre.[2]

   xxxvij. Item[k] les avantditz Alexandre etc. [l]et ces compaignons,
traitours a roy et a roiaume,[l] durant le[m] temps de la dite proteccion[3]
en anientissement de la dit appell' fauxement counseilleront et firent
le roy comander par ces lettres as[i] diverses chivalers, esquiers et[n]
viscontz et autres sages[o] ministrez des[h] diverses countees a[h] lever et
p. 171 assembler tout le[m] poair / qils purroient pur venir ove le dit duc Dirl'
encountre les avantditz iij. seignurs appellantz pur eux sodaignement
guerrer et destruer.

   xxxviij. Item[p] durant le temps de la dicte proteccion les avantditz
Robert de Veer etc. [q]et ces autres compaignons[q] firent le roy par ces
lettres notifier a dit duc Dirl' coment il et autres estoient appellez de
tresoun par les ditz Thomas duc de Glouc' etc.,[r] Richard conte
Darundell' etc.[s] et Thomas conte de Warrewyk' et coment le roy avoit
de ceo done jour as dictes parties tanqe a prochein parlement et coment
il avoit pris en[t] especiall' proteccion ambedeux parties ovesqe toutz
lour gentz, biens et chateux, et outre estoit contenuz es dictes lettres
du roy qe si le dit duc Dirl'[u] avoit sufficiant poair qil ne lerroit daler
avant ove tout la[v] poair[w] qil purroit assembler et[x] le roy luy encounter-
oit ovesqe tut sa[y] poair, et qe le roy ovesqe luy ymetteroit en aventure
soun corps roial, et qe le roy estoit en grant perill' de luy mesme et
de[z] tout soun roiaume sil nestoit eide et[aa] socure par le dit duc Dirl',
et qe le dit duc Dirl' devoit ceo[bb] moustrer a toutz les gentz qi estoient

---

[a] R.P., faulx chivaler de Londres.   [b-b] R.P. names Nevill, de Vere and de la
Pole as above, p. 238 and n.   [c-c] R.P. om.   [d] R.P. om.   [e-e] R.P. om.
[f] R.P. encrochant ency.   [g-g] R.P. names de la Pole, Tresilian and Brembre as
above, p. 238 n.   [h] R.P. de.   [i] R.P. a.   [j-j] R.P. bones seignurs et leaux.
[k] Treson' in the margin.   [l-l] R.P. names the other appellees as above, p. 238 n.;
there follows in R.P. mesfesours et traytours.   [m] R.P. la.   [n] R.P. ses.
[o] R.P. ses.   [p] Treson' in the margin.   [q-q] R.P. names de la Pole, Nevill, and
Brembre as above, p. 238 n.   [r] R.P. conestable d'Engletere.   [s] R.P. et de Surr'.
[t] R.P. inserts sa.   [u] R.P. om.   [v] R.P. son dit.   [w] R.P. inserts et venir au
roi. Et tost apres firent le roi escrier au dit duc d'Irland, qe il prendroit le chaump'
ovesqe tut son poair.   [x] R.P. inserts qe.   [y] R.P. soun.   [z] R.P.; MS. om.
[aa] R.P. ne.   [bb] R.P.; MS. soy.

35. Also, the aforesaid Nicholas Brembre etc. by assent and counsel
of the aforesaid Alexander etc. and others his fellows, accroaching to
themselves royal power, caused it to be cried and proclaimed in the said
city of London that, upon pain of forfeiture of whatever might be
forfeited to our said lord the king, no person should make so bold as
to speak or utter any word or expression in disapprobation of the said
misfeasors and traitors or any of them.[1]

36. Also, the aforesaid Alexander etc., Robert de Vere, etc., and the
others, traitors to the king and to the realm, caused the king to instruct
his council to appoint as sheriffs certain persons throughout England
who were named to him by the said misfeasors and traitors, with the
intent that they should cause such persons as they should name to
attend parliament as knights of the shire; to the undoing of the good
and lawful lords and worthy commons of the realm and also of the
good laws and customs of the land.[2]

37. Also, the aforesaid Alexander etc. and his fellows, traitors to the
king and to the realm, during the time of the said protection,[3] in order
to frustrate the said appeal, falsely counselled and caused the king to
command by his letters sundry knights, esquires, and sheriffs and other
discreet ministers of sundry counties to levy and assemble all the power
they could to join with the said duke of Ireland against the aforesaid
three Lords Appellant to bring sudden war and destruction upon them.

38. Also, during the time of the said protection the aforesaid Robert
de Vere etc. and the others his fellows caused the king by his letters to
signify to the said duke of Ireland that he and others were appealed of
treason by the said Thomas duke of Gloucester etc., Richard earl of
Arundel etc., and Thomas earl of Warwick, and that the king had
awarded a day therefore to the said parties at the next parliament and
that he had taken into his special protection both parties with all their
people, goods, and chattels, and it was further contained in the king's
said letters that if the said duke of Ireland had sufficient power he
should not fail to march on with all the force he could muster and the
king would meet him with all his own power and that with him the king
would hazard his royal person and that the king was in great danger for
himself and for all his realm if he were not aided and succoured by the
said duke of Ireland, and that the said duke of Ireland was to show this

[1] A reference to a proclamation forbidding Londoners to speak ill of the king,
the queen, or of those about the king (Riley, *Memorials*, p. 500; *Book of London
English*, ed. Chambers and Daunt, pp. 92–3; and above, pp. 214–16).

[2] In Aug. 1387 the sheriffs were disobliging when asked to manipulate parliamentary elections in the royal interest (Walsingham, *Hist. Ang.*, ii. 161); this
article gives the Appellants' version of the sequel. For comment see A. Steel,
'The sheriffs of Cambridgeshire and Huntingdonshire in the Reign of Richard II',
in *Proc. Cambridge Antiquarian Soc.*, xxxvi (1934–5), 31; and R. Virgoe, 'The
Crown and Local Government: East Anglia under Richard II', in *Reign of Richard
II*, pp. 221–2.

[3] The protection granted to the parties to the Appeal immediately upon the
king's meeting with Gloucester, Arundel, and Warwick on 17 Nov. 1387; see
above, p. 238.

1388 assemblez ove^a luy, et qe le roy paieroit toutz les gages et costages du^b dit duc Dirl' et de^c toutz les gentz par luy assemblez.[1] Par force des^b quelles lettres et malveis et ^{d}traiterouse excitacion^d sibien du^e dit duc Dirl'^{f} come de ces adherentez et toutz les autres mesfesours et traitours, le dit duc Dirl' assembla grant nombre des^b gentz darmes et darchers,^{g} sibien des countees de Lancastre,^{h} Cestre et^h Gales come des autres lieux du^b roiaume, a destruer et ^{i}a mort mettre^i les avantditz seignurs et toutz autres ^{j}qi feurent assentantz al fesance^j des ditz ordenance, estatut et commissioun,^{k} en defesance du roy et de soun roiaume.

xxxix. Item^l lavantdit^m Robert de Veer duc Dirl' faux traitour a roy et a roiaume assembla grant nombre^n des gentz darmes et ^{o}darchers, sibien des^o countees de Lancastre, Cestre et Gales ^{p}come des^p plousours autres lieux, al entente davoir ^{q}destruitz traiterousement ove^q tout sa poair les ditz^r Thomas duc de Glouc' conestable Dengl', Henry etc.,^{s} Richard etc.,^{t} Thomas etc.^{u} et Thomas etc.^{v} et autres loialx lieges nostre seignur le roy sibien en defesance et anientissement de nostre dit seignur le roy ^{w}com des ditz loialx seignurs,^{w} et issint chivacha ^{x}le dit duc Dirl'^{x} ove grant poair et force des^y gentz darmes et ^{z}darchers des countees avantditz^z par my le^{aa} roiaume tanqe ^{bb}ils viegnent a^{bb} un lieu qest^{cc} appelle ^{dd}Rottecotebrigge qest pres^{dd} de Coteswold et,^{ee} accrochantz a luy roial poair, il^{ff} fist desplaier^{gg} le baner du roy en sa compaignie,[2] encountre lestat du roy et de sa corone. A quele temps le dit duc Dirl' et sa compaignie par la grace de Dieux feurent de lour male purpos destourbez.

Nunc procedendum est ad articulos contra dominum Simonem Burle, dominum Johannem Baucham, dominum Jacobum Berneres, et dominum Johannem Salesbury, milites, per prefatos dominos et regni communitatem prolatos.[3]

j.^{hh} Primerement les comunes du roiaume ^{ii}empeschent et accusent^{ii} qe Simond de Burley^{jj} chivaler, Johan Beauchamp chivaler, Johan Salesbury chivaler, et James Berneres chivaler, ovesqe Alexandre ercevesqe Dever' etc.,^{kk} Robert de Veer duc Dirl', Michel de la Pole

---

^{a} *R.P.* a. ^{b} *R.P.* de. ^{c} *R.P.; MS.* a. $^{d-d}$ *R.P.* traiterouses exitations. ^{e} *R.P.* de le. ^{f} *R.P. om.* ^{g} *R.P.* archers. ^{h} *R.P. inserts de.* $^{i-i}$ *R.P.* mettre a mort. $^{j-j}$ *R.P.* queux furront de l'assent del fesance. ^{k} *R.P. inserts* et. ^{l} Treson' *in the margin.* ^{m} *R.P.* le dit. ^{n} *R.P.* poair. $^{o-o}$ *R.P.* archers de. $^{p-p}$ *R.P.* et de. $^{q-q}$ *R.P.* traiturousement destruz a. ^{r} *R.P. inserts* seignurs. ^{s} *R.P.* count' Derby. ^{t} *R.P.* count' d'Arondel et de Surr'. ^{u} *R.P.* count' de Warr'. ^{v} *R.P.* counte marescall'. $^{w-w}$ *R.P.* et de tut soun roialme. $^{x-x}$ *R.P. om.* ^{y} *R.P.* de. $^{z-z}$ *R.P.* archers de countee de Cestre. ^{aa} *R.P.* la. $^{bb-bb}$ *R.P.* il vient pres d'. ^{cc} *R.P.* qe l'ein. ^{dd} *R.P.* Rottot brige pres. ^{ee} *R.P.* en. ^{ff} *R.P. om.* ^{gg} *R.P.* esplaier. ^{hh} *The numerals here printed at the beginning of the articles of impeachment are in the margin of the MS. Many are wholly or in part bled off.* $^{ii-ii}$ *W* acusent et empeschent; *R.P.* accusont et empeschont. ^{jj} *MS. and W; R.P.* Beurle. ^{kk} *W and R.P. om.*

[message] to all the people who were assembled with him and that the 1388
king would pay all the wages and costs of the said duke of Ireland and
of all the people assembled by him.[1] By force of which letters and of
the wicked and traitorous instigation as well of the said duke of Ireland
as of his adherents and all the other misfeasors and traitors, the said
duke of Ireland assembled a great number of men-at-arms and archers,
as well of the counties of Lancaster, Chester, and Wales as of other
places in the realm, to destroy and put to death the aforesaid lords and
all others who were in agreement with the making of the said ordinance,
statute, and commission; to the undoing of the king and of his realm.

39. Also, the aforesaid Robert de Vere, duke of Ireland, false traitor
to the king and to the realm, assembled a great number of men-at-arms
and archers as well of the counties of Lancaster, Chester, and Wales as
of several other places with intent to have traitorously destroyed with
all his power the said Thomas duke of Gloucester constable of England,
Henry etc., Richard etc., Thomas etc. and Thomas etc., and other loyal
subjects of our lord the king, as well to the undoing and destruction of
our said lord the king as of the said loyal lords; and so the said duke of
Ireland rode forth with a great power and force of men-at-arms and
archers from the counties aforesaid through the realm until they came
to a place called Radcot Bridge, near Cotswold, and accroaching to himself royal power he caused the king's banner to be displayed in his
company,[2] contrary to the dignity of the king and of his crown. At
which time the said duke of Ireland and his company were by God's
grace baulked of their wicked purpose.

It is now time to pass to the articles exhibited by the
above-mentioned lords and the commons of the realm against
Sir Simon Burley, Sir John Beauchamp, Sir James Berners,
and Sir John Salisbury.[3]

1. First the commons of the realm impeach and accuse Simon Burley
knight, John Beauchamp knight, John Salisbury knight, and James
Berners knight, in that they, together with Alexander archbishop of
York etc., Robert de Vere duke of Ireland, Michael de la Pole earl

---

[1] On the subject-matter of this article and the next, cf. above, p. 256 and n.

[2] On 20 Dec. 1387.

[3] The impeachment of Burley, Beauchamp, Berners, and Salisbury began on 12
Mar.; the articles were delivered in writing, but by the Commons alone, on 17
Mar. (below, p. 288). These events happened, therefore, after the trial and judge-
ment of the five principal accused and that of Blake and Usk. All the accused
were chamber knights; for Burley see also below, p. 275 n.; for Salisbury and
Beauchamp, above, pp. 228–30 and n.

The text of the MS. between here and p. 306 below has been collated with
W.A.M. 12227 (= W), for which see above, pp. xlviii–li, and as far as p. 278
below with that in R.P., iii. 241–3.

1388 conte de Suff', Robert Tresilyan[a] justice, et Nichol Brembre chivaler, atteintz en cest present parlement de hautes tresouns, veiantz la tendresse del age nostre seignur le roy et la innocence de sa roial persone luy firent entendre come pur verite tantz des fauces choses[b] par eux countre loialte et bone foy ymaginez et controvez qe entierement eux luy firent de tout a eux doner son amour,[c] ferme foy et credence et haier ces loialx[d] seignurs et[e] lieges par queux il duist [f]avoir estee de droit pluis governee.[f] Et auxint accrochantz[g] a eux roial poair en defranchisantz nostre seignur le roy de sa sovereignete, emblemissantz et amenissantz sa[h] prerogative et regalie, luy firent cy avant obeiser qil fuist jurre destre governe, conseille et demesne par eux et qil lez meinteindra et sustiendra a viver et a[i] murrer ove eux, la ou le roy duist estre de pluis franc condicion qe nul autre de son roiaume; et[j] issint ont mys le roy [k]pluis en[k] servage encontre son honour et regalie et contre[l] lour ligeance, come traitours. Par vertue de[m] quele serement sibien les malveistez et tresouns southescriptz[n] come toutz les autres malfaites[o] et tresouns ajuggez envers[p] les[q] v. traitours atteintz[r] en ceste present parlement sont avenuz.[1]

ij. Item la ou Alexandre ercevesqe etc.,[s] Robert de Veer etc.,[t] Michel de la Pole etc.,[u] Robert Tresilyan etc.,[v] Nichol Brembre etc.,[w] Johan Blake etc.,[x] et Thomas Husk[y] sont ajuggez[z] en ceste present parlement de diversez hautes tresouns, si come [aa]est contenuz pleinement[aa] en les appelles, accusementz et processe[bb] faitz en ceste present parlement, les ditz comunes diont, accusont et empeschent les avantditz Simond, [cc]Johan', Johan,[cc] et James[dd] qils come traitours et enemys du roy et du roiaume feurent sachantz, conseillantz, eidants, abettantz, confortantz [ee]et assentantz[ee] a toutz les ditz traitours ensi atteintz en toutz les[ff] traisouns avantditz;[gg] et[hh] les ditz Simond et Johan Beauch' feurent principalx fesours de toutz les traisouns avantditz.[ii]

iij. Item les ditz Simond, John Beauch', Johan Salesbury, et James, apercevantz[jj] qe [kk]le mair et les[kk] bones gentz de Loundres avoient outrement refusez en presence du roy daccomplir [ll]les malveis purpos de[ll] prodicion touchaunt le murdre des seignurs et comunes en[mm] darrein parlement, par lour traiturose accrochement fauxement ove les seignurs[nn] traitours atteintz conseilleront nostre seignur le roy et tant firent qe nostre seignur le roy soy eloignast hors du[oo] dit parlement par plusours[pp] jours et fist certifier qil[qq] ne voloit unqes aprocher au[rr] dit parlement ne comuner ove les ditz seignurs et comunes des

---

[a] W and R.P. here and subsequently Tresilian.   [b] MS. inserts et; W and R.P. om.   [c] R.P. inserts et.   [d] W and R.P. foialx.   [e] R.P. om.   [f–f] W de droit pluis avoir estre governee.   [g] R.P. encrochantz.   [h] W and R.P. insert roial.   [i] R.P. om.   [j] R.P.; MS. and W om.   [k–k] R.P. and W; MS. en pluis.   [l] W and R.P. encontre.   [m] W and R.P.; MS. om.   [n] W desouthescriptz; R.P. desouz escriptz.   [o] W malveistes; R.P. malveistees.   [p] W vers.   [q] R.P. inserts ditz.   [r] W om.   [s] R.P. d'Everwyk.   [t] R.P. duc d'Irland.   [u] R.P. counte de Suff'; W (for the last five words) Michel etc.   [v] W and R.P. justice.   [w] W and R.P. chivaler.   [x] W and R.P. om.   [y] R.P. Usk.   [z] W and R.P. insert et atteinz (R.P. atteintz) traitours.   [aa–aa] W pleinement est contenuz; R.P. est pleinement

of Suffolk, Robert Tresilian justice, and Nicholas Brembre knight, 1388 attainted of high treasons in this present parliament, seeing the tenderness of the age of our lord the king and the innocence of his royal person, caused him to apprehend as truth so many false things by them against loyalty and good faith imagined and contrived that they entirely engrossed in all things his love, firm faith, and belief and caused him to hate his loyal lords and subjects by whom he ought of right rather to have been governed. And moreover accroaching to themselves royal power by disfranchising our lord the king of his sovereignty, and impairing and diminishing his prerogative and regality they made him so far obey them that he was sworn to be governed, counselled, and guided by them, to maintain and support them and to live and die with them, whereas the king ought to be of a free condition above any other in his realm; and so they put the king more in servitude against his honour and regality, contrary to their allegiance and as traitors. By virtue of which oath have occurred as well the wickedness and treasons below written as all the other misdeeds and treasons adjudged against the five traitors attainted in this present parliament.[1]

2. Also, whereas Alexander archbishop etc., Robert de Vere etc., Michael de la Pole etc., Robert Tresilian etc., Nicholas Brembre etc., John Blake etc., and Thomas Usk have been adjudged in this present parliament of sundry high treasons (as is fully contained in the appeals, accusations, and process made in this present parliament), the said commons say, accuse and impeach the aforesaid Simon, John, John, and James that as traitors and enemies of the king and of the realm they, with full knowledge and consent were counsellors, aiders, abettors, and comforters to all the said traitors so attainted in all the treasons aforesaid; and the said Simon and John Beauchamp were principal actors in all the treasons aforesaid.

3. Also, the said Simon, John Beauchamp, John Salisbury, and James, perceiving that the mayor and good people of London had utterly refused in the king's presence to accomplish the wicked and treasonable project touching the murder of the lords and commons in the last parliament, by their traitorous accroachment together with the traitorous lords [now] attainted, falsely counselled our lord the king and so far prevailed that our lord the king absented himself for several days from the said parliament and made it known that he would never come near the said parliament nor treat with the said lords and

contenu.   *bb* R.P. processes.   *cc–cc* W Johan Salesb', Johan Beauch'; R.P. John Beauchamp, John Salesbury.   *dd* apercevantz qe le mair e les bones gentz *deleted after this word.*   *ee–ee* W and R.P.; MS. om.   *ff* W lour.   *gg* W om. *hh* W inserts qe.   *ii* R.P. adds ovesqe les dit traitours de ce atteintz; W adds etc. *jj* W perceverantz; R.P. perceitvantz.   *kk–kk* R.P. les maire et.   *ll–ll* W le malveys purpos de; R.P. les malveises purposes et.   *mm* W au; R.P. a.   *nn* W and R.P. om.   *oo* R.P. de le.   *pp* W 'lusous'.   *qq* R.P. q'.   *rr* W and R.P. le.

---

[1] This article was adjudged a matter of treason by the lords in parliament (R.P., iii. 243). Cf. Articles 1 and 2 of the Appeal (above, pp. 240–2).

1388 busoignez du roiaume pur nul peril, perde ne meschief qi purront[a]
aucunement avenir a luy et[b] a soun roiaume sil[c] ne fuisse primerement
asseurez par les ditz[d] seignurs et comunes qils ne duissent riens dire ne
faire en le dit parlement vers[e] lez ditz Simond, [f]Johan, Johan,[f] et James,
et les ditz traitours atteintz; mes[g] qils duissent aler et proceder avant
touchaunt le processe[h] qi fuist lors comence envers[i] Michel de la Pole;[j]
a grant arrerissement du roy et du[k] roiaume et encountre[l] les aunciens
ordenances et libertes du parlement.[m]1

iiij. Item la ou au[n] darrein parlement tenuz a Westm'2 Michel de la
Pole counte de Suff' en plein parlement pur plusours[o] causes des-
honestez par luy faitz countre[p] le roy et sa regalie fuist descharge del
p. 172 office du[q] chaunceller et le grant seal le roy[r] pris de luy, / le dit Simond
adonqes conestable de Dovorr', accrochant a luy roial poair,[s] par son
procurement et abettement luy fist reavoir le grant seal pur ensealer
la[t] patente de Dovorr' pur son singuler profit, quele fuist subversion
de tout la ley du roiaume a[u] grant desheritison del corone le[v] roy,
sicom est contenu en la[w] dite patente, quele est de record en la[w]
chauncellerie.[x]3

v. Item la ou au[y] darrein parlement Michel de la Pole[z] fuist atteint
de[aa] certeins mesprisons des queux il fuist [bb]empeschez par les comunes
du roialme[bb] en ycelle parlement devant le roy et toutz les seignurs et
piers [cc]du roiaume[cc] en le dit parlement et comande au[dd] prison tanqe
il eust fait fyn et raunsoun au[dd] roy, la[ee] vient le dit Simond come
conestable de Wyndesore et[ff] par sa subtilite et abettement[gg] suist
au[y] roy qil avoit le dit conte en sa garde a Wyndesore, a cause qe le roy
moult fuist conversant illeoqes, et pur faire le dit conte estre meisnale[hh]
et pres du roy pur conseiller le roy et autrement eider de perfourner
touz les faux tresouns avantditz,[ii] et puis luy lessa aler et eschaper
hors du roiaume, paront execucion ne poet estre fait des juggementz
renduz countre[jj] le dit counte.[kk]4

vj. Item apres qe le duc de Glouc' et autres seignurs appellantz
eient afferme lour appellez a Westm' en presence du roy vers les v.
traitours atteintz,5 vient un prelat du roiaume a Simond de Burley[ll]
chivaler et luy empria de conseiller et prier le roy de comander Robert

[a] R.P. purroit; W purroient.   [b] R.P. ou.   [c] R.P. si.   [d] W and R.P.
avantditz.   [e] W envers; R.P. encontre.   [f-f] W and R.P. Johan Beauchamp,
Johan Salesbury.   [g] W salvant; R.P. sauvant.   [h] W and R.P.; MS. om.
[i] R.P. inserts sire.   [j] W inserts counte de Suff'.   [k] R.P. de tout son.   [l] W
contre.   [m] W adds etc.   [n] R.P. a.   [o] W and R.P. diverses.   [p] R.P.
encontre.   [q] R.P. de.   [r] R.P. inserts feust.   [s] W and R.P.; MS. om.
[t] W and R.P. le.   [u] R.P. en.   [v] R.P. du.   [w] W le.   [x] W adds etc.
[y] R.P. a.   [z] W and R.P. add counte de Suff'.   [aa] R.P. des.   [bb-bb] W. and R.P.,
but in R.P. la comune for les comunes; MS. atteint.   [cc-cc] R.P. om.; W om. the
next four words.   [dd] W and R.P. a.   [ee] W om.   [ff] From R.P.; MS. and W
om.   [gg] W inserts et.   [hh] R.P.; MS. meynable; W meinable.   [ii] W suisditz;
R.P. desusditz.   [jj] R.P. encontre.   [kk] W adds etc.   [ll] MS. and W; R.P.
Beûrle.

---

1 Cf. Articles 15–16 of the Appeal (above, pp. 250–2 and n.).

commons of the business of the realm for any peril, loss, or mischief 1388
that might in any way happen to him and his realm, unless he were first
assured by the said lords and commons that in the said parliament
they would say or do nothing against the said Simon, John, John, and
James and the said traitors [now] attainted; but they were to proceed
and go forward with the process then begun against Michael de la Pole;
to the great detriment of the king and of the realm and contrary to the
ancient ordinances and liberties of parliament.[1]

4. Also, whereas at the last parliament held at Westminster[2] Michael
de la Pole earl of Suffolk was in full parliament, by reason of many
discreditable acts committed by him against the king and his regality,
dismissed from the office of chancellor, and the king's Great Seal taken
from him, the said Simon, being then constable of Dover, accroaching
to himself royal power by his procurement and abetment caused him
to resume possession of the Great Seal to seal the patent of Dover for
his own peculiar benefit, which was subversive of all the law of the land
and to the great disherison of the king's crown, as is contained in the
said patent, which is of record in the chancery.[3]

5. Also, whereas at the last parliament Michael de la Pole was
attainted of certain misprisions whereof he was impeached by the commons of the realm in that parliament before the king and all the lords
and peers of the realm in the said parliament and committed to prison
until he should have made fine and ransom to the king, there came the
said Simon as constable of Windsor and by his subtlety and abetment
made suit to the king to have the said earl in his custody at Windsor,
since the king was much there, and to have the said earl as a household companion and near the king to counsel the king and otherwise
to help to perform all the false treasons aforesaid, and afterwards let
him go and escape from the realm, wherefore execution cannot be
made of the judgements rendered against the said earl.[4]

6. Also, after the duke of Gloucester and the other Lords Appellant
had affirmed their appeals at Westminster in the presence of the king
against the five traitors [now] attainted,[5] a prelate of the realm came to
Simon Burley knight and prayed him to counsel and beg the king to

[2] The parliament of 1 Oct.-28 Nov. 1386.

[3] A reference to letters patent, dated 16 Oct. 1386 and warranted under the
signet, which granted Burley, as constable of Dover castle, the profits of pleas of
trespass and other actions heard in his court and the right to use the writ of
attaint (*Cal. Pat. R., 1385-9*, p. 225). Pole was not in fact dismissed from the
chancellorship until 23 Oct. 1386.

[4] The commons accuse Burley of responsibility for the escape of Pole to the
Continent towards the end of 1387, on the grounds that it was to the custody
of Burley, as constable of Windsor castle, that Pole was committed after his
impeachment in Oct. 1386. Between that committal, however, and the escape in
question there supervened for Pole nearly a year of liberty and prominence at
court. See above, p. 178 and n., 214; and below, p. 320 and n.

[5] A reference to the meeting in Westminster Hall on 17 Nov. 1387 (above,
pp. 212-14). The prelate mentioned in this article was probably Robert Wikeford,
archbishop of Dublin (ibid., p. 206).

1388 de Veer duc Dirl' qil ne face ne procure estre fait tant^a lever^b des gentz darmez et darchers^c deinz le roiaume, quele purra torner en destruccion du roy et du^d roiaume, et le dit Simond respondy en grant manere qe sil parle^e pluis de ceste matere il luy ferroit avoir grant malgre et dedignacion du^d roy quele ne purra susteigner. Issint fuist le dit Simond ^{f}abbettour, mayntenour^f et sustenour ^{g}du dit^g traiturouse purpos le dit duc.

vij. Item^h la ou le dit Simond fuist chamberleyn nostre seignur le roy en sa tendre age et tenuz de luy counseiller pur le mielx en profit de luy et de soun roiaume, le dit Simond par^i malveis engyn et procurement counseilla nostre seignur le roy davoir deinz soun hostelle grant nombre^j des aliens, Beaumers et autres, et de les doner grantz dons des revenuz et commodites du roiaume, paront nostre seignur le roy est grandement enpoverez et le poeple^k outrement oppressez.^{l1}

viij. Item les ditz Simond, Johan Beauch', Johan Salesbury, et James, ove ^{m}les v.^{m} traitours atteintz, conspireront et ymagineront traiterousement la mort et destruccion de ceux qi furent^n assentantz^o a la fesance de la commission et estatut^p ^{q}fait en la^q darrein parlement.^{r2}

ix. Item les ditz Simond, Johan Beauch', Johan Salesburi, et James furent^n eidantz et abettantz au^s roy qe le counte de Suff' fuist si longement^t en loffice du^u chaunceller pur accomplir lour ^{v}malveis et traiturouse purpos,^{v} si qe tout le roiaume fuist en perille de perdicion par cause de malveis^w governaille endementiers^x qil estoit chaunceller etc.^{y3}

x. Item la ou les ditz Simond, Johan Beauch', Johan Salesbury, et James avoient conissance de les traisouns faitz par les^z traitours atteintz, ills deussent avoir fait notice as bons seignurs et piers du roiaume de lour ditz traisouns traiterousement ymaginez,^{aa} et ceo ne firent point mes ^{bb}counseillerent et sustiendrent^{bb} les ditz traitours en ^{cc}lours ditz traisouns etc.^{cc4}

xj. Item le dit Simond apres ceo qe les seignurs appellantz avoient estee a Westm'^{5} et afferme lour appelle ^{dd}vers les^{dd} traitours suisditz en presence du roy et puis nostre seignur le roy estoit a soun manoir de Shene,^{ee} le dit Simond envoia pur le mair de Dovorr' et luy mesna en presence du roy illeoqes et disoit au^{ff} roy qe le dit meir duist amesner^{gg} au roy sil busoigne mille hommes defensables^{hh} de v.

---

^{a} *From W and R.P.; MS.* tout. ^{b} *W and R.P. insert* de poair. ^{c} *R.P.* archers. ^{d} *R.P.* de. ^{e} *W* parloit. $^{f-f}$ *W* meintenour abettour. $^{g-g}$ *W* del; *R.P.* de le. ^{h} *R.P. inserts* par. ^{i} *R.P. inserts* son. ^{j} *W* plente; *R.P.* pleinte. ^{k} *W and R.P. insert* du roialme. ^{l} *W adds* etc. $^{m-m}$ *W* Robert de Veer duc de Irland, Alexandre ercevesqe Dev', Michel de la Pole counte de Suff', Robert Tresilian justice et Nichol Brembre chivaler. *R.P. also gives the names, but the text is defective at this point.* ^{n} *R.P.* feuront. ^{o} *R.P.; MS.* assentance; *W* assent'. ^{p} *R.P.; MS. and W* estatuz. $^{q-q}$ *W* faitz en le; *R.P.* faitz z̄. ^{r} *W adds* etc. ^{s} *R.P.* a. ^{t} *R.P.* longe. ^{u} *R.P.* de. $^{v-v}$ *R.P.* malveises et traiterouses purposes. ^{w} *W* mal. ^{x} *R.P.* dementiers. ^{y} *R.P.* om. ^{z} *R.P. inserts* ercevesqe et autres. ^{aa} *W adds* et controvez. $^{bb-bb}$ *R.P.* conseilleront et susteindront. $^{cc-cc}$ *W* lour traisons suisditz etc.; *R.P.* lour tresons. $^{dd-dd}$ *W* vers le; *R.P.* devers les v. ^{ee} *MS. and W insert* et.

order Robert de Vere duke of Ireland not to effect or cause to be 1388
effected so great a levy of men-at-arms and archers within the realm as
might redound to the destruction of the king and of the realm, and the
said Simon answered in haughty fashion that if he spoke further of this
matter he would cause him to incur such despite and ill-will on the part
of the king as he could not endure. And thus the said Simon was an
abettor, maintainer, and supporter of the said traitorous purpose of the
said duke.

7. Also, whereas the said Simon was chamberlain of our lord the
king in his tender age and bound to counsel him for the best to the
profit of himself and of his realm, the said Simon by wicked design and
procurement counselled our lord the king to have in his household a
great number of aliens, Bohemians, and others, and to give them great
gifts out of the revenues and commodities of the realm; whereby our
lord the king is greatly impoverished and the people utterly oppressed.[1]

8. Also, the said Simon, John Beauchamp, John Salisbury, and
James, with the five traitors [now] attainted, conspired and treacherously plotted the death and destruction of those who consented to the
making of the commission and the statute made in the last parliament.[2]

9. Also, the said Simon, John Beauchamp, John Salisbury, and
James aided and abetted the king in bringing it about that the earl of
Suffolk was so long in the office of chancellor, in order to achieve their
wicked and traitorous purpose, so that all the realm was in danger of
ruin by reason of bad government during the time that he was chancellor etc.[3]

10. Also, whereas the said Simon, John Beauchamp, John Salisbury,
and James had knowledge of the treasons committed by the traitors
[now] attainted, they ought to have informed the good lords and peers
of the realm of their said traitorously conceived treasons, and this they
did not do, but gave counsel and support to the said traitors in their
said treasons etc.[4]

11. Also, after the Lords Appellant had attended at Westminster[5]
and affirmed their appeal against the abovesaid traitors in the presence
of the king and afterwards our lord the king was at his manor of Sheen,
the said Simon sent for the mayor of Dover and brought him into the
king's presence there and told the king that the said mayor would bring
to the king, if the need arose, a thousand fencibles from the Cinque

---

[ff] R.P. a.   [gg] R.P. mesner.   [hh] W and R.P. insert dez (R.P. des) gentz.

---

[1] Burley was tutor to the young Richard II, and as sub-chamberlain during the
hereditary chamberlainship of Robert de Vere was effectively in control of that
office (Tout, *Chapters*, iii. 331 and n.; vi. 45, 47). For his part in negotiating the
Anglo-Bohemian marriage treaty of 1381, see *Perroy*, pp. 145-6, 149 n., 153-4.
[2] An accusation depending for its force on a knowledge of Article 27 of the
Appeal (above, p. 260). It was adjudged a matter of treason by the lords in
parliament (*R.P.*, iii. 243).
[3] Pole was chancellor from 13 Mar. 1383 to 23 Oct. 1386.
[4] For comment see Bellamy, *Law of Treason*, p. 221.
[5] On 17 Nov. 1387 (above, pp. 212-14).

1388 Portez,[1] en excitant et confortant le roy countre^a loppinion et appelle des ditz^b seignurs appellantz.^{c}

xij. Item la ou le dit Simond ad demure entour la persone ^{d}nostre seignur^d le roy a temps de sa juvente tanqe a^e certein temps qil fuist defendu la presence du roy par bone conseill' le^f roy par^g son malveis^h governaille entour sa persone et ^{i}certeins autres^i malfaites, apres il revient au^j compaignie du roy sanz assent du^k bone conseill'.[2] Et par procurement du dit Simond, Robert de Veer adonqe conte Doxenford fuist ^{l}mesne au^l compaignie du roy,^{m} le quelle conte^n puis celle temps fist diverses tresouns des queux il est atteint, et le dit Simond fuist abettour, procurour, counseillour et meintenour de les^o pluis de les tresons suisditz. Et pur pluis enfourmer sy prist de^p done de lavantdit conte^n le chastelle et seignurie de Lounhales ove les appurtenances en Gales a avoir a ly et a^q ces heires pur^r toutz jours pur lencre du dit counte.^{s} Et par celle cause fist nostre seignur le roy grantier et doner au dit conte^s terrez et tenementz a la value de cynke centz^t marcz par an a avoir a le dit conte^s et a ces heires a^u toutz jours, queux furent^v au^w seignur Coucy^x etc.^{y}[3]

xiij. Item ^{z}le dit^z Simond, Johan Beauchamp', Johan Salesbury, et James, ovesqe les traitours atteintz,^{aa} furent^v procurantz et sustenanz ^{bb}a lour^{bb} poair de faire debate et contrariouse severance^{cc} entre nostre seignur le roy et les bones seignurs et piers du roiaume et la bone cominalte^{dd} dycelle, en destruccion du roy et du roiaume, et sustenantz mal governaille entour la persone nostre seignur le roy et retreihantz le bon et ^{ee}roial coer du roi^{ee} des seignurs et piers du roiaume ^{ff}et comunes dycellez.^{ff}

xiiij. Item la ou a^{gg} darrein parlement estoient faitz certeins com-missions^{hh} et estatut par assent du roy et^q des seignurs espirituelles et temporelles et par les^{ii} comunes du roiaume pur^{jj} bon governaille du roy et du roiaume et ^{kk}certeins peins^{kk} limite en ycelle estatut devers ceux^{ll} qi destourberent^{mm} lexecucion du dit commission, les ditz Simond, Johan Beauch', Johan Salesbury et James destourberent^{mm} lexecucion du dit commissioun en tant qils counseilleront le roy daler^{nn}

^{a} W and R.P. encontre. ^{b} W om. ^{c} W adds etc. $^{d-d}$ R.P. et ovesqe.
^{e} R.P. au. ^{f} R.P. du. ^{g} R.P. pur; *reading in W uncertain.* ^{h} W mal.
$^{i-i}$ W autres certeins. ^{j} R.P. a la. ^{k} R.P. de. $^{l-l}$ R.P. mesme en la.
^{m} R.P. adds nostre seignur. ^{n} R.P. duc. ^{o} R.P. le. ^{p} W del. ^{q} W om.
^{r} W a. ^{s} R.P. duc. ^{t} MS. mille; W and R.P. for last two words D. ^{u} R.P.
pur. ^{v} R.P. feuront. ^{w} R.P. a. ^{x} W Courcy; R.P. de Coucy. ^{y} R.P.
om. $^{z-z}$ W lez ditz; R.P. les ditz. ^{aa} W avantditz; R.P. avant ditz atteintz.
$^{bb-bb}$ R.P.; MS. and W om. ^{cc} R.P. inserts par. ^{dd} W also cominalte.
$^{ee-ee}$ R.P.; MS. om. du roi; W honurable coer nostre seignur le roy. $^{ff-ff}$ R.P.
et la commune d'ycell'; W et co⟨mun⟩es dycell' etc. ^{gg} R.P.; MS. om.; W au.
^{hh} W and R.P. commission. ^{ii} R.P. inserts bones. ^{jj} R.P. inserts la.
$^{kk-kk}$ W certein peine; R.P. certeyne peyne. ^{ll} R.P.; MS. and W queux.
^{mm} R.P. destourberont. ^{nn} daler *repeated in MS.*

[1] Burley was constable of Dover castle and warden of the Cinque Ports.
[2] In June 1379 the care of the king's person was taken from Burley, the king's

Ports;[1] instigating and encouraging the king against the opinion and 1388 appeal of the said Lords Appellant.

12. Also, whereas the said Simon remained in attendance upon the person of our lord the king in the days of his youth until a certain time when he was forbidden the king's presence by the king's good council owing to his evil government of the king's person and to certain other misdeeds, he afterwards returned to the king's company without the assent of the good council.[2] And by the contrivance of the said Simon, Robert de Vere, then earl of Oxford, was brought into the king's society, which earl after that time committed sundry treasons whereof he is attainted, and the said Simon was abettor, procurer, counsellor, and maintainer of most of the treasons abovesaid. And (for greater particularity) in this way he received of the gift of the aforesaid earl the castle and lordship of Lyonshall, in Wales, with the appurtenances, to hold to himself and his heirs in perpetuity, for the advancement of the said earl. And on this account he caused our lord the king to give and grant to the said earl lands and tenements formerly belonging to the Sieur de Coucy etc. to the yearly value of 500 marks, to hold to the said earl and his heirs in perpetuity.[3]

13. Also, the said Simon, John Beauchamp, John Salisbury, and James, together with the traitors [now] attainted, contrived and did their utmost to maintain a state of dispute, opposition, and division between our lord the king and the good lords and peers of the realm and the good commonalty of the same; to the undoing of the king and of the realm; and supported evil government about the person of our lord the king and caused the king's good and royal heart to be withdrawn from the lords and peers of the realm and the commons of the same.

14. Also, whereas in the last parliament there were made certain commissions and a statute with the assent of the king, of the lords spiritual and temporal and of the commons of the realm for the good government of the king and of the realm and certain penalties specified in that statute for those who disturbed the execution of the said commission, the said Simon, John Beauchamp, John Salisbury and James disturbed the execution of the said commission inasmuch as they

---

tutor, and given to John Cobham (Tout, *Chapters*, iii. 349 and n.). Burley remained sub-chamberlain.

[3] In 1382, Robert de Vere and Philippa, his wife, who was the daughter of Enguerrand de Coucy, were granted a share in Enguerrand's lands, to hold during Philippa's life; de Vere, however, was to hold during his mother's life, if he and his mother should survive Philippa. In 1383, the king granted to de Vere a fee simple interest in the lands, if Philippa were to die without issue (*Cal. Pat. R., 1381–5*, pp. 177, 314). De Vere's grant to Burley of the castle and lordship of Lyonshall (in Herefs.) was made before Aug. 1384 (ibid., p. 447). For the more extravagant reports of Burley's cupidity which were current at the time, see Knighton, *Chronicon*, ii. 294, and C. D. Ross, 'Forfeiture for treason in the reign of Richard II', in *E.H.R.*, lxxi (1956), 564–5 and n., and on the grants to de Vere, *R.P.*, iii. 207.

1388 en lontisme paiis, cestassavoir Notyngham, Cestre, et aillours, pur
assembler grant poair des[a] gentz darmes et archers[b] pur occier et
destruer traiterousement les seignurs et autres nomez[c] en mesme la
commissioun et certeins chivaleres des countes, sergeanz du[d] ley et
[e]autres nomez en le darrein[e] parlement,[1] et ceo par cause de la faisance
et user du dite commissioun, en destruccion du roy et du roiaume et
anientisement de toutz bones ordenancez faitz en parlement.[f]

xv. Item la ou la ley de la terre est fait en[g] parlement par le roy
et les[c] seignurs espirituelx et temporelles et tout la cominalte[h] du
roiaume, les ditz Simond, Johan Beauch', Johan Salesbury et James
ont estee comunes destourbours de la ley qe la ley [i]de la terre[i] ne poet
avoir soun cours et plousours foitz ont destorbez les justices, sergeantz
et autres sages du ley par grevouse et haynouse manaces[j] et autrement,
siqe les justices en lour juggementz et les[k] sergeantz et autres / sages
du ley noseront pur doute ajugger,[l] pleder, faire ne user la ley solonc
leffect dycelle pur pour des[m] ditz Simond, Johan Beauch', Johan
Salesbury et James, issint accrochantz[n] a eux roial poair, come les
justices, sergeantz et autres sages du ley sceyvont moustrer[o] pluis
a plein.[p]

xvj. Item la ou [q]les ditz[q] Alexandre ercevesqe Dever', [r]Michel de la
Pole counte de Suff', Robert de Veer duc Dirl'[r] traitours sont atteintz
par appelle[s] suisdit de tresoun de ceo qils accrocheront a eux roialx
poair et firent nostre seignur le roy promettre au[t] roy Franceys par ses
lettres et messages pur eide et afforcement aver pur accompler cestes[u]
hautes tresons, prodicions et murdres dont[v] ils sont atteintz de doner
et rendre au dit roy Franceys la ville et le chastel de Caleys et toutz
autres chastelx et forcelettes[w] en la marche de Pycardie et Artoys,
les ditz Simond, Johan Beauch' et[x] Johan Salesbury[y] furent[z] conissantz
et counseillantz a cestes hautes tresouns et assentantz qe [aa]vij. saufcondites serroient faitz[aa] par le roy Fraunceys [bb]au dit John Salesbury
et a John Lancastre pur aler de par dela de tretir ovesqe le roi
Franceys[bb] pur accomplir[cc] les ditz traisouns et autres contenuz en les
articles suisditz.[dd]2

p. 173

Sequitur modo processus et execucio dicti parliamenti secundum modum curialium apud Westmonasterium in

---

[a] R.P. om.   [b] W darches.   [c] W om.   [d] R.P. de.   [e-e] W autres queux
furent au darrein; R.P. autres queux feuront a darrein.   [f] W adds etc.   [g] W
inserts plein.   [h] W also cominalte.   [i-i] W om.   [j] W and R.P. manace.
[k] W om.   [l] R.P.; MS. a jugement; W ajugg'.   [m] R.P. de les.   [n] R.P.
accrocheront; W acroch⟨er⟩ent.   [o] W inserts et enformer; R.P. et enfourmer.
[p] W adds etc.   [q-q] W om.   [r-r] W Robert de Veer etc., Michel de la Pole
etc.; R.P. Michel de Pole et Robert de Veer duc Dirl'.   [s] R.P. l'appell.
[t] R.P. a.   [u] R.P. om.   [v] R.P.; MS. and W om.   [w] R.P. forteresses.
[x] Interlined.   [y] e James deleted after this word.   [z] R.P. feuront.   [aa-aa] R.P.
un saufconduyt serroit fait; W vij saufconduct' ser' faitz.   [bb-bb] R.P.; MS. and
W om.   [cc] W inserts et perforner; R.P. et perfournir.   [dd] W adds etc.

advised the king to go to distant places, that is to say Nottingham, 1388
Chester, and elsewhere, to assemble a great force of men-at-arms and
archers for the traitorous slaughter and destruction of the lords and
others named in the same commission and certain knights of the shire,
serjeants at law, and others named in the last parliament,[1] and this by
reason of the making and user of the said commission; to the undoing
of the king and of the realm and the nullifying of all good ordinances
made in the parliament.

15. Also, whereas the law of the land is made in parliament by the
king and the lords spiritual and temporal and the whole commonalty
of the realm, the said Simon, John Beauchamp, John Salisbury, and
James have been common disturbers of the law, so that the law of the
land cannot take its course, and they have many times disturbed the
justices, serjeants, and others learned in the law by grievous and odious
threats and otherwise, so that the justices in their judgements and the
serjeants and others learned in the law dared not, for fear, deliver
judgement, plead, or carry out or use the law according to its intention,
for dread of the said Simon, John Beauchamp, John Salisbury, and
James who thus accroached to themselves royal power, as the justices,
serjeants, and others learned in the law can more fully show.

16. Also, whereas the said traitors, Alexander archbishop of York,
Michael de la Pole earl of Suffolk, Robert de Vere duke of Ireland, have
been attainted of treason by the appeal abovesaid in that they
accroached to themselves royal power and caused our lord the king to
promise to the French king by his letters and messages, in order to gain
his aid and support for the accomplishing of these high treasons,
betrayals, and murders whereof they are attainted, to give and
surrender to the said French king the town and castle of Calais and all
other castles and fortresses in the march of Picardy and Artois, the said
Simon, John Beauchamp, and John Salisbury were aware of these high
treasons and counselled them, and agreed that seven safe-conducts
should be made by the French king for the said John Salisbury and
John Lancaster to go overseas to treat with the French king for the
accomplishing the said treasons and others contained in the articles
abovesaid.[2]

Now follows the account, composed in French after the
manner of those employed in the king's service about the
court at Westminster, of the process in this parliament and

---

[1] These 'others named' were perhaps those chosen to negotiate with the king
on behalf of the parliament of Oct.–Nov. 1386 while he was at Eltham; for
Richard's proposal that a deputation be sent, see Knighton, *Chronicon*, ii. 216.
For the king's movements in 1387, see above, pp. 178–80, 184–6.

[2] This article was adjudged a matter of treason by the lords in parliament
(*R.P.*, iii. 243). It refers to Articles 28–32 of the Appeal (above, pp. 260–2).

1388 obsequio domini regis famulancium Gallico sermone conscriptus, prout plane sequitur post premissa.

[a]Le[1] duc[a] de Gloucestre conestable Dengl', le counte de Derby, le counte Darundell', le counte de Warr', et[b] le counte [c]de Notyngham[c] marchalle Dengl' appellantz viendrount ove lour grant retenue le[d] primere jour de cest parlement, cestassavoir le Lundy prochein apres [e]la feste Purificacion[e] nostre Dame,[f] a Westm' et illoeqes eux proferont prest devant le roy pur meyntener lour appelle vers Alexandre ercevesqe Deverwyk, Robert de Veer duc Dirl', Michel de la Pole conte de Suff', Robert Tresilian faux justice et Nichol Brembre faux chivaler du[g] Loundres des plousours treisouns par eux faitz a[h] roy et a son roiaume, des queux tresouns les pointz adonqes feurent leuz[i] devant le roy en plein parlement.[2] A quelle jour par comandement du roy et assent de tout le parlement les ditz ercevesqe, duc Dirl', conte de Suff' et[j] Robert Tresilyan feurent solempnement[k] demaundez, et ne[j] viegnont[l] point. Et le Mardy[m] prochein furent autre foithe demaundez en plein parlement, [n] et ne veignent pas. Et le Meskerdy lors proschein ensuant furent autrefoitz demandez, et ne veignent point; issint a celle jour lour defautes furent recordez par le roy en plein parlement.[n] Et puis apres le Joefdy le xj. jour de Feverer lors prochein,[3] le roy seant en plein parlement et toutz ces[o] countes et barons et piers du roiaume entour ly et auxi toutz les comunes du roiaume esteantz devant luy, en presence des ditz duc de Glouc', conte de Derby, conte Darundelle, conte de Warr', et conte marschalle, monseignur Johan Deverose seneschalle del hostelle de[p] roy par comandement du[q] roy dona juggement en tiele manere, cestassavoir qe les ditz duc Dirl', conte de Suff' et[r] Robert Tresilyan soient traignez et penduz come traitours du roy et du roiaume et ils et lour heires desheritez pur toutz jours, et qe les temporaltees du[s] dit ercevesqe soient seises en le[t] mayn le roy al oeps du roy;[4] a rendre de quelle juggement toutz les prelatz du [u]parlement soi retraihent[u] pur saver lour regularite.[5] Et puis le Lundy lors[r] proschein le roy mesmes soy venoit en parlement et seant en soun see en presence de toutz seignurs temporelx comanda son dit seneschalle dire en noun du roy [v]qe le[v] fuist la volunte du roy qe Nichol Brembre suisdit fuisse arrayne ycelle jour: et puis le roy soy absenta. Et puis le dit Nichol fuist amesne en plein parlement par le[w] cont de Kent conestable del Tour[x] et ces ministres et illoeqes fuist arreyne et toutz les articles de tresoun queux luy feurent surmys et des queux il fuist appellez ovesqe

[a-a] *From W. MS. Duc.*   [b] *W; MS. om.*   [c-c] *W; MS. om.*   [d] *W* a.
[e-e] *W* le feste del Purificacion de.   [f] *W; MS. om.*   [g] *W* de.   [h] *W* au.
[i] *W; MS.* liez.   [j] *W* om.   [k] *Two letters in this word are interlined.*   [l] *W* viegnent.   [m] *W inserts* lors.   [n-n] *W; MS. om.*   [o] *W* ceux.   [p] *W* le.
[q] *W* de.   [r] *W* om.   [s] *W; MS.* des.   [t] *W* la.   [u-u] *W* roialme soy retreterent hors du parlement.   [v-v] *W* qil.   [w] *Interlined.*   [x] *W inserts* de Loundres.

[1] The beginning of the Monk's second narrative of the Merciless Parliament, for which see above, pp. xlvii–li, 234 n.

the execution of its judgements. After the foregoing articles 1388
it runs:

The[1] duke of Gloucester constable of England, the earl of Derby, the
earl of Arundel, the earl of Warwick, and the earl of Nottingham
marshal of England, appellants, came with their great retinue to Westminster on the first day of this parliament, that is to say on the Monday
next after the feast of the Purification of Our Lady [3 February] , and
there presented themselves before the king, ready to maintain their
appeal against Alexander archbishop of York, Robert de Vere duke of
Ireland, Michael de la Pole earl of Suffolk, Robert Tresilian false justice,
and Nicholas Brembre false knight of London of the many treasons
committed by them against the king and against his realm, of which
treasons the points were then read before the king in full parliament.[2]
On which day, by command of the king and with the assent of the
whole parliament, the said archbishop, the duke of Ireland, earl of
Suffolk, and Robert Tresilian were solemnly called, and came not. And
on the Tuesday following [4 February] they were once more called in
full parliament, and came not. And on the Wednesday then next following [5 February] they were once more called, and came not; therefore
on that day their defaults were recorded by the king in full parliament.
And then afterwards on Thursday the 11th day of February then next
following,[3] the king being seated in full parliament and all his earls and
barons and peers of the realm about him and also all the commons of
the realm standing before him, in the presence of the said duke of
Gloucester, earl of Derby, earl of Arundel, earl of Warwick, and earl
marshal, Sir John Devereux, steward of the king's household, by the
king's command delivered judgement in this fashion, that is to say that
the said duke of Ireland, earl of Suffolk and Robert Tresilian should be
drawn and hanged as traitors to the king and the realm and they and
their heirs disinherited for ever and that the temporalities of the said
archbishop should be seized into the king's hand to the king's use;[4]
at the delivery of which judgement all the prelates of parliament withdrew to save their conformity with religious rule.[5] And afterwards, on
the Monday then next following [17 February] , the king himself came
into the parliament and, taking his seat in the presence of all the lords
temporal, commanded his said steward to declare in the king's name
that it was the king's will that Nicholas Brembre abovesaid should be
arraigned on that day: and afterwards the king withdrew his presence.
And afterwards the said Nicholas was brought in full parliament by the
earl of Kent, constable of the Tower, and his officers, and was there
arraigned and all the articles of treason which were laid to his charge

---

[2] The articles were read by Geoffrey Martin, a clerk of the Crown (*Favent*,
p. 15; *Cal. Pat. R., 1385-9*, p. 513).   [3] Correctly, on Thurs., 13 Feb.
[4] For the full sentences see *R.P.*, iii. 237; cf. below, p. 308 and n.
[5] Cf. *R.P.*, iii. 236-7, placing the prelates' withdrawal on 5 Feb.

1388 les autres traytours par les ditz cynk seignurs appellantz feurent lieux[a]
devant luy en plein parlement, a quelle il demaunda counseille, et fuist
ouste par la ley du parlement.[1] Et apres il demanda copies[b] de les[c]
articles et jour de respounse; et ne puist[d] avoir.[2] Et sur ceo [e]a present[e]
il fuist chace de respoundre a chescun article par soy 'Coupable' ou
'Noun coupable', et le dit Nichol respoundy 'De rien coupable'. A
quelle le duc de Glouc' et ces ditz[f] compaignouns responderont en plein
parlement qe le dit Nichol fuist et est faux traitour au roy et a[g] roiaume
et ceo voillent perfourner[h] et meintener come le parlement voloit
agarder.[3] Et le dit Nichol profra de[f] le defendre ovesqe soun corps, et
fuist [i]par parlement ouste.[i] Et puis le Maresdy touz les seignurs appellantz devant le roy en plein parlement ont ewages les[j] gauns et toutz
les seignurs[k] piers du roiaume et plousours chivalers et esquiers illoeqes
gageront ensi lour gauntes et getteront devant le roy a[g] nombre de ccc.
gauntz et v. qe le dit Nichol est[l] faux traitour a[g] roy et a[g] soun[f]
roiaume sanz les [m]aprendre arere.[m]

Et[n] Meskerdy apres les[o] piers de tout le roiaume soy aviseront quelle
juggement vodroient doner devers le dit Nichol. Endementiers[p] Robert
Tresilyan fuist pris hors de Westm'[4] et amesne en plein parlement et
illoeqes luy[q] fuist declare par le dit seneschal en ycelle parlement
comentz le dit Robert Tresilyan fuist appelle ovesqe les autres de si
[r]hautes tresouns[r] par [s]les ditz duc Glouc' etc.[s] et jour luy fuist assigne
et sur ceo proclamacion fait parmye tout le roiaume de respoundre a[t]
dit jour de parlement, a quelle jour il ne venoit point et fuist solempnement appellez et sic primo,[u] secundo et tercio en plein parlement;
issint qe par son defaute fuist agarde qe le dit Robert Tresilyan soit
traigne et [v]penduz etc. et qe ces[v] terres et tenementz, biens et chateux
soient forfaitz a roy pur toutz jours.

[w]Mors Tresilian:[w] Par quoy sanz respounse du dit Robert Tresilyan[5]
il fuist ajugge[u] en absence du roy en plein parlement qil serra mesne
a la Tour de Loundres et dilleoqes traigne a Tybourne et illeoqes
penduz; et comaunde fuist a[x] marschalle de prendre garde de luy et
faire execucion ycelle jour et qe les mair, viscountes et[y] aldremantz
de Loundres soient eidantz a ceo perfourner. [z]Et ensi fuist[z] etc.

Et le Joefdy lors proschein ensuant le roy vient en plein parlement et comanda a toutz[aa] seignurs de[bb] parlement qils aleront[cc]
a juggement de Nichol Brembre: et puis le roy se issa de parlement.

[a] W leuz. [b] W la copie. [c] W des. [d] W poet. [e-e] W om. [f] W om.
[g] W au. [h] MS. and W; recte pursuier? Cf. above, p. 240 (pursuir). [i-i] W
ostee par parlement. [j] W lour. [k] W inserts et. [l] W fuist. [m-m] W arere
prendre. [n] MS. inserts qe; W om. [o] W le. [p] W et dementiers, followed
by mesme le mesqerdy. [q] Interlined. [r-r] W haut treson. [s-s] W le dit duc
de Glouc' et sez compaignons. [t] W au. [u] W om. [v-v] W penduz et ses.
[w-w] A marginal heading in MS.; W om. [x] W al. [y] Interlined. [z-z] W om.
[aa] de expunged after this word. [bb] W du. [cc] W alerent.

---

[1] Cf. the declaration of the lords on 4 Feb. that the Appeal belonged to the
laws and course of parliament (ibid., p. 236); and for comment, Bellamy, Law
of Treason, pp. 168n., 169.

and whereof he was appealed with the other traitors by the said five
Lords Appellant were read before him in full parliament, whereupon
he asked for counsel, which request was by the law of parliament rejected.[1] And afterwards he asked for copies of the articles and for a day
to answer; and was refused.[2] And thereupon he was compelled then and
there to answer to each several article 'Guilty' or 'Not Guilty'; and the
said Nicholas answered 'Guilty of nothing'. Whereat the duke of
Gloucester and his said companions answered in full parliament that the
said Nicholas was and is a false traitor to the king and to the realm, and
this they would make good and maintain as the parliament should
award.[3] And the said Nicholas offered to make his defence to it with his
body, which was disallowed by the parliament. And afterwards, on
Tuesday [18 February], before the king in full parliament all the Lords
Appellant threw down their gauntlets and then and there all the peers
of the realm and many of the knights and esquires, by likewise flinging
down their gauntlets before the king to the number of 305 and refusing
to take them back, wagered battle that the said Nicholas is a false
traitor to the king and to his realm.

And afterwards, on Wednesday [19 February], the peers of the
whole realm deliberated what judgement they would deliver with
respect to the said Nicholas. Meanwhile Robert Tresilian was taken
outside Westminster[4] and brought into full parliament, and there it
was declared to him by the said steward in that parliament how the
said Robert Tresilian nad been appealed with the others of such high
treasons by the said duke of Gloucester etc. and a day had been
assigned to him, and proclamation thereupon made throughout the
realm, for him to answer on the said day of parliament, on which day
he came not and was solemnly called (and so a first, second, and third
time) in full parliament; so that by his default it was awarded that the
said Robert Tresilian should be drawn and hanged etc. and that his
lands and tenements, goods and chattels should be forfeited to the king
in perpetuity.

Death of Tresilian. Wherefore without any answer from the said
Robert Tresilian,[5] it was adjudged in full parliament and in the king's
absence that he should be taken to the Tower of London and thence
drawn to Tyburn and there hanged; and the marshal was commanded
to take charge of him and to execute judgement that day, and the
mayor, sheriffs, and aldermen of London were to assist in carrying it
out. And so it was etc.

And on the Thursday then next following [20 February], the king
came in full parliament and commanded all the lords of parliament to
proceed to judgement on Nicholas Brembre: and the king then went

[2] Brembre asked also for the opportunity (denied to him) of responding, i.e.
of answering the allegations in detail (*Favent*, p. 16).

[3] Cf. *R.P.*, iii. 238, where this offer comes after Brembre's offer of battle.

[4] Cf. below, p. 310.

[5] Tresilian was invited to speak of events *since* his condemnation which made
the sentence inappropriate and refused to do so (below, p. 312 and n.).

1388 Et donqes vient Brembre et a^a luy furent reherces^a plusours materes^b
de^c tresouns des queux il fuist appellez par les ditz seignurs et enpesche
p. 174 par tut le comune de^d roiaume,[1] et ou il respoundy ^{e}a de primes^e
'De rien coupable' trove fuist par toutz les piers de^d roiaume coupable.
Issint fuist ajugge en mesme le^f manere come Tresilian etc.; et ycelle
jour fuist^a traignez et penduz etc.

Et le Lundy ^{g}et le jour^g de Mars lors proschein[2] monseignur Robert
Beleknapp, monseignur Johan Holte, monseignur William Bourgh',
monseignur Roger Fulthorp,' monseignur Johan Cary, et Johan
Loketon, justices de ley, feurent arrayne en plein parlement de^c hautes
articles et pointz ^{h}de tresoun^h et enpesches par les comunes queux^i
feurent lieux^j en Latyn et puis en Englys;[3] as queux articles chescun
justice par soy avoit son respounse. Et puis les ditz^k justices feurent
remys a la Tour de Loundres.

Et le Maresdy^l proschein[4] Johan Blake et Thomas Uske^m feurent
arraynez en le dit parlement devant le duc Deverwyk ^{n}esteant lieutenant le roy^n en absence du roy et illoeqes furent enpesches par les
comunes des^o plusours hautes pointz de tresoun, as queux ils respoun-
derent severalment; mes Blake longe temps estoit muez et ne voloit
parler par longe temps pur saver ^{p}le heritage^p de soun heir, et puis le
seneschalle le roy, supposant luy faire celle^q en fraude et collusion issint
qe le roy ne duist mye aver le forfaiture de ces terrez, luy comaunda de
respoundre, reherceant celle qil navera lavantage de ces terres coment
qil soy tiegne muts; et donqes il respoundy tres sagement; et les^r
respounse feurent reportez, et puis feurent remandes a prison.[5] Et^s
Meskerdy apres les ditz Blake et Uske,^{m} porce qe lour respounse ^{t}feurent
'Coupables',^{t} avoient juggement par assent du roy en plein parlement:
cestassavoir qe Blake serra traigne del Tour de Loundres tanqe a
Tybourne et illoeqes penduz; et le dit Uske^u serra auxint traigne et
penduz et son^v test coupe et mys sur Neugate.[6] Et ensi ^{w}fuist fait^w
ycelle jour etc.

Et le Joefdy lors proschein[7] les justices feurent^x en une prive
chambre, et les seignurs^y piers du roiaume ne poent accorder de lour
juggement:[8] issint les ditz justices feurent remys a la^z Tour. Et ycelle
jour levesqe de Chichestre fuist enpecche par les comunes en plein

---

^{a} W om. ^{b} W maneres. ^{c} W dez. ^{d} W du. $^{e-e}$ W adeprimes.
^{f} W la. $^{g-g}$ W le (the first letter over an erasure) seconde jour. $^{h-h}$ W dez
tresons. ^{i} W inserts pointz. ^{j} W luez. ^{k} W om. ^{l} W Mesqerdy.
^{m} W Husk. $^{n-n}$ W lieutenant. ^{o} W de. $^{p-p}$ W leritance. ^{q} W ceo.
^{r} W lour. ^{s} W inserts le. $^{t-t}$ W fuist 'Coupable'. ^{u} W Husk. ^{v} W sa.
$^{w-w}$ W furent. ^{x} W inserts a Westm'. ^{y} W inserts et. ^{z} W le.

---

[1] For the idea that the Commons accused (i.e. impeached) Brembre (and the
other principal accused), see below, p. 298, and R.P., iii. 238.

[2] The next Mon. was 24 Feb., but proceedings against the judges did not begin
until Mon., 2 Mar. This mistake means that all proceedings in parliament from
Mon., 2 Mar. to Fri., 6 Mar. inclusive are dated a week too early in the above
account. Moreover, the judges were not brought into parliament on the Tues.

out of the parliament. And then Brembre came and there were recited 1388
to him several matters of treason whereof he was appealed by the said
lords and impeached by all the commons of the realm;[1] and though he
at once replied 'Guilty of nothing', he was by all the peers of the realm
found guilty. Therefore it was adjudged in the same manner as for
Tresilian etc.; and the same day he was drawn and hanged etc.

And on the Monday and the Tuesday then following[2] Sir Robert
Bealknap, Mr. John Holt, Mr. William Burgh, Mr. Roger Fulthorpe,
Mr. John Cary, and John Lockton, justices of the law, were arraigned
in full parliament and impeached by the commons of high articles and
points of treason, which were read out in Latin and then in English,
to which each justice made his several answer.[3] And afterwards the said
justices were remitted to the Tower of London.

And the next Tuesday[4] John Blake and Thomas Usk were arraigned
in the said parliament before the duke of York, who in the king's
absence was his lieutenant, and were there impeached by the commons
of many high points of treason to which they severally replied, but
Blake remained for a long time mute and, in order to save the inheritance of his heir, would not speak, and then the king's steward, supposing him to be acting thus in fraud and collusion so that the king should
not have the forfeiture of his lands, commanded him to answer,
repeating that despite remaining mute he would have no profit of his
lands; and then he answered quite discreetly; and the answers were
recorded, and afterwards the accused were remanded to prison.[5] And
afterwards on Wednesday the said Blake and Usk, since their answer
had been 'Guilty', received judgement by assent of the king in full
parliament, that is to say, that Blake should be drawn from the Tower
of London to Tyburn and there hanged, and the said Usk should also
be drawn and hanged and his head severed and set up on Newgate.[6] And
so it was done the same day etc.

And the Thursday then following,[7] the justices were in a privy
chamber and the peers of the realm could not agree upon their
judgement:[8] and accordingly the said justices were remitted to
the Tower. And on the same day the bishop of Chichester was
impeached by the commons in full parliament of certain points of

following their first appearance. See above, pp. l-li.

[3] The main grounds of the impeachment of the judges were their answers to
the questions put to them by Richard in 1387, and on 2 Mar. the commons
delivered a copy of the questions and answers; it was no doubt these that were
read. The judges severally offered the defence that they had acted under duress.
See *R.P.*, iii. 238-9, and above, pp. 196 ff.

[4] Correctly, on Tues. 3 Mar.

[5] Hitherto Blake and Usk had been in the custody of, respectively, the duke
of Gloucester and the earl of Arundel (*R.P.*, iii. 240). For the charges against
them and their response, see ibid.

[6] Cf. *R.P.*, iii. 240, recording, in addition, sentences of disinheritance and
forfeiture; see also below, pp. 314-16.

[7] Correctly, on Thurs., 5 Mar.   [8] *Favent*, p. 20, is less discreet.

1388 parlement de certeinz pointz de tresoun.[1] Et le Vendredy[a] proschein[2]
lercevesqe de Canterbirs et toutz les prelatz feurent en plein parlement
et en lour presence les ditz enpecchementz feurent rehercez par le
seneschalle a[b] dit evesqe; et il respoundy as eux. Et les comunes
prieront qil soit arestu[c] pur ceo qil conust parcelle, et les prelatz
countreplederont. Issint prieront dysser pur enparler,[d] et issint firent;
et puis viendrent en parlement toutz les[e] ditz justices, et illeoqes
feurent ils et chescun de eux ajugges destre traignez et penduz come
traitours et lour terres,[f] biens et chateux forfaitz a[g] roy pur toutz
jours. Et puis reviendrent[h] le[i] dit ercevesqe de Canterbirs et toutz
les prelatz, horspris levesqe de Chichestre, et lercevesqe de Canterbirs
pria a toutz les seignurs et comunes de[j] parlement pur [k]la mercie[k]
de Dieux et en oevere de charite granter respit del execucion des
corps de[l] justices avantditz. Et puis levesqe de Ely chaunceller Dengl'
disoit qe le roy ad[m] grauntee as[n] justices lour vies, et comanda en
noun du roy qe execucion de lour corps cesse. Et puis le seneschalle
comanda de mesner les ditz justices a la[o] Tour areremayn.[p] Et ensi
[q]fuist fait.[q][3]

Et [r]puis le Maresdy[r] le x. jour de Marcz le roy fuist en[s] parlement
et les comunes luy granteront[t] une demi xv[me] a estre levez de [u]les lays[u]
gentz a la xv[ev] de Paschqe[w] sur condicion qe tout passe pur la[o] viage
sur la[o] mer quelle le conte Darundelle ad empris a[x] perfourner, si Dieux
luy eide, et a nulle autre oeps.[4]

Et le Joefdy lors proschein ensuant[y] le dit conestable de la Tour
mesna en parlement Simond de Burley,[z] Johan Beauch' chivaler,
Johan Salesbury chivaler, et James Berneres chivaler, Richard
Metford[aa] clerk, Nichol Slake clerk, [bb]Richard Clyfford clerk,[bb] et
Johan Lyncol' clerk de[cc] comandement du roy, et illeoqes devant
le dit[dd] duc Deverwyk lieutenant le[ee] roy [ff]en absence du roy[ff] en
presence de toutz les[gg] seignurs temporelx les comunes du roiaume
enpescherent primerement le dit Simond de plusours hautez pointz
de tresoun; as queux le dit Simond respoundy de poyns[hh] en point
pluis sagement et luy[dd] profra chivalrousement de defendre ovesqe
son corps qil[ii] unqes ne fuist traitour come il est enpesche par les
comunes: et a ceo ne fuist resceu mes[jj] chace par[kk] parlement a
respoundre 'Coupable' ou 'Noun coupable',[ll] et il respondy 'De rien

---

[a] W inserts lors.   [b] W au.   [c] et expunged.   [d] W emparler.   [e] Interlined.   [f] W inserts et tenementz.   [g] W au.   [h] W; MS. viendroit.   [i] W lez.
[j] W du.   [k-k] W pite et mercy.   [l] W dez.   [m] W avoit.   [n] W inserts ditz.
[o] W le.   [p] W; MS. a remayn.   [q-q] W fuist etc.   [r-r] W le mesqerdy puis.
[s] W inserts le.   [t] W granterent.   [u-u] W leys.   [v] W quinzisme.
[w] W inserts lors proschein.   [x] W de.   [y] W om.   [z] W inserts chivaler.
[aa] W Mitford.   [bb-bb] W om.   [cc] W du.   [dd] W om.   [ee] Written in the
MS. above de, which is not deleted; W du.   [ff-ff] Added in the margin but
marked for insertion here.   [gg] Interlined.   [hh] W point.   [ii] W qe.   [jj] W
inserts fuist.   [kk] W inserts le.   [ll] W om.

treason.[1] And on the Friday following[2] the archbishop of Canterbury 1388
and all the prelates were in full parliament, and in their presence the
said impeachments were recited by the steward to the said bishop; and
he replied to them. And the commons prayed that he should be
arrested, because he confessed to some of the impeachments, and the
prelates entered a counter-plea. They therefore prayed leave to withdraw and imparl; and this they did; and afterwards all the said justices
came into parliament, and there they and each of them were adjudged
to be drawn and hanged as traitors and their lands, goods, and chattels
forfeited in perpetuity to the king. And then the said archbishop of
Canterbury returned, and all the prelates, except the bishop of
Chichester, and the archbishop of Canterbury prayed all the lords and
commons of parliament, for God's mercy and as a work of charity, to
grant a stay of execution upon the bodies of the justices aforesaid. And
then the bishop of Ely, chancellor of England, said that the king had
granted the justices their lives, and in the king's name he commanded
that execution on their bodies be stayed. And then the steward commanded that the said justices should be taken back to the Tower. And
so it was done.[3]

And then on Tuesday, 10 March, the king was in parliament and the
commons granted him a half-fifteenth, to be levied from the laity at the
quinzaine of Easter [12 April], on condition that the whole of it was
devoted to the naval expedition which the earl of Arundel had undertaken, with God's help, to carry out and to no other purpose.[4]

And on the Thursday then next following [12 March] the said constable of the Tower by the king's command brought into parliament
Simon Burley, John Beauchamp knight, John Salisbury knight, and
James Berners knight, Richard Medford clerk, Nicholas Slake clerk,
Richard Clifford clerk, and John Lincoln clerk, and there, before the
said duke of York, the king's lieutenant in the absence of the king, in
the presence of all the lords temporal, the commons of the realm
impeached first of all the said Simon of many high points of treason;
to which the said Simon answered very discreetly, point by point and
offered, as a knight, to defend himself by his body against the charge
that he had ever been a traitor as it was laid in the commons' impeachment: and he was not admitted to do this but constrained by the parliament to answer 'Guilty' or 'Not guilty'; and he answered 'Guilty of

---

[1] Cf. *R.P.*, iii. 241, delaying the impeachment of the bishop until 6 Mar. Cf.
below, pp. 316-17; see also above, p. xlvii.

[2] Correctly, Fri., 6 Mar. On the order of events cf. *R.P.*, iii. 240-1, where it is
implied that the justices were dealt with before Rushock; so too below, pp.
316-17. Whatever the correct order, it is to be understood that the prelates were
present at the day's proceedings against Rushock — at the end of which judgement was deferred — but absent from the judgement against the justices.

[3] For the sequel see below, p. 336 and n.

[4] An exceptional grant in that it was made before the end of parliament.
See also below, pp. 350-2 and nn.

1388   coupable'.[1] Et puis le dit Simond fuist comande arreremayn*a* a la*b* Tour.

Et puis Johan Beauch', Johan Salesbur', et James Berneres*c* illoeqes en mesme la manere feurent enpesches par les ditz*c* comunes de*d* plusours hautez *e*pointz de tresoun;*e* as queux ils respounderont severalment 'De rien coupable'. Et puis ils feurent remandez a la*b* Tour; et les *f*clercs pur celle jour auxi feurent a Tour remandez*f* sanz enpeschement ou respounse dycelles.

Et puis le Marsdy proschein les comunes doneront les articles en escript, et les ditz Simond, Johan, Johan et*g* James respounderont de novelle a chescun article 'De rien coupable'. Et le dit Simond fuist si malade qil fuist supporte a le barre par monseignur Baudewyn Radyngton[2] de lune partie et Johan Durant esquier de lautre partie. Et puis feurent remandez a le Tour de Loundres.

Et le Vendredy lors proschein le roy seant en plein parlement et toutz les prelatz, *h*ducs, countez*h* et barouns entour luy et les comunes esteant devant luy, les ditz comunes prieront le roy de grauntier pur quiete et tranquillite du roiaume qe toutz les seignurs*i* si bien temporelx come espirituelx ferroient une serement en manere qensuit:*j*[3]

'Soient toutz les seignurs du parlement si bien prelatz come autres jurrez en plein parlement qils garderont et ferront garder la bone pees, quiete et tranquillite du roiaume, et si ascun vuille faire encountre cella ils luy contresteront*k* et destourberont*l* a tout lour poair. Et si ascuns gentz voillent riens faire encountre les corps de les v. seignurs, cestassavoir Thomas duc de Glouc', Henry conte de Derby, Richard conte Darundelle et de Surr', Thomas conte de Warr', et Thomas conte marschalle, ou ascun de eux, ils esteront*m* ove les ditz seignurs jesqes a lentier fyn de ceste present parlement et eux mayntiendront et sustiendront a tout lour dit poair a viver et a morir ove eux encountre toutz, nulle persone nautre chose except en manere avantdit salvant toute foithe lour ligeance vers nostre seignur le roy et la prerogative de sa corone et les leys et bone custumez du roiaume.

p. 175   'Item en mesme la manere soient / jurrez toutz les seignurs, chivalers et autres entour la persone le roy. Item en mesme la manere soient jurrez les comunes du parlement affaire en manere avantdit. Item les mairs, aldermans et baillifs des citees et burghes soient jurrez en mesme la manere. Item qe les viscountes ⟨et⟩*n* chivalers des countes pernent autiel serement de les gentils deinz mesmes le*o* countes. Et sur ceo briefs soient mandez a chescun counte, cite et borghes parmy le roiaume, deinz queux briefs soit compris la forme et manere des

---

a W; MS. a remayn.   *b* W le.   *c* W om.   *d* W dez.   *e–e* W tresons.
f–f W ditz clerks auxi.   *g* Interlined.   *h–h* W countes duces.   *i* du parlement expunged after this word.   *j* ⟨Not⟩a de juramento *in the margin.*   *k* W; MS. contristerent.   *l* W; MS. destourberent.   *m* W esteeront.   *n* MS. om.   *o* W lez.

---

[1] i.e. Burley was required to plead 'Guilty' or 'Not Guilty' to each article, but before submitting to this requirement he tried to enter separate pleas to the

nothing'.[1] And afterwards the said Simon was committed again to the 1388
Tower.

And afterwards John Beauchamp, John Salisbury, and James Berners
were in the same manner there impeached by the said commons of
many high points of treason; to which they severally answered 'Guilty
of nothing'. And afterwards they were remanded to the Tower; and for
that day the clerks also were remanded to the Tower without having
been impeached or having made their answer.

And afterwards on the next Tuesday [17 March], the commons
delivered the articles in writing, and the said Simon, John, John, and
James once more replied to each article 'Guilty of nothing'. And the
said Simon was so ill that he was supported at the bar by Sir Baldwin
Raddington[2] on one side and John Durant esquire on the other. And
then they were remanded to the Tower of London.

And the Friday then next following [20 March], the king sitting in
full parliament and all the prelates, dukes, earls, and barons about him
and the commons standing before him, the said commons prayed the
king to grant, for the quiet and tranquillity of the realm, that all the
lords, as well temporal as spiritual, should make an oath in manner
following:[3]

'Let all the lords of parliament, as well prelates as others, be sworn
in full parliament that they will keep and cause to be kept the good
peace, quiet, and tranquillity of the realm, and if any man is minded to
act against this, they will oppose and discomfort him to the utmost of
their power. And if any are disposed to do anything against the persons
of the five lords, that is to say Thomas duke of Gloucester, Henry earl
of Derby, Richard earl of Arundel and of Surrey, Thomas earl of
Warwick, and Thomas earl marshal, or any of them, they will take their
stand with the said lords until this present parliament is wholly ended,
and will maintain and support them to the best of their said power, to
live and die with them against everyone, no person or thing excepted,
in manner aforesaid, saving always their allegiance to our lord the king
and the prerogative of his crown and the laws and good customs of the
realm.

'Also in the same manner let there be sworn all the lords, knights,
and others about the king's person. Also in the same manner let there
be sworn the commons of the parliament, to act in manner aforesaid.
Also let there be sworn in the same manner the mayors, aldermen, and
bailiffs of cities and boroughs. Also let the sheriffs and knights of the
shires receive the like oath from the gentry in the counties. And in this
regard let writs be directed to every county, city, and borough throughout the realm, in which writs let there be comprised the form and

several parts of certain of them. Cf. below, p. 318, and *R.P.*, iii. 243. For the
articles see above, pp. 268-78. For 'point' as a legal term of art, see M. D. Legge,
' "Hamlet" and the Inns of Court', in *Studies in Language and Literature in
Honour of Margaret Schlauch* (Warsaw, 1966), pp. 213 ff.
    [2] Controller of the wardrobe and possibly a kinsman of Burley (Tout, *Chap-
ters*, iv. 196-9).   [2] Cf. *R.P.*, iii. 244; *Cal. Cl. R., 1385-9*, pp. 405-6.

1388 serementz avantditz et qils ne doygnent nulle foy ne credence a nulle parlance en contrarie.' Et le roy granta.

Sur qoy toutz les seignurs sibien temporelx come espirituelx et toutz les chivalers des countes, citezeins des citees, burgeys des burghes venuz au parlement par brief et auxint toutz autres chivalers et esquiers esteantz en le dit parlement[1] firent le dit serement sur la croys de Canterbirs.

Et puis les ditz comunes granterent au roy un demy quinsime a lever a le quinsime de Pasqe prochein ensuant pur le viage quele[a] Richard conte Darundelle admiralle Dengleterre ad empris de faire sur le meer; et auxint granterent la custume et subside des leyns, quirs et peaux lanuz et treys soldz del tonelle et xij d. del livere a durer tanqe a la feste de Pentecoste proschein.[2]

Et les[b] comunes prieront au roy qe luy plerroit qe les ditz v. seignurs purroient avoir xx. mille liveres pur[c] lour grauntz despencez qils firent pur salvacion du roiaume et en destruccion des traitours atteintz. Et le roy[d] graunta ovesqe lie[e] coer.[3] Et donqes les ditz comunes prieront qe x. mille liveres ent soient paiez as[f] v. seignurs devant la[g] feste de Pentecoste proschein de les subsides avantditz. Et puis ajourna le parlement tanqe a la quinsime de Pasqe proschein.[4]

A quele quinsime le Lundy les seignurs et comunes viendront a Westm' et illeoqes les nouns de[h] chivaleres, citezeins et burgeys furent appellez par le rolle. Et le Meskerdy apres le roy seant en plein[i] parlement et toutz les prelatz, ducs, countes[j] et barons entour luy, les comunes luy mercierent de la bone conclusion et graciouse volunte a darrein continuance en parlement, et puis prieront juggement de ceux qi sont enpesches et ensement qe les Beaumeres soient[k] voidez du roiaume.[5]

[l]*Privacio vite Simonis de Burlee.*[l] Et puis tout temps tanqe a la Marsdy proschein apres la[g] feste Phelippe et Jacob touz les seignurs et piers du roiaume furent ententifs[m] entour le juggement de monseignur[n] Simond de Burlee.[6] A quele Marsdy le duc de Glouc' seant lieutenant du roy en parlement, les ducs, countes,[o] barons et piers du roiaume par assent du roy ajuggerent le dit Simond, pur ceo qil fuist trove coupable en plusours pointes de tresoun, destre treigne del

---

[a] W; MS. om.   [b] prieront *deleted after this word.*   [c] W en guerdon de.
[d] W; MS. om.   [e] W lee.   [f] MS. *inserts* x, *which has not been deleted; W inserts* ditz.   [g] W le.   [h] W dez.   [i] W om. ·   [j] W kontes.   [k] W; MS. soiez.   [l-l] *A marginal heading in MS.; W* om.   [m] W; MS. ententif.
[n] W S⟨ire⟩.   [o] W kountes et.

---

[1] i.e. knights and squires who had come to Westminster in the retinues of the lords attending parliament; for these see above, p. 280.

[2] The tax on movables was in fact granted on 10 Mar.; for the grant of the custom and subsidy on wool, woolfells, etc., and of tunnage and poundage on 20 Mar., see *R.P.*, iii. 244; see also above, p. 286 and n.

[3] This grant was not made until 2 June, the lords and commons making it a condition of their renewal on that day of the custom and subsidy on wool,

manner of the oaths aforesaid and that people give no faith or belief 1388
to any utterance to the contrary.' And the king granted it.

Whereupon all the lords, as well temporal as spiritual, and all the
knights of the shires, citizens of cities, and burgesses of boroughs that
were come by writ to the parliament and also all other the knights and
esquires present in the said parliament[1] made the said oath upon the
cross of Canterbury.

And afterwards the said commons granted to the king a half-fifteenth
to be levied at the quinzaine of Easter next following [12 April] for the
naval expedition that Richard earl of Arundel, admiral of England, had
undertaken to make; and they further granted the custom and subsidy
upon wool, hides, and woolfells and 3s. the tun and 12d. in the pound,
to continue until the feast of Whitsuntide next [17 May].[2]

And the commons prayed the king that he might be pleased for the
five lords to have £20,000 for the great expenses they had laid out for
the salvation of the realm and the undoing of the traitors attainted.
And the king granted it with a glad heart.[3] And then the said commons
prayed that £10,000 thereof should be paid to the five lords before the
feast of Whitsuntide next out of the subsidies aforesaid. And afterwards
[the king] adjourned the parliament until the quinzaine of Easter next
[12 April].[4]

At which quinzaine, on the Monday [13 April], the lords and
commons came to Westminster and there the names of the knights,
citizens, and burgesses were called by the roll. And the Wednesday after
[15 April], the king being seated in full parliament and all the prelates,
dukes, earls, and barons about him, the commons thanked him for the
happy conclusion and gracious disposition experienced at the last
sitting in parliament, and afterwards they prayed judgement upon those
who were impeached and likewise that the Bohemians should be
expelled from the realm.[5]

Simon Burley deprived of his life. And afterwards, during all the
time until the Tuesday next after the feast of St. Philip and St. James,
all the lords and peers of the realm applied themselves to judgement
upon Sir Simon Burley.[6] On which Tuesday [5 May], with the duke of
Gloucester sitting as the king's lieutenant in parliament, the dukes,
earls, barons, and peers of the realm by the assent of the king passed
judgement upon the said Simon, because he was found guilty in many
points of treason, that he should be drawn from the Tower of London

woolfells, etc. until 24 June 1389. The grant of the subsidy, however, was to be
effective from Sat. in the octave of Whitsun (23 May) 1388, and the grant to the
Appellants by implication from the same day (*R.P.*, iii. 245, 248; below, p. 294;
see also *Cal. Pat. R., 1385–9*, p. 456).

[4] Cf. *R.P.*, iii. 245, and below, p. 320.

[5] Cf. below, p. 322, where the date given for the petition for judgement on the
knights is 13 Apr. For the petition for the expulsion of Bohemians see *R.P.*,
iii. 247.

[6] So too *R.P.*, iii. 243. For the dramatic events of the intervening period see,
however, below, pp. 328–30.

1388 Tour ^{a}de Loundres^a a Tybourne et illeoqes penduz et coupe la teste.[1]
Et nostre seignur le roy, pur ceo qe le dit Simond servist le roy al
temps de sa juvente et auxint servist le noble prince piere le roy et la
princesse miere le roy et ensement a cause qil fuist chivaler del gartour,
relessa a dit Simond son traire et^b pendre et agarda qe son teste serra
coupe jouste le Tour.[2] Et Wauter Clopton' chief justice du roy dona
juggement du dit Simond, et le juggement renduz le dit Simond fuist
amesne ces mayns liez luy arere parmy la citee du^c Loundres tanqe
a le Tour de Loundres et illeoqes fuist decoupe la teste et enterre a
Newabbeye illeoqes.^{d}[3]

Et puis le Marsdy le xij^{me} jour de Maii Johan Beauchamp' chivaler,
James Berneres chivaler et Johan Salesbur' chivaler furent mesnes a
le barre en plein parlement devant le duc Deverwyk president du roy
et devant toutz seignurs temporelx en le dit parlement et illeoqes fuist
reherce par le dit Wauter Clopton' a Johan Beauchamp', James
Berneres,^{e} et Johan Salesbury coment ils furent empesches et accuses
par les comunes en parlement des plusours articles de treson, queux
furent liveres en escript et as queux les ditz Johan, James, et Johan
avoient lour respounse; et responderont 'De rien coupable': et les
comunes replieront 'Coupable'. Et sur ceo lez^f ducs,^{g} countes, barons
et piers du roiaume ont examinez ove bone deliberacion les articles
suisditz; et ^{h} sont trovez^h coupables en ascuns des pointz de tresoun.[4]
Sur quoy les ditz ducs, countes, barons et piers du roiaume ajuggent
et agardent par assent du roy qe les ditz Johan Beauchamp',^{i} James^j
et Johan serroient treignez et penduz et coupez les testes. Et pur ceo
qe les avantditz Johan Beauchamp' et James furent grantz gentils du
roiaume et le dit Johan Beauchamp' fuist seneschalle del hostelle ^{k}de
roy,^{k} lour fuist relesse le traire et pendre et qe lour testes serroient
coupes jouste le Tour de Loundres, et qe le dit Johan Salesbury soit
treigne et penduz pur ceo qil^l fuist trove coupable de tresoun sibien
de cea le^m meer come de la.[5] Et sur ceo furent mesnez de Westm'
parmy Loundres tanqe a la^n Tour, et illeoqes fuist execucion fait solonc
la purport du juggement avantdit.^{o}

Et ycelle jour levesqe de Chichestre fuist solempnement appellez
troys foithe^p doier soun juggement;^{q} et al tierce foithe^p il vient et

---

$^{a-a}$ W om. ^{b} prendre *deleted after this word.* ^{c} W de. ^{d} W om.
^{e} W om. ^{f} W; MS. le. ^{g} W duks. $^{h-h}$ W trovez sont. ^{i} W om.
^{j} furent grantz gentils *written after this word but deleted.* $^{k-k}$ W om.
^{l} W qe. ^{m} W la. ^{n} W le. ^{o} Nota qualem mortem subierunt J. Beac',
Jacobus Berners et Johannes Salesbury *in the margin.* ^{p} W foitz. ^{q} W
inserts en plein parlement.

---

[1] Cf. *R.P.*, iii. 243, recording, in addition, sentences of disinheritance and forfeiture. Burley was found guilty of the charges in Article 8 of the impeachment
(for which see above, p. 274), and these were declared matters of treason.
[2] Cf. *R.P.*, iii. 243; see also Tout, *Chapters*, iii. 331 and n., and above, p. 274
and n.

to Tyburn and there hanged and his head severed.[1] And our lord the 1388
king, for the reason that the said Simon served the king in the time of
his youth and also served the noble prince the king's father and the
princess his mother, and likewise because he was a knight of the Garter,
remitted to the said Simon the drawing and hanging and awarded that
he should be beheaded next the Tower.[2] And Walter Clopton, the king's
chief justice, delivered judgement upon the said Simon, and, judgement
given, the said Simon was led, with his hands bound behind him,
through the city of London to the Tower of London and was there
beheaded and buried in New Abbey hard by.[3]

And afterwards on Tuesday 12 May, John Beauchamp knight, James
Berners knight, and John Salisbury knight were brought to the bar in
full parliament before the duke of York, the king's president, and
before all the lords temporal in the said parliament and there it was
recited by the said Walter Clopton to John Beauchamp, James Berners,
and John Salisbury how they were impeached and accused by the
commons in parliament of many articles of treason, which were
delivered to them in writing and to which the said John, James, and
John had their answer and answered 'Guilty of nothing': and the commons replied 'Guilty'. And thereupon the dukes, earls, barons, and
peers of the realm examined with good deliberation the articles abovesaid and they were found guilty in some of the points of treason.[4]
Whereupon the said dukes, earls, barons, and peers of the realm
adjudged and awarded by assent of the king that the said John Beauchamp, James, and John should be drawn and hanged and their heads
severed. And for the reason that the aforesaid John Beauchamp and
James were great gentlemen of the realm and the said John Beauchamp
had been steward of the king's household, the drawing and hanging
were remitted in their case and they were to be beheaded next the
Tower of London, and John Salisbury was to be drawn and hanged
because he was found guilty of treason as well on this side the sea as
beyond it.[5] And thereupon they were taken from Westminster through
London to the Tower, and there execution was done according to the
purport of the judgement aforesaid.

And on the same day the bishop of Chichester was thrice solemnly
called to hear his judgement and at the third call he came and stood at

---

[3] The Cistercian house of St. Mary Graces. Burley's acquisition of property
intended by Edward III for the endowment of this house was an occasion of
scandal at the time of his death (*Cal. Pat. R., 1385-9*, pp. 468, 539; see also
N. B. Lewis, 'Simon Burley and Baldwin of Raddington', in *E.H.R.*, lii (1937),
pp. 662-9).

[4] Beauchamp and Berners were found guilty of the charges in Article 1 of the
impeachment, and Salisbury of, in addition, the charges in Article 16; and these
were declared matters of treason (*R.P.*, iii. 243; above, pp. 268-70, 278).

[5] See below, p. 332 and n., and for the full sentences, *R.P.*, iii. 243. Salisbury
was not in fact sentenced to beheading: he was to undergo the lingering death
effected by strangulation at this time; see Bellamy, *Crime and Public Order in
England in the Later Middle Ages*, p. 187.

1388   esteit a le barre. Et le dit[a] Wauter Clopton juggement dona en manere qensuit:

'Il est bien conuz a vous qe vous estez accusez par les comunes du roiaume, as quelles vous avetz eu vostre respounce,[1] et les accusamentz et respounse sont[b] bien examinez par les piers du roiaume ove bone deliberacion: et [c]trove est qe vous estez[c] coupable de tresoun, sur qoy toutz les piers du roiaume, seignurs temporelx, par assent du roy ajuggent vous come traitour au roy et a son roiaume et qe toutz vos terres et tenementz, biens et chateux soient forfaites au roy. Et quant a lexecucion de vostre corps le roy soi avisera.'[2]

Et puis le second jour de Juyn le roy seant en plein parlement et toutz les seignurs temporelx et espirituelx esteant entour luy et les comunes esteantz a le barre, le counte de Warr' et le counte de Salesbirs amesneront monseignur Johan Holand frere au roy nostre seignur apparaille come counte en parlement, et Thomas Hobile esquier porta lespee du dit monseignur Johan Holand, et le roy prist lespee et seinta le dit monseignur Johan et luy noma counte de Huntyngdon',[d] pur quele le[e] roy graunta xx. liveres de prendre del counte de Huntyngdon' par les mayns des viscountes illeosqes qi pur le temps y serront pur

p. 176   son title et[f] noun de[g] counte et auxi ij. mille marcz par an en / meintenance et supportacion de son estat, a avoir des terres et rentes a tout sa vie; de quele grant une chartre fuist lieu:[3] et puis le dit counte de Hontyngdon'[h] fist son homage au roy. Et tout ceo qe fuist[i] grante au counte de Huntyngdon' fuist al instance de tout la comune et seignurs du roiaume et ovesqe speciale grace de roy.

Et ycelle jour les comunes graunteront a roy la subside des leyns, quirs, peaux lanuz, treys soldz del tonelle de vin et xij. deners del livere tanqe a la[j] feste de seint Johan le Baptistre proschein de illeoqes tanqe a mesme la[j] feste lors en un an proschein ensuiant.[4]

Et puis le Meskerdy le tierce jour de Juyn en le moustre de Weymoust'[k] le roy renovella son serement et toutz seignurs du roiaume luy firent homage[l] de novelle et en outre toutz les ditz seignurs et comunes du parlement firent illeoqes serement.[5]

Et puis le Joefdy proschein le roy seant en plein parlement moult les comunes et les seignurs de lour grant naturesse et grant donz avantditz amercia[m] et prometta a eux et a toutz les seignurs en parlement

---

[a] W; MS. om.   [b] W om.   [c-c] W trove estes.   [d] Nota de Johanne Holand comite de Huntyngdon' effecto *in the margin.*   [e] MS. and W om.   [f] MS. and W de.   [g] W; MS. om.   [h] fuist al instance *deleted after this word.*   [i] *Repeated in* W.   [j] W le.   [k] W Westm'.   [l] moustre *deleted after this word.*   [m] W om.

---

[1] On 6 Mar. (above, pp. 284–6 and n.).

[2] In fact the lords temporal were to consider Rushock's fate. The sentence included disinheritance and the confiscation of temporalities in addition to forfeiture. Before the end of the parliament the bishop was exiled to Cork, where he was to be permitted to receive 40 marks a year 'si ascun de ses amys luy voille tant doner'; translation to the see of Kilmore followed later in the year.

the bar. And the said Walter Clopton delivered judgement in manner following:

'You are well aware that you are accused by the commons of the realm to whom you have had your answer,[1] and the accusations and answer have been thoroughly examined by the peers of the realm with good deliberation: and it is found that you are guilty of treason, whereupon all the peers of the realm, lords temporal, by assent of the king, adjudge you as traitor to the king and to his realm and that all your lands and tenements, goods and chattels are forfeit to the king. And as for execution upon your body, the king will consider further.'[2]

And afterwards, on 2 June, the king being seated in full parliament and all the lords temporal and spiritual standing about him and the commons standing at the bar, the earl of Warwick and the earl of Salisbury brought into parliament Sir John Holland, brother of our lord the king, in the robes of an earl, and Thomas Hobyle esquire carried the sword of the said Sir John Holland, and the king took the sword and girded the said Sir John and named him earl of Huntingdon, for which the king granted him £20, to be taken from the county of Huntingdon by the hands of the sheriffs there for the time being, for his style and title of earl and also 2,000 marks yearly for the maintenance and support of his estate, to be received from lands and rents for his whole life; of which grant a charter was read:[3] and afterwards the said earl of Huntingdon did his homage to the king. And all that was granted to the earl of Huntingdon was at the instance of all the commons and lords of the realm and with the king's especial grace.

And on the same day the commons granted to the king until the feast of St. John the Baptist next [24 June], and from then until the same feast in the year next following, the subsidy on wool, hides, and woolfells, 3s. on the tun of wine and 12d. in the pound.[4]

And afterwards on Wednesday 3 June in the monastery of Westminster the king renewed his oath and all the lords of the realm did homage to him afresh, and furthermore all the said lords and commons of the parliament made oath there.[5]

And afterwards on the Thursday following [4 June], sitting in full parliament the king heartily thanked the commons and the lords for their great benevolence and lavish grants aforesaid and promised them

See *R.P.*, iii. 244; *Cal. Pat. R., 1385-9*, p. 453, and below, p. 332.

[3] For the charter see *R.P.*, iii. 251. The grant of 2,000 marks (= £1,333. 6s. 8d.) per annum was to Holland and his heirs by Elizabeth, his wife (for whom see above, p. 192). The sum included the value of the lands already held by Holland of the king's gift. In the event the last 700 marks (= £466. 13s. 4d.) came, not from lands and rents, but from the petty custom (*Cal. Pat. R., 1385-9*, pp. 494-5). Cf. below, p. 342.

[4] These grants were to be effective from Sat. in the octave of Whitsun (23 May) 1388 (above, p. 290 n.).

[5] The king renewed his coronation oath, the prelates their fealty, the lords temporal their homage; and prelates, lords temporal, and commons took the oath mentioned here and given *in extenso* below (p. 306). See *R.P.*, iii. 251-2.

1388 destre bon roy et seignur a eux et a chescun de eux, et comanda les
comunes de suier lour briefs de lour gages. Et ensi fina le parlement.[a]

Sequitur perdonacio super premissis:[1]

Item priont les comunes qe la [b]ou au[b] darrein parlement [c]par cause[c]
des grantz et horribles meschiefs et perils [d]qe lors[d] estoient eschuez
pur[e] malveys governance qi fuist entour la persone du roy par tout
soun temps devant par Alexandre[f] ercevesqe Deverwyk, Robert de
Veer[f] duc Dirl', Michel de la Pole[f] counte de Souff', Robert Tresilian[g]
justice, et Nichol Brembre chivaler, et autres lour adherentz et autres,
paront le roy et tout son roiaume estoient molt pres davoir estee de
tout anientz et destruitz, et pur celle cause et pur eschuer tielx perils
et meschiefs pur temps avenir estoit fait par estatut en le[h] dit parlement
[i]certeins ordeignances[i] et une commission as diverses seignurs pur le
bien, honour et sauvete du roy, sa regalie et de tout son roiaume,
[j]quele commission est aillours suis escript.[j][2] Et sur ceo les avantditz
Alexandre, Robert, Michel, Robert, et Nichol, et lour adherentz et
autres avantditz, veiantz lour dite[k] malveys governance y serroit
aperceu et eux par celle cause de legere estre puniz par bone justice
affaire[l] et auxi lour malveys faitz et purpos devant usez estre destourbez
par les ditz seignurs assignez par commission, come desuis, firent,
conspirerent et purposeront[m] plusours horribles tresouns et malveistes
encountre le roy et les avantditz seignurs ensi assignez et encountre
toutz autres seignurs et comunes queux furent assentantz al faisance des
dites ordeignances[n] et commissioun, en defesance du roy, sa regalie
et de tout soun roiaume: Sur quoy Thomas duc de Glouc' uncle de[o]
roy nostre dit seignur et fitz au roy Edward iij.[p] (qe Dieux assoille),
Richard counte Darundelle, et Thomas conte [q]de Warr',[q] apercevans
les malveistes et purposes des traitours avantditz, soy assemblerent[r]
en forcible manere pur salvete de lour persones pur moustrer et declarer
les ditz treisouns et malveis purpos[s] et ent[t] mettre remedie, come
Dieux le voloit, et viendrent[u] en presence du roy nostre dit seignur et
affermerent[v] envers les v.[w] traitours appellez[x] de[y] hautes tresouns
par eux faitz au roy et a son roiaume; sur quele appelle le roy nostre

---

[a] W adds Burton'. Explicit.   [b-b] W; MS. au an; R.P. and S.R. ou a.
[c-c] R.P. pur causes; S.R. par causes.   [d-d] R.P. q' alors; S.R. qalors.   [e] S.R.
par.   [f] R.P. and S.R. insert alors.   [g] R.P. and S.R. insert nadgairs.   [h] S.R.
la.   [i-i] W certeins ordenance; R.P. and S.R. certeine ordenance.   [j-j] W lez
tenures de quele commission sy ensuent etc.; R.P. and S.R. les tenures de (S.R.
des) quelles commission et estatut cy ensuent (S.R. ensuient); followed in R.P.
by the introductory words of the commission and statute and in S.R. by the text
of the commission and the introductory words of the statute.   [k] S.R. dites.
[l] R.P. and S.R.; MS. and W affaires.   [m] W, R.P., and S.R., purposerent.
[n] R.P. ordenance.   [o] W, R.P. and S.R. du.   [p] W, R.P., and S.R. om.
[q-q] W om.   [r] R.P. assembleront.   [s] R.P. and S.R. purposes.   [t] W, R.P.,
and S.R. de ent.   [u] R.P. viendront.   [v] R.P. affermeront.   [w] R.P. and S.R.
ditz cynk.   [x] R.P. appell.   [y] S.R. des.

and all the lords in parliament that he would be to them and to each 1388
one of them a good king and lord, and bade the commons sue out their
writs for their wages. And so ended the parliament.

Next follows the pardon in respect of the foregoing proceedings:[1]

The commons pray that whereas at the last parliament by reason
of the great and horrible mischiefs and perils which had then befallen
through the bad government which had been exercised about the king's
person throughout all his time hitherto by Alexander archbishop of
York, Robert de Vere duke of Ireland, Michael de la Pole earl of
Suffolk, Robert Tresilian justice, and Nicholas Brembre knight and
other their adherents and others, whereby the king and all his realm
came very near to being wholly undone and destroyed, and for this
reason and in order to avoid such perils and mischiefs for the future
there were made by statute in the said parliament certain ordinances
and a commission to divers lords for the weal, honour, and safety of the
king, his regality, and of all his realm; which commission is written
elsewhere above.[2] And hereupon the aforesaid Alexander, Robert,
Michael, Robert, and Nicholas and their adherents and others aforesaid,
seeing that their said bad government would in these circumstances be
discovered and they themselves would in consequence easily suffer
punishment by the doing of good justice, and also that the evil deeds
and purpose they had hitherto practised were baulked by the appointment of the said lords by commission, as above, committed, conspired,
and purposed many horrible treasons and wickednesses against the
king and the aforesaid lords so appointed and against all the other lords
and commons who had assented to the making of the said ordinances
and commission, to the undoing of the king, his regality, and all his
realm. Whereupon Thomas duke of Gloucester, uncle of the king our
said lord and son to King Edward III (whom God assoil), Richard earl
of Arundel, and Thomas earl of Warwick, perceiving the wickednesses
and purposes of the traitors aforesaid, assembled in forcible fashion for
the safeguarding of their persons to show and declare the said treasons
and wicked purpose and to apply a remedy therefor, as God willed it,
and came into the presence of the king our said lord and made affirma-
tion against the five traitors appealed of high treasons by them committed against the king and against his realm; upon which appeal the

[1] There follow, not the 4 pardons granted at the end of the parliament, but the
4 petitions of the commons to which the pardons were the response and which
were recited in them. The Monk, however, and no doubt his source, omitted
from the 1st petition the text of the letters patent of 19 Nov. 1386 announcing
the appointment of the continual council established in the current parliament
and that of the statute enacting the commission of appointment of this council.
See *R.P.*, iii. 248-50 and *S.R.*, ii. 43 ff., with which, and with W.A.M. 12227
(= *W*) the text from here to p. 306 below has been collated.

[2] Above, pp. 166 ff.

1388 dit seignur ajourna les parties suisditz tanqe a ceste present parlement et
les prist en sa salve proteccion, come en le record[a] sur mesme lappelle
pleinement appiert.[1] Et puis en grant rebellite et encountre la dite
proteccion les ditz traitours ove lour adherentz et autres avantditz,
continuantz lour malveis purposes suisditz[b] ascuns de eux assemblerent[c] grant poair pur avoir destruit les ditz duc et[d] countz appellantz
et autres loialx lieges du roy et pur accomplier lour treisouns et [e]mal-
veis purpos[e] suisditz. Sur quoy [f]les ditz[f] duc de Glouc', Henry conte de
Derby, les ditz countz Darundelle et de Warr', et Thomas conte
marschalle, veiantz loverte destruccion du roy nostre dit seignur et de
tout soun roiaume si les malveis purposes des traitours avantditz et lour
adherentz ne fuissent destourbez, qe ne poet avoir este fait alors sinoun
ove[g] forte mayn, pur le bien et salvete du roy nostre dit seignur et de
tout son roiaume soy [h]assembleront forciblement et chivacheront et
pursueront[h] tanqe ils avoient destourbez [i]la dite[i] poair quillee[j] par les
traitours et lour adherentz suisditz queux v.[k] traitours sont atteintz en
ceste[l] parlement de tresouns et malveistez suisditz a la suite et appelle des
ditz duc de Glouc', countes de Derby, Darundelle, Warr', et marschalle,
[m]et accusament des comunes du roiaume:[m][2] qe please a nostre dit tres
redoute seignur le roy daccepter, approver et affermer en ceste present
parlement tout ceo qe fuist fait en le darrein parlement, come desuis,
et qanqe ad estee fait depuis le[n] darrein parlement par force de lestatut,
ordenance ou commissioun avantditz, et auxi tout ceo qe les avantditz
duc de Glouc', countes Darundelle et de[o] Warr' firent, tout ceo qe
mesmes ceux duc et countes et les ditz countes de Derby et marschalle
firent ou ascun de eux fist ou ascun autre[p] de lour compaignie ou de
eide de eux ou de lour adherentz ou dascun de eux[q] touchant les
assemblez, chivachez, appelles et pursuites avantditz come chose fait
al honour de Dieux, salvacioun du roy nostre dit seignur, meyntenance
de sa corone, et salvacion de tout son roiaume, et dordiner et establier
qe les ditz duc de Glouc', countes[r] Darundelle, Warr', et marschalle,
ne nulle de eux ne nulle qad estee de lour retenue, compaignie, force,
eide, counseille ou assent ou dascun de eux en les choses avantditz,
ne nulle autre persone pur ascune chose suisdite ne soit empesche,
moleste ne greve a suite de[s] roy ne de partie qeconqe nen autre manere
par cause dascun assemblee, chivache, combatement, lever de[t] penons
ou de[u] baneres, desconfiture, mort de homme, enprisonement dascun
persone,[v] prise, amesner ou detenue des chivalx ou autres[w] bestez,
prise et[x] emporter des biens et[y] hernoys, armures, chateux ou autres
moebles qeconqes, arsures des maysons ou dautres possessions ou biens
qeconqes, assaut, baterie, robberies, larcyns, vener ou demurer ove[z]

---

[a] *R.P. and S.R. insert* fait.   [b] *R.P. and S.R. om.*   [c] *R.P.* assembleront.
[d] *MS. and W insert* autres.   [e-e] *R.P.* malveises purpos; *S.R.* malveis purposes.
[f-f] *S.R.* le dit.   [g] *R.P. and S.R.* a.   [h-h] *MS. and R.P.; W and S.R.* assemblerent . . . chivacherent . . . pursuerent.   [i-i] *S.R.* le dit.   [j] *MS. and W;*
R.P. quelle; *S.R.* quille.   [k] *W, R.P., and S.R.* cynk.   [l] *W, R.P., and S.R.*
insert present.   [m-m] *R.P. and S.R. om.*   [n] *R.P. and S.R. insert* dit.
[o] *R.P. om.*   [p] *MS.* autres.   [q] *S.R. inserts* en ou; *R.P.* ou.   [r] *R.P. and*

king our said lord adjourned the parties abovesaid until this present 1388
parliament and took them into his safe protection, as in the record
made upon the same appeal fully appears.[1] And afterwards in great
rebellion and against the said protection the said traitors with their
adherents and others aforesaid, continuing their wicked purposes abovesaid, as to some of them assembled great power with a view to destroying the said duke and earls, the appellants, and other loyal subjects of
the king, and to accomplishing their treasons and wicked purpose
abovesaid. Whereupon the said duke of Gloucester, Henry earl of
Derby, the said earls of Arundel and of Warwick and Thomas earl
marshal, seeing the manifest destruction of the king our said lord and of
all his realm if the wicked purposes of the traitors aforesaid and their
adherents were not baulked, which could not then have been done
except by force, for the weal and safeguarding of the king our said lord
and of all his realm, assembled in forcible fashion and continued to ride
and pursue until they had thwarted the said power gathered by the
traitors and their adherents abovesaid, which five traitors are attainted
in this parliament of the treasons and wickednesses abovesaid at the
suit and appeal of the said duke of Gloucester, earls of Derby, Arundel,
and Warwick and earl marshal and on the accusation of the commons
of the realm:[2] That it may please our said most dread lord the king to
accept, approve, and affirm in this present parliament all that was done
in the last parliament, as above, and so much as has been done since
the last parliament by force of the statute, ordinance, or commission
aforesaid, and also all that the aforesaid duke of Gloucester and earls
of Arundel and Warwick did, and all that the same duke and earls and
the said earl of Derby and earl marshal or any one of them did or any
other of their company or of their aid or of their adherents or of any
one of them, touching the assemblies, ridings, appeals, and pursuits
aforesaid, as a thing done to the honour of God, the safeguarding of the
king our said lord, the maintenance of his crown, and salvation of
all his realm, and to ordain and establish that there shall not be any
impeachment, molestation, or harassment, at the suit of the king
or of any party whatsoever or in any other manner, of the said duke
of Gloucester, earls of Arundel and Warwick, and earl marshal or of
any of them or of anyone who has been of their joint or several retinue,
company, force, aid, counsel, or assent in the matters aforesaid or of
any other person for anything abovesaid by reason of any assembly,
riding, skirmish, raising of pennons or of banners, rout, homicide,
imprisonment of any person, taking, leading away, or detaining of
horses or of other beasts, taking and carrying off of goods and harness,
armour, chattels, or other movables whatsoever, burning of houses or
of other possessions or goods whatsoever, assault, battery, robberies,

---

S.R. insert de Derby.   *ˢ W and R.P.* du.   *ᵗ R.P. and S.R.* des.   *ᵘ S.R.* des.
ᵛ MS. and W insert pur.   *ʷ R.P. and S.R.* dautres.   *ˣ S.R.* ou.   *ʸ W, R.P.*
and S.R. om.   *ᶻ MS.* ou.

---

[1] Ibid., p. 238; *R.P.*, iii. 229.   [2] Cf. above, p. 284.

1388 force et armes[a] en presence[b] du roy au parlement ou counseils ou aillours, leve des gentz ou exciter les genz a lever forciblement encountre la pees par lettres, commissions ou autre fait qeconqe ou dascun autre chose qe poet estre surmys qe eux ou ascun de eux [c]deussent ou deust[c] avoir fait ou purpose davoir fait du comencement de[d] mounde touchant ascuns des materes suisdit devant le fyn de ceste present parlement par nulle ymaginacion, interpretacion ou autre colour qeconqe; / mes soient ent quites et descharges a toutz jours; forspris qe le roy soit respondu de toutz les biens et chateux queux [e]furent a[e] ceux queux furent[f] atteintz en ceste present parlement ou a ascun de eux, et queux biens et choses furent[g] prises par qeconqe persone le primere jour de Janver darrein passe ou[h] puis en cea.[i1]

p. 177

Item qe nulle persone qad este entour la persone le roy nautre persone qeconqe soit empesche, moleste ne greve par appelle, accusement ou en autre manere a cause de mal governance ou mal conseille entour la[j] persone le roy en ascune temps devant [k]le fyn de[k] ceste present parlement ou a cause dascun autre chose qad estee[l] declarre en ceste present parlement pur treisoun ou mesprison', forspris ceux qi sont atteintz et ajuggez en ceste present parlement et forspris Johan Rypon' clerk,[2] Henry Bowet clerk,[3] William Mounkton' clerk,[4] Johan Lancastre chivaler,[5] Henry Ferrers chivaler,[6] Richard Clifford clerk,[7] Richard Metford[m] clerk,[8] [n]Nichol Slake clerk,[9] Johan Lyncoln' clerk,[n10] Johan Holcotes,[o11] Nichol Southwell',[12] James Lustrak,[13]

---

[a] *R.P. and S.R. insert* ou arme.　　[b] *W in error inserts* du presence.　　[c-c] *R.P. and S.R.* deust ou deussent; *MS.* deussent au deust.　　[d] *W and R.P.* du.　　[e-e] *S.R.* feuront as.　　[f] *R.P. and S.R.* sont.　　[g] *R.P.* furont.　　[h] *W, R.P., and S.R.; MS.* en.　　[i] *In R.P. and S.R. the king's reply to the foregoing petition follows.*　　[j] *S.R.* le.　　[k-k] *W, R.P., and S.R.; MS.* en.　　[l] *W; MS.* est; *R.P. and S.R.* este.　　[m] *W* Mitford.　　[n-n] *W reverses the order of the names; R.P. and S.R.* Johan Lincoln de Grymmesby clerk, Nichol Slake clerk.　　[o] *R.P. and S.R. insert* esquier.

---

[1] From 4 Jan. 1388 the chattels of the five principal accused had officially been in royal custody (*Cal. Cl. R., 1385-9*, p. 463). See also below, p. 324. The first petition ends at this point. It was granted with the addition of pardons for justices, ministers, and others whom the Appellants had taken but subsequently allowed to go free, or at whose escape they had connived, between 14 Nov. 1387 and the end of the parliament (*R.P.*, iii. 249).

[2] For whom see above, p. 202 and n.

[3] A well-rewarded royal clerk and ecclesiastical lawyer, who accompanied Bishop Despenser on his crusade and gave evidence on his behalf in parliament. Early in 1388 he was Richard II's proctor at the papal curia. See Rymer, *Foedera*, vii. 569; A. B. Emden, *Biographical Register of the University of Cambridge to 1500* (Cambridge, 1963), pp. 83-4; John Le Neve, *Fasti Ecclesiae Anglicanae, 1300-1541* (revised edn., London, 1962-7), i. 7. For the suggestion that Bowet was used in the Anglo-French negotiations of 1387, see *Palmer*, p. 119.

[4] Described as the parson of Kirklington, by Ripon (Yorks.) (*Cal. Cl. R., 1381-5*, pp. 605, 618, 621). He was pardoned in 1390 (*Cal. Pat. R., 1388-92*, p. 228).　　[5] For whom see above, p. 262.

thefts, coming or remaining with force and arms in the king's presence at the parliament or councils or elsewhere, raising of people or exciting people to rise forcibly against the peace by letters, commissions, or any other deed, or of any other thing that it may be surmised that they or any one of them should have done or purposed to have done from the beginning of the world touching any of the matters abovesaid before the end of this present parliament, by any imagination, interpretation, or other colour whatsoever, but they shall be thereof quit and discharged for ever; except that the king shall be answered for all the goods and chattels which belonged to those or to any one of those who were attainted in this present parliament, and which goods and things were taken by any person on the first day of January last past or afterwards until now.[1]

Also, that no person who has been about the king's person nor any other person whatsoever, shall be impeached, molested, or harassed by appeal, accusation, or in any other manner by reason of bad government or bad counsel about the king's person at any time before the end of this present parliament or by reason of any other thing that in this present parliament has been declared for treason or misprision, except those who are attainted and adjudged in this present parliament and except for John Ripon clerk,[2] Henry Bowet clerk,[3] William Monkton clerk,[4] John Lancaster knight,[5] Henry Ferrers knight,[6] Richard Clifford clerk,[7] Richard Medford clerk,[8] Nicholas Slake clerk,[9] John Lincoln clerk,[10] John Holcote,[11] Nicholas Southwell,[12] James Lustrake,[13]

[6] Lord of Groby (Leics.). He was summoned to the Merciless Parliament but died on 3 Feb., its 1st day. His offence was involvement in the negotiations for the ransoming of Jean de Bretagne, for which see above, p. 188 and n., and p. 256. See *Cal. Inq. p.m.*, xvi. 546-51; *Lords' Reports on the Dignity of a Peer*, iii. 725; *Palmer*, pp. 118-19; and for Ferrers's service on commissions of the peace etc., *Cal. Pat. R., 1381-5*, pp. 70, 85, 142, etc.; ibid., *1385-9*, pp. 254, 386, etc. Richard II stayed at Groby just before the council at Nottingham in Aug. 1387 (Tuck, *Richard II and the English Nobility*, p. 228).

[7] A clerk of the king's chapel. Clifford, who had been in custody since the beginning of the year, was released on the last day of the parliament, pledged to appear at the next parliament, and the same is true of 3 others in the above list: Medford, Slake, and Lincoln. See above, pp. 228-30, and below, p. 340 and n.

[8] At the time of his arrest in Jan. 1388, the king's secretary.

[9] At the time of his arrest in Jan. 1388, the dean of the king's chapel.

[10] At the time of his arrest in Jan. 1388, a chamberlain of the Exchequer.

[11] Holcote's arrest, to secure his appearance before the council, was ordered on 16 July 1387 (*Cal. Pat. R., 1385-9*, p. 389). He was released from the Fleet prison on 19 May 1389 (*Cal. Cl. R., 1385-9*, pp. 583-4).

[12] For whom see above, p. 262.

[13] Lustrake brought safe-conducts from Charles VI for the king, de Vere, and others in the course of the Anglo-French negotiations in the autumn of 1387 (Walsingham, *Hist. Ang.*, ii. 170); and for the safe-conducts, above, p. 262.

For Lustrake see also *Cal. Cl. R., 1381-5*, pp. 627-8, 635; ibid., *1385-9*, pp. 20, 31; ibid., *1389-92*, pp. 8, 416; and *Diplomatic Correspondence of Richard II*, ed. Perroy, pp. 177-8. The name suggests a Gascon origin: Lustrake = Listrac (Gironde).

1388 Henry Clerk de Thakstede,[a][1] Simond[b] Shiryngham,[2] Johan Fitz Martyn,[c][3] William Chestreton' persoun de Ratelsden',[4] frere Richard Roughton' del ordre de freres[d] Menours[5] et Thomas soun frere,[e] et toutz ceux qi[f] sont dela la meer avesqe[g] les traitours ou[h] voillent aler a eux en apres.

Item que nulle qad este de retenue, compaignie, fors, eide, counseille, assent ou adherence[i] de ceux qi sont atteintz ou ajuggez en ceste present parlement ou dascun de eux [j]forspris ceux[j] qi[f] sont forspris[k] devant soit enpesche, moleste ne greve al[l] suite de[m] roy ne [n]de partie[n] ne en autre manere par cause dassemble,[o] chivache, combatement, leve de[p] penons ou des[q] baneres, desconfitures,[r] mort de homme, enprisonement dascun persone,[s] prise, amesner ou detener[t] des chivalx ou dautres bestez, [u]prise et emporter[u] des biens, hernois, armurez, chateux ou autres moebles qeconqes, arsures des maisouns [v]et autres[v] possessions ou biens qeconqes, assaut, baterie, robberyes, larcyns, vener ou demurer ove[w] force et armes ou arme en presence du roy en parlement, counseils ou aillours, lever des gentz ou exciter les gentz a lever forciblement[x] encountre la pees par lettres, commissions ou autre fait qeconqe encountre lentent ou pursuit des avantditz duc de Glouc', countes [y]Darundelle, Derby,[y] Warrewyk, et marschalle, quelle entent et pursuit sont declarres par lour appelle en ceste present parlement, ou dascune autre chose qi poet estre surmys qe eux ou ascune de eux [z]duissent ou duist[z] aver fait ou purpose daver fait puis [aa]comencement du[aa] mounde, touchant ascun[bb] des matieres encountre lentent ou pursuite suisditz declarrez en lappelle suisditz etc.[cc][6]

Item que les appellez,[dd] pursuites, accusamentz, processez,[ee] juggementz et execucions[ff] faitz et renduz en ceste present parlement soient approvez, affermez et establiez come chose fait duement pur le bien et profit du roy nostre dit seignur et de tout soun roiaume nient contreesteant[gg] qe les seignurs espiruelx et procuratours [hh]du clergie[hh] soy absenterent[ii] hors du parlement a temps des ditz juggementz[jj] pur

[a] W, R.P. and S.R. Thaxstede.   [b] W, R.P., and S.R. Symkyn.   [c] W, R.P., and S.R. insert clerk or clerc.   [d] MS., W, and S.R. frere.   [e] W confrere.   [f] W queux.   [g] W, R.P., and S.R. ovesque.   [h] R.P. and S.R. et touz (S.R. toutz) autres q'.   [i] MS. and W adherent; R.P. and S.R. adherdance.   [j-j] W, R.P., and S.R.; MS. om.   [k] R.P. and S.R. insert a.   [l] R.P. and S.R. a.   [m] W and R.P. du.   [n-n] R.P. and S.R. dautre partie queconque.   [o] R.P. and S.R. dascun assemble.   [p] R.P. and S.R. des.   [q] R.P. and S.R. de.   [r] R.P. descomfiture.   [s] MS. and W insert pur.   [t] W, R.P., and S.R. detenue.   [u-u] R.P.; S.R. pris et emporter; MS. pris et enportez; W prise et emport'.   [v-v] W et dautres; R.P. and S.R. ou dautres.   [w] W, R.P., and S.R.; MS. a de.   [x] R.P. and S.R. insert et.   [y-y] R.P. and S.R. de Derby, Arundell.   [z-z] R.P. and S.R. deust ou deussent; W deussent ou deust; MS. duissent au duist.   [aa-aa] R.P. and S.R. le comencement de.   [bb] W, R.P., and S.R. ascuns.   [cc] R.P. and S.R. om.; in these sources the king's reply to the petition follows at this point.   [dd] purseutes deleted after this word.   [ee] W and R.P. processe.   [ff] R.P. execucion.   [gg] R.P., W, and S.R.; MS. tout reesteant.   [hh-hh] R.P. and S.R. des seignurs espirituels (S.R. espiritueles).   [ii] R.P. and S.R. absenteront.   [jj] R.P. and S.R. insert renduz.

Henry clerk of Thaxted,[1] Simon Shiryngham,[2] John Fitz Martin,[3]   1388
William Chesterton parson of Rattlesden,[4] Brother Richard Roughton of
the order of Friars Minors,[5] and Thomas his brother and all those who
are beyond the sea with the traitors or will go to them in the future.

Also that none who has been of the retinue, company, force, aid,
counsel, assent, or adherence of those who are attainted or adjudged
in this present parliament or of any of them, except those before
excepted, shall be impeached, molested, or harassed at the suit of the
king or of a party or in any other manner, by reason of any assembly,
riding, skirmish, raising of pennons or banners, routs, homicide,
imprisonment of any person, taking, leading away, or detaining of
horses or of other beasts, taking and carrying off of goods, harness,
armour, chattels, or other movables whatsoever, burning of houses and
other possessions or goods whatsoever, assault, battery, robberies,
thefts, coming or remaining with force and arms or armed in the
presence of the king in parliament, councils, or elsewhere, raising of
people or exciting people to rise forcibly against the peace by letters,
commissions, or any other deed whatsoever against the intent or pursuit
of the aforesaid duke of Gloucester, earls of Arundel, Derby and
Warwick, and earl marshal, which intent and pursuit are declared by
their appeal in this present parliament, or of any other thing which it
may be surmised that they or any of them should have done or purposed to have done since the beginning of the world touching any of
the matters against the intent or pursuit abovesaid declared in the
appeal abovesaid etc.[6]

Also, that the appeals, pursuits, accusations, processes, judgements,
and executions made and delivered in this present parliament shall be
approved, confirmed, and established as a thing duly done for the weal
and profit of the king our said lord and of all his realm, notwithstanding that the lords spiritual and proctors of the clergy absented themselves from the parliament at the time of the said judgements for the

[1] Perhaps the clerk serving the chantry at Thaxted, for which see P. Morant,
History and Antiquities of Essex (2 vols., London, 1768), ii. 443 and n.; cf.
Registrum Simonis de Sudbiria, diocesis Londoniensis, A.D. 1362–1375, ed. R. C.
Fowler, C. Jenkins, and S. C. Ratcliff (Canterbury and York Soc., 2 vols., 1916–
38), ii. 44.   [2] For whom see above, p. 205 n., and *Letter Book H*, p. 146.

[3] *Alias* John Taverner. He is described as a clerk of Lincs. His properties in
Lincoln were taken into custody on 28 Feb. 1389 but restored on 7 July 1390
(*Cal. Fine R., 1383–91*, p. 284; *Cal. Inq. Misc.*, v. 185; *Cal. Cl. R., 1389–92*,
p. 192; and see also *Cal. Pat. R., 1381–5*, p. 554).

[4] Chesterton was later pardoned for misprision of treason. He was probably
the clerk who sent a defamatory letter about Thomas Arundel, chancellor and
bishop of Ely, to the pope in the course of the Merciless Parliament (*Cal. Pat.
R., 1388–92*, p. 92; below, p. 337 n.).

[5] Br. Richard Roughton, O.F.M. was Robert de Vere's confessor (*Cal. Pat. R.,
1385–9*, p. 65). Br. Thomas Roughton, O.F.M., mentioned ibid., p. 236, was
presumably the brother who is next in the above list.

[6] The end of the second petition, which was granted without any additions.
For the beneficiaries of this pardon, see below, p. 342 and n.

1388 loneste et salvaction de lour estat, come contenu est en un protesta-
cion par[a] mesmes les seignurs espirituelx et procuratours livere en ceste
present parlement,[1] et qe par ymaginacioun et[b] interpretacion ou autre
mocion qeconqe nulle dycelles soient reversez, enfreintez ou anullez
en ascune manere: et si ascun face pursuite denfreindre, anuller ou
reverser ascuns des pointez suisditz, quele pursuite soit de record, soit
ajugge et eit execucion come traitour et enemy du roy et du[c] roiaume:
porveu [d]tote foithe[d] qe ceste acceptacion, approve, affermance[e] et
establissement touchantz[f] les assembles, appelles, pursuites, accusementz, processez,[g] juggementz et execucions suisdit eiant et tiegnent
force et vertue en cestes cases issintz escheuz[h] et avenuz ou declarrez
soulement et qils ne soient treitz en ensample nen consequencie en
temps avener ne qe la dite commissioun fait au[i] darrein parlement soit
treite en ensample nen consequencie en temps avener, mes[j] touchantz[k]
les matieres suisditz[l] qils estoisent[m] fermement [n]pur temps qi passe
est[n] desicome ils[o] estoient si profitables[p] au roy, sustenance et meyntenance de sa corone et salvacion de tout le[q] roiaume et faitz de si
grant necessite;[r] coment qe diverses pointz sont declarrez pur tresoun
en ceste present parlement autres queux[s] ne furent declarrez par estatut
devant,[p] qe nulle justice eit poair de rendre juggement dautre cas de
tresoun nen[t] autre manere qils navoient devant le comencement de
ceste present parlement etc.[u][2]

Item qe nulle des[v] traitours atteintz par [w]appelles suisditz[w] ou
accusement[x] des comunes qi sont unqore en vie ne soient reconseillez
ne restitutz a la ley par[y] pardoun nen autre manere salvant la grace et
pardoun qi est fait en ceste present parlement. Et si ascun pursuie de
les reconseiller ou les faire pardoun avoir ou les restituer a la ley en
ascun manere et ceo soit[z] duement et overtement[aa] par record prove,
soit ajugge et eit execucion come traitour et enemy du roy et du[bb]
roiaume.[3] Et si[cc] ascune chartre de pardoun ou licence de repairer en
Engleterre ou autre grant soit fait as ditz traitours ou ascun de eux
destre restituit a la ley ou demourer en Engleterre ou aillours qe limite
[dd]nest a[dd] eux en ceste present[ee] parlement qe toutz tielx chartres
et grantez soient voides et de nulle value. Et si ascuns des ditz traitours
revieigne ou soi tiegne en Engleterre ou aillours deinz le poair et
seignurie le roy nostre dit seignur ou ascuns de ses lieges par qeconqe
voie ou si ascuns des ditz traitours qi sont limitez a demorer en certeins

[a] R.P. and S.R. pur.   [b] W, R.P., and S.R. om.   [c] R.P. and S.R. de.
[d-d] W and R.P. toute foitz; S.R. tout foitz.   [e] R.P.; S.R. affirmançe; MS. and
W afferme.   [f] W, R.P., and S.R. touchant.   [g] W processe.   [h] S.R.; R.P.
eschuz; MS. escheies; W escheiez.   [i] R.P. and S.R. a.   [j] R.P. and S.R. insert
qanqe est fait.   [k] W touch'; R.P. and S.R. touchant.   [l] MS. and W insert
mes.   [m] R.P. and S.R. for the last two words estoise.   [n-n] R.P. and S.R.
om.; but see S.R. ii. 49n.   [o] R.P. and S.R. eles.   [p] MS. and W insert et.
[q] R.P. son.   [r] R.P. and S.R. insert et.   [s] R.P. and S.R. q'.   [t] W, R.P.,
and S.R.; MS. nien.   [u] R.P. and S.R. om.   [v] S.R. de.   [w-w] R.P. and S.R.
l'appell susdit; W apell' suisdite.   [x] R.P. accusementz.   [y] R.P. and S.R.;
MS. and W de.   [z] R.P. and S.R. om.   [aa] R.P. and S.R. insert et.   [bb] R.P.

honour and safeguard of their estate, as is contained in a protestation 1388
by the same lords spiritual and proctors delivered in this present parliament,[1] and that by imagination and interpretation or any other motion
none of the same shall be reversed, infringed, or annulled in any
manner: and if any makes pursuit to infringe, annul, or reverse any of
the points abovesaid, such pursuit being of record, he shall be adjudged
and have execution as a traitor and enemy of the king and of the realm:
provided always that this acceptance, approval, confirmation, and
establishment touching the assemblies, appeals, pursuits, accusations,
processes, judgements, and executions abovesaid shall have and hold
force and virtue only in these cases thus befallen and come to pass or
declared and that they shall not be drawn in example or precedent in
time to come, and that the said commission made at the last parliament
shall not be drawn in example or precedent in time to come; but touching the matters abovesaid that they shall stand firmly for the time that
is past inasmuch as they were so profitable to the king, support and
maintenance of his crown, and salvation of all the realm, and done out
of such great necessity; and although sundry points are declared for
treason in this present parliament other than were declared by statute
before, that no justice shall have power to deliver judgement of any
other case of treason or in any other manner than he had before the
beginning of this present parliament etc.[2]

Also, that none of the traitors attainted by the appeals abovesaid or
the accusation of the commons who are still alive shall be reconciled
or restored to the law by pardon or in any other manner, saving the
grace and pardon which is made in this present parliament. And if anyone pursues to reconcile them or to cause them to have pardon or to
restore them to the law in any manner, and this is duly and manifestly
proved by record, he shall be adjudged and have execution as a traitor
and enemy to the king and to the realm.[3] And if any charter of pardon
or licence to repair to England or any other grant is made to the said
traitors or to any of them to be restored to the law or to abide in
England or elsewhere than is limited to them in this present parliament,
that all such charters and grants shall be void and of no validity. And if
any of the said traitors return or have his being in England or elsewhere
within the power and lordship of the king our said lord or any of his
lieges by any way, or if any of the said traitors who are limited to abide

and S.R. de.   *cc W, R.P., and S.R.; MS. om.*   *dd–dd W; MS.* nest au; *R.P.*
and S.R. est a.   *ee R.P. and S.R. om.*

---

[1] On Wed., 5 Feb. (*R.P.*, iii. 236–7).

[2] The 3rd petition ends at this point. To it and to the 4th and final one, the
king returned a single, affirmative answer. The import of the 3rd petition was
that for the future judges were to follow the Statute of Treasons of 1352 (25
Edward III, statute 5, *cap.* 2, for which see *S.R.*, i. 319–20).

[3] Cf. Article 10 of the Appeal, where the grant by the accused of pardons for
treasons is itself deemed treason (above, p. 246).

1388 lieux ^{a}soient trovez^a hors ou passe le lieu a luy ^{b}limites, come desuis,^{b} soit fait de luy come de traitour du roy et du^c roiaume.^{d}

Sequitur forma juramenti:[1]

Vous jurrez qe vous nassenterez ne^e suffreres en qanqe en vous est qe ascun juggement, estatut ou ordenance faitz^f ou renduz en ceste present parlement soit ascunement ^{g}adnulle, reverse ou repelle^g en ascun temps avener, et^h outre qe vous sustiendres les bones leys et usages du roiaume avant ces heures faitz et uses et firmement garderez et ferrez garder la bone pees et^i quiete et tranquillite en le roiaume sanz les destourber en ascun manere a vostre poair: si Dieux vous eide et ces seintez.^{j}

Sequitur jam perdonacio concessa Londoniensibus:[2]

Item priont les comunes ^{k}de Loundres^k qe please a nostre seignur p. 178 le roy granter general pardoun a toutz les citezeins de Loundres et / a chescun de eux de toutz maneres des^l tresouns, felonies et de toutz autres choses pur^m queux homme perdroit vie ou membre ou forferoit terrez ou tenementz dont ils sont enditez, rettes,^{n} empesches ou accusez puis le primere jour Doctobre lan du regne^o le roy qore est sisme tanqe au^p darrein jour de Maii lan unsisme nostre^q seignur le roy; forspris ceuz queux sont ajuggez, emprisonez, atteintz ou autrement accuses par la^r cominalte^s en ceste present parlement et forspris ceux queux sont exceptez en le^t pardoun.^{j}

Expletis igitur premissis videndum est^u quomodo alia transierunt in anno presenti.[3] Nam primo die Februarii amoti erant ab eorum officio quatuor justiciarii, scilicet dominus Robertus Beleknapp', dominus Johannes Holte,^{v} dominus Willelmus Borgh, et dominus Rogerus Fulthorp, et missi in Turrim London'. Item eodem die amotus est dominus Johannes Cary capitalis^w baro in scaccario et ad Turrim London' causa custodie demandatur; et quidam Johannes Loghton serviens ad legem missus est pariter cum

---

$^{a-a}$ R.P. and S.R. soit trove.　　$^{b-b}$ R.P. and S.R. limite.　　^{c} R.P. and S.R. de.　　^{d} W adds etc.; in R.P. and S.R. the king's reply to the two foregoing petitions follows.　　^{e} R.P. ne ne.　　^{f} R.P. fait.　　$^{g-g}$ R.P. anullez, reversez, ou repellez.　　^{h} R.P. inserts en.　　^{i} R.P. om.　　^{j} W adds etc. $^{k-k}$ R.P. om.　　^{l} R.P. de.　　^{m} W and R.P.; MS. par.　　^{n} R.P. inserts appellez. ^{o} R.P. inserts nostre seignur.　　^{p} R.P. a.　　^{q} R.P. inserts dit.　　^{r} R.P. le. ^{s} W also cominalte.　　^{t} R.P. la general.　　^{u} Interlined.　　^{v} dominus Johannes Loghton' deleted after Holte.　　^{w} B (a false start?) expunged after this word, which is at the end of a line.

in certain places are found outside or overstep the place to them limited, 1388
as above, it shall be done with him as with a traitor to the king and to
the realm.

The following is the form of the oath:[1]

You shall swear that you will not assent or suffer, so far as in you
lies, that any judgement, statute, or ordinance made or rendered in this
present parliament shall in any way be annulled, reversed, or repealed
in any time to come, and further that you will support the good laws
and customs of the realm made and used before these times and will to
the best of your power firmly keep and cause to be kept the good
peace, quiet, and tranquillity of the kingdom without disturbing them
in any manner. So help you God and his saints.

Next follows the pardon granted to the Londoners:[2]

Also the commons of London pray that it may please our lord the
king to grant a general pardon to all the citizens of London and to each
of them for all manner of treasons and felonies and for all other things
for which a man might lose life or limb or might forfeit lands or tenements whereof they are indicted, accused, impeached, or charged from
1 October in the sixth year of the reign of the present king [1382] to
the last day of May in the eleventh year of our lord the king [1388];
with exception of those adjudged, imprisoned, attainted, or otherwise
accused by the commonalty in this present parliament and of those
excepted in the pardon.

The foregoing matters disposed of, we must look at the
progress of other events during this year.[3] On 1 February
four justices, Sir Robert Bealknap, Sir John Holt, Sir William
Burgh, and Sir Roger Fulthorpe, were removed from office
and sent to the Tower of London. The same day saw the
removal of Sir John Cary, chief baron of the exchequer,
and his committal for safe custody to the Tower of London,
to which, in common with these judges, one John Lockton,

[1] i.e. the oath taken by the prelates, lords temporal, and the Commons on
3 June 1388 (above, p. 294). The text has been collated with *R.P.*, iii. 252 and
with W.A.M. 12227 (= *W*).

[2] What follows is the petition to which the pardon granted to the citizens of
London towards the end of the Merciless Parliament was the response. John
Northampton, John More, and Richard Northbury were in fact excluded from
this pardon, and forfeitures and escheats incurred during the period which it
covered were unaffected by it (*R.P.*, iii. 248).

[3] The Monk is about to resume his own narrative of the Merciless Parliament,
interrupted on p. 236 above, but first he refers to changes in the judiciary which
preceded the opening of the parliament; on this passage see above, p. li.

1388 illis in Turrim London'.[1] Quo eciam die creati sunt novi justiciarii, scilicet Walterus Clopton' capitalis justiciarius in banco regis et Robertus Charleton' capitalis justiciarius[a] in communi banco.[2]

Item in pleno parliamento facta trina proclamacione[3] istorum dominorum de prodicione per prefatos dominos appellatorum, et quia non comparuerunt set se a parliamento subdole subtraxerunt, xiij. die Februarii ad illorum judicium processerunt, condempnantes eos tanquam proditores trahi et suspendi et eorundem bona mobilia et inmobilia confiscari et heredes eorum perpetuo exheredari; ac quiscumque[b] eos capere posset illos impune occideret.[4] Dominum vero Alexandrum Nevylle utpote notissimum proditorem adjudicarunt; temporalia sua ac[a] eciam cetera bona sua mobilia et inmobilia confiscarunt, nolentes enim propter reverenciam sue dignitatis sentenciam mortis in ipsum dictare, set domino pape aliisque prelatis ecclesie causam sue deposicionis reliquerunt discutere ac eciam terminare.[5] Dictus vero archiepiscopus in latibulis interim latitabat quia comparere publice non audebat.

Item xvij. die Februarii dominus Nicholaus Brembre coram dominis in pleno parliamento fuit adductus et ad articulos contra eum objectos affirmative vel negative breviter respondere[c] fuit coactus; qui super hoc peciit sibi consilium adhiberi, set nequaquam fuit sibi concessum. Tunc vero ille negavit ea esse vera que sibi opponebantur, et hoc satis fuit paratus probare duello contra quemlibet opponentem excepto rege et aliis de ejus prosapia oriundis. Ad hec fuit sibi responsum quod in hujusmodi bellum non procederet, presertim ubi testes ea deposuerint esse vera que sibi obiciebantur (quia profecto omnes de communitate acclamabant omnia fore vera que sibi fuerunt objecta) et hoc predicti

---

[a] Interlined.   [b] Recte quicumque (Winterbottom).   [c] MS. responderer.

[1] Cf. Cal. Cl. R., 1385–9, pp. 382–3, the committal to the Tower, on 1 Feb., of every person in the Monk's list except Fulthorpe.
[2] Charlton was appointed on 30 Jan. and Clopton the following day (Cal. Pat. R., 1385–9, p. 400; Cal. Cl. R., 1385–9, p. 383).
[3] On 3, 4, and 5 Feb. (R.P., iii. 236–7; above, p. 280).
[4] Cf. R.P., iii. 237 and above, p. 280, omitting the substance of the last clause.

a serjeant at law, was also dispatched.[1] On this day, too, new 1388
justices were appointed, Walter Clopton to be chief justice
of the King's Bench and Robert Charlton chief justice of the
Common Pleas.[2]

When proclamation made three times[3] in full parliament
for those lords who were appealed of treason by the above-
mentioned lords had failed to secure their appearance (they
having craftily withdrawn from attendance), the parliament
proceeded on 13 February to judgement upon them,
condemning them, as traitors, to be drawn and hanged; their
goods, movable and immovable, were to be forfeited, and
their heirs disinherited in perpetuity; and anybody who
could capture them might kill them with impunity.[4] Alexander Nevill had judgement against him as a most notorious
traitor; his temporalities and also all his goods, movable
and immovable, were confiscated, but out of respect for
his high office the parliament was unwilling to pronounce
sentence of death upon him and left it to the pope and
other high dignitaries of the Church to debate and finally
decide the question of deposing him.[5] Meanwhile the archbishop himself skulked in hiding, not daring to show himself
in public.

On 17 February Sir Nicholas Brembre was brought in full
parliament before the lords and forced to answer with a
short affirmative or negative the articles propounded against
him. He thereupon asked that he might be allowed counsel,
but his request was utterly refused. He then denied the truth
of the charges laid against him, and he was quite ready to
substantiate his denial by battle against any adversary except
the king and others springing from the royal line. In reply to
this he was told that in such cases battle would not lie,
especially where witnesses deposed to the truth of all the
charges against him (for indeed the whole commons kept
on crying out that all those charges were true), and the

[5] Nevill was also disinherited. On 13 Feb. the lords deferred a decision on his
person, but the Monk's belief that his fate was the subject of negotiations at
Rome is confirmed by his translation on 30 Apr. to the see of St. Andrew's.
Before the parliament opened he had fled north, whence, at the second attempt,
he escaped overseas to Brabant, and there he died on 16 May 1392. See *R.P.*,
iii. 237; Knighton, *Chronicon*, ii. 292; *Historians of the Church of York*, ed.
J. Raine (R.S., 3 vols., 1879-94), ii. 424; below, pp. 344, 492.

1388 domini manu propria vellent probare.¹ Set finito isto die ulterius in ista materia minime processerunt.

Sequenti vero die sedente rege*a* in parliamento et predicti quinque domini principales appellatores steterunt deorsum ex alia parte (prout semper fecerunt in cunctis articulis superius expressatis quandocumque coram rege sive locum ejus tenente aliquem de prodicione notarunt) perlectis articulis prelibatis contra dominum Nicholaum Brembre et alios manifeste exhibitis² rex eundem dominum Nicholaum multipliciter excusavit, protestando ipsum numquam scivisse eum fore proditorem nec in predictis articulis ipsum culpabilem vel reum umquam fuisse in quantum ipse cognovit. Ad hec predicti domini projectis cirotecis suis cum aliis infinitis assistentibus affirmarunt ea esse vera que sibi erant objecta. Tandem ad sedandum lites et discordias super predictis in hoc ultimo convenerunt ut certi domini terminarent an super articulis contra eum propositis esset dignus morte aut non; propter quod pro examinacione dictorum articulorum electi sunt xij. magni domini, scilicet dux Ebor', comes Cancie, comes Sar', comes Northumbr', et alii barones pro implecione numeri supradicti, qui super hoc habita deliberacione nullam causam mortis invenientes in articulis sepedictis cum tali responsione ad prefatos dominos sunt regressi;³ qui contra eos indignacionem propterea conceperunt.

Set tunc ex insperato innotuit illis quomodo Robertus Tresilyan erat in sanctuario Westm':⁴ mox predicti domini ceteris omissis pro tempore ad dictum sanctuarium cum multitudine glomerosa celeriter adierunt; at dux Glouc' accepta clava protinus dictum Robertum Tresilyan arrestavit et ipsum defendebat ab hiis qui in eum irruere crudeliter satagebant. Et profecto nisi iste casus casualiter accidisset proculdubio gravis discordia inter predictos dominos tunc*b* exorta fuisset. Sicque xix. die arestatum

---

a Interlined.   *b Interlined.*

¹ Cf. above, p. 282, delaying the Appellants' explicit offer of battle until 18 Feb.

² Cf. *R.P.*, iii. 238, where a reading of the articles touching Brembre himself, on 17 Feb., is recorded.   ³ On 19 Feb.

⁴ Tresilian was found in one of the sacrist's houses in Westminster, within the sanctuary (M. Aston, *Thomas Arundel* (Oxford, 1967), p. 346 and n.; and for the

Lords Appellant were willing to prove it by personal 1388
combat.[1] But the day came to an end with no further progress made in the matter.

Next day [18 February], with the king seated in the parliament and the five chief lords who were the appellants standing
below and facing him (as they did throughout the proceedings on all the articles set out above whenever the king or his
deputy was present at their efforts to brand anybody as a
traitor), the above-mentioned articles publicly propounded
against Sir Nicholas Brembre and others were read over,[2]
when the king offered a large number of different arguments
in exculpation of Sir Nicholas whom, he protested, he had
never known to be a traitor or to be, as far as he himself
was aware, guilty or chargeable in the terms of the articles.
In reply the lords flung down their gauntlets, as did countless
other of those present, and declared that the charges against
him were true. To settle all disputes and differences over the
matter it was in the end agreed that certain lords should
decide whether on the articles laid against him he did or
did not deserve death; twelve great lords, namely the duke of
York, the earl of Kent, the earl of Salisbury, the earl of
Northumberland, and others to make up the specified
number were accordingly chosen to scrutinize the articles,
and finding after considering the matter that they disclosed
no occasion for the death penalty, returned[3] with a report to
that effect to the lords, who were consequently moved to
indignation against them.

But at this point the unexpected news arrived that Robert
Tresilian was in the sanctuary of Westminster;[4] and the lords
speedily dropped everything else for the moment to hurry
there, accompanied by a densely packed crowd: taking a
mace, the duke of Gloucester forthwith arrested Robert
Tresilian and shielded him from those who were making
savage efforts to set upon him. There is no doubt that, but
for this chance occurrence, serious disagreement would have
arisen between the lords on this occasion. This, then, was the

bounds of the sanctuary, N. H. MacMichael, *Sanctuary at Westminster* (Westminster Abbey Occasional Papers, xxvii, 1971), pp. 9–14; see also *Favent*, p. 17).
The wool staple, to which he was taken, was by the Palace of Westminster, outside what is now New Palace Yard (*Chronica Johannis de Reading et Anonymi
Cantuariensis, 1346–1367*, ed. Tait, p. 298). See also below, pp. 332, 498.

1388 Robertum Tresilyan dicti domini de sanctuario predicto
violenter funestis manibus abstraxerunt et in domum lanarum
extra sanctuarium adduxerunt, *a*interrogantes eum sollicite
an sanctuarium*b* ecclesie Sancti Petri Westmon' regis et regni
proditorem salvaret; quibus constanter dixit quod salvaret
talem quia pro hujusmodi criminosis potissime fuit illa
libertas ecclesie predicte concessa.[1] Qui putantes ipsum in
sui ipsius salvacionem hoc asseruisse ideo fidem suis dictis
nequaquam dederunt*a* set abhinc coram toto parliamento
ipsum protinus perduxerunt, *c*ubi fuit sibi recitatum
quomodo fuerat trina proclamacione vocatus et quia non
venit judicio parliamenti erat adjudicatus tanquam proditor
trahi et suspendi. Quibus ipse dixit quod processus contra
eum habitus erat erroneus et invalidus et per consequens
annullandus; et hoc per jura sua vellet probare.[2] Set confestim fuit contra eum replicatum quod factum sive judicium
parliamenti manet irrevocabile quia per debitum processum
fuit taliter contra eum pronunciatum. Unde*c* confestim data
sentencia super eum, scilicet trahi et suspendi, ilico ipsum
rapuerunt ad Turrim London' et eodem die a Turri eadem
per medium civitatis usque Tybourne ad furcas super cratem
erat tractus et indilate suspensus; qui nullo metu sive pudore
seu mortis timore voluit fateri ipsum umquam proditorem
fuisse.

Istis denique sic peractis iterato redierunt domini predicti
ad judicium domini Nicholai de Brembre: miseruntque pro
duobus de qualibet arte London', quibus vellent informari
an esset culpabilis super contentis in articulis supradictis vel
non; qui circa verba superflua vacantes demum sine effectu
ad propria redierunt. Tunc vero miserunt dicti domini pro
majore London'[3] et pro quibusdam senioribus ac recordatore[4]
ejusdem civitatis ut ipsi deponerent super credulitate eorum,
scilicet an credebant ipsum scire de predictis prodicionibus

a-a In the margin but marked for insertion here.   *b* An erasure, covered by
a dash, follows.   *c-c* In the lower margin but marked for insertion here.

---

[1] The charters on which the Abbey based its claim to rights of sanctuary supported Tresilian's case (below, p. 324 and n.).

[2] This was Tresilian's response to an invitation to plead against his sentence
(*R.P.*, iii. 238; *Favent*, p. 17; cf. above, p. 282).

manner of Robert Tresilian's arrest on 19 February by the 1388 above-named lords, in whose fell clutches he was forcibly dragged from the sanctuary and taken to the Wool House outside. They were at pains to ask him whether the sanctuary of St. Peter, Westminster, gave immunity to a traitor against the king and the realm: he answered steadily that it did, since it was for such offenders in particular that the privilege had been conferred upon the church of Westminster.[1] Supposing him to have made this assertion in order to save himself, the lords put no faith in what he said, but at once haled him away to face the whole parliament and to have recited to him how he had been three times called by proclamation and, because he did not appear, condemned by judgement of the parliament to be drawn and hanged as a traitor. His answer to this was that the proceedings against him were founded in error and had no force and should accordingly be quashed; and this he wished to prove in accordance with his rights.[2] But he was met by the swift retort that the action or judgement of the parliament was irrevocable, since it was by due process that it had pronounced against him as it had. Sentence was quickly passed on him, namely to be drawn and hanged, and he was at once hustled off to the Tower of London. On the same day he was drawn on a hurdle from the Tower through the city to the gallows at Tyburn and hanged out of hand; but no fear or shame or dread of death altered his refusal to admit that he had ever been a traitor.

This episode concluded, the lords returned once more to considering their judgement on Sir Nicholas Brembre, and sent for two representatives from each of the London crafts, through whom they wished to learn whether or not he was guilty of the matters comprised in the articles mentioned above; but after spending some time in needless chatter these people at length returned home with nothing accomplished. The lords then sent for the mayor of London[3] and certain of the aldermen, together with the recorder,[4] who were to depose to their personal belief, to say, that is, whether they believed that Brembre was or was not aware of the treasons

---

[3] Nicholas Exton.   [4] William Cheyne.

1388 supra specificatis vel non; qui dixerunt ipsum putantes pocius de hujus⟨modi⟩ scire quam nescire. Protinus conversi ad recordatorem dixerunt: 'Quid dicit lex tua in casu isto?' Quibus ipse dixit: 'Pro certo ille qui scivit talia atque celavit et non detexit merito puniretur vite privacione etc.' Igitur xx. die Februarii in pleno parliamento condempnatus est dominus Nicholaus Brembre trahi et suspendi.[1] Eodem modo fecerunt de eo sicut factum est de Roberto Tresilyan, et dum tractus fuisset ad furcas dixit cum fratribus per viam devote Placebo et Dirige et ab omnibus veniam postulavit: sicque cum ingenti contricione vitam finivit. Ejus revera contricio et devocio cunctos pene astantes ad lacrimas provocabant.[2]

Item xxj. die Februarii domini et communitas in pleno parliamento ordinarunt unum navigium ad proficiscendum in mare, ac ejus capuducem Ricardum comitem Arundell' statuerunt.

Item xxij. die Februarii, scilicet Cathedra Sancti Petri, p. 179 venit / rex ad monasterium Westm' et intererat processioni ibidem cum clericis de sua capella et monachis intermixtis: demum finita missa cum vesperis, quia Quadragesima erat,[3] ad manerium suum de Kenyngton' rediit comedendum.

Item quarto die Marcii in pleno parliamento adjudicati fuerunt trahi et suspendi Johannes Blake et Thomas Usk, qui cum magna contricione cordis summaque penitencia mortem suscepit dicensque cum traheretur valde devote Placebo et Dirige, vij. Psalmos Penitenciales, Te Deum laudamus, Nunc dimittis, Quicumque vult, et alios in articulo mortis devocionem tangentes.[4] Cujus contricio fuit aliis in exemplum corrigere suorum vitam retrahendo se a malo et ad bonum se quantocius convertendo. Demum iste Thomas Usk fuit suspensus ac incontinenti depositus ac post xxx. mucronis ictus fere decapitatus. Semper usque ad mortem numquam fatebatur se deliquisse contra Johannem Northampton' set erant omnia vera que de eo

---

[1] For the full sentence see *R.P.*, iii. 238; and for a comment on the charge of concealment of treason, Bellamy, *Law of Treason*, p. 221.

[2] Cf. *Favent*, p. 18.

[3] Outside Lent, dinner was taken between the High Mass — the Mass attended by the king — and Vespers; in Lent, it was taken after Vespers.

above specified; and they said that they supposed he was 1388
aware rather than ignorant of them. Turning at once to the
recorder the lords asked him, 'What, in that case, does that
law of yours say?' 'Without doubt', he told them, 'anyone
who, having knowledge of such matters, concealed instead
of disclosing them, would be, and would deserve to be,
punished by the loss of his life etc.' And so on 20 February
Sir Nicholas Brembre was condemned in full parliament to be
drawn and hanged;[1] and they dealt with him as they had
done with Robert Tresilian. As he was being drawn to the
gallows he devoutly recited the Placebo and Dirige with the
friars along the way and asked pardon of everyone; and thus,
with great contrition, brought his life to an end. Indeed, his
contrition and piety moved almost all the bystanders to
tears.[2]

The lords and commons gave orders in full parliament on
21 February that a naval expedition should put to sea, and
appointed Richard earl of Arundel to command it.

On 22 February, the feast of St. Peter's Chair, the king
visited Westminster Abbey and with the clerks of his chapel,
who mingled with the monks, took part in the procession.
Eventually when Mass (which, because it was Lent, was immediately followed by Vespers)[3] was over, he went back
to his Kennington manor to dinner.

Sentence of drawing and hanging was passed on 4 March
in full parliament on John Blake and also on Thomas Usk,
who met his death with great contriteness of heart and
supreme penitence, reciting with the utmost piety, as he
was drawn to the gallows, the Placebo and Dirige, the
Seven Penitential Psalms, the Te Deum, Nunc dimittis,
Quicumque vult, and other hymns that bear upon devotion
in the hour of death.[4] His contrition was an example to
others to amend their lives by drawing back from evil
and turning forthwith to good. Eventually Thomas Usk
was hanged and immediately taken down and, after about
thirty strokes of the axe, beheaded. To the very end he
refused to admit having wronged John Northampton, of
whom he maintained that every word was true that he

[4] A repertoire betraying Usk's clerical status. On the sentences against Usk and
Blake and their trial, cf. above, p. 284 and nn.

1388 predicaverat coram rege in quodam consilio habito apud Radynggum anno elapso.[1]

Item quinto die Marcii domini et communitas regni episcopum Cicestr' sunt satis aspere allocuti, quia secundum justiciarios jam in Turri London' inclusos illis debuit dixisse apud Notyngham quod nisi illi judicarent illos falsissimos proditores regi et regno qui ultimo parliamento conati sunt potestatem regalem super se assumere et illam a rege auferre proculdubio illos manifeste convinceret fore nequissimos proditores dignos utique trahi et suspendi. Ad hec omnes existentes in parliamento*[a]* contra eum graviter sunt commoti et simile judicium sibi dedissent nisi ob reverenciam sancte matris ecclesie ac ordinis clericalis sueque dignitatis ab hoc protunc proposito destitissent: unde postea super hoc librato consilio quid facerent cum tali nephando episcopo demum considerabant quod potestas secularis antequam fuerit degradatus et rite omni honore et gradu ecclesiastico fuisset privatus nequaquam posset in ipsum sentenciam traccionis et suspensionis proferre; nichilominus tamen omnia ejus bona mobilia et inmobilia fuerant confiscata et temporalia vero sua eciam in manu regis fuissent assumpta.[2]

Item sexto die Marcii predicti justiciarii coram toto parliamento fuerunt producti et adjudicati trahi et suspendi et omnia eorum bona mobilia et inmobilia confiscari.[3] Set ad peticionem clericorum aliorumque dominorum temporalium rex eis vitam concessit: sicque in Turrim London' iterum demandantur. Quo eciam die predicti domini et plena communitas Anglie iterato episcopum Cicest' dure et aspere sunt aggressi in tantum quod nisi clerici forcius cum eo protunc stetissent vitam suam eo die indubie amisisset. Set demum illis cessantibus de premissis mox ad alia divertissent, scilicet ad gubernacionem regis et pro subsidio habendo ad sustentandum navigium in mari isto tempore

---

[a] graviter *deleted after this word.*

[1] The council in question was held at Reading, but in 1384; above, pp. 90 ff.

[2] For the sentence on Thomas Rushock, bishop of Chichester, pronounced on 12 May, see above, p. 294 n.; and for the nature of the proceedings against him on 5–6 Mar., see above, p. 287 n.

[3] The judges were also disinherited. For their names see above, p. 306, and for their trial, the open sessions of which were on 2 and 6 Mar., *R.P.*, iii. 238–9, 240–1; cf. above, pp. 284 and n., 286.

had spoken before the king in a council held at Reading in 1388 the previous year.[1]

On 5 March the lords and commons of the realm launched a scathing verbal attack upon the bishop of Chichester, who, according to the justices now confined in the Tower of London, was supposed to have told them at Nottingham that unless they held those persons to be the falsest of traitors to king and kingdom who in the last parliament had tried to take the royal power upon themselves and to remove it from the king, he would undoubtedly show them up as thoroughly wicked betrayers who richly deserved drawing and hanging. This provoked everyone attending the parliament into strong feeling against him, and they would have passed a tit-for-tat sentence upon him, had not reverence for Holy Mother Church, the priestly order, and the bishop's exalted rank made them forbear on this occasion from their purpose. When, later, they gave thought to the question what they should do with a bishop so depraved, they finally decided that until he had been degraded and formally stripped of all ecclesiastical dignity and status the secular power could in no circumstances pronounce sentence of drawing and hanging upon him; but none the less, his goods, movable and immovable, were all confiscated and his temporalities, too, were taken into the king's hand.[2]

The justices themselves were brought before the whole parliament on 6 March and condemned to be drawn and hanged, with confiscation of all their goods, movable and immovable.[3] However, upon the petition of the clergy and of others from among the lords temporal, the king granted them their lives. They were thus once more committed to the Tower of London. On the same day the aforesaid lords and the full commons of England renewed their attack upon the bishop of Chichester with such severity and bitterness that if the clergy had not on this occasion taken up a firm stand in his support he would undoubtedly have lost his life that day. Eventually, however, the subject was dropped and attention was turned to such other affairs as the guidance to be given to the king and the provision of a subsidy to maintain a naval expedition at sea in the coming

1388 autumpnali,[1] ac ad alias materias pro regni comodo declarandas.

Item xij. die Marcii predicti clerici et milites[2] de Turri London' coram toto parliamento fuerunt adducti et ad objecta negative vel assertive respondere compulsi virtute parliamenti. E quibus dominus Simon Burle super diversis articulis sibi impositis, presertim in primo articulo, varie respondebat eo quod quedam concessit et quedam constanter negavit.[3] Hoc advertentes illi de communitate bene notabant; quodque ipse presensit; ex post negative ad omnia dedit responsa et magno modo asserens se velle probare manu propria non esse vera ea que fuerant sibi objecta. Ceteri vero milites, scilicet domini J. Beauchamp', James Berneres et J. Salesbury ad omnes articulos eisdem impositos negative eciam respondebant. ⟨De⟩[a] clericis namque nichil egerunt. Per quatuor enim dies postea super[b] regni gubernacione et super expedicione comitis Arundell' tractaverunt.[c4]

Quo eciam die et tempore in pleno parliamento magnus rumor exuberavit de Lollardis et eorum predicacionibus ac libris eorum Anglicis, quibus idiotas et simplices pravis eorum doctrinis diversimode perverterunt ac enormiter quosdam eorum opinionibus quasi per totam Angliam locupletes fallaciter infecerunt. Super hiis autem erant citati ad comparendum coram magistro Thoma Southam subcollectore domini pape xx. die Marcii: quo die venerunt presentibus ibidem quibusdam episcopis ac aliis tam in theologia quam in legibus graduatis; eratque inter alios frater Willelmus Botelesham de ordine Predicatorum doctor in theologia [d]et episcopus Landavensis,[d] dixeruntque Lollardi cum dictum episcopum ibidem vidissent quod non tenebantur coram eis comparere neque respondere, quia ibidem judices minime habuerunt, eo quod predictus

---

[a] MS. om.   [b] Written above de, which is expunged.   [c] Written after a false start, va (for vacaverunt?), had been expunged.   [d-d] In the margin but marked for insertion here.

---

[1] A reference to the grant of a half-fifteenth on 10 Mar.; see above, p. 286 and n.

[2] See above, pp. 228–30. This reference, which leaps over all the matter copied by the Monk from the Chancery roll of proceedings in the Merciless Parliament to the preliminaries of his own account, shows how much of an interpolation the former is.

autumn,[1] as well as the announcement of further measures 1388 for the welfare of the kingdom.

The above-mentioned clerks and knights[2] were brought from the Tower of London on 12 March to face the whole parliament, by whose authority they were compelled to answer the accusations against them with a simple negative or affirmative. Sir Simon Burley, who was one of them, varied his replies to the different articles laid against him, and particularly to the first, admitting some points while steadfastly denying others.[3] This, when they noticed it, was by no means lost on the commons; indeed he himself became conscious of it and thenceforward returned negative answers to all the charges, declaring with spirit that he was ready to prove in personal combat that the accusations made against him were not true. The remaining knights, Sir John Beauchamp, Sir James Berners, and Sir John Salisbury, likewise entered denials of all the articles laid against them. No action was taken about the clerks: the next four days were spent in discussions about the government of the kingdom and the earl of Arundel's expedition.[4]

At this time — indeed on this day — a great deal of talk broke out in full parliament about the Lollards and their preaching and the books in the English language, whereby in all sorts of ways they led astray the feeble-minded and the simple with their pernicious doctrines and in outrageous fashion contrived by misleading arguments to taint with their opinions even some of the well-to-do up and down the country. In this connection they were cited to appear before Master Thomas Southam, the pope's sub-collector, on 20 March. When, on that day, they attended, there were present certain of the bishops and other graduates in divinity and canon law, who included Brother William Bottlesham of the order of Friars Preachers, a doctor of divinity and bishop of Llandaff. On sight of the bishop the Lollards declared that they were not bound to appear or make any answer before that tribunal, which did not contain any judges, since the

---

[3] For the first charge against Burley, see above, pp. 268-70, and for procedure on 12 Mar., ibid., pp. 286-8 and n.

[4] The Monk refers to the next 4 days of parliamentary business, i.e. Fri., 13, and Mon.-Wed., 16-18 Mar.; but cf. *R.P.*, iii. 243, and above, p. 288.

1388 episcopus erat frater et apostata,[1] ceteri vero erant in-
sufficientes eos audire seu eciam dictam materiam terminare.
Sicque iminente festo Paschali prorogatum fuit negocium
usque lapsum festi predicti.

Quo in tempore naute de Dertemouthe ceperunt vij. naves
magnas ac quatuor naves minores vino sale et aliis mercimoniis diversis onustas.

Item xix. die Marcii ob reverenciam diei Dominice Palm-
arum instantis et solempnitatis Paschalis jam accedentis
protelatum fuit parliamentum usque in quindenam festi
predicti,[2] et ut perficerentur ea que in dicto parliamento
erant tacta et mota et adhuc remanserunt[a] indecisa, super
crucem archiepiscopi jurarunt quod in quindena Pasche
revenirent et ea finaliter terminarent. Concesserunt tamen
ante recessum eorum domino regi unam dimidiam quintamdecimam, et clerus concessit eciam sibi unam dimidiam
decimam; concessum est eciam domino regi a mercatoribus
xij. denarii de libra, iij. solidi de dolio, et liij. solidi iiij. denarii
de lanis, de quibus sepedicti v.[b] domini rege acceptante perciperent xx. milia marcarum pro eorum expensis.[3]

[c]Item post cepcionem parliamenti domini et comunes
regni miserunt ad villam de Hull pro Michaele de la Pole ut
ad parliamentum veniret; qui hoc caute comperiens antequam
potuit arestari fugam arripuit et ad partes transmarinas
celeriter se divertit ac duci Hibernie ilico se conjunxit; qui
sumpto sano consilio statimque habito salvo conductu ad
regem Francorum pariter adierunt et cum eo manserunt per
totum annum sequentem.[c4]

Item circa finem mensis Marcii Francigene quoddam
fortalicium [d]vocatum Poylle[d] in marisco juxta Cales' situatum
dolo quorundam Pycardorum in eo existencium in magnum

---

[a] The letters eru in this word are written over an erasure.   [b] Interlined.
[c-c] In the lower margin.   [d-d] Added in the margin.

---

[1] A conclusion deriving from the Lollard tenet 'quod religiosi viventes in
religionibus privatis non sint de religione christiana', for which see *Fasciculi
Zizaniorum*, ed. Shirley, p. 281; see also Aston, *Thomas Arundel*, p. 324, and
McFarlane, *Lancastrian Kings and Lollard Knights*, p. 193.

[2] Parliament was prorogued on 20 Mar. until 13 Apr., but lords and commons
were resummoned for 12 Apr. (*R.P.*, iii. 245). For the oath to which the Monk
refers in his next words, see above, pp. 288–90.

bishop was a friar and an apostate[1] and the rest not qualified 1388
to hear them or to determine the matter. With Easter almost
upon them the business was adjourned until that feast should
be over.

It was at this time that the seamen of Dartmouth captured
seven large vessels and four smaller ones with cargoes of wine,
salt, and other merchandise.

Out of deference to Palm Sunday [22 March], now imminent, and the approaching Easter festival, the parliament
was on 19 March prorogued until the quinzaine of Easter
[12 April].[2] To secure the completion of business already
touched upon or introduced in the parliament but still
remaining undetermined, the members swore on the archbishop's cross to return on the quinzaine and finally dispose
of it. Before withdrawing, however, they granted the king a
half-fifteenth, and the clergy granted him a half-tenth. From
the merchants he received a grant of 12d. in the pound, 3s.
the tun, and 53s. 4d. on wool. Out of this the five Lords
Appellant, with the king's approval, were to be paid 20,000
marks for their expenses.[3]

After the opening of the parliament the lords and commons
of the realm had sent to Hull to secure the attendance of
Michael de la Pole, but he was wary enough to learn their
intention and before he could be arrested took to flight,
losing no time in making his way overseas, where he
promptly joined the duke of Ireland. After judicious consultation they soon obtained a safe conduct and went off together to the French king, with whom they remained
throughout the year that followed.[4]

About the end of March the French, through the trickery
of some Picards among the inmates, inflicted a heavy loss on
the English king by capturing a fortress called the Poil which

[3] The grant, not of 20,000 marks but of £20,000, was made on 2 June. The
rate per sack of the wool subsidy mentioned was that on exports carried by alien
merchants; the denizen rate was 50s. See above, p. 290 and nn.

[4] A reference to Pole's second escape to the Continent, after the king's
consent, on 17 Nov. 1387, to his trial in parliament; for his route see Froissart,
Chroniques, xii. 286. The search for Pole in Hull was put in hand on or about 20
Dec. (*Issues of the Exchequer, Henry III to Henry VI*, ed. Devon, p. 234). For
Pole's death see below, p. 404; and for de Vere's escape overseas late in 1387,
above, pp. 222-4.

1388 dampnum regis Anglorum ceperunt[1] ac eciam usque adhuc
possident et tenent.

Item[a] circa principium mensis Aprilis venit ad regem
dominus Johannes Holand miles et frater regis[b] narrans de[c]
tractatu inter ducem Lancastr' et regem Hispannie habito
(prout supra premittitur folio x[mo].);[2] et ob spem finalis concordie idem dux intendit morari apud Bayonam per tempora
longiora donec suum consequatur effectum.

Item xiij. die Aprilis[3] parliamento resumpto illi de communitate pecierunt instanter dictos milites in Turri London'
detentos adjudicari; qui hoc audientes celeriter procurarunt
dominum Ricardum Scrop, dominum Johannem Coboham
et dominum Johannem Deverose[4] milites transire ad illos
ut iterato possent respondere super articulis memoratis:
quorum peticioni dicta communitas nullatenus adquievit.
Tunc divertebant se ad alia, scilicet ad mercandisas diversas,

p. 180 decernentes utile fore regno ut / unusquisque sua mercimonia
libere vendere poterit ubicumque sibi placuerit non obstante
libertate cuicumque civitati concessa. Placuit istud universis,
et ut sic fieret postea per parliamentum fuit decretum.[5]

Item xvij. die Aprilis[6] quedam generosa[d] mulier rem
nephariam in absencia sui mariti habuit cum quodam presbitero; unde suasu dicte mulieris virum suum de transmarinis
partibus redeuntem prefatus presbiter insanus occidit in lecto
suo jacentem. Illi vero incontinenti [e]summo mane[e] in aurora
et in eodem lecto dormientes fuerant intercepti et de tanto
facinore palam convicti presbiter in carcere fuit detrusus,[f]
ubi penas condignas sustinuit usque ad mortem, mulier vero
die quo supra juxta Bermundesey ad furcas fuit combusta.[7]

[a] Cave in the margin opposite this passage but partly bled off.   [b] Interlined.
[c] Interlined.   [d] Added in the margin.   [e-e] Added in the margin.   [f] fuit
and the first two letters of detrusus are marginal additions.

[1] See Cal. Pat. R., 1385-9, pp. 495, 522; and for the situation of Poil, History
of the King's Works, ed. H. M. Colvin (London, 1963-   ), i. 456.
[2] Above, p. 194 and n., Lancaster's envoy in these negotiations was in fact
Sir Thomas Percy (below, p. 344). Holland left Lancaster's company in the early
summer of 1387 (Russell, English Intervention, pp. 485-6).
[3] Cf. above, p. 290 (15 Apr.).   [4] For these three see above, p. 232.
[5] A reference to the statute 11 Richard II, cap. 7; but this was not enacted
until 14 May (below, p. 334 and n.).
[6] The date is in fact that of the final episode in the story here related.
[7] The people concerned were Andrew Wanton, his wife, Elizabeth, and his

stands in the marshes near Calais;[1] indeed they have it in their 1388 possession to this day.

Sir John Holland, the king's brother, arrived at the court about the beginning of April to report on the negotiations conducted between the duke of Lancaster and the king of Spain (described above, ten folios back);[2] in view of his hope of a final agreement the duke proposed to wait some further time at Bayonne until his object was achieved.

When the parliament reassembled, the commons presented on 13 April[3] an urgent petition that it should proceed to judgement on the knights confined in the Tower of London, who, on hearing of this, hastily contrived to send by the medium of Sir Richard Scrope, Sir John Cobham, and Sir John Devereux[4] a request for a second opportunity of replying to the articles mentioned above: but to this request the commons utterly refused to agree. The parliament then turned its attention to other business concerning various commodities and decided that it would be in the interest of the realm for everybody to be free to sell his wares wherever he chose, notwithstanding the privileges that any city enjoyed by grant. This was universally approved, and it was decreed by the parliament that so for the future it should be.[5]

17 April.[6] In her husband's absence, a woman of family was guilty of criminal connection with a priest, and in the upshot, on the husband's return from overseas, the besotted priest was persuaded by the woman to kill him as he lay in his bed. The pair were quickly seized very early one morning as, with dawn breaking, they slept in the same bed; and after they had been publicly convicted of the monstrous deed the priest was clapped in prison, there to be subjected to condign punishment that ended only with his death, while the woman was burned at the stake near Bermondsey on the day mentioned above.[7]

chaplain, Robert Blake. The chaplain, together with John Bal, a servant of Wanton's, was convicted of the murder, and the wife of 'consent and aid', at the gaol delivery of Winchester Castle in July 1387, when the woman's execution was respited, because of her pregnancy, until the next gaol delivery, in Feb. 1388. Her case was meanwhile removed into the King's Bench, where judgement was given at the quinzaine of Easter 1388 that execution should proceed. See P.R.O., J.I., 3/174, rot. 2; ibid., K.B., 27/508, Rex rot. 4; and V.C.H. Hants., iii. 96. (I am indebted for these references to Mr. Hector.) The penalty of burning inflicted on the woman shows that her offence was deemed to be petty treason (Bellamy, Law of Treason, pp. 226 ff.).

1388   Quo in tempore fuit proclamatum London' quod omnes habentes bona illorum qui se retraxerunt contempnentes ad parliamentum venire sive illorum qui sunt condempnati ad mortem ea cancellario et thesaurario exhiberent, revelarent et dictis officiariis sursum liberarent, sub forisfactura omnium suorum bonorum etc.[1]

Item xviij. die Aprilis misit rex pro cartis et privilegiis Westmon' apud Kenyngton' et in presencia cancellarii,[2] episcopi Wynton',[3] domini Johannis Deverose seneschalli domini regis et aliorum magnorum tunc ibidem existencium ejus jussu erant perlecta, et profecto istis de causis. Cancellarius quoque Anglie pro nichilo[a] reputabat quemquam de sanctuario extrahere confugientem ad illud, ejusque bona tanquam si essent fisco regio merito nichilominus confiscanda absque consciencia vellet ea quadam violencia asportare; quibus contrarium cavetur quod non solum rei sanguinis ac aliis criminibus quibuscumque irretiti dicta inmunitate gauderent cum bonis omnibus eorundem verum eciam eadem libertate alii infames cujuscumque condicionis, licet sint rei majestatis regie obnoxii, inibi potirentur.[4] Ad ista vero episcopus[b] quasi concludendo respondit satis versute: 'Ergo et si rex a quoquam ibi occideretur, adhuc libertate ista pensata salvaretur ibidem; quod esset absurdum. Immo pocius totum privilegium ejusdem loci melius foret destruere quam talia enormia sustinere.' In hoc ultimo et in omnibus aliis fuit derisus, quia non est compertum quod aliquis regum precedencium[c] in tam sacro loco taliter suam vitam finiret nec est presumendum in posterum ita fieri debere contrariis penitus annullatis. Ad hec vero rex applaudebat, asserens

---

[a] par *expunged after this word.*   [b] *Interlined.*   [c] *A short erasure, covered by a dash, follows.*

---

[1] Cf. above, p. 300 n.   [2] Thomas Arundel, since 3 Apr., archbishop of York.
[3] William of Wykeham, bishop of Winchester 1367–1404.
[4] The privilege of sanctuary at Westminster rested on putative charters of Edgar and Edward the Confessor, which granted life and limb, but not explicitly possessions, to offenders against the king and the king's majesty. In 1378, after discussion in parliament, fraudulent debt and trespass were excepted from the scope of sanctuary at the Abbey, but the privilege in cases of felony was confirmed. Thus in 1388 the monks had a good case. The content and vocabulary of the above passage suggest that the Monk had a written source, the work of someone well versed in the legal technicalities; very likely he had the entire

Proclamation was made in London at this time that all 1388
who had in their possession goods belonging to those who
had withdrawn themselves and disdained to attend the parliament or to those who had been condemned to death should,
on pain of forfeiture of all their own goods etc., produce
and disclose them to the chancellor and the treasurer and
deliver them up to those officers.[1]

The king sent on 18 April for the charters and evidences
of Westminster's privileges to be brought to Kennington,
where they were read by his order in the hearing of the
chancellor,[2] the bishop of Winchester,[3] Sir John Devereux,
the king's steward, and other prominent persons in attendance. The occasion was as follows. The chancellor of England
himself thought it nothing for a fugitive to be dragged out of
sanctuary, and he was prepared without compunction to use
a measure of force to remove that fugitive's goods as if,
despite the violation of sanctuary, they were properly forfeit
to the royal exchequer. But provision is to the contrary, that
not only should the blood-guilty and those accused of any
other offence whatever, together with all their possessions,
enjoy the immunity concerned, but others with a bad name,
whatever their station and even though they may be open
to the charge of treason against the king, should in sanctuary
be awarded the same rights.[4] In his reply the bishop, with
some astuteness, affected to draw an inference from this:
'So, even if the king were to be killed in the sanctuary by
somebody, his slayer would still be safe there, if this right
were conceded; and that would be absurd. No, rather than
suffer such outrageous consequences it would be better to
do away altogether with the privilege attaching to the place.'
By this last argument as indeed by all the others, he exposed
himself to ridicule, since none of the kings of the past is
known to have ended his life that way in a spot so hallowed,
and it is not to be supposed that such a thing need happen
in the future, even if all objections to sanctuary were over-
ruled. This indeed was the view favoured by the king, who

dossier which the monks of Westminster took to Kennington in 1388. See P. H.
Sawyer, *Anglo-Saxon Charters: An Annotated List and Bibliography* (London,
1968), nos. 774, 1039, 1043; *R.P.*, iii. 51 (cf. ibid., 37); and Aston, *Thomas
Arundel*, pp. 346–7, and above, pp. 142–4.

1388 omnes illos extractores Roberti Tresilian de sanctuario Sancti
Petri Westmon' cum consencientibus et agentibus fore profecto excommunicacionis sentencia innodatos.

Ecce quomodo nobilis rex ecclesiam Dei veneratur et
diligit! Quam affectuose et sollicite satagit ejus libertates
defendere ac eciam conservare! Verum nullus episcoporum tantum zelat pro juribus ecclesie quantum ipse, unde
multociens, nisi ipse solus fuisset, suas libertates forsitan
perdidisset. Patet namque de quodam scutifero Lollardo,
qui denegavit debitas solvere decimas abbati de Osneye;
quare ad prosecucionem dicti abbatis fuit captus et in
carceribus aliquamdiu detentus. Ille vero per brevia regia a
Michaele de la Pole tunc temporis cancellario[1] cum favore
habita et concessa de carcere nitebatur evadere et totum
processum predicti abbatis penitus annullare; quod audiens
abbas predictus conquestus est archiepiscopo Cantuar', qui
confestim regem adivit et narravit sibi totum processum,
rogansque eum obnixe ne permitteret talia procedere contra
ecclesiasticas libertates. Cui rex ait: 'Volumus quod jura
ecclesiastica omnino serventur illesa;[a] ideo non obstantibus
nostris brevibus quibuscumque procedatis canonice secundum jura vestra contra eum et involvatis eum censuris
ecclesiasticis tam acerbe et tamdiu quousque reatum suum
agnoscat et libenter promittat dicto abbati satisfacere super
dampnis premissis et super hoc inveniat sufficientes fide-
jussores stare mandatis ecclesie; contradictores vero in
hac parte quoscumque monicione premissa ab hujusmodi
molestacionibus desistere compellatis. Procedatis namque in
causis ecclesiasticis secundum jura vestra, quia revera nolumus
nec intendimus in aliquo juri ecclesiastico derogare.' Liquet
profecto clare ex premissis quanta reverencia et veneracione
habet ecclesiam Dei rex iste, quia nisi mediacione dicti
archiepiscopi ipse taliter concessisset[b] prefatus abbas totum
processum et jus suum forsitan amisisset eo quod secularis
potestas et laicalis aviditas contra eum fortiter decertabant.

[a] *In the margin but marked for insertion here.*   [b] MS. concessissit.

---

[1] Pole was chancellor from 13 Mar. 1383 to 23 Oct. 1386. The astute squire
no doubt applied for a writ of prohibition, halting the case in the ecclesiastical
courts.

maintained that all those who had dragged Robert Tresilian 1388
out of the sanctuary of St. Peter, Westminster, together with
those who had acquiesced or taken part in the act, were involved forthwith in a sentence of excommunication.

How this noble king reveres and loves God's Church!
How sympathetically and anxiously he exerts himself to
champion her liberties and preserve them! Why there is not
a bishop so jealous as he is for the rights of the Church, so
that on many occasions, but for him and him alone, she
might have lost her privileges. So much is apparent from the
case of the Lollard squire who refused to pay to the abbot
of Osney the tithes due to him and was in consequence
arrested at the suit of the abbot and kept for some time in
confinement. Having by favour obtained the issue of certain
royal writs by Michael de la Pole, chancellor at the time,[1] he
strove to secure his release from prison and the complete
annulment of the whole of the abbot's process against him.
When he heard of this, the abbot complained to the archbishop of Canterbury, who hurried to the king and told him
the whole story, earnestly begging him not to allow
behaviour of this sort to be carried on against the liberties
of the Church. 'It is our will', the king told him, 'that the
rights of the Church shall be preserved entirely unimpaired.
You are therefore, notwithstanding any writs of ours, to proceed against this man, under canon law in accordance with
your rights, and to implicate him in the censures of the
Church for as long and with as much severity as will make
him admit his offence and freely promise to satisfy the
abbot's claim for redress and in this matter find adequate
sureties that he will abide by the behests of the Church; those
who would gainsay you in this, whoever they are, you are
to compel, after first warning them, to cease such harassment. In ecclesiastical causes you are to proceed in accordance with your rights, because in truth we neither wish nor
intend to detract in any way from the right of the Church.'
From the foregoing it is very clear in what awe and reverence
this king of ours holds God's Church, since but for this concession made at the archbishop's intervention, the abbot
might have lost the whole of his process and also his right, for
worldly power and lay cupidity fought strongly against him.

1388 In multis enim casibus antea sicut nunc rex iste sepe pro ecclesia et tuicione suorum jurium clipeum defensionis objecit; que omnia hic propter prolixitatem omitto.

Predicti vero domini super eorum appellacionibus finem facere cupientes per unam quindenam et amplius laborabant quomodo execucionem possent habere de illis qui olim circa regem steterunt et illum interim*a* nequiter gubernabant, set non valebant deducere ad effectum propter potenciam procuratam pro parte adversa quod ardencius peroptabant.[1] Unde xxvij. die Aprilis in pleno parliamento ex parte Simonis de Burle surrexit dux Eboracen', asserens dictum Simonem fidelem fuisse hominem in cunctis negociis tam regi quam regno; et si quis hoc vellet negare vel contradicere, ipse affirmaret ipsum falsum dixisse, et hoc probaret duello. Cui respondit dux Gloucestr' quod sue ligiancie fuit falsus, et hoc optulit *b*se probaturum,*b* si fuisset opus, manu sua dextera sine multis racionibus. Ad hec dux Ebor' excanduit dixitque fratri suo quod menciebatur: cui dux Gloucestr' verba consimilia confestim retorsit; sicque affati unus irruisset in alium nisi rex utpote clemens et benignus eos cicius pacificasset. Igitur protelatum fuit negocium postea per quinque dies sequentes:[2] interim pro isto et aliis gravaminibus ubique in regno communitas ejusdem habuit colloquium cum domino nostro rege, cui promisit pius rex ea velle concedere que cedere poterunt ad comodum sibi et regno.

Illo quoque tempore Flandrenses miserunt ad regem Francorum pro pace habenda cum Anglicis et cum omnibus aliis sibi propinquis; qui ab eisdem accepta ingenti summa pecunie concessit eis ilico quod petebant.[3] Illi vero statim miserunt quosdam valentes de suis ad tractandum cum consilio domini regis super premissis; qui per totum fere tempus

---

a Interlined.   *b-b* Written over an erasure.

---

[1] Cf. *Favent*, p. 21, recording a division in the ranks of the Appellants at this juncture: Gloucester, Arundel, and Warwick supported the demand of the Commons for a capital sentence on Burley, but Derby and Nottingham wished his life to be spared.

[2] i.e. on the next 5 days of parliamentary business: Burley's case was not considered in full parliament between Tue., 28 Apr. and Mon., 4 May inclusive.

[3] If so, Charles VI authorized negotiations on the part of the leading Flemish

As in this, so in many earlier cases this king repeatedly 1388
interposed a buckler of defence on behalf of the Church
to safeguard her rights, but to avoid prolixity I omit them
here.

The lords above-mentioned, anxious to press their appeals
to a conclusion, worked for a fortnight or more on means
to have execution done upon those who had formerly surrounded the king and at that time exerted an evil influence
on him, but owing to the strength enlisted for the opposition
they were unable to realize their fervently cherished desire.[1]
Thus on 27 April, the duke of York rose in full parliament on
behalf of Sir Simon Burley, who, he declared, had been in
all his dealings loyal to the king and the realm; and to anybody who wished to deny or gainsay this, he would himself
give the lie and prove his point in personal combat. In reply
the duke of Gloucester said that Burley had been false to
his allegiance, and this he offered to prove, if need were,
with his own sword-arm and without multiplying arguments.
At this the duke of York turned white with anger and told
his brother to his face that he was a liar, only to receive a
prompt retort in kind from the duke of Gloucester; and after
this exchange they would have hurled themselves upon each
other had not the king with characteristic mildness and goodwill, been quick to calm them down. This matter was accordingly put off for the next five days:[2] and in the meantime
the commons discussed it, and other causes of complaint up
and down the country, with the king who, always mindful
of his duty, undertook to make whatever concessions would
tend to his own and his kingdom's advantage.

The Flemings sent messengers at this time to ask the king
of the French for leave to make peace with the English and
with all the rest of their neighbours; upon receipt from them
of a very large sum of money he met their request there and
then.[3] They at once dispatched some of their leading men to
negotiate terms with the king's council; the envoys were here

towns that had no licence from Philip the Bold, duke of Burgundy and count
of Flanders. On 15 May, however, on the eve of the conference at Calais which
the Monk mentions below, and under pressure from the English, the Flemings
asked Philip the Bold to participate (*Handelingen van de Leden en Van de Staten
ven Vlaanderen (1384-1405)*, ed. W. Prevenier (Commission royale d'histoire,
Brussels, 1959), pp. 425-6). See also Knighton, *Chronicon*, ii. 270-1.

1388 parliamenti jugiter affuerunt, et quamvis aliqui eorum ad eorum patriam redierunt, nichilominus tamen*a* unus eorum affuit semper presens pro eorum negociis expediendis.

p. 181 Rex vero et ceteri domini multum zelabant pro vita domini Simonis de / Burle miseruntque ad comunes ducem Ebor' et dominum Johannem Coboham ut iterato dictus Simon omnino admitteretur respondere ad articulos supradictos. Responderunt communes hoc nequaquam fieri posse modo quia ejus responsiones sunt perpetualiter in recordo redacte. Ad hec dictus J. Coboham intulit, dicens ipsum fuisse infirmum protunc et ideo micius et graciosus est agendum cum eo. Ista et alia plura inseruit pro eo set non fuerunt ab illis admissa.[1]

Item xx. die Aprilis concessum est in parliamento transmittere quosdam Cales' ad tractandum de pace cum Flandrensibus et quosdam apud Pruissiam ad tractandum eciam cum eisdem de pace.[2] Sequenti vero die misit rex duos milites ad communes, rogans illos ut ob reverenciam Sancti Georgii universa quiescerent usque xxv. diem Aprilis; quodque gratanti animo concesserunt.

Item xx. die Aprilis coram magistro Thoma Southam subcollectore domini pape et aliis episcopis ac magistris in theologia aliisque graduatis examinati fuerunt quatuor Lollardi super predicacionibus eorum et quomodo senciebant de fide et aliis articulis; in quibus male se habebant, et profecto in multis inventi sunt culpabiles; quorum duo ad unitatem fidei sunt conversi, alii vero duo in carceribus sunt projecti quousque fuerit determinatum quid de illis facerent juxta canonicas sancciones.

Item quinto die Maii non obstantibus precibus et suasionibus regis et regine aliorumque magnorum fuit dominus Simon Burle per processum parliamenti adjudicatus trahi et suspendi ac postremo decapitari, set quia fuit miles de la Gartere omnia fuerunt sibi remissa solummodo decapitacione excepta;[3] sicque de Westmonasterio ligatis post terga manibus

---

a Interlined.

[1] Cf. above, pp. 286-8, 318; and for the articles, presented by the commons in writing on 17 Mar., above, pp. 268 ff.

[2] For the embassy for the negotiations at Calais see Rymer, *Foedera*, vii. 581-2; cf. P.R.O., E.364/22, mm. 22^V, 23, and ibid., E. 403/519, 16 May, 5 June;

almost without interruption throughout the duration of the 1388
parliament, and though some of them returned home, there
was always one of them on hand to forward their business.

In deep concern for the life of Sir Simon Burley, the king
and the rest of the lords sent the duke of York and Sir John
Cobham to the commons to ask that he should at least be
admitted to answer a second time to the articles above-
mentioned. The commons replied that this was now impossible since his answers were a matter of definitive written
record. Here Sir John Cobham interrupted to say that he had
been a sick man at the time and that he ought on that
account to be treated with more gentleness and indulgence,
but this, like a number of other arguments in his favour interposed by Sir John, was not accepted by the commons.[1]

It was agreed in parliament on 20 April that envoys should
cross to Calais for peace talks with the Flemings and that
others should go to Prussia for similar negotiations.[2] On the
following day the king sent to the commons two knights with
a request, that out of veneration for St. George all business
should remain in abeyance until 25 April; and to this they
willingly agreed.

It was also on 20 April that before Master Thomas Southam,
the pope's sub-collector, and a tribunal including bishops,
masters in theology, and other graduates, four Lollards were
questioned about their preaching and their religious views and
also upon other articles; they did not acquit themselves well
and on many points were found unquestionably guilty. Two
of them were converted to the unity of the Church, but the
other two were thrown into prison until it should be decided
what, under the canonical sanctions, was to be done with them.

On 5 May, despite the entreaties and arguments of the king
and queen and other exalted persons, Sir Simon Burley was
condemned by parliamentary process to be drawn and
hanged and finally beheaded; but since he was a knight of
the Garter, the whole sentence, except only for the beheading, was remitted;[3] and so, with his hands tied behind him, he

and for that appointed to treat with the Prussian towns of the German Hanse,
with which there had been virtually no commercial intercourse since 1385, *Cal.
Cl. R., 1385-9*, p. 403; Rymer, op. cit., vii. 581; E. Power and M. M. Postan,
Studies in English Trade in the Fifteenth Century (London, 1933), pp. 107-8.
See also below, p. 368 and n.   [3] Cf. above, p. 292.

1388 gradiens via regia per medium civitatis London' usque Tour-
hull', ubi fuit decapitatus et in Nova Abbacia ibi deprope
est sepultus. Duodecimo vero die Maii domini Johannes
Beauchamp', Jacobus Berneres, et Johannes Salesbury consimilem sentenciam acceperunt: relaxata sunt omnia dictis
J. Beauch' et J. Berneres decollacione excepta, quia erant
generosi valde ac^a quia prefatus J. Beauchamp' fuit paulo
ante seneschallus hospicii domini nostri regis.[1] Igitur isti duo
transierunt modo quo supra et juxta Turrim London' fuerant
decollati: J. vero Beauchamp' sepultus est apud Wyrcestr'
in monasterio Sancte Marie et J. Berneres apud Westmonasterium est humatus in capella Sancti Johannis Baptiste.
J. vero Salesbury, eo quod fuerat appellatus de prodicione
facta per eum tam infra regnum quam extra,[2] de Turri
London' per medium civitatis usque Tybourne fuit tractus
et ibi suspensus, sepultusque est apud Westmonasterium
juxta J. Berneres in prelibata capella. Quo eciam die
episcopus ^{b}Cicestr' amisit temporalia sua et omnia bona sua
mobilia et inmobilia^b judicio parliamenti.[3]

Dux vero Glouc' et dominus Johannes Coboham onerarunt
consciencias suas eo quod Robertum Tresilyan de sanctuario
Westmon' violenter extraxerint: xv. die Maii venerunt et
submiserunt se^c domino abbati, promittentes se satisfacere
juxta posse. Ulterius processerunt in parliamento domini
et comunes de regis gubernacione et que persone pro ejus
regimine circa se haberentur. Demum convenerunt quod duo
episcopi London' et Wynton'[4] et comes Warwyk' ac domini
J. Coboham et Ricardus Scrop' jugiter sibi astarent, nichilque
faceret sine consensu eorum; item dominum Petrum de
Courteneye statuerunt camerarium domini regis, quem rex
grato animo acceptavit.[5]

Quo in tempore papa peciit subsidium a clero, set illi
de parliamento hoc sagaciter advertentes ordinarunt quod

^{a} MS. at. $^{b-b}$ Underlined in red, apparently by Parker; and there is a contemporary pointing hand in the margin. ^{c} Interlined.

---

[1] Cf. above, p. 292 and n.; and for Beauchamp's removal from office on 31
Dec. 1387, above, p. 228.
[2] A reference to Article 16 of the impeachment, for which see above, pp.
278 and 293 n.
[3] Cf. above, p. 294 n.

was marched from Westminster along the king's highway 1388 through the city of London to Tower Hill, where he was beheaded, being buried in New Abbey close by. On 12 May Sir John Beauchamp, Sir James Berners, and Sir John Salisbury received a similar sentence, of which all except the beheading was remitted for Sir John Beauchamp and Sir James Berners because they were of gentle birth and because Sir John Beauchamp had shortly before been steward of the king's household.[1] These two therefore made the journey described above and were beheaded near the Tower of London, John Beauchamp being buried at Worcester in St. Mary's Abbey and James Berners in the chapel of St. John the Baptist at Westminster. Because he had been appealed of treason committed both within the realm and outside it,[2] John Salisbury was drawn from the Tower of London through the city to Tyburn and there hanged: he was buried at Westminster near James Berners in the above-mentioned chapel. On the same day the bishop of Chichester, as a result of a judgement in parliament, lost his temporalities and all his goods, movable and immovable.[3]

The duke of Gloucester and Sir John Cobham had it heavily on their consciences that they had dragged Robert Tresilian by force out of the Westminster sanctuary. They came on 15 May and submitted themselves to the abbot, promising to make satisfaction so far as lay in their power. In the parliament the lords and commons pursued the subject of control over the king and the choice of persons to surround him and guide him. It was finally agreed that two bishops, London and Winchester,[4] the earl of Warwick, and Sir John Cobham and Sir Richard Scrope should be in constant attendance upon him and that he should do nothing without their consent. Sir Peter Courtenay was appointed the king's chamberlain, and the king was well pleased to accept him.[5]

The pope just now demanded a subsidy from the clergy, and with a shrewd eye to the situation members of the

[4] Respectively Robert Braybrooke and William of Wykeham. It is, however, unlikely that any councillors were appointed for the king before the concluding stages of the parliament.

[5] Courtenay was appointed chief chamberlain, in the place of Robert de Vere, on 12 Feb. 1388 (*Cal. Pat. R., 1385-9*, p. 383). He was a kinsman of the king and formerly a knight of the chamber.

1388 faceret translaciones episcoporum videlicet quod Elyens' ad Eborac', Dunelmens' ad Elien', Bathoniens' ad Dunelmens' et^a Salesburien' ad Bathonien' ecclesias concederet pertransire et dominum Johannem Waltham clericum privati sigilli in Sar' episcopum confirmaret; que omnia domino pape fuerunt directa.[1] Papa vero super istis consultus annuit peticioni eorum et transtulit archiepiscopum Eboracen' ad archiepiscopatum Sancti Andree in Scocia, set quia tota fuit scismatica ibidem habere introitum non potuit nisi manu forti eosdem Scotos viriliter debellasset.

Item xiiij.^{mo} die Maii ordinatum est in pleno parliamento quod omnes amici regno Anglie ac omnes regis ligii homines ubicumque in Anglia libere possent emere et vendere secundum statutum Edwardi tercii anno nono non obstante privilegio aut statuto.[2] Sicque per hoc civitas London' et alie civitates utrobique in Anglia suas libertates, immo quantum ad hoc sua privilegia, perdiderunt et non inmerito, quia in principio parliamenti quidam merceri, aurifabri, pannarii et alii inquieti in civitate London' porrexerunt billas in dicto parliamento contra piscarios et vinetarios, asserentes eos fore vitallarios, judicantes eos indignos tam celebrem regere civitatem.[3] Isti namque turbatores eorum perversis adinvencionibus et maliciis illam pocius nituntur destruere quam permittere,^{b} ut apparet, sua libertate gaudere, nam majorem eorum Nicholaum Exton' pecierunt deponi et manifeste contra eorum privilegia et statuta per extraneum judicem

^{a} *Interlined.* ^{b} *Interlined.*

---

[1] These requests were for the translation of Thomas Arundel from Ely to York, of John Fordham from Durham to Ely, of Walter Skirlaw from Bath and Wells to Durham, and of Ralph Erghum from Salisbury to Bath and Wells. Urban VI acceded to them in bulls issued on 3 Apr. 1388, the date on which he also provided John Waltham, keeper of the privy seal, to the see of Salisbury and translated Alexander Nevill, archbishop of York, to St. Andrews. Even so the caritative subsidy of a half-tenth for which he had asked the English clergy eluded him. See Rymer, *Foedera*, vii. 573–7; *Cal. Papal Letters*, iv *(1362–1404)*, pp. 272–3; *Perroy*, pp. 305 ff. Cf. *Favent*, p. 22; R. G. Davies, 'The Episcopate and the Political Crisis in England of 1386–1388', in *Speculum*, li (1976), 674 ff.

[2] A reference to 11 Richard II, *cap.* 7, confirming 9 Edward III, statute 1, *cap.* 1, and 25 Edward III, statute 3, *cap.* 2; these statutes established free trade for foreigners and denizens within the realm in victuals and all other merchandise. See *R.P.*, iii. 247; *S.R.*, i. 270, 314–15; ii. 53–4; *Letter Book H*, p. 325. The crucial issue was the trade in victuals. By confirming the statutes of 1335 and

parliament laid it down that he should effect translations 1388
among the bishops and agree that Ely should move to
York, Durham to Ely, Bath to Durham, and Salisbury to
Bath, while Master John Waltham clerk of the privy seal
should be confirmed in the bishopric of Salisbury; and all
these proposals were conveyed to the pope.[1] After taking
counsel the pope met the request and translated the archbishop of York to the archbishopric of St. Andrew's in
Scotland, but since that entire country was in schism he
could not gain admittance there except by the drastic
expedient of first subjugating the Scots in hard-fought
battle.

It was enacted in full parliament on 14 May that all
persons in friendship with the English kingdom and all the
king's subjects throughout England were to be free to buy
and sell in conformity with the statute of 9 Edward III, any
privilege or statute notwithstanding.[2] As a result, London
and other cities in various parts of England lost their liberties
— indeed, for the matter of that, their privileges, as they
deserved to do, for at the beginning of the parliament certain
mercers, goldsmiths, drapers, and other restless elements in
the city of London presented in the parliament bills of
complaint against the fishmongers and the vintners, whom
they described as victuallers, unfitted in their judgement to
control a city so illustrious.[3] These trouble-makers, with their
wrong-headed new doctrines and their ill-natured behaviour,
apply their efforts rather to the city's undoing than to
letting it enjoy its liberties, as events show, for they
petitioned that their mayor, Nicholas Exton, should be
deposed and (in flagrant breach of the citizens' privileges and
statutes) examined and have judgement passed upon him

1351 in preference to that of 1382 (6 Richard II, statute 1, caps. 10-11), which
had more recently established free trade within the realm in victuals, the Merciless
Parliament left dormant the issue of whether or not victuallers might hold judicial
office; another clause in the statute of 1382 (cap. 9) took this freedom from them
(S.R., ii. 28). But see also below, p. 366. In London the freedom of non-
citizens to sell fish and other victuals in the City had been established by an ordinance of the mayor and aldermen of 31 July 1384 (Letter Book H, p. 244).

[3] An attempt to use the statute of 1382 to exclude fishmongers and vintners
from office in London. The fishmongers were unquestionably victuallers; the
vintners traded on an altogether larger scale and had interests in the non-victualling
export trade.

1388 examinari ac eciam judicari.[1] Set nequaquam fuerant in hujusmodi exauditi.

Item de istis justiciariis de nece dominorum*a* convictis domini et tota communitas regni sollicite in isto parliamento tractarunt:[2] demum sic finaliter concordarunt, scilicet quod ad Hiberniam in exilium pro perpetuo mitterentur et quod procul abinvicem separentur,*b* quod eciam de locis suis inibi limitatis sub pena mortis ultra tria miliaria non exirent quodque annuatim certam summam pecunie de fisco regio pro eorum sustentacione quilibet eorundem haberet.

Item*c* xxvij. die Maii quidam clericus[3] provisione pape fovens litem contra alium racione cujusdam beneficii tunc vacantis venitque ad sanctuarium Westmon' gracia tuicionis sue persone; qui sepius tempore istius parliamenti porrexit cancellario tunc Elien' episcopo[4] billas diversas, rogans attencius quatenus ad jus suum vellet habere respectum. Cancellarius vero ad suas supplicaciones minime advertebat, quia pocius stetit cum suo adversario quam cum illo; propter quod dictus clericus confecit unam magnam litteram in qua multa convicia inseruit de cancellario antedicto aliaque nova in eadem tangencia statum regni stulte et insipienter expressit. Hanc quidem litteram cuidam Romepete tradidit ad bajulandum suo socio in Romana curia commoranti: bajulus vero habens facere cum cancellario prescius de insertis in predicta littera de eodem episcopo*d* contentis illam sibi
p. 182 ad captandum / sue dominacionis benivolenciam presentavit. Qua perlecta misit illum perlegi coram toto et pleno parliamento; qua audita protinus omnes exarserunt in iram, adjudicantes ipsum vita indignum tanquam falsissimum proditorem

---

a Sc. approbanda *or some such word.*   *b* Sic, for separarentur.   *c* Nota de clerico *in the margin.*   *d* Written above the word which precedes it here.

---

[1] A reference to the claim of the citizens of London to be impleaded only in courts within the City, deriving from Henry I's charters for the City, for which see C. N. L. Brooke, G. Keir, and S. Reynolds, 'Henry I's charter for the City of London', in *Journal of the Society of Archivists*, iv (1970–3), 575–6. Nicholas Exton, mayor since 1386, was a fishmonger. Cf. *Cal. Pat. R., 1385–9*, p. 514.

[2] For this charge see *R.P.*, iii. 240, and for the judgement against the justices on 6 Mar. 1388, above, pp. 286, 316. The decision to exile them was reached in the last days of the parliament, after the feast assigned by the Monk to 1 June (below, p. 340 and n.; *Favent*, p. 23). Bealknap and Holt were exiled to Drogheda, Fulthorpe and Burgh to Dublin, Cary and Lockton to Waterford. Each was restricted to movement to within 2 or 3 leagues of his place of exile.

by a judge from outside.[1] They were quite unable, however, to gain a hearing for such demands as this.

There was anxious discussion in this parliament by the lords and by the entire commons of the realm about the justices who had been convicted of [countenancing] the death of the lords.[2] It was finally agreed that they should be banished for life to Ireland, where they were to be widely separated from one another and were moreover not to move, on pain of death, more than three miles from the places expressly designated for them; and each of them was to receive yearly for his maintenance a certain sum of money from the royal exchequer.

On 27 May a clerk,[3] who on the strength of a papal provision had instituted proceedings against another about a benefice then vacant, went into sanctuary at Westminster for his personal safety. Several times in the course of this parliament he had addressed to the chancellor, then bishop of Ely,[4] sundry bills earnestly begging him to consider the justice of his case. But the chancellor, whose sympathies lay rather with his opponent than himself, paid no attention to his entreaties. The clerk accordingly concocted a lengthy letter in which he incorporated a good deal of abuse of the chancellor and was also so stupid and unwise as to recount news which touched on matters of state. This letter he handed to a Rome-bound traveller for delivery to an associate of his staying at the papal curia: but the bearer, having some business with the chancellor, and with advance knowledge of the remarks about him included among the contents, made a bid for his lordship's goodwill by presenting the letter to him. After reading it, the chancellor sent it to be read out to a full meeting of the whole parliament, where it was heard in a blaze of immediate and universal indignation, the writer

Bealknap and Fulthorpe were each granted £40 per annum for life, Holt and Burgh, £26. 13s. 4d. each, and Cary and Lockton £20 each. See *R.P.*, iii. 244; *Cal. Cl. R., 1385-9*, pp. 515-16.

[3] Probably William de Chesterton, parson of Rattlesden (Suff.), in the diocese of Norwich; if so the benefice in contention was Yaxley (Hunts.), in the diocese of Lincoln (*Cal. Pat. R., 1388-92*, p. 92; *Cal. Papal Letters*, iv (*1362-1404*), pp. 372, 379). For the episode see also Aston, *Thomas Arundel*, p. 348; and for Chesterton, above, p. 302.

[4] The chancellor, Thomas Arundel, had been provided to the see of York on 3 April 1388 but did not receive the temporalities until 14 Sept.

1388 qui tam audacter regni secreta presumeret propalare; non
obstante sanctuario supradicto ipsum vellent festinanter
vita privare, set confestim miserunt pro abbate ut ad eos in
propria persona veniret. Qui venit et[a] astitit coram eis;
statimque sibi erat tota materia declarata, qui[b] per mollia
verba nitebatur eos sedare et dictum clericum de eorum
manibus liberare. Illi vero econtrario magnis vocibus ex-
clamantes dixerunt sanctuarium non debere ipsum salvare,
quia deliquit in eo; et si vellet tenere quod tales salvaret
posset esse causa destruccionis regni tocius, quod absit.
Plura et alia verba fuerunt sibi prolata, set demum onerarunt ipsum[b] abbatem prefatum clericum custodire usque in
diem quartum[b] sub pena sua temporalia amittendi ut
interim discuteretur per parliamentum qualem penam
clericus sepedictus subiret. Quod audiens clericus antedictus preparavit se tam Deo quam mundo ac si continuo
moreretur et collocavit se juxta feretrum Sancti Edwardi
opem et juvamen ab ipso jugiter implorando.

Penultimo vero die Maii sub manucapcione liberati sunt
de Turri London' milites, scilicet[b] domini Willelmus Elmham, Thomas Trivet, et Nicholaus Daggeworthe, sub hac
forma quod compareant in proximo parliamento responsuri
ad ea que volunt illis opponere domini supradicti.[1] Quo
eciam die comunes et domini de parliamento pecierunt
prefatum clericum sibi de sanctuario Westmon' liberari aut
in eodem debere pro suis delictis puniri, quia esset absurdum quod delicta remaneant impunita; constat namque
istum contra omnes existentes in regno graviter deliquisse in
revelando regni secreta in exteras regiones, nec tales quampluribus videtur debere defendere aut fovere sanctuarium
prelibatum, set pocius ipsum quantocius ejicere ac seculari
judici tradere puniendum. Rex autem in contrarium sen-
tenciavit, asserens loca privilegiata censuris fore vallata et
si quis hiis contravenerit potest de facili illis involvi, et

---

[a] *An erasure, covered by a dash, follows.*   [b] *Interlined.*

[1] *Cal. Cl. R., 1385-9*, pp. 397-8. The 3 knights had been in custody since
1 Jan. (above, p. 228).

who thus recklessly ventured to publish state secrets being 1388
condemned as the falsest of traitors and unfit to live. Despite
his having taken sanctuary, they would have been ready to
deprive him of his life without more ado, but they did send
an urgent summons to the abbot to wait upon them in
person. When he arrived and faced them, he was at once given
a full account of the affair, whereupon he tried by means of
conciliatory language to calm them down and to save the clerk
from their clutches. They for their part were loud and emphatic in their contention that sanctuary ought not to save
him, since it was in sanctuary that his offence was committed;
and if the abbot wanted to hold that sanctuary provided
safety for people of that sort, it could well cause the ruin of
the whole realm, which Heaven forfend. After several other
arguments had been put to him, they finally made the abbot
responsible, on pain of losing his temporalities, for guarding
the clerk for the next three days, so that the parliament
might meanwhile debate the question what punishment he
should suffer. On hearing of this, the clerk made his arrangements for this world and the next, as if he might die at any
moment, and took up a position by the shrine of St. Edward,
whose help and succour he implored without ceasing.

On 30 May the three knights, William Elmham, Thomas
Trivet, and Nicholas Dagworth, were released under mainprise from the Tower of London with the proviso that they
were to appear in the next parliament to answer whatever
charges the Lords Appellant wished to bring against them.[1]
The commons and the lords of the parliament demanded on
the same day that the clerk mentioned above should be
delivered up to them out of the sanctuary of Westminster
or that he must be punished within the sanctuary for his
misdeeds, since it would be ludicrous for those misdeeds to
remain unpunished; it was beyond dispute that he had committed a serious offence against every inhabitant of the kingdom by disclosing its secrets for transmission to foreign parts,
and to very many people it seemed that, rather than protect-
ing or harbouring persons like him, the sanctuary ought
forthwith to expel him and surrender him to a secular judge
for punishment. The king took a contrary view, maintaining
that these privileged places were hedged about by the Church's

1388 quamdiu eisdem sic fuerit involutus omnia facta sua postmodum ante absolucionem habitam in periculum sue anime*a*
indubie vergere dinoscuntur; 'et ideo de loco sacro quemquam*b* extrahere vel ibidem punire nobis non est; igitur
relinquendum est illius arbitrio puniendum qui habet custodiam dicti loci.' Ulterius promisit illis rex alloqui abbatem
de ista materia et omnia per Dei graciam feliciter terminare.
Set istis non obstantibus, primo die Junii clamosis vocibus
iterato dictam materiam quidam domini et alii de communitate nepharie resumebant, et omnino dictum clericum
tanquam proditorem vellent habere punitum; inter quos erat
dominus Radulphus Basset, qui numquam loquebatur bonum
de ecclesiastica libertate. Protestando dixit melius fore quod
non staret lapis super lapidem[1] in prefato loco quam sic tales
proditores foveret qui taliter secreta regni transmittebant
ad exteras regiones; et revera si permittatur modo tales
salvare, tale inconveniens in posterum forsitan sequeretur
quod ⟨si⟩*c* rex ibidem occideretur a casu (quod absit) ejus
occisor impune inibi plena libertate gauderet, quod omnino
foret absonum racioni.[2] Plura hiis similia contra dominum
abbatem hinc inde diversimode proponebant: postremo jusserunt ipsum dictum clericum custodire usque ad proximum
parliamentum sub pena qua incumbit. *d*j. die Junii*d* rex fecit
grande convivium dominis universis; quo finito comes
Arundell' peciit licenciam a rege eundi ad mare,[3] qua optenta
confestim accinxit se ad iter et x. die Junii cum suis classem
intravit. Item de mense Maii quidam ex nostris in partibus
occidentalibus ceperunt ij. barges, in quibus habuerunt circa
lxxx. homines bene armatos. Item circa finem Maii clerici
in Turri London' inclusi facta securitate de veniendo ad
proximum parliamentum de Turri prefata fuerant liberati.[4]

---

a The letter d has been expunged after this word.   *b* Interlined.   *c* MS.
om.   *d-d* Written above Quo eciam die, which is not deleted.

---

[1] Cf. Matt. xxiv. 2; Mark xiii. 2; Luke xix. 44; xxi. 6.
[2] Cf. above, p. 324, where the identical argument is attributed to William of
Wykeham. For Ralph, Lord Basset of Drayton (d. 1390) see G.E.C., ii. 3.
[3] Cf. Favent, pp. 22-3, who says that the banquet took place on Sun., 31 May,
at Kennington. On 2 June Arundel was given power to conclude a treaty with
the duke of Brittany (Rymer, Foedera, vii. 586-7). See also below, pp. 350-2
and nn.

powers of censure, in which anybody infringing the privileges 1388 might easily find himself involved, and for as long as he was so involved it was notorious that until he obtained absolution all his subsequent actions indisputably tended to imperil his soul; 'it is not, therefore, for us to drag anybody out of a holy place or punish him in it; and his punishment must accordingly be left to the discretion of the person who has the keeping of that place.' The king further undertook to speak to the abbot about the matter and by God's grace to bring the whole affair to a satisfactory conclusion. In spite of this, however, certain of the lords, with support from some of the commons, mischievously took up the matter again on 1 June with a great deal of noise, being wholly set upon getting the clerk punished as a traitor; they included Sir Ralph Basset, who never had a good word to say for the privileges of the Church. By way of protestation he argued that it would be better that there should not be left one stone in the sanctuary standing upon another[1] than that it should shelter traitors of this kind who thus communicated state secrets to foreign parts; indeed if it were allowed on this occasion to save such people, the consequences for the future might be so awkward that if by some chance (which he prayed God would avert) the king were killed in the sanctuary, his slayer would enjoy there complete impunity and liberty; and this would be totally at odds with common sense.[2] Further arguments of this sort, with differences of presentation, were put to the abbot from all sides: in the end he was ordered, subject to the prescribed penalty, to keep the clerk in his custody until the next parliament. On 1 June the king entertained all the lords at a great banquet, at the end of which the earl of Arundel asked leave to make his departure for the coast;[3] having obtained it he at once prepared for the journey and embarked with his forces on 10 June. A further event in May was the capture in the west by some of our country-men of two barges carrying eighty well-equipped fighting men. About the end of May the clerks who had been confined in the Tower of London were released after security had been given for their appearance at the next parliament.[4]

[4] Richard Clifford, John Lincoln, Richard Medford, and Nicholas Slake were released on 4 June, the last day of the parliament (*Cal. Cl. R., 1385-9*, p. 414).

1388 Item secundo[a] die Junii dominus Johannes Holand frater regis
ad peticionem dominorum et communitatis factus est comes
Huntyngdon' [b]dotatusque est a rege cum illo comitatu mille
libris per annum.[b1]

Item iij. die Junii apud Westmon' completa missa solempni
et sermone finito coram magno altari in sede regia eatenus
inibi preparata regnique principibus astantibus ceterisque
dominis universis positis eciam libro et cruce super parvulam
mensam altaris rex suum juramentum quod olim in sua coronacione prestitit renovavit: domini vero tam[c] spirituales quam
temporales ea que domino regi solebant in sua coronacione
prestare cum omni subjeccione ac grato animo[c] sibi exhibu-
erunt.[2] [d]Hiis expletis confestim omnes episcopi sub una stola
coadunati sentenciam excommunicacionis fulminabant in
illos qui hujusmodi sacramentum in posterum presump-
serint violare seu regem contra dominos concitare aut ipsum
eorum falsis suggestionibus provocare;[d] et ad instanciam
dominorum et communitatis omnia que facta erant in presenti parliamento rex pro perpetuo inviolabiliter ratificavit.
Sequenti vero die rex valefaciens et regracians omnibus
unicuique tribuit facultatem ad propria remeare. [e]Et ut omnia
que in dicto parliamento erant gesta firmiter et inviolabiliter
quacumque revocacione cessante pro perpetuo permanerent
et starent irrevocabiliter ⟨et⟩[f] inconcusse quoddam statutum
proinde ediderunt quatinus omnes qui cum predictis dominis
surrexerunt atque illi qui in auxilium ducis Hibernie de comitatibus Cestr', Salopie et Wallie advenerunt starent in gracia
ab omni forisfaccione immunes; contravenientes sive imposterum impugnantes aliquod istorum consimilem penam
subirent qualem tulerunt hii paulo superius nominati.[e3]
Sicque quarto die Junii parliamentum erat finitum.

Rex vero deinceps per totum autumpnum venacioni
indulsit. Circa medium vero mensis Junii magister Alexander

---

[a] Aliter primo *written above this word.* [b-b] *In the margin but marked*
for insertion here. [c] *An erasure, covered by a dash, follows.* [d-d] *In the*
lower margin but marked for insertion here. [e-e] *In the lower margin but*
marked for insertion here. [f] MS. *om.*

---

[1] For the grant to Holland, which was in fact of lands to the value of 2,000
marks (£1,333. 6s. 8d.) per annum, see above, p. 294 and n.

On the petition of the lords and commons Sir John Holland, 1388
the king's brother, was on 2 June created earl of Huntingdon, and with the earldom received from the king an endowment of £1,000 a year.[1]

At the conclusion of a solemn Mass and sermon at Westminster on 3 June, the leading men of the kingdom and all
the rest of the lords stood by while the king, for whom a
royal throne had been prepared for the purpose before the
high altar and a book and cross laid upon a small altar table,
renewed the oath which he had taken long ago at his coronation, whereupon the lords, both spiritual and temporal,
offered to him in full and cheerful submission the allegiances
which it was customary to swear to their lord king on that
occasion.[2] This done, the bishops, assembled under a single
stole, at once fulminated sentence of excommunication
against those who should thereafter dare to break their oath
or to rouse the king's anger against the lords or use false
insinuations to excite him; and at the request of the lords
and commons the king ratified irrevocably and for all time
everything that had been done in the present parliament. In
bidding them farewell on the following day the king expressed
his thanks and gave everybody leave to return home. In order
that all the proceedings of this parliament should for ever
remain and stand firm and inviolate, irrevocable and un-
shakable, and beyond the operation of any repeal, a statute
was published providing that all who rose with the Lords
Appellant and those who came from Cheshire, Shropshire,
and Wales to the aid of the duke of Ireland should be admitted
to grace and excused any kind of forfeiture, but that those
who infringed or in time to come called in question any of
the provisions should undergo the same punishment as was
suffered by the people named just above.[3] And so, on 4 June,
the parliament came to an end.

From now until the end of the autumn the king took his
pleasure in the chase. About the middle of June Alexander

[2] Cf. above, pp. 294, 306. Robert Braybrooke, bishop of London, was the
celebrant at the Mass on this occasion, and 13 bishops were present (Liber Niger
Quaternus, fo. 88ᵛ).
[3] Cf. the official record, omitting the explicit reference to the supporters of
de Vere (R.P., iii. 248-50; S.R., ii. 49). See also above, pp. 296 ff.

1388 Nevyll' quondam archiepiscopus Eboracen' erat captus in navicula juxta Novum Castrum super Tyne, ubi erat in custodia majoris dicte ville usque xxviij. diem Novembris, quo die cum uno solo presbitero et valetto aufugit; quo divertit nescitur.[1] Et cito post in isto mense Junii juxta Tuttebury captus est Johannes Ripon' clericus; qui xix. die mensis Junii, indutus vestibus stragulatis sicuti erat captus, ligatis pedibus sub ventre equi London' adducitur et in Turri London' carcerali custodie demandatur.[2]

Finito vero parliamento, ut supradictum est, dominus Thomas Percy expeditis negociis pro quibus a duce Lancastr' fuit missus rediit Bayonem cum pleno responso.[3] Item xxix. die Junii Scoti manu armata cum duabus turmis, una in parte orientali et alia in parte occidentali, Angliam depopulaturi[a] intrarunt; totam patriam ex omni parte rapinis et incendiis usque Tynemouth' vastarunt, homines vero quos potuerunt capere vesana inclemencia occiderunt, amplius quam cccc. de valencioribus viris ceperunt, at circa medium mensis predicti cum preda magna nullis resistentibus in Scociam sunt reversi. Revera per c. annos elapsos numquam per ipsos [b]ea parte[b] tot dampna erant commissa. Item xxvij. die Julii rex tenuit consilium apud Oxon' in quo fuit ordinatum quod rex[c] ix. die Septembris apud Cantebrigiam celebraret aliud parliamentum. Item circa principium mensis Augusti galee ex parte Francorum conducte apud Kyrkelee Rode et apud Portesmouth' combusserunt domos circa loca maritima constructas. Item primo die Augusti apud Haulton'[4] apparuerunt mira prodigia, nam due stelle circa horam vesperorum ceperunt in partibus austrinis clarescere et in medio inter eas visum est celum aperire[d] ac angelos luciferos quasi per unam horam in
p. 183 aere volitare. Demum in / celum subito redierunt.

Item viij. die Augusti papa[e] recessit de Luca;[5] proposuit

---

[a] MS. depopulaturam.   [b-b] Interlined.   [c] Interlined.   [d] Sic MS.; recte aperiri (Winterbottom).   [e] Interlined.

[1] Nevill went to Brabant (below, p. 492).
[2] The janitor of the Tower was paid for Ripon's keep from 12 July (P.R.O., E. 403/521, 19 Nov.). Ripon's colourful clothes, forbidden to a clerk, were a form of disguise. See also above, p. 300.   [3] Above, p. 194 and n.
[4] Perhaps Halton (Cheshire), belonging to the duchy of Lancaster.
[5] Correctly, not Lucca but Perugia, where Urban had been since 2 Oct. 1387 (above, p. 202 and n.). There follows one explanation among several current at the time or later of how it was that Urban VI entered Rome in Sept. 1388 and

Nevill, the former archbishop of York, was captured in a small 1388
vessel off Newcastle upon Tyne, in the custody of whose
mayor he remained until 28 November, when, accompanied
by a single priest and a servant, he made his escape; it is not
known where he went.[1] A little later in this same June the
clerk John Ripon was caught near Tutbury and on the 19th,
wearing the striped garments in which he had been arrested
and with his feet tied together under his horse's belly, he was
brought to London and lodged in prison in the Tower.[2]

The parliament having come to an end, as described above,
Sir Thomas Percy, who had dispatched the business on which
he had been sent by the duke of Lancaster, returned to
Bayonne with a comprehensive reply.[3] On 29 June the Scots,
bent on creating havoc, made an armed incursion into England
in two bodies, one in the east and the other in the west;
pillage and fire devastated the entire countryside all round as
far as Tynemouth; the people they could lay hands on were
slaughtered with maniac savagery, and more than 400 men of
substance were taken prisoner before, about the middle of
the month, they returned unresisted to Scotland with enormous plunder. Not for the past hundred years, indeed, had so
much mischief been done by them in that region. The king
held a council at Oxford on 27 July at which it was laid down
that he should hold another parliament at Cambridge on 9
September. About the beginning of August galleys chartered
on behalf of the French set fire at Kirkley Road and at Portsmouth to buildings erected near the sea-shore. Amazing
marvels were presented to view at Haulton[4] on 1 August,
when, about the time of Vespers two stars began to shine in
the southern sky and midway between them the heavens were
seen to open and angels carrying lights to flit about in the air
for about an hour before all at once returning into the heavens.

On 8 August the pope left Lucca,[5] intending to make the

was received there without ceremony; for others see *Theoderici de Nyem De
Scismate Libri Tres*, ed. Erler, p. 121 and n.; and *William Thorne's Chronicle of
Saint Augustine's Abbey, Canterbury*, ed. Davis, pp. 663-4. Peter de Tartaris,
alias Peter Romanus, abbot of Monte Cassino (1374–1395), was an Urbanist and
chancellor to Ladislas of Durazzo, king of Sicily. The Monk's reference to
disorder in the Cassinese lands at this time is confirmed in Erasmus Gattula,
Ad Historiam Abbatiae Cassinensis Accessiones (Venice, 1734), pp. 462 ff.; see
also idem, *Historia Abbatiae Cassinensis per Saeculorum Seriem Distributa*
(Venice, 1733), pp. 504, 511 ff.

1388 quoque transire Neapolim per Montem Cassinum, ubi jacuit Sanctus Benedictus. Romani vero putantes ipsum velle venisse Romam cum magno comitatu contra eum certis miliariis exierunt ut cum gaudio introducerent illum in urbem, set ille obliquavit viam versus Romam volens transire per montem predictum usque Neapolim; quod comperientes Romani continuo illum spreverunt et ad urbem quantocius repedarunt. Papa namque misit ad abbatem Montis Cassini rogans attente quod possit transire pacifice juxta eum, habitoque responso ab abbate predicto quo presensit per illum habere transitum minime foret tutum, ad urbem Romam demum quasi invitus accessit pretermissis honoribus et ceteris universis que a Romanis debuit habuisse si primitus cum illis voluerit accessisse.

De Scotis. Item xij. die Augusti Scoti numero triginta milia pugnatorum iterato Angliam invaserunt ut terram Dei nutu afflictam iterum novis dispendiis magis affligant,[1] veneruntque ad portas Novi Castri, ubi homines nostros viriliter sunt aggressi, sic quod ex ut⟨r⟩aque parte quidam ceciderunt interfecti. Erat namque principalis dux eorum comes de Duglas, qui responsa obprobriosa domino Henrico de Percy protulit existenti protunc in dicta villa Novi Castri, qui commotus ad ea verba similia eidem retorsit, promittens sibi indubie obviare antequam Scociam contingeret pervenire.[2] Tandem Scoti retraxerunt se at aliqualiter deprope sua tentoria exstruxerunt. Ordinarunt, inquam, ut magna pars eorum retro a tergo irruerent et caudam nostrorum hominum defalcarent. Consimilem ordinacionem excogitabant nostri in ipsos: nam dominus Henricus Percy in faciem eorum cum suis invaderet et dominus Matheus Redeman[3] cum aliis sibi adjunctis sequeretur eos a tergo, ut sic tali

---

[1] The Scots invaded on the West March under Robert, earl of Fife, and on the East March under James, earl of Douglas. The Monk relates the course of events in the east which culminated, at Otterburn, in the death of Douglas but the defeat of the English under Henry Percy the younger, who was warden of the East March. Clearly, his account is derived from a written source, probably a newsletter; the vivid detail of the account of the English *débâcle* on the front commanded by Sir Henry Percy suggests an eye-witness who was present there. The probable date of the battle is 5–6 Aug. (when the moon was new), and, if so, the Monk has misdated the Scottish invasion of England; nor does he record the fact that Newcastle and Otterburn were stages on the return journey of the Scots from the furthest point of their raid, near Durham. See R. White, *History of the Battle*

journey to Naples by way of Monte Cassino, where St. Benedict lay buried. Supposing him to mean to visit Rome, the
Romans, with a numerous company in attendance, came out
some miles to meet him and to escort him amid rejoicing into
the city, but he turned off the road to Rome, wishing to
travel by Monte Cassino as far as Naples; and as soon as they
discovered this the Romans, disgusted with him, went back
to their city. The pope had sent to the abbot of Monte
Cassino an urgent request to be allowed a peaceable passage
through his neighbourhood, but when he received from the
abbot a reply which prompted foreboding that it would be
anything but safe to obtain a passage by way of Monte
Cassino, he went after all to Rome, as it were against his will,
and in the absence of the courtesies and all the other atten-
tions he was to have had from the Romans if he had been
willing to arrive in their company in the first place.

The Scots. On 12 August the Scots, mustering 30,000
fighting men, again invaded England to inflict once more
upon a country already, by the will of God, sorely stricken
further and greater injury.[1] They reached the gates of Newcastle, where they launched a spirited attack upon our forces,
with losses in killed on each side. Their commander-in-chief,
the earl of Douglas, sent to Sir Henry Percy, who was in
Newcastle at the time, an abusive message by which he was
stung into a retort in similar language, undertaking that
before it was Douglas's fortune to reach Scotland the pair
would certainly meet.[2] At length the Scots withdrew and
pitched their tents some little way off. Their plan, I may say,
was that their main strength should fall back and deliver an
assault from behind to cut off our rear. Against them our
people had thought out a similar plan: Sir Henry Percy was
to make a frontal attack with his troops while Sir Matthew
Redmayne,[3] joined by other commanders, was to take the

---

of Otterburn (London, 1857), pp. 22 ff., 132-3 (where, however, the suggested
date is 19-20 Aug.), and Campbell, in *Europe in the Late Middle Ages*, ed. Hale,
Highfield, and Smalley, p. 210. (I owe the White reference to Mr. Campbell.)

[2] Douglas, having captured Percy's pennon, boasted that he would put it on
the walls of Dalkeith Castle; in reply, Percy vowed that the pennon would not
leave Northumberland (Froissart, *Chroniques*, xiii. 211).

[3] A prominent figure in the defence of the Marches at this time and said by
Froissart (op. cit., xiii. 228) to have been captain of Berwick.

1388 astu eos confunderent universos ac[a] victoriam reportarent.
Set dominus Henricus Percy incaute irruit in eos circa horam
vesperorum suis indispositis protunc ad pugnam; tamen
comitem de Duglas viriliter in suo tentorio interfecit.[1]

Capcio domini Henrici de Percy. Scoti vero ad voces ex-
clamancium excitati, qui sua arma non deposuerunt, in
nostros, qui passim et inordinate venerant ad conflictum,
statim irruunt animose. Sic, inquam, nostros tam acriter
debellarunt quod dictum dominum Henricum et ejus fratrem
Radulfum[2] ibidem ceperunt et de nostris magnam stragem
fecerunt et ex illis quosdam valentes secum captivos duxerunt; sicque ibidem ex nostris quingenti et l.[b] in ore gladii
perierunt[3] et eo amplius, quia episcopus Dunelm'[4] non venit
ad succursum prout inter eos erat condictum. Erat namque
tunc satis prope cum magna armatorum sequela, set propter
noctis tenebras renuit ad locum illum accedere, immo cum
suis mox ad villam Novi Castri perrexit, ubi revera si expectasset ortum solis mulieres illum lapidibus obruerent propter
mortem viris suis inflictam in pugna prefata, quia si eum
innata animositas ad audaciam provocasset tam illos quam
captivos ab hujusmodi clade forsitan liberasset. Set quid?
Istud infortunium contigit Anglicis nostris protunc apud
Otrebourne primo propter impetuosum animum et excessi-
vam audaciam domini[c] Henrici de Percy, que causabant
nostros propter festinanciam prodire ad bellum sine ordinacione, secundo quia nox nostros Anglicos delusit in tantum
⟨quod⟩[d] quando ipsi percuterent Scotum incaute propter unius
lingue consonanciam profecto Anglicum ceciderunt. Tercio
defuit illis auxilium et juvamen secundum quod inter eos et
episcopum Dunelm' fuerat concordatum, prout supra est
tactum. Set non sic pugnavit alio latere dominus Matheus
Redeman, quia Scotis inspectis viriliter est eos aggressus,

---

[a] *Interlined.*   [b] et l. *added later.*   [c] *Interlined.*   [d] *MS. om.*

[1] Douglas was slain in open combat, and only English sources attribute the feat
to Percy himself (cf. Walsingham, *Hist. Ang.*, ii. 176; Knighton, *Chronicon*, ii.
297).
[2] Ralph Percy's captor was Sir John Maxwell of Pollock; Henry Percy's, Sir
John de Montgomery of Egglesham; see Froissart, op. cit., xiii. 222-3, 226-7.
[3] Cf. Ecclus. xxviii. 22 (xxviii. 18): 'multi ceciderunt in ore gladii'.
[4] Walter Skirlaw. Perhaps he would have done better had he been in possession
of his see: he received the temporalities on 13 Sept. (below, p. 355 n.).

enemy in the rear, so that by this stratagem the whole 1388
Scottish army would be thrown into confusion and victory
would be won. But Sir Henry Percy was so rash as to make
his assault about the time of Vespers without on this occasion drawing up his troops in battle formation; yet by a
heroic effort he dispatched the earl of Douglas in his own
tent.[1]

Capture of Sir Henry Percy. Roused by the noise of shouting voices, the Scots who had not laid aside their weapons,
immediately made a spirited attack upon our men, who over
the whole front had straggled into action in irregular order.
So it was, I say, that the Scots severely defeated our troops,
capturing Sir Henry Percy and his brother Ralph[2] and doing
tremendous slaughter among our men, of whom they carried
off some doughty soldiers as their prisoners; and so it was
that five hundred and fifty or more of our people perished
'by the edge of the sword'[3] because the bishop of Durham[4]
failed to come to their aid in the way previously concerted
between them. He was quite close at hand at the time, with a
large armed force under his command, but owing to the
darkening night declined to approach the spot: on the contrary
it was not long before he and his force reached Newcastle,
where, if he had waited for sunrise, he would certainly have
been overwhelmed by the stones flung by women avenging
the slaughter suffered by their husbands in the battle, for if
any fighting instincts had prompted boldness he might perhaps have saved both them and the prisoners from disaster.
But why dwell on it? The calamity that befell our countrymen on this occasion at Otterburn was due in the first place
to the heady spirit and excessive boldness of Sir Henry Percy,
which caused our troops to go into battle in the disorder
induced by haste; in the second place because the darkness
played such tricks on the English that when they aimed a
careless blow at a Scotsman, owing to the chorus of voices
speaking a single language it was an Englishman that they
cut down; and in the third place they were disappointed of
the help and support arranged between them and the bishop
of Durham, as is mentioned above. But on the enemy's other
side Sir Matthew Redmayne fought a very different battle.
After reconnoitring the Scots he delivered an assault so

1388 sic quod turpiter vertuntur in fugam, jussitque omnes occidi absque redempcione, illis solummodo exceptis qui pro cassidibus suis valeant solvere centum marcas; persecutusque est eos usque ad fines*a* Scocie occidendo et letaliter vulnerando, cepitque inter alios dominum Jacobum de Lyndissey virum nominatissimum tocius Scocie utique in suis actibus prepollentem,[1] et rediit cum triumpho ad sua. Ceciderunt de Scotis tam in una parte quam in alia amplius quam quingenti. Scoti vero qui dominum Henricum Percy et suos vicerunt campum custodientes usque ad horam primam diei sequentis hanelabant semper dictum dominum Henricum Percy occidere; set comes de Dombarr' a mortis interitu ipsum salvavit. Demum audita strage suorum per dominum Matheum Redeman facta statim cum festinacione cum suis captivis in Scociam redierunt. Rex vero hiis auditis ira incaluit volens vindicari de Scotis: xxij. die Augusti ea de causa apud Northampton' suum consilium convocavit, affectans namque ad partes illas transire et Scotos universos delere. Set quia jam hiemps vicina instabat, illi de consilio decreverunt fore consulcius expectare quousque veniat novus annus et interim ea omnia que sunt necessaria pro tam summo *b*et arduo*b* negocio cum discrecione previa ordinare: placuit vero istud consilium universis utpote sanum et bonum.[2]

Facta comitis Arundell in mari. Comes vero Arundell' statim postquam pervenit ad mare[3] transtulit se navigando ad aquam de Sequana, ubi combussit unam magnam navem de Tour'. Abinde recessit versus le Trade,[4] ubi cepit vj. naves sale onustas. Item velificando juxta portum de Rochell' cepit duas naves vino et aliis mercimoniis oneratas. Applicuit tandem apud insulam de Baas, ubi fecit milites, scilicet

---

a Written above partes, which is not deleted.   *b–b* Interlined.

---

[1] Cf. Froissart, *Chroniques*, xiii. 232 ff. The only certain facts are that Lindsay was a prisoner after Otterburn (in the earl of Northumberland's custody) and Redmayne at liberty (*Cal. Cl. R., 1385–9*, p. 535; *Rot. Scot.*, ii. 95; below, p. 400). For Sir James Lindsay of Crawford (d. 1396), see *D.N.B.*, xi. 1178–80.

[2] On 20 Aug. — the date may mean that the Monk has misdated the council — at Northampton, the king appointed Henry Percy, earl of Northumberland, and John, Lord Nevill of Raby, wardens of the Marches and issued commissions of

resolute that they ignominiously turned tail and he gave 1388
orders for every man of them to be killed with no quarter
given except to those who could pay 100 marks for their
helmets. Before returning home in triumph he had continued
the chase as far as the Scottish border, dealing death and
mortal wounds all the way, and his prisoners included Sir
James Lindsay, the most renowned figure in all Scotland,
with some powerful achievements to his credit.[1] Scottish
killed, in one area or the other, amounted to over 500. Those
Scots who had defeated Sir Henry Percy and his forces kept
the field until the first hour of the following day, thirsting
all the while for the blood of Sir Henry Percy, but the earl of
Dunbar saved him from being put to death. When they eventually heard of the slaughter of their compatriots by Sir
Matthew Redmayne, they at once hurried back to Scotland
with their prisoners. At the news of these events the king was
aflame with anger and with the desire to be revenged on the
Scots, and, all anxiety to march north and destroy them to
a man, he consequently called a meeting of his council for
22 August at Northampton. Owing, however, to the near
approach of winter the councillors decided that it would be
advisable to wait for the new campaigning season to come
round and meanwhile to make judiciously in advance all the
arrangements needed for an undertaking so important and so
difficult: this was the course that appealed to all of them as
sound and advantageous.[2]

Exploits of the earl of Arundel at sea. On reaching the sea[3]
the earl of Arundel at once sailed across to the River Seine,
where he fired a large vessel of Tours. From here he withdrew to 'le Trade',[4] where he captured six ships laden with
salt; and cruising off the port of La Rochelle he took two
ships with cargoes of wine and other goods. Landing subsequently on the island of Batz, he conferred knighthood on

array for the northern counties (*Rot. Scot.*, ii. 95; and see Storey, in *E.H.R.*
lxxii (1957), 600).
   [3] On 10 June (above, p. 340). For this expedition see Jones, *Ducal Brittany,
1364-1399*, pp. 108-12. The Monk's account conceals Arundel's failure to
achieve his main purpose: an invasion of France with the assistance of John de
Montfort, duke of Brittany. His knowledge of the earl's itinerary points to the use
of a written source, the author of which was probably in the earl's company.
   [4] Probably Le Havre.

1388 dominum le Despenser et alios generosos;[1] combussitque ibidem cxl. naves parvas et magnas, commorans ibidem x. diebus. Et abhinc ad insulam de Bay[2] pervenit, ubi pro redempcione duarum insularum, scilicet Scermith et Bayn, aurum, vinum et carnes bovinas habunde recepit; mansitque ibidem viij[to]. diebus; et post hec ad insulam de Use pervenit ac predam bestiarum[a] juxta castrum ipsius agebat deduxitque ad naves, qua dimissa per patrias et per loca navigans sua cum classe demum apud portum de Rochell' salve pervenit. In cujus villa erant pro ipsius tuicione dux de Barre, vicecomes de Tolkars, marescallus Francie[3] et dominus de Pounce, cum m. et c. hominibus armorum, cum quibus optulit se quantocius pugnaturum si eos ad hoc audacia animaret. Cui dixerunt se velle cum eo congredi si xij. diebus voluerit expectare;[4] qui ad istas promissiones factus est alacer et jocundus; festivus non obstantibus eorum gonnis et machinis, velint nolint, cum suis descendit in terram, ubi propter spem belli milites de novo creavit: mansitque apud villam de Burgnoff' xiiij. diebus et combussit ibidem quatuor bonas villas, destruxit eciam ibidem domos et alia instrumenta quibus vinum facerent et x. milia dolia vacua igne

p. 184 consumpsit. Demum ad insulam de Reyth accessit, / pro cujus redempcione mille francos et mille oves, lx. magnas bestias et lxvj. dolia vini accepit. Venitque apud Hastyngg' in Anglia cum suis secundo die Septembris.[5]

Item circa principium mensis Septembris capitaneus Cales'[6] cum aliis capitaneis Anglicis ibidem in partibus in Flandriam equitavit, cepit magnam predam bestiarum, et rediit Cales'. Altera die equitavit in Pycardiam, ubi eciam diversorum animalium predas agebat et Cales' omnia reducebat: tanta quoque copia bestiarum erat tunc Cales' quod una ovis vendebatur pro duobus grossis, set

[a] Interlined.

---

[1] Arundel knighted 7 persons on 28 June (P.R.O., E. 101/41/4; see also ibid., 5). For Thomas Despenser, b. 22 Sept. 1373, and later (1397–9) earl of Gloucester, see G.E.C., iv. 278–80.   [2] Belle Isle.

[3] Louis de Sancerre, marshal of France 1369–1402. When Arundel began to threaten La Rochelle, Louis de Sancerre was besieging Bouteville, then in English hands; this enterprise he abandoned in order to assist the defendants of La Rochelle. See 'Recueil des Documents concernant le Poitou', in Archives Historiques du Poitou, xxi (1891), 380 n.

Lord Despenser and other gentlemen,[1] and in the course of a 1388
stay of ten days set fire to 140 vessels, large and small. From
there he proceeded to the island of the Bay,[2] where he received gold, wine, and beef in lavish quantities for the ransom
of the two islands of Noirmoutier and Bouin: he stayed here
eight days. After this he went to the island of Yeu, where the
beasts that formed his booty were driven to the neighbourhood of the castle before being brought down to the ships.
On leaving this island he coasted with his fleet through the
area and its settlements, eventually reaching the port of
La Rochelle without mishap. Lodged in the town for its
defence were the duc de Bar, the vicomte de Thouars, the
marshal of France,[3] and the sire de Pons, disposing of 1100
men-at-arms, with whom the earl offered to do battle as soon
as might be if their courage inspired them to it. They replied
that if he would wait twelve days they would come to grips
with him;[4] whereupon, put by their undertaking into a brisk
and cheerful mood, and in high spirits despite their guns and
other engines of war, he disembarked under their noses with
his troops and in expectation of action conferred further
knighthoods. During a stay of fourteen days at Bourgneuf he
burned down four flourishing towns in the neighbourhood,
where he also destroyed buildings and other equipment used
for making wine and fired 10,000 empty tuns. Finally he
visited the island of Ré for the ransom of which he received
1,000 francs, 1,000 sheep, 60 larger cattle, and 66 tuns of
wine. He arrived at Hastings in England with his forces on
2 September.[5]

About the beginning of September the captain of Calais,[6]
in company with other English captains in the neighbourhood, made a mounted raid into Flanders and took considerable booty in cattle before returning to Calais. On another
occasion he raided Picardy and made further hauls there of
assorted livestock, all of which he brought back to Calais.
So great, indeed, was the abundance of animals in Calais at
this time that sheep were sold for two groats apiece, but the

---

[4] Or did 12 days intervene between Arundel's arrival at La Rochelle and Louis
de Sancerre's arrival to relieve it? Cf. Froissart's belief (*Chroniques*, xiii. 275)
that the arrival of Louis de Sancerre precipitated Arundel's re-embarkation.

[5] Correctly, 3 Sept.   [6] William Beauchamp.

1388 capitaneus predictus non permisit*a* quod aliqua bestia *b*ullo foro*b* in Angliam venderetur. Item ix.*c* die Septembris ecclesia Sancti Pauli London' sanguine humano erat polluta per ministros ejusdem civitatis, nam primo percusserunt quendam ibidem usque ad sanguinis effusionem qui ob tuicionem sue persone confugiebat ad illam, deinde violenter illum extrahentes in porta de Ludgate incarcerarunt. Stetitque ecclesia predicta irreconsiliata fere per septimanam.

Parliamentum apud Cantebrig'. Item x. die Septembris[1] apud Cantebrig' rex suum parliamentum incepit. Primo namque ante omnia statuerunt quod episcopi omnes provisione pape translati ad sedes suas transirent et possessionem corporalem per eorum vicarios assumerent indilate.[2] Quo facto dominum Johannem Waltham clericum privati sigilli domini nostri regis in Sar' episcopum consecrarunt.[3] Statuerunt eciam quod stapula lanarum moveret se de Middelbourgh et apud Cales' se quantocius stabiliret: nichilominus remansit ibidem ultra diem assignatum per magnum tempus usque ad tercium diem Februarii, erat namque dies hujus limitacionis primus dies Decembris proximo futurus.[4] Item illi de communitate in isto parliamento de signis dominorum graviter sunt conquesti 'eo quod ea gestantes propter suorum potenciam dominorum in tam cervicosam superbiam sunt elati quod varias extorsiones in patria circumcirca ausu temerario committere non verentur; unde pauperes in curiis principum et aliorum ubicumque dilaniant et confundunt, mediocres vero et alios indifferenter in quibuscumque locis ubi jus redditur jure suo expoliant et enervant, quia jus cum justicia racionis*d* tramite procedere non permittunt: hec itaque et alia profecto*e* signorum audacia committere non formidant.' Hiis quoque auditis prefati domini, generalitatem hujus querimonie elidere cupientes, jusserunt ipsos in specie

---

a A word has been deleted after this word.   *b-b* Interlined; and a word has been deleted between these two.   *c* Aliter viij. written above this word. *d* Aliter equitatis written above this word.   *e* Interlined.

---

[1] Correctly, 9 Sept. The proceedings took place at Barnwell Priory. See, on this parliament, J. A. Tuck, 'The Cambridge Parliament, 1388', in *E.H.R.*, lxxxiv (1969), 225-43. The fact that Abbot Colchester visited the prior of Ely on or about 7 Oct. suggests that he attended in person. Br. Thomas Merks was with him on the visit to Ely (W.A.M. 24538).

captain would not allow the sale at any price of any beast for 1388 export to England. On 9 September the church of St. Paul in London was profaned by human blood shed by city officers who, when their quarry had taken sanctuary there to safeguard his person, first dealt him blows that drew blood and then dragged him out by force and imprisoned him in Ludgate. The church remained unreconciled for about a week.

Parliament at Cambridge. The king opened his parliament at Cambridge on 10 September.[1] The very first decision was that all those bishops who had been translated by papal provision should proceed to their sees and at once assume corporal possession through their vicars general.[2] This done, John Waltham, keeper of the king's privy seal, was consecrated bishop of Salisbury.[3] A further decision was that the wool staple should be moved from Middelburg and immediately established at Calais: it nevertheless remained at Middelburg until 3 February, long after the day appointed for the transfer, the date specified having been 1 December next.[4] At this parliament the commons complained bitterly about the badges issued by the lords, 'since those who wear them are, by reason of the power of their masters, flown with such insolent arrogance that they do not shrink from practising with reckless effrontery various forms of extortion in the surrounding countryside; fleecing and discomfiting the poor in every court, including those of the greatest, and indiscriminately robbing the middle and other classes of their rights and reducing them to helplessness wherever justice is dispensed, since they do not allow right to go hand in hand with justice along the paths of reason; and it is certainly the boldness inspired by their badges that makes them unafraid to do these things and more besides.' After listening to this the lords, anxious to dispose of the generalized nature of the complaint, told the commons to come down to cases and to

[2] See above, p. 334 and n. The bishops of Bath and Wells and Durham received their temporalities on 13 Sept., York his on 14 Sept., and Ely his on 27 Sept.

[3] On 20 Sept.

[4] The removal of the staple to Calais, in fulfilment of a promise made by the king in the Merciless Parliament, was ordered on 24 Oct., but on 15 Nov. the date was put back until 2 Feb. (*R.P.*, iii. 250; *Cal. Cl. R., 1385-9*, pp. 537, 541, 618-19; see also T. H. Lloyd, *The English Wool Trade in the Middle Ages* (Cambridge, 1977), p. 231).

1388 illis tradere hujusmodi malefactores talia committentes, et
taliter eos castigarent quod similia perpetrare ceteri perti-
mescant.[1] Ista promissio illis non placuit, immo omnino
vellent quod predicta signa deponerent si pacem et tranquillitatem in regno habere exoptent. Ad hec rex, affectans
ut tranquillitas foret in regno pro bono pacis et ut aliis daret
exemplum, optulit se deponere sua signa; quod summe
placuit communitati predicte: set domini post multa convicia
et verba probrosa illis de communitate prolata noluerunt
consentire ad id quod eorum aviditas flagitabat, quare inter
eos dissensio est exorta. Rex autem vidit eos sic adinvicem
discordare propter deposicionem signorum predictorum;
volens comune dissidium evitare eos primo ad concordiam
revocavit, postea vero, ut omnis materia dissencionis radicitus
exstirpetur, concessit dominis sepedictis uti eorum signis
usque in proximum parliamentum, prout in Gallico ydiomate
hic seriosius continetur:[2]

Primerement qe touz lez liverees appellez signes si bien de nostre
seignur le roy come dautres seignurs comencez usez puis le primer an
del noble roy Edward tierce (qe Dieu assoille) et touz autres menuz
liverees come chaperons ne soient desoremes donez ne portez mes
soient oustes sur payne allimite en ceste present parlement.

Mes le roy voet par assent dez seignurs en parlement qe la matere
touchant ceste article soit continue en lestat qorest tanqe a proschein
parlement en espoir damendement faire par luy et les seignurs de son
conseille en le mesne temps, salvant lestat du roy et dez seignurs et de
touz autres estatz du parlement.

Item qe touz lez gildes et fraternites et lour comune boistes soient
oustes et adnullez pur touz jours et les biens et chateux en possessioun
disposez pur la guerre par discrecion des seignurs du parlement, salvant
toute foitz chaunteries ordeinez dauncien temps pur lalmes de lour
fondours et autres amortisez par licence du roy et autres choses ordenez
al honour de seint esglise et encres de divine servise, sanz livere, con-
federacie, meintenaunce ou riotes en arrerissement du ley.[3]

Item qe chaunceller, tresorer, chamberleyn, seneschal del houstelle
le roy, gardein del prive seal, justices et chief baron del escheqer et
touz autres seignurs du conseille le roy et clerke dez rollez soient

_____

[1] Cf. above, p. 82.

[2] There follows the unique text of the commons' petitions in the parliament
at Cambridge, headed by their petition against liveries, to which alone is the reply
of the king and council also given.

[3] This was, no doubt, the petition that precipitated the official inquiry into the

hand over to them those offenders who did such things, who 1388 would be so punished that their colleagues would be scared off similar behaviour.[1] So far from being satisfied with this undertaking, the commons were firm in their demand that if the lords wanted to have peace and quiet in the kingdom they must drop the use of badges altogether. Out of a desire for domestic tranquillity the king thereupon offered, for peace' sake and in order to set an example to others, to discard his own badges — an offer which gave the utmost satisfaction to the commons. But after launching a great deal of abuse and vituperation at the commons the lords refused to agree to their eagerly pressed demand; and the two sides were at odds. Seeing the discord between them over the question of dropping the badges, and anxious to avoid a general split, the king first summoned them back to harmony and then, in order to root out completely all matter for controversy, he allowed the lords to go on using their badges until the next parliament; witness the contents of the following detailed account in French:[2]

First, that all the liveries called 'badges', as well of our lord the king as of other lords, of which the use has begun since the first year of the noble king Edward the Third (whom God assoil) and all other lesser liveries, such as hoods, shall henceforward not be given or worn but shall be abolished upon the pain specified in this present parliament.

But it is the king's will, with the assent of the lords in parliament, that the matter touching this article shall be continued in its present state until the next parliament in the hope that in the meantime amendment will be effected by him and the lords of his council, without prejudice to the dignity of the king and of the lords and of all other estates of the parliament.

Also, that all gilds and fraternities and their common chests shall be abolished and done away with for all time and the goods and chattels in their possession laid out upon the war at the discretion of the lords of parliament, saving always chantries ordained in ancient time for the souls of their founders and others acquired in mortmain by royal licence and other things ordained to the honour of Holy Church and the increase of divine service, without livery, confederacy, maintenance, or riots in hindrance of the law.[3]

Also that the chancellor, the treasurer, the chamberlain, the steward of the king's household, the keeper of the privy seal, the justices, the chief baron of the exchequor, and all other the lords of the king's

gilds of 1388-9, for which see T. and L. T. Smith, *English Gilds* (E.E.T.S., 1870), 1 ff. See also *Letter Book H*, p. 336, and Tuck, art. cit., pp. 237-8.

1388 firmement serementez qe nul soit mys en office de justice de la pees
ne fait viscounte, eschetour, baillif, nautre ministre ne officer le
roy par nul don ne brocage ne nul qe pursuie destre en office par luy
ou par autre eins les pluis bons et loialx a lour scient.[1]

Item qe lez justices dez assisez et justices de la pees eient poair
denquere et terminer auxibien al suite del roy come de partie par
bille ou par lettre du roy de touz manerez de meintenance, extor-
cions et oppressions faitz ou affaire al poeple et dez dons prises par[a]
jurours pur verdit dit ou a dire.[b] Et purceo qe diverses opinions sont
en quel cas meintenance doit estre ajugge et en quele nemye, de-
clarissement ensuyt: cest assavoir quant ascun seignur espirituelle ou
temporelle ou dame ou femme de religioun ou qeconqe autre de
quele estat ou condicion qil soit emprent ou susteigne ascun querele
dautre homme a qi il nest pas partie cosyn nalye pur avoir lentierte
ou partie de ceo qest en demande ou embrace ou procure enquestes
a passer[2] en querels dont il nest partie pur lower, done ou promesse,
et quant ascuns soy assemblent en grantz routes et multitude de
poeple outre lour degre et estat en feires, marches, cessions dez
justices, courtz, lovedaies et autres lieux et maynteygnent et sus-
teignent faux provisours ou autres en lour esglises ou provendres ove
p. 185 grant poair en destourbaunce de la ley ou en affray du poeple, ou /
feignent diverses querels par autres de lour assent devers plusours
lieges du roiaume et a eux facent assaut, manassent, batent ou
oustent de lour terres countre droit et processe de ley et lour tiegnent einz ove grant poair siqe les ditz lieges nosent pursuier la ley ne
defendre lour droit pur doute de mort, et quant ascuns mayngtenent
ou retiegnent devers eux ascuns persons enditez ou[c] utlages pur
felonie ou comunes larons ou murdrez ou autres felons, siqe lez
officeres du roy, come viscountes, baillifs, nautres officeres, nose faire
lour offices come duissent de droit pur paur de lour meintenance[d] et
supportacioun. Et fait a entendre qen lez cases suisditz soit ajugge
meintenance;[3] et pur ceo soit ordeine en ceste present parlement
qe si ercevesqe, evesqe, abbe ou priour ou autre homme ou femme de
religioun, duc, counte, baron, bacheler, esquier ou autre, de quele
estat ou condicion qil soit, soit atteint, face fyn au roy devant les
justices ou il serra atteint et au partie pleintif ses damages au double
et qe ceste tiegne lieu et force en temps avenir soulement.

---

[a] MS. et.   [b] Et du roy de touz maneres de meintenance *deleted after this
word.*   [c] ulag *deleted after this word.*   [d] MS. meintentenance.

---

[1] Cf. 12 Richard II, *cap.* 2 (*S.R.*, ii. 55).
[2] i.e. the passing of verdicts by inquests.
[3] Maintenance, in the strict sense, was the supporting of another's plea without
an arrangement to share the profits. The petition uses the term in a broader sense,
to cover also the offences of champerty (supporting a plea in consideration of a
share in the profits) and conspiracy to abuse legal procedure and frustrate the

council and the clerk of the rolls shall be straitly sworn that none 1388
shall be put into the office of justice of the peace, or made sheriff,
escheator, bailiff, or other minister or officer of the king by reason
of any gift or bribe, and that none who by himself or by another
makes suit to be in office [shall be appointed] save only those who
to their knowledge are the best and most law-worthy.[1]

Also that justices of assize and justices of the peace shall have
power to inquire into and to determine, at the suit both of the
king and of a party, by bill or by the king's letters, all manner of
maintenance, extortions, and oppressions practised or to be practised
upon the people, and gifts taken by jurors for verdict delivered or
to be delivered. And because there are different opinions about the
cases in which maintenance ought or ought not to be adjudged, the
definition follows: that is to say when any lord, spiritual or temporal, lady, woman of religion, or any other of whatsoever estate
or condition he be, takes up or supports another's quarrel to which
he is not a party by reason of blood or marriage, in order to have
the whole or a part of that which is claimed, or instigates or
procures for reward, gift, or promise the passing[2] of inquests in
quarrels to which he is not a party; and when any gather together
in great routs and multitudes of people in excess of their degree
and condition in fairs, markets, sessions of justices, courts, love-
days, and elsewhere and maintain and support false provisors or
others in their churches or prebends with great power, to the
disturbance of the law or to the intimidation of the people; or
feign sundry quarrels by the agency of others in collusion with
them against many lieges of the realm and practise against them
assault, menaces, and battery or oust them from their lands contrary to right and process of law and occupy those lands with great
power so that the said lieges dare not pursue the law or defend
their right for fear of death; and when any maintain or retain
about them any persons indicted or outlawed for felony or any
common thieves, murderers, or other felons, so that the king's
officers, such as sheriffs, bailiffs, and other officers, dare not
perform their offices, as of right they ought, for fear of their
maintenance and support; and let it be understood that in the cases
abovesaid it shall be adjudged maintenance.[3] Be it therefore
ordained in this present parliament that if any archbishop, bishop,
abbot, or prior or any other man or woman of religion, duke, earl,
baron, bachelor, esquire, or other, of whatsoever estate or condition
he be, is attainted, he shall make fine to the king before the
justices where he is attainted and to the party complainant double
his damages, and that this shall take place and effect for time to
come only.

course of justice. All three had been statutory offences since 1293. See *Select
Cases in the Court of King's Bench under Edward I*, iii., ed. G. O. Sayles (Selden
Soc., 58), liv ff.

1388   Item[1] qe touz estatuz dez laborers, artificers et vitaillers faitz en
temps le roy Edward iij. aiel nostre seignur le roy qorest nient repellez
soient affermez en ceste present parlement,[2] adjoustantz qe nulle
laborer ne servant homme ne femme, de quele estat ou condicion qil
soit, departe hors del ville ou il demoert au fyn del terme pur servir
ou demurrer en autre ville sanz lettre patent enseale desouz le seal a
ceo assigne, quele seal lez justices de la pees deliverent a le pluis suffisant de chescun hundred come lour serra enforme par bons enquestez
devant eux en le counte ou en le hundred, [a]fesant expresse mencion
del noun du fesour en la dite lettre et le noun de soun mestre, tesmoignant
ou il vorra aler et soun departer bone et resonable,[a] pur ensealer les ditz
lettres as ditz laborers et servantz quant il serra duement requis sanz
rien ent prendre pur le seal. Et si la dite lettre soit desavowe par cely
qest suppose ent le fesour ou prove pur feint ou faux eit cely laborer ou
servant adonqes lemprisonement de xl. jours; et si nul servant ou laborer
soit trove sanz tiel lettre en cite, burghe, ville, haut chimyn ou autre
lieu qeconqe, meintenant soit arestutz par qeconqe persone qi ly vorra
arester et soit mesne a le proschein gaole a demurrer illeoqes xl. jours,
et endementiers soit proclamacion fait parmy lez countes ou il est pris
si ascun luy vorra chalenger pur soun servant,[3] et si nul viegne de luy
chalenger deinz le dit terme soit tenuz de servir a luy qi luy ensi prist sil
luy voet avoir pur soun servant, et qe le dit laborer ou servant eit lettre
patent desouz le seal de viscounte de forrein counte tesmoignant soun
emprisonement et ou il vorra aler et qe nul luy recette outre un jour en
soun realer en sa paiis sur grant peyne a paier au roy sil ne soit malade.

Item qe le dit seal eit scripture del noun del counte et del hundred
ou de wapentake et en mye le seal soit mys une signe par avys des
seignurs, et qe chescun citee ⟨et⟩[b] burghe eit autiel seal.

Item qe ceux qi se feignent hommes travaillez par de la et illeosqes
estre emprisonez portent ovesqe eux une lettre patent desouz le seal
du capitan du marche ou dascun chastelle illeosqes tesmoignant lour
emprisonement en lour estre par dela sur la peyne suisdit.[4]

Item chescun qi va mendinant qest able de servir ou de laborer qe
soit fait de luy come de celuy qi departe de ville sanz lettre come desuis
est dit, sauvez gentz de religioun.[5]

[a-a] *This passage is misplaced and appears in the translation in what seems to be its proper place.*   [b] *MS. om.*

---

[1] The following petitions formed the basis of 12 Richard II, *caps.* 3-10. The
statute, however, required every vill to have a pair of stocks and decreed that a
servant or labourer illicitly travelling without letters patent should be confined,
not in prison, but in the stocks; it exempted servants travelling on the business of
their lords and masters from the requirement to carry letters patent; it required
artisans who were not needed in their own employments to labour in the harvest,
and made other changes of detail in the several clauses. See *S.R.*, ii. 56-9; Tuck,
in *E.H.R.*, lxxxiv (1969), 228-9; and N. Ritchie, 'Labour Conditions in Essex in
the Reign of Richard II', in *Essays in Economic History*, ed. E. M. Carus-Wilson,
ii (London, 1962), pp. 91 ff.

Also[1] that all the statutes of labourers, artificers, and victuallers 1388 made in the time of King Edward III, grandfather of our lord the king that now is, and not repealed shall be affirmed in this present parliament,[2] with the addition that no labourer or serving-man or woman, of whatsoever estate or condition he be, shall at the end of his term depart out of the town where he dwells to serve or dwell in another town without sealed letters patent under the seal for that purpose assigned (which seal the justices of the peace shall deliver to the man in each hundred best qualified, as they shall be informed by good inquisitions taken before themselves in the county or in the hundred, to seal the said letters to the said labourers and servants upon due request without taking anything for the seal), the said letters making express mention of the name of the executant and of his master and testifying whither the labourer wishes to go and that his departure is for good and reasonable cause. And if the said letters are disavowed by him who is supposed to be the executant thereof or are proved to be forged or false, then that labourer or servant shall have forty days' imprisonment; and if any servant or labourer is found in city, borough, town, highway, or other place whatsoever without such letters, he shall be straightway arrested by any person that will arrest him and taken to the nearest gaol, there to remain for forty days, and proclamation shall meanwhile be made throughout the counties where he is taken, in case anyone wishes to claim him as his servant, and if none comes to claim him within the said term, he shall be bound to serve him who thus took him, if he wishes to have him for his servant;[3] and that the said labourer or servant shall have letters patent under the seal of the sheriff of the foreign county, testifying his imprisonment and whither he wishes to go and that none shall harbour him for more than one day in his journey back to his own country, under great penalty to be paid to the king, unless the labourer be sick.

Also that the said seal shall have inscribed upon it the name of the county and of the hundred or wapentake, and in the middle of the seal shall be set a device by advice of the lords and that every city and borough shall have a similar seal.

Also that those who give themselves out to be men who have travelled out of the realm and have there been imprisoned shall carry with them letters patent under the seal of the captain of the march or of some castle there, testifying their imprisonment during their being out of the realm, under the penalty abovesaid.[4]

Also that with every person that goes begging, being able to serve or labour, it shall be done as with him who departs from his town without letters, as is abovesaid, people of religion excepted.[5]

---

[2] Cf. 12 Richard II, *cap.* 3, which confirmed the relevant unrepealed statutes of Richard II's reign as well as those of his grandfather's reign — an important change, since it was only by the enactment of 2 Richard II, statute 1, *cap.* 8 that the Ordinance of Labourers of 1349 became a statute. (*S.R.*, ii. 11, 56).

[3] Cf. 12 Richard II, *cap.* 3. [4] Cf. 12 Richard II, *cap.* 8.

[5] Cf. 12 Richard II, *cap.* 7.

1388   Item qe nul mendinant impotent de servir naille hors de la ville ou il fuist nee et qe touz ceux qen cites et autres villes recettent ou retiegnent tiels mendinantz, forspris les religious et lez voegles lepers et couchantz sur litz en maladie, soient amerciez devant lez justices de la pees ou les mairs, baillifs, conestables del lieu et qe lez ditz justices, mairs, baillifs et conestables soient sermentez de loialment enquerer et due execucion faire de les premissez.

Item qe nul laborer, servant ne lour fille ne fitz ne soit mys en artifice sil soit requis a servir entour la charue et housbondrie; et si nul covenant ^{a}ou lien^a de prentice soit fait au^b contrarie soit tenuz pur nulle.[1]

Item qe nul servant, laborer ne servant de nul artificer ne de vitailler ne porte baselard ne daggere nespeie sur forfaiture dycelle et qe viscountes, mairs, baillifs et conestables eient poair darester touz lez contrevenantz a cestes ordenances et les baselardes, daggers et espeies suisditz seiser et garder tanqe al venue dez justices de la pees ensemblement ove lez nouns de ceux qi eux porterent.[2]

Item qe lez gardeins de lez gaols soient chargez de resceiver tielx laborers, servantz, mendinantz et vegarantz en prisons et lez deteigner illeosqes sanz meinprise ou lesser en baille sur peine de paier au roy cent soldz.

Item qe lez ditz ordeinances tiegnent si bien lieux en cites, burghes, ⟨et⟩^{c} villes deins franchise come dehors.[3]

Item qe les justices enquergent et terminent en lour cessions si lez ditz mairs, baillifs et conestables ont fait duement lez ditz arestes et execucions et recettes dez laborers, servantz et mendinantz et ceux qi sont trovez en defaute encourgent grant peine allimite en ceste present parlement et qe touz lez fyns et amerciementz devant lez ditz justices faitz soient levez par le viscounte et liverez as deux persones esluz par le counte devant lez ditz justices en sustenance de la guerre et supportacion del counte ou ils serront levez.[4]

Item qe touz ceux qi aillent en pelrinage come mendinantz soit fait de eux come dez laborers come desuis.[5]

Item qe les justices de la pees facent lour cessions en chescun counte solonc lordinance fait en autres estatuz, pernantz gages, cest assavoir iiij$s$. le jour et le clerke del justice ij$s$., de fynes et amerciementz

p. 186 faitz devant / eux par les mayns lez ditz deux hommes esluz^d et qils continuent lour cessions en chescun quarter de lan^e par trois jours ^{f}au meyns.^{f}[6]

    $^{a-a}$ MS. en lieu. ^{b} MS. ou. ^{c} MS. om. ^{d} MS. esluy. ^{e} MS. counte.
$^{f-f}$ Added later.

---

[1] Cf. 12 Richard II, *cap.* 5.   [2] Cf. 12 Richard II, *cap.* 6.
[3] Cf. with this sentence and the next, 12 Richard II, *cap.* 9. The principles of imprisonment without bail and free of charge were anticipated in 34 Edward III, *cap.* 9 (*S.R.*, i. 366).
[4] Cf. 12 Richard II, *cap.* 10, which added 6 justices to each of the existing commissions of the peace, sitting quarterly, but ignored the request that fines be

Also that no beggar impotent to serve shall go out of the town where 1388
he was born and that all those who in cities and other towns harbour or
retain such beggars, with the exception of people of religion, the blind
lepers, and such as lie in their sick beds, shall be amerced before the
justices of the peace or the mayors, bailiffs, or constables of the place
and that the said justices, mayors, bailiffs, and constables shall be sworn
to inquire according to the law and to make due execution of the foregoing.

Also that no labourer or servant or his daughter or son shall be set
to any craft if he is required to serve at the plough and at husbandry;
and if any covenant or bond of apprenticeship to the contrary be made
it shall be held null.[1]

Also that no servant, labourer, or servant of any craftsman or
victualler shall carry baselard, dagger, or sword upon pain of forfeiture
of the same, and that sheriffs, mayors, bailiffs, and constables shall have
power to arrest all who contravene these ordinances and to seize and
keep until the coming of the justices of the peace the abovesaid base-
lards, daggers, and swords, together with the names of those who
carried them.[2]

Also that the keepers of gaols shall be charged to receive into prison
such labourers, servants, beggars, and vagrants and to keep them there
without mainprise or admission to bail upon pain of paying to the king
100s.

Also that the said ordinances shall hold place as well in cities,
boroughs, and towns and within liberties as outside them.[3]

Also that the justices shall inquire and determine in their sessions
whether the said mayors, bailiffs, and constables have duly made the
said arrests and executions and have received the custody of the
labourers, servants, and beggars, and those found in default shall incur
the great penalty specified in this present parliament; and that all the
fines and amercements made before the said justices shall be levied by
the sheriff and delivered to two persons, chosen by the county before
the said justices, for the sustaining of the war and for the upkeep of the
county where they are levied.[4]

Also that with those who go on pilgrimage as beggars it shall be done
as with the labourers abovesaid.[5]

Also that the justices of the peace shall hold their sessions in each
county according to the ordinances made in other statutes, taking their
wages, that is to say 4s. a day and the clerks of the justices 2s., out of
the fines and amercements made before them, by the hands of the said
two chosen men, and that they shall continue their sessions in each
quarter of the year for three days at the least.[6]

applied to the costs of war. The labour legislation of 1388 was not in fact included in the commission of the peace until June 1390, when J.P.s were charged
with the enforcement of *caps*. 3, 6, and 10 of the Statute of Cambridge (R.
Sillem, 'Commissions of the Peace, 1380-1485', in *B.I.H.R.*, x (1932-3), 83;
see also Ritchie, in *Essays in Economic History*, ed. Carus-Wilson, ii. 92, n. 3).

[5] Cf. 12 Richard II, *cap*. 7.   [6] Cf. 12 Richard II, *cap*. 10.

1388   Item soit ordeine dez termez usuels qe le mestre hyne pregne pur lan entier x*s*., et charetter x*s*., bercher x*s*., bouerer vj*s*. viij*d*., vacher vj*s*., viij*d*., porcher vj*s*., femme laborer vj*s*., deye vj*s*., chacer del charue vij*s*., au pluis et chescun autre laborer et servant solonc lour degre et*a* meyns en paiis ou ils soloient prendre meyns.[1] Et qe nul servant de artificere ne de vitaillers deinz cites, burghes nautres villes ne pregne pluis qe lez laborers suisnomez solonc lour estat sanz courtesie ou regard par covenant. Et si nul donne ou pregne a contrarie a primere foith' qil serroit atteint celuy qi prent ou donne paie au roy lexcesse issint pris et al seconde foitz double lexcesse et al tierce foitz treble lexcesse et le pernour sil neit riens de paier eit lemprisonement de xl. jours.

Item qe lestatut fait lan quinte nostre seignur le roy qorest, cest assavoir le seconde chapitre, contenant qe nul face emporter nenvoier or nargent par dela et qe le roy ne grante licence a nully de amesner, nemporter ou envoier or ou argent hors du roiaume si noun a souldiers le roy queux sont dela la meer . . .*b*[2]

Item qe lestatut fait lan seconde le roy qorest, cest assavoir le quinte chapitre, qi comence 'Item dez controvours de faux novels*c* et controvours des orribles et faux mensonges de prelatz, duckes, countes, barons et autres etc.' soit revoqe en ceste present parlement.[3]

Item qe touz maneres dez tenantz si bien deinz franchise come dehors et ceux qi tiegnent terrez en villenage et autres tenantz a volunte si bien dez seignurs come dez autres horspris villeins de sanke soient contributories as despencez des chivalers venantz au parlement pur lour countes et a touz maneres charges en supportacion del comune poeple, horspris en le counte de Kent soit leve en la manere come ad estee avant ses heures.[4]

Item qe nul viscounte soit charge sur son acompte en lescheqer*d* le roy dez fermes ou dez autres choses certeins ou de noun certeins ou de riens forspris de ceo qil poet lever duement duez au roy sanz perde du dit viscounte, non obstantz lez charges dez viscountes avant ses heures usez, et qe lez barouns de lescheqer eient poair sanz suier brief

---

a MS. au.   *b* This paragraph is evidently incomplete.   *c* MS. moneye.
d d. expunged after this word.

---

[1] Cf. 12 Richard II, *cap.* 4.

[2] The paragraph is incomplete. The reference is to 5 Richard II, statute 1, *cap.* 2 (*S.R.*, ii. 17) and the commons no doubt petitioned for its confirmation. Though not confirmed, the statute remained operative within the limits convenient to the government; see 2 Henry IV, *cap.* 5 (*S.R.*, ii. 122).

[3] A reference to 2 Richard II, statute 1, *cap.* 5. Reaffirming the substance of 3 Edward I, *cap.* 34, this provided that persons guilty of uttering the slanders which it described should be imprisoned until they produced the authors of the slanders. 12 Richard II, *cap.* 11 left their punishment to the discretion of the Council. See *S.R.*, i. 35; ii. 9, 59.

Also be it ordained concerning the usual terms that the master hind 1388 shall take for the entire year 10*s.*, the carter 10*s.*, the shepherd 10*s.*, the oxherd 6*s.* 8*d.*, the cowherd 6*s.* 8*d.*, the swineherd 6*s.*, the woman labourer 6*s.*, the dairymaid 6*s.*, the driver of the plough 7*s.*, at the most, and every other labourer and servant according to their degree, and less in the region where they were accustomed to take less.[1] And that no servant of craftsman or of victuallers within cities, boroughs, or other towns shall take more than the labourers above named, according to their estate, without courtesy or reward by covenant. And if any give or take contrariwise, the first time that he shall be attainted the taker or giver shall pay to the king the excess so taken, and at the second time double the excess, and at the third time treble the excess, and the taker, if he has nothing wherewith to pay, shall have forty days' imprisonment.

Also that the statute made in the fifth year of our lord the king that now is [1381-2], that is to say the second chapter, containing that none shall cause gold or silver to be carried or sent out of the realm and that the king shall not grant licence to any to take away, carry, or send gold or silver out of the realm except to soldiers of the king who are beyond the sea . . .[2]

Also that the statute made in the second year of the king that now is [1378-9], that is to say the fifth chapter, which begins 'Also of devisors of false news and devisors of horrible and false lies about prelates, dukes, earls, barons, and others etc.', be revoked in this present parliament.[3]

Also that all manner of tenants, both within liberties and without, and those that hold lands in villeinage and other tenants at will both of lords and others, excepting villeins by blood, shall be contributory to the expenses of knights coming to parliament for their shires and to all manner of charges in support of the common people, except that in the county of Kent the money shall be levied in the same manner as it has hitherto been.[4]

Also that no sheriff shall be charged upon his account at the king's exchequer with farms or other things, certain or uncertain, or with anything except that which he can duly levy as owing to the king without loss to the said sheriff, notwithstanding the charges upon sheriffs hitherto used; and that the barons of the exchequer shall have power, without suing a writ out of the chancery, to discharge

---

[4] A request for the continuance of the exemption of tenants in Kentish gavelkind from liability to contribute to the wages of the knights of the shire and for unequivocal recognition of the liability of the free tenants of lords summoned individually to parliament, and of other tenants of such lords unless of villein status. 12 Richard II, *cap.* 12 provided that, if a lord purchased land hitherto liable to contribute, the liability would continue. See *S.R.*, ii. 59; L. C. Latham, 'Collection of the wages of the knights of the shire in the fourteenth and fifteenth centuries', in *E.H.R.*, xlviii (1933), 455 ff., and for some of the issues involved, H. M. Cam, *Liberties and Communities in Medieval England* (Cambridge, 1944), pp. 236 ff.

1388 del chauncellerie ent descharger lez ditz viscountes par lour serement par vertue de celle ordenance.[1]

Item lestatut fait lan du regne le roy qorest sisme qi comence 'Item ordinatum est et statutum quod nec in civitate London' nec in aliis civitatibus, burgis, villis vel portubus maris per totum regnum predictum aliquis vitelarius officium judiciale[a] exerceat neque occupet quovismodo nisi in villis ubi alia persona sufficiens ad hujusmodi statum habendum reperiri non poterit: [b]dum tamen[b] idem judex pro tempore quo in officio illo steterit ab exercicio vitallarii, sub pena forisfacture victualium suorum sic venditorum, penitus cesset et se abstineat per se et suos omnino ab eodem' soit conferme et qil tiegne lieu auxibien en la citee de Loundres come aillours en avantage du roy et du roiaume et en eide de bone governance de la dit citee sur haute peyne allimite contre eux qi aillent a contrarie.[2]

Item soit ordeigne qe nul homme de quel estat ou condicion qil soit, greindre ne meindre, passe le meer devers le court de Rome hors du roiaume Dengleterre, par licence ou sanz licence, pur soi providre dascun benefice de seint esglise ove cure ou sanz cure en le dit roiaume. Et si ascun le face et par vertue de[c] tiel provisioun accepte ascun benefice ou face accepter en mesme le roiaume qal cel temps mesme le provisour soit hors de proteccion le roy et mesme le benefice voide syqe bien lice a patroun de mesme le benefice espirituel ou temporel presente a ycelle une clerke able a sa volunte.[3]

Item qe si nul tannere, corriour, sentere, nautre persone qeconqe vende pealx ou quirs fauxement overez ou nient covenablement corroiez ou tannez qe lez ditz pealx et quirs soient forfaitz au roy. Et si nul achate tielx pealx, quirs, botes ou solers et soy sente greve eit suite devers le vendour et recovere ses damages a treble et en mesme la manere soit fait as vendours des draps lynnes et dautres et de pelure et dautres peltries etc.

Item qe nul pistour ne braseour soit amercie al quarte defaute einz eit corporel penaunce sanz redempcion solonc lez estatutz avant sez heures faitz, scilicet pistor collistrigium et braciator castigatorium,[d] et qe viscountes en lour torn et seneschalles dez seignurs tenauntz lez letes en hundrede facent due execucion sur peine allimite en ceste present parlement, et qe justices de la pees eient poair denquerre de touz contrevenantz si bien al suite du roy come de partie; et si ascun seneschalle de franchise ou ascun autre officer soit atteint de ceo qil nad fait due punissement solonc le purport de lez estatutz avant ses heures

[a] S.R. inserts decetero habeat.   [b-b] S.R. in quo tamen casu.   [c] Inter-lined.   [d] MS. castigorium.

[1] i.e. sheriffs were not to be held accountable for sums which could not be

the said sheriffs thereof upon their oath by virtue of this ordinance.[1]   1388

Also that the statute made in the sixth year of the king that now is [1382-3], which begins 'Also it is ordained and enacted that neither in the city of London nor in other cities, boroughs, towns, or ports of the sea throughout the realm aforesaid shall any victualler exercise or in any wise occupy any judicial office except in towns where no other sufficient person can be found to hold such office: and then provided always that the same judge for as long as he shall continue in that office, shall utterly cease and abstain, by himself and his, from the exercise of victualling, under pain of forfeiture of his victuals so sold,' shall be confirmed and that it shall hold place as well in the city of London as elsewhere to the profit of the king and of the realm and in furtherance of the good government of the said city, under the great penalty prescribed for those who go against it.[2]

Also be it ordained that no man of whatever estate or condition he be, great or small, shall pass over sea to the court of Rome out of the realm of England, with or without licence, to provide for himself any benefice of Holy Church, with or without cure, in the said realm. And if any do so, and by virtue of such provision accept or cause to be accepted any benefice in the same realm that thereupon such provisor shall be outside the king's protection and such benefice void so that it shall be entirely lawful for the patron of such benefice, spiritual or temporal, to present to the same a competent clerk at his will.[3]

Also that if any tanner, currier, souter, or other person whatsoever sell skins or hides falsely worked or not properly curried or tanned, the said skins and hides shall be forfeit to the king. And if any buy such skins, hides, boots, or shoes and feel himself aggrieved, he shall have his suit against the vendor and recover treble damages; and in like manner it shall be done with the vendors of linen and other cloths and of furs and other peltry.

Also that at his fourth default no baker or brewer shall be amerced but shall have corporal punishment without ransom according to the statutes heretofore made, to wit the baker, the pillory and the brewer the whipping-post, and that sheriffs at their tourns and lords' stewards holding hundred leets shall make due execution, upon the pain specified in this present parliament, and that justices of the peace shall have power to inquire of all contraveners as well at the suit of the king as of a party; and if any steward of a franchise or any other officer is attainted of having failed to administer due punishment according to the intent of the statutes heretofore made, he shall pay to the king

---

levied on account of the enlargement of franchises. See Tuck, in *E.H.R.*, lxxxiv (1969), 239.

[2] A reference to 6 Richard II, statute 1, *cap.* 9 (*S.R.*, ii. 28). See also above, p. 334 and nn.

[3] Cf. 12 Richard II, *cap.* 15 (*S.R.*, ii. 60, and below, p. 430; see also p. 382).

1388 faitz, paie fyn au roy solonc le discrecion dez justices et damages au partie pleintif au double etc.[1]

Ista postmodum et alia plura[2] hiis adjuncta fuerunt in statutum redacta London'que ac aliis plerisque locis eciam proclamata. In isto itaque parliamento clerus concessit domino regi unam decimam et una quintadecima concessa est sibi a populo laicali.[3]

Circa festum sancti Michaelis magistri Nicholaus Stoket,[a] Walterus Sibyle et Thomas Gray de Eboraco venerunt de Prusia, referentes pacem esse firmatam inter nos et illos ac ampliora privilegia Anglicis mercatoribus concessisse quam ibi actenus habuerunt: nam antea suas negociaciones non[b] poterant mercatores inibi exercere nisi in confinio et in uno loco quasi in remotissimo angulo terre illius, nunc vero istorum tractatu libere possunt emere et vendere in omni loco terre predicte.[4]

Sexto die Octobris dominus Thomas Tryvet miles[5] coegit equum suum currere in terra nuperius exarata, et casualiter inter sulcos cespitans ipsum Thomam cadendo oppressit et ita confregit quod vix per novem horas postea supervixit. Quo eciam die in pleno parliamento fuerat proclamatum ut si quis contra eum vellet opponere de prodicione seu de alio crimine notabili propter quod mortis supplicio merito puniretur, crastina die veniret et proponeret ac secundum allegata et probata sentenciam judicialem subiret. Set Deus hanc sentenciando prevenit. Ceteri namque milites,[6] qui aliquamdiu

---

[a] *Added in the margin after* Nicholaus, *which ends a line.*　　　[b] *Interlined.*

---

[1] The commons were asking for (but did not obtain) a stiffening of the Assize of Bread and Ale, attributed to 51 Henry III, exemplified in letters patent in 1379, and subsumed in the ordinances and statutes relating to the sale of victuals which were not included in the definitive commission of the peace of 1380. This authorized amercement as the punishment even after the 3rd offence, provided the offence in question was of a minor nature: corporal punishment was required only if such offences were committed 'pluries', without intention of amendment. The Assize provided other means for the corporal punishment of brewers (assumed to be women) beside the whipping post: the tumbril and the trebuchet. See *S.R.*, i. 199-200; *Cal. Pat. R., 1377-81*, p. 335; *R.P.*, iii. 84; Sillem, in *B.I.H.R.* (1932-3), x. 99.

[2] 12 Richard II, *caps.* 1, 13-14, and 16 were not derived from the petition just recited.

[3] The lay grant was for the defence of the realm (*Cal. Fine R., 1383-91*,

a fine according to the justices' discretion and to the party complain- 1388
ing double his damages etc.[1]

These provisions, and a number of others in addition,[2]
were later drawn up into a statute and proclaimed in London
and several other places. In this parliament the clergy granted
the king a tenth, while the laity made him a grant of a fifteenth.[3]

Masters Nicholas Stoket, Walter Sibyle, and Thomas Gray
of York returned from Prussia about Michaelmas [29 Sep-
tember] to report that peaceable relations had been established between us and the Prussians, who had given to English
merchants more extensive privileges than they had hitherto
enjoyed there: for whereas in the past these merchants had
been unable to pursue their business except on the borders
and in one very remote corner of the country, as a consequence of the negotiations they are now free to buy and sell
in every part of it.[4]

On 6 October, when Sir Thomas Trivet[5] put his horse to
the gallop over some newly ploughed land, his mount happened to stumble between the furrows and fell with its
weight on top of him, crushing him so badly that he lived
barely nine hours more. On that very day proclamation was
made in full parliament that anybody who wished to accuse
him of treason or of any other outstanding crime that would
properly be visited with the death penalty, was to appear and
put his case on the following day when the accused would be
subjected to a judicial decision in accordance with what was
alleged and proved. But God forestalled any such judgement
with his own. The rest of the knights,[6] who had been for

---

pp. 265-9). For the tenth granted by the clergy of the southern province in convocation on 12 Oct. 1388, on more stringent conditions, see ibid., p. 264, and
Tuck, in *E.H.R.*, lxxxiv (1969), 241.

[4] The Anglo-Prussian treaty of 21 Aug. 1388 gave reciprocal privileges to
English merchants in Prussia and Prussian merchants in England (Rymer, *Foedera*,
vii. 599-601; Power and Postan, *Studies in English Trade in the Fifteenth Century*,
p. 108). See also above, p. 330.

[5] For whom see above, pp. 228 and n., 338. The following episode occurred
while Trivet was riding to join the king's household at Barnwell (*Vita Ricardi II*,
p. 120).

[6] William Elmham and Nicholas Dagworth. With Trivet, they had been released
from custody on 30 May 1388, bailed to appear at the next parliament (above,
p. 338).

1388 in custodia erant detenti quia *prima facie* erant quodammodo dominis predictis suspecti, pristine libertati eo
die fuerant restituti preterquam in curia domini regis
nequaquam manerent. Consimilem vero graciam dominus
Ricardus Metford, dominus Ricardus Clifford,*b* dominus
p. 187 Nicholaus / Slake et dominus Johannes Lincoln clerici[1]
reportarunt.

Quo in tempore *venerunt nova quomodo* dux Lancastr'
copulavit filiam suam Katerinam*b* filio et heredi regis
Hispannie, pro cujus copulacione multam immo et magnam
copiam auri recepit, set pax inter regnum Anglie et Hispannie
nullatenus per hoc potuit optineri quia in tantum erat rex
Hispannie regi Francorum confederatus quod nullo modo
sine ejus assensu pax inter nos potuit reformari.[2] Item circa
principium mensis Octobris venerunt Scoti juxta Berewycum
ut ibi predas abigerent bestiarum; quibus confestim homines
nostri occurrerunt et ipsos in fugam coegerunt, quos ipsi
prosequentes quosdam occiderunt ex illis et quosdam circa
quingentos ceperunt. Item xij. die Octobris[3] Londonienses
ut moris est *celebrata eleccione novi majoris* dominum
Nicholaum Tuyford aurifabrum in eorum majorem communiter elegerunt.

Item de mense Octobris rex Francorum congregata multitudine armatorum contra ducem Geldr'*[4] processit, venitque

---

In the right-hand margin: Vide plura de isto duce Gel⟨dr'⟩ deorsum in margine
ad i⟨stum⟩ signum ☙; *and in the lower margin the following passage*: Mortuo duce
Brabancie quedam matrona generosa in ejus ducatum successit; quem dux Geldr'

---

*a–a Interlined.   b Interlined.   c–c In the upper margin but marked for
insertion here.   d–d Added in the margin.*

---

[1] For whom see above, p. 340 and n.
[2] The betrothal of Catalina, Lancaster's younger daughter, to Henry, son and
heir of Juan I of Castile, took place at Palencia, probably on 17 Sept. 1388. As
part of the same settlement of outstanding dynastic issues, Lancaster renounced
his claim to the throne of Castile and received, in return, an indemnity of £100,000
and an annual pension of £6,600. Juan I had in fact refused to make a peace
treaty with England which did not embrace France. See Russell, *English Intervention*, pp. 504 ff., and, on the negotiations at Bayonne that preceded the
marriage alliance, above, p. 194 and nn.
[3] Correctly, 13 Oct. (*Letter Book H*, p. 335).

some time under arrest because appearances at first made   1388
them objects of some suspicion to the Lords Appellant,
were restored on the same day to their former liberty, except
that they were in no circumstances to remain about the royal
court. Comparable indulgence was won for themselves by the
clerks, Richard Medford, Richard Clifford, Nicholas Slake,
and John Lincoln.[1]

News now arrived of the match made by the duke of Lancaster between his daughter Katherine and the son and heir
of the king of Spain, a match for which he reaped numerous,
and indeed substantial, rewards in gold, but by which peace
could not possibly be achieved between the kingdoms,
England and Spain, because the Spanish king was so much in
league with the king of the French that without the latter's
approval there was no way in which peace could be restored
between us.[2] About the beginning of October the Scots
appeared in the neighbourhood of Berwick to carry out a
cattle-raid; our men were quick to confront them and put
them to flight, in the subsequent pursuit killing some of them
and capturing others to the number of about 500. On 12
October[3] the people of London held the customary election
of a new mayor: the common choice for that office fell on
Sir Nicholas Twyford, a goldsmith.

In this same October the king of the French collected an
army and marched against the duke of Guelders.*[4] Arrived

---

*In the right-hand margin: See further concerning this duke of Guelders, in
the lower margin at this symbol ♨; and in the lower margin, the following passage:
On the death of the duke of Brabant a certain noblewoman succeeded to the

---

[4] William of Jülich, duke of Guelders 1371-1402, who had been, since June
1387, England's ally. On their campaign against him in the autumn of 1388,
Charles VI and the French in fact avoided Brabant. It is, however, true that they
suffered losses both in Guelders and on the return journey, after the conclusion of
peace between the king of France and the duke of Guelders in the treaty of
Körenzig, on 12 Oct. 1388. The regency of Philip the Bold, duke of Burgundy,
and of John, duke of Berry, his brother, was ended in Nov. 1388. See *Chronique
du religieux de Saint-Denys*, ed. Bellaguet, i. 528 ff.; H. Laurent and F. Quicke,
*Les Origines de l'état bourguignon: l'accession de la maison de Bourgogne aux
duchés de Brabant et de Limbourg (1383-1407)*, i (Brussels, 1939), pp. 161-2,
220 ff.

1388 in Brabanciam, ubi inter quingentos et sexcentos amisit
de suis: tandem Parisius cum verecundia est reversus, ubi
non post multos dies ex more tento parliamento illi de
communitate ducem de*a* Berry et ducem Burgundie de
eorum regis consilio amoverunt, affirmantes eos illorum
regem nequiter gubernasse et semper bellum, non pacem,
optasse et propter hoc eos penitus destruxisse; unde ceteris
postpositis finaliter concludendo dixerunt se velle omnino
pacem habere.

Item xvij. die Octobris apud Novum Castrum obiit dominus J. Nevyll';[1] quo eciam die apud Cantebrig' parliamentum
erat finitum. *b*Quo in tempore dux Lancastr' cum suis venit
Burdegal.'*b* Item post principium mensis Novembris[2] venit
rex Westmon' et optulit feretro Sancti Edwardi unum anulum
aureum in quo est rubea gemma inclusa magni precii et
valoris. Item xvj. die Novembris Johannes Haule de Dertemouthe quinque naves hominibus armorum bene munitas

jure hereditario vendicavit,[3] ac in maximo apparatu in Brabanciam cum exercitu
suo secessit, firmans castella et cetera fortalicia inibi circumquaque. Mulier vero
misit pro succursu ad regem Francorum, qui venit splendide in comitiva
armatorum suorum ad subigendum ducem predictum: dux quoque vias suas
quibus transiret obstruxit, unde rex Francorum plures ibi de suis amisit. Expost
enim mediantibus amicis inter utrosque ambo convenerunt sub hac forma, quod
dux Geldr' per unum annum integrum non gestaret arma contra regem Francorum
nisi imperator aut rex Anglorum ea de causa sibi misissent, in quorum presencia
infra annum contra eum liceret arma gestare, non obstante convencione premissa.[4]
Quibus rite peractis dux ipse disposuit adire Terram Sanctam; et in eundo a quibusdam suis emulis fuit captus et quinquaginta millibus marcarum redemptus,
datis obsidibus viam tenuit quam accepit, *c*nec illam*c* propter hoc minime preter-
misit.[5] Formam convencionis inter ipsum et regem Francorum domino regi
fideliter destinavit.

a Interlined.   *b–b* A marginal entry which occurs at this point in the MS.
but without an exact indication of the place for its insertion.   *c–c* Interlined.

[1] John, Lord Nevill of Raby (d. 1388), for whom see G.E.C., ix. 502-3; see
also Cal. Inq. p.m., xvi. 725 ff.

[2] On 14 Nov. (Liber Niger Quaternus, fo. 86). The king was to have the use
during his lifetime of the ring mentioned in this passage, and it was to be worn
by his successors at their coronation.

[3] A partisan reference to the claim of Duke William of Guelders to the succession in Brabant following the death of Duke Wenzel of Brabant in 1383. Wenzel
had ruled in the right of Joanna, his wife, by whom he was survived. William
derived his hereditary claim from the marriage of his father, William III of Jülich,
whom he succeeded in that duchy in 1393, to Marie, youngest of the sisters of
the Duchess Joanna. He had more limited claims on certain dependent territories
of Brabant which were situated in the duchy of Jülich; for these see Vaughan,

in Brabant, he lost between 500 and 600 men before return- 1388 ing humiliated to Paris, where, at a parliament held according to custom a few days later, the commons removed the dukes of Berry and Burgundy from the king's council, declaring that they had misguided the king, had consistently preferred war to peace, and had on this account utterly ruined the commons, whose own pre-eminent desire could be summed up as wholly for peace.

Sir J. Nevill[1] died at Newcastle on 17 October, the day on which the Cambridge parliament came to an end. The duke of Lancaster came with his retinue to Bordeaux at this time. Early in November[2] the king visited Westminster and presented to St. Edward's shrine a gold ring set with a very costly and valuable ruby. On 16 November John Hawley of Dartmouth sent to sea five ships with a strong complement

duchy, to which the duke of Guelders had claims based on hereditary right.[3] Summoning his utmost resources, he established himself and his army in the heart of Brabant, stiffening the defences of the castles and other strongholds all round him. The woman sent for help to the king of the French who came in majestic array at the head of his army to put the duke down; but the latter blocked the roads on the line of approach so that the French king lost a number of his men on the way. Through the mediation of friends of both parties, the pair subsequently reached an agreement whereby the duke was to abstain for one whole year from bearing arms against the king of the French unless the emperor or the English king sent expressly asking him to do so: in company with them it would be permissible for him, notwithstanding the agreement, to bear arms within the year against the French king.[4] These matters duly concluded, the duke arranged a journey to the Holy Land; on his way there he was taken prisoner by some of his enemies. Ransomed at the cost of 50,000 marks, he handed over hostages and continued the journey he had undertaken without in the least allowing the circumstances to make him abandon it.[5] The terms of the agreement between himself and the king of the French he loyally reported to our own king.

Philip the Bold, p. 97. See also Laurent and Quicke, op. cit., pp. 106 ff., 138 ff.

There follows a reference to the war between Duke William and the Duchess Joanna which occasioned the French intervention in Guelders in 1388.

[4] The Treaty of Körenzig, for which see above, p. 371 n. In it, Duke William of Guelders undertook to give a year's notice of hostilities against the king of France, and to indulge in these only if his obligations to the king of England required him to do so (*Gedenkwaardigheden uit de Geschiedenis van Gelderland*, ed. I. A. Nijhoff (6 vols., 1830-75), iii. no. 132; *Chronique du religieux de Saint-Denys*, ed. Bellaguet, i. 548 ff.).

[5] In Nov. 1388 the duke departed, not for Outremer, but to take part in the crusade in Prussia. For his capture at Pomeranian hands on 13 Dec. see R. Ernsing, *Wilhelm III von Jülich als Herzog von Geldern (1372-1393)* (Paderborn and Münster, 1885), pp. 76 ff. He returned to Guelders in Oct. 1389, but his envoy was in England in Mar. 1389 (P.R.O., E. 403/521, 13 Mar.).

1388 misit in mare; ceperuntque secundo die viij. naves vino de la Rochelle et aliis mercimoniis diversis onustas, et tercio die ad villam de Dertemouthe salvi et incolumes pervenerunt. Habueruntque in jam dictis navibus ix^c. dolia vini, ceperunt eciam in illis homines armorum iiij^{xx}.

Item circa finem mensis Novembris electi sunt per consilium domini regis episcopus Dunelm', magister J. Schepeye, magister Ricardus Rounhale, dominus J. Deverose, dominus J. Clanvowe, et dominus Nicholaus Daggeworth' ad tractandum de pace cum Francis; et quinto die Decembris versus Cales' transierunt omnes excepto J. Deverose.^{a1} Franci vero, quia non habuerunt salvum conductum, ad eos apud Cales' descendere formidabant,^{2} propter quod negocium usque post festum Natalis Domini exstitit protelatum.^{b} Item de mense Decembris capitaneus ville de Chireborgh^3 cum suis hominibus armorum in Franciam equitavit, venitque ad quandam villam ubi erant nundine; omnes res venales ibidem^c que erant alicujus valoris cum universis captivis secum asportavit et ad Chireborgh predictam sine resistencia secum adduxit. Item eodem mense capitaneus de Berewyk equitavit cum suis usque Scoticum mare,^{4} cepitque captivos et predam magnam nimis, et omnia ad villam de Berewyk sine molestacione cujusque adduxit.

Item^d relatum est tunc temporis de quodam milite Francigena existente in Terra Sancta, ubi habuit in visione quod transiret ad quoslibet Christianos in Europe partibus habitantes ut ipsi omnino dimitterent eorum bella et ad pacis redeant unitatem: ob hanc igitur^e causam venit ipse Burdegal', ubi dux Lancastr' tenuit suum Natale, volensque cum eo in Angliam transire causa predicta.^{5} Rex quoque Anglie tenuit suum Natale apud Eltham in multis hastiludiis

---

^{a} *A short space, covered by a dash, follows.* ^{b} Quo eciam tempore misit rex igitur duci Lancastr' ut sub sua ligiancia ad eum veniret *deleted after this word.* ^{c} *Interlined.* ^{d} Ca⟨ve⟩ *in the margin but damaged.* ^{e} *Interlined.*

---

^{1} Ambassadors were appointed to treat with the French about a truce or a final peace on 26 Nov. 1388; Sheppey is not named in the procuration. Ronhale, Clanvow, Skirlaw (bishop of Durham), and Dagworth left England a week or more after the date in the text. The mission was a response to an approach made initially by Philip the Bold, duke of Burgundy, on behalf of the king of France as long ago as Dec. 1387; the proposal then was for a truce during which the king of Armenia would use his good offices to secure a final peace. See P.R.O., E. 364/22,

of men-at-arms; on the second day out they captured eight 1388
vessels laden with wine of La Rochelle and other miscellaneous goods, and on the third day they returned safe and
sound to Dartmouth. The captured ships contained 900 tuns
of wine, and the prisoners taken included 80 men-at-arms.

About the end of November the choice of the king's
council for negotiators with the French about peace fell
upon the bishop of Durham, Master John Sheppey, Master
Richard Ronhale, Sir John Devereux, Sir John Clanvow, and
Sir Nicholas Dagworth, of whom all, except Sir John
Devereux, crossed to Calais on 5 December.[1] Having no safe-
conduct, the French were afraid to come as far as Calais to
meet them;[2] and the business was accordingly postponed
until after Christmas. During December, too, the captain of
Cherbourg[3] made a mounted raid with his men-at-arms into
France. Coming into a town where a fair was in progress, he
carried off every article on sale that was worth anything
and having made all the people his prisoners took his captures
back to Cherbourg unresisted. During the same month the
captain of Berwick conducted a mounted raid with his forces
as far as the Scottish sea,[4] taking prisoners and an enormous
amount of booty, all brought back with him to Berwick
without interference from anyone.

There were reports at this time about a French knight who,
while he was in the Holy Land, was bidden in a vision to visit
all the Christian inhabitants of Europe, urging them to abandon their wars altogether and to return to the unity of peace.
This mission brought him to Bordeaux, where the duke of
Lancaster (with whom, in pursuit of his purpose, the knight
wished to travel to England) spent his Christmas.[5] The king of
England for his part kept Christmas at Eltham, with numerous

mm. 21[V], 25; ibid., 23, mm. 26, 33; Mirot and Déprez, in *B.E.C.*, lx (1899),
p. 209, no. 498; Rymer, *Foedera*, vii. 610–12; cf. ibid., p. 637. The negotiations
took place at Leulingham, between Calais and Boulogne. For the truce signed
there on 18 June 1389 see below, p. 398.

[2] A safe-conduct for the French ambassadors was issued on 16 Nov. (Rymer,
op. cit., vii. 608).

[3] William Scrope (*Cal. Pat. R., 1385–9*, pp. 129–30).

[4] i.e. the Firth of Forth. The captain of Berwick was Sir Ralph de Lomley.

[5] Cf. Froissart (*Chroniques*, xiii. 301–2), who witnessed a joust between 5
English knights of Lancaster's household and 5 French knights at Bordeaux in the
New Year, 1389.

1388 et jocundis solaciis congruentibus festivitati predicte. Item modicum ante festum Natalis Domini quidam de Dertemoutha et Fowy sulcantes maria xxv. naves magnas et parvas vino plene*a* onustas ceperunt et sine dampno ad propria redierunt.

1389   xvj. die Januarii obiit frater Johannes Tymeworthe abbas de Burgo Sancti Edmundi; et die xxviij. ejusdem mensis conventus ejusdem loci processit per viam scrutinii ad eleccionem et fratrem Willelmum Cratefeld monachum de gremio ejusdem ecclesie in sui abbatem assumpsit.[1]

Quo in tempore dominus Nicholaus Daggeworthe veniens de Cales' exposuit domino regi et suo consilio quomodo Francigene voluerunt simul habere Scociam in tractatu eorum inter nos et illos de pace. Ad hoc ex parte nostra fuit responsum quod hoc non erat opus ibi cum illis tractare 'ex quo nobis ita vicini*b* existunt quod nos sicco pede ad illos possumus venire ac consimiliter ipsi ad nos: igitur si voluerint nobiscum de pace tractare, veniant ad nos sicuti solebant et ea que volunt proponere pacifice*c* audiemus.'[2] Ad hec Francigene dixerunt se velle super isto articulo cum eorum rege consulere, sicque fecerunt; propter quod illi ex parte nostra ibidem missi diu postea Cales' morabantur reditum expectantes Francorum.

Item xx. die Januarii rex tenuit suum magnum consilium apud Westmonasterium, ad quod magne persone tocius Anglie pro majori parte*d* cum aliis valentibus personis de communitate venerunt, in quo multa fuerunt proposita ac eciam ventilata que in apertum minime prodierunt. Tamen ordinatum est quod comes Notyngham' cum aliis viris cordatis sibi adjunctis haberet custodiam marchie orientalis versus Scociam et *e*comes Northumberl⟨and'⟩,*e* dominus de Beaumond, dominus de Clifford et alii domini illius patrie custodirent occidentalem plagam Scocie contiguam usque festum Sancti Petri ad Vincula, quo tempore, Deo favente, rex cum toto suo retenemento Scociam adiret et illorum

---

a MS. pleno.   *b* An erasure, covered by a dash, follows.   *c* Interlined.
d venerunt deleted after this word.   *e-e* In the margin but marked for insertion here; the final letters have been lost at the edge of the MS.

---

[1] The election received the royal assent on 1 Feb. 1389 and the temporalities were restored on 8 Oct. (*Cal. Pat. R., 1388-92*, pp. 4, 112; see also ibid., p. 45).

tourneys and pleasant pastimes suitable for the season. 1388
In the course of a cruise, seamen from Dartmouth and
Fowey captured just before Christmas twenty-five ships
of varying sizes, with full cargoes of wine, and returned
home unscathed.

Brother John Timworth, abbot of Bury St. Edmunds, died 1389
on 16 January; and on the 28th the convent proceeded to an
election by ballot, when their choice of abbot fell on Brother
William Cratfield, a monk from the bosom of the abbey.[1]

Sir Nicholas Dagworth arrived at this time from Calais
and explained to the king and council that the French
wanted to have Scotland included in the peace negotiations
between them and ourselves. To this the reply on our side
was that it was unnecessary for discussion of this with the
Scots to be at Calais, 'since they are such near neighbours of
ours that we can visit them dry-shod, as they can us: if,
therefore, they want peace talks with us, let them come to
us, as they have always done, and we will listen quietly to
what they have to say.'[2] The French said in answer that upon
this point they wished to consult their king; and this is what
they did; with the consequence that our envoys hung about
at Calais for a long time afterwards, waiting for the return of
the French.

On 20 January the king held his great council at Westminster, which was attended by most of the great from all
over England, together with other worthies drawn from the
commons, and at which several matters were raised and
discussed that were not disclosed. It was ordered, however,
that the earl of Nottingham, assisted by other men of mettle,
should take charge of the Eastern March towards Scotland,
and that the western districts bordering Scotland should
be safeguarded by the earl of Northumberland, Lord Beaumont, Lord Clifford, and other local magnates, until the
feast of St. Peter's Chains [1 August], when, under God's
favour, the king with his entire following would march
on Scotland and take vigorous action to tame completely

[2] The truce of Leulingham provided for the Scots and they, though reluctant
to participate, accepted the terms (Froissart, *Chroniques*, xiii. 316–17; below, p.
398 and nn.). The Monk may have drawn at this point on the actual text of the
council's instructions to the English envoys.

1389 ferocitatem viriliter perdomaret.[1] Concessumque est eis quod
ad vadia domini regis haberent sexcentas lanceas per idem
tempus et duo milia sagittariorum *ultra illos quos illi in
dicta patria poterunt colligere et habere.*[2] Item ad instanciam dominorum tunc ibidem presencium rex contulit
ducatum Aquitannie duci Lancastr' et ducatum Hibernie
duci Gloucestr' suis avunculis. Quicquid dictum est non erant
ibi pro tempore nisi locum tenentes, prout quidam dicunt
et pro vero affirmant, eo quod ista pertinent ad coronam,
unde rex non potuit talia ab illa pro perpetuo alienare.[3]

In principio mensis Februarii misit rex pro abbate Westm'
ad comparendum coram eo ibidem responsurus super querelis
et gravaminibus que illi de capella Sancti Stephani contra
eum nequiter intentabant. Dixerunt namque ipsum agere in
curia Romana post prohibicionem regis ad privacionem sive
inhabilitacionem suorum beneficiorum et hac de causa
monachum quendam ad dictam curiam destinasse.[4] Super
istis dati sunt judices ad sentenciandum: judices vero tale
judicium super eum dederunt, quod si foret verum ita eum
fecisse prout illi asseruerunt merito temporalia sua amitteret
indilate et corpus suum in carceribus poneretur ubi rex
p. 188 voluerit assignare. / Istud fuit deductum tandem coram
consilio domini regis abbate presente, qui diversimode
excusavit se, promittensque illis si fuerit oportunum suum
monachum a curia revocare. Rex vero hiis auditis, quamvis
abbas contra prohibicionem deliquerit prosequendo causam
suam in curia contra illos de capella prefata, nichilominus
totum remisit, volens ecclesiam suam ea parte servare

a-a In the margin but marked for insertion here.

---

[1] On 8 Mar. 1389, Thomas Mowbray, earl of Nottingham, was appointed
warden of the East March for one year, from 1 June 1389, and on 3 Mar. 1389,
Henry Percy, earl of Northumberland, Roger Clifford, John, Lord Roos, and
Ralph, Lord Nevill, were appointed wardens of the West March from 15 June
1389; in the event, only the appointments of Roos and Nevill took effect in the
West March; they did so from 15 June 1389 (*Rot. Scot.*, ii. 94, 96; *Cal. Documents relating to Scotland*, ed. Bain, iv. 389; Storey, in *E.H.R.*, lxxii (1957),
612 and nn.).
[2] Cf. Nottingham's indenture, promising him £12,000 p.a. in time of war and
requiring him to find 400 men-at-arms and 800 archers on the East March for the
months of June and July 1389 (P.R.O., E. 101/73/2/38). Roos and Nevill were
promised £6,000 p.a. in time of war (ibid., E. 403/524, 17 July). For the men
actually retained by Nottingham on the East March, see ibid., E. 364/30, m. 28.

the savage spirit of the Scots.[1] In the meantime they were to 1389
be allowed, in addition to the forces which they might be
able to raise and maintain locally, 600 spearmen and 2,000
archers, their wages paid by the king.[2] At the request of the
lords present at this council the king conferred the duchy
of Aquitaine on the duke of Lancaster and the dukedom of
Ireland on another uncle, the duke of Gloucester. Whatever
the words used, the grantees were only temporary lieutenants,
as some people say and, indeed, lay down for truth, since
these fiefs are appurtenances of the Crown, so that the king
had no power to alienate them from it in perpetuity.[3]

At the beginning of February the king summoned the
abbot of Westminster to appear before him and to answer
the complaints and accusations maliciously levelled against
him by the clergy of St. Stephen's Chapel. They alleged that
after the issue of a royal writ of prohibition he was moving
in the Roman curia to secure their being deprived of, or
disqualified from, their benefices and that with this object
he had dispatched a monk to the curia.[4] Judges were
appointed to pronounce upon the matter: the judgement
they delivered on the abbot was that if it was true that
he had behaved as the complainants declared, he would
deserve to lose his temporalities forthwith and to suffer
bodily imprisonment wherever the king chose to specify.
Now at last there was trial of the facts before the king's
council in the presence of the abbot, who offered various
arguments in his defence, and undertook that, if circumstances favoured it, he would recall his monk from the curia.
When he heard this, the king, despite the abbot's offence
against the prohibition in proceeding in the curia against the
clergy of the chapel, nevertheless remitted all penalty out of
his desire to keep his church safe from harm or loss in that

[3] Cf. below, p. 518 and n. Lancaster was not created duke of Aquitaine until
Mar. 1390, when the grant was for his life. The lordship of Ireland, recently forfeited by de Vere, was not conferred on Gloucester at this time; but in 1392 he
was appointed the king's lieutenant in Ireland, though not for life or heritably.
See below, pp. 414, 486.

[4] The allegation was correct: Br. John Borewell had been at the curia since
Dec. 1387, promoting the cause of the abbot and convent of Westminster against
the canons of St. Stephen's Chapel in the protracted phase which had opened
when the latter refused to submit to papal judgement in favour of the Abbey in
1381, for which see above, p. 38 n.; and see also *Monks*, p. 118.

1389 indempnem. Constat namque quod ista causa,*a* que adhuc vertitur et agitatur inter abbatem et conventum Westmon' et decanum dicte capelle infra palacium regium situate, habuit incepcionem parum ante mortem regis Edwardi tercii a conquestu ac magnis sumptibus dictorum religiosorum hucusque continuata. Interim vero dicti religiosi sustinuerunt ea de causa dispendia non modica et jacturas, videlicet in amissione suorum temporalium tempore Michaelis de la Pole cancellarii domini regis, quamvis rex nichil percepit de eisdem tamen circa prosecucionem eorundem erat eis satis dampnosum. Causa discordie fuit ista: nam predicti religiosi ea vellent exercere ibidem in illos et alios infra palacium prefatum degentes que ordinarie jurisdiccionis sunt secundum quod antiquitus dinoscitur eos fecisse; set postea multorum precibus et instancia pariter inclinati propter bonum pacis et concordie triginta octo personas ejusdem collegii exemerunt[1] et plura hiis ampliora illis postmodum processu temporum concesserunt, nec tamen eorum aviditati satisfacere potuissent quin in omni tractatu aliquod novum concedendum semper illis callide porrexerunt, prout in eorum tractatibus plenius continetur.*b* Religiosi vero causam in curia ventilarunt et *c*pro eis*c* tres sentencias reportarunt, ipsis suspensis a divinis cum eorum capella, in qua suspensione diu postea usque ad ista tempora perstiterunt; qui semper dictis religiosis dampna et incomoda regi et universis regni dominis profecto interim nepharie procurabant, immo vigilanter et attrociter incitabant isto tempore dominum regem, ducem Gloucestr', dominum Thomam archiepiscopum Eboracen' cancellarium Anglie, et alios generosos contra prefatos religiosos ad inducendum eos causam et prosecucionem suam dimittere et eorum

---

a Interlined.   *b* MS. continentur.   *c-c* Interlined.

[1] Clement VI exempted the dean and canons of St. Stephen's from the jurisdiction of the ordinary, and the abbot and convent of Westminster (who claimed parochial and ordinary jurisdiction in their precinct) had not pressed a claim to jurisdiction over the college itself in the face of this privilege — a wise acquiescence represented by the Monk as an explicit grant of exemption to the 38 members of the college. The dispute was about jurisdiction over other residents in the Palace of Westminster. The 1st of the 3 papal judgements in the Abbey's favour referred to by the Monk in the following account was the excommunication and suspension of the dean and canons by Urban VI on 23 June 1378,

respect. It is well known that this ecclesiastical cause, which 1389 is still simmering briskly between the abbot and convent of Westminster on the one hand and the dean of the above-named chapel in the royal palace on the other, had its origin shortly before the death of King Edward III and has been carried on to this day at high cost to the monks, who in this period have had to endure through it great expense and sacrifice, namely in the loss of their temporalities when Michael de la Pole was the king's chancellor; for though the king took nothing out of the temporalities, the proceedings for their recovery were costly enough. The occasion of the dispute was that, in accordance with what is recognized to have been their practice in ancient times, the religious would have liked to exercise over the St. Stephen's clergy and others established within the palace the jurisdiction proper to an ordinary, but afterwards, bowing alike to entreaties and to pressure from many quarters, for the sake of peace and har-mony they exempted 38 members of the college[1] and later, in the course of time, made to St. Stephen's further and more lavish concessions without, however, being able to satisfy the other party's greed sufficiently to prevent them from ever-lastingly putting forward some cunning new demand at every discussion, as is more fully contained in the [record of the] negotiations. The monks aired their cause in the Roman curia and obtained three judgements in their favour, the St. Stephen's clergy and their chapel being suspended from the celebration of divine service; and this suspension had now con-tinued for a long time, throughout which they contrived in their malice endless damage for the religious and, indeed, trouble for the king and all the great men in the kingdom — at this very time they were watchfully and ruthlessly setting the king, the duke of Gloucester, Thomas archbishop of York and chancellor of England, and other noblemen against the monks, who were to be induced to drop the pursuit of their

following their refusal to answer a citation to the papal court; for the others see above, p. 38 n. The dean and canons submitted to papal judgement on or about 15 June 1393, and the dispute was finally compromised on 10 Aug. 1394. See W.A.M. Bk. 12, fos. 31 ff.; W.A.M. 18435; Liber Niger Quaternus, fo. 118; *Cal. Papal Letters*, iv (1362-1404), p. 462; and *V.C.H. London*, i. 567-8. It is clear that the Monk wrote with some of the voluminous records of the dispute before him.

1389 ordinacioni submittere indilate; quodque factum multum displicuit religiosis predictis, quia quos antea habuerunt dominos et amicos nunc eorum mala informacione, nolentes eos submittere eorum dominacionibus prout illi eorum potestatibus ⟨se⟩[a] subdiderunt, de amicis ad inimicicias sunt conversi.

Papa vero super ordinacione facta in ultimo parliamento commotus, eo quod nullus transiret ad curiam Romanam ad impetrandum beneficium majus vel minus, igitur reservavit omnia beneficia vacancia sive vacatura in manu sua,[1] scribens domino regi super benediccione sua quod non impediret citatos nominaliter sive personaliter venire ad curiam responsuri quare beneficia de jure aliis debita illicite[b] occupare presumunt. Set quia[b] predicta ordinacio parliamenti nequaquam fuerat executa ideo universa ut antea inconcusse steterunt.

Item xiij. die Februarii obiit magister Adam Houton' episcopus Meneven'; ad quam favore domini regis electus est dominus Ricardus Metford', set papa eleccionem cassavit et fratrem Gilbertum episcopum Herefordensem ad ecclesiam prefatam transferre curavit ac magistrum Johannem Trevenant in Herefordensem episcopum confirmavit.[2]

Circa finem mensis Februarii missus est per regem et suum consilium comes Arundell' in Walliam, ubi usus est illa gravissima inquisicione vocata traillebaston';[3] nam Wallici protunc adinvicem dissidebant, qua de causa fuit ipse directus ad partes illas; erat namque quidam magnus Wallicus et generosus super diversis extorsionibus multipliciter impetitus, unde missus in carceribus prima nocte revera diem extremum claudebat; propter quod Wallici nimium sunt commoti. Item xxv. die Marcii erat Thomas quondam Elien' episcopus[b] in Eboracensi ecclesia installatus. Quo in tempore Scoti[c]

---

[a] *MS. om.*   [b] *Interlined.*   [c] *et, partly erased, follows this word in MS.*

[1] For the ordinance see below, p. 430. In 1395 Boniface IX revoked the reservations of Urban VI (*Registrum Johannis Trefnant episcopi Herefordensis, A.D. 1389-1404*, ed. W. W. Capes (Canterbury and York Soc., 1916), pp. 90 ff.).

[2] Gilbert was translated to St. David's and Trefnant provided to Hereford on 6 May 1389. For Gilbert, a Dominican, see *B.R.U.O.*, ii. 765-6; for Trefnant, an auditor of papal causes and himself a royal clerk, ibid., iii. 1900-1. See also *Diplomatic Correspondence of Richard II*, ed. Perroy, no. 118 and n., and for

cause and to submit it forthwith to the decision of these 1389 magnates. This conduct was greatly to the distaste of the religious, inasmuch as their former patrons and friends were now, by the misrepresentations of their adversaries, converted from friendship to hostility because the monks declined to imitate their opponents' deference to authority by submitting themselves to their lordships.

Perturbed by the ordinance made in the last parliament that none should go to the Roman curia to sue for any benefice, great or small, the pope reserved in his own hands all benefices now vacant or becoming so,[1] and wrote to the king requesting him, as he valued the papal blessing, not to prevent cited parties from appearing in the curia, either in name or in person, to show cause for their presuming unlawfully to occupy benefices that ought of right to belong to others. Since, however, the parliamentary ordinance was not carried out, everything remained as it had been before, without any disturbance.

The death occurred on 13 February of Master Adam Houghton, bishop of St. David's, to which Sir Richard Medford was elected with the king's backing, but the pope quashed the election, took steps to translate Brother [John] Gilbert, the bishop of Hereford, to St. David's, and confirmed Master John Trefnant as bishop of Hereford.[2]

About the end of February the earl of Arundel was sent by the king and his council into Wales, where he conducted the very severe form of inquiry known as 'trailbaston',[3] the reason for his dispatch to those parts being internal discord at this time between the Welsh themselves. A prominent Welshman of gentle birth who on many counts faced charges of a variety of acts of extortion, was committed to prison, where he did not survive his first night; and there was great consequent unrest among the Welsh. Thomas, formerly bishop of Ely, was installed at York on 25 March. About this time the Scots

Medford, above, p. 230 and n.

[3] The traditional name for a general commission of oyer and terminer such as was granted on 18 Feb. 1389 to Arundel and designed to deal with the kinds of offences that faced him in Wales (*Cal. Pat. R., 1388–92*, pp. 55–6; A. Harding, 'Early Trailbaston Proceedings from the Lincoln Roll of 1305', in *Medieval Legal Records edited in Memory of C. A. F. Meekings*, ed. R. F. Hunnisett and J. B. Post (London, 1978), pp. 144 ff).

1389 patriam juxta Caerliell' plane vastarunt, homines, mulieres
et eciam pueros occiderunt, et quos ceperunt eos nudos cum
eorum preda in Scociam abduxerunt. Electus namque Sancti
Augustini[1] circa finem mensis Novembris a papa confirmatus
in fine mensis Marcii in Anglia applicuit et a domino rege
honorifice est susceptus et omnia que ab eo peciit optinuit
graciose.

Bulla papalis super mutacione jubilei. Item octavo die
Aprilis papa de consilio fratrum suorum propter vite hominum brevitatem statuit annum jubileum fore deinceps de
triginta tribus annis in triginta tres annos et ut proximus
annus jubileus inciperet in anno a Nativitate Domini
millesimo ccc. nonagesimo[a] proximo futuro. Tenor vero sue
bulle talis est:

Urbanus etc. ad perpetuam rei memoriam. Salvator noster,[2] unigenitus Dei filius, de sinu patris in uterum dignatus est descendere
matris, in qua et ex qua nostre mortalitatis substanciam divinitati[b] sue
in supposisti unitate ineffabili unione conjunxit, id quod fuit permanens
et[c] quod non erat assumens, ut haberet[d] unde hominem lapsum redimeret et pro eo satisfaceret Deo patri. Ubi enim venit plenitudo
temporis, misit Deus filium suum, [e]natum ex muliere, factum sub lege,[e]
ut eos qui sub lege erant redimeret, ut[f] adopcionem reciperent filiorum;[3] ipse namque, 'factus nobis a Deo sapiencia et[g] justicia,[h] sancti-
ficacio et redempcio',[4] 'non per sanguinem hircorum aut vitulorum set
per proprium sanguinem introivit semel in sancta, eterna redempcione
inventa';[5] non enim corruptibilibus,[i] auro et argento, set sui ipsius agni
[j]immaculati et incontaminati[j] precioso sanguine nos redemit,[6] quem in
ara crucis [k] pro nobis[k] innocens immolatus non guttam sanguinis
modicam (que tamen propter unionem ad verbum pro redempcione
tocius humani generis suffecisset) set copiose velud quoddam pro-
fluvium noscitur effudisse, ita ut a planta pedis usque ad verticem[l] nulla
sanitas reperiretur[m] in eo.[n7] Quantum ergo exinde, ut nec supervacua,
inanis[o] aut superflua tante effusionis miseracio redderetur, thesaurum
militanti ecclesie acquisivit, volens suis thesaurizare filiis pius pater,
ut sic sit infinitus thesaurus hominibus, quo qui usi sunt Dei amicicie

---

[a] *Written above* xxxix, *which has been deleted.*   [b] *C; MS.* divinitatis.
[c] *C; MS.* eciam.   [d] *C; MS.* habeat.   [e-e] *C* factum sub lege, natum ex muliere;
Vulg. factum ex muliere.   [f] *C and Vulg.; MS.* et.   [g] *C om.*   [h] *Vulg. inserts*
et.   [i] *C and Vulg.; MS.* corruptibili.   [j-j] *C* incontaminati et immaculati.
[k-k] *C om.*   [l] *C inserts* capitis.   [m] *C* inveniretur.   [n] *C* ipso; *Vulg., for the
last five words* non est in eo sanitas.   [o] *C; MS.* manus.

[1] William Welde; for his election see above, p. 180.
[2] This bull repeats much of the language of Clement VI's *Unigenitus Dei
filius* of 27 Jan. 1343, in Extrav. Commun. V. ix. 2, for which see *Corpus Juris*

wrought downright havoc in the countryside about Carlisle, 1389
slaughtering men, women, and even children, and carrying off
naked to Scotland, with their booty, those they made prisoner.

The abbot-elect of St. Augustine's,[1] who had received
papal confirmation about the end of November, landed in
England at the end of March, to meet a flattering reception
by the king who graciously granted his every request.

Papal bull on a change in the jubilee. In consideration of
the shortness of human life the pope decreed on 8 April,
with the advice of his brethren, that the jubilee year should
henceforward fall every thirty-three years and that the next
such year should begin in the year of Our Lord 1390 then
next following. Here is the text of his bull:

Urban etc. for everlasting remembrance. Our Saviour,[2] the only-
begotten Son of God, deigned to come down from the Father's bosom
into the womb of a mother, in whom and from whom by an unutter-
able union he joined the stuff of our mortality in unity of person with
his godhead, taking upon him that which was abiding and that which
was not, that he might have the means of redeeming Man after his fall
and making satisfaction on his behalf to God the Father. For when the
fullness of the time was come, God sent forth his Son, made of a
woman, made under the law, to redeem them that were under the law,
that they might receive the adoption of sons;[3] and he 'who of God is
made unto us wisdom and righteousness and sanctification and redemption',[4] 'not by the blood of goats and calves, but by his own blood,
entered in once into the holy place, having obtained eternal redemption
for us';[5] for he redeemed us not with corruptible things, as gold and
silver, but with his very own precious blood, as of a lamb without
blemish and without spot,[6] which blood, when, an innocent victim, he
was sacrificed for us upon the altar of the cross, he is known to have
shed not in one small drop (though that, because of the union with
the Word, would have sufficed for the redemption of all mankind)
but lavishly, as might be some torrent, so that from the sole of his
foot even unto his head there was no soundness found in him.[7] How
great therefore is the treasure which (so that the compassion of such an
outpour should not be rendered needless, purposeless, or superfluous)
like a devoted father, seeking to lay up riches for his children, he
thereby won for the Church militant, that thus there might be a
treasure unto men that never faileth, which they that use become the

Canonici, ed. Friedberg (2 vols., Leipzig, 1879–81), ii. 1304–6, from which it is
here cited as *C*. Had the dating clause of the bull been abbreviated before the text
reached the Monk? Cf. below, p. 460.

[3] Cf. Gal. iv. 4–5.   [4] 1 Cor. i. 30.   [5] Heb. ix. 12.
[6] Cf. 1 Pet. i. 18–19.   [7] Cf. Isa. i. 6.

1389   participes ^{a}sunt effecti.^{a1} Quem quidem thesaurum non 'in sudario
p. 189   repositum'^{2} / non in agro absconditum^3 set per beatum Petrum celi
clavigerum ejusque successores suos in terris vicarios commisit, fidelibus
salubriter dispensandum et propriis^b et racionabilibus causis, nunc
pro totali, nunc pro parciali remissione pene temporalis^c pro peccatis
debite, tam generaliter quam specialiter, prout cum Deo expedire
cognoscerent, vere penitentibus et confessis misericorditer applicandum.
Ad cujus quidem^d thesauri cumulum beate ^{e}et gloriose^e Dei ^{f}genitricis
Marie et omnium electorum^f a primo justo usque ad ultimum merita
adminiculum prestare noscuntur; de cujus consumpcione seu diminu-
cione^g non est aliquatenus formidandum, tam propter infinita Christi,
ut predictum est, merita quam pro eo quod quanto plures ex ejus
applicacione trahuntur ad justiciam, tanto magis accrescit ipsorum
cumulus meritorum. Quod felicis recordacionis Bonefacius papa viij^{us}
predecessor noster primo^h pie, ^{i}prout indubitanter^i credimus, considerans et debita^j meditacione revolvens, quantum^k apud homines
gloriosi principes terre Petrus et Paulus, per quos evangelium Christi
Rome^l resplenduit^4 et per quos ecclesia religionis sumpsit exordium,^{5}
qui facti Christiani populi per evangelium genitores, ^{m}gregis dominici^m
pastores, fidei lucerne, ecclesiarum columpne, pre ceteris apostolis
peculiari quadam prerogativa in ipso Salvatore fidei virtute precellunt,
quorum uni, scilicet^n apostolorum principi, sicut beato^o dispensatori
claves ^{p}celestis regni^p commisit, alteri, tanquam ydoneo doctori magis-
terium ecclesiastice erudicionis injunxit, in speciali veneracione haberi
debeant et debita honorificencia honorari,^{q} pro ipsorum memoria
recolenda crebrius, et reverencia a cunctis Christi fidelibus eis devocius
exhibenda,^{r} ipsorumque patrocinio favorabilius^s assequendo, incon-
sumptibilem thesaurum^t pro excitanda et remuneranda devocione
fidelium voluit aperire, decernens^6 de fratrum suorum consilio, ut
omnes qui ^{u}in anno^u a Nativitate Domini millesimo ccc^{mo}. et quolibet
anno centesimo tunc^v secuturo, ad dictorum apostolorum basilicas de
urbe accederent reverenter, ipsasque, si Romani ad minus triginta, si
vero peregrini aut forenses fuerint^w quindecim, diebus continuis ^{x}vel
interpolatis^x saltem semel in die, dum^y tamen vere penitentes et
confessi existerent, personaliter visitarent, suorum omnium obtinerent
plenissimam veniam peccatorum. Et deinde felicis recordacionis
Clemens papa vj. predecessor noster de fratrum suorum consilio ex
certis causis ad annum quinquagesimum reduxit, statuens^7 de fratrum

$^{a-a}$ *Vulg.* facti sunt. ^{b} *C; MS.* pro piis ^{c} *C* temporalibus. ^{d} *C; MS.*
om. $^{e-e}$ *C om.* $^{f-f}$ *C* genitricis omniumque electorum. ^{g} *C*
minucione. ^{h} *C om.* $^{i-i}$ *C* sicut indubie. ^{j} *C* attenta. ^{k} *C; MS.*
quanta. ^{l} *Breviary* Roma. $^{m-m}$ *C; MS.* gregisque dominice. ^{n} *C; MS.*
sicut. ^{o} *C* bono. $^{p-p}$ *C* regni coelorum. ^{q} *C* venerari. ^{r} *C*
adhibenda. ^{s} *C; MS.* favorabili. ^{t} *C inserts* huiusmodi. $^{u-u}$ *C; MS. om.*
^{v} *C* extunc. ^{w} *C; MS. om.* $^{x-x}$ *C; MS.* aut interpolatim. ^{y} *C; MS.*
dummodo.

^{1} Cf. Wisd. vii. 14. ^{2} Luke xix. 20. ^{3}Cf. Matt. xxv. 25.

friends of God.[1] This treasure, not 'laid up in a napkin'[2] or hidden in 1389 the earth,[3] he gave in trust to be dispensed to the faithful for their salvation by the blessed Peter, keeper of the keys of heaven, and his successors, God's vicars on earth, and to be for proper and reasonable causes applied out of compassion, sometimes for entire and sometimes for partial remission of the temporal penalty due for their sins, both generally and specially, as by God's grace should be seen to be expedient, to the truly penitent and confessed. To the heaped abundance of this treasure the merits of the blessed and glorious Mary mother of God, and of the elect from the first of the righteous to the last, are known to contribute; there need be no fear of its consumption or dimunition, not only because of the boundless merits of Christ, as aforesaid, but also because the greater the number of those who by its application are brought to righteousness, the greater grows the abundance of the merits themselves. All of which our predecessor Pope Boniface VIII of happy memory first took into devout consideration, as we verily believe, bestowing due thought on the reflection of how great is the debt of special reverence and proper honour owed by mankind to the glorious princes of the earth, Peter and Paul, through whom the Gospel of Christ shone forth at Rome[4] and through whom the Church acquired the beginnings of religion,[5] who, becoming through the Gospel begetters of Christ's people, shepherds of the Lord's flock, lamps of the faith, and pillars of the churches, surpass the other apostles in possessing by virtue of their faith a peculiar prerogative in the eyes of the Saviour himself, for to one of them, to wit the chief of the apostles, as his blessed steward, he entrusted the keys of the heavenly kingdom, and on the other, as a fitting teacher, he enjoined the mastery of the Church's learning. In order, therefore, that their memory might be the more often cultivated, veneration the more devoutly accorded to them by all the faithful of Christ, and their patronage the more favourably acquired, Pope Boniface sought to throw open this inexhaustible treasure so as to stimulate and to reward the devotion of the faithful, ordaining[6] with the advice of his brethren that all who in the year 1300 from our Lord's birth, and in every hundredth year that should follow, should come in reverence to the said apostles' basilicas in the city and should in person attend the same, after true penitence and confession, at least once in each of thirty days, if they were Romans, or, if they were strangers or foreigners, once in each of fifteen days, in continuous or interrupted succession, should obtain the fullest pardon for all their sins. And afterwards our predecessor Pope Clement VI of happy memory, with the advice of his brethren, for certain reasons reduced the interval to fifty years, decreeing[7] with the advice

[4] Cf. the 4th lesson at Mattins, St. Peter's and St. Paul's day (Sermon of St. Leo the pope).   [5] Cf. the Collect for the same day.

[6] In *Antiquorum habet fida*, 22 Feb. 1300 (*Les Registres de Boniface VIII*, ed. G. Digard, M. Faucon, A. Thomas, and R. Fawtier (Bibliothèque des Écoles françaises d'Athènes et de Rome, 4 vols. 1884-1939), ii. 3875).

[7] In *Unigenitus Dei filius*.

1389 suorum consilio ut universi Christi[a] fideles qui vere penitentes et confessi in anno a Nativitate ejusdem Domini[a] millesimo ccc[mo]. quinqua-
gesimo tunc[a] proximo[b] futuro, et deinceps perpetuis futuris temporibus
de quinquaginta in quinquaginta annos,[c] predictas ipsorum[d] Petri et
Pauli[e] basilicas ac Lateranensem ecclesiam causa devocionis modo
[f]premisso visitarent,[f] plenissimam omnium peccatorum suorum veniam
consequerentur:[g]

Nos, considerantes quod etas hominum amplius in dies labitur
pauciores et desiderantes quamplurimos participes fieri indulgencie
memorate, cum plurimi ad annum quinquagesimum propter vite
hominum brevitatem non perveniant,[h] et ut cunctorum populorum[i]
augeatur devocio, fides resplendeat,[j] spes vigeat et caritas vehemencius
invalescat,[k] ac attendentes quod anno tricesimo tercio Salvatoris
Domini nostri Jesu Christi ipse noster Salvator pro nobis eterno Patri
Ade debitum solvit et veteris piaculi caucionem pio cruore[l] detersit,
destructisque mortis vinculis victor ab inferis resurrexit[1] et per quadraginta dies per multa argumenta suis apparens discipulis videntibus illis
ascendit in celum[2] ac demum dona carismatum per inmissionem
Sancti Spiritus in filios adopcionis effudit, et quod numero hujusmodi
triginta trium annorum, qui fuerunt totum tempus vite ipsius nostri
Salvatoris quibus conversatus in mundo miro clausit ordine sui moras
incolatus,[3] plurima eciam alia et grandia divinarum scripturarum
misteria adaptari possunt, et ut jugis ipsius Salvatoris et eorum que
pro humani salute generis gessit ac verbis docuit et exemplis fidelibus
insit memoria, de fratrum nostrorum consilio ex supradictis et aliis
justis causis ad annum tricesimum tercium reducimus per presentes,
statuentes de eorundem fratrum nostrorum consilio et apostolice pleni-
tudine potestatis ut universi Christi[m] fideles [n]vere penitentes et confessi
qui in[n] anno a Nativitate ejusdem Domini[m] millesimo ccc[mo]. nonagesimo
proximo[o] futuro et deinceps perpetuis[p] temporibus de triginta tribus
annis in triginta tres annos[q] predictas ipsorum[r] Petri et Pauli[s] basilicas
[t]ac Lateranensem et Sancte Marie Majoris de urbe ecclesias,[t] que[u]
ob ipsius reverenciam Virginis inter alias predicte urbis ecclesias
devotissime honoratur, ad quam causa devocionis populi confluit
multitudo et quam, ut cunctus populus ipsius precibus Virginis et
meritis, que pre sanctis omnibus ab eodem Salvatore nostro meruit
exaudiri, hujusmodi consequatur indulgencie largitatem, in hoc ex
hujusmodi et aliis certis causis racionabilibus censuimus honorandam,
causa devocionis modo premisso[v] visitaverint plenissimam omnium
peccatorum suorum veniam consequantur; ita videlicet, ut, quicumque

[a] C om.   [b] C proxime.   [c] C annis.   [d] C eorundem.   [e] C inserts
apostolorum.   [f-f] C praedicto visitaverint.   [g] C consequantur.   [h] MS.
perveniat.   [i] C fidelium.   [j] C splendeat.   [k] C (in the corresponding phrase)
incalescat.   [l] From the Exultet; MS. tenore.   [m] C om.   [n-n] C qui vere
poenitentes et confessi in.   [o] C proxime.   [p] C inserts futuris.   [q] C (in the
corresponding phrase) annis.   [r] C eorundem.   [s] C inserts apostolorum.
[t-t] C et Lateranensem ecclesiam.   [u] Written above devotissime, which is deleted.
[v] C praedicto.

of his brethren that all the faithful of Christ who after true penitence
and confession should in the year 1350 from our said Lord's birth then
next to come and every fifty years thereafter for all future time attend
the aforesaid basilicas of Peter and Paul and the Lateran church for
reasons of devotion in the manner above should obtain the fullest
possible pardon for all their sins:

We, considering that the age of mankind is more and more declining
into fewness of days, and desiring that as many as possible shall be
made partakers of the above-mentioned indulgence, inasmuch as very
many, because of the shortness of human life, never reach their fiftieth
year; and in order that the devotion of all peoples may be increased,
that faith may shine forth, hope flourish, and charity go from strength
to strength; and mindful that it was in the thirty-third year of the
Saviour, our Lord Jesus Christ, that our Saviour himself paid on our
behalf Adam's debt to the everlasting Father and wiped clean with his
pious blood the bond of expiation for the ancient crime, and, having
broken the chains of death, rose victorious out of hell,[1] and showing
himself by many infallible proofs forty days to his disciples, while they
beheld, went up into heaven[2] and at length by sending the Holy Ghost
upon them poured out the gifts of grace on the sons of his adoption;
and mindful, too, that to this number of thirty-three years, which were
the whole time of the life of our Saviour that he passed in the world
before bringing to an end in wondrous order the tarrying time of his
sojourn,[3] many other great mysteries of the divine scriptures can also
be applied; and so that in the faithful there may be abiding memory
of the Saviour himself and of what he did and by word and example
taught for the salvation of mankind; with the advice of our brethren,
for the abovesaid and for other righteous causes by these presents do
reduce the interval to thirty-three years, ordaining, with the advice of
our same brethren and out of the fullness of apostolic authority, that
all the faithful of Christ, being truly penitent and confessed, who in
the year 1390 from our Lord's birth next coming and thereafter every
thirty-three years for all time shall out of devotion attend in the
manner above the aforesaid basilicas of the same Peter and Paul, the
Lateran church, and that of St. Mary Major (which, because of the
veneration accorded to the Virgin herself is among all the churches of
the city most devoutly honoured and frequented by the people in great
numbers because of their devotion, and which, in order that all the
people, by the prayers and merits of the Virgin, who before all the
saints has earned a hearing from our Saviour, may achieve the bounty
of the present indulgence, we have for these and other reasonable
causes thought fit to honour in this regard) shall gain the fullest
possible pardon for all their sins; so, that is to say, that whosoever

---

[1] Cf. the Easter Eve *Exultet.*
[2] Cf. Acts i. 3, 9-10, and the Ascension Day Mass.
[3] Cf. the second stanza of the hymn *Pange lingua*, composed for the Mass and
office of Corpus Christi.

1389 [a]voluerit hujusmodi indulgenciam assequi, si Romanus, ad minus triginta continuis vel interpolatis saltem semel in die, si vero peregrinus aut forensis extiterit, modo simili quindecim diebus ad dictas basilicas et ecclesias accedere teneatur;[a] adicientes ut hii[b] eciam qui pro ea consequenda[c] ad easdem[d] basilicas et ecclesias[e] attendentes[f] post iter [g]arreptum co⟨n⟩tingerent[h] legittime impediri[g] quominus ad urbem illo anno valeant pervenire, aut in via vel dierum pretaxato numero non completo in dicta urbe decesserint, vere penitentes, ut premittitur, et confessi, eandem indulgenciam consequantur; omnes nichilominus et singulas indulgencias per nos et[i] predecessores nostros Romanos pontifices tam prenominatis quam aliis basilicis et ecclesiis[j] de dicta urbe concessas ratas et gratas habentes, ipsas auctoritate apostolica confirmamus et approbamus ac eciam innovamus et presentis scripti patrocinio communimus. Nulli ergo etc. nostre reduccionis, constitucionis, adjeccionis, confirmacionis, approbacionis et innovacionis infringere etc. Data Rome apud Sanctum Petrum vj. Idus Apriles anno xj[mo].

Item isto anno dominus papa constituit duo festa nova in
p. 190　ecclesia Dei fore solempnia ubique / in toto orbe terrarum, scilicet festum Visitacionis beate Marie cum visitaret Elizabeth post Annunciacionem per Gabrielem archangelum sibi factam, quodque tantis indulgenciis sublimavit quantisque festum Corporis Christi actenus illustratur, et festum beate Anne matris genetricis Dei Marie, quod eciam, ut premittitur, celebre statuit venerari.[1]

In[k] principio mensis Maii rex tenuit suum consilium apud Westmonasterium; in quo proposuit et declaravit pro se ipso affirmans ipsum fore plene et perfecte etatis ad modum heredis petentis hereditatem cum ipse pervenerit ad vicesimum primum annum;[2] unde quesivit a dominis universis[3] an posset super se rite suscipere[l] solum regni gubernaculum

---

[a-a] *C* voluerint indulgentiam huiusmodi assequi, se Romani, ad minus xxx., si vero peregrini aut forenses modo simili xv. diebus ad praedictas basilicas et ecclesiam accedere teneantur.　[b] *C* ii.　[c] *C; MS.* consequendi.　[d] ecclesias *deleted after this word.*　[e] *C* ecclesiam.　[f] *? Recte* accedentes, *as in the (generally inferior) text of this bull from the exemplar addressed to the archbishop of Prague to be found in C.C.C.C. MS. 512, fos. 162–3; C* accedent. [g-g] *C* arreptum impediti legitime.　[h] co⟨n⟩tingerent *Winterbottom;* co⟨n⟩tigeret *MS. Cf. p. 52.*　[i] *C* vel.　[j] *C; MS.* ecclesias.　[k] *In the margin opposite this passage, a contemporary pointing hand.*　[l] *The letter* s *is blotted out after this word.*

---

[1] On 8 April 1389, Urban VI instituted the feast of the Visitation, and this was reaffirmed by Boniface IX later in the year (R. W. Pfaff, *New Liturgical*

would obtain this indulgence shall, if he is a Roman, be bound to 1389
attend the aforesaid basilicas and churches at least once in each of
thirty days, successive or not, or, if he is a stranger or foreigner, in
like manner in each of fifteen days; with this further addition that
they who, setting out for the same basilicas and churches to obtain
the indulgence, may chance after beginning their journeys to be lawfully hindered from reaching the city that year or may, being truly
penitent and confessed, as aforesaid, die either on the road or in the
city before completing the prescribed number of days of attendance,
shall obtain the same indulgence; holding to be valid and acceptable,
none the less, all and singular indulgences granted by us and our predecessors pontiffs of Rome as well to the above-named basilicas and
churches as to others of the said city, we confirm and approve the
same by apostolic authority and moreover renew and reinforce them
by the support of the present writing. To none, therefore, [let it be
permitted] to infringe [this written page containing] our reduction,
ordinance, addition, confirmation, approval, and renewal. Given at
Rome at St. Peter's, 8 April in the eleventh year [1389].

The pope further established in this year two new feasts
to be ceremoniously observed everywhere in God's Church
throughout the entire world, namely the feast of the Visitation of the blessed Mary (when she visited Elizabeth after the
Annunciation made to her by the archangel Gabriel), which
he dignified by indulgences as lavish as those hitherto distin-
guishing the feast of Corpus Christi, and the feast of the
blessed Anne, mother of Mary mother of God, for which he
ordained the same ceremonious veneration.[1]

At the beginning of May the king held a council at Westminster, at which he introduced a statement on his own
behalf, declaring that his attainment of fully completed age
put him in the position of an heir claiming his inheritance on
reaching his twenty-first year.[2] He therefore asked the whole
body of lords[3] whether or not he could properly assume sole

---

Feasts in later Medieval England (Oxford, 1970), p. 40 and n.; *Magnum Bullarium Romanum Augustae Taurinorum Editum*, iv (1859), pp. 602–4). The reference to the feast of St. Anne is puzzling. Urban VI ordered the observance of this feast in England in a bull dated 30 June 1381 and published by Archbishop William Courtenay on 18 May 1383 (Wilkins, *Concilia*, iii. 178–9).

[2] The council met in the Marcolf chamber in the Palace of Westminster on 3–4 May. The king, born on 6 Jan. 1367, was 22. The proclamation giving effect to his assumption of power is dated 8 May (Rymer, *Foedera*, vii. 618–19).

[3] A phrase betraying the fact that this was a great council (Tout, *Chapters*, iii. 454 and n.).

1389 aut non. Qui respondentes dixerunt omnes quod bene potuit
et deberet super se tale onus assumere. Quibus ipse ait:
'Optime scitis quomodo per istos duodecim annos ex
quo factus sum rex fui per alios gubernatus ac eciam totum
regnum; et bene perpendi populum meum semper de
anno in annum diversis imposicionibus fore vexatum,
et in nullo propter hoc regnum nostrum vidimus robora-
tum. Igitur, ex quo suscepimus onus, dignum arbitramur
eciam accipere et regimen, cum simus tam perfecte etatis
quatinus negligencia quacumque remota (Domino auxi-
liante) circa salutem et comodum populi nostri et regni
intendimus de cetero assidue laborare ut subditi nostri
deinceps quiecius vivere valeant et regnum nostrum uberius
prosperetur ac in posterum in melius reformetur.' Sicque
consequenter cancellarium et thesaurarium de officiis eorum
amovit[1] necnon et omnes alios officiarios tam majores
quam minores, eciam illos de ultra mare, quosdam ad tempus
et quosdam pro perpetuo, ab eorum officiis previa discrecione removit, et presertim illos qui nuper per dictos dominos
regnum et regem regentes fuerant in quibusvis officiis con-
stituti; item ejecit de familia sua circiter quadringentos, et
precipue illos qui per predictos dominos in suam curiam
fuerant introducti aut eis aliquo amicicie federe copulati.[a]
Cancellarium suum constituit episcopum Wynton'[2] et suum
thesaurarium episcopum Exonien'[3] ac portitorem sui privati
sigilli magistrum Edmundum de Stafford.[4]

Item quarto die Maii obiit Thomas Brompton' episcopus
Roffens'.[5] Item circa finem mensis Maii comes Arundell'
peciit licenciam a rege transeundi ad Terram Sanctam; quam
demum cum magna instancia optinuit, set non multum post
ex causa extitit revocata. Dominus Johannes Holand comes

---

[a] Cave *in the margin opposite this passage.*

---

[1] Respectively, Thomas Arundel, archbishop of York, and John Gilbert, bishop
of Hereford. Each was removed from office on 4 May.
[2] William of Wykeham. He and the new treasurer and keeper of the privy seal
were appointed on 4 May. Cf. Walsingham, *Hist. Ang.*, ii. 181.
[3] Thomas Brantingham.

control of the kingdom; and when they all said in reply 1389
that he certainly could, and should, shoulder the burden,
he went on: 'You are very well aware of the way in which
throughout the twelve years since I became king I, and
the entire kingdom too, have been under the control of
others. I have carefully pondered the extent to which, year
after year, my people have been unendingly harassed by all
kinds of imposts and I have not seen that this kingdom of
mine is in any respect the stronger in consequence. Now,
therefore, that I have taken up the burden, I think it is fitting
that I should also assume the conduct of affairs, since I have
reached an age of maturity at which I mean, to the exclusion
of all negligence, with God's help to work tirelessly for
the future at the well-being and profit of my people and
my kingdom, so that my subjects may henceforward live
in greater peace and my kingdom enjoy a more ample
prosperity and a future of salutary reform.' In pursuance
of this he removed the chancellor and the treasurer from
office[1] and, following in the footsteps of prudence, dismissed from their posts, in some cases temporarily and
in others permanently, all other officials, great and small,
including those serving overseas, with special attention to
recent appointments to office by the lords controlling the
king and the kingdom. He further expelled from his household about four hundred persons, notably those who had
been brought into the court by those lords or were linked to
them by any covenant of friendship. As his chancellor he
appointed the bishop of Winchester,[2] as his treasurer the
bishop of Exeter,[3] and as keeper of the privy seal Master
Edmund Stafford.[4]

The death occurred on 4 May of Thomas Brinton, bishop
of Rochester.[5] About the end of the same month the earl
of Arundel asked the king for leave to make the journey
to the Holy Land, and after much solicitation it was granted;
but shortly afterwards a reason was found for revoking it.
Sir John Holland, earl of Huntingdon and brother to the

[4] A royal clerk, for whom see B.R.U.O., iii. 1749-50.
[5] The Monk's date is consistent with that of Brinton's will, 29 Apr. 1389
(Sermons of Thomas Brinton, Bishop of Rochester (1373-1389), 2 vols. (ed.
M. A. Devlin, Camden 3rd ser., lxxxv-vi), ii. 503-4).

1389 Huntyngdon' et frater regis factus est admirallus et custos
ville et castri de la Brest.*[a][1] Item xiiij. die Junii electus de
Burgo Sancti Edmundi[2] a Cosmate Gentili episcopo Bonon'
erat in curia[b] benedictus; et xx. die ejusdem mensis idem
episcopus Cosmas Gentilis magistrum Johannem Trevenant
in episcopum Hereforden' et magistrum Edmundum monachum de Burgo Sancti Edmundi in episcopum Landavensem
solempniter ibidem in curia consecravit, transtulit namque
papa fratrem Willelmum Botelesham de ecclesia Landavensi
ad ecclesiam Roffensem.[3]

Item xvij. die Junii erat festum Corporis Christi, quo die
dominus papa ob reverenciam tanti festi indulgencias olim
dicto festo concessas egregie duplicavit, decernens ut omnes
eo die reverenter ad ecclesiam confluentes vere penitentes
et confessi ubi primo percipiebant c. dies jam pro perpetuo
perciperent dies ducentos, sicque omnes alias indulgencias
pertinentes festo predicto duplicando per ordinem provide
ampliavit.[4] Item statuit ut ubicumque tempore interdicti
apertis ecclesie valvis pulsatisque campanis licite eo die ob
reverenciam Corporis Christi divina valeant celebrari non
obstante quacumque constitucione: item omnibus sequentibus corpus Domini in eundo et redeundo dum portatur ad
infirmum, dummodo sint vere contriti et confessi, centum
dies indulgencie concessit perpetuis temporibus duraturos.

Item dictum est supra in precedenti anno quomodo
ordinatum fuit quod quidam domini sua patrimonia in partibus borealibus undecumque habentes illas plagas ab invasione
hostium custodirent;[5] set profecto illa ordinacio effectualiter
non processit, nam domini boreales Scotica bella magis
experti voluerunt habere homines et pecunias sufficientes ad

---

a The rest of this paragraph and the whole of the next are written in the lower
margin of pp. 190 and 191 of the MS. with no indication of the place for insertion in the text.   *b* Interlined.

---

[1] Holland was appointed admiral on 18 May 1389 and captain of Brest on
1 June (Rymer, *Foedera*, vii. 622; Tout, op. cit., p. 455 n.). Both offices had been
vacated by the earl of Arundel.

[2] William Cratfield, abbot of Bury St. Edmunds, 1390-1415. See above, p. 376,
and for Cosmas Gentilis, ibid., p. 203 n.

[3] Bottlesham (for whom see above, p. 318) was not translated to Rochester
until 27 Aug. 1389. Mr. Edmund Bromfield was consecrated at Rome on 20 Jan.
1390 (John Le Neve, *Fasti Ecclesiae Anglicanae, 1300-1541*, revised edn., xi. 22).

king, was created admiral and keeper of the town and castle 1389
of Brest.[1] In the Roman curia the abbot-elect of Bury St.
Edmunds[2] received the papal blessing on 14 June from
Cosmas Gentilis, bishop of Bologna, and on the 20th of the
same month the same bishop solemnly consecrated Master
John Trefnant as bishop of Hereford and Master Edmund,
a Bury St. Edmunds monk, as bishop of Llandaff, from
which see the pope had translated Brother William Bottlesham to Rochester.[3]

The feast of Corpus Christi fell on 17 June, when the
pope, out of veneration for this important feast, made an
outstanding gesture by doubling the indulgences hitherto
accorded to it, decreeing that henceforward all who on that
day, being truly penitent and confessed, devoutly attended
church should evermore receive two hundred days' indulgence where they previously used to receive one hundred;
and he thoughtfully increased, by doubling them in their
turn, all the other indulgences associated with the feast.[4]
He further ordained that during periods of interdict it should
be everywhere lawful on that day, in view of the reverence
attaching to Corpus Christi, for church doors to be opened,
the bells to be rung and divine service to be celebrated,
despite the provisions of any constitution; and to all those
following the Host as it is borne to and from the sick he
granted for all time to come a hundred days' indulgence on
condition of their being truly contrite and confessed.

The account of the preceding year given above told how it
was decreed that certain nobles whose family estates lay in
various northern districts were to defend that region from
every attack;[5] but in the event this decree was ineffective,
because those northern lords who had most experience of
war with the Scots wanted men and money adequate to the

Though a monk of Bury St. Edmunds by origin, he was abbot of La Grande Sauve
(diocese of Bordeaux) at the time of his elevation (*B.R.U.O.*, i. 276). The Monk's
date for Trefnant's consecration is confirmed in *Registrum Johannis Trefnant*,
ed. Capes (Canterbury and York Soc., 1916), p. 3.

[4] It was Martin V who, in *Ineffabile sacramentum* (1429), doubled the indulgences given by Urban IV for the feast of Corpus Christi in *Transiturus* (1264);
but the Monk's reference to a decree of Urban VI on this matter is not to be dismissed lightly, for a fellow monk, Br. John Borewell, was at the curia at this
time (above, p. 379 n.).

[5] Above, pp. 376–8. (The Monk's year began on 25 Mar.)

1389 custodiam plage predicte, quodque fuit illis negatum. Igitur comes Notyngham, dominus de Nevyll',[1] et ceteri valentes de patria xxv. die Junii cum mille et quingentis armatorum Scociam intraverunt et parum ibi profecerunt quia majorem potenciam contra eos paratam quantocius invenerunt, quam invadere non audebant propter multitudinem inibi congregatam. Scoti vero parum vel nichil de illis curantes xxix. die Junii circa xxx[ta]. milia pugnatorum per aliam viam Angliam bellicose intrantes patrias ex omni parte usque Tynemouthe vastarunt, mandantes priori dicti loci ut daret eis redempcionem pro cellis et aliis bonis ejus ibi deprope existentibus, alias ea consumerent incendiis et rapinis; quod utique fecerunt non obstante quod rex fuerat de hujusmodi premunitus.[2] Comes vero Northumbr' providens qualiter istis dominis potuit verisimiliter evenire caute retraxit se et venit ad regem et factus est sui consilii capitalis: comes quoque de Notyngham cum suis, auditis dampnis que Scoti toti patrie inferebant, festinus accessit ad Berewycum et ibidem se recipiebat. Domini namque Matheus Redeman et Thomas Ogle[3] in redeundo Scotos a tergo viriliter insequentes ducentos ex eis occiderunt pariter et ceperunt: dominus eciam de Nevyll' quandam patriam in Scocia numquam perantea equitatam vastavit et predas inde ad sua presidia abigebat. Causa namque discordie inter boreales[a] dominos erat ista: quia vero omnes sunt generosi et nobiles, quamvis unus illorum erat comes alius baro et quidam eorum sunt domini vocitati, nichilominus in percepcione pecunie affectaverant[b] esse pares; quodque fuit eis negatum, et ideo ad eorum propria divertebant. Sicque tota illa patria exceptis castellis incustodita manebat; quare Scoti liberam habilitatem habebant facere suum velle quantum ad destruccionem patrie antedicte.

Dictum est supra quomodo rex Francorum misit domino regi Anglie pro treugis habendis inter ipsos quatinus ut infra

[a] *Written above* discordie, *which has been deleted.*   [b] *MS.* assectaverant.

---

[1] Thomas Mowbray, earl of Nottingham, and Ralph, Lord Nevill, were wardens of, respectively, the East and the West March (above, p. 378 n.). The major cause of dissension in the March in the summer of 1389 was the anger of Henry Percy, earl of Northumberland, at Mowbray's appointment (*Proceedings and Ordinances of the Privy Council of England*, i, ed. H. Nicolas (London, 1834),

defence of the area, and this was refused them. On 25 June 1389 the earl of Nottingham, Lord Nevill,[1] and the rest of the local gentry invaded Scotland with 1,500 men-at-arms but made little headway, since they at once found in readiness against them superior forces which, by reason of the great numbers they mustered, they dared not attack. The Scots, paying little or no attention to the invaders, stormed 30,000 strong into England on 29 June by another route and devastated the country over a wide area extending as far as Tynemouth, where they sent the prior a demand that he should ransom his cells and other property in the neighbourhood or have them wasted by fire and pillage, a threat which, despite the king's having been apprised of it, they actually proceeded to carry out.[2] The earl of Northumberland, foreseeing how matters were likely to turn out for the invading English nobles, discreetly withdrew and joined the king, in whose council he was awarded a pre-eminent place. News of the damage the Scots were inflicting on the whole countryside sent the earl of Nottingham hurrying with his forces to Berwick, where he established himself. In the course of their own return journey Sir Matthew Redmayne and Sir Thomas Ogle[3] carried out a spirited attack on the Scottish rear, killing or capturing 200 of the enemy; while Lord Nevill laid waste a region of Scotland never previously raided and drove off booty from it to his camp. The reason for dissension among the northern lords was this: all were of noble or gentle blood, though one might be called an earl, another a baron, and others 'lords', but when it came to drawing money, they aspired to equality; this was refused them, and they accordingly broke away to their homes. The whole area, with the exception of the castles, was thus left unprotected, so that the Scots had complete freedom to do what they liked by way of ravaging the countryside.

I have told above how the king of the French sent to the king of England to suggest a truce between them during which

12[b]-12[d]; J. A. Tuck, 'Richard II and the Border Magnates', in *Northern History*, iii. (1968), 44-5).

[2] The dependencies of Tynemouth Priory were on Coquet Island and in Tynemouth itself.

[3] Correctly, Sir Robert Ogle (d. 1409), for whom see *G.E.C.*, x. 26-7.

1389 treugas habitas possent comodius et consulcius de finali pace tractare: annuit enim rex Anglie votis suis misitque Cales' quosdam viros discretos parumper supra notatos[1] ad tractandum cum illis quos dictus rex Francorum illuc providerat destinare, sicque tractabant ibidem cum Francis usque in finem mensis Junii, quo in tempore aliqualiter concordati placuit utrique parti firmam treugam habere usque ad finem trium annorum tam per terram quam per mare et quod ista treuga non solum extenderet se ad ista duo regna set eciam ad amicos ambarum parcium tam ultra mare quam citra ac eciam ad Scotos si voluerint resarcire dampna que nobis subdole intulerant et ea regi Anglorum servare que tenentur de jure antiquo sibi servare; treuga vero per aquam inciperet xv. die mensis Augusti ab ortu solis.[2] Igitur ad captandam securitatem treuge predicte transierunt Parisius ex parte nostra magister Ricardus Rounhale doctor in legibus, dominus Johannes Clanvowe et dominus Nicholaus Daggeworthe, milites, habitaque securitate treuge predicte a rege Francorum Cales' redierunt. Istam treugam fieri procurarunt rex Armenie et Robertus Gebenens' antipapa, qui multum affectat unam sinodum convocatam habere ad sedandum istud scisma quod in ecclesia Dei jam fere per xij. annos duravit; set Urbanus noster referens se verum esse papam frustra foret tunc, ut asserit, sinodum congregare.[3]

Primo die Julii venerunt London' tres de Francia viri[4] missi per regem Francorum et ejus consilium in Scociam ad explorandum a Scotis an vellent predicte treuge communiter assentire et omnia que deberent regi Anglorum facere forent parati implere aut contra eum bella proponerent ulterius p. 191 continuare vel quid finaliter / vellent agere in premissis eorum inquirerent ultimam voluntatem. Sicque fuit missum

[1] Above, p. 374; and for the French approach, not explicitly recorded by the Monk in his surviving text, see ibid., n.

[2] On land and sea the truce of Leulingham of 18 June 1389 was to begin on 15 Aug., except between the Loire and the Rhone, where it was to begin on 1 Aug. The Monk's summary goes beyond the published text of the truce in so far as it related to Scotland. See Rymer, *Foedera*, vii. 622 ff.; below, p. 402 and n.

[3] A passage tending to confirm the existence in the months preceding the truce of Leulingham of proposals for a conference to discuss the Schism, at which Clement VII was to be represented; see J. J. N. Palmer, 'England and the Great Western Schism, 1388-1399', in *E.H.R.*, lxxxiii (1968), 516-17. For Leo VI of Armenia's part in the truce, see *Cal. Pat. R., 1385-9*, p. 503.

negotiations for a final peace might be conducted with 1389 greater convenience and deliberation. The king of England agreed to this request and sent to Calais, to negotiate with the envoys whom the French king had arranged to dispatch thither, the judicious persons named a little above.[1] Their discussions with the French went on until the end of June, by which time a measure of agreement was reached and both sides were content to have a strict three-year truce by land and sea, the truce to extend not only to the two contracting kingdoms but also to the friends of both parties on either side of the sea, and moreover to the Scots if they were willing to make good the damage inflicted on us by their treachery and to honour the obligations to the king of England which they are bound by ancient right to observe. At sea the truce was to begin at dawn on 15 August.[2] Master Richard Ronhale, LL.D., Sir John Clanvow, and Sir Nicholas Dagworth, knights, went to Paris on our behalf to take security in respect of this truce and returned to Calais after receiving it from the French king. The people who brought about the truce were the king of Armenia and Robert of Geneva, the antipope; Robert was anxious that a synod should be convened to settle the schism which had now persisted in God's Church for about twelve years; but on our side Urban, declaring himself to be the true pope, maintained that no purpose would be served by convoking a synod at that time.[3]

Three Frenchmen[4] arrived in London on 1 July on their way to Scotland, whither they had been sent by their king and his council to find out from the Scots whether they wished to associate themselves with the agreement for a truce and were ready to fulfil all their obligations to the English king, or whether they proposed to continue further a state of war with him; and to obtain the Scots' last word about the action they meant to take in this connection. A similar mission

---

[4] Mr. Peter Fresnel, Hennart de Campbernart, and a 3rd person, described as a squire, whose name is not recorded; they received a safe-conduct from Richard II on 3 July. Nicholas Dagworth, who accompanied them, arrived in London, from France, on 13 July and left for Scotland the next day. See P.R.O., E. 364/23, m. 33; *Calendar of Documents relating to Scotland*, ed. Bain, iv. 395; cf. *Bower*, ii. 415; *Rot. Scot.*, ii. 98-9; Rymer, *Foedera*, vii. 631.

1389 duci Britannie, set ipse in omnibus que rex Francorum ab eo petebat minime adquievit; quare jam de novo inter illos durissimum exortum est bellum. Unde rex Anglie in auxilium ducis predicti concessit duo milia virorum utique strenuorum in armis et duo milia sagittariorum, propriis tamen stipendiis ducis predicti; insuper idem rex concessit ut alii de regno suo quicumque[a] ad predictum ducem proprio capite vellent transire plenam tribuit libertatem.[1]

Item tercio die Julii apud Shene rege presente fuit bellum muscarum minutarum que Latine sciniphes et Anglice gnattes vocantur.[2] Tanta namque strages fuit illarum quod per modios poterant dimetiri. Item sexto die Julii Thomas dominus de Clifford[3] subito arreptus paralisi diem clausit extremum. Item ix. die Julii rex Anglie plures de curia sua amovit, quia forte erant predictis dominis satis familiares. Quo in tempore dominus Henricus Percy et frater suus Radulphus factis redempcionibus fuerunt a Scottorum manibus liberati: nam dictus dominus Henricus liberavit dominum Jacobum de Lyndeseye ac ultra hoc solvit pro redempcione sua vij. milia marcarum; frater suus Radulphus solvit pro se quingentas marcas.[4] Item xiij. die Julii in Cancia orta tempestate tonitrui et fulguris unde pro majori parte ecclesia et villa de Maufeld fuerant igne consumpte.

In fine mensis Julii[5] venerunt London' pacis nostri tractatores; qui confestim adierunt regem, exponentes sibi quomodo et sub qua forma capta erat treuga: deinde quarto die Augusti venit London' comes Sancti Pauli ad captandum securitatem a rege super observacione treuge predicte, quare dominus rex cum suo consilio ix. die Augusti venit Westm' et decimo die ejusdem mensis facta securitate firmavit treugam prefatam.[6] Hiis igitur rite peractis accessit rex ad manerium suum de Eltham ubi splendide convivavit comitem predictum et alios milites qui causa pretacta cum illo venerunt;

---

[a] voluerint *deleted after this word.*

[1] An improbable but not quite impossible story. For Anglo-Breton relations in this period see Jones, *Ducal Brittany, 1364–1399*, pp. 116 ff. In principle the truce of Leulingham included Brittany and conservators were appointed for the duchy (Rymer, *Foedera*, vii. 629).
[2] Cf. Walsingham, *Hist. Ang.*, ii. 186–7; Knighton, *Chronicon*, ii. 311.

was sent to the duke of Brittany; but he refused to agree to any of the claims made upon him by the French king, and the grim struggle between them broke out afresh. For the duke's support the king of England contributed 2,000 men-at-arms of high quality and 2,000 archers, who were, however, to be paid by the duke himself; the king further agreed to give full freedom of action to any others of his subjects who might wish to join the duke as volunteers.[1]

At Sheen on 3 July, while the king was there, there was a battle of the little flies known in Latin as 'sciniphes' and in English as 'gnats'. So great was the slaughter that the corpses could be measured in pecks.[2] On 6 July Thomas, Lord Clifford,[3] was seized by a sudden paralysis and brought his life to a close. On 9 July the king dismissed several members of his court because they happened to be rather intimate with the Lords Appellant. It was about this time that on payment of their ransom Sir Henry Percy and his brother Ralph were set free from the clutches of the Scots, Sir Henry releasing Sir James Lindsay and also paying a personal ransom of 7,000 marks, while his brother Ralph paid 500 marks for his own liberty.[4] On 13 July, when a thunderstorm broke over Kent, the church and town of Mayfield were in large measure destroyed by fire.

At the end of July[5] our representatives in the peace negotiations arrived in London and hurried to the king with a report of the manner and form in which the truce had been concluded: the count of St. Pol next arrived in London, on 4 August, to take security from the king for his observance of the truce, and the king, who had come to Westminster with his council on the 9th, gave the security and confirmed the truce on 10 August.[6] The formalities duly concluded, the king proceeded to his manor of Eltham, where he sumptuously feasted the count and other knights who had come

[3] Correctly, Roger, Lord Clifford; he died on 13 July 1389 (*Cal. Inq. p.m.*, xvi. 827-45; *G.E.C.*, iii. 292).

[4] The king contributed £3,000 to Percy's ransom (*Calendar of Documents relating to Scotland*, ed. Bain, iv. 420; *Issues of the Exchequer, Henry III to Henry VI*, ed. Devon, pp. 239, 244). For James Lindsay see above, p. 350 and n.

[5] A date confirmed by P.R.O., E. 364/22, mm. 21ᵛ, 25; ibid., 23, m. 26.

[6] See Rymer, *Foedera*, vii. 636-8. Waleran, count of Ligny and St. Pol, was accompanied by Jean d'Estouteville and Yves Derian.

1389　demum licencia captata infra paucos dies prefatus comes et alii qui cum illo aderant suum remearunt ad regem.

Post hec venit rex ad manerium suum de Shene, ubi xv. die Augusti celebrato consilio episcopum Exonien'^{a} ab officio thesaur⟨ar⟩ie absolvit et fratrem Gilbertum jam episcopum Meneven' in suum thesaurarium reassumpsit.[1] Et ex post in pluribus locis multa consilia celebravit, videlicet apud Wyndesoram, Sar', et alibi ubi sibi contigerat declinare.[2]

Item in ista estate Burdegalis decessit dominus Johannes Harpedene miles, seneschallus Aquitannie; cui substituit rex dominum Henricum Percy.[3] Item modicum ante finem mensis Augusti erat dominus Johannes Rypon' clericus de Turri London' penitus liberatus, ^{b}set parum post in eandem usque proximum parliamentum erat reductus.^{b4} Quo in tempore predicti tres viri de Francia venerunt de Scocia, qui ibidem cum Scotis et Anglis tractabant sic quod treuga inter nos et illos pariter sit firmata.[5] Item ix. die Augusti obiit frater Willelmus Brydford abbas Sancte Marie de Eboraco; cui successit frater Thomas Steynesgreve.[6]

Item in mense Septembris ac eciam antea in diversis locis Anglie pestilencia circuivit, juvenes potissime consumens:[7] quam ob rem rex existens in austrinis partibus vidensque quosdam de suis subita morte prosterni festinus gressus suos acceleravit versus Wyndeshoram, ubi ad eum Scoti venerunt et predictam treugam, non deductis dampnis nobis per eosdem illatis, firmarunt.[8] Quodque plures nostrorum grave cordi tulerunt, quia, ut dictum est, non satisfecerunt

---

^{a} Johannem *in the margin in a later hand.*　　$^{b-b}$ *In the margin but marked for insertion here.*

---

[1] Gilbert was not appointed until 20 Aug. (*Cal. Pat. R., 1388-92*, p. 95). Brantingham's retirement was on account of age and infirmity (ibid., p. 102).

[2] For the council at Windsor on 20 Aug. 1389, see also *Proceedings and Ordinances of the Privy Council*, ed. Nicolas, i. 6 ff. There is also evidence of a council at Clarendon on 13 Sept. and one at Westminster on 24 Sept. (ibid., p. 11; P.R.O., E 403/524, 23 Aug.).

[3] Harpeden died before 20 Aug. 1389; his successor was in fact William le Scrope. In 1393, Sir Henry Percy was appointed the duke of Lancaster's lieutenant in Aquitaine, and on 9 June 1394 the king's lieutenant there. See *Carte*, i. 176, 177, 178, 179.

[4] Ripon appeared before the council at Westminster, on 25 Aug., 1389, but he was not freed from the Tower until 1393 (*Cal. Cl. R., 1389-92*, p. 17; ibid., *1392-96*, p. 69). See also above, p. 344.

with him on his mission. A few days later the count and 1389
those accompanying him took their leave and returned to
their own king.

After this the king visited his manor at Sheen, where a
council was held on 15 August and the bishop of Exeter was
relieved of his post as treasurer, to which the king restored
Brother [John] Gilbert, now bishop of St. David's.[1] He
subsequently held a number of councils at several places,
including Windsor and Salisbury and others at which he
happened to stop.[2]

In the course of the summer Sir John Harpeden, seneschal
of Aquitaine, died at Bordeaux; and to replace him the king
appointed Sir Henry Percy.[3] Shortly before the end of
August the clerk, Sir John Ripon, was set completely free
from the Tower of London, but he was soon afterwards
taken back there to await the next parliament.[4] The three
Frenchmen mentioned above arrived about this time on their
return journey from Scotland, where their conversations with
the Scots and English had brought about the establishment of
the truce between us and the Scots too.[5] The death took
place on 9 August of Brother William Bridford, abbot of St.
Mary York; he was succeeded by Brother Thomas Stonegrave.[6]

In September, and indeed earlier, plague spread through
various parts of England, its victims being chiefly among the
young.[7] It was for this reason that the king, who was in the
south of the country at the time, seeing members of his own
circle struck down by sudden death, hurriedly bent his steps
towards Windsor, where the Scots visited him and confirmed
the truce without any allowance for the damages inflicted
by them on us.[8] This gave rise to considerable heart-burning
among our countrymen since, as they pointed out, the Scots

[5] See above, p. 398 and n. Nicholas Dagworth, who accompanied these envoys
to Scotland, returned to London on 12 Sept. (P.R.O., E. 364/23, m. 33).

[6] The election received the royal assent on 20 Sept. 1389 (Cal. Pat. R., 1388-
92, p. 113).

[7] Cf. Walsingham, Hist. Ang., ii. 186.

[8] The Scottish envoys, Sir Adam de Glendonwys and Sir Henry Douglas, had
been seen by the king by 4 Oct. 1389. The English claimed, in addition to
compensation for breaches of the Anglo-Scottish truce of 1386, payment of the
sum of £16,000 outstanding on the ransom of David Bruce (David II) in 1357.
See Rot. Scot., ii. 99, 101-2; Rymer, Foedera, vii. 526-7, 638-9, 651-3.

1389 pro dampnis nobis illatis et, quod pejus est, ea pacifice permissum est eis tenere durante treuga que antea a nobis
violenter manu rapida extorserunt. Unus illorum namque in
civitate decessit, set quia scismaticus nec penituit nec ab
errore suo[a] converti voluit ejus cadaver insepultum aliquandiu
jacebat quousque fratres Predicatores illud rapientes et
nequiter sepelissent mala hora sua.

Item[b] de mense Septembri circa festum[c] Nativitatis beate
Marie obiit Parisius dominus Michael de la Pole quondam
comes Southfolch'.[1] Item xiij. die Octobris cives London'
processerunt ad eleccionem novi majoris; et electus est
Willelmus Venour grocerus.[2] Attamen quamvis major pars
tenuit cum isto Willelmo Venour nichilominus aurifabri,
pannarii et merceri ac alii eisdem confederati instancius
Adam Bamme aurifabrum[a] in eorum majorem diutine postul-
arunt; set non prevaluerunt. Constat namque per hoc civitatem (quod dolendum est) esse divisam; que autem divisio
a tempore Johannis Northampton' quondam majoris London'
usque ad istud tempus continuatur.

Obitus domini Urbani pape sexti. Item xv. die Octobris
Rome obiit papa Urbanus sextus; et secundo die Novembris
cardinales elegerunt Neapolitanum cardinalem[d] Bonefacium
nonum vocitatum.[3] Quo in tempore rex cum consilio suo
privato elegit sibi vicecomites per Angliam universaliter
fecitque sibi jurare ut bene et fideliter in eorum officiis se
haberent; qui solebant antea per cancellarium, thesaurarium,
clericum privati ⟨sigilli⟩[e] et per barones de scaccario prefici
et ordinari; unde de isto facto plures in curia admirabantur.[f][4]
Item xvij. Octobris in valvis ecclesie Sancti Pauli bulle papales
erant affixe declarantes quomodo illud divorcium factum in
curia Romana per dominum Johannem Ripon clericum inter
Robertum le[g] Veer ducem Hibernie et ⟨Philippam⟩[h] filiam
domini Ingelramy [i]domini de Coucy[i] et Ysabelle amite
domini regis fuit invalidum et nullum.[5] Secundo quoque die
Novembris Bonifacius ix.[j] electus est in papam.

---

[a] *Interlined.*   [b] *In the margin opposite this entry, a contemporary pointing
hand.*   [c] Na' festum *deleted after this word.*   [d] Neapolitanum *repeated but
deleted.*   [e] *MS. om.*   [f] *MS.* admirabant.   [g] *Sic MS.*   [h] *MS. blank.*
[i-i] *In the margin but marked for insertion here.*   [j] *Written in MS. above*
Bonifacius.

made no reparation for the losses they had caused us and, what 1389 was worse, were allowed for the period of the truce peaceable possession of what they had previously wrested from us by crude violence and rapine. One of the Scottish envoys happened to die in the city, but since he was an unrepentant schismatic who refused to be converted from his error, his corpse lay for some time unburied until, in an evil hour for them, the Friars Preachers seized it and wickedly gave it burial.

In September, about the feast of the Nativity of the Virgin [8 September], Sir Michael de la Pole, sometime earl of Suffolk, died in Paris.[1] On 13 October the citizens of London proceeded to the election of a new mayor: their choice fell on William Venour, a grocer.[2] Yet though a majority supported Venour, the goldsmiths, drapers, and mercers and their associates kept up a long and insistent demand for Adam Bamme, a goldsmith, as their mayor; but they did not get their way. These proceedings testify to the regrettable split which has persisted until now from the period of John Northampton's mayoralty.

Death of Pope Urban VI. On 15 October Pope Urban VI died in Rome, and on 2 November the cardinals elected a Neapolitan cardinal whose title was Boniface IX.[3] About this time the king, assisted by his privy council, chose the sheriffs who were to serve throughout England and made them take an oath to himself that they would behave well and loyally in office. Since it had hitherto been the custom for sheriffs to be appointed and controlled by the chancellor, the treasurer, the clerk of the privy seal, and the barons of the exchequer, the king's action caused widespread surprise in the court.[4] On 17 October papal bulls were posted on the doors of St. Paul's declaring null and void the divorce effected in the Roman curia by the clerk, John Ripon, between Robert de Vere duke of Ireland and [Philippa] daughter of Enguerrand Sire de Coucy and Isabel the king's aunt.[5] On 2 November Boniface IX was elected pope.

[1] Pole died on 5 Sept. 1389 (*Cal. Pat. R., 1388-92*, pp. 517-18). He had forfeited his earldom on 13 Feb. 1388. [2] Cf. *Letter Book H*, p. 348.
[3] The new pope was Perinus Tomacellus, cardinal-priest of S. Anastasia and known as 'Neapolitanus' (Eubel and van Gulik, *Hierarchia Catholica Medii Aevi*, i. 23).
[4] For the mode of appointment of sheriffs, see 14 Edward III, statute 1, *cap.* 7 (*S.R.*, i. 283). See also above, p. 266 and n. [5] See above, pp. 188-90.

1389   Quo in tempore dominus rex executus est illam gravissimam
p. 192 inquisicionem contra usurpatores corone sue / vocatam
traillebastoun' in Estsex' scilicet Cancia et alibi; unde quamplures[a] fuerant indictati et quidam vinculis mancipati. Nam
isti de banco domini regis ad diversos comitatus perrexerunt
semper inquirendo pro utilitate et comodo domini regis,
ut dixerunt;[1] attamen in quibusdam comitatibus nichil
comodi attulerunt, quia homines illorum comitatuum noluerunt eorum vicinos gravare: ministri vero de banco predicto
ea de causa vocarunt eos infideles domino regi. Set audito
adventu domini ducis Lancastr' ab hujusmodi insolitis
continuo quieverunt.

Quo eciam tempore episcopus Dunolm' W. Skyrlowe
missus in Flandriam ad componendum et tractandum de pace
cum Flandrensibus, mox rex Francorum mandavit eis ne
aliquo modo cum Anglicis de pace tractarent absque ejus
auctoritate et licencia si in[b] quiete in posterum vellent vivere
aut in pace.[2] Item xix. die Novembris dux Lancastr' apud
Plommouth' cum suis[c] sanus et incolumis applicuit. Item xxij.
die Novembris dominus Baldewynus miles duxit in uxorem
relictam domini Nicholai Brembr'.[3] Et xxv. die ejusdem
mensis dominus Johannes Golafre miles duxit in uxorem
filiam domini de Mohoun, que quondam fuit copulata
domino filio Walteri.[4]

Item ix. die Decembris[5] rex tenuit suum consilium apud
Radynggum; quo die versus villam predictam cum multitudine
copiosa venit dux Lancastr'. Rex namque fere ad duo miliaria
erga eum equitavit et ab eo et ab aliis universis in osculo pacis
satis honorifice fuit exceptus. Et accedentes ad consilium

---

[a] The last six letters of this word are interlined.   [b] Interlined.   [c] et in
deleted after this word.

[1] A reference to inquiries into waste at the king's expense and other offences
set on foot in Aug., Sept., and Oct. 1389 (Cal. Pat. R., 1388-92, pp. 140-2).
In Michaelmas Term 1389 the King's Bench sat at Brentwood and Wycombe, but
with these exceptions stayed at Westminster. On 'trailbaston' see above, pp. 82 n.,
383 n.
[2] Skirlaw, Mr. Richard Ronhale, and others were appointed on 5 Nov. 1389
to treat with the Flemings. Skirlaw accounted for an embassy in Picardy lasting
from 10 Nov. to 18 Dec. Preparatory negotiations had taken place in Oct. 1389.
See P.R.O., E. 364/23, m. 33ᵛ; Mirot and Déprez, in B.E.C., lx (1899), p. 210,
no. 503; Rymer, Foedera, vii. 648-9; Handelingen van de Leden en Van de

Meanwhile the king set on foot in Essex, Kent, and else- 1389
where the very rigorous inquiry, directed against usurpers of
the royal authority, which is known as 'trailbaston'; and a
very large number of persons were in consequence indicted
and some clapped in irons: the justices of the King's Bench
journeyed into various counties conducting ceaseless inquiries
to further the interests and advantage of the king, as they
said.[1] But in some counties their efforts were unavailing,
because the inhabitants were unwilling to embarrass their
neighbours, and were for that reason described by the dignitaries of the Bench as disloyal to the king. News of the
coming of the duke of Lancaster put an abrupt end to these
unusual proceedings.

During the same period Walter Skirlaw, the bishop of
Durham, had been sent to Flanders to negotiate a peace
settlement with the Flemings, to whom, however, the French
king promptly issued a warning against talking peace with the
English without his permission and authority if they wished
to pass their future in peace and quiet.[2] On 19 November the
duke of Lancaster landed safe and sound at Plymouth with
his companions; on the 22nd Sir Baldwin [Raddington]
married the widow of Sir Nicholas Brembre;[3] while on the
25th of the same month Sir John Golafre married Lord
Mohun's daughter, who had formerly been the wife of Lord
Fitz Walter.[4]

The king held a council at Reading on 9 December;[5] and
on that day the duke of Lancaster arrived there with a
numerous following. The king rode out about two miles to
meet him, and by the king and all the rest of the company
he was welcomed courteously enough and with a kiss of
peace. When they came to the council, the duke's very first

Staten van Vlaanderen (1384–1405), ed. Prevenier, nos. 98, 100.

[3] She was Idonea, daughter of John Stody, a London vintner; for the prob-
ability that her new husband was Sir Baldwin Raddington, controller of the
wardrobe, 1381–97, see Tout, *Chapters*, iv. 197 n.

[4] She was Philippa, daughter of Sir John de Mohun (*G.E.C.*, v. 479–80). For
the death of her 1st husband, Walter, Lord FitzWalter, in 1386, see above, p. 190;
and for Golafre, a chamber knight, Harvey, *Westminster Abbey and its Estates
in the Middle Ages*, p. 378. An entry in *Cal. Pat. R., 1388–92*, p. 154 suggests that
the marriage took place before 13 Nov. 1389.

[5] Correctly, 10 Dec. (*Proceedings and Ordinances of the Privy Council*, ed.
Nicolas, i. 17).

1389 primo ante omnia incepto sermone pacem dominorum*a* cum domino rege idem dux non sine causa, ut dicebatur, iterum renovavit et rigorem sui animi quem erga comitem Northumbr' actenus gerebat ad instanciam domini regis gratanter remisit, prebens aliis exemplum in hoc quomodo deposito rancore pacifice viverent et quiete;[1] quia nil utilius regno quam pax et concordia continue habita et possessa. Demum consilio pro eo die finito diem parliamenti ante eorum recessum statuerunt die Lune proxima post festum Sancti Hillarii.

Item xiij. die Decembris[2] dux Lancastr' venit Westmon' cum honorabili comitiva militum, dominorum, et aliarum venerabilium personarum: exivit enim contra eum major cum senioribus London'. Abbas vero et conventus Westmon' in suis froccis usque ad portam monasterii versus Toothull' processionaliter exierunt et in ecclesiam usque magnum altare, cantando responsorium 'Honor virtus', solempniter adduxerunt. Dicta vero oracione ab abbate factisque suis oblacionibus confestim ad Sanctum Paulum equester accessit et demum in suum hospicium se recepit.

Item xiiij. die Decembris obiit dominus Nicholaus abbas de Waltham juxta London':[3] quo eciam tempore*a* obiit abbas de Theokesbury.[4] Rex itaque tenuit suum Natale apud Wodestoke, ubi ultimo die Decembris[5] comes Penbrok' juvenis fere xvij. annorum volens probare equum suum cum alio milite domino Johanne Sancti Johannis vocato erga proximum hastiludium factoque concursu miles prefatus *b*⟨ad j⟩ussum magistri dicti comitis lanceam ⟨suam⟩ a latere projecit: pars vero illius que ⟨era⟩t in sua manu terram attingendo*c* ⟨se⟩*d* fi⟨geb⟩at, alia sursum prominebat, in quam ⟨equu⟩s dicti comitis effrenatus illum impe⟨tuo⟩se impulit*e*

---

a Interlined.   *b-b (p. 410)* Written in the margin; incaute lanceam suam gerens comitis femuri imposuit *deleted in the text. Parts of the marginal entry at the edge of the MS. have been lost.*   *c MS.* attigendo.   *d* ⟨se⟩ Winterbottom; MS. om.   *e* Written above invexit, which has not been deleted.

---

[1] See above, p. 22 and n.

[2] The feast of St. Lucy. But the responsory mentioned by the Monk — *Honor, virtus et potestas et imperium* — was the responsory for Trinity Sunday; it was traditionally associated with the votive Mass at ceremonial crown-wearings (H. G. Richardson, 'The coronation in medieval England', in *Traditio* xvi (1960), 130).

proceeding, in the opening words of his speech, was to 1389
restore once more (and not, it was said, without cause)
peaceful relations between the Lords Appellant and the king,
while he himself, at the king's urgent request, willingly
dropped the grudge he had hitherto borne against the earl of
Northumberland, thereby setting others an example of how,
by laying their bitterness aside, they might live in peace and
quiet;[1] for nothing benefits a kingdom more than the un-
broken possession and enjoyment of peace and harmony.
Before they withdrew at the end of the day's proceedings in
council, they fixed a day for a parliament on Monday after
St. Hilary [17 January 1390].

On 13 December[2] the duke of Lancaster, with a distinguished escort of knights, gentlemen, and other persons of
standing, visited Westminster: the mayor and aldermen of
London went out to meet him, and the abbot and convent
of Westminster, wearing their frocks, walked in procession
to the Tothill gate of the monastery, from which, singing
the responsory 'Honor virtus', they ceremoniously conducted
him into the church and up to the high altar. When the abbot
had said a prayer, the duke made his offering and shortly
afterwards rode off to St. Paul's before taking up his quarters
in his own house.

On 14 December the death occurred of Nicholas abbot of
Waltham near London:[3] the abbot of Tewkesbury[4] also died
about this time. The king kept Christmas at Woodstock,
where, on the last day of December,[5] the earl of Pembroke,
a youth of about seventeen, with an eye to the next tournament, set out to prove his horse against another knight, Sir
John St. John. As the riders met, this other knight, in
obedience to an order from the earl's instructor, threw his
lance to one side: as it reached the ground, the handle end
stuck, leaving the other pointing upwards, and the earl's
horse, careering on unchecked, ran him against this, which

[3] Nicholas Morice had been abbot of Waltham Holy Cross since 1371.
[4] Thomas Chesterton, for whom see W. Dugdale, *Monasticon Anglicanum*
(6 vols. in 8, London, 1817–30), ii. 55–6.
[5] Correctly, on 30 Dec. (*Cal. Inq. p.m.*, xvi. 885–923). John de Hastings, earl
of Pembroke, the victim of the tragedy now related by the Monk, was born on
11 Nov. 1372. For the extraordinary ill-luck of the Hastings earls of Pembroke
in the 14th century, see Walsingham, *Hist. Ang.*, ii. 195.

1389 et prope virilia ingredi⟨ens⟩ et*a* corpus lacerans sic quod sibi vulnus ⟨morta⟩le inflixit; amotaque casside con⟨fe⟩stim loquelam amisit;*b* sicque comes graviter vulneratus non post magnam horam diem clausit extremum. Confestim lacrime succedunt ridentibus, nam ex hoc facto tota curia nimia anxietate turbatur. Dolent communiter omnes ejus mortem: rex namque cum suis ineffabili dolore concutitur: regina vero mesta cum aliis mulieribus satis lugubris in suo thalamo residens flebilem duxit vitam: famuli quoque dicti comitis consternati quid facere poterint*c* profecto ignorant, cum*d* mori pocius quam vivere protinus affectabant. Demum suis exsequiis solempniter celebratis apud Hereford' juxta patrem suum honorifice sepelitur.[1] Miles vero qui eum ledebat fuge subsidio continuo se commisit, qui si diucius in curia ibidem expectasset proculdubio mortis excicium incurrisset.[2]

1390 Item xiij. die Januarii apud Croydon' capti sunt et in marchelsia*e* inclusi xvj. homines diversarum arcium mechanicarum periti; quidam autem illorum erant operarii, qui volentes insurgere in viros ecclesiasticos et in alios laicos vicinos eorum et eos morti tradere affectabant et aliam surrexionem aliis premissis nequiorem suscitare proposuissent nisi celerius eorum consilium fuisset denudatum.[3] Sicque tres illorum mense Februarii postea erant tracti et apud furcas suspensi.

Item xvij. die Januarii apud Westmon' cepit rex suum parliamentum; et duravit usque in secundum diem Marcii: quodque finitur duris *f*statutis ibidem editis.*f* Quo in tempore dominus papa cardinales omnes superstites quos Urbanus deposuit restituit pristine dignitati et dominum Adam per ipsum eciam restitutum*g* in suum consiliarium pre ceteris*h* elegit.[4] Creati sunt eciam*i* per papam tres alii cardinales; et unus illorum erat Cosmatus Gentilis, qui jamdudum fuerat in Anglia domini Urbani sexti collector.

a Interlined.   *b* See note b–b on p. 408.   *c* Sic MS.; cf. p. 204.
d Written over an erasure.   *e* MS. marchessia.   *f–f* Added in the margin.
g constituit suum primarium deleted after this word.   *h* illum deleted after this
word.   *i* Interlined.

---

[1] In the church of the Friars Preachers. Later the body was removed to the church of the Grey Friars in London (*G.E.C.*, x. 396 n.).

tore its way through his groin into his body and dealt him 1389 a mortal wound. His helm was removed, but he was soon past speech and it was not much above an hour before the sorely stricken earl had breathed his last. At once laughter gave place to tears, and the whole court was shocked by the occurrence into perturbation. The earl's death was a grief shared by all: the king and his circle were shaken by a sorrow beyond words; the queen, in company with the other ladies, sat sad and dejected in her chamber and passed her days in weeping; while to the earl's servants, too much dismayed to know at all what to do, immediate death seemed preferable to continued life. The last solemn rites were later performed at Hereford, where the earl was given honourable burial beside his father.[1] As for the knight who caused the fatal injury, he immediately took to flight; if he had lingered about the court he would certainly have met his death.[2]

On 13 January sixteen men practising various handicrafts 1390 were arrested at Croydon and lodged in the marshalsea; some of them were workmen whose intention was to rise against the clergy and their lay neighbours and put them to death; and if their plot had not been so swiftly laid bare they planned to raise another revolt even more wicked than that described above.[3] Thus it was that later, during February, three of them were drawn and hanged.

The king began his parliament at Westminster on 17 January; it lasted until 2 March, and by its end some harsh legislation had been promulgated. During this time the pope restored to their former dignity all the cardinals whom Urban had deposed, and chose Adam [Easton], also reinstated, as his chief adviser.[4] Three other cardinals were also created by the pope, one of them being Cosmas Gentilis, for some time Pope Urban VI's collector in England.

[2] John of St. John received the king's pardon in 1391 (*Cal. Pat. R., 1388-92*, p. 469).

[3] Above, pp. 2 ff.; and see *Cal. Pat. R., 1388-92*, p. 215.

[4] Adam Easton and 2 other cardinals deposed by Urban VI in 1385 — probably the only survivors — were restored by Boniface IX on 18 Dec. 1389 (Eubel and van Gulik, *Hierarchia Catholica Medii Aevi*, i. 22-4). In the same consistory Boniface IX created 4 new cardinals, one of whom was Cosmas Gentilis Megliorato, papal collector in England (ibid., pp. 24, 40). See also above, p. 106 and n.

1390   *Statutum contra provisores.* Item xxix. die Januarii factum fuit et confirmatum in parliamento statutum odiosum*a* contra provisores, scilicet quod omnes transeuntes ad curiam Romanam pro beneficiis optinendis sive impetrandis eo ipso neque illo neque alio expost in regno gauderet,*b* corpusque ejus nichilominus voluntati regie subjaceret, per hoc enim volentes excludere papam a collacione quorumcumque beneficiorum et legittimis patronis collaciones eorundem contradere et conferre. Eodem modo ordinarunt de majoribus dignitatibus ecclesiarum, scilicet vacante archiepiscopatu, episcopatu seu abbacia sive alia dignitate quacumque eligibili quod suis eleccionibus*c* omnino gauderent prohibicione*d* pape in hac re nequaquam obstante.[1] Quod postquam aures
p. 193 pape insonuit graviter tulit cordi. Qua de causa statuerunt / certos ambassiatores destinare ad curiam, quosdam videlicet clericos et quosdam milites, personas irregulares, ut hii beneficia ecclesiastica parvipendentes forcius penes papam in hac causa instarent.[2]

Item in isto parliamento plura hiis moverunt, scilicet de artificibus, de operariis, et de diversis servientibus quatinus ut omnes isti et singuli meliori foro cuicumque servirent de eorum artificiis et serviciis deinceps quam antea impenderunt, ut tactum est supra in parliamento tento apud Cantebrigiam:[3] set quia imposiciones*e* rerum venalium quibus ipsi viverent minus eque taxarunt, ad suum effectum minime pervenerunt.

Item parum ante finem mensis Februarii dominus Ricardus Meteford' recepit litteras papales super episcopatum Cicestren' *f*et cito post in episcopum consecratus est.*f*[4]

Item in isto parliamento dominus Johannes Holand comes

---

a ac *deleted.*   *b Recte* gauderent.   *c A letter is blotted out after this word.*   *d A marginal correction of* auctoritate.   *e MS.* posiciones.   *f-f In the margin but marked for insertion here.*

---

[1] Cf. below, pp. 418 ff.; and W. A. Pantin, *The English Church in the Fourteenth Century* (Cambridge, 1955), pp. 84 ff.

[2] For this embassy, which did not set out until mid-summer, see below, p. 430 and n. The one clerical member was a royal clerk: his 'irregularity' made it unlikely that he would in fact receive a timely papal offer of a benefice. For Boniface IX's reactions to the Statute of Provisors of 1390, see Lunt, *Financial Relations of the Papacy with England, 1327–1534,* ii. 391 ff.

[3] Above, pp. 360 ff. and nn. The parliament of 1390, in confirming this

Statute against provisors. On 29 January the detestable 1390
statute of provisors was enacted and confirmed in the parliament, laying it down that every person going to the Roman
curia to obtain or secure the grant of a benefice should be
thereby precluded from enjoying either it or, from that time
forward, any other benefice in the realm, and that his body
should be none the less subject to the king's will. The object
was to bar the pope from the collation of all benefices
whatsoever and to bestow such collation on the lawful
patrons. It was likewise ordained, in regard to the higher
ecclesiastical dignities, that when an archbishopric, bishopric,
abbacy, or any other elective office whatever fell vacant,
there should be full enjoyment of the election procedure,
notwithstanding any papal prohibition in the matter.[1]
When this reached the ears of the pope, he took it very much
to heart, and for this reason the parliament decided to send
to the curia accredited ambassadors, some of them clerics
and some knights, but all persons bound by no religious rule,
so that in their disregard of ecclesiastical preferment they
would be the more emphatic in their dealings with the pope
over this matter.[2]

Further business propounded in this parliament concerned
artisans, workmen, and servants of various kinds, who were
all in future to be employed in their crafts and services at a
lower rate of pay than hitherto, as is mentioned above in the
account of the Cambridge parliament.[3] Since, however, the
imposts on retail goods on which the workpeople lived were
inequitably assessed, the legislation failed of its intended
effect.

Shortly before the end of February Richard Medford
received his papal letters concerning the bishopric of
Chichester and was soon afterwards consecrated bishop.[4]
In the course of this parliament the earl of Huntingdon,

---

legislation in 13 Richard II, statute 1, *cap.* 8, modified it in one respect: henceforward, at Easter and Michaelmas, J.P.s were to publish the lawful wages of
artisans and labourers, regulated according to the price of food, which was also to
be at the justices' discretion (*S.R.*, ii. 63; *R.P.*, iii. 268-9). For the price-levels
referred to by the Monk in his next sentence, see Ritchie, in *Essays in Economic
History*, ed. Carus-Wilson, ii. 95-6.
[4] Medford was provided on 17 Nov. 1389 and consecrated on 10 Apr. 1390.
See also *Diplomatic Correspondence of Richard II*, ed. Perroy, no. 118 and n.

1390 Huntyngdon' factus est camerarius domini regis et ejus sub-
camerarius dominus Thomas Percy effectus est.[1] Item in fine
istius parliamenti dux Lancastr' per dominum regem et
assensu tocius parliamenti in ducem Aquitannie nichil inde
reddendo erectus est; et dominus ⟨Edwardus⟩[a] filius et heres
ducis Eborac' factus est comes Rotelandie, cui eciam rex
contulit castellum de Okeham cum suis pertinenciis universis.[2] Item statutum est in eodem quod curia mareschallie
deinceps non admitteret placita forinseca set staret contenta
ad lites et querimonias dicte curie pertinentes [b]infra virgam
tantummodo emergentes.[b][3] Consimiliter de curia constabu-
larie et mareschallie non extenderet se ad lites terrarum sive
bonorum mobilium seu immobilium set directe ea que ad
arma pertinent solummodo intenderet et non ad alia ullo
modo.[4] Item quinto die Marcii venit ventus magnus a plaga
occidentali domos suo tegimento spolians et concuciens,
arbores quoque violenter ad terram prostravit, dampna non
modica intulit post futuris plangenda. Quo in tempore
venerunt London' ambassiatores domini pape comendantes
ipsum domino regi et regno.[5]

Item x. die Marcii misit rex Westmon' unum par sotu-
larium de rubeo velvetto gemmis margarit' ad modum florum
deliciarum confect', a papa Urbano vj.[c] parum ante ejus
obitum benedictorum, ad reponendum ibidem cum aliis
ornamentis regalibus ad regis coronacionem spectantibus
in prefato monasterio custoditis. Constat namque quod rex
statim post coronacionem suam domum revestiarii intraret,
ubi sua regalia deponeret et alia indumenta sibi per suos
cubicularios adaptata assumeret, et abhinc via proximiori
in palacium suum rediret; set econtra fuit factum in coronacione istius regis, et male, nam quidam miles vocatus dominus

[a] MS. blank.   [b-b] In the margin but marked for insertion here.   [c] Written
in MS. above Urbano.

---

[1] Holland's appointment was made not later than 22 Feb. (Cal. Pat. R., 1388–
92, p. 194).
[2] Lancaster was appointed duke of Aquitaine for his life, to hold from Richard
II and his heirs as kings of France, on 2 Mar. and did homage to the king in parliament the same day; Edward of York was created earl of Rutland and granted the
castle and lordship of Oakham on 25 Feb. and he too did homage in parliament
on 2 Mar. (Rymer, Foedera, vii. 659–60; R.P., iii. 263–4). For the form of the
grant to Lancaster, see Tout, Chapters, iii. 464 n.

Sir John Holland, was made king's chamberlain and Sir 1390
Thomas Percy became under-chamberlain.[1] At the close of
the parliament, the duke of Lancaster was advanced by the
king, with the approval of the whole parliament, to the dukedom of Aquitaine, for which he was to render nothing; and
Sir [Edward] son and heir of the duke of York was created
earl of Rutland, having also conferred on him by the king the
castle of Oakham with all its appurtenances.[2] In the same
parliament it was ordained that in future the court of the
marshalsea should not entertain foreign pleas but should be
restricted exclusively to those suits and plaints belonging to
its competence which should arise within the verge.[3] The
court of the constable and marshal of England was likewise
not to extend its jurisdiction to actions concerning land or
movable or immovable goods but was to apply itself specifically to matters of chivalry alone and in no way to anything
else.[4] On 5 March there was a great westerly gale which
stripped roofs, rocked whole buildings, and flung trees flat
on the ground, creating havoc for posterity to bewail. The
pope's envoys, sent to commend him to the king and the
kingdom, arrived in London at this time.[5]

The king sent to Westminster on 10 March a pair of red
velvet shoes, with fleurs-de-lis worked on them in pearls,
which had been blessed by Pope Urban VI shortly before his
death; they were to be deposited with the rest of the royal
insignia associated with the king's coronation that are kept
in the monastery. It is generally accepted that immediately
after his coronation the king should go into the vestry, where
he should take off the regalia and put on the other garments
laid out ready for him by his chamberlains before returning
by the shortest route to his palace, but at the coronation of
the present king the contrary was done, with deplorable
results; for when the coronation was over, a certain knight,

[3] A reference to 13 Richard II, statute 1, *cap.* 3, restricting the jurisdiction of
the steward and marshal to a radius of 12 miles from the household (*S.R.*, ii. 62;
R.P., iii. 267).

[4] 13 Richard II, statute 1, *cap.* 2 prohibited the trial in the court of the constable and marshal of cases determinable by the common law (*S.R.*, ii. 61-2; cf.
R.P., iii. 265). For this statute see Keen, in *T.R.H.S.*, 5th ser., xii (1962), 98.

[5] In fact Damian de Cataneis, Boniface IX's envoy, was in England as early as
Dec. 1389; he stayed until May 1390 (*Diplomatic Correspondence of Richard II*,
ed. Perroy, no. 111 and n.); see also *Perroy*, p. 311.

1390 Simon Burlee peracta coronacione assumpsit regem ^asuis regalibus sic vestitum^a inter sua brachia per portam regiam palacium ingrediens, turbis hinc inde occurrentibus et illum prementibus, in eundo unum de sotularibus regalibus benedictis per incuriam ibidem amisit.[1] Igitur nostrates caveant imposterum ne ullatenus permittant regem cum insigniis regalibus amplius extra ecclesiam exire set, ut moris est, completa coronacione divertat in domum revestiarii, ut predicitur, et ibi sua regalia ornamenta honeste deponat.

Et quia supra proxime feci aliqualem mencionem de parliamento, igitur hic addam aliqua, prout sequitur:[2]

Nostre^b seignur le roi a soun parlement tenuz a Weymoust'^c Lundy proschein apres la^d feste de seint Hiller lan de son reigne treszisme oie la grevouse compleint de sa comune en mesme le parlement des outrageouses meschiefs et damages qi sont avenuz a son dit roialme purceo qe tresons, murdres et rapes des femmes sont trop comunement faitz et perpetrez et cele^e pluis purceo qe chartres ^fdes pardons^f ont estee trop legerement grantez en tieux cases; la^g comune pria a nostre seignur le roi qe tieux chartres ne fuissent mes grantez; a qei nostre seignur le roi respondy qil vorroit salver sa liberte et regalie come ces progenitours ont fait devant ces heures meis pur la^h quiete et pais nurrir deinz son roialme delassent des grands et noebles en mesme le parlement esteantz ad grante qe nul chartre de pardon desore soit allowe devant qeconqes justices pur murdre, mort de homme occiz par agaite, assalt ou malice purpense, tresoun ou rap de femme, si mesme le murdre ou mort de homme occiz par agaite, assalte ou malice purpense, tresoun ou rap de femme ne soient especifiez en mesme la chartre; et siⁱ chartre de mort de homme soit^j allegge devant qesconqes justices^k en quele chartre ne soit especifie qe cely de qi mort ascun tiel soit arreigne fuist murdres ou occiz par agaite, assaute ou malice purpense enquergent les justices par bone enqueste de^l visne ou le^m mort fuist occiz, sil fuist murdry ou occiz par agaite, assalte ou malice purpense, et sils trovent qil fuist murdrie ou occiz par agaite, assaut ou malice purpenseⁿ soit la chartre disalowe et soit fait outreⁿ solonc ceo qe la ley demande. Et si ascun prie au roi pur chartre de pardoun pur murdre, mort de homme occiz par agaite, assalt ou malice purpense, tresoun ou rap

---

^{a-a} *In the margin but marked for insertion here.* 　　^b Gallicum *in the margin.* ^c *S.R.* Westm'. 　　^d *S.R.* le. 　　^e *S.R.* ceo le. 　　^{f-f} *S.R.* de pardon. 　　^g *S.R. inserts* dite. 　　^h *S.R. inserts* greindre. 　　ⁱ *S.R. inserts* la. 　　^j *S.R.; MS. om.* ^k *MS. inserts* pur murdre mort. 　　^l *S.R.* del. 　　^m *S.R.* la. 　　ⁿ *The letter* s *(a false start) is blotted out after this word.*

---

[1] A grievous loss, since the shoes were part of the regalia worn by Alfred at his coronation in Rome by Leo IV and later by Edward the Confessor at his

Sir Simon Burley, took the king up in his arms, attired as he 1390 was, in his regalia, and went into the palace by the royal gate with crowds milling all round him and pressing upon him, so that on the way he lost one of the consecrated shoes through his thoughtlessness.[1] Our people must therefore take good care in future that the king is not allowed for a moment to leave the church wearing the regalia but that the practice is observed whereby, when the coronation is over, he goes to the vestry and there decently puts off his royal insignia.

As I made some mention just now of the parliament, I will here amplify it by adding the following:[2]

Our lord the king, at his parliament held at Westminster on Monday next after the feast of St. Hilary, the thirteenth year of his reign [17 January 1390], hearing the grievous complaint of his commons in the same parliament of the outrageous mischiefs and damages which have happened to his said realm because treasons, murders, and rapes of women are very commonly done and perpetrated and the more so because charters of pardon have been very easily granted in such cases; the commons prayed our lord the king that such charters should be no more granted; whereto our lord the king answered that he would save his liberty and regality, as his progenitors have hitherto done but to nourish quiet and peace within his realm, by the assent of the great men and nobles present in the same parliament, he has granted that no charter of pardon from henceforth shall be allowed before any justices for murder or for the death of a man slain by ambush, assault, or malice aforethought, treason, or rape of a woman, unless the same murder, death of the man slain by ambush, assault, or malice afore-thought, treason or rape of a woman be specified in the same charter; and if a charter for homicide be alleged before any justices in which charter it is not specified that he of whose death any such is arraigned was murdered or slain by ambush, assault, or malice aforethought, the justices shall inquire by a good inquest of the neighbourhood where the dead man was slain, whether he was murdered or slain by ambush, assault, or malice aforethought, and if they find that he was murdered, or slain by ambush, assault, or malice aforethought, the charter shall be disallowed and further it shall be done as the law demands. And if any be a suitor to the king for a charter of pardon for murder, death of a man slain by ambush, assault, or malice aforethought, treason, or rape

coronation and entrusted by Edward to Westminster Abbey. See Richard of Cirencester, *Speculum Historiale*, ii. 26 ff.; *Flete*, p. 71; and for the monks' resolve to approach the king on the subject when he came of age, ibid., p. 19.

[2] There follows the text of 13 Richard II, statute 2, *cap.* 1, enacted in the parliament of 17 Jan. to 2 Mar. 1390; this has been collated with that in *S.R.*, ii. 68-9. See also below, p. 430.

1390
p. 194

de femme, si le chamberleyn endose tiel bille ou face endoser, mette le noun de celuy qi pria pur tiel^a chartre sur ^{b}mesme la bille sur^b / peyne de mil marcz; ^{c}et si le southchamberlein endose tielle bille face semblablement sur peyne de cynk centz marcz; et qe nulle autre qe chamberleyn ou southchamberlein endose ne face endoser nulle tiele bille sur peyne de mil marcz;^{c} et qe^d tiel bille soit envoie et directe a gardeyn du prive seal et qe nul garant du prive seal soit fait pur tiel chartre avoir si noun qe le gardeyn de prive seal eit tiele bille endose ou signe par le chamberleyn ou southchamberleyn, come desuis est dite. Et qe nul chartre de pardoun de tresoun ne de autre felonie passe la chancellerie sanz garant de^e prive seal forsqe en cas ou le chanceller le puisse granter de son office sanz ent parler au roi. Et si celuy a qi prier^f ascun chartre de pardoun pur murdre, mort de homme tue par agaite, assaut ou malice purpensee, treson ou rap de femme soit grantee, soit erchevesqe ou duk, paie au roi mille livres, et sil soit evesqe ou count paie au roi mil marcz,^{g} et sil soit clerk bachiler ou autre de meindre estat, de quele condicion qil soit paie au^h roi cc. marcz, et eit lemprisonement dun an.

Item[1] come le noble roi Edwarde aiel nostre seignur le roi qore est a son parlement tenuz a Westm' ^{i}a les^i oetaves ^{j}de la^j Purificacion de^k Nostre Dame lan de son reigne vint et quint ^{l}fist reciter^l lestatut fait a Cardoil^m en temps soun aiel le roi Edward fitz au roi Henry touchant lestate de seint esglise Dengleterre,[2] le dit aiel nostre dit^n seignur le roi qore est de lassent des grands de soun roialme en mesme le parlement tenuz le dit an vynt et quint esteantz al honour de Dieux et de seint esglise et de tout soun roialme ordeigna et establist qe francs eleccions des ^{o}ercheveschies, eveschies^o et touz autres dignitees et benefices electives en Engleterre se tiendroient ^{p}des lors^p en manere come ils^q furent granteez par ses progenitours et par lez auncestres dautres^r seignurs foundours et qe^s toutz prelates et autres gentz de seint esglise qavoient avoesons de qeqonqes benefices de done le roi ou de cez progenitours ou dautres seignurs et donours husent franchement lour collacions et presentementz; et sur ceo certein punissement estoit ordeigne en mesme lestatut pur ceux qi acceptont aucun dignitee ou benefice au contraire de^t dit estatut fait a Westm' le dit an vynt et quint, come devant est dite: le quele estatut nostre seignur le roi ad feit reciter en ceste present parlement al requeste de sa comune en mesme le parlement, le^u tenour^v de quele estatut est tiel come cy ensuyt:

^{w}*Statutum contra provisores.*^{w} Come jadys en^x parlement de bone

^{a} *S.R.; MS.* celle. $^{b-b}$ *MS. repeats these words at the top of p.* 194.
$^{c-c}$ *S.R.; MS. om.* ^{d} *MS. inserts* nul. ^{e} *S.R.* du. ^{f} *S.R.; MS.* par.
^{g} *S.R. inserts* et sil soit abbe, prior, baron' ou baneret paie au roi cynk centz marcz. ^{h} *S.R.* ou. $^{i-i}$ *S.R.* al. $^{j-j}$ *S.R. del.* ^{k} *S.R. om.* $^{l-l}$ *S.R.; MS. om.* ^{m} *S.R.* Kardoile. ^{n} *S.R. om.* $^{o-o}$ *S.R.; MS.* ercevesqes, evesqes.
$^{p-p}$ *S.R.* delors. ^{q} *S.R.* eles. ^{r} *S.R.* des autres. ^{s} *S.R. om.* ^{t} *S.R.* du.
^{u} *S.R.* la. ^{v} *A letter has been blotted out after this word.* $^{w-w}$ *A marginal heading in MS.; S.R. om.* ^{x} *S.R. inserts* le.

of a woman, if the chamberlain endorse or cause to be endorsed such 1390 bill he shall set upon the bill the name of him that made suit for such charter upon pain of 1,000 marks; and if the under-chamberlain endorse such bill he shall do likewise on pain of 500 marks; and that no one other than the chamberlain or under-chamberlain shall endorse or cause to be endorsed any such bill on pain of 1,000 marks; and that such bill shall be sent and directed to the keeper of the privy seal and that no warrant of privy seal for having such a charter shall be made unless the keeper of the privy seal has such a bill endorsed or signed by the chamberlain or under-chamberlain, as abovesaid. And that no charter of pardon for treason or for other felony shall pass the chancery without a warrant of privy seal except in the case where the chancellor can grant it of his office without speaking thereof to the king; and if he at whose suit any charter of pardon for murder, death of a man slain by ambush, assault, or malice aforethought, treason or rape of a woman, is granted be an archbishop or duke, he shall pay the king £1,000; and if he be bishop or earl, he shall pay the king 1,000 marks; and if he be clerk, bachelor, or other of lesser estate, of whatsoever condition he be, he shall pay the king 200 marks and suffer one year's imprisonment.

Item:[1] whereas the noble king Edward, grandfather of our lord the king that now is, at his parliament held at Westminster at the octaves of the Purification of Our Lady in the twenty-fifth year of his reign [9 February 1351], caused to be rehearsed the statute made at Carlisle in the time of his grandfather King Edward son of King Henry touching the estate of the Holy Church of England,[2] the said grandfather of our said lord the king that now is with the assent of the great men of his realm, being in the same parliament held in the said twenty-fifth year, to the honour of God and of Holy Church and of all his realm, ordained and established that free elections of archbishoprics, bishoprics, and all other dignities and benefices elective in England should hold from henceforth in the manner in which they were granted by his progenitors and by the ancestors of other lords as founders, and that all prelates and other people of Holy Church who had advowsons of any benefices by gift of the king or of his progenitors or of other lords and donors should freely have their collations and presentations; and thereupon a certain punishment was ordained in the same statute for those who accept any dignity or benefice contrary to the said statute made at Westminster in the said twenty-fifth year, as aforesaid; which statute our lord the king has caused to be recited in this present parliament at the request of his commons in the same parliament, the tenor whereof is such as here follows:

Statute against Provisors. Whereas aforetime in the parliament of

[1] There follows the text of the second Statute of Provisors (13 Richard II, statute 2, *caps.* 2-3), in which the text of the first Statute of Provisors (25 Edward III, statute 4) is also rehearsed. This text has been collated with that in S.R., i. 316-18 and ii. 69-74. See also above, p. 412.

[2] 35 Edward I, *caps.* 1-4 (S.R., i. 150-2).

1390   memorie sire Edwarde roi Dengl', aiel nostre seignur le roi qorest, lan
de soun reigne trentisme[a] quint a Kardoille tenuz oie la peticion mys
devant le dit aiel et soun conseil en le dit parlement par la cominalte
de soun roialme contenant qe come seint esglise Dengleterre[b] estoit
foundu en lestate[c] de prelacie deins le roialme Dengl' par le dit aiel et
ces progenitours et conts et barons et noebles de soun roialme et lour
auncestres pur eux et le poeple enfourmer de la ley Dieu et pur faire
hospitaliteez, almoignes et autres oeveres de charite es lieux ou lez
esglises furent fonduz pur les almes des foundours et de lour heires et
de toutz Chrestiens; et certeins possessions tant en fees, terres et rentz
come en avoesons qi se extendent a grante value par les ditz foundours
feurent assignes as prelates et autres gentz de seint esglise du dit roialme
pur celle charge sustener, et nomement des possessions qi feurent
assignez as ercevesqes, evesqes, abbes, priours, religiouses et autres gentz
de seint esglise par[d] les rois du dit roialme, contz, barons et autres
noebles de soun roialme; mesmes les rois, conts, barons et autres[e]
noebles come seignurs et avowes eussent et aver deussent la garde des
tilx voidances et les presentementz et collacions des benefices esteantz
des[f] tielx prelacies et les ditz rois en temps passe soloient aver [g]la
greindre[g] partie de lour consels pur la salvacion du roialme qant ils ent
eurent meister de tielx prelates et clercs issint avances; le pape de Rome
accrochant a luy la seignurie des[h] tielx possessions et benefices mesmes
les benefices dona et granta as aliens qi unqes ne [i]demoerront en[i]
roialme Dengleterre et as cardinalx qi y demuerer ne purront[j] et as
autres tant aliens come denizeins autre si come il ust este patroun ou
avowe des ditz dignites et benefices, come il ne feust de droit solonc la
ley de Engleterre; par les queux sils feussent soeffretz a peyne demur-
reroit aucun benefice en[k] poy de temps en le dit roialme qil ne serroit
es mayns des aliens et denizeins par vertue de tilx provisions contre
la bone voluntee et disposicioun des foundours des[l] mesmes les
benefices et issint les eleccions des [m]erceveschies, eveschies[m] et
autres religious faudroient et les almoignes, hospitalitees et autres
oevres de charite qi serroient [n]faitz es ditz lieux serroient[n] sustreitz,
le dit aiel et autres lays patrons en temps de tieux voidances perdroient
lour[o] presentementz, le dit conseil periroit, et biens sanz nombre
serroient emportez hors du roialme, en adnullacion de lestat de seint
esglise Dengleterre et disheritison du dit aiel et des conts, barons
et noebles et en offence et destruccion des leys et[p] droiturs de soun
roialme et grant damage de soun poeple et subversion de lestate de
tout soun roialme suisdit et econtre[q] la bone disposicion et voluntee
des primers foundours; de lassent des counts, barons, noebles et tout
la dite cominalte a lour instante requeste considerez les damages et

---

[a] *S.R. ii. 69 inserts* et; *MS. and S.R. i. 316 om.*   [b] *From S.R.; MS. om.*
[c] *S.R.* estat.   [d] *S.R.; MS.* pur.   [e] *MS. and S.R. ii. 70; S.R. i. 316 om.*
[f] *MS. and S.R. i. 316* des; *S.R. ii. 70 de.*   [g-g] *S.R. i. 316* la grein⟨u⟩re; *S.R.*
ii. 70 le greinour.   [h] *S.R.* de.   [i-i] *S.R. i. 316* dem⟨ur⟩erent el.   [j] *MS.*
and S.R. ii. 70; S.R. i. 316 purroient.   [k] *Written above* de, *which has been*
expunged.   [l] *S.R.* de.   [m-m] *MS. and S.R. ii. 70; S.R. i. 316* ercevesqes

good memory of Edward king of England, grandfather of our lord the 1390
king that now is, held at Carlisle in the thirty-fifth year of his reign
[1306-7], upon the hearing of the petition put before the said grandfather and his council in the said parliament by the commonalty of
his realm, containing that whereas the Holy Church of England was
founded in the estate of prelacy within the realm of England by the
said grandfather and his progenitors and the earls, barons, and nobles of
his realm and their ancestors to inform them and the people of the law
of God and to perform hospitalities, alms, and other works of charity,
in the places where the churches were founded, for the souls of the
founders, their heirs, and all Christians; and certain possessions as well
in fees, lands, and rents as in advowsons, which extend to a great value,
were assigned by the said founders to the prelates and other people of
the Holy Church of the said realm to sustain the same charge, and
especially of the possessions which were assigned to archbishops,
bishops, abbots, priors, religious, and all other people of Holy Church
by the kings of the said realm, earls, barons, and other nobles of his
realm, the same kings, earls, barons, and other nobles, as lords and
patrons have had and ought to have the keeping of such voidances and
the presentations and collations of the benefices being of such prelacies;
and the said kings in times past were wont to have the greater part
of their councils, for the safeguard of the realm, when they had need of
such, from such prelates and clerks so advanced; the pope of Rome
accroaching to himself the lordship of such possessions and benefices
gave and granted the same benefices to aliens which did never dwell
in the realm of England and to cardinals who may not dwell here
and to others, as well aliens as denizens, as if he had been patron or
advowee of the said dignities and benefices (as he was not of right
according to the law of England); whereby if they should be suffered,
there would within a short time be scarcely any benefice within the said
realm which would not be in the hands of aliens and denizens by virtue
of such provisions contrary to the goodwill and disposition of the
founders of the same benefices and so the elections to archbishoprics,
bishoprics, and of other religious should fail and the alms, hospitalities,
and other works of charity which should be done in the said places
should be withdrawn, the said grandfather and other lay patrons in the
time of such voidances should lose their presentations, the said council
should perish, and numberless goods should be carried out of the realm,
in annihilation of the estate of the Holy Church of England and disherison of the same grandfather and the earls, barons, and nobles and
in offence and destruction of the laws and rights of his realm and to the
great damage of his people and subversion of the estate of all his realm
abovesaid and contrary to the good disposition and will of the first
founders; by the assent of the earls, barons, nobles, and of all the said
commonalty at their instant request, after consideration of the damages

evesches; ercevesqes *deleted in MS. before* ercevechies.   [n-n] *S.R. ii. 70; MS.*
om.; S.R. i. 316 as *for* es.   [o] *MS. and S.R. i. 316; S.R. ii. 70* lours.
[p] *S.R. i. 316; MS. and S.R. ii. 70 om.*   [q] *S.R.* countre.

1390 grevances suisditz en le dit plener parlement fuist purvieu, / ordeine
p. 195 et establie qe les ditz grevances, oppressions et damages en mesme le
roialme des adonqes mes ne serroient suffretz en ascun manere. Et ja
monstre soit a nostre seignur le roi en ceste parlement tenuz a Westm'
as oetaves de la Purificacion de^a nostre Dame lan de soun reigne Dengle-
terre^b vyntisme quint et de France duzisme par le^c grevous pleint de
tout la comune de soun roialme qe les grevances et meschiefs suisditz
sabondent de temps en temps a pluis grant damage et destruccion de
tout le roialme pluis qe unqes ne furent;^{d} cest assavoir qore de novel
nostre seint piere le pape par procurement des clercs et autrement ad
reserve et reserve de jour en autre a sa collacion generalment et especialment si bien ercheveschies, eveschies, abbeies et^e priories come toutz
dignites et autres benefices Dengleterre qi sont de lavowerie des^f gentz
de seint esglise et les donne auxibien as aliens com as denizeins et prent
de toutz tiels benefices les primers fruites et autres profitz plousours
et grante partie de^g tresore de^h roialme si est emporte et despendue
hors du roialme par les purchasours de^i tieux graces; et auxint par tiels
reservacions prives plousours clercs avancez en ceste roialme par lour
verrois patrouns qont tenuz lour avancementz ^{j}pesiblement par long
temps^j sont sodeinement oustez; sur qoi ^{k}la dite^k comune ad prie a
nostre seignur le roi qe desicome le droit de la corone Dengleterre et
le^l ley du dit roialme sont tielx qe sur meschiefs et damages qe si
aveignent^m a soun roialme il doit et est tenuz par soun serement de
lacorde de soun poeple en soun parlement faire ent remedie et ley en
oustant^n meschiefs et damages ^{o}qensi aveinont, qe luy pleise de ceo
ordeigner remedie; nostre seignur le roy, veiant les meschiefs et
damages^o suisnomez et eiant regarde a^p dit estatut fait en temps son dit
aiel et a les causes contenuz en ycelle, le^q quele estatut tient ^{r}tout jour
en^r sa force et ne fuist unqes defait ne adnulle en nulle point, et par
tant ^{s}il est^s tenuz par soun serement de le faire garder come la ley de
soun roialme, coment qe par suffrance et negligence ad este puis
attempte a contraire, et ^{t}eiant auxint^t regarde a les grevouses pleintz
a luy faitz par soun poeple en ces diverses parlementz cea en arere
tenuz, voillant les tres grandes damages et meschiefs qi sont avenuz
et aveignent^u de jour en autre a lesglise Dengleterre par la dite cause
remedie ent ordeigner,^{v} par assent de toutz les grandes et la^w cominalte
de soun dit roialme al honour de Dieux et profit de la dite esglise
Dengleterre et de tout soun roialme ad ordeine et establie qe les francs
eleccions des ercheveschies, eveschees et de^x toutz autres dignitees
et benefices electifs en Engleterre se tiegnent desore en manere come
ils feurent grantez par les progenitours nostre dit seignur le roi et par
les auncestres des autres seignurs foundours. Et qe toutz prelates
et autres gentz de seint esglise qont avowesons de qeconqes benefices

^{a} *S.R. ii. 70 om.* ^{b} *S.R.; MS. om.* ^{c} *S.R.* la. ^{d} *MS. and S.R. ii. 71;*
S.R. i. 317 firent. ^{e} *S.R.; MS. om.* ^{f} *S.R. i. 317* de. ^{g} *S.R. i. 317* du.
^{h} *S.R. i. 317* del. ^{i} *S.R. ii. 71* des. $^{j-j}$ *S.R. i. 317* par long temps pesiblement.
$^{k-k}$ *MS. and S..R. i. 317* la dite; *S.R. ii. 71* le dit. ^{l} *S.R.* la. ^{m} *S.R.* aveign-
ont. ^{n} *S.R. inserts* les. $^{o-o}$ *S.R.; MS. om.* ^{p} *S.R. ii. 71* au; *S.R. i. 317* al.

and grievances abovesaid, in the said full parliament it was provided, 1390
ordained, and established that the said grievances, oppressions, and
damages in the same realm should from henceforth not in any manner
be suffered. And now it is shown to our lord the king in this parliament
held at Westminster at the octaves of the Purification of our Lady in
the 25th year of his reign of England and of France the twelfth [9
February 1351] by the grievous complaint of all the commons of his
realm that the grievances and mischiefs abovesaid do at all times
abound to the greater damage and destruction of all the realm more
than ever were before, viz. that now of late our Holy Father the Pope
by procurement of clerks and otherwise, has reserved and daily reserves
to his collation generally and specially as well archbishoprics,
bishoprics, abbeys, and priories as all dignities and other benefices of
England which are of the avowry of the people of Holy Church, and
gives the same as well to aliens as to denizens and takes of all such
benefices the first fruits and many other profits, and a great part of the
treasure of the realm is thus carried away and spent outside the realm
by the purchasers of such graces; and furthermore by such privy
reservations many clerks, advanced in this realm by their true patrons,
who have peaceably held their advancements for a long time, are
suddenly ousted; whereupon the said commons have prayed our lord
the king that since the right of the Crown of England and the law of the
said realm are such that upon the mischiefs and damages which befall
his realm he ought, and is bound by his oath, with the accord of his
people in his parliament, to make remedy and law therefor, for the
voiding of the mischiefs and damages which thus befall, that it may
please him thereupon to ordain remedy; our lord the king seeing the
mischiefs and damages above-mentioned and having regard to the said
statute made in the time of his said grandfather and to the causes
contained in the same, which statute continues to retain its force and
was never undone or annulled in any point, and therefore he is bound
by his oath to cause the same to be kept as the law of his realm
(although by sufferance and negligence attempts have since been made
to the contrary), and also having regard to the grievous complaints
made to him by his people in sundry of his parliaments heretofore held,
wishing to ordain remedy for the very great damages and mischiefs
which have befallen and daily befall the Church of England from the
said cause, by the assent of all the great men and the commonalty of
his said realm, to the honour of God and the profit of the said Church
of England and of all his realm, has ordained and established that the
free elections to archbishoprics, bishoprics, and all other dignities and
benefices elective in England shall from henceforth hold in the manner
in which they were granted by the progenitors of our said lord the king
and by the ancestors of the other founding lords. And that all prelates
and other people of Holy Church who have advowsons of any benefices

q MS. *and S.R. i. 317* le; *S.R. ii. 71* la. $r-r$ *S.R.* touz jours. $s-s$ *S.R.* est il.
$t-t$ *S.R.* auxint eiant. u *S.R. ii. 71* veignent; *S.R. i. 317* viegnont. v *S.R.;*
MS. ordeine. w MS. *and S.R. i. 317* la; *S.R. i. 71* le. x *S.R. i. 317 om.*

1390 [a]de doun[a] nostre seignur le roi et de ces progenitours ou dautres seignurs et donours pur faire [b]divine service[b] et autres charges ent ordeignez eient lour collacions et presentmentz franchement en manere com ils estoient feoffez par lour donours. Et en cas qe daucun ercheveschee, eveschee, dignite ou autre qeconqe benefice soit reservacion, collacion ou provisioun fait par la court de Rome en destourbance dez eleccions[c] ou presentacions suisnomez qa mesme[d] temps des voidances qe tiels reservacions, collacions ou[e] provisions deussent prendre [f]leffecte qe a[f] mesme la voidance nostre seignur le roi et ces heirs eient et enjoicent pur celle foitz les collacions as ercheveschies, eveschies et autres benefices[g] electives qi sont de sa avowerie au tielx come cez progenitours avoient avant qe franc eleccion fuist grante desicome les eleccions furent primes grantes par les progenitours le roi sur certein forme et condicion, come a demander du roi congie deslier et puis apres la eleccion davoir soun assent royal, et ne mye en autre manere, les quels condicions nient gardez la chose doit par resoun resorter a sa primere nature. Et qe si daucun[h] meason' de religion del avowerie du[i] roi soit tiel reservacion, collacion ou provision fait en desturbance de franc eleccione eit nostre seignur le roi et ses heirs a celle foitz la collacion a doner celle dignite a persone covenable. Et en cas qe reservacion, collacion ou provision soit fait a la court de Rome de nul esglise, provendre ou autre benefice qi sont del avowerie dez gentz de seint esglise dont le roi est avowe paramont immediate qa mesme le temps de voidance a quele temps la reservacion, collacion ou provision deussent prendre effecte, come desuis est dite, qe le roi et ses heirs de ceo eient le[j] presentement ou collacion a celle foitz et issint de temps en temps a toutz les foitz qe tiels gentz de seint esglise serront destourbez de lour presentementz ou collacions par tiels reservacions, collacions ou provisions, come desuis est dite. Save a eux le droit de lour avowesons et presentementz qant nul collacion ou provision de la court de Rome ent ne soit fait ou qe lez dites gentz de seint esglise oisent ou[k] voillent a mesmes les benefices presenter ou collacion faire et lour presentees puissent leffecte de lour collacions et presentementz enjoicer; et en mesme la manere eit chescun autre seignur de quele condicion qil soit les presentementz ou collacions a les[l] measons de religion qi sont de sa avowerie et as benefices de seint esglise qi sont p. 196 appurtenantz a mesmes les measons; et si tiels avowes / ne presentent point as[m] tiels benefices deinz le[j] dymy an apres tiels voidances[n] ne levesqe de lieu ne le[o] donne par laps du[p] temps deins un moys apres le dymy an, qadonqes le roi eit ent les presentementz et collacions come il ad [q]des autres[q] de savowerie demesne. Et en cas qe les presentes du[r] roi ou les presentes [q]des autres[q] patrouns de seint esglise ou de lour[s] avowes ou ceux[t] as[u] qeux le roi ou tiels patrons ou avowes suisditz

---

[a-a] S.R. des douns.   [b-b] S.R. divines services.   [c] S.R. inserts collacions.
[d] S.R. i. 317 inserts les; S.R. ii. 71 le.   [e] S.R. et.   [f-f] S.R. i. 317 effect
qe a; S.R. ii. 71 effect de.   [g] S.R. dignites.   [h] S.R. dascun; MS. aucun.
[i] S.R. i. 318 le.   [j] MS. and S.R. i. 318 le; S.R. ii. 72 la.   [k] S.R. et.

by gift of our lord the king and of his progenitors or of other lords and
donors, to perform divine services and other charges thereof ordained,
shall have their collations and presentations freely in the manner in
which they were enfeoffed by their donors. And in case reservation,
collation, or provision of any archbishopric, bishopric, dignity, or other
benefice is made by the court of Rome in disturbance of the elections
or presentations above named, that at the same time of voidance when
such reservations, collations, or provisions are due to take effect, our
lord the king and his heirs at the same voidance shall have and enjoy
for that occasion the collations to archbishoprics, bishoprics, and other
benefices elective which are of his avowry such as his progenitors had
before free election was granted, inasmuch as elections were first
granted by the king's progenitors upon a certain form and condition,
as to demand 'congé d'élire' from the king and subsequently after the
election to have his royal assent, and in no other manner; which conditions not being kept, the thing ought by reason to resort to its first
nature. And that if any such reservation, collation, or provision of any
house of religion of the king's avowry is made in disturbance of free
election, our lord the king and his heirs shall have for that time the
collation to give this dignity to a suitable person. And in case reservation, collation, or provision of any church, prebend, or other benefice
which is of the avowry of people of Holy Church whereof the king is
immediate advowee paramount is made at the court of Rome, that at
the same time of the voidance at which the reservation, collation, or
provision are due to take effect, as abovesaid, the king and his heirs
shall have the presentation or collation thereof for that occasion, and so
from time to time whensoever such people of Holy Church shall be
disturbed of their presentations or collations by such reservations, collations, or provisions, as abovesaid; saving to them the right of their
advowsons and presentations, when no collation or provision of the
court of Rome is made thereof or where the said people of Holy
Church venture to, or will, present, or make collation to the same
benefices, and their presentees may enjoy the effect of their collations
and presentations; and in the same manner every other lord, of whatsoever condition he be, shall have the presentations or collations to the
houses of religion which are of his avowry and to the benefices of
Holy Church which are appurtenant to the same houses; and if such
advowees do not present to such benefices within the half-year after
such voidances and the bishop of the place do not give the same by
lapse of time within a month after the half-year, that then the king shall
have the presentations and collations thereof as he has of others of his
own avowry. And in case the presentees of the king or the presentees
of other patrons of Holy Church or of their advowees, or those to
whom the king or such patrons or advowees abovesaid shall have given

^{l} S.R.; MS. lour. ^{m} S.R. a. ^{n} S.R. ii. 72 voidance. ^{o} S.R. la.
^{p} S.R. i. 318 de. $^{q-q}$ S.R. dautres. ^{r} S.R. le. ^{s} S.R. ii. 72
lours. ^{t} S.R.; MS. oeux. ^{u} S.R. i. 72 a.

1390 averont donez benefices appurtenauncez a lour presentementz ou collacions soient destourbez par tiels provisours issint qils ne puissent aver
possession[a] des[b] tiels benefices par vertue des presentementz et
collacions issint a eux faitz, ou qe ceux qi sont en possession[c] des tiels
benefices soient empesches sur lour ditz possession[d] par tiels provisours,
adonqes soient lez ditz provisours et lour procuratours, executours et
notairs atthachez par lour corps et mesnez en respons, et sils soient
convictes demurgent en prisone sanz estre lessez a meinprise ou[e]
baille ou autrement deliverez tanqe ils eient[f] fait fyn et redempcion
a[g] roi a sa volunte et gree al partie qi se sentera greve; et nient meyns
avant qils soient deliverez facent pleine renunciacion et trovent suffi-
ceant suertee qils nattempteront tiele chose en temps avener ne nul
proces sueront par eux ne par autres[h] devers nully en la dite court de
Rome ne nul par aillours pur [i]nul tiel emprisonement ou renunciacion[i]
ne nul autre chose dependant de eux. Et en cas qe tiels provisours,
procuratours, executours et notairs ne soient trovez qe lexigende courge
devers eux par due proces et qe briefs issent de prendre lour[j] corps
quele part qils soient trovez auxi bien a la suite le roi come de partie,
et qen le mesne temps le roi [k]eit les profitz[k] de[l] tiels benefices issint
occupiez par tiels provisours, forspris abbeies, priories et autres measons
qont college ou covent, et en[m] tiels measons eient les covent et college[n]
lez profitz, savant toutfoitz a nostre seignur le roi et as autres seignurs
lour ancien droit. Et eit cest estatut lieu auxi bien de reservacions,
collacions et provisions faitz et grantez en temps passe devers toutz
ceux qi nount[o] unqore adeptz corporel possession de[p] benefices a eux
grantez par mesmes les reservacions, collacions ou[q] provisions come
devers toutz autres en temps[r] avenir; et doit cest estatut tiegnir lieu
comenceant as[s] oeptaves suisditz.[1]

Et outre ceo nostre[t] seignur le roi qorest de lassent des graunds de
son roialme esteant en ceste present parlement ad ordeine et establie
qe de toutz ercheveschies, eveschies et autres dignites et benefices
electives et autres benefices de seint esglise[u] qi comenceront[v] destre
voides de fait le xxix. jour de Januer lan du regne[w] nostre[x] seignur le
roi[y] treszime ou puis ou qi se voideront en temps avenir deinz le
roialme Dengleterre, le dit estatut fait le dit an xxv. soit fermement
tenuz pur toutz jours et mys en due execucion de temps en temps en
toutz pointz. Et si aucun face[z] acceptacioun daucun benefice de seint
esglise au[aa] contraire de cest estatut et ceo duement provee et soit de
par de la, soit[bb] exile et banny hors du roialme pur toutz jours et ces
terres, tenementz, biens et chateux forfaitz au roi; et sil soit deins le
roiaume soit[cc] auxi exile et banny [dd]et encourge autiel forfaiture[dd]

[a] S.R. ii. 72 possessions.   [b] S.R. i. 318 de.   [c] S.R. i. 318 possessions.
[d] S.R. possessions.   [e] S.R. en.   [f] S.R. averont.   [g] S.R. au.   [h] S.R.
i. 318 autre.   [i-i] S.R. nuls tielx emprisonementz ou renunciacions.   [j] S.R.
ii. 72 lours.   [k-k] S.R.; MS. om.   [l] S.R. ii. 73 des.   [m] S.R.; MS. in.
[n] S.R. colleges.   [o] S.R. ne sont.   [p] S.R. des.   [q] S.R. et.   [r] a expunged
after this word.   [s] S.R. i. 318 a les; S.R. ii. 73 al.   [t] S.R. inserts dit.
[u] S.R. inserts qeconqes.   [v] S.R. comencerent.   [w] S.R.; MS. om.   [x] S.R.

benefices belonging to their presentations or collations, are disturbed 1390
by such provisors, so that they may not have possession of such
benefices by virtue of the presentations and collations so made to them,
or those who are in possession of such benefices are impeached upon
their said possession by such provisors, then the said provisors, and
their proctors, executors, and notaries shall be attached by their bodies
and brought to answer; and if they are convicted, they shall remain in
prison without being admitted to mainprise or bail or otherwise
delivered until they have made fine and ransom to the king at his will
and satisfaction to the party feeling himself aggrieved; and nevertheless
before they are delivered they shall make full renunciation and find
sufficient surety that they will not attempt such a thing in future nor
sue any process, by themselves or by others, against any man in the said
court of Rome or anywhere else for any such imprisonment or
renunciation or any other thing depending thereon. And in case such
provisors, proctors, executors, and notaries are not found, the [writ of]
exigent shall run against them by due process and writs shall issue to
take their bodies wherever they are found, as well at the king's suit as
at the party's, and that meanwhile the king shall have the profits of
such benefices so occupied by such provisors, except abbeys, priories,
and other houses that have colleges or convents, and in such houses the
convents and colleges shall have the profits, saving always to our lord
the king and to other lords their ancient right. And this statute shall
hold good as well of reservations, collations, and provisions made and
granted in times past, against all those who have not yet obtained corporal possession of the benefices granted to them by the same reservations, collations, or provisions, as against all others in the future; and
this statute is to hold good from the octaves abovesaid.[1]

And furthermore our lord the king that now is, with the assent of the
great men of his realm attending this present parliament, has ordained
and established that for all archbishoprics, bishoprics, and other dignities
and benefices elective and other benefices of Holy Church which shall
begin to be void in fact on 29 January in the 13th year of the reign of
our lord the king [29 January 1390] or thereafter, or shall fall vacant in
future within the realm of England, the said statute made in the said
25th year shall be firmly held for ever and put into due execution from
time to time in all points. And if anyone accept any benefice of Holy
Church contrary to this statute, and this is duly proved and he is beyond
the sea, he is to be exiled and banished from the realm for ever and his
lands, tenements, goods and chattels forfeited to the king; and if he is
within the realm he is also to be exiled and banished and to incur such

inserts dit.   [y] *S.R. inserts* Richard.   [z] *S.R. inserts* ascun.   [aa] *S.R.* a.
[bb] *S.R.* demurge.   [cc] *S.R. inserts* il.   [dd-dd] *S.R.* come devant est dit et
encourge mesme la forfaiture. *There follows in MS.* et qe lour procuratours,
executours et notairs et somenours encourge mesme la forfaiture. *Of this clause*
qe *to* somenours *has been deleted.*

---

[1] i.e. 9 Feb. 1351. The recital of 25 Edward III, statute 4 ends here.

1390   come desuis est dite; et preigne soun chymyn issint qil soit hors du
roialme deins sys semayns procheins apres tiel acceptacion, et si aucun
recept aucun tiel banny venant de^a par de la ou esteant deinz le roialme
apres les sys symaignes avantditz, conissant de ceo, soit auxi^b exile et
banny et encourge autiel forfaiture come desuis^c est dite. Et qe lour
procuratours, ^{d}executours et notairs^d et somenours eient la forfaiture
et peyne suisditz. Purveu nepurqant qe toutz iceux as queux nostre
seint piere le pape ou ces predecessours ont purveu aucun erchescheie,
eveschie ou autre dignite ou benefices electifs ou autres benefices de
seint esglise del patronage dez gentz de seint esglise a cause de voidance
devant le dit xxix. jour de Januar' et ent feurent en corporel possession
devant le^e mesme le xxix. jour eient et enjoient lour ditz ercheveschies,
eveschies, dignitees et benefices peisiblement pur lour vies, nient
contresteant les estatutz et ordeinances^f avantditz. Et si le roi envoie
par lettre ou en autre manere al court de Rome al excitacion dascun
persone ou si aucun autre envoie ou prie a mesme la court paront le^g
contraire de cest estatut soit fait touchant^h erchescheie, eveschie,
dignite ou autre benefice de seint esglise deins le dit roialme, si celui
qi fait tiel excitacion ou tiel prier soit prelate de seint esglise paie a^i
roi la^j value de ces temporaltes par^k an, et sil soit seignur temporel
paie au roi la^l value de cez terres et possessions nient moebles dun an;
^{m}et sil soit autre persone destate pluis bas paie au roi la value du benefice pur quel tiel prier soit fait et eit la prisone dun an.^{m} Et est
lentencion de cest estatut qe de toutz dignites et benefices^n de seint
esglise qestoient voidez de fait le^o dit xxix. jour de Januer qeux sont
donez ou as qeux soit purveu par lappostoil devant mesme le xxix.
jour qe ceux as qeux tiels douns ou provisions soient faitz puissent
franchement des tiels douns et provisions suer execucion sanz offence
de cest estatut. Purveu toutz foitz qe de nul dignite ou benefice qestoit
pleine le dit xxix. jour de Januer null^p a cause daucun doun, collacion,
reservacion ou^q provision ou autre^r grace dappostoil^s qeconqe nient
execut devant le dit xxix. jour ^{t}de Januer^t ne sue ent execucion sur les
peines contenuz en ceste present estatut.

Item ^{u}est ordeine^u et establie qe si aucun port ou envoie deins
le roialme en^v le poair nostre dit seignur le roi aucuns somons, sen-

p. 197   tences / ou escomengementz envers aucune persone de quele condicion qil soit par^w cause de la mocion, fesance, assent ou execucion du
dit estatut dez provisours, soit il pris et arestuz et mys en prisone
et forface touz cez terres et tenementz, biens^x et chateux pur toutz
jours et outre encourge la peine de vie et de membre. Et si aucun
prelate face execucion dez tiels somons, sentences ou excomenge-
mentz, qe ces temporaltees soient prises et demourgent es mayns
nostre dit seignur le roi tanqe due redresse et coreccion ent soit fait.

---

^{a} MS. le. ^{b} S.R. auxint. ^{c} S.R. devant. $^{d-d}$ S.R. notairs, executours.
^{e} S.R. om. ^{f} S.R. ordinance. ^{g} S.R. qe la. ^{h} S.R. inserts ascun. ^{i} S.R.
au. ^{j} S.R. le. ^{k} S.R. dun. ^{l} S.R. le. $^{m-m}$ S.R.; MS. om. ^{n} ceux
as quex [sic] tiels douns ou provisions soient faitz puissent franchement deleted

forfeiture as abovesaid and take his way so that he be out of the realm 1390
within six weeks after such acceptance, and if anyone receives any such
banished person coming from overseas or being within the realm after
the aforesaid six weeks, being aware thereof, he shall also be exiled and
banished and incur such forfeiture as abovesaid; and that their proctors,
executors, notaries, and summoners suffer the forfeiture and penalty
abovesaid. Provided nevertheless that all those to whom our Holy
Father the pope or his predecessors have provided any archbishopric,
bishopric, or other dignity or benefices elective or other benefices of
Holy Church of the patronage of the people of Holy Church by reason
of voidance before the said 29 January and who were in corporal
possession thereof before the same 29 January shall have and enjoy
their said archbishoprics, bishoprics, dignities, and benefices peaceably
during their lives, notwithstanding the statutes and ordinances aforesaid. And if the king sends by letter or otherwise to the court of Rome
at the instance of any person, or if any other person sends or sues to
the same court, whereby anything is done contrary to this statute
touching any archbishopric, bishopric, dignity, or other benefice of
Holy Church within the said realm, if he that makes such instance or
suit is a prelate of Holy Church, he shall pay to the king the value of his
temporalities for one year, and if he is a temporal lord, he shall pay to
the king the value of his lands and immovable possessions of one year;
and if he is another person of lower estate he shall pay to the king the
value of the benefice for which such suit is made and suffer imprisonment for one year. And it is the intent of this statute that of all dignities
and benefices of Holy Church that were in fact void on the said 29
January which are given or to which provision has been made by the
pope before the same 29 January that they to whom such gifts or
provisions have been made may freely sue execution of such gifts and
provisions without infringing this statute. Provided always that of no
dignity or benefice that was filled on the said 29 January may any man,
because of any gift, collation, reservation, or provision or other papal
grace whatsoever that was not executed before the said 29 January, sue
execution thereof upon the pains contained in this present statute.

Also it is ordained and established that if any man brings or sends
within the realm in the power of our said lord the king, any summonses,
sentences, or excommunications against any person of whatsoever condition he may be, by reason of his moving, making, assenting, or execut-
ing the said statute of provisors, he is to be taken, arrested, and put in
prison and forfeit all his lands and tenements, goods and chattels for
ever and moreover incur the penalty of life and limb. And if any prelate
makes execution of such summonses, sentences, or excommunications,
that his temporalities shall be taken and shall remain in the hands of
our said lord the king until due redress and correction is thereof made.

after this word.   *o* S.R.; MS. de.   *p* S.R.; MS. om.   *q* S.R. et.   *r* S.R.
dautre.   *s* S.R. de l'appoistoill'.   *t–t* S.R. om.   *u–u* S.R. ordeigne est.
v S.R. ou.   *w* S.R. a.   *x* S.R. bien.

1390 Et si aucun persone de meindre estate qe prelate, de quele condicion qil
soit, face tiel execucion, soit pris,[a] arestuz et mys en prisone et eit[b]
lenprisonement[c] et face fyn et ranceon solonc la discrecion de[d] conseil
nostre dit seignur le roi.

[e]Affirmato statuto contra provisores jam edito, ut predictum est, ordinabant illi de consilio domini regis tr⟨es⟩
personas domino pape destinar⟨e⟩ que beneficia omnimodo
ecclesiastica refutarent, videlicet duos milites et unum clericum ho . . .[f] qui de mense Julii iter arripientes ante festum
Sancti Michaelis Romam venerunt.[e][1]

1388   Ceste article ensuant des provisours fuist fait a Cantebrigge lan du
reigne le roi Richard puis le conqueste seconde duszisme en la manere
come ensuit:[2]
   Item qe nul liege du roi de quele estat ou condicion qil soit, greindre
ou meindre, passe le meer nenvoie hors du roialme Dengleterre par
licence ou sanz licence, sanz especiale congie du roi mesmes pur[g] soy
providre ou purchacer aucun benefice de seint esglise ove cure ou sanz
cure en le dit roiaume; et si aucun le face et par vertue de tiel provision
accept par luy ou par autre aucun benefice en mesme le roialme qe a
celle temps mesme le provisour soit hors du[h] proteccion du roi et
mesme le benefice voide; si qe bien lise a patron de mesme le benefice,
si bien espirituele come temporele, presenter a ycelle une clerc able
a sa volunte.

1390 Unum eciam satis rigide statutum est in isto parliamento,[3]
quod quicumque dolose aut insidiose occiderit hominem
numquam cartam domini regis pro tali scelere commisso
ullatenus optineret set penam olim[i] pro talibus transgressori-
bus limitatam omnino subiret.
   Quo in tempore solempnia hastiludia Francigene juxta
Cales' celebrarunt; propter quod quidam valentes milites de

---

[a] S.R. inserts et.   [b] S.R.; MS. om.   [c] S.R. emprisonement.   [d] S.R. du.
[e-e] This passage was added later and is partly in the margin: the space of one and
a half lines left for it proved inadequate.   [f] MS. ho followed by four minim
strokes. The word is at the edge of the MS. and the final letters are now lost.
Recte honestum ?   [g] The letter s (a false start?) expunged after this word.
[h] S.R. de.   [i] Written above the line.

---

[1] See above, p. 412. The ambassadors were John Cheyne and William Farindon,
knights, and Alan de Newerk, clerk; Cheyne left London on 15 June; Newerk on
20 July (Diplomatic Correspondence of Richard II, ed. Perroy, no. 120 and n.).
For Newerk's career as a royal clerk, see B.R.U.O., ii. 1354-5.

And if any person of less estate than a prelate, of whatever condition he may be, makes such execution, he shall be taken, arrested, and put in prison and suffer imprisonment and make fine and ransom according to the discretion of the council of our said lord the king.

Upon the enactment of the Statute of Provisors, as I have set out just above, the king's council gave orders for dispatching to the pope three persons who would utterly reject all offers of ecclesiastical benefices, namely two knights and a cleric [of integrity], who set out in July and arrived in Rome before Michaelmas [29 September].[1]

The following article concerning provisors was enacted at Cambridge in the 12th year of King Richard the Second since the Conquest. This is how it went:[2]

Also that no liege man of the king, of whatever estate or condition he may be, great or lowly, shall pass over the sea nor send out of the realm of England, with or without licence, in the absence of special leave from the king himself, to provide or purchase for himself any benefice of Holy Church, with or without cure, within the said realm; and if anyone do so and by virtue of such provision accept by himself or by another any benefice within the same realm, that at that time the same provisor shall be outside the king's protection and the same benefice void; so that it shall be quite lawful for the patron of the same benefice, as well a spiritual as a temporal person, to present to it a competent clerk at his pleasure.

There was also a somewhat severe enactment in this parliament[3] providing that whoever committed homicide by treachery or ambush should never in any degree obtain the king's pardon for perpetrating his crime but should without fail undergo the penalty traditionally prescribed for such offenders.

During this period the French held a ceremoniously conducted tournament near Calais; and in consequence some of

[2] There follows the text of 12 Richard II, *cap.* 15; cf. *S.R.*, ii. 60, with which the text has been collated, and above, p. 366 and n. The text, with this French preface, probably reached the Monk as part of a dossier on the second Statute of Provisors, 1390, just recited.

[3] i.e. in the parliament of 17 Jan.–2 Mar. 1390. The Monk refers to 13 Richard II, statute 2, *cap.* 1. For the text see above, pp. 416–18, and for comment, J. M. Kaye, 'The Early History of Murder and Manslaughter', in *Law Quarterly Rev.*, lxxxiii (1967), 391 ff.

1390 nostris, illuc eciam probi armigeri pariter accesserunt.[1]

Divulgatum est tunc temporis quomodo Saraceni in Turkeya et alibi terras et loca Christianorum penitus destruxerunt et tributarios eos fecerunt; tamen Deum unum vel deos eos colere aut qualemcumque sectam servare voluerint permiserunt, dumtamen eis tributa solverent indilate nonnumquam negata. Consequenter quoddam oppidum in Barbaria sive in Affrica situatum, quod jam tarde Januenses callide conquisierant ac[a] cum ceteris Christianis existentibus in eo jam tenuerant, obsederunt:[2] unde nonnulli domini nobiles milites et armigeri valentes de Anglia petiverunt licenciam a rege illuc transire causa succurrendi locum prefatum; inter quos fuerunt potissime nominati, scilicet comes Devonie, dominus W. Nevyle, dominus J. Clanvowe, magister hospitalis Sancti Johannis,[3] et alii viri famosi qui lesionem sue bone fame minime sustinerent.

Tandem imminente solempnitate Paschali rex cum suis quasi per unum mensem jugiter in jocundis solaciis huic tempori congruentibus persistebat. Demum celebrato festo Sancti Georgii in principio mensis Maii fiebant solempnia hastiludia apud Smethefeld, ubi namque affuerunt rex et regina, duces et ducisse, comites et comitisse, cum aliis Anglie nobilibus utriusque sexus ac popularibus infinitis.

Quarto vero die Maii comes Derbeye Henricus filius et heres ducis Lancastr', optenta licencia tam a rege quam a patre suo, dirigens se versus mare cum suis proponensque cum sua honorabili comitiva succurrere dictos Christianos a paganis obsessos aliorum auxilio Christianorum: set frustra. Nam venit Cales', ubi diu expectavit pro habendo salvum conductum pro se et suis a rege Francorum set illud sub ea

---

[a] *Interlined.*

[1] For the tournament at St. Ingelvert in Mar. and Apr. 1390 see Froissart, *Chroniques*, xiv. 105 ff., and *Chronique du religieux de S. Denys*, i. 674 ff. Froissart, however, gives May as the month; cf. ibid., p. 406.

[2] A reference to the siege of El Mahadia, chief port of Tunis, from July to Sept. 1390. The Saracens were not the besiegers: they were besieged by a crusading force raised on the initiative of the Genoese. See J. Delaville le Roulx, *La France en orient au xive siècle* (Bibliothèque des Écoles françaises d'Athènes et de Rome, 1st ser., t. 44-5 (1886), i. 166 ff., and below, pp. 448-50.

[3] Respectively, Edward Courtenay, earl of Devon 1377-1419; Sir William

our own gallant knights, and worthy squires too, made their 1390
way thither.[1]

It became generally known at this time how the Saracens
in Turkey and elsewhere had completely destroyed the
lands and settlements of the Christians, whom they laid
under tribute, nevertheless allowing them to worship the
One God or other gods and to preserve whatever sects they
wished, provided that the tribute was promptly paid, though
it was sometimes withheld and for this reason the Saracens
had laid siege to a town in Barbary or Africa which the
Genoese by slow but skilful methods had lately captured
and were now occupying in company with other Christians
already in the place.[2] A number of Englishmen, nobles,
knights, and gallant squires, accordingly begged leave of
the king to go out to the relief of the town; among them
were men of the greatest distinction, including the earl
of Devon, Sir William Nevill, Sir John Clanvow, and the
master of the hospital of St. John,[3] as well as other famous
men who would be the last to endure any injury to their
reputations.

With Eastertide [3 April] at hand, the king and his court
abandoned themselves for a month or so on end to the
pleasant pastimes proper to the season. When the feast of St.
George [23 April] had been celebrated, there was a formal
tournament in early May at Smithfield, attended by the king
and queen, dukes and duchesses, earls and countesses, and
the English nobility of both sexes, besides innumerable
members of the populace.

On 4 May Henry earl of Derby, son and heir of the duke of
Lancaster, took leave of the king and of his father the duke
and set out for the coast with the intention of going with his
distinguished companions, and with help from others of the
faith, to the relief of the Christians beleaguered, as
mentioned above, by the pagans: but he was foiled. Arrived
in Calais, he waited there a long time for a safe-conduct from
the French king for himself and his party, but he failed

Nevill, Sir John Clanvow, chamber knights, and Br. John Radyngton, master of
the Hospital of St. John of Jerusalem, *c.*1382–96. Radyngton, however, is said in
Cal. Cl. R., 1389–92, p. 126, to have been visiting Rhodes at this time. For Nevill
and Clanvow see also below, p. 480 and n.

1390 forma qua petebat nullatenus potuit optinere: igitur in Angliam repedavit.[1]

Quarto quoque die Maii dominus de la Welle[2] et dominus David Lyndeseye[a] miles Scoticus bene armati primo cum lanceis acutissimis in[b] equis hostiliter concurrerunt, deinde cum securibus, postremo cum daggeres, pedestres certarunt; que omnia peregerunt satis strenue secundum relata.

Item octavo die Maii consecratus est frater Alexander ⟨Bache⟩[c] in episcopum Assavensem apud Westmonasterium ab archiepiscopo Cantuar',[3] qui [d]fuit et[d] est confessor domini regis, de ordine Predicatorum, magister in theologia. Ad istam solempnitatem accesserunt rex et regina ac alii nobiles generosi. Erat nempe frater iste, quando primo venit ad regem, satis humilis et devotus in gestu, vultu, in victu, in questu, et in omnibus suis actibus perspicue moderatus; nec voluit equitare, set de uno loco ad alium sequendo curiam pedester transire; episcopatum vero primitus recusabat. Set parum postea mutata voluntate cepit insolencius agere contra universa premissa, ut jam[e] rei effectus probavit.

Eo namque die venit London' dux Geldr', quem rex die sequenti leta fronte suscepit et eum splendide convivavit ac cum inmensis solaciis tripudiis variisque eciam[e] instrumentorum gaudiis ministravit, [f]studuitque eum in omnibus[f] honorifice deservire. Demum xj. die Maii audita morte domini Radulphi domini de Basset,[4] qui fuit unus de militibus de la gartere, confestim dominus rex loco ipsius prefatum ducem Geldr' subrogabat. Traxitque moram hic predictus dux quasi per unum mensem et ab universis Anglie primatibus gratanter susceptus demum optenta licencia a

---

[a] In the margin but marked for insertion here.   [b] Interlined.   [c] MS. blank.   [d-d] Interlined.   [e] Interlined.   [f-f] Written over an erasure.

---

[1] Henry, earl of Derby was at Calais from c.13 May to 5 June 1390 (Expeditions by Henry, earl of Derby, pp. 9 ff.; F. R. H. Du Boulay, 'Henry of Derby's Expeditions to Prussia, 1390-1 and 1392', in Reign of Richard II, p. 162). See also below, p. 440.

[2] John, Lord Welles, d. 1421, for whom see G.E.C., xii (2). pp. 441-3. His encounter with Lindsay, the challenger, took place in London on 6 May; Welles was unhorsed. See Calendar of Documents relating to Scotland, ed. Bain, iv. 404;

completely to get it in the form asked for and so returned 1390 to England.[1]

It was also on 4 May that Lord Welles[2] and a Scottish knight, Sir David Lindsay, armed cap-à-pie, first of all jousted on horseback with unrebated lances, and then continued the combat on foot with battle-axes and finally with daggers, performing spiritedly enough throughout, according to report.

At Westminster on 8 May, Brother Alexander [Bache] was consecrated bishop of St. Asaph by the archbishop of Canterbury.[3] A member of the order of Friars Preachers and a master in divinity, he was, and still is, the king's confessor. The king and queen and other high-born nobles were present at the ceremony. When this friar first came to the king, his behaviour, his expression, his standard of living, and his attitude to personal gain were quite humble and devout and there was a transparent modesty in everything he did; refusing to ride, he followed the court from place to place on foot; and at first he declined to be made a bishop. But shortly afterwards he suffered a change of heart and began to behave with an arrogance that, as the event has now proved, ran counter to all this.

The duke of Guelders arrived in London on the same day, to be greeted on the next with a smiling welcome from the king, who feasted him sumptuously and plied him with the most lavish entertainments, including dancing and a pleasing variety of instrumental music, and was at pains to pay him every flattering attention. Eventually, on 11 May, having had news of the death of Ralph, Lord Basset,[4] who had been a knight of the Garter, the king at once replaced him in the order by the duke of Guelders. His stay here lasted about a month, at the end of which, having been cordially received by all the leading men of this country, he took leave of the

Rymer, *Foedera*, vii. 671-2; *Wyntoun*, iii. 47-50. See also *Issues of the Exchequer, Henry III to Henry VI*, ed. Devon, p. 243.

[3] Alexander Bache, for whom see *B.R.U.O.*, iii. 2146. He remained Richard II's confessor until his death; this occurred between 13 Aug. and 15 Sept. 1394.

[4] The probable date of death of Ralph Basset of Drayton is 10 May 1390 (*Cal. Inq. p.m.*, xvi. 963-75).

1390 rege et aliis dominis patrie ad propria cum multis donis et muneribus remeavit.[1]

Item xxviij. die Maii comes Notyngham Anglicus et comes de Morryf[2] Scoticus in equis concurrebant armati sexies cum lanceis valde acutis; et quia in hiis comes Notyngham magis egregie se habebat quam comes de Morrif, laus sibi fuerat attributa. Consimili modo dominus Petrus de Courteneye eques et armatus cum sua secabili lancea concurrebat versus quendam militem de Scocia satis strenuum ac valentem et lauream reportavit. Quo facto dominus rex prohibuit talia hastiludia fieri in suo regno ac[a] certis de causis penitus interdixit.[3]

p. 198 Post hec mense Junii consilio celebrato decretum est in eodem quod episcopus Dunelm' transiret Cales' tractaturus cum Francigenis de pace finali, fuitque ibidem tractando usque xiij. diem Julii.[4] In quo tractatu plura fuerunt petita ex utraque parte, que omnia erant in scriptis redacta et ambobus regibus presentata ut ipsi predicta cum eorum consilio consulcius terminarent.

Consilio apud Westmonasterium terminato, dominus rex ante recessum suum de London' fecit solempnia hastiludia proclamari apud Smethefeld fieri x. die Octobris, protestans quod ipse cum certis[b] sibi[c] adjunctis omnes adventantes citissime liberaret.[5] Confestim post rex transtulit se Glovern' multum appetens proavum suum ibi jacentem transferre; ubi occurrebant ei Cantuarien' archiepiscopus, episcopus London' et quidam alii episcopi cum clericis et juris peritis super attestacione[d] miraculorum domino pape dirigenda,

---

[a] *A short erasure follows.*   [b] *A letter has been blotted out after this word.*
[c] *The letters* adi *expunged after this word.*   [d] domino pape *deleted after this word.*

---

[1] For the visit of Duke William I of Guelders to England in May 1390, see P.R.O., E. 403/530, 24 Apr., 4 May; L. A. J. W. Baron Sloet, 'De Reis van Willem van Gulik, Hertog van Gelre en Graaf van Zutfen, naar Londen, in het jaar 1390', in *Bijdragen voor Vaderlandsche Geschiedenis en Oudheidkunde*, 3rd ser., i (1882), 319-36; H. Laurent and F. Quicke, *Les Origines de l'état bourguignon: l'accession de la maison de Bourgogne aux duchés de Brabant et de Limbourg (1383-1407)*, i (Brussels, 1939), pp. 375-7.

[2] Respectively, Thomas de Mowbray, earl of Nottingham and earl marshal (d. 1399), and John Dunbar, earl of Moray (d. 1391/2). For the legend which later accrued to their encounter, see *The Scots Peerage*, ed. J. Balfour Paul (9 vols., Edinburgh, 1904-14), vi. 300. See also Rymer *Foedera*, vii. 666; *Calendar of*

king and other English noblemen and returned home with 1390
numerous gifts and presents.[1]

On 28 May the English earl of Nottingham and the Scottish earl of Moray,[2] armed and mounted, jousted six courses
with unrebated lances; the earl of Nottingham, having
acquitted himself in them with greater distinction than the
earl of Moray, was awarded the honours. In a similar combat,
Sir Peter Courtenay, armed and on horseback, jousted,
lance edged, with a Scottish knight, who was not wanting in
vigour or mettle, and carried off the laurels of victory. At
the conclusion of this tournament the king gave orders that
contests of this kind should not take place in his kingdom
and for certain reasons put a complete ban on them.[3]

At a council subsequently held in June it was resolved that
the bishop of Durham should cross to Calais to treat with the
French about a final peace: he was there about this business
until 13 July.[4] In the course of the talks a number of demands
were put forward by each side; these were put into writing
and submitted to the two kings so that they might consider
and dispose of them in consultation with their councils.

When the council at Westminster was over, but before his
departure from London, the king proclaimed a formal tournament to be held at Smithfield on 10 October, declaring that
he and his associates would provision all comers with the
utmost promptitude.[5] Soon afterwards the king proceeded to
Gloucester, the resting place of his great-grandfather, whose
translation he was very anxious to effect. Here he was met by
the archbishop of Canterbury and the bishop of London and
other bishops, with clergy and lawyers in attendance, to
consider dispatching to the pope testimony about miracles,

Documents relating to Scotland, ed. Bain, iv. 411.

[3] i.e. in future tournaments lances were to have blunt points.

[4] Walter Skirlaw, bishop of Durham, and others were appointed to treat with
the French for a truce or final peace on 8 Apr. 1390 and given their instructions
at 2 councils held in that month. Skirlaw left London on 13 Apr. and returned on
15 July. The conference opened at Leulingham on 4 July. See P.R.O., E. 364/24,
m. 34; *Proceedings and Ordinances of the Privy Council*, ed. Nicolas, i. 19-24;
Rymer, *Foedera*, vii. 667-9; H. Moranvillé, 'Conférences entre la France et
l'Angleterre (1388-1393)', in *B.E.C.*, 1 (1889), 358-9. For the protocol referred
to by the Monk in his next sentence see ibid., pp. 367-9.

[5] See below, p. 450; and for the provisioning that preceded the tournament,
Cal. Pat. R., 1388-92, p. 302.

1390 primo discutiendo per eos utrum sint vera miracula seu con-
ficta; super quo negocio prius papa misit episcopo London'
quandam bullam ad inquirendum veritatem dictorum
miraculorum et ad certificandum sibi quomodo rei veritas
se habeat in negocio antedicto.[1]

Quo peracto rex cum suis rediit ad manerium suum de
Wodestok, et archiepiscopus divertit Sar' causa visitandi
ecclesiam illam tam in capite quam in membris, primo enim
facta citacione primo, secundo et tercio pro episcopo Sar'[a]
quod compareret et humiliter admitteret visitacionem sui
archiepiscopi; coram quo tandem comparuit procurator prefati episcopi, asserens suum episcopum habere tale privilegium
se non debere visitari a quoquam:[2] unde orta est grandis discordia inter eos. Quo in tempore magister Thomas Montagu
fuerat in decanatu Sar' installatus et fecit residenciam suam
ibi tunc quasi incipiendo, qui prefatum archiepiscopum in
suam domum excepit et ipsum diversis et lautis ferculis
deservivit; et mediantibus amicis inter archiepiscopum et Sar'
episcopum ad concordiam sunt reducti. Sicque pacificati [b]ac
completa visitacione ibidem[b] archiepiscopus continuavit
ulterius in provincia sua sibi decreta suam visitacionem.

Pestilencia. Circa principium mensis Junii immensus calor
succrevit et duravit fere usque mensem Septembris. Qua de
causa propter aeris corrupcionem magna mortalitas hominum
causabatur. Continuata est ista epidemia in diversis partibus
Anglie, quamvis universaliter non desevit, usque festum
sancti Michaelis et pocius juvenes quam senes consumpsit.[3]
Obierunt tamen isto tempore pestilenciali milites famosi,
scilicet dominus Guido de Bryan,[4] dominus Degr' de Seys,[c5]

---

[a] ad comparend' *deleted after this word.*   [b-b] *Added in the margin.*   [c] et
interlined after this word.

---

[1] The mandate to the bishop of London was probably the papal response to
Richard II's application to the curia for Edward II's canonization in 1387; see
Perroy, p. 301.

[2] In fact John Waltham, bishop of Salisbury, disputed Archbishop Courtenay's
right to visit the bishop or diocese of Salisbury by metropolitical authority unless
the diocese of Canterbury and other dioceses of the province not visited since the
last metropolitical visitation of Salisbury were first visited. Courtenay did, however, visit the bishop on 11 July, and, thereafter, the diocese. See I. J. Churchill,
*Canterbury Administration: the Administrative Machinery of the Archbishopric
of Canterbury Illustrated from Original Records* (2 vols., London, 1933), i. 326-9.
Thomas Montague, whom the Monk mentions in this passage, was tenant of

after having first discussed among themselves whether the   1390
miracles are genuine or fictitious. The pope had earlier
addressed a bull concerning this matter to the bishop of
London, directing him to inquire into the genuineness of
these miracles and to certify to the pope the true facts of the
case.[1]

This business concluded, the king returned with his entourage to his manor of Woodstock; and the archbishop went off
to Salisbury to carry out a visitation of that church, head and
members alike, having begun by citing the bishop of Salisbury a first, second, and third time to appear and humbly
submit to visitation by his archbishop. When at last the
bishop's proctor appeared before him, it was to declare that
the bishop enjoyed the privilege of exemption from visitation by anybody;[2] and this led to considerable discord
between the parties. Master Thomas Montague had at this
time been installed as dean of Salisbury and had taken up residence by way of entering upon his office. He received the
archbishop in his house and provided him with elegant and
varied entertainment; and harmony was restored by the intercession of friends between the archbishop and the bishop of
Salisbury. Peace thus secured, the visitation of Salisbury was
completed and the archbishop went on with his programme
of visitation in the province committed to his charge.

Plague. About the beginning of June intensely hot
weather set in and continued until nearly September.
This was the cause, owing to the rankness of the air, of
a great and deadly pestilence, which was epidemic in various
parts of England (though it never raged everywhere) until
Michaelmas, its victims being rather the young than the
old.[3] Even so, some illustrious knights died in this time
of plague, namely Sir Guy de Brien,[4] Sir Digory Seys,[5]

'Steynoresplace', in King Street, belonging to the sacrist of Westminster (Liber
Niger Quaternus, fo. 88ᵛ; and see also *V.C.H. Wilts.*, iii. 170, 176).

[3] Cf. Walsingham, *Hist. Ang.*, ii. 197.

[4] A magnate who had served Edward III and Richard II in the chamber and
household and in other capacities (Tout, *Chapters*, vi. 43, 48; *G.E.C.*, ii. 361-2).
He died on 17 Aug. 1390 (*Cal. Inq. p.m.*, xvi. 959-62). An entry dated 28 July
1390 on *Cal. Pat. R., 1388-92*, p. 293 suggests that his death may have been
expected. See also *Cal. Papal Letters*, iv *(1362-1404)*, p. 393.

[5] In 1387 keeper of Queenborough castle (*Cal. Pat. R., 1385-9*, p. 381). He
was dead by 9 Nov. 1390 (*Cal. Cl. R., 1389-1392*, pp. 209-10).

1390 dominus Thomas Beauchamp:[1] isti fuerunt milites nominati. Decesserunt eciam alii non ita utique excellentes, videlicet dominus Johannes de Arundell',[2] *a*dominus Johannes Hanneslegh et dominus David Craddok,[3] milites strenui set non tam notorie approbati sicut illi pretacti.*a* Et dominus papa in ista estate confirmavit eleccionem abbatis de Waltham,[4] electo ejusdem monasterii in Anglia existente. Item xxij. die Julii dominus Henricus comes Derbeye frustratus voto transeundi in Barbariam optenta licencia transivit in Prussyam.[5]

Item xxiiij. die Julii venit rex Leycestr' ubi eum dux Lancastr' cum maxima jocunditate recepit, convivia instauravit, atque gaudia gaudiis aggregavit; sicque per aliquot dies continue ludis et exhillaracionibus vacaverunt. Demum celebrato ibidem consilio dux Lancastr' rogavit pro Johanne Northampton' et suis sociis quod possent redire et morari London' ac*b* uti eorum mercimoniis prout olim fecerunt ibidem. Ad quem rex ait: 'O dulcissime avuncule, non est in potestate mea hoc facere modo, ut estimo.' 'Immo', ait dux, 'ista et majora facere valeatis; absit enim quod vestra potestas esset in tantum restricta quod nequiretis concedere ligiis vestris graciam temporibus oportunis cum res se expostulat id faciendi.' Ad hec rex aliquantulum substitit, dicens: 'Si sic facere potero, *c*alii sustinuerunt magnam miseriam: itaque*c* scio quid faciam amicis meis existentibus jam in partibus transmarinis.' Hiis dictis concessit rex Johanni Northampton' ad rogatum ducis Lancastr' liberum ingressum et egressum in London'*b* quandocumque sibi placuerit *d*dumtamen continuam moram non trahat ibidem neque domicilium per se vel per mediam personam in predicta civitate teneat ullo modo, set sicut extraneus potest se in illa habere

---

a-a Deleted in MS. *b* Interlined. *c-c* Interlined.
d-a(p. 442) Deleted in MS. and enclosed within the syllables Vac . . . at.

---

[1] Was this Thomas Beauchamp of Ryme (Dorset), for whom see *Cal. Cl. R.*, *1385–9*, pp. 482–3, and ibid., *1389–92*, pp. 188, 279? If so he died after 8 July 1390.

[2] The son of John, Lord Arundel (d. 1379), who was the brother of Richard, earl of Arundel (d. 1397) (*G.E.C.* i. 253). He died on 14 Aug. 1390 (*Cal. Inq. p.m.*, xvi. 951–2).

[3] A royal servant and diplomat. He was appointed mayor of Bordeaux in 1387

and Sir Thomas Beauchamp,[1] all knights of repute. Others 1390
not so unquestionably eminent who succumbed were Sir
John Arundel,[2] [Sir John Hanneslegh, and Sir David
Craddock,[3] gallant knights all but not so well or so favourably known as those mentioned above]. In the course of the
summer the abbot-elect of Waltham[4] had his election confirmed by the pope without himself leaving England. On 22
July Henry earl of Derby, baulked of his desire to go to
Barbary, left for Prussia, having first obtained leave of the
king.[5]

On 24 July the king arrived at Leicester, where the duke
of Lancaster gave him the warmest of welcomes, providing
banquets and plying him with such a succession of festivities
that several days on end were devoted to amusement and
gaiety. Eventually a council was held, and on behalf of John
Northampton and his associates the duke of Lancaster put
in a request that they might return to London to live and
to follow their trades there as they had in the past. 'My
dear uncle', replied the king, 'it is not in my power, I think,
to do that now.' 'On the contrary,' said the duke, 'you could
do that and more. God forbid that your power should be
so cramped that you could not extend grace to your liege
subjects when the circumstances call for such action.' At
this the king hesitated for a moment and said: 'If I can do
what you say, there are others who have suffered great hard-
ship; so that I know what to do for my own friends who are
now overseas.' This talk was followed by the king's grant to
John Northampton, at the instance of the duke of Lancaster,
of freedom to enter and leave London at will [provided that
he did not take up continuous residence there or in any
way maintain, either in person or by an agent, any establishment in the city; but his position there was to be just such

and in Feb. 1390 a conservator of the Anglo-French truce (*Carte*, i. 175, 176).
See also Tout, *Chapters*, vi. 60, 63.

[4] William Neel. The king licensed the visit of his proctors to Rome, to obtain
confirmation of his election, on 10 Feb. 1390 (*Cal. Pat. R., 1388-92*, p. 190;
cf. ibid., p. 189).

[5] Derby embarked at Boston, and his wardrobe accounts suggest that he did
so on 19 July (*Expeditions by Henry, earl of Derby*, p. xxxvi). See also above,
pp. 432-4.

1390 consimili modo et ille.*a*1 Sociis suis vero in predicta civitate
habitare permisit facta*b* satisfaccione prius hiis precipue
quos gravius offendebant. Abhinc rex Notyngham accessit,
scilicet xxviij. die Julii, ubi aliquamdiu moram traxit.2

Quo in tempore dux Lancastr' optinuit a rege ut in Eborac'
et in provinciis circumadjacentibus posset exercere illam
terribilem inquisicionem contra usurpatores corone traillebaston' vocatam:3 subest causa. Nam propter quendam
Willelmum Bekwyth idem dux id fieri procuravit, eo quod
prefatus Willelmus vendicabat quandam ballivam sive custodiam*c* habere in foresta de Knaresbourgh secundum quod
progenitores sui ibidem actenus habuerunt, quodque fuit
sibi negatum.4 Ministri vero*b* ducis Lancastr' deputarunt
ibidem alium servientem sui loco, prout eis melius videbatur,
alium namque scilicet*b* in alienis partibus oriundum; et ideo
magis odium grassabatur. In tantum dictum Willelmum
eorum factis exacerbarunt quod plures dicti facti incentores
manu propria interfecit, et minas et insidias dictis ministris,
quia ipsum exlegarunt, apposuit, ut eos gravaret quomodocumque posset, tandem cum paucis silvarum latibula expeciit ut
ipsum de suis inimicis salvaret. Set quid? Dies sessionis
instabat; nam prefatus dux in sua inquisicione omnes amicos
fautores consiliarios receptatores*b* ac benefactores dicti
Willelmi tam in Eboraco quam alibi in patria indictavit. Illi
vero qui redditibus et possessionibus habundabant perdicionis
causa se duci gratis dederunt: alii vero qui pauca habebant
ad nemora cum sepedicto Willelmo pariter confluebant. Set

---

a See note d–a on p. 440.   *b Interlined.*   *c vendicabat deleted after this
word.*

---

1 The words cancelled in the MS. are in fact needed for an adequate summary
of the letters patent granted to John Northampton at Leicester on 28 July 1390;
moreover, Northampton was permitted to travel anywhere in the realm and he
received partial restitution of his forfeited goods (*Cal. Pat. R., 1388-92*, p. 297).
For Northampton's full pardon, in Dec. 1390, see also below, p. 454. The
sentences of exile from London against John More and Richard Northbury were
revoked on, respectively, 30 July and 20 Oct. 1390, and it is to these pardons that
the Monk refers in his next sentence. Northbury's pardon is said to have been
granted at the request of the duke of Lancaster. See *Cal. Pat. R., 1388-92*, pp.
296, 311. For the king's visit to Leicester, see also Knighton, *Chronicon*, ii. 313.
2 On 2 Aug., however, letters patent were dated at Oakham castle (*Cal. Pat. R.,
1388-92*, p. 298; see also ibid., pp. 292-3, 297).
3 A reference to the commission of oyer and terminer granted, not to

as is permitted to a stranger].[1] His associates were allowed to 1390
live in the city after making amends, in particular to those
they had most seriously offended. From here the king moved
on 28 July to Nottingham, where he stayed for some time.[2]

During this period the duke of Lancaster obtained from
the king authority to conduct in York and the surrounding
areas the fearsome inquisition, aimed at usurpers of the
royal power, which is known as 'trailbaston'.[3] The occasion
was as follows. It was on account of one William Beckwith
that the duke got these proceedings instituted, Beckwith
having asserted his claim to a bailiwick or wardenship in
the forest of Knaresborough hitherto held by his ancestors,
and his claim having been rejected.[4] Instead of him, the
duke's ministers, acting for the best as they saw it, appointed
somebody else to the office — a man moreover who was not
a native of those parts — and ill-feeling was in consequence
all the more prevalent. So embittered was Beckwith by
their behaviour that with his own hand he killed several
of the people who had inspired it and subjected the ministers
themselves, in revenge for outlawing him, to threats and
ambushes calculated to harass them in every way possible,
and eventually went with a few companions into hiding
in the woods to gain safety from his adversaries. Need I
say more? The sitting-day was at hand; and in his inquisition
the duke had indicted all Beckwith's friends, supporters,
counsellors, harbourers, and benefactors in York and
elsewhere in the countryside. Those with considerable
income or property to lose required no further inducement
to give themselves up to the duke; others, whose possessions
were few, flocked into the forest to join Beckwith. But

Lancaster, but to Robert de Swylyngton and others, to inquire into treasons,
felonies, etc. in the lordship and liberty of Knaresborough on 10 Mar. 1390 (*Cal.
Pat. R., 1388-92*, pp. 269-70). This, a special and not a general commission, was
not a commission of trailbaston in the strict sense; see above, p. 383 n. Cf. *Vita
Ricardi Secundi*, p. 131.

[4] The office in question was probably that of the bailiff of Bilton Park or that
of the bailiff of Ockendon, both in Knaresborough Chase and both held at one
time by a John Beckwith (*John of Gaunt's Register, 1372-6*, ed. S. Armitage-
Smith (Camden, 3rd ser., xx-xxi), i. 527, 626; ii. 1093). For the intermittent riots
in Yorks. led by William Beckwith and his family since 1387, see J. G. Bellamy,
'The Northern Rebellions in the later Years of Richard II', in *Bulletin of the
John Rylands Library*, xlvii (1964-5), 255 ff. See also below, pp. 486, 516.

1390 quid profuit illis qui se subdiderunt, cum aliam graciam ab eo non poterant optinere nisi ut dictum Willelmum omnino perquirerent et illum sibi adducerent viribus undecumque quesitis? Quod audiens dictus Willelmus volens se et suos salvare ad densiora nemora cum quingentis aliis qui ejus causa fuerant indictati transtulit se indefesse: sicque primi in vinculis perstiterunt et alii in solitudine aberrantes vitam incertam duxerunt. Fuerat namque numerus indictatorum p. 199 sui causa fere mille secundum / quod a fidedignis fuit relatum. Semper talium laudabilis exitus commendatur, rarissime tamen visus.

Item quinto die Augusti erat magna tempestas pluvie cum clamosis tonitruis et coruschacionibus micantibus intermixtis, duravitque hec timorosa tempestas ultra duas horas et tam vehemens erat pluvia quod nulla domus adeo bene cooperta que potuit ejus violenciam sustinere quin una via vel alia aqua intraret.[a]

Octavo die Augusti comes Derbeye applicuit in Prussya aput villam de Dansk, ubi statim audivit certa nova de mareschallo Prussye quomodo ipse cum suo exercitu iter arripuit versus regnum de Lectowe.[1] Quo accepto dictus comes confestim venit ad villam de Conyngghesbrok paratisque ibidem cum celeritate possibili quinquaginta lanceis et sexaginta sagittariis cum victualibus pro se et suis, transactaque mora ibidem unius diei gressus suos accelerat post mareschallum predictum; qui diebus quinque per loca deserta illius patrie equitavit antequam potuit ad eum attingere. Quem demum super rivum de Memble cum suo exercitu invenit exspectando victualia sua que venirent ad eum

---

[a] *In the margin a pointing hand and the following note:* in isto loco, scilicet viij. die Augusti, processus comitis Derbeye inscriberetur. Vide infra ad tale signum o+o. *The passage so marked is accordingly printed here in its proper chronological place.*

---

[1] Henry of Derby and his advance party landed in fact at Rixhöft, north of Danzig, and on 9 Aug. His main force, however, landed at Danzig. The purpose of his expedition was to join forces with the Teutonic Knights under their marshal, Engelhardt Rabe ('the marshal of Prussia') and move against Skirgiello, regent in Lithuania for Vladyslav II of Poland-Lithuania. This enterprise was deemed a crusade because Samogitia, part of Lithuania, was still pagan; the fighting took place here. The Anglo-German forces were allied with Vitold ('King of Wytort'), Skirgiello's cousin and rival for the regency. Henry of Derby joined

where was the gain for those who surrendered, when the only 1390
favour they could win from the duke was to muster forces
from every quarter to hunt down Beckwith and bring him
back? When he heard of this, Beckwith, seeking safety for
himself and his companions, together with 500 others who
had been indicted on his account, moved with undiminished
energy into more thickly wooded country: and thus the first
group remained prisoners and the rest led a precarious life
of wandering in the wilderness. The number of those indicted
on Beckwith's account, according to trustworthy reports,
was about a thousand. A happy outcome for events like these
always wins approval but is very seldom seen.

There was a great rainstorm on 5 August, accompanied by
a combination of deafening thunder and vivid lightning; this
terrible storm lasted over two hours and so torrential was the
rain that no house was well enough roofed to stand up to its
violence without admitting the water by one way or another.

On 8 August the earl of Derby landed in Prussia at the
town of Danzig, where he at once received reliable news that
the marshal of Prussia, with his army, had taken the field
against the king of Lithuania.[1] On hearing this the earl proceeded immediately to Königsberg, where with all possible
speed he got ready a force of fifty lances and sixty bowmen,
with food supplies for himself and his men, and after a single
day's stay in the town hastened his steps in the marshal's wake.
Not until he had ridden for five days through the desolate
country of those parts could he catch up with the marshal,
whom, however, he at last found with his army waiting beside
the River Memel for the provisions which were to reach him

forces with Marshal Rabe on 22 Aug., and Vilna, whither Skirgiello retreated,
was taken on 4 Sept. The siege of the citadel of Vilna was abandoned on or about
7 Oct. Derby reached Königsberg on the return journey on 20 Oct. and there,
contrary to the Monk's account, he stayed until 9 Feb. For his itinerary see
Expeditions by Henry, earl of Derby, pp. xxxvi-vii; and for the campaign,
Du Boulay, in *Reign of Richard II*, pp. 156 ff. The detail of the above account
betrays the use of a written source; so too peculiarities of punctuation not characteristic of the Monk's own composition. This source, it seems clear, was also used
by Walsingham; cf. *Hist. Ang.*, ii. 197–8. Its author was ill-informed about Derby's
movements after the earl reached Königsberg on the return journey and probably
left his company at that point. His interest in and access to the roll of the marshal
of the Teutonic Knights may be a clue to his sphere of duty in the Anglo-German
army. (I am indebted to Dr. M. B. Parkes for help with the palaeography of this
passage.)

1390 per aquas; qui postquam comitis adventus sibi innotuit assumpto secum rege de Wytort cum multitudine copiosa de suis venit ei obviam, quem leta fronte et vultu jocundo satis honorifice suscepit, referens sibi regem de Lectowe[1] longe ante, scilicet per tres menses, pro defensione sue patrie, ut didicit, in lato campo cum tota sua potencia extitisse ac omnia passagia ad eum introeuncia preoccupasse super rivum p. 200 predictum sic quod nullus / in suum regnum intraret sine bellicoso insultu. Verumptamen dictus mareschallus habuit bonos exploratores et satis fideles, qui adduxerunt illum et ejus exercitum ad passagium magis accommodum pro se et suis quam ipse putavit, quamvis ipse cum suis vij. diebus continuis equitaret antequam ad dictum passagium perveniret ac eciam in ipso itinere per idem tempus eorum victualia pro se et eorum equis secum usque ad dictum passagium cariare necessario oporteret.[2] Veneruntque ad dictum passagium, ubi invenerunt vij. duces cum magna multitudine armatorum vexilloque regis de Lectowe vocat⟨i⟩ Skyrgall' palam expanso: igitur facto congressu cum paganis passagium predictum super eos Christiani adipiscuntur, ceperuntque ex illis tres duces, tres vero alios occiderunt, et plures quam ccc. de melioribus eorum gladio peremerunt, prout ipsimet fatebantur. Pro istis namque sic peractis comes predictus ope suorum et precipue sagittariorum meruit multas grates. Ibi etenim moriebatur dominus Johannes de Loudham miles, cujus anime etc.[3] Rex de Lectowe Skyrgall' cum alia magna potencia erat prope super unum montem juxta predictum passagium, vidensque illud per Christianos adeptum fugit cum suis in forciorem civitatem sue terre vocatam le Wylle. Christiani vero multis laboribus fatigati statuerunt nocte illa quiescere super rivum predictum expectando victualia eorum et alia armamenta que ad eos venirent per aquam.

Quo in tempore in auxilium Christianorum venit quedam potencia valde bellicosa de Lyfland; quibus in unum redactis ad civitatem in qua rex de Lectowe latebat in magna potencia sunt aggressi, illam igne et ferro viriliter devastantes.

---

[1] The Monk did not know, though doubtless the marshal did, that Skirgiello was regent, not king. Cf. Walsingham, op. cit., ii. 198.

[2] The crossing was at the confluence of the Wilia with the Memel.

by water. When he was told of the earl's arrival, the marshal, 1390 taking with him the 'king of Wytort' and a large party of his own men, came to meet him and, with his face wreathed in a smile of pleasure, welcomed him with all appropriate courtesy. He reported that he had learned how the king of Lithuania[1] had been in the field with his entire strength for as long as three months previously in defence of his territories and had pre-emptively occupied all the Memel crossings giving access to them, so that nobody could enter his kingdom except by armed assault. But the marshal had competent and thoroughly trusty scouts who guided him and his army to a crossing more suitable for their purpose than he had thought, though it was only after seven days' uninterrupted riding that they reached it and they had perforce to carry with them on their journey food for themselves and their horses.[2] Upon their arrival at the crossing, they found there seven dukes with a large armed force flaunting the standard of the king of Lithuania (whose name was Skirgiello). Battle was joined with the heathen, from whom the Christians won possession of the crossing, capturing three dukes and killing three others, while more than 300 of the enemy's best troops, as they themselves admitted, fell to their swords. For the results thus achieved the earl earned copious thanks in consequence of the help given by his men and particularly by his bowmen. In this battle Sir John Loudham died, on whose soul [God have mercy].[3] Skirgiello, the king of Lithuania, with another numerous army, was close by, on a hill overlooking the crossing, and seeing it in the hands of the Christians he took flight with his troops into a city of some strength in his country known as Vilna. Exhausted by their many efforts, the Christians decided to rest for the night on the river bank while they waited for the food supplies and other equipment which were to reach them by water.

There now arrived to help the Christians a force of high fighting quality from Livonia and when this had been incorporated they moved off in great strength to attack the city in which the king of Lithuania had gone to ground and set to work with a will to lay it in ruins with fire and steel.

---

[3] For Loudham see *Expeditions by Henry, earl of Derby*, pp. 303-4, and *Cal. Inq. p.m.*, xvi. 1017, where the date of his death is given as 28 Aug. 1390.

1390 Demum Christiani dictam civitatem ceperunt, captisque et occisis in ea quatuor hominum milibus, secundum quod fuit inventum in rotulo mareschalli: nam interfectus *a*fuit ibidem*a* frater regis Polanye ac vexillifer regis de Lectowe, qui videns stragem suorum confestim fugit in castellum. Causa capcionis predicte civitatis erat prefatus comes, qui revera ibidem cum suis egregie se habebat et primus omnium vexillum suum apposuit super muros ejusdem.

Christiani quoque castellum ad quod rex de Lectowe fugiendo intravit per quinque septimanas strenue obsederunt et profecto illud optinuissent si victualibus habundassent et votiva sanitate vigerent, set illi de Lyfland ac eciam Prussiani varias egritudines incurrebant, propter quod ibidem circa obsidionem stare diucius minime valuerunt: unde Pruyssiani et illi de Lyfland relicta obsidione in propriam patriam sunt reversi. Mareschallus Pruyssianorum duxit secum in Pruyssiam captivos de Lectowe octo milia ut faceret eos Christianos: magister vero de Lyfland duxit secum captivos de Lectowe tria milia et quingentos secundum estimacionem rotuli mareschalli.

Die namque octavo postquam prefatus mareschallus et dictus comes pervenerunt cum suis ad civitatem de Conyngysbrok' in Pruyssia, venerunt nova quod rex Polanie et de Crakowe paravit se cum ingenti exercitu Pruyssie patriam debellare; quod audiens idem mareschallus ilico suum exercitum congregavit rogans dictum comitem obnixe quatinus ut cum eo in defensionem dicte patrie contra prefatum regem Polanie et de Crakowe vellet procedere. Annuit comes votis suis, sicque die crastina de Conyngesbrok' recedentes contra regem Polanie cum eorum exercitu perrexerunt.*b*

p. 199 Quo in tempore dux Bourbon' de Francia collecto grandi exercitu de diversis partibus Europe apud Januam transfretavit in Barbariam ubi cum predictis Christianis bellum iniit cum paganis. Primo victoriam optinuit de predictis paganis, set secunda vice ex adverso venit intollerabilis copia paganorum cum magna audacia ⟨et⟩*c* Christianos compulit fugere ad naves eorum in multo discrimine personarum; sicque Christiani qui

---

a–a Interlined.   *b* The passage referred to in the note on p. 444 above ends here, and the present text returns to the point in the MS. where the interpolation is suggested.   *c* MS. om.

The Christians eventually took the city, in which prisoners 1390 and killed amounted to 4,000 men, according to the findings of the marshal's roll. The dead included the brother of the king of Poland and the standard-bearer of the king of Lithuania, who on seeing the destruction of his forces fled precipitately into the citadel. The capture of the city was due to the earl, who, together with his men, indeed behaved in this attack with great distinction and was the very first to plant his standard on the city walls.

For five weeks, the Christians vigorously pressed the siege of the citadel into which the king of Lithuania had withdrawn in his flight, and they would certainly have gained possession of it if they had had plenty of food and the good health they would have wished, but the Livonians, and the Prussians too, contracted various ailments that made them quite unable to remain any longer to prosecute the siege, which they consequently abandoned to return to their own countries. The marshal of the Prussians took back with him to Prussia 8,000 Lithuanian prisoners to be made into Christians, while the master of Livonia took with him 3,500, according to the reckoning of the marshal's roll.

On the eighth day after the arrival of the marshal and the earl with their troops in Königsberg in Prussia, news reached them that the king of Poland and Krakow was preparing, with a huge army, the conquest of the Prussian homeland. When he heard this, the marshal at once assembled his own army and made an urgent appeal to the earl to agree to march with him in defence of his country against the king of Poland and Krakow. The earl fell in with his wishes; and on the following day they left Königsberg and marched with their troops against the king of Poland.

It was during this period that the French duke of Bourbon gathered at Genoa a large army, drawn from various parts of Europe, and sailed to Barbary, where, with these Christians, he opened hostilities against the heathen, over whom he won an initial victory. But in a second engagement the bold charge of an irresistible horde of heathen forced the Christians to flee in great bodily peril to their ships. Those who escaped with their lives from the

1390 vivi evaserunt a manibus paganorum ad propria sunt reversi de eorum evasione Deum multipliciter collaudantes.[1]

Item x^mo. ⟨die⟩^a Octobris apud Smethefeld erant solempnia hastiludia; qua de causa de pluribus partibus ad civitatem London' comites et valentes milites accesserunt. Inter alios venit comes Sancti Pauli cum uxore sua sorore domini regis[2] cum aliis strenuis de Francia; venit eciam comes dictus Ostrevantz[3] cum aliis Alemannis in nobili apparatu, nam omnia utensilia pro se et suis secum adduxit per aquam. Causa horum hastiludiorum fuit hec: nam dux Geldr' dum esset hic in Anglia[4] multum affectavit videre regem nostrum armatum, promisitque iccirco^b in suo recessu revenire et dictis hastiludiis interesse ^c die et loco,^c set impeditus non potuit perficere quod optabat. Durabant namque ista hastiludia per tres dies; laus quoque prime diei domino regi fuit concessa.[5]

Veniente itaque festo translacionis sancti Edwardi rex fuit in monasterio Westmon' ad primas vesperas et ad completorium cum tota sua capella; ad matutinas eciam media nocte aderat cum sua capella; ad processionem vero in die erat,^d et ad magnam missam in choro residebat cum sua capella circumdante corona. Parum post^d principium magne misse^d intravit regina solempniter coronata in chorum et in aquilonali parte secessit. Officium quoque divinum episcopus London' peregit.

Eo eciam die^d London' processerunt ad eleccionem novi majoris, ac Adam Bamme aurifabrum in eorum majorem concorditer elegerunt.[6] Post hec rex perrexit Wyndeshoram, ubi diversis cibariis satis laute prefatos dominos convivavit.

---

^a MS. om.   ^b Written above the line.   ^c-c In the margin but marked for insertion here; recte die et loco predicto?   ^d Interlined.

---

[1] A not wholly accurate account of the Barbary crusade. The crusaders, having embarked at Marseilles, sailed via Genoa, where their leader, Louis II, duke of Bourbon, made a courtesy call. During their 2-month siege of El Mahadia, in Tunis, they enjoyed some successes but eventually negotiated a truce and re-embarked under its protection. See Delaville le Roulx, *La France en orient au xive siècle*, i. 171–94; L. Mirot, *Le Siège de Mahdia (1390)* (Paris, 1932), pp. 12 ff.; and above, p. 432.

[2] Waleran de Luxemburg, count of Ligny and St. Pol (d. 1415) and Maud, his wife (d. 1392). She was the daughter of Thomas de Holland, earl of Kent, and Joan of Kent, who married secondly Edward, prince of Wales, and was the mother

clutches of the heathen returned to their homes offering 1390
manifold praises to God for their deliverance.[1]

A formal tournament was held at Smithfield on 10
October, providing the nobles and gallant knights of many
areas with a reason for visiting London. Among them was
the count of St. Pol with his wife, the king's sister,[2] and
with other doughty warriors from France; the count of
Ostrevantz, so called,[3] also came with other Germans, all
splendidly turned out, since he had brought all the gear for
himself and his party with him by sea. The occasion for this
tournament was that the duke of Guelders during his stay
here in England[4] had been very anxious to see our king
accoutred for combat, and for that reason had promised on
his departure that he would return and attend a tournament
at this time and place; but he was prevented from carrying
out his wish. The tournament lasted three days, on the first
of which the honours were awarded to the king.[5]

When the feast of the Translation of St. Edward [13 Oct-
ober] came, the king, accompanied by his entire chapel,
attended Prime, Vespers, and Compline at Westminster
Abbey; with his chapel he was also present for Matins at
midnight and at the procession during the day. At High Mass
he sat in the choir with his chapel, wearing his crown. Shortly
after High Mass began, the queen, solemnly crowned, entered
the choir and withdrew to the north side. The divine office
was performed by the bishop of London.

On the same day the people of London proceeded to
the election of a new mayor: they were agreed in choosing
Adam Bamme, a goldsmith.[6] The king now left for Windsor,
where with suitable elegance he regaled his distinguished
guests with an assortment of dainties. Here he created the

---

of Richard II (*G.E.C.*, iv. 325; vii. 153). For Maud see also below, p. 488; and for
Waleran, above, p. 400.

[3] William, count of Ostrevantz (d. 1417), for whom see also below, p. 452 n.
For his attire cf. Froissart, *Chroniques*, xiv. 257. See also Rymer, *Foedera*, vii.
683, and Laurent and Quicke, *Les Origines de l'état bourguignon: l'accession de
la maison de Bourgogne aux duchés de Brabant et de Limbourg (1385-1407)*,
i. 390-1.   [4] Cf. above, pp. 434-6.

[5] Cf. Froissart (*Chroniques*, xiv. 261-2), who assigns the honours on the 1st
day to the count of St. Pol and the earl of Huntingdon and on the 2nd day —
when the king came armed — to the count of Ostrevantz and Hugh Despenser.

[6] Cf. *Letter Book H*, pp. 358-9.

1390 Comitem de Ostrevantz militem de la gartere fecit ibidem, contulitque eidem per annum quingentas marcas: propter quod frendent Francigene ipsum comitem cum cachinno turpiter irridentes eo quod fecisset homagium et fidelitatem regi Anglorum;[1] de quorum improperio comes ipse parum curavit quamvis percepit illos multum exinde dolere et grave cor erga illum habere palam conspexit. Erat namque comes predictus filius Alberici domini Selandie.[2] Expletis quoque festis et conviviis satis honorifice eisdem exhibitis receptisque muneribus a rege et ab aliis ducibus et dominis Anglie, Alemanni et Franci optenta a domino rege licencia sua ad propria remearunt.

Major vero civitatis London' in suo officio solidatus fecit proclamari per totam civitatem London' quod nullus extraneus venderet aut ad vendendum staret in civitate ultra pulsacionem xj. in signo. Et quia sequebatur magna caristia presertim bladi in ista sequenti yeme et deinceps, cum modius frumenti protunc vendebatur xxij. denariis, ipse vero major predictus, pervigil in officio suo existens, si quos pistores, braciatores et alios vitalarios excedere modum videbat, habendo respectum ad singula eos secundum qualitatem delicti acriter puniebat.[3]

Item quasi in principio mensis Novembris apud Westmonasterium in cancellaria domini regis fuit publice proclamatum ut si qui contra episcopum Dunelm'[4] modo facta translacione episcopum Eliensem vel alios quondam in magno parliamento super diversis articulis diffamatos vellent opponere, venirent secure et proponerent in proximo parliamento ac utique super hujusmodi justiciam reportarent.

Parliamentum. Duodecimo die Novembris apud Westmonasterium tenuit rex suum parliamentum; duravitque usque in tercium diem[a] Decembris. In quo multa erant proposita set pauca ad effectum deducta. Primo tactum fuit in eo de precio lane ubicumque in Anglia secundum verum valorem pensando melioritatem illius juxta quam

---

[a] Septembris *deleted after this word.*

[1] Cf. *Chronique du religieux de S. Denys,* ed. Bellaguet, i. 688; Froissart, *Chroniques,* xiv. 264-5.
[2] Count William's father was Albert of Bavaria, count of Hainault, Holland, and Zealand, 1389-1404.

count of Ostrevantz a knight of the Garter and conferred 500 1390
marks a year on him: this caused some gnashing of French
teeth and ill-bred sneers at the count for having done homage
and fealty to the English king.[1] Their offensiveness was of
small concern to the count although he was aware that they
were considerably nettled and he could see plainly enough
that they nursed a grudge against him. The count was the
son of Alberic lord of Zealand.[2] When the festivities were
over and the guests had been entertained with appropriate
courtesy at a series of banquets and had received presents
from the king and from others among the English dukes and
lords, the Germans and Frenchmen took their leave of the
king and returned to their homes.

When he had been confirmed in his office, the mayor
of London caused a proclamation to be made throughout
the city that no stranger should make, or stand ready to
make, any sale in the city after the clock had struck eleven.
In consequence of a great dearth, especially of corn, which
followed in the subsequent winter and after it, when a
measure of wheat sold for 22d., the mayor behaved with
great vigilance in the exercise of his office and punished, with
a severity that took account of the facts of individual cases,
and the nature of the offence, all the bakers, brewers, or
other victuallers he saw overstepping the mark.[3]

About the beginning of November it was publicly proclaimed in the king's chancery at Westminster that all with
anything to lay to the charge of the bishop of Durham[4]
(now, following his translation, bishop of Ely), or of others
who had been accused on various counts in the great parliament some time before, should come forward without fear
of the consequences and state it in the next parliament,
when they could be sure of obtaining justice.

Parliament. On 12 November, the king held his parliament
at Westminster; it lasted until 3 December. In it many topics
were raised but few of them led to any decisive action. The
first question discussed concerned the price of wool and how
it was to be related throughout England to its true worth in

---

[3] i.e. offenders against the Assize of Bread and Ale were suitably punished. See
also below, p. 474 and n.

[4] John Fordham, for whom see above, pp. 230, 332–4 and n.

1390 fideliter taxaretur ac eciam ita venderetur ab omnibus utrobique taxa premissa omnino servata.[1] Puto istud minime
observari. Preterea statutum est in eo pro perpetuo quod
stapula lane staret in Anglia et deinceps nullatenus foret
extra.[2] Concessum est domino regi eciam in isto parliamento quod ipse de mercatoribus perciperet xij. denarios
de libra. Item ad peticionem communitatis concessum est
J. Northampton' omnia bona sua mobilia et immobilia tam
in civitate quam extra penitus rehabere et ita libere stare
in civitate London' sicut antea stetit paucis annis elapsis.[3]
Permissum est libere per parliamentum domino pape conferre
omnia beneficia in curia vacancia in futurum non obstantibus quibuscumque statutis in contrarium promulgatis.[4]
Cetera communitas permisit dominis terminare; sicque ad
propria redierunt.[5]

In festivitate Sancti Edmundi Regis et Martiris fuit rex in
monasterio Westmon' ad vesperas et ad matutinas in nocte;
in die vero erat ad processionem et ad magnam missam:
deditque conventui pro suo labore decem marcas.[a]

p. 200 Dominus rex tenuit suum Natale aput Eltham satis
solempne; deinde continuavit moram suam in partibus occidentalibus, nunc apud Gloverniam et nunc apud Bristolliam,
tamen pro majori parte Bristollie moram traxit usque post
1391 lapsum festi Pasche. Circa medium mensis Februarii dominus
Henricus Percy, dominus de Beaumont et dominus de Clifford[6] optenta a rege licencia transierunt mare, affectantes

[a] *In the MS. the marked passage mentioned in the note on p. 444
above follows here.*

[1] For the ensuing measures designed to secure these ends, see *R.P.*, iii. 278;
Cal. Cl. R. 1389-92, pp. 214, 238; cf. ibid., p. 226; and for wool prices at this
time, T. H. Lloyd, *The Movement of Wool Prices in Medieval England* (*Economic
History Review* Supplement, no. 6, 1973), pp. 20, 49.
[2] The wool-staple was moved from Calais to the towns mentioned in the
Statute of Staple of 1354, with effect from 9 Jan. 1391. The grant of poundage,
to which the Monk refers, was made for 3 years, on 3 Dec., conditionally on the
enforcement of home staples, a condition applying also to the subsidies on wool,
woolfells, and the tonnage on wine imports granted at the same time. See *R.P.*,
iii. 278, 279; *S.R.*, i. 332-43, 348; Lloyd, *English Wool Trade in the Middle Ages*,
pp. 207-8, 232.
[3] The consequence of the annulment, on 2 Dec. 1390 and in response to a
common petition, of all judgements against Northampton (*R.P.*, iii. 282-3; *Cal.
Pat. R., 1388-92*, p. 335; *Letter Book H*, p. 359).
[4] As far as we know, the parliament of Nov.-Dec. 1390 made no such ordinance.

terms of its quality, which was to determine its fair valua- 1390
tion and the conditions of its sale, with strict regard to that
valuation, by all traders everywhere.[1] I fancy that this goes
unheeded. It was also laid down for all future time in this
parliament that the wool-staple should be established in England and that henceforward it should in no circumstances be
out of the country.[2] In this same parliament the king was
granted the right to take from merchants 12d. in the pound.
At the petition of the commons John Northampton was given
the right to resume full possession of all his goods, movable
and immovable, both within and outside the city, and to
enjoy in London the same position of freedom as he had
done a few years earlier.[3] The pope was freely allowed by
the parliament to collate to all benefices falling vacant in
future within the Roman curia, any statutes published to the
contrary notwithstanding.[4] The remaining business was left
by the commons for the lords to complete; and so they
returned to their homes.[5]

On the feast of St. Edmund, King and Martyr [20 Novem-
ber], the king attended Vespers and midnight Matins at
Westminster Abbey; and on the day itself he was present at
the procession and at High Mass. He presented the convent
with 10 marks for its pains.

The king kept Christmas with some ceremony at Eltham,
following it with a prolonged stay in the west, now at Gloucester and now at Bristol, though it was at Bristol that he
passed most of his time until Easter had come and gone. 1391
About the middle of February Sir Henry Percy, Lord
Beaumont, and Lord Clifford,[6] having obtained the king's
leave, went overseas in pursuance of their desire to visit

That of Nov.-Dec. 1391 accorded a discretionary power to the king in the enforcement of the Statute of Provisors of 1390, and that power may have been
used to exempt benefices vacated at the curia from the penalties of the statute
(below, p. 482 and n.; cf. *Vita Ricardi Secundi*, p. 132; and W. T. Waugh, 'The
Great Statute of Praemunire', in *E.H.R.*, xxxvii (1922), 182, 183 and n.).

[5] Cf. *R.P.*, iii. 283, recording the presence of the Commons until the dissolution of the parliament, on 3 Dec.

[6] Respectively, Henry Percy, earl of Northumberland (d. 1408); Thomas, Lord
Clifford; and John, Lord Beaumont (d. 1396). Percy was captain of Calais and
went overseas for its defence (*Carte*, ed. ii. 161, 163; *Cal. Pat. R., 1388-92*,
p. 376). Clifford received the king's licence to go overseas on 11 Jan. 1391 and
died in Prussia (ibid., p. 363; below, p. 480).

1391 visere exteras regiones.*ᵃ* Transacto festo Pasche rex venit Wyndeshoram festum sancti Georgii celebraturus; quo peracto consilium tenuit apud Radynggum, multum desiderans videre regem Francorum et colloquium habere cum illo, quomodo scilicet pax inter eos posset finaliter stabiliri.[1] Ad hoc erat responsum protunc *ᵇ*⟨ex⟩ parte dominorum ibidem ea vice ⟨pre⟩sencium quia ex quo*ᵇ* archiepiscopus Cantuar' et alii domini non erant presentes ibidem protunc, ut deberent, ad ea que illis proponebantur respondere negabant quousque omnes quorum intererat insimul convenissent. Unde prorogatum fuit hoc consilium usque Westmonasterium,[2] ubi post multas examinaciones et viarum salutarium perquisiciones fuit diffinitum quod ante omnia mitterentur ad regem Francorum et ejus consilium certi milites ut ipsi diligencius ab eis primo inquirerent quomodo et sub qua forma vellent tractare et si rex eorum ex assensu parcium Cales' descenderet[3] an manu armata veniret vel cum paucis equitibus more pacis ad dictam villam vellet accedere; ceteris pro tempore pretermissis: hiis ergo certitudinaliter habitis dominus noster rex*ᶜ* sciret quomodo in premissis expedicius se haberet. Igitur super isto negocio directi sunt nuncii ad regem Francorum milites, scilicet dominus Lodowycus Clifford, dominus Thomas Percy, dominus Nicholaus Sharnesfeld, et dominus Nicholaus Daggeworth, viri valentes et famosi; qui redeuntes dixerunt regem Francorum manu potenti velle ad prefatum locum venire si deberet venire, aliter namque propter maliciam sue plebis non audebat equitare vel se movere ad locum tam remote distantem, quantum vero ad tractatum asserebant eos velle tractare

---

ᵃ An erasure follows.   *ᵇ⁻ᵇ In the margin (and damaged at the edge) but marked for insertion at this point;* protunc *is followed by a short erasure.* *ᶜ Two letters have been blotted out after this word.*

---

[1] On 14 Feb. 1391, Richard II's envoys, Thomas Percy and Lewis Clifford, had agreed with Charles VI's envoy, the duke of Bourbon, on a meeting between the two kings on 24 June 1392, each king to be accompanied by 400 knights and squires. Later, Richard asked Charles VI to agree to a preparatory conference in advance of their own meeting, and the king accepted Richard's proposal that the duke of Lancaster should come to France for this purpose; in these negotiations the English envoys were probably Lewis Clifford and Sir Thomas Blount. In the following paragraph, the Monk confuses the reason underlying this further approach to Charles VI in 1391 with concern about details of the conference between the two kings which had already been settled in Feb., and he is confused

foreign parts. Easter [26 March] over, the king came to 1390
Windsor to celebrate the feast of St. George [23 April],
after which he held a council at Reading, being very anxious
to see the king of France and to have conversations with
him about the means of establishing a definitive peace
between them.[1] The answer made to this suggestion by the
lords present at Reading on this occasion was that since the
archbishop of Canterbury and other lords were not there as
they should have been, they themselves declined to comment
on the proposal until there had been a meeting of all the
interested parties. The council was accordingly adjourned to
Westminster,[2] where, after considerable study and search for
the advantageous course, it was determined that, to begin
with, certain knights should be sent to the king of the French
and his council to make careful inquiries of them in the first
place about the manner and form of procedure under which
they wished to negotiate, and whether the French king, if,
after agreement between the parties, he travelled to Calais,[3]
would come with an armed force or would be willing to make
his way to the town peace-time fashion, in company with a
few knights. The remaining problems were to be shelved for
the moment: when he was sure of the answers to the above
questions, the king would know what attitude to adopt for
the best in this matter. The knights sent as envoys on this
business to the king of the French were Sir Lewis Clifford,
Sir Thomas Percy, Sir Nicholas Sarnesfield, and Sir Nicholas
Dagworth, men of worth and reputation. On their return
they reported that the French king wished to come to the
meeting-place with a powerful force, if he had to come
at all; in no other conditions, owing to the rancour of the
French populace, did he dare to ride abroad or transport

---

about the identity of the envoys used in these several missions. See Moranvillé,
in *B.E.C.*, 1 (1889), 359-60, 369-71; *Diplomatic Correspondence of Richard II*,
ed. Perroy, no. 129 and n., and for the diplomatic background, J. J. N. Palmer,
'The Anglo-French Peace Negotiations 1390-1396', in *T.R.H.S.*, 5th ser., xvi
(1966), pp. 81 ff. See also below, p. 490.

[2] A great council had in fact been summoned some two weeks before the
council at Reading, to meet in London on 26 Apr. (P.R.O., E. 403/533, 8 Apr.).

[3] It had already been agreed that the conference should be either at Leulingham or between Guines and Ardres, the choice to depend on whether Charles
VI stayed at Boulogne or St. Omer. Leulingham was a hamlet between Boulogne
and Calais, and Richard II was to stay at Calais.

1391 eo modo quo vellent. Duravit iste tractatus ex utraque parte per magnum tempus et vicissim prodierunt nuncii amborum ex parte regnorum magnis laboribus et expensis eorundem et adhuc sine effectu profecto tempus concordie consumebant.[1]

Circa principium mensis Maii comes Derbeye sanus et hillaris in Angliam applicuit.[2] Tercio die Maii aput Toothull' erat duellum inter duos felones, scilicet inter appellatorem et defensorem: victus est appellator quamvis habuerit justiorem querelam. Nam sponte fatebatur coram omnibus quod alio anno ejus suasu et hortatu quidam fugitivus ⟨qui⟩[a] ad sanctuarium Sancti Petri Westmon' confugiebat exivit sicque dolose fuit comprehensus et tandem suspensus. Qui ipsum jam pugnando acriter infestavit ac impedivit quominus posset victoriam optinere, prout sibi videbatur, pro vero; hanc autem assercionem fore validam jurejurando firmavit sicut ipse in die Judicii vellet animam suam salvam habere coram summo Deo.[b] Item circa principium mensis Maii[3] dominus Johannes Waltham episcopus Sar' factus est thesaurarius domini regis.

Circa medium mensis Junii venit in Angliam nuncius pape abbas Nonantulensis ordinis sancti Benedicti et die sancti Johannis Baptiste accessit ad regem apud manerium suum de Shene cum suis nobilibus existentem; a quo fuit satis honorifice receptus. Primo quidem idem abbas ex parte domini pape regem salutavit, tradens ei bullam papalem cujus tenor una cum credencia prefati nuncii ac responsione domini regis sequitur proxime seriatim:

p. 201   Bonefacius episcopus servus servorum Dei carissimo filio Ricardo regi Anglie illustri salutem et apostolicam benediccionem. Ad nostri presenciam regrediens quem misimus nobilis vir Damianus de Cathaneis miles Januen', consiliarius et nuncius noster, nobis tua magnifica et rege fideli digna munera perferens simul et suavissimas litteras detulit[4] et quam hilariter quamque benigne illum susceperis et de eximia devocione quam tuo tuorumque more majorum ad Deum et ad sanctam ejus

---

[a] MS. om.   [b] In the margin but damaged at the edge: ⟨Not⟩a dolos perversis ⟨m⟩odicum valere. ⟨Vi⟩de inferius de ⟨Johan⟩ne Paule in ⟨quart⟩o folio sequenti [i.e., MS. p. 207; below, p. 498].

[1] See further below, p. 478.
[2] Derby landed at Kingston-upon-Hull (Expeditions by Henry earl of Derby, pp. 98, 99).   [3] On 2 May.

himself to a spot so remote. As for the negotiations, the 1391
envoys said that the French were willing to conduct them as
the English pleased. The negotiations between the parties
went on for a long time: at great cost in effort and money,
envoys set out from each kingdom in turn; and the period
of truce was being used up, still with nothing achieved.[1]

About the beginning of May the earl of Derby landed in
England in excellent health and spirits.[2] On 3 May there was
a trial by battle at Tothill between two felons, approver and
accused: the approver was defeated, though his was the more
righteous quarrel. He had publicly volunteered a statement
that in a previous year a fugitive who had fled to the sanctuary of St. Peter, Westminster, had been persuaded and
encouraged by the accused man to come out, only to be
treacherously seized and ultimately hanged. In the present
fight the accused set up a savage attack and prevented the
approver from winning victory for what he held to be the
truth: that his allegation was well founded he was prepared
to confirm upon oath, as he would have his soul saved before
God on high on the Day of Judgement. About the beginning
of May[3] John Waltham, bishop of Salisbury, became the
king's treasurer.

The abbot of the Benedictine house of Nonantola arrived
in England as papal nuncio about mid-June and visited the
king, then, in company with his nobles, at his manor of
Sheen, on St. John the Baptist's Day [24 June], to meet a
properly courteous welcome. He began by greeting the king
on the pope's behalf and handed him a bull, of which the
tenor here follows, together with the nuncio's credence and
the king's reply, all in their order.

Boniface, bishop, servant of the servants of God, to his most dear
son, Richard, the illustrious king of England, greeting and the apostolic
blessing. On his return to our presence from his mission the noble
Damian de Cataneis, knight of Genoa, our counsellor and nuncio,
brought to us your gifts, of a splendour befitting a loyal sovereign, and
at the same time delivered your very agreeable letter;[4] he also told us
of the gladness and kindness with which you received him and the
outstanding devotion, so characteristic of yourself and your forebears,

---

[4] For some of the gifts, see *Diplomatic Correspondence of Richard II*, ed.
Perroy, p. 215; and for the mission of Damian de Cataneis, above, p. 414 and n.

1391 Romanam ecclesiam ac personam nostram per multiplices et commendabiles effectus gerere comprobaris et nonnulla alia ex tue celsitudinis parte exposuit seriose. Nos autem et in predictis litteris contenta et hujusmodi exposita intelleximus diligenter; munera vero animo suscepimus hilari etsi preciosissima et jocundissima forent illa non magis ponderantes quam preclarum mittentis affectum et proinde tibi uberes gracias exsolventes; set quos nobis pro tue serenitatis parte stricte recommendavit habere intendimus casibus occurrentibus propensius commendatos. Verum inter eandem ecclesiam et quemlibet catholicum principem tanta connexio esse debet ut semper, prout casus requirit, sese mutuis et honestis vicissitudinibus foveant[a] atque juvent, sic tamen quod in quovis facto ipsa equitas non ledatur nec derogatur juri aut ecclesiastice libertati. Et propterea, dilectissime fili, cum intelleximus fide digno relatu quod quidam non que Dei set que sua, et forsan non sic sua, sunt perversa ambicione querentes perastutis modis et reprobis viis tue sublimitati suggerere nisi fuerunt, ac tandem effecerunt, quod quoddam statutum regium, si tamen ita dici debeat, contra libertatem hujusmodi dudum editum et saniori consilio non servatum tua serenitas innovavit,[1] celsitudinem tuam, cujus salutem honorem et statum zelamur, attente requirimus et hortamur, tibi nichilominus paternis consiliis suadentes, quatinus regali providencia[b] considerans quod illi tales non salutem tuam, non honorem, non tui status corroboracionem ex hoc querunt, set pocius labem infigere clarissime fame tue, et quod majores tui, temporibus illis quibus presidentes ecclesie belligerantibus contra majores eosdem vel palam totis viribus assistebant, numquam simile quidem[c] temptarunt[2] et quod hii tales que aput eosdem majores non fuissent ausi[d] temptare spe falsa te seducentes obtinuerunt in hoc quod querebant, velis graviori et justiori consilio dare ordinem cum effectu quod hujusmodi statutum penitus deleatur ac taliter provideatur ne quidem[c] ipsi tale post hec[e] et ceteri sint ad similia tardiores. Circa que dilecto filio Nicholao abbati monasterii Nonantulen' ordinis sancti Benedicti Mutinen' dioc⟨esis⟩ apostolice sedis nuncio, quem utpote virum fidelem prudentem et admodum nobis carum ad tui presenciam presencialiter destinamus, indubiam fidem adhibere poterit regia celsitudo. Datum Rome aput Sanctum Petrum xviij. Kalendas Maii pontificatus nostri anno secundo.

Postea dictus nuncius suam credenciam coram rege et

---

[a] *MS.* fovent.   [b] *The words* aliter prudencia *are written above this word.*
[c] *Recte* quid *(Winterbottom).*   [d] *MS.* ausu.   [e] *Sc.* temptent *or some such verb.*

---

[1] A reference to the first Statute of Provisors, 1351, and its re-enactment in 1390 (above, pp. 418 ff.).
[2] A reference (not entirely well judged) to Anglo–papal relations *temp.* Boniface VIII (1294–1303), during the Anglo-French struggle of Edward I's reign.

which its many praiseworthy manifestations prove you to bear towards
God, his Holy Roman Church, and our own person, and described in
detail your Highness's position respecting some other matters. We have
ourselves given careful consideration both to the contents of your letter
and to this report: as for the gifts, which we received with great
pleasure, we value them no more, despite their surpassing costliness
and charm, than the sender's evident affection; and for them we offer
you our profuse thanks. The persons for whom the nuncio, on your
serenity's behalf, closely sought our favour, we mean, as opportunity
offers, to regard as preferentially recommended. Indeed, between the
Church and every catholic prince there ought to be such close ties that
whenever circumstances require it there should be honourable reci-
procity of help and support, provided, however, that in whatever is
done justice does not suffer and that there is no impairment of the law
or of the Church's liberty. And it is on this account, dearly beloved son,
that, having learned from trustworthy reports that certain men whose
wayward ambition is set not upon the things that are God's but upon
those that are their own (and perhaps not, even so, their own) have by
cunning and discreditable ways and means made strenuous efforts,
ultimately successful, to prompt your eminence to bring about your
serenity's renewal of a certain royal statute (if indeed it should be so
described) published long ago to the prejudice of that liberty and in
the light of wiser counsels allowed to lapse,[1] we earnestly request and
urge your highness, for whose well-being, honour, and estate we are
full of zeal, offering none the less our fatherly advice to persuade you
(having regard in your royal prudence to the fact that for men of the
sort described the object in all this is not your well-being, your honour,
or the buttressing of your estate but rather to impose a blot upon your
fair fame; to the fact that your ancestors, at times when the heads of
the Church were with all their strength openly supporting those who
were at war with those ancestors,[2] never attempted anything even
resembling this; and finally to the fact that such men as these, using
false hopes to lead you astray, have in the pursuit of their aims achieved
what they would never have ventured to try with your ancestors) to
be pleased to act upon weightier and more righteous counsel and give
effective orders that this statute is to be completely abrogated and such
provision made as will prevent these men themselves from repeating
their attempt in future and will make others slow to imitate it. In this
connection your royal highness may give unquestioning credence to
our beloved son, Nicholas, abbot of the monastery of Nonantola, of
the order of St. Benedict, in the diocese of Modena, nuncio of the
apostolic see, whom, as a man of loyalty and prudence standing high
in our affection, we are sending to your presence to wait upon you in
person. Given in Rome at St. Peter's on 14 April in the second year
of our pontificate [1391].

Addressing the king and the nobles who were present on

1391 nobilibus tunc ibidem existentibus secundum quod sequitur explicavit:[1]

Illustrissime principum, sanctissimus dominus noster papa salutat serenitatem vestram et eisdem transmittit apostolicam benediccionem, desiderio audire desiderans[2] sepe de serenitate vestra et ipsius statu nova felicia, nec inmerito, cum inter ceteros mundi principes attenta devocione majestatis vestre erga fidem sacrosanctam *a*aliter sacratissimam*a* orthodoxam sanctam Romanam ecclesiam matrem vestram et sanctissimum dominum nostrum prefatum vos sibi ascripserit in carissimum singularissimum immo unicum filium, et illum filium in quem spem suam firmissimam posuit, sicut et predecessores suos Romanos pontifices Christi vicarios in serenissimos progenitores vestros, maxime sanctos,[3] sacratissime Christiane fidei et sancte matris ecclesie tutissimos et fortissimos*b* defensores posuisse cognoscit, qui progenitores numquam nisi veris summis pontificibus adheserunt. Ulterius attentis vestrorum et vestra devocionibus supradictis, percepto per litteras excellencie vestre vestrique consilii[4] quedam condita fore statuta in detrimentum ecclesiastice libertatis admiracionem concepit non modicam, attentis fide scienciis virtutibus et prudenciis quibus vestra serenitas vestrumque regnum decorari noscuntur. Et velut bonus pater*c* emendacionem et salutem animarum filiorum suorum desiderans per quendam magnificum et egregium comitem primo et per alios istarum parcium successive admonuit et exortatus fuit*d* statutarios dictorum statutorum quod dicta statuta in quantum ledebant ecclesiasticam libertatem de medio tollerent, nec per hec, ut satis expresse tangit dominus noster, nisi que sunt contra ecclesiasticam libertatem. Non enim intendit dominus noster, sicut nec debet, vestram minuere coronam seu potenciam, non tollere quin quecumque statuta in regno vestro condere valeatis non faciencia contra ecclesiasticam libertatem: immo coronam et potenciam vestram quantum sibi est possibile conservare et augmentare paratus et ad hoc se cognoscit multipliciter obligatum. Et quoniam propterea licet expectans diucius non senciit statutarios antedictos justis monitis obtemperasse prefatis, ut eosdem aliquantulum ulterius admoneret et ne res hec non tolleranda ad alios transiret in exemplum, nil innovando nec processus aliquos faciendo, que jura contra statuta et statuentes contra ecclesiasticam libertatem statuunt expressit, a

a–a These words argue an archetype in which they were written above sacrosanctam.   *b* The words aliter continuos are written above this word.   *c* Cf. pastor in the version which Walsingham cites (Hist. Ang., ii. 200).   *d* MS. inserts et.

---

[1] Variant readings betray the Monk's use of a written source for the following speech, and a version of this was also used by Walsingham (*Hist. Ang.*, ii. 200-1). Cf. below, p. 470, where the king in his reply to the pope seems to refer to a written copy of the speech. On the diplomatic points see P. Chaplais, 'English Diplomatic Documents to the end of Edward III's Reign', in *The Study of Medieval Records*, ed. D. A. Bullough and R. L. Storey (Oxford, 1971), pp. 27 ff.

this occasion, the nuncio next developed the theme of his 1391
instructions as follows:[1]

Most illustrious of princes, our most Holy Father the pope greets
your serenity and sends you his apostolic blessing; with desire does he
desire[2] to have frequent glad tidings of your serenity and of your
serenity's estate, and justifiably so, when among all the princes of the
world it is you whom (contemplating your majesty's devotion to the
sacred orthodox faith, the Holy Roman Church your mother and our
most holy Lord himself) he has taken unto himself for his most
beloved, his special, nay his unique son — the son in whom he has
reposed his just such utterly confident hope as he knows his predecessors, too, pontiffs of Rome and vicars of Christ, reposed in your
most serene (and above all your sanctified)[3] forebears as the surest and
most valiant (or enduring) defenders of the sacred Christian faith and of
holy mother Church, those forebears who never gave their support to
any but the true supreme pontiffs. Contemplating further the devotion
shown by you and yours, when he gathered from the letters of your
excellency and your council[4] that certain statutes have been set up to
the detriment of the Church's liberty, he felt no little astonishment, in
view of the faith, the knowledge, the virtues, and the discretion which
are well known to grace your serenity and your serenity's realm. And
so, like a good father who desires the chastening and the salvation of
the souls of his sons, he conveyed to the authors of these statutes, first
through an august and prominent nobleman and subsequently through
a succession of other persons from those parts, his warning and exhortation to do away with these statutes in so far as they were damaging to
the Church's liberty, referring thereby, as our lord quite explicitly does,
only to those measures which are directed against that liberty. For it is
not our lord's intention, nor, indeed, is it consistent with his duty, to
detract from your crown or your authority or to take away from you
the power to set up in your realm any statutes that do not operate
against the Church's liberty: on the contrary, he is ready, so far as it is
possible for him, to preserve and enhance your crown and your authority and he acknowledges his manifold obligations to do so. When,
therefore, after a long wait, he realized that the above-mentioned
statute-makers had not heeded his righteous admonishment, in order to
administer some further slight warning and to prevent their intolerable
behaviour from becoming a model for others, without taking any unprecedented action or initiating any proceedings, he rehearsed the
provisions of the canon law against statutes, and the makers of statutes,
inimical to the Church's liberty, having been impelled to do so by more

[2] Cf. Luke xxii. 15. [3] Edward the Martyr and Edward the Confessor.
[4] A reference to the protest about provisions dated 26 May 1390, carried to
the curia in the summer of that year by the envoys referred to on pp. 412 and
430 above (Rymer, Foedera, vii. 672-5; Diplomatic Correspondence of Richard
II, ed. Perroy, no. 120). For this phase in Anglo–papal relations see Perroy, pp.
319 ff.

1391 pluribus et pluribus eciam propulsatus, pronunciando ipsa statuta, prout
jura pronunciant, nulla et irrita pro ea parte vel toto in quantum faciunt
contra ecclesiasticam libertatem.[1] Et quoniam nec sic idem dominus
noster animos ipsorum statuencium immutari persensit[a] et cum magna
amaritudine mentis intelligens[2] hec in fame vestre celsitudinis expresse
in statuto predicto vestrorum et regni vestri denigracionem non modicam redundare, idem dominus noster propterea tactus dolore cordis
intrinsecus me servulum suum ad majestatem vestram presencialiter ecce
transmittit, exhortatur, rogat et requirit quod vestra majestas, inspectis
et devocione predicta[b] animarum vestre et statuencium predictorum
salute honoribus domini nostri ac vestro, dignemini statuta ipsa prout
sunt nulla in quantum, ut supra, tolli et de vestris capitularibus aboleri
mandare, maxime statuta Quare impedit et Premuniri facias[3] et hiis
similia. Offert enim dominus noster quod si dicti statutarii vel alii sen-

p. 202 tirent se a sanctitate sua in aliquo aggravatos mittant / ad dominum
nostrum sufficientes ambassiatores vel nuncios allegaturos causas
gravaminum, quoniam idem dominus noster quantum cum Deo poterit
est promptus complacere majestati vestre eciam regno vestro. Et in
quantum (quod absit) dicti statuentes non tollerent statuta predicta
facta, ut prefertur, contra ecclesiasticam libertatem, idem dominus
noster salvo honore pastoralis officii et salvis honestate ecclesie et
animarum salute illa sub dissimulacionis pallio transire non posset.

Ulterius, illustrissime princeps, idem dominus noster vestre majestati
significat quomodo a jam inter regem Francie et antipapam sunt tenti
et habiti certi tractatus[4] et inter eos est finaliter ad infra dicenda
pacta deventum, videlicet quod rex idem promittit antipape transmittere secum, qui jam pronunciavit in suo anticonsistorio ad urbem
se esse venturum, duces Burgundie et Torene[5] cum forcia sua et istorum
ducum ad partes Italie, qui eum, ut promittunt, ponent in sede beati
Petri urbemque vastabunt et omnia sanctuaria tollent et ea ad partes
Gallicas asportabunt, et antipapa promittit dictum regem de Romano
imperio coronare[6] et duci Burgundie multa magnalia et duci Torene

---

[a] persenciit *in the margin; but* persensit *is not deleted.*   [b] MS. predictis.

[1] Phrases seeming to mitigate the force of Boniface IX's annulment of the 1st
and 2nd Statutes of Provisors, together with the Statute of Carlisle of 1307, on
4 Feb. 1391, for which see *Magnum Bullarium Romanum*, iv. 606-10; *Cal. Papal
Letters*, iv *(1362-1404)*, p. 277. Cf. the king's interpretation below, p. 470.

[2] Cf. 'Estuans intrinsecus ira vehementi in amaritudine loquar mee menti'
(*Die Gedichte des Archipoeta*, ed. H. Watenphul and H. Krefeld (Heidelberg,
1958), x. 1.

[3] i.e. the statutes of 1353 and 1365 now known as Praemunire (27 Edward III,
statute 1, *cap.* 1, and 38 Edward III, statute 2, *caps.* 1-4); *quare impedit* and *praemunire facias* were writs used in their enforcement. See *S.R.*, i. 329, 385-7;
Waugh, in *E.H.R.*, xxxvii (1922), 182 n.

[4] A reference to meetings between Charles VI and Clement VII at Avignon in
the winter of 1389-90, for which see E. Jarry, 'La "Voie de Fait" et l'alliance
franco-milanaise (1386-1395)', in *B.E.C.*, liii (1892) 220-1. On the accuracy of
the following account of their outcome see J. J. N. Palmer, 'English Foreign

and yet more persons, and pronounced the statutes, as the canon law   1391
pronounces them, null and void, either wholly or in part, so far as they
operate against that liberty.[1] And since not even so was our lord aware
of any change of heart in the statute-makers, and since he recognizes,
with great bitterness of spirit, that these matters redound to the serious
blackening of your highness's reputation, as it is portrayed in this
statute, and of the reputation of your family and your kingdom, the
deep distress of his innermost heart has caused him to send me, his
humble servant, here to appear in person before your majesty, and
urges, begs, and requires your majesty to consider the devotion above-
mentioned, the salvation of your own soul and of the souls of the
statute-makers, and our lord's honour and your own, and to see fit to
command that these statutes, as being null in so far etc. (as above),
and in particular the statutes of Quare impedit and Premuniri facias,[3]
and the like, shall be done away with and deleted from your codes. If
the statute-makers or any other persons feel themselves to be in any
respect aggrieved by his holiness, our lord offers them the opportunity
of sending to him properly accredited ambassadors and envoys to state
the occasion of their grievances, since he is ready to do all in his power,
under God, to gratify your majesty and your majesty's kingdom. Any
failure (which Heaven avert) on the part of the statute-makers to do
away with these statutes, brought into being, as aforesaid, in contravention of the Church's liberty, our lord could not allow to pass under
the cloak of dissimulation without injury to the honour of his pastoral
office, the self-respect of the Church, and the salvation of human souls.

Next, most illustrious prince, our lord informs your majesty that
negotiations recently held between the king of France and the anti-
pope[4] have ended in their reaching an agreement whereby the king
promises the anti-pope (who has just declared in his anti-consistory that
he intends to come to Rome) that he will send with him into Italy the
dukes of Burgundy and Touraine,[5] accompanied by the royal forces and
their own, to establish him, as they have undertaken to do, in the seat
of the blessed Peter, to sack the city itself, and make away with all its
shrines and transfer them to places in France. For his part, the anti-
pope promises to crown the king as Roman emperor;[6] to do many

<hr />

Policy, 1388-99', in *Reign of Richard II*, pp. 86 ff. By 24 June 1391, the pope
knew, but perhaps the nuncio did not, that the French expedition to Italy, the
kernel of the Franco-Clementist agreement, had been postponed; for England's
part in bringing this about, see ibid., pp. 95 ff.

[5] Respectively, Philip the Bold, duke of Burgundy, the French king's uncle,
and Louis, duke of Touraine, later duke of Orleans, the king's brother.

[6] A *rapprochement* between Wenzel of Bohemia, king of the Romans and
claimant to the imperial throne since the death of the Emperor Charles IV in
1378, and Boniface IX in Nov. 1390 added point to Clement VII's stance, for
which there is other evidence, that the Empire was vacant. Rumours that Clement
intended to 'transfer' the Empire to France had long been current. See E. Delaruelle, E.-R. Labande, and P. Ourliac, *L'Église au temps du grand schisme et de la
crise conciliaire (1378-1449)* (1962), p. 73; Jarry, in *B.E.C.*, liii (1892), 228-9;
Valois, ii. 309 and n.

1391 quod investiet eum de omnibus terris quas ecclesia Romana habet in
Italie partibus, et quendam alium dominum[1] promisit coronare regem
Tuscie et Lombardie, Lodowycum vero, qui se pretendit ducem Andegavie, persecutorem regni Sicilie promisit per vim armorum ponere in
pacifica possessione dicti regni.[2] Quare idem dominus noster attendens
fidem et devocionem progenitorum vestrorum et vestram erga fidem
catholicam sanctam ecclesiam matrem vestram et Romanos pontifices
qui fuerunt per tempora ad celsitudinem vestram velut ad carissimum et
singularissimum immo unicum filium recursum confidentissimum
habet, exhortatur et rogat majestatem eandem ut ad defensam
Christiane fidei et sancte matris ecclesie se exponat. Attendere enim
debet ipsa majestas quam prejudiciale esset toti Christianitati si
antipapa per tirannidem papalia jura teneret et posset rex Francie dici
dicta jura tenere; et scire debet vestra serenitas quantum summi pontifices Gallici regnum Anglie et ejus jura semper conati fuerunt cum omni
eorum potencia spirituali et temporali diminuere atque deprimere;
et attendere debet vestra majestas quod prejudiciale foret toti mundo
quod eciam imperium per tirannidem teneretur et maxime per Gallicos,
in quos jam de Germanis in suo secreto anticonsistorio dicitur antipapam transtulisse; et eciam quoad specialem statum vestre corone
domino nostro videtur quod debeatis inspicere. Nostis enim innatum
odium inter Anglicos et Gallicos, nostis cupiditatem Gallicorum et
superbiam, qui si (quod absit) obtinerent predicta nedum odiosos sibi
set totum mundum curarent possetenus usurpare nec regnum vestrum
maneret exemptum. Ita quod respectu Dei fidei ecclesie et vestro eciam
vestra majestas debet predicta respicere et de oportunis remediis providere. Et quoniam domino nostro relatum est ipsum regem cum vestra
corona velle tractare concordiam, cognoscit suam et suorum astuciam,
qui ad hoc tendunt ut habita cum vestra majestate concordia liberius
possint usurpare predicta et usurpatis eis cum eorum versuciis et
fallaciis conventa frangere et omnia vestra postea usurpare. Quare
suadet dominus noster quod respectu fidei, extra quam predictus rex
et sui esse noscuntur tanquam scismatici ac excommunicati et heretici
cum quibus participare et tractare non licet nisi super reducendo eos
ad fidem et ad obedienciam debitam et devotam, quod nulla alia sit
vestra cum illis communio. Si tamen vestra sublimitas deliberaverit
omnino velle tractare cum illis eo casu dominus noster vestram
majestatem exhortatur et rogat quod nulla fiat conclusio nisi ipse

[1] Giangaleazzo Visconti of Milan, father-in-law of Louis, duke of Touraine.
A treaty between the dukes of Burgundy and Touraine on the one part and
Giangaleazzo on the other in Mar. 1391 provided for the recognition of the latter
as lord of Lombardy and the March of Treviso if Clement VII should crown an
emperor (L. Mirot, *La Politique française en Italie de 1380 à 1422*, i: *les prélimi-
naires de l'alliance florentine* (Paris, 1934), pp. 22 ff.).

[2] Louis II, duke of Anjou, had been crowned king of Sicily by Clement VII in
Nov. 1389 and was at this time in Italy, trying to make good his claim against

wonders for the duke of Burgundy; and to invest the duke of Touraine 1391
with all the lands that the Church of Rome has in Italy; to crown
another nobleman[1] king of Tuscany and Lombardy; and as for Louis,
the self-styled duke of Anjou, who claims the kingship of Sicily, the
anti-pope has promised to put him by force of arms into peaceable
possession of that kingdom.[2] In view, therefore, of the loyalty and
devotion shown by you and your forebears to the catholic faith, to
your holy mother the Church and to the Roman pontiffs over the
years, our lord betakes himself with the utmost confidence to your
highness as to his best-loved, his particular, nay his unique son, and
urges and implores your majesty to declare yourself for the defence of
the Christian faith and holy mother Church. Your majesty should
consider how damaging it would be to the whole of Christendom if the
anti-pope held the papal rights by sheer despotism and if the king of
France could be said to control those rights; your serenity must know
how hard supreme pontiffs of French origin have always tried, to the
limit of their power, spiritual and temporal, to weaken and disparage
the realm of England and its rights; your majesty should reflect that it
would be damaging to the whole world for the Empire too to be held
by sheer despotism, especially by the French, to whom it is said that
the anti-pope in his secret anti-consistory has just transferred it from
the Germans; and it also seems to our lord that you should look carefully at the effect on your own crown. You are aware of the inborn
hatred between the English and the French, you are aware of the
covetousness of the French and of their arrogance: if (as Heaven forfend) they gained their present objective, they would see to it that so
far as their power sufficed they would seize dominion over the whole
world, let alone the objects of their hatred, and your own kingdom
would not be excluded. Out of regard for God, for the faith, for the
Church and for yourself, your majesty ought therefore to look at this
situation and make timely provision to remedy it. Our lord has been
told that the king of France wishes to negotiate an agreement with
your crown: in this he recognizes the guile of that king and his people,
who aim at an agreement with your majesty in order that once they
have it they will be freer to effect the seizures above described, and,
this done, with characteristic cunning and treachery to break the
compact and proceed to seize everything you possess. Our lord
therefore suggests that out of regard for the faith, outside which the
French king and his people are recognized to lie, as schismatics, ex-
communicates, and heretics with whom it is unlawful to deal or treat
except on the subject of bringing them back into the faith and into a
proper and devout obedience, that you should have no other kind of
intercourse with them. But if your sublimity decides, in spite of everything, upon willingness to negotiate with them, in that case our lord
urges and begs your majesty that there shall be no settlement unless

Ladislas of Durazzo, who had the support of Boniface IX; for the assistance
afforded him by the anti-pope, see *Valois*, ii. 169–70.

1391 Francie rex promittat pro se et omnibus suis per solempnia capitula
et pacta debitis penis et roboracionibus vallata vestre serenitati quod
nullas gentes armigeras mittet vel de partibus suis in Italiam alias venire
permittet et quod de factis Romane ecclesie et Romani imperii vel
alicujus partis Italie nullo modo se impediet ipse vel sui directe vel
indirecte per se vel alios publice vel occulte, et quod ipse rex Francie
in nullo favebit antipape in partibus Italie cum gentibus vel pecuniis
publice vel occulte contra dominum nostrum papam et ecclesiam
sanctam Dei, et similiter per omnia se de Romano imperio nullatenus
intromittent: alias penas incurrant^a appositas et pax intelligatur esse
fracta. Esset eciam desiderium domini nostri, illustrissime principum,
quod vestra serenitas per solempnes ambassiatores studeret inducere
dominum imperatorem ut pro Dei reverencia et sancte matris ecclesie
(ac imperialis dignitatis et sui interesset honoris) una cum majestate
vestra concurreret in omnibus supradictis nec se permitteret decipi a
fallaciis et versuciis et blandis ac largis oblacionibus Gallicorum, quas
quousque eis placeret observarent, set pocius fraternitate inter
majestates ambas existente ad predicta forcius colligata resistatis hiis
que cupide et inique ac fallaciter cogitant, ita quod Gallici cognoscentes
se non posse iniqua sua desideria^b et desistant a dictis iniquis
cogitacionibus et ad obedienciam sancte ecclesie et domini nostri redire
procurent. Et quoniam quoad supradictum transitum faciendum jam
dicebatur gentes parari, idem dominus noster exhortatur et rogat quod
ipsa vestra majestas ad suam defensam prestet tale subsidium quod
cum ipso et aliis subsidiis aliorum fidelium sanctam ecclesiam et statum
suum valeat a Gallicorum insultibus defensare.

Ore, serenissime princeps, hec sunt que dominus noster michi
imposuit pronunc me vestre debere exponere majestati; alia dicenda
dicam suis temporibus.

Sequitur responsio domini regis ad premissa:[1]

Beatissime pater, debita filiali recommendacione premissa vestre
sanctitatis litteras per ipsius nuncium, virum utique religiosum Nicholaum abbatem monasterii Nonantulen' ordinis sancti Benedicti Mutinen'
dioc⟨esis⟩, honorifice presentatas et credenciam in eisdem litteris sibi
commissam quam nobis oraculo vive vocis exposuit pleno collegimus
p. 203   intellectu. In quarum serie litterarum / et effectu dicte credencie post
nonnulla vestre benignitatis et paterne dileccionis eloquia (quorum
obtentu necnon et^c hillari recepcione munusculorum ex parte nostra
per honorabilem virum Damianum de Cathaneis militem Januen' ad
vestre sanctitatis presenciam transmissorum, que non magis quam

---

^{a} *Altered in MS. from* incurrent. ^{b} *Sc.* obtinere *or some such verb.*
^{c} *L om.;* ex *follows in MS.*

[1] The text of the following letter has been collated with that in Edinburgh
University, Laing MS. iii. 351a, fos. 139^V-140^V (cited hereafter as *L*). See also
Diplomatic Correspondence of Richard II, ed. Perroy, no. 133.

the king of France promises your serenity on behalf of himself and his 1391
subjects by means of solemn articles and contracts hedged about with
appropriate penalties and sanctions, that he will send no armed forces,
and will suffer no others to pass from his territories, into Italy; that he
will not involve himself in any way in the affairs of the Roman Church
or of the Roman Empire or any part of Italy, either he or his, either
directly or indirectly, either in person or by his agents, either openly
or secretly; that he will in no respect support the anti-pope inside Italy,
whether with men or money, openly or secretly, against our lord the
pope and the holy Church of God; and that under similar detailed
prohibitions the French will not meddle in the slightest degree with the
Roman Empire: otherwise they are to incur the attendant penalties and
the peace is to be understood to have been broken. It would be our
lord's further wish, most illustrious of princes, for your serenity to seek
by means of a formal embassy to persuade the emperor, of his veneration for God and Holy Mother Church (and it would be in the interest
of the imperial dignity and his own honour), to act in concert with your
majesty in all the foregoing matters and not to let himself be deceived
by the wiles and cunning or the smooth and lavish offers of the French,
which they would honour only as long as it pleased them, but rather by
drawing tighter to meet this crisis the existing bonds of brotherhood
between your two majesties you may together oppose the greedy,
wicked, and treacherous plans of the French, so that they, realizing
that their unrighteous desires outrun their power, may abandon their
evil designs and bring about their return to their obedience to Holy
Church and to our Lord. Since there are recent reports that forces are
being got ready to make the crossing into Italy, our lord urges and
begs that your majesty will supply for his defence such help that with
it and with similar help from others of the faithful he will be able to
protect Holy Church and his own estate against attack by the French.

This, most serene prince, completes the oral statement which our
lord charged me to make on the present occasion to your majesty:
what remains to be said I will say at the appropriate times.

The king's answer to the foregoing was as follows:[1]

Most blessed father, after our dutiful filial commendations, We have
laid to heart the letters from your holiness which your nuncio, the right
religious Nicholas abbot of the Benedictine monastery of Nonantola
in the diocese of Modena, has done us the honour of presenting to us,
and also the instructions given to him in the same letters, which he has
developed in an oral statement to us. In the course of these letters and
in the tenor of the instructions, after a number of expressions of your
benevolence and fatherly affection (by reason of which, as well as by
your gratified acceptance of the humble gifts conveyed on our behalf
to your holiness in person by the noble Damian de Cataneis, knight of
Genoa, which your holiness was so gracious as to welcome with no

1391 mittentis affectum eadem sanctitas dignabatur amplecti, nedum filialis devocionis integritas erga vestre sanctitatis personam quamplurimum excitatur, et merito, set et nostra precordia inmense exultacionis jubilum ilico resonabant) paterne exhortacionis, rogacionis et requisicionis verba percepimus in effectu ad quatuor inductiva: primo[a] videlicet ut ordinem velimus impendere quod statutum illud contra libertatem ecclesie dudum, ut asseritur, editum et per nos postea innovatum, ut dicitur, penitus deleatur,[1] quodque statuta (ut verbis utamur nobis expositis) Quare impedit et Premuniri facias et hiis similia tolli mandaremus de medio et de capitularibus aboleri; secundo[b] pensatis inter adversarium nostrum Francie et malediccionis alumpnum antipapam illicitis paccionibus[c] tam contra vestre sanctitatis personam quam contra Romanum imperium et terras ecclesie in partibus Italie et regnum Sicilie factis et initis necnon et periculis que exinde verisimiliter sequerentur ut faceremus circa hoc de oportuno remedio provideri, et in casu quo foret ex parte nostra tractatus de pace cum Gallicis quod nulla inde conclusio fieret nisi certa pacta, penis vallata debitis, roborentur que beatitudinis vestre personam Romanum imperium terras ecclesie et regnum Sicilie supradicta servarent ab injuriis et invasionibus quibus almam personam vestram et loca predicta Gallici supradicti nituntur in dies infestare; tercio[d] quod carissimum fratrem nostrum imperatorem per ambassiatores nostros studeremus inducere ut pro honore ecclesie et imperialis dignitatis nobiscum in hac parte concurrat nec decipi se permittat a fallaciis et blandis promissionibus Gallicorum; quarto[e] cum circa invasionem hujusmodi gentes parate dicantur ad transitum faciendum in proximo quod ad vestre sanctitatis defensam tale subsidium prestare velimus ut cum ipso et subsidiis aliorum fidelium sanctam ecclesiam et statum celsitudinis vestre possitis a Gallicorum insultibus defensare. Nos itaque attendentes, sicut in dictis litteris et adjuncta credencia[2] continetur oblatum, quod non est intencionis vestre sicut nec debetis, ut clare subjungitur, nostram potenciam vel coronam minuere, immo illas quantum est possibile conservare ac eciam augmentare, et ad hoc vestra clemencia se esse multipliciter obligatam agnoscit, de quo apostolice celsitudini tota mente referimus plenitudinem graciarum, cupientes quoque pro parte nostra similiter ut et vestre altitudinis honor et status[f] ecclesie in suis libertatibus conserventur, ad quod pariter nos astrictos esse cognoscimus, habito super premissis deliberato consilio ut devotus ecclesie filius ad ea sic duximus respondendum.[g] In primis, sicut statuta regni nostri non nisi in parliamento conduntur sic nec absque auctoritate parliamenti revocari poterunt nec deleri; quare ad complacenciam vestre sanctitatis in proximo parliamento nostro libenti animo faciemus habito in ea parte cum statibus regni nostri deliberato consilio, quod absque

---

[a] j. *in the margin.*   [b] ij. *in the margin.*   [c] *MS. and L. insert* non.   [d] iij. *in the margin.*   [e] iiij. *in the margin.*   [f] *MS. inserts* et, *which L omits.*   [g] Responsio *in the margin.*

[1] Cf. above, pp. 462–4 and n.   [2] See above, p. 462 n.

more warmth than the affection of the sender, not only was the full
measure of our filial devotion towards your holiness's person quickened
in the highest degree, and rightly so, but a song of boundless joy echoed
in our heart) we remarked the words of fatherly exhortation, entreaty,
and request which in effect introduce four suggestions: first, that we
should consent to issue an order that the statute, allegedly published
long ago against the Church's liberty and subsequently, it is said,
renewed by us, should be completely abrogated,[1] and that we should
command that the statutes (to use the terms of the statement made to
us) of Quare impedit and Premuniri facias and their like should be done
away with and deleted from our codes; secondly, that in view of the
unlawful compacts made and entered into between our adversary of
France and that foster-child of malediction, the anti-pope, both against
your holiness's person and against the Roman Empire, the Church's
Italian lands, and the kingdom of Sicily, and also in view of the dangers
likely to follow therefrom, we should cause provision to be made for
timely countermeasures, and that in the event of our engaging in peace
negotiations with the French there should be no final settlement
without a firm undertaking, hedged about with appropriate penalties,
which would safeguard your beatitude's person, the Roman Empire,
the Church's lands, and the kingdom of Sicily against the wrongs and
encroachments with which the French daily strive to harass your
gracious person and the regions above named; thirdly, that we should
seek through our envoys to persuade our very dear brother the emperor, for the honour of the Church and of the imperial dignity, to act
in concert with us in this matter and not let himself be deceived by the
wiles and the smooth promises of the French; and fourthly, since
invasion forces are said to be ready for an early crossing into Italy,
that we will supply for your holiness's defence such help that with it
and with similar help from others of the faithful you can protect Holy
Church and your highness's own estate against attack by the French.
We have carefully noted the assurance offered in your letters and in the
instructions annexed to them[2] that it is not your intention nor, as is
expressly added, is it consistent with your duty to detract from our
authority or our crown but, on the contrary, to preserve and even
enhance them, as far as possible, and your clemency recognizes your
manifold obligations to do so: for this we render with all our heart
to your apostolic highness our thanks in full measure, being on our side
desirous that your highness's honour and the estate of the Church shall
likewise be preserved in possession of their liberties, and recognizing
our reciprocal commitment to this principle. After mature consideration of the circumstances we have decided that this is the answer
which as a devout son of the Church we should make. In the first
place, just as the statutes of our realm are laid down only in parliament, so they cannot be repealed or annulled except with parliament's
authority. In our desire to satisfy your holiness, we will therefore in
our next parliament carefully consider the subject with the estates
of our realm and gladly do whatever can be done in this matter without

1391 diminucione corone nostre circa hoc fuerit faciendum: ex eo namque
quod per dictum nuncium petebatur statuta Quare impedit et Premuniri
facias, ut premittitur, aboleri admiracionis causa consurgit maxime cum
ab aliis summis pontificibus numquam fuerunt hec petita, quoniam
constat illa statuta eciam inter laicos patronos regni nostri subditos
super jure patronatus eorum et aliis*a* legem tribuere ab antiquissimis
temporibus observatam.[1] Verum, piissime pater, attento quod, sicut
ultra in se dicta credencia continebat, in casu quo per sanctitatem
vestram statuentes hujusmodi senciant se gravatos in aliquo causis
hujusmodi gravaminum per ipsorum ambassiatores aut nuncios allegatis,
intenditis nobis et regno nostro vestri gracia quantum cum Deo poteritis
complacere, speramus quod habita super premissis communicacione
benevola via poterit inveniri utrique parti placabilis absque eo quod
detrahatur honori ecclesie aut corone nostre quevis diminucio subse-
quatur. Si vero tractatus pacis per Gallicos offeratur hac vice qui
concludi poterit et secure firmari ut guerrarum dispendia, per que
populi Christiani sanguis effunditur, valeant evitari de cetero, nostre
intencionis existit ante conclusionem eandem pro desiderio beatitudinis vestre tales condiciones apponere que comode et honeste per
partem nostram poterunt obtineri. Quantum autem ad missionem
ambassiatorum nostrorum ad presenciam fratris nostri predicti ex
causa plenius expressata superius scire dignetur eadem vestra sanctitas
quod effectualiter in hac parte prevenimus beatitudinis vestre vota.[2]
Ceterum non deficiet quin scietur in proximo si inter nos et dictum
adversarium nostrum pax erit vel longa treuga firmata; in cujus eventu
bene placet nobis quod per subditos nostros de subsidio jam dicte
sanctitati valeat subveniri, quatenus comode fieri possit, ut vestre
benignitati complacenciam impendamus. Set si inter nos et Gallicos
guerre denuo suscitentur, tam gravia expensarum onera oportebit nos
et regnum nostrum ea occasione subire quod iidem subditi aliunde non
poterunt amplius onerari: verumptamen speratur quod stantibus guerris
eisdem Gallici per nostrates erunt adeo infestati quod non vacabit eis
(Deo volente) contra vestre sanctitatis personam vel ecclesiam*b* aut
alia comminata perficere nec*c* talia attemptare.*d*

Istis itaque sic peractis mansit nuncius papalis in Anglia
usque mensem Novembris, in cujus principio dominus rex
sine ulteriori dilacione suum parliamentum voluit inchoare
in quo dictus nuncius responsum congruum obtineret prout
sibi erat promissum.

a MS. and L al'; cf. Higden, ix. 257: aliter.   *b* There may be a lacuna in the
text at this point (Winterbottom).   *c* L aut.   *d* L adds Scriptum etc. in
palacio nostro Westmonasterii xxx. die Julii anno etc. quartodecimo [sic]. (For
quartodecimo read quintodecimo.)

---

[1] i.e. the Statutes of Praemunire of 1353 and 1365 reinforce the ancient
custom that in England the secular courts have jurisdiction over all issues affecting

disparagement of our crown. The request made by the nuncio that the 1391 statutes of Quare impedit and Premuniri facias should be done away with occasioned very great surprise, inasmuch as this is a demand never yet made by other supreme pontiffs because it is well understood that even as between lay patrons who are subjects of our kingdom those statutes transmit a law on the right of patronage and other matters that has been observed from very ancient times.[1] But since we have noted, most godly father, the intention, further contained in the said instructions, that if the authors of such statutes feel themselves in any respect aggrieved by your holiness and will by their ambassadors and envoys state the grounds of their grievances, you mean to exercise your grace to do all that, under God, you can do to meet the wishes of ourselves and our realm, we hope that after a friendly exchange of views on the foregoing matters a way can be found, acceptable to both sides, which will avoid any derogation from the Church's honour and will not lead to any impairment of our crown. If this time we are offered by the French a peace treaty which can be concluded and confirmed with assurance, so that it will henceforward be possible to escape the waste of war by which Christian blood is spilled, it is our intention, before it is so concluded, to attach to it such conditions conforming with your beatitude's desires as can be usefully and honourably secured by our side. As for the dispatch of our ambassadors to the court of our brother the emperor for the purpose elaborated above, may it graciously please your holiness to know that in this respect we have effectually anticipated your beatitude's wishes.[2] It cannot fail to be very soon known whether between us and our adversary abovesaid a peace, or a protracted truce, is going to be established; if it is, we are quite content that our subjects may come to the rescue of your holiness with the full measure of help that is conveniently practicable, so that we can meet your benignity's wishes. If, however, hostilities break out afresh between us and the French, it will be necessary for us and our realm to shoulder for that reason such a heavy burden of cost that our subjects will be unable to accept from elsewhere any addition to the load: none the less it is hoped that so long as a state of war subsists, the French will be so harassed by our people that, God willing, they will have no time to carry out operations against your holiness's person or the Church, or their other threats, or to make any attempt of that kind.

These matters disposed of, the papal nuncio remained in England until November, at the beginning of which the king meant to inaugurate without further delay the parliament in which the nuncio was to be given the suitable reply he had been promised.

disputes between patrons.
[2] A reference to the dispatch of George Felbrigge, a chamber knight, to Wenzel of Bohemia at the beginning of May or a little earlier (P.R.O., E. 403/533, 6 May).

1391 *Caristia.* Modicum ante principium istius anni orta est magna caristia bladi in Anglia, ita ut modius frumenti aliquando London' vendebatur duobus solidis et aliquando viginti denariis. Verumptamen major London' egregie se habuit in ista penuria: nam taliter rexit victualia in civitate protunc quod unusquisque comode posset vivere, licet cariori foro.[1] Et profecto nisi extrinseci subsidia in isto articulo prestitissent, tota plaga London' cum suis provinciis adjacentibus fame et inedia exciciali tabesceret annona sublata. Incepitque ista caristia circa medium mensis Marcii et duravit usque ad maturitatem frugum novorum.[a]

p. 204 Contigit quoque in ista estate aput Conynggesbourgh' in Pruissya quod quidam presbiter volens celebrare, ex insperato dominus Willelmus Duglas miles Scoticus in ecclesiam illius intravit; quem videns dictus presbiter noluit perficere quod incepit: requisitus cur reliquit opus inceptum respondit dicens se nolle celebrare in presencia scismaticorum. Ad hec dictus Willelmus Duglas excanduit et multo furore repletus hoc asseruit sibi fore maliciose procuratum per dominum de Clifford', unde minas sibi et aliis Anglicis intentavit;[2] quo tandem egresso presbiter missam celebravit. Qua finita dictus Willelmus Duglas [b]cum suis[b] Anglicos in aperta strata furibundus invasit, quendam armigerum mutilavit; armiger vero recepto vulnere irruit in eum ense nudo et letaliter vulneravit, qui ex eo vulnere cecidit interfectus; occubueruntque simul cum eo alii duo Scoti. Fuerunt eciam ibidem in illa civitate domini de Anglia protunc, scilicet dominus Despenser,[3] dominus filius Walteri,[4] [c]dominus de Beaumond,[5] dominus Clifford',[c]* et dominus de Bourcer';[6]

* Duo isti subtracti non erant ibi secundum quosdam *in the margin.*

[a] *Recte* novarum *(Winterbottom).*   [b-b] *In the margin but marked for insertion here.*   [c-c] *Underlined (for deletion) in MS.*

[1] On the price of corn, cf. *Vita Ricardi Secundi*, p. 132; and above, p. 452. In Feb. 1391, Adam Bamme, the mayor, made available £400 from the Orphan Fund of the City for the purchase of corn against the coming summer (*Letter Book H*, pp. 361–2; *Cal. Select Pleas and Memoranda of the City of London, 1381–1412*, ed. Thomas, pp. 174–5).

[2] For the antecedent quarrel between Sir William Douglas and Thomas, Lord Clifford, see Du Boulay, in *Reign of Richard II*, p. 171. For Clifford see also above, p. 454 and n.

Dearth. Shortly before the beginning of this year there had 1391
arisen in England a great dearth of corn, so that in London a
measure of wheat sold at times for 2*s.* and at others for 20*d.*
The mayor of London, however, distinguished himself by his
conduct in this time of shortage, managing foodstuffs within
the city during this period in such a way that everybody
could survive comfortably, though at increased cost.[1] And
indeed, if people outside had not lent their aid at this point,
the whole London area and its neighbouring districts, deprived
of their food supply, would have wasted away from the deadly
effects of hunger and starvation. The dearth began about the
middle of March and lasted until the new crops were ripe.

It happened in the course of this summer that just as a
priest at Königsberg in Prussia was proposing to celebrate
Mass, a Scottish knight, Sir William Douglas, unexpectedly
came into his church. At sight of him, the priest refused to
complete the office he had started: and being asked why he
had abandoned the task he had begun he replied that he
would not celebrate in the presence of schismatics. Sir
William blazed with anger at this, and in the intensity of
the passion that filled him declared that the affair had been
arranged through the spite of Lord Clifford, whom, with the
other Englishmen, he made the target for a volley of threats.[2]
After he had withdrawn, the priest celebrated Mass; and
when it was over, Douglas, supported by his men, made a
furious attack on the Englishmen in the street outside and
maimed a squire, who, however, on receiving his injury,
hurled himself with drawn sword at Douglas and dealt him
a mortal wound that struck him lifeless to the ground; and at
the same time there fell with him two other Scots. The English nobles present in the city at this time were Lords Despenser,[3] Fitz Walter,[4] Beaumont,[5] Clifford and Bourgchier;*[6]

*The two removed from the list were not there according to some sources *in
the margin opposite the names of Beaumont and Clifford, which have been deleted.*

---

[3] Thomas, Lord Despenser (d. 1400), for whom see above, p. 352 n. He was
licensed to go to Prussia on 20 May 1391 (*Cal. Pat. R., 1388-92*, p. 413).
[4] Walter, Lord Fitz Walter (d. 1406), for whom see *G.E.C.*, v. 480-2.
[5] John, Lord Beaumont (d. 1396), for whom see *G.E.C.*, ii. 61.
[6] John, Lord Bourgchier (d. 1400), for whom see *G.E.C.*, ii. 247.

1391 qui accepto vexillo animavit illos et Anglicos alios transire ad campum, quibus ibidem existentibus adheserunt Alemanni, Boemici et illi de Geldr': Scotis vero solummodo Francigene ⟨se⟩[a] adjunxerunt. Tandem ad instanciam cujusdam magni illius patrie quieverunt a bello quamvis animo manebant perseveranter discordes.

Quo in tempore magna clades pestilencie in partibus occiduis et aquilonaribus Anglie fere per totam estatem invaluit,[1] in tantumque[b] aput Eboracum desevit quod xij. milia hominum morte consumpsit. Item xviij. die Julii clerici London' fecerunt ludum satis curiosum aput Skynnereswell' per dies quatuor duraturum, in quo tam Vetus quam Novum Testamentum oculariter ludendo monstrabant.[2] Item xxvj. die Julii cesus est comes Darmenak in Lombardia cum suis a facie exercitus comitis Virtutum:[3] nam prepropere bello se inmiscuit, quia si expectasset dominum Johannem Haukewode, qui in ejus succursum jam venire paraverat, forsitan vivus habito bono consilio evasisset; nunc autem ipse cum aliis ad numerum xj. milium perierunt, plures eorum ad montes fugerunt, ubi a rusticis illius patrie armati fuerunt capti, qui pro inmenso calore armorum prius introrsus nimium calefacti subito post deposicionem eorundem vitam perdentes miserabiliter sunt extincti. Johannes vero Haukewode, audito rumore de comite Darmenak quomodo cum suis interiit, noluit inire certamen cum tam magno exercitu triplo majori suo, callide retraxit se et suos ac sanus pervenit Padue, quamvis hostes ejus eum in eundo multipliciter infestassent; nam ripas fluminum per loca fregerunt et totam patriam circumcirca inundaverunt ne liberum transitum versus Paduam[c] optineret; ipse tamen cum suis salvus evasit et de suis ultra quatuor non amisit. Item de mense Augusti in partibus borealibus erat tempestas tonitrui fulguris et pluvie inaudita.

---

[a] ⟨se⟩ Winterbottom; MS. om. [b] The last three letters of this word are interlined. [c] MS. Padue.

---

[1] Cf. Walsingham, Hist. Ang., ii. 203-4.   [2] Above, p. 94 n.

[3] The correct date is 25 July. John, count of Armagnac, was killed before the walls of Alessandria by the forces of Giangaleazzo Visconti, lord of Milan ('the count of Vertus'). In the following account of the episode, the Monk, in common with other chroniclers, delays Sir John Hawkwood's retreat towards Padua until after the death of Armagnac; in fact he withdrew well before that event.

of whom the last-named, catching up the standard, urged his 1391
fellow nobles and other Englishmen to go to the scene. On
their arrival they were supported by men from Almain,
Bohemia, and Guelders; but the Scots were joined only by
the French. Under persuasion by one of the prominent men
of that country, they eventually stopped fighting, though at
heart they remained implacably opposed.

A great calamity at this time was the plague which almost
throughout the summer prevailed in western and northern
England.[1] At York it raged so violently that it killed 12,000
people. On 18 July the clerks of London staged at Skinners
Well a rather elaborate play, timed to last four days, in which
scenes from both the Old Testament and the New were
presented in dramatic form.[2] In Lombardy the count of
Armagnac and his men were smitten before the army of the
count of Vertus on 26 July.[3] He had rushed over-hastily
into action when by waiting for Sir John Hawkwood, who
was in instant readiness to come to his help, he might perhaps
have profited from good advice and escaped with his life. As
it was, however, he perished in company with as many as
11,000 others; large numbers fled into the hills, where, still
wearing their armour, they were captured by the local
peasantry. They had earlier become overheated in the swel-
tering conditions inside the armour, and upon its removal
their lives were miserably snuffed out. When John Hawkwood heard reports of the way in which the count of
Armagnac and his men had met their deaths, he declined to
join battle with so large an army, three times the size of his
own, and carried out a skilful withdrawal of his forces and
reached Padua in good fettle, despite the manifold harass-
ments to which he was subjected on the march by the enemy,
who, to deny him a free passage towards Padua, breached
river-banks here and there and flooded the whole surrounding
countryside; but none the less he escaped unscathed with his
men, of whom he did not lose above four. During August
there occurred in the north an unprecedented storm of
thunder, lightning, and rain.

Hawkwood was at the time a *condottiere* in the pay of Armagnac's ally, Florence.
See Bueno de Mesquita, *Giangaleazzo Visconti, Duke of Milan (1351-1402)*, pp.
130-2. For the phrase 'a facie', cf. 1 Kgs. (1 Sam.) vii. 10.

1391   Circa[1] principium vero Septembris rex tenuit suum consilium aput Cantuariam, ubi secundum condictum Francigene
ad tractandum de pace eciam confluissent si promissa servassent, et quia non comparuerunt confestim rex finem imposuit
consilio. Set antequam abinvicem discesserunt dux Gloucestr'
in presencia omnium qui aderant licenciam peciit a rege et
obtinuit eundi ad terram Prussye:[2] quo facto unusquisque
ad propria remeavit. Circa festum Nativitatis beate Marie
venerunt Francigene aput Eltham ad tractandum de pace
cum rege; qui accepto responso in Franciam sunt reversi.

Dux namque Gloucestr' modicum ante recessum suum
versus Prussyam misit ad ecclesiam Sancti Petri Westmon'
unum nobile vestimentum de panno aureo rubei coloris,
cum aurifragiis de nigro velvetto contextis[a] cum litteris grossis
sub hac figuracione 'T.A.' compositis cum cignis [b]de margarytis[b] ejusdem quantitatis intermixtis miro immo diverso modo
insutis, ac artificiose insertis vestimentum predictum mirifice
adornabant.[3] Fueruntque ejusdem vestimenti iij. cape j.
casula ij. tunicelle iij. albe cum stolis et manipulis unius secte.
Contulit eciam eodem die unum jocale argenteum et
deauratum ac subtiliter fabricatum, in cujus medio situatur
una fistula de berillo satis capax ad collocandum in ea Corpus
Dominicum cum in processione deferri immineat. Donavit
eciam ij. pelves argenteas et deauratas artificiose compositas
pro manuum locione ad magnum altare; item ij. candelabra,
scilicet ymagines argenteas et[c] deauratas vultus angelicos
preferentes; item unum thuribulum argenteum et deauratum
magni valoris. Ceterum hec omnia erant per eum antea
ecclesie predicte collocata; set per indenturam postea
reaccepit, et obligavit se heredes et executores suos obligacione pervalida dicte ecclesie quatinus ut omnia bona
premissa post mortem suam in adeo bono statu sepedicte

[a] *Underlined in MS.; cf.* brudatis *in the indenture and inventory, for which
see below, p. 480, n. 1.* [b-b] *Interlined.* [c] *A short erasure follows.*

[1] The following paragraph relates to a stage in the Anglo-French negotiations
referred to on pp. 456–8 above, but the dating is confused. A council was held at
Canterbury on 20 Aug. The king was at Eltham on 13–14 Sept. and again on 20
Sept., and it was probably on the latter occasion that he met the French envoys:
Jean de Saquainville, lord of Blaru, and Bègue de Villaines are known to have
been in England in the 2nd half of Sept. See P.R.O., E. 403/533, 12 Aug.; *Cal.
Pat. R., 1388–92*, pp. 476, 481; Moranvillé, in *B.E.C.*, 1 (1889), 360 n.

About[1] the beginning of September the king held his 1391
council at Canterbury, where, according to the agreed
arrangement, the French, too, if they had kept their
promises, would have joined those present for peace talks:
and as they failed to appear the king speedily put an end to
the council. Before the councillors went their several ways
the duke of Gloucester, in the presence of all who attended,
asked and received the king's leave to go to Prussia;[2] and this
done everybody returned home. About the feast of the
Nativity of the Virgin [8 September] the French came to
Eltham for peace talks with the king; and after receiving his
answer they went back to France.

Shortly before his departure for Prussia the duke of
Gloucester sent to the church of St. Peter, Westminster, a
splendid vestment of cloth of gold, red in colour, with or-
phreys of black velvet embroidered with the capital letters
T.A. in monogram interspersed with swans carried out in
matching pearls stitched on in a remarkable way, or rather
variety of ways, and cunningly worked in, so as to add
wonderfully to the beauty of the vestment.[3] It was composed
of three copes, a chasuble, two tunicles, and three albs, with
stoles and maniples, all matching. On the same day he also
presented a cleverly made jewel of silver and gilt, having in
the middle of it a beryl cylinder spacious enough to contain
the Host·when it is intended to be carried in procession.
Further gifts were two silver and gilt basins of skilful work-
manship for the washing of the celebrant's hands at the high
altar; two candelabra in the form of silver and gilt images
with angels' faces; and a silver and gilt censer of great value.
All these gifts had been bestowed by him upon the church of
Westminster on an earlier occasion; but he subsequently took
them back by indenture, entering on behalf of himself,
his heirs, and executors, into a stringently drawn bond in the
church's favour that after his death all the foregoing goods

[2] Cf. Rymer, *Foedera*, vii. 705–6. The licence is dated at Westminster, 16
Sept. 1391. Gloucester was given power to treat with the Grand Master of the
Teutonic Order on behalf of Richard II.

[3] 'T.' and 'A.' were the initial letters of Thomas of Woodstock and Eleanor
('Alianora'), his wife; she was the daughter of Humphrey de Bohun, earl of
Hereford, Essex, and Northampton (d. 1373), and the device on the Bohun badge
was a swan.

1391 ecclesie restituerentur quo ea accepit; que jam in ultima
donacione predictorum bonorum sunt rupte voluntarie per
eum et pro perpetuo annullate.[1]

Igitur xxvj. die Septembris postquam commendasset se
beato Petro et sancto Edwardo predicte ecclesie patronis
prefatus dux Gloucestr' iter suum arripuit versus Pruyssyam,
et circa medium mensis Octobris mare intravit; transivitque
cum eo comes Staffordie, qui in ista estate filiam ducis predicti duxit in uxorem.[2] Circa principium mensis Octobris[3]
dominus Thomas Arundell' Eborac' archiepiscopus factus
est cancellarius domini regis. Item xvij. die Octobris venit
Damianus de Cathaneys nuncius domini pape in Angliam.
[a]Item xvij. die Octobris dominus Johannes Clanvowe miles
egregius in quodam vico juxta Constantinopolim in Grecia
diem clausit extremum: quam ob causam dominus Willelmus
Nevyle ejus comes in itinere, quem non minus ⟨quam⟩[b]
se ipsum diligebat, inconsolabiliter dolens numquam postea
sumpsit cibum, unde transactis duobus diebus sequentibus
in eodem vico lamentabiliter expiravit. Erant isti milites
inter Anglicos famosi viri nobiles et strenui ac eciam de
genere claro producti.[4] Item in ista estate in quadam insula
versus Jerosolim obiit cum magna contricione dominus de
Clyfford' miles juvenis fortis et audax.[a][5]

Parliamentum. Tercio die Novembris aput Westmonasterium tenuit rex suum parliamentum; duravitque in secundam
diem Decembris; in quo plura fuerunt mota et quedam ad
effectum deducta. Primo namque quia stapula de lana
modicum profuit domino regi isto anno jam transacto, ideo
p. 205 statutum est ut dicta stapula a festo Pasche proximo / futuro
staret deinceps continue aput Calesiam.[6] Statutum vero
contra provisores editum noluerunt isti de parliamento

[a-a] *In the lower margin.*   [b] *MS. om.*

---

[1] Gloucester had given the benefactions mentioned in this paragraph to Westminster Abbey on 1 Dec. 1387, the abbot and convent promising in return to
keep his anniversary and that of his wife, and this agreement was made by indenture. Subsequently, and no doubt on recalling his gifts, the duke released the
monks from their obligation. Was this episode connected with the coolness
between Gloucester and the Abbey mentioned above (p. 380)? See W.A.M. 9474*;
Liber Niger Quaternus, fos. 85ᵛ, 100; J. Wickham Legg, 'On An Inventory of the
Vestry in Westminster Abbey taken in 1388' in *Archaeologia* lii (1890), 284–5.

should be restored to it in as good condition as he had 1391
received them; but now in the final disposition of this
property both indenture and bond were arbitrarily broken
by him and rendered permanently void.[1]

After commending himself to St. Peter and St. Edward,
patrons of the church of Westminster, the duke set out on
26 September for Prussia, putting to sea about mid-October.
With him travelled the earl of Stafford, who during the summer had married the duke's daughter.[2] Thomas Arundel,
archbishop of York, became the king's chancellor about the
beginning of October;[3] and on the 17th Damian de Cataneis
arrived in England as a papal nuncio. It was also on 17
October that in a village near Constantinople in Greece the
life of Sir John Clanvow, a distinguished knight, came to its
close, causing to his companion on the march, Sir William
Nevill, for whom his love was no less than for himself, such
inconsolable sorrow that he never took food again and two
days afterwards breathed his last, greatly mourned, in the
same village. These two knights were men of high repute
among the English, gentlemen of mettle and descended from
illustrious families.[4] During this summer, on an island on the
way to Jerusalem, there died, deeply penitent, Lord Clifford,
a young knight of great courage and daring.[5]

Parliament. The king held a parliament at Westminster
on 3 November which lasted until 2 December. Several
matters were raised, and some brought to fruition. In the
first place, since the wool-staple had been of small profit
to the king in the preceding year, it was ordained that from
the following Easter [14 April 1392] onwards it should
be set up permanently at Calais.[6] Those who attended the
parliament refused any repeal of the statute of provisors;

---

[2] Thomas de Stafford, 3rd earl of Stafford (d. 1392), married Anne, the eldest
of Gloucester's 3 daughters (*G.E.C.*, xii (1), 179–80; ibid., v. 729)'.
[3] In fact on 27 Sept.
[4] See McFarlane, *Lancastrian Kings and Lollard Knights*, pp. 165–6, 230–2,
and above, p. 432. I am indebted to Mr. Andrew Prescott for the suggestion that
the words 'inter Anglicos' point to the Monk's use of a written source, possibly
a news-letter, at this point.
[5] The probable date of Thomas, Lord Clifford's death is 4 Oct. 1391 (P.R.O.,
C. 136/71/17; cf. *G.E.C.*, iii. 292).
[6] Until the next parliament (which proved to be that of Jan.–Feb. 1393) wool
leaving England was to be taken to Calais; but there were also to be home staples
in places designated by the council (*R.P.*, iii. 285; and see above, p. 454 and nn.).

1391 ullatenus revocare; ob reverenciam tamen summi pontificis volunt bene permittere quoslibet causa voti solvendi vel salutis anime causa transire ad sedem apostolicam et suas devociones facere utrobique:[1] aliud responsum ab eis non potuit papalis nuncius obtinere, sicque recessit;[2] set Damianus hic remansit. Item isti de parliamento inter cetera ordinarunt quod omnia perquisita religiosorum nondum illis ante festum Michaelis[a] per regem confirmata confestim elapso illo festo universa ad manus regias[b] cum suis juribus integraliter devenirent;[3] sicque ad fiscum regium infinitas pecunias ante festum sancti Michaelis habunde[c] officiarii, cancellarius scilicet et thesaurarius, cumularunt. Plura alia fuerunt ordinata in isto parliamento que in aperto nondum cercius venerunt.[4]

Dominus Thomas dux Gloucestr' tendens versus Prussyam multa pericula et jacturas sustinuit in mari, nam remige destituto inter fluctus fuit ad diversa loca jactatus. Demum incidit in mare quoddam nigerrimum et quasi, ut videbatur, immobile, ubi propter aeris densitatem omnes existentes in aliis navibus cum eodem ilico ab eo fuerunt segregati; propter quod aliquas naves cum suis bonis onustas ibidem amisit in diversis locis pelagi spaciosi absortas, ibi quoque protunc perdidit homines, equos optimos, pannos eciam magni valoris et jocalia precii inaudati: nec mirum, cum venti neque mocio aquarum illos juvare de tam periculoso loco ullatenus valuerunt. Dux vero in tam infausto loco terribiliter constitutus et de vita sua quodammodo desperatus varia Deo et ejus sanctis obnixe emisit vota pro salvacione sui ipsius et suorum. Confestim de illa maris ingluvie divina favente virtute fuit

----

[a] festum Michaelis: cf. below, p. 508.   [b] A short erasure follows.   [c] dicti expunged after this word.

----

[1] Liberties which had never been in doubt. In fact the king was given a discretionary power in the enforcement of the Statute of Provisors until the next parliament (*R.P.*, iii. 285; and see above, p. 454 and n., and below, p. 512 and n.).

[2] He left on or after 12 Dec. (*Diplomatic Correspondence of Richard II*, ed. Perroy, p. 230).

[3] A reference to 15 Richard II, *cap.* 5, requiring property held by nominees to the use of religious to be amortized before 29 Sept. 1392 (and also bringing gilds, fraternities, and the common property of towns within the scope of the legislation on mortmain) (*S.R.*, ii. 79–80; and for comment, J. M. W. Bean, *The Decline of English Feudalism, 1215–1540* (Manchester, 1968), pp. 125–6;

but out of respect for the supreme pontiff they were quite 1391
willing to allow anybody to visit the apostolic see for the
purpose of discharging a vow or securing the salvation of his
soul, and to perform his devotions there or in this country.[1]
The papal nuncio could get no other answer out of them, and
with this he departed;[2] but Damian stayed on here. The
parliament further laid down, among other things, that all
property acquired by people of religion and not confirmed to
them by the king before Michaelmas [29 September 1392]
should, without exception, pass forthwith after that feast in
its entirety and with all its rights into the hands of the
Crown.[3] As a consequence ministers, namely the chancellor
and the treasurer, had by Michaelmas accumulated untold
sums of money to fill the royal treasury to overflowing.
Several other ordinances were made in this parliament which
have not yet been authoritatively disclosed.[4]

On his voyage towards Prussia Thomas duke of Gloucester
suffered many hazards and losses at sea. When he had
dropped his pilot, he was storm-tossed by the waves from one
place to another until he eventually entered waters enveloped
in darkness and, as it seemed, almost motionless. Here, owing
to thick fog, all his fellow travellers in the other ships quickly
became separated from him, and as a result he lost a number
of vessels with their goods aboard, all swallowed up at different points in the expanse of ocean, and his losses on this
occasion moreover included men, very fine horses, cloths of
great value, and jewels of unheard-of costliness. Nor was this
surprising, when neither wind nor current served to help
them out of jeopardy. Placed in this luckless and alarming
situation, and near to despairing of survival, the duke
urgently poured out to God and his saints all sorts of vows
for the deliverance of himself and his companions. The divine
power was exercised in his favour and he was swiftly and

J. L. Barton, 'The Medieval Use', in *Law Quarterly Rev.* lxxxi (1965), 562 ff.;
and S. Raban, 'Mortmain in Medieval England', in *Past and Present*, 62 (Feb.
1974), 14).

[4] A reference to acts of the parliament still unpublished after the proclamation
of the statutes of this parliament in the counties in or about the beginning of Mar.
1392. For an example see the ordinance relating to the king's archers referred to
in *Cal. Pat. R., 1391–1396*, p. 96; and for the proclamation in the counties,
P.R.O., E. 403/536, 4 Mar.

1391 miraculose ereptus et in mare magis notum, scilicet prope
Scociam, est appulsus. Demum parum ante festum Natalis
Domini dux ipse cum suis omnibus qui cum ipso remans-
erant sanus et incolumis applicuit aput Bamburgh'.[1]

Dominus noster rex tenuit suum Natale aput[a] Langeleye
in Chilterne; ad quem accesserunt Aquitannenses, dicentes
quod ab antiquo solebant gubernari per reges Anglorum et
nullatenus per alios super se ad nutum regium constitutos,
solo principe Wallie vero[b] herede regni Anglorum excepto.
Hec et alia habuerunt dicti Aquitannenses in scriptis redacta
diversis sigillis munitis, que omnia tradiderunt domino nostro
regi; que postquam ex ordine perlegisset percepit evidenter
hiisdem litteris ducem Lancastr' nollent in eorum dominum
sive rectorem habere; habitoque super hoc consilio dictas
litteras suo sigillo sigillatas duci Lancastr' una cum voluntate
sua et hominibus supradictis per quendam suum secretarium
destinavit.[2] Quibus perceptis et visis ac audita domini regis
voluntate post multa verba dictis Aquitannensibus irrever-
enter prolata litteram suam patentem super ducatum
Aquitannie sibi a domino rege concessam coram eis perlegit
statimque confregit. Sicque quievit Aquitannicorum
commocio.

Item xxij. die Decembris abbas Westmon' intravit aquam et
iter arripuit versus Romam; habuitque licenciam a rege
absentare se ab Anglia per duos annos, cupiens interim[c] se
a debito liberare.[3]

1392 Duodecimo die Februarii[4] tenuit rex suum consilium aput
Westmonasterium; duravitque usque in quintumdecimum
diem ejusdem mensis; in quo domini temporales (ac eciam
viri ecclesiastici) vehementer insteterunt contra dominum
Alexandrum Nevyle et ducem Hibernie ita quod nullatenus
ad pristinum statum reverterentur neque in terram Anglie
revenirent causa more quovis pacto, asserentes ista a domino
rege ea racione petisse ut inde murmur populi sedaretur.

---

[a] Ch *deleted after this word.*   [b] reg' *deleted after this word.*   [c] *Written
over an erasure.*

---

[1] Cf. Walsingham, *Hist. Ang.*, ii. 202.
[2] On 30 Nov. 1390, in response to Gascon protest, Richard II revoked the
resumption of previous grants of lands and revenues in Aquitaine executed earlier
in the year, on the occasion of the grant of the duchy to Lancaster; the Monk

miraculously snatched from the sea's greedy maw and carried 1391
into more familiar waters off the Scottish coast. Eventually
the duke, with all who had not become separated from him,
landed safe and sound at Bamburgh shortly before Christmas.[1]

The king kept Christmas at Langley in the Chilterns, where
he was visited by representatives from Aquitaine, who
claimed that from times long past they had been accustomed
to be governed by the English Crown and not by third parties
set in authority over them by the exercise of the king's will,
with the single exception of the prince of Wales as the true
heir to the English throne. The Aquitanians had written statements, variously sealed, embodying these and other matters,
all of which they handed to the king; and when he had read
through the whole series it was crystal-clear to him from
these documents that the Aquitanians would not consent to
have the duke of Lancaster as their lord or ruler. After consultations about the matter, he caused the documents, under
his own seal, and a statement of his decision to be conveyed
to the duke of Lancaster by one of his secretaries, who was
accompanied by the Aquitanians.[2] On seeing and examining
the documents and learning the king's decision, the duke
addressed the Aquitanians at great length and with scant
courtesy and then read out to them and forthwith tore up
the king's patent granting him the duchy of Aquitaine. So
turmoil was replaced by calm in Aquitanian affairs.

On 22 December the abbot of Westminster took ship to
begin his journey to Rome: he had the king's leave to be
away from England for two years, in the course of which he
wanted to clear himself of debt.[3]

The king held at Westminster on 12 February[4] a council 1392
which lasted until the 15th. The temporal lords (and the
ecclesiastics, too) were most emphatic in their insistence that
Alexander Nevill and the duke of Ireland should not be restored
to their former positions and should on no account return to
England to stay. The reason advanced for making this demand
of the king was the need to silence popular murmuring.

has misdated and misunderstood this episode. See Rymer, *Foedera*, vii. 662,
687–8; Armitage-Smith, *John of Gaunt*, pp. 370–2; *Palmer*, pp. 154–6.

[3] In fact Colchester went to the curia partly on the king's business; cf. P.R.O.,
E. 403/536, 13 Dec., where he is described as 'in secreto nuncius regis'. See also
Liber Niger Quaternus, fo. 87ᵛ.   [4] So too P.R.O., E. 403/536, 16 Dec.

1392 Annuit eis rex benigne petitis et concessit quod sine spe revertendi pro perpetuo de regno Anglie relegarentur: unde dicti domini singuli et universi regraciantes ei multum feceruntque eidem sacramentum de novo quod vellent secum stare contra quoscumque offensores ac hostes externos seu internos, promittentesque eum juvare universaliter pro viribus contra omnes, concessa sibi tunc plena potestate regendi suum regnum ad libitum cunctis temporibus post futuris.[1]

Concessit eciam tunc dominus rex duci Gloucestr' custodiam tocius Hibernie per tres annos sequentes, quibus de fisco regio perciperet annuatim x. libras; finitis vero dictis tribus annis ipse deinceps suis propriis sumptibus et expensis illam sua industria gubernaret, reddendo singulis annis domino regi quingentas libras; et si quid de ferocibus Hibernensibus possit adquirere, [a]sibi et[a] suis heredibus maribus succederet sine contradiccione in evum.[2] Item eodem consilio durante electi fuerunt ad tractandum cum Francigenis dux Lancastr', episcopus Dunolm' et alii valentes et industriosi.[3]

Quo in tempore aput Castrum Bernardi fuit dolose per prodicionem cujusdam Thome Blande Willelmus Bekwyth occisus.[4] Item xxv. die Februarii dux Lancastr' cepit licenciam a rege transeundi versus Cales', et circa principium mensis Marcii venit Cales': fueruntque ibidem nostri tractatores de pace cum Francigenis aput Seint Homeres in Francia per quinque septimanas et amplius (habentes tamen recursum continuum semper interim ad Calesiam) et profecto satis modicum inibi profecerunt. Sicque quasi inanes et sine spe concordie circa principium mensis Aprilis in Angliam redierunt.[5]

[a-a] *Interlined.*

---

[1] Cf. the petition of the commons in parliament on 2 Dec. 1391 that the king should be as free in his regality, liberty, and dignity as any of his predecessors (*R.P.*, iii. 286).

[2] Gloucester was not appointed the king's lieutenant in Ireland until 29 Apr. 1392 or a little later, and by 23 July 1392 the appointment, for 15 years, had been superseded (*Cal. Cl. R., 1389–92*, p. 463; Rymer, *Foedera*, vii. 722; *Roll of the Proceedings of the King's Council in Ireland . . . A.D. 1392–3*, ed. J. Graves (R.S., 1877), p. 255, where, however, the king's letter is assigned to 1393). (For advice on this passage I am indebted to Professor G. O. Sayles.)

[3] The envoys other than Lancaster and Walter Skirlaw, bishop of Durham, were Richard Ronhale, John Holland, earl of Huntingdon, and Thomas Percy (P.R.O., E. 403/536, 4 Mar.).

The king graciously agreed to their demand and accepted that 1392
the banishment of the two from England should be permanent and should preclude any hope of return. For this the
lords, one and all, expressed their deep gratitude, renewing
their oaths of readiness to support him against any attackers
and enemies whatever, foreign or domestic, and promising
every assistance to the limit of their power against all comers;
while at the same time the king was accorded full power to
rule his kingdom as he pleased for all time to come.[1]

The king granted to the duke of Gloucester at this time the
keeping of the whole of Ireland for the next three years, in
each of which he was to draw from the royal treasury £10.
When the three years were ended, however, he was thenceforward to govern the country at his own costs and charges
and by his own efforts, paying the king £50 yearly, while
anything he won from the wild Irish was to pass incontest-
ably to himself and his male heirs in perpetuity.[2] Those
chosen during the same council to negotiate with the French
were the duke of Lancaster, the bishop of Durham, and other
estimable and skilful persons.[3]

It was at this time that at Barnard Castle William Beckwith
was craftily brought to his death through the treachery of
one Thomas Bland.[4] On 25 February the duke of Lancaster
took leave of the king to cross to Calais, where he arrived
about the middle of March. Our representatives there for
peace talks with the French spent five weeks or more at St.
Omer in France (with constantly repeated visits to Calais
throughout the period); but it was scanty progress indeed
that they made there; and thus, empty-handed and with no
hope of agreement, they returned to England about the
beginning of April.[5]

[4] Cf. *Annales Ricardi Secundi*, ed. H. T. Riley (R.S., 1866), pp. 160–1, attri-
buting responsibility for Beckwith's death to friends of Sir Richard Rokeley, for
whom see Bellamy, in *Bulletin of the John Rylands Library*, xlvii (1964–5), 256.
See also *Cal. Pat. R., 1391–6*, p. 265; above, p. 442 and n., and below, p. 516.

[5] Ronhale, however, did not return until 20 Apr. (P.R.O., E. 364/26, m. 54).
For the conference, which took place at Amiens, see Moranvillé, in *B.E.C.* 1
(1889), 360–2, 371 ff., and *Palmer*, p. 145. The French envoys were the dukes
of Berry, Burgundy, and Bourbon. See also above, p. 456 and n., and below, pp.
490–2. St. Omer was one of two places (the other being Boulogne) chosen as
possible places of residence for the French king during the conference of kings
planned for June 1392.

1392 Dominus noster rex tenuit suum Pascha aput Eltham. Item xxiij. die Aprilis dominus noster rex aput Westmonasterium fecit solempnes, immo sumptuosas, exequias pro sorore sua

p. 206 Matilda / comitissa Sancti Pauli[1] in cereis et luminaribus circa feretrum illius, in pannis nigris et aureis ac pauperum distribucione (nam in ista erogacione quilibet pauper accepit ad minus iiij. denarios), item in vexillis et labaris circa feretrum *ejusdem erectis,* que mirifice rutilarunt; erant enim depicta in illis omnia arma regum Christianorum, ducum eciam et comitum Anglicorum: que omnia excepta pauperum distribucione precepto domini regis ecclesie Westmon' erant relicta. Item vij. die Maii venit dux Gerlie locuturus cum rege; fuerat namque London' et cum rege quasi per totum mensem predictum.

Consilium aput Stamford'. Quo eciam mense, scilicet xxv. die, dominus rex aput Stamford' tenuit suum consilium ita magnum sicut parliamentum, nam de omnibus comitatibus Anglie venerunt milites et viri periciores tocius Anglie,[2] quos dux Gerlie intuens stupefactus dicebat se numquam vidisse tam nobilem nec tam generosam communitatem alicujus regni, asserens eos una die sufficere dimicare contra totum mundum habito bono regimine; item suspirando affirmabat nullum regem sub sole tantam ac talem communitatem habere: et ideo hortabatur dominum regem confidere in Domino ac in jure suo, et nullo modo eum cum falsissimis Francigenis concordare nec ad verba illorum tam ampullosa expavescere, quia si contingat eum in Francia equitare ac regi Francorum bellum dare, ipsumque cum ejus hominibus armorum in ejus adjutorium sibi occurrere lato in campo viriliter contra suos adversarios dimicantem paratum invenire, nullo pavore concussum.[3] Hec et hiis similia, immo hiis majora, postquam predictus nobilis dux Gerlie fuerat prosecutus, finem imposuit verbis suis; cujus animositatem viri strenui et cordati multa laudum commendacione attollunt, desides vero et vecordes illam postponunt.

a-a MS. erectis ejusdem.

[1] For whom see above, p. 450 and n. For the funeral see Harvey, *Westminster Abbey and its Estates in the Middle Ages*, p. 378 n.

[2] Cf. Walsingham, *Hist. Ang.*, ii. 206; Knighton, *Chronicon*, ii. 318-19, and *Cal. Cl. R., 1389-92*, pp. 562-3. For the attendance of knights see also P.R.O.,

The king kept Easter [14 April] at Eltham; and on 23
April caused the funeral rites of his sister Maud, countess
of St. Pol,[1] to be performed with great ceremoniousness and,
indeed, lavish expenditure at Westminster, with candles and
lights around the bier, black and gold hangings, doles to the
poor (each of whom received in this bestowal of charity at
least 4*d*.), and banners and standards set up about the bier
and making a wonderfully brilliant display, emblazoned as
they were with all the arms of the kings of Christendom and
the dukes and earls of England. All these things, with the
exception of the alms distributed to the poor, were by the
king's order left in the possession of the church of Westminster. The duke of Guelders arrived on 7 May to talk
with the king: he was in London and in the king's company
for almost the whole month.

Council at Stamford. It was also in this month, namely
on the 25th, that the king held at Stamford a council as well
attended as a parliament, for from every county there came
to it those knights and other gentlemen with the greatest
wealth of experience in the whole of England.[2] They presented a sight to astonish the duke of Guelders, who said he
had never in any kingdom seen commoners of such
impressiveness and breeding, and declared that, well led, they
were equal to a conflict on one and the same day against the
entire world. He added, with a sigh, that no king under the
sun had commoners of such numbers and quality, and he
therefore urged the king to put his trust in the Lord and in
his own right and not to come to any kind of agreement with
those arch-deceivers, the French, or be dismayed by their
bombastic language, for if it ever came about that the king
was campaigning in France and joined battle with the French
king, he would find the duke ready to come to his aid in the
field with his men-at-arms and to fight it out man to man
against his enemies, unshaken and unafraid.[3] After pursuing
these and similar, indeed even stronger, arguments, the noble
duke of Guelders concluded his observations. His ardent
spirit has been highly praised and approved by men of mettle
and courage, but the indolent and chicken-hearted disparage it.

E. 403/538, 12 July. The council was summoned for 24 May.
    [3] Cf. above, p. 372 and n. The bellicose speech is entirely in character.

1392 Igitur[a] incepto consilio in presencia dictorum militum dux
Lancastr' voluntatem Francorum lucide explicavit, dicens
illos primo peciisse regem Anglorum eis remittere jus et
clamium suum totaliter que aliquo modo habuit vel habere
poterat ad regnum Francorum pro perpetuo et quod flores
deliciarum de suis armis omnino deponeret; secundo petiverunt ducatum Normannie et comitatum de Artoys pro
perpetuo eciam eis remitti cum suis appendiciis universis;
tercio quod omnia ea que in Acquitannia quocumque titulo
adquisierunt vel ad manus eorum quomodocumque deven-
erunt et in manibus eorundem erant pronunc dux Berrye
ad totam vitam suam tantum pacifice possideret sine
calumpnia seu impugnacione quacumque, mortuo vero duce
de Berrye predicto Aquitannia et Vasconia integre cum suis
pertinenciis universis rediret ad ducem Lancastr' et heredes
suos in perpetuum, ita tamen quod dux ipse et heredes sui
pro tota Aquitannia regi Francorum redderet homagium
consuetum.[1] Ista vero in nullo placuerunt communitati
Anglie, quia dixerunt stultum fore et nimis dampnosum regi
et sue corone ut pro comodo unius persone tantas et tam
pulcras dominaciones perpetualiter amitteret,[b] que regibus
Anglorum per tam longa tempora cum suis juribus hereditarie
subjacuerunt. Super hiis namque contencionibus dominus
rex de consilio ducis Lancastr' non obstante communitate
sua in quibusdam vellet condescendere peticionibus Gallicorum, et hoc propter bonum pacis, et in quibusdam non,
quia vellet eorum peticiones modificare ita ut singulos ex
utraque parte pacificaret: unde super isto negocio direxit
quosdam nuncios ad Gallicos ut capta treuga ipsi ex utraque
parte interim melius de hujusmodi deliberarent; quod et
factum est.[2] Nam firmata erat treuga inter Anglicos et
Francos a festo sancti Michaelis proximo nunc futuro usque

---

[a] In the margin, a hand pointing to this passage.　　　　[b] MS. amittere.

[1] The English proposed that Berry should hold Poitou for life of the duke of
Aquitaine, and that after his death the county should be added to the duchy.
See on these negotiations Moranvillé, in B.E.C., 1 (1889), 371; Palmer, in T.R.H.S.,
5th ser., xvi (1966), 87 n.; and Vale, English Gascony, 1399-1453, p. 28 nn.
[2] The envoys on this occasion included John Gilbert, bishop of St. David's,
William Montague, earl of Salisbury, Thomas Percy, and Richard Ronhale. Ron-
hale left London on 25 June. On 5 May 1392, before the council at Stamford,
Richard had confirmed the extension of the truce of 1389 until 29 Sept. 1393;

When the council began, the duke of Lancaster in the presence of the knights above-mentioned gave a clear account of the objectives of the French, explaining that their first demand was that the English king should renounce for ever all right or claim that he in any way had or might have to the French throne and that he should drop the fleurs-de-lis altogether from his arms; secondly, they demanded that the duchy of Normandy and the county of Artois, with all their appanages, should also be surrendered to them in perpetuity; thirdly, that everything in Aquitaine that they had acquired by any title whatever or that had in any way come into their possession and was at present in their hands should be peaceably held, for his lifetime only, by the duke of Berry without claim or dispute, but after the death of the duke of Berry Aquitaine and Gascony with all their appurtenances should revert in their entirety to the duke of Lancaster and his heirs for ever, though on the understanding that the duke and his heirs would do the customary homage to the French king for the whole of Aquitaine.[1] These terms were not at all to the liking of the English commons, who said that it was absurd, besides being extremely damaging to the king and the Crown, that for the benefit of a single person he should suffer the permanent loss of such extensive and such fair domains, which, with their attendant rights, had for so long been hereditarily subject to the kings of England. In the clash of opinions over this, the king, advised by the duke of Lancaster and in spite of the commons, would have liked, in the interests of peace, to make some concessions to the demands of the French and to refuse others, since he wanted to secure such modifications in the terms as would appease all members of both parties. He accordingly dispatched envoys on this business to the French, so that a truce might be called during which both sides could improve their consideration of the matter; and this was in fact done.[2] A truce was proclaimed between the English and French, to last from the Michaelmas [29 September] then next to come until the same feast in

and he repeated his confirmation on 20 July (Rymer, *Foedera*, vii. 714-22, 728-9; see also P.R.O., E. 364/26, m. 54; ibid., E. 403/538, 11 July).

1392 ad illud et idem festum anno revoluto. Sicque a tumultibus bellicis interim quieverunt.

^aItem circa finem Maii obiit in Brabancia aput Lovayn magister Alexander Nevyll' quondam archiepiscopus Eboracensis.^{a1} Item isto anno fuit statutum quod omnes habentes bona sive redditus^b ad valorem xl. librarum in Anglia milites efficerentur.² Quo in tempore dominus rex consilio sui cancellarii et thesaurarii omnes suas curias de London' ad Eboracum^c removit: putabant isti officiarii per hoc non modicum dampnificare civitatem London' set pocius propter hoc multa majora dampna intulerunt regi et hominibus regni quam jam dicte nobili civitati, nam pauperes propter earundem curiarum remocionem sua placita perdiderunt, tum quia non habebant expensas eundi ad tam locum remotum, tum quia propter earum tam subitam amocionem ^d⟨n⟩escientes consulere seipsos ⟨super⟩ causis eorum ita fuerunt animo ⟨co⟩nsternati et attoniti quod quodam⟨m⟩odo facti sunt pene insensati.^{d3} Incitabant quoque isti officiarii dominum nostrum regem contra Londonienses propter quasdam sediciones inter illos et quosdam suorum famulorum nuperius perpetratas. Favebant instanter parti istorum officiariorum dux Lancastr' et comes Huntyngdon'. Volentes igitur tanquam iniquitatis filii⁴ (isti scilicet officiarii cum aliis sibi adjunctis) omnem maliciam quam poterant excogitare Londoniensibus ostendere, conceperunt unum breve regium contra Londonienses prefatos satis terribile et valde horribile, sic quod aures audientis faceret pertinnire.⁵ Continebat namque articulos graves quamplures et precipue de gentibus in civitate valde nocivos, insuper precipiendo mandantes quatinus proximo die post festum Nativitatis Sancti Johannis Baptiste etc., prout sequitur:

Ricardus⁶ Dei gracia rex Anglie et Francie et dominus Hibernie majori et vicecomitibus necnon omnibus et singulis aldermannis

---

^{a–a} *Added in the margin.*   ^b redditus *repeated but deleted the second time.*
^c *The letters* re *(a false start for* removit*) have been expunged after this word.*
(This is the end of a line.)   ^{d–d} *Added in the margin and damaged at the edge.*

---

¹ Nevill died on 16 May (*Historians of the Church of York*, ed. Raine, ii. 424).
² For writs ordering this distraint but covering only 7 counties and London, see *Letter Book H*, p. 378; *Cal. Cl. R., 1392–6*, p. 82.
³ Cf. *Vita Ricardi Secundi*, p. 133; and for the writs effecting the removal of the courts to York see *Cal. Cl. R., 1389–92*, pp. 466–7, 565; *Cal. Pat. R., 1391–6*,

the following year. And so, for the time being, there was rest 1392 from the turmoil of war.

About the end of May the death occurred at Louvain in Brabant of Alexander Nevill, sometime archbishop of York.[1] During this year it was ordained that all possessors of property or rents in England worth £40 [a year] should take up knighthood.[2] On the advice of his chancellor and the treasurer the king removed all his courts from London to York: the ministers thought thereby to deal a damaging blow to the city of London, but it was rather upon the king and the people of the kingdom that far greater damage was in consequence inflicted than on London, since through the removal of the courts the poor had to abandon their pleas, not only because they had not the money to travel to a place so far away but also because, owing to the suddenness of the transfer and their inability to be their own advisers about their lawsuits, they were so dismayed and shocked that they could be said to be almost out of their minds.[3] The ministers concerned had set the king against the Londoners because of certain acts of mutiny they had recently committed against some of the ministers' underlings. Emphatic in their support of the ministers' case were the duke of Lancaster and the earl of Huntingdon. In their desire, natural in children of wickedness[4] (I mean the ministers and others associated with them), to show the Londoners all the ill-will they could think of, they composed against them a royal writ so fearsome and utterly hair-raising as to cause 'the ears of whosoever heard it to tingle'.[5] It contained a large number of articles, of a serious nature and highly and specially damaging about the people of the city, and moreover an order and command that on the day after the Nativity of St. John the Baptist [25 June] etc., as follows:

Richard[6] by the grace of God king of England and France and lord of Ireland to the mayor and sheriffs and to all and singular the aldermen

p. 65; *Letter Book H*, p. 378; and for the ensuing events, C. M. Barron, 'The quarrel of Richard II with London, 1392-7', in *Reign of Richard II*, pp. 178-9.
    [4] Cf. 2 Kgs. (2 Sam.) iii. 34; vii. 10; 1 Chron. xvii. 9; Hos. x. 9, etc.
    [5] Cf. 1 Kgs. (1 Sam.) iii. 11; 4 Kgs. (2 Kgs.) xxi. 12; Jer. xix. 3.
    [6] Cf. Close Roll, 15 Richard II (P.R.O., C. 54/233, cited as *Cl. R.*), m. 3. See also *Cal. Cl. R., 1389-92*, p. 466; *Letter Book H*, p. 377; *Lords' Reports on the Dignity of a Peer*, iii. 741.

1392 London' salutem. Quibusdam certis de causis nos specialiter moventibus, vobis precipimus firmiter injungentes quod quacumque excusacione cessante et omnibus aliis pretermissis in propriis personis vestris una cum viginti et quatuor personis concivibus vestris de validioribus et magis*a* sufficientibus communariis dicte civitatis sitis coram nobis et consilio nostro aput Notyngham in crastino Sancti Johannis Baptiste proximo futuro, plenam et sufficientem potestatem communitatis dicte civitatis nostre*a* vobiscum tunc deferentes, ad respondendum pro vobis et communitate predicta super hiis que vobis ex parte nostra ibidem exponentur et ad faciendum ulterius et recipiendum quod per nos et dictum consilium nostrum tunc*a* contigerit ordinari. Et hoc sub *b*pena forisfacture*b* vite et membrorum ac omnium que nobis forisfacere poteritis nullatenus omittatis aliquibus concessionibus, libertatibus, privilegiis seu consuetudinibus in contrarium concessis sive usitatis non obstantibus. Proviso semper quod vos pro custodia civitatis nostre predicte*a* ac pace et tranquillitate ejusdem pro tempore absencie vestre sic ordinetis prout vos nobis vestro periculo inde respondere volueritis. Et habeatis ibi hoc breve. Teste meipso aput Staunford xxix. die Maii anno regni nostri quintodecimo.

Sequitur retornacio[1] super breve predicto:

p. 207   Nos Johannes Hende major et aldermannus civitatis London', Johannes Shadworth' et Henricus Vannere vicecomites et aldermanni ejusdem civitatis et omnes alii et singuli aldermanni civitatis predicte, videlicet Johannes Hadlee, Willelmus Venour, Adam Bamme, Willelmus Baret, Johannes Frossh', Willelmus More, Johannes Loveye, Adam Karlill', Thomas Vyvent, Johannes Franceys, Willelmus Shyryngham, Henricus Bamme, et Robertus de Excestr' prior ecclesie Sancte Trinitatis London', Thomas Wilford', Drugo Barantyn, Willelmus Olyver, Willelmus Wotton', Adam de Sancto Ivone, Gilbertus Magh'feld', Willelmus Brampton', et Thomas Neuton', una cum viginti et quatuor personis concivibus nostris de validioribus et magis sufficientibus communariis dicte civitatis, videlicet Johanne Walcote, Johanne Furneux, Rogero Elys, Willelmo Evote, Hugone Boys, Johanne Wade, Johanne Sybyll', Willelmo Hyde, Henrico Yevele, Ricardo Whityngton', Johanne Wodecok, Willelmo Parker, Thoma Panton', Thoma Knolles, Johanne Frankeleyn, Johanne Forster, Willelmo Radewell', Thoma Weyland', Johanne Cosyn, Johanne Mokkyng', Willelmo Frenyngham, Johanne Sandhirst, Johanne Ragenhull', et Hugone Sprot, parati sumus coram vobis excellentissimo domino et domino nostro rege et consilio vestro aput Notyngham in crastino sancti Johannis Baptiste in brevi domini regis nobis directo specificato ad respondendum, faciendum et recipiendum quod dictum breve exigit et requirit secundum formam ejusdem brevis.

---

a Cl. R.; MS. om.   *b–b Cl. R.* forisfactura.

of London greeting. For certain particular causes us specially moving 1392 we order you, firmly enjoining, that, ceasing every excuse and deferring all else, in your proper persons and in company with twenty-four persons, your fellow-citizens, from among the ablest and best-qualified of the commoners of the said city, you appear before us and our council at Nottingham on the morrow of St. John the Baptist next to come [25 June], bringing then with you full and sufficient power of the commonalty of our said city, to answer for yourselves and the commonalty aforesaid touching what shall there be laid before you on our behalf and further to do and receive what by us and our said council shall then happen to be ordered. And this, under pain of forfeiture of life and limb and of all that you shall be able to forfeit to us, you are in no wise to omit, any concessions, liberties, privileges, or customs to you granted or by you exercised to the contrary notwithstanding. Provided always that for the safeguard of our city aforesaid and for the peace and tranquillity of the same during the time of your absence you are to take such order as you will therefor answer to us at your peril. And you are to have there this writ. Witness myself at Stamford the 29th day of May in the fifteenth year of our reign [1392].

The return[1] to the above writ was as follows:

We, John Hende mayor and alderman of the city of London, John Shadworth and Henry Vanner sheriffs and aldermen of the same city, and all and singular the other aldermen of the city aforesaid, namely John Hadley, William Venour, Adam Bamme, William Barret, John Fresh, William More, John Lovey, Adam Carlisle, Thomas Vivent, John Francis, William Sheringham, Henry Bamme, and Robert de Exeter prior of the church of Holy Trinity London, Thomas Wilford, Drew Barentin, William Oliver, William Wotton, Adam de St. Ives, Gilbert Maghfeld, William Brampton, and Thomas Newton, in company with twenty-four persons, our fellow citizens, from among the ablest and best-qualified commoners of the said city, namely John Walcot, John Furneaux, Roger Ellis, William Evote, Hugh Boys, John Wade, John Sibile, William Hyde, Henry Yevele, Richard Whittington, John Woodcock, William Parker, Thomas Panton, Thomas Knolles, John Franklin, John Forster, William Radwell, Thomas Weyland, John Cousin, John Mokkynge, William Frenyngham, John Sandhurst, John Ragenhull, and Hugh Sprot, are ready, before you our most excellent lord and our lord king and your council at Nottingham on the morrow of St. John the Baptist specified in the writ of our lord the king to us directed, to answer, to do and to receive what the said writ demands and requires, according to the form of the same writ.

[1] In the sense of 'reply'. The Londoners did not 'return' the king's writ: to do so would have signified assent to the waiver of the City's customary customs and liberties demanded in it, as one of the bases on which the case was to proceed. See also below, p. 498, and for the following text, *Letter Book H*, pp. 377–8.

1392   Causa autem que instigavit regem versus Londonienses
secundum quosdam erat ista. Notum est regem quandoque
pecuniis indigere; igitur misit ipse rex quibusdam civibus
London' ut ipsi super certo jocali magni precii sibi accom-
modarent quinque milia marcarum sive librarum. (Et prevale-
bat adhuc jocale predictum summam petitam.) Verumptamen
ipsi excusarunt se, asserentes eos modicum lucrari post eorum
perditam libertatem, cum in civitate extranei gaudent tanta
libertate sicut illi, et ideo pretermissis comodis nullatenus
possunt ad tam magnam summam venire.[1] Rex autem super
hac re non modicum stupefactus consuluit tandem quendam
Lombardum super isto casu, qui confestim promisit regi
satisfacere votis suis et in crastino venit ad regem cum prelibata summa; et quesivit rex ab eo quomodo tam cito tam
magnam summam adquirere potuisset, cui ille ait, 'A diversis
mercatoribus London' mutuavi.' Quod audiens rex animum
indignatum deinceps versus Londonienses gerebat eo quod
uni extraneo cicius quam sibi vellent tantam summam
pecunie mutuare.[2]

Paule.[3] Item de mense Maii[a] quidam domicellus familiaris
et serviens ad opera diversa ecclesie Westmon' nomine
Johannes Paule pro morte cujusdam hominis indictatus circa
medium mensis Maii erat captus et sepius coram judice de
banco domini regis pro illo homicidio impetitus numquam[b]
de illa felonia potuit se congrue excusare. Ideo xxiiij[to]. die
Maii fuit pro illo delicto adjudicatus ad furcas suspendi.
Cum vero duceretur ad furcas fatebatur se dignum morte
pati quia erat falsus et ingratus Deo et ecclesie Westmon';
primo[c] quia cautelose quosdam allexit exire de sanctuario
Sancti Petri Westmon' et postea erant capti et suspensi;
secundo[d] autem suasit quosdam eciam de sanctuario predicto
exire qui incontinenti fuerant comprehensi et coram judice

---

[a] *Interlined.*   [b] se *expunged after this word.*   [c] j. *in the margin.*   [d] ij.
in the margin.

---

[1] A reference to the legislation of 1388, for which see above, p. 334 and n.

[2] Cf. Walsingham, *Hist. Ang.*, ii. 207–8.

[3] For the following case see P.R.O., K.B., 27/524, m. 11[v], recording the indictment of John Paule in 1377 for felonies, his outlawry at the Middlesex eyre in
1378 after failure to respond to 5 demands that he put in an appearance, and his
final appearance in the King's Bench on 17 May 1392 and condemnation there.

According to some people the occasion prompting the 1392 king's anger with the Londoners was this. The king is known to be from time to time in need of money; and it was for this reason that he sent to certain London citizens asking for a loan of 5,000 marks (or £5,000) on the security of a very valuable jewel. (And this jewel was worth even more than the sum requested.) But the citizens offered excuses, declaring that since the loss of their privileged position they had prospered but little, seeing that outsiders enjoyed in the city the same freedom as themselves, so that owing to the interruption in their profits they were quite unable to reach so large an amount.[1] More than a little taken aback by this, the king eventually turned for advice on the situation to a certain Lombard, who at once promised to satisfy the king's wants and on the following day came to him with the specified sum. Asked by the king how he had been able in such a short time to raise so much money, he said, 'I borrowed it from various London merchants.' After hearing this the king nursed a grudge against the Londoners for being readier to lend so large a sum of money to a foreigner than to himself.[2]

Paule.[3] May also saw the arrest, about the middle of the month, of John Paule, a household servant and odd-job man at the church of Westminster indicted for homicide. In the course of frequent appearances on this charge before a King's Bench judge he was never able to clear himself properly of this felony, and on 24 May he was sentenced to hang for his crime. When he was being led to the gallows, he confessed that he deserved to suffer death for his treachery and ingratitude to God and the church of Westminster, first in deceitfully luring out of the sanctuary of St. Peter, Westminster, certain persons who were afterwards arrested and hanged; secondly in inducing to leave the sanctuary some others who were immediately apprehended and, upon their judicial conviction

On this occasion Paule pleaded that at the time of his outlawry in 1378 he had been in sanctuary at Westminster Abbey and fearful of leaving it 'propter quosdam emulos suos'. The bailiff of the abbot of Westminster's liberty delivered him to the King's Bench in 1392, in response to a royal precept. If Paule is to be identified with the adversary of the approver mentioned above (p. 458), he left sanctuary in or after 1378 and may have been living outside it at the time of his arrest in 1392. (I owe the plea roll reference to Mr. Hector.)

1392 de crimine convicti ad perpetuos carceres fuerant mancipati; tercio[a] prodidit nequiter Robertum Tresylian tempore parliamenti quando domini temporales contra quosdam regnicolas erant moti in sanctuario occulte latitantem, de quo dicti domini violenter extraxerunt et a Turri London' usque ad furcas per medium civitatis tractum aput Tybo⟨u⟩rne illico suspenderunt.[1] Ecce quomodo Deus remunerat tales falsarios, immo possent dici pocius ecclesiarum violatores ac eciam illarum libertatum nequissimi effractores! Patet namque quod dolus et fraus nemini patrocinari deberet. (Vide supra de ista materia in fine quarti folii.[2])

In ista estate diversis partibus Anglie domorum ac villarum incendia multipliciter invaluerunt. Nam aput Lederede ignis discurrens nunc ad istam partem ville nunc ad aliam saltando ultra quasdam domos fere totam villam consumpsit preter illas domos quas ignis per saltum transilierat, que miraculose ab incendio sunt servate. Fuerunt quoque et alie domorum combusciones in locis diversis, scilicet aput Basyngstoke, aput Kymbalton', et aput Sanctam Mariam de Otery, que[b] multa dispendia intulerunt hominibus tam degentibus in eisdem quam easdem possidentibus.[c]

Decimo nono die Junii major London' Johannes Hende draper, Johannes Shadworth' mercerus et Henricus Vanner' vinetarius, vicecomites London' cum aldermannis et communariis dicte civitatis superius nominatis accinxerunt se ad iter in apparatu satis honesto veneruntque ad villam de Notyngham parum ante festum Nativitatis Sancti Johannis Baptiste. Et in proximo die post festum predictum, sedente rege in solio suo regali, cum suo consilio et dominis spiritualibus et temporalibus, in quorum omnium presencia cancellarius Anglie[3] causam consilii proncunciavit et ostensa causa cur dominus rex amovit curias suas et cetera que concernebant predictum consilium confestim convertit se ad Londonienses et satis rigide est illos[d] allocutus, dicens eos regem parvipendere ex quo ejus breve neglexerant retornare,[4] deinde quantum ad regimen civitatis multos defectus illis

---

[a] iij. in the margin.   [b] Interlined.   [c] A word has been erased after this word.   [d] dicens deleted after this word.

---

[1] Cf. above, pp. 310-12.   [2] Ibid., p. 458 (=MS., p. 200).

on criminal charges, committed to prison for life; and thirdly
in that when, at the time of the parliament, feeling among
the temporal lords was running high against some of their
fellow countrymen, he wickedly betrayed Robert Tresilian's
secret hiding-place in the sanctuary from which he was
forcibly dragged out by the lords before being drawn from
the Tower through London to the gallows and hanged out of
hand at Tyburn.[1] Mark how God pays back such dissemblers,
or rather, to give them a preferable name, such profaners of
churches and violators of ecclesiastical privilege! It is plain
that guile and cheating ought not to win immunity for anybody. (On this topic see above, at the end of the fourth folio
back.[2])

During this summer fires in buildings and whole towns
were very prevalent in various parts of England. At Leatherhead flames spread rapidly to one part of the town after
another and, though they sometimes skipped individual
buildings, consumed almost all the town with the exception
of the buildings over which the fire had leaped and which
were thus miraculously saved from burning. There were also
other outbreaks in various places, namely Basingstoke, Kimbolton, and Ottery St. Mary, to the heavy cost of both occupants and owners of the buildings affected.

On 19 June the mayor of London, a draper named John
Hende, and the sheriffs, John Shadworth, a mercer, and
Henry Vanner, vintner, together with the above-named aldermen and commoners of the city, set about making their
journey in some style and reached Nottingham shortly before
the Nativity of St. John the Baptist [24 June]. On the day
after the feast, when the king had seated himself on the royal
throne, with his council and the lords spiritual and temporal
in attendance, the chancellor of England[3] announced to the
entire company the occasion for this council. Having stated,
among other relevant matters, the reason for the king's
removal of his courts, he at once rounded on the Londoners
and addressed them with marked severity, declaring that their
neglect to return the king's writ showed contempt for him;[4]
moving on to the government of the city he had a number of

---

[3] Thomas Arundel.   [4] Cf. above, p. 495 n.

1392 imposuit; et in quibusdam culpabiles fuerunt inventi, ut dicebatur. Tandem Johannem Hende absolvit de officio majoritatis sue, et missus est ad castrum de Wyndeshore; Johannem vero Shadworth' et Henricum Vanner' amovit de officiis eorum et misit eos ad diversa castella, unum aput Odyham et alterum ad castrum de Walyngford':[1] ceteri jussi sunt ad civitatem eorum redire. Interim custodiam civitatis London' habuit Willelmus Staundon' et gerebat vices majoris usque principium mensis Julii; quo in tempore precepto domini regis factus est custos civitatis London' *a*dominus Edwardus Dalyngrugge miles;*a* et Londonienses gratanter illum admiserunt.[2] Rex vero ante recessum Londoniensium p. 208 de Notyngham / constituit duos vicecomites London', Gilbertum Magh'feld' scilicet et Thomam Newton': steterunt-que isti vicecomites in officiis eorum usque in finem anni, et tunc electi fuerunt de novo per Londonienses.[3] Rex vero tunc omnes libertates ab olim Londoniensibus concessas ex toto et plenarie revocavit.[4]

Circa principium mensis Julii obiit comes Staffordie, juvenis nondum habens xx. annos.[5] Quo in tempore rex Francorum Carolus ferebatur*b* insania; nam quosdam de suis domesticis in suo furore transfodit, qui continuo prop-ter mortis violenciam vitam cum hujus mundi gaudio ocius relinquebant;[6] unde confestim a suis captus fuit et ligatus. Set postea, secundum quosdam, convaluit ipse de sua infirmitate et exercuit tirannidem in populo suo atrocius quam umquam antea fecerat, secundum relata, immo eciam secundum veridica et probata.*c* Eodem mense captus fuit dominus Johannes Beeltoft in Lombardia, quem sic captum

---

a-a In the lower margin but marked for insertion at this point.   *b* Recte feriebatur? So too in the sidenote.   *c* Memorandum quod in ista estate Carolus ⟨r⟩ex Francorum insania ferebatur ⟨et q⟩uosdam de suis domesticis ⟨a⟩trocissime perimebat: tandem ⟨a⟩ suis fuit captus et ligatus *in the margin but damaged at the edge*.

---

[1] The writs committing Hende, Shadworth, and Vanner to their several prisons are dated 25 June 1392 (*Cal. Cl. R., 1392–6*, p. 2).

[2] Dallingridge, who is described as a king's knight, was appointed warden of the City on 25 June (*Cal. Pat. R., 1391–6*, p. 100). Standon, a grocer, did not become mayor until 13 Oct. 1392 but may have been appointed locumtenens when Hende left for Nottingham on 19 June (Barron, in *Reign of Richard II,*

shortcomings to charge them with; and of some of these, it 1392
was reported, they were found guilty. Eventually John Hende
was relieved of his mayoralty and sent to Windsor castle;
John Shadworth and Henry Vanner were removed from
office and sent to different castles, one to Odiham and the
other to Wallingford:[1] the rest of the citizens were ordered to
return to London. For the time being the keeping of the city
was in the hands of William Standon, who deputized as
mayor until the beginning of July, when by the king's order
Sir Edward Dallingridge became warden of London: willingly
accepted as such by the citizens.[2] Before the Londoners left
Nottingham the king appointed as the two sheriffs of London
Gilbert Maghfeld and Thomas Newton: and these two
remained in office until the end of the year, when they were
re-elected by the Londoners.[3] The king then utterly and completely revoked all the liberties granted to the Londoners
from antiquity onwards.[4]

The death occurred about the beginning of July of the
earl of Stafford, a young man not yet twenty years old.[5]
At this time Charles, king of the French, went into a transport of insanity; in his frenzy he ran his sword through some
of his menservants, who, put to a sudden and violent death,
prematurely quitted this life and the joys of this world.[6]
The king was therefore speedily seized and bound by his
attendants. Some sources say, however, that he later recovered from his malady and played the despot over his
people more savagely than he ever had done in the past,
according to report — or rather according to true and established fact. In the same month Sir John Beltoft was captured
in Lombardy; and after taking him prisoner his enemies,

p. 183 n.). On 26 June Dallingridge was appointed escheator in London (*Cal.
Fine R., 1391-9*, p. 49). See also *Letter Book H*, p. 379.
    [3] Maghfeld and Newton were appointed sheriffs of London and Midd. on 25
June 1392, reappointed on 22 July, and elected by the warden and citizens for a
further year on 21 Sept. 1392 (*Cal. Fine R., 1391-9*, pp. 49, 54; *Letter Book H*,
p. 385).
    [4] Cf. below, p. 502. In fact the City lost its liberties on 22 July 1392 (Barron,
in *Reign of Richard II*, p. 87).
    [5] Thomas de Stafford, 3rd earl of Stafford, died on 4 July 1392 (*G.E.C.*,
xii (1), p. 180). He was 24 years or more old.
    [6] Cf. *Chronique du religieux de S. Denys*, ed. Bellaguet, ii. 20, 25. The king
killed 4 men but enjoyed a measure of recovery after 3 days.

1392 emuli sui, scilicet ribaldi, nequiter occiderunt: erat enim miles egregius et fortissimus preliator.[1]

Preterea[2] xviij. die Julii aput Wyndeshore rex existens circa Anglie magnates ad eum ibidem et alios avide confluentes magnas fecit expensas. Ibi venerunt ipso rege jubente xxiiij. aldremanni et quadringenti alii de civitate London' comunarii vocati: in quorum omnium presencia, scilicet prelatorum, dominorum, et supradictorum, Johannes Hynde dudum major, Johannes Shadeworth' et Henricus Vannere nuper vicecomites London' submiserunt se et sua domino regi, quamvis J. Shadeworth' reluctari nitebatur primo valde constanter, demum tamen submisit se pro meliori ut alii faciebant. Tunc enim, secundum quosdam, abstulit ab eis libertates quascumque quas protunc habebant, deditque eciam eis[a] libere ad propria remeare nullam eis molestiam ea vice ulterius inferendo: quibus reversis dominus rex cum suo consilio dominum Edwardum Dalyngrugge amovit de officio custodie sue ac loco ejus substituit dominum Baldewynum de Radyngton' militem, qui satis rigide in dicto officio se habebat. Demum mediantibus amicis pro eis et precipue domina regina Anglie, que iteratis vicibus, immo multociens, prostravit se ad pedes domini regis tam ibi quam aput Notyngham, obnixe et sedule deprecando pro dicta civitate London' et pro statu civium ejusdem quatinus ut ipse suam indignacionem ab eis averteret ne tam celebris civitas cum tam numerosa plebe in ea degente pereat inconsulte, scilicet calore iracundie emulorum suorum, ad hec clemens et benignus rex pietate motus ad instanciam domine regine aliorumque suorum procerum et magnatum remisit eis omnia que in eum deliquerunt sub ista condicione, quod infra decem annos proximo sequentes solvant ei aut ejus certis attornatis quadraginta milia librarum, et hoc ad verum

[a] Sc. licenciam or some such word.

---

[1] For Beltoft see also Cal. Cl. R., 1389-92, p. 265; ibid., 1392-6, p. 532; Cal. Pat. R., 1388-92, p. 116.

[2] The following passage contains some inaccuracies. On 18 July, in response to a writ of Edmund, duke of York, the mayor, sheriffs, and 22 aldermen for the years 1389-90, together with the mayor and sheriffs lately removed from office, and the aldermen for the current year, appeared at Eton before the commission of oyer and terminer appointed to inquire into defaults in the government of the

ruffians that they were, foully murdered him. He was an outstanding knight and the doughtiest of fighters.[1]

On[2] 18 July the king, then at Windsor, laid out large sums
of money on the entertainment of the English notables who
thronged there eagerly to meet him and other people. Here
came at the king's command twenty-four aldermen and 400
others, described as commoners, of the city of London: and
before this entire assembly, that is to say the prelates, the
lords, and the persons mentioned above, John Hende, the
former mayor, and John Shadworth and Henry Vanner, the
ex-sheriffs of London, made submission of their persons and
their property to the king, though at first John Shadworth
made very determined efforts to resist before eventually
deciding he had better knuckle under like the others. According to some people it was on this occasion that the king
withdrew from the Londoners all the privileges they then
possessed and left them free to return to their homes without
subjecting them at this time to any further harassment. After
their return to London the king and his council removed
Sir Edward Dallingridge from his post as warden and replaced
him by Sir Baldwin Raddington, who behaved somewhat
severely in the office. At length through the intercession, on
behalf of the Londoners, of friends, conspicuous among them
the queen (who more than once, indeed on many occasions,
both at Windsor and at Nottingham, prostrated herself at the
king's feet in earnest and tireless entreaty for the city and the
welfare of its citizens that he would cease to direct his anger
against them and would not let so famous a city and its
teeming masses perish without due consideration simply
because of the burning passion of its enemies), the king's
mild and kindly nature was moved by pity, and persuaded
by the queen and by others among his nobles and prominent
men he forgave the Londoners all their offences against him
on condition that within the next ten years they paid him or
his unquestionable attorneys £40,000 in real terms of jewels

City and submitted to the king's judgement. The commission's verdict was given
on 22 July, and that day the Londoners appeared before the king and council in
Windsor castle and were told of the appointment of Sir Baldwin Raddington as
warden and of other arrangements for the government of the City. On the same
day Hende, Shadworth, and Vanner were released on bail. See *Letter Book H*,
p. 386; *Cal. Cl. R., 1392-6*, pp. 87-9; Barron, op. cit., pp. 186-8.

1392 valorem, videlicet in jocalibus aut in pecunia numerata, et
quod venirent erga eum et exciperent eum aput Wandles-
worthe decenti apparatu, unaqueque ars dicte civitatis
in secta sua et in equis, et per medium dicte civitatis honorifice perducerent eum usque Westmon' die ad hoc prefixo,
qui fuit xxj. mensis Augusti.[1] Londonienses vero consenserunt ista premissa pro eorum modulo percomplere ac in
omnibus pro posse votis regiis obedire. Quid ultra? Venit
dies prefixus; rex[a] de manerio suo de Shene in regio apparatu
iter suum sumpsit versus London'; erga quem exierunt
Londonienses ex omnibus artibus civitatis ejusdem, equestres
omnes, usque Wandleworth' et quelibet ars in propria sua
secta; qui pre multitudine a ponte London' protendebantur
ultra villam de Kenyngeton', et annumerantur ad xxij. milia
equitum: erat quoque numerus peditum infinitus. In primo
namque occursu aput Wandelesworth' optulerunt domini
regi Londonienses gladium et claves civitatis predicte, deinde
ad portam pontis London' presentarunt domino regi duos
equos electos vocatos courceres: unus illorum erat albi
coloris et alter rubei coloris, cum sellis argenteis ac splendide
deauratis; ibi eciam dederunt domine regine unum pulcrum
palefridum cum sella aurea adornatum. Erat autem pons
London' et cetere strate eminenciores dicte civitatis [b]diver-
sorum pannorum aureorum, sericorum aliorumque bistinc-
torum[b] lucide perornate. Procedebat ulterius, venit in
Stratam Piscariam, ubi venerunt[c] duo juvenes preclari forma
decori specie cum duobus thuribulis aureis thurificantes eum
honorifice, prout decebat. Et processit parumper, venit in
vicum qui vocatur Chepe; ibi de quadam alta structura descenderunt quasi duo angeli in specie puerorum, ut erant,
quendam cantum egregie et suaviter modulantes ac in eorum
manibus duas aureas coronas habentes magni valoris: primus
vero coronam quam in manu sua gestabat posuit super caput
regis; alter quoque coronam quam ipse gerebat imposuit

---

[a] In the margin, a hand pointing to this passage.   [b-b] Sic MS.   [c] venerunt
repeated but deleted the second time.

[1] Cf. below, p. 510. Pardons for offending citizens of London were not issued
until 19 Sept., and for them the Londoners probably paid £10,000 (Cal. Pat. R.,
1391-6, pp. 130, 171, 226; Letter Book H, pp. 380-1; Barron, op. cit., p. 194

or specie, and that on the day appointed for his progress,
which was 21 August, they should come out to meet him and
receive him at Wandsworth with appropriate pomp, each city
craft in its own livery and mounted on horseback, to escort
him with all honour through the city to Westminster.[1]
The Londoners agreed to carry out these conditions to the
letter, so far as they could, and to comply in all respects to
the best of their ability with the king's wishes. What is there
to add? The appointed day came; the king set out in royal
splendour from his manor of Sheen on the road to London;
to meet him representatives of every craft in the City, all
mounted, came out as far as Wandsworth, each craft in its
own livery; the throng was so great that it stretched from
London Bridge beyond Kennington, mustering 22,000 horse-
men and an uncountable number on foot. At the first
encounter at Wandsworth the Londoners handed to the king
a sword and the keys of the city; at the gate of London
Bridge they presented him with two carefully chosen horses
of the kind called 'coursers', one white and the other a bay,
with saddles of silver magnificently gilded: and here also
they gave to the queen a beautiful palfrey adorned by a
gold saddle. London Bridge itself and the chief city streets
were gaily decorated with [banners of] assorted cloths
of gold, silks, and other double-dyed fabrics. The king
went on his way, and when he reached Fish Street there
appeared two young men of fine figure and handsome
appearance carrying two gold thuribles with which, as was
fitting, they did him honour by censing him. A little further
on he came to the street known as Eastcheap, and here
there descended from a lofty structure two 'angels' in the
shape of boys (which is what they were) carolling a melody
with singular art and sweetness and having in their hands
two gold crowns of great costliness: the first boy placed
on the king's head the crown he was carrying in his hand,
and the crown borne by the other was set by him on the

---

and n.). For the 10-year term, see also H. Suggett, 'A Letter describing Richard
II's reconciliation with the City of London, 1392', in *E.H.R.*, lxii (1947), p. 213.
For the festivities on 21-2 Aug. see Barron, op. cit., pp. 190-1 and references
cited there. The Monk fails to record a meeting between the king and Londoners
in Westminster Hall after the festivities on 21 Aug.; for this see Knighton,
Chronicon, ii. 320-1; *E.H.R.*, lxii, loc. cit.

1392 capiti regine. Sicque abhinc lento passu coronati venerunt ad Temple Barre, ubi presentarunt sibi unam tabulam auream valentem centum marcas. Abhinc recto tramite perrexerunt usque ad portam monasterii Westm', ubi occurrebat ei prior et conventus revestiti et albis capis induti cum crucibus, cereis, thuribulis, et textibus: quos videns rex et regina ilico descenderunt de equis et depositis coronis osculati sunt textus. Deinde in revertendo versus ecclesiam, conventus cantabat responsorium 'Agnus in altari'; demum venientes ante magnum altare conventus canebat antiphonam 'Solve jubente'.[1] Dominus rex interim super gradus marmoreos devote genuflexit et post ipsum venit regina et similes devociones peregit. Dicta collecta pro rege conventus intrabat ad feretrum Sancti Edwardi cum illa antiphona 'Ave, Sancte rex Edwarde'. Completa oracione ac factis suis oblacionibus rex in suum palacium est reversus.

Mox Baldewynus de Radyngton' custos London' ex parte Londoniensium invitavit dominum regem ad prandium erga diem crastinum. Annuit rex: convivio celebrato Londonienses optulerunt domino regi unam tabulam mensalem argenteam ac deauratam longitudine novem pedum, valentem quingentas marcas.[a] Istis sic decursis, quadam die non longe postea in magna aula Westmon' sedens rex in sua sede regia concessit prefatis Londoniensibus omnes libertates quas ab eis abstulerat exceptis tribus, que sunt iste:[2] quod non legarent redditus suos aut tenementa personisve aliquibus conferant ut inde fierent cantarie aut fraternitates sine domini regis licencia speciali[3] (unde quidam affirmant per hoc omnes cantarias seu fraternitates eo modo exortas nec per cartam domini regis specialiter roboratas, presertim London', fore omnino invalidas pro perpetuo et extinctas); item quando fiunt placita London' super rebus mundanis et per

---

[a] In the margin, a hand pointing to this passage.

---

[1] Respectively a responsory in the Mass for the commemoration of St. Edward, king and confessor, and an antiphon for that of St. Peter. Ave sancte rex Edwarde, mentioned later, was an antiphon in the former Mass.

[2] The City regained its liberties on 19 Sept. 'until further order', but without the exceptions which the Monk proceeds to enumerate (Cal. Pat. R., 1391-6, p. 173; cf. Letter Book H, p. 381). Quite probably he confuses the terms of the

head of the queen. And so, wearing their crowns, they went 1392 from there at a stately pace to Temple Bar, where they were presented with a gold table worth 100 marks before proceeding by the direct route to the gate of the monastery at Westminster. Here the king was met by the prior and convent in new clothes and wearing white copes, with crosses, candles, censers, and Gospels: on seeing them the king and queen at once dismounted and, laying aside their crowns, kissed the Gospels. On the way back to the church the convent sang the responsory 'Agnus in altari' and upon their eventual arrival before the high altar the antiphon 'Solve jubente'.[1] Meanwhile the king knelt reverently on the marble steps and after him came the queen and performed similar devotions. When the collect for the king had been said, the convent went into St. Edward's shrine to the accompaniment of the antiphon 'Ave, Sancte rex Edwarde'. When he had finished his prayers and made his offerings, the king returned to his palace.

Soon afterwards Baldwin Raddington, the warden of London, invited the king on behalf of the Londoners to a banquet on the following day. The king accepted: and when the banquet was held the Londoners presented to the king a silver and gilt table nine feet long and worth 500 marks. One day, shortly after these events had run their course, the king took his seat on the royal throne in the great hall at Westminster and granted to the Londoners all the privileges he had withdrawn from them, with three exceptions, which were as follows.[2] They were not to bequeath their rents or tenements or to bestow them on anybody for the purpose of endowing chantries or fraternities unless they had the king's special licence.[3] (Some people maintain that in consequence all chantries and fraternities originating in such endowments and not expressly confirmed by royal charter, especially in London, are completely and permanently invalid and dissolved.) In the second place, when pleas concerning secular matters are held in London and it happens that a wrongful

---

final restoration of liberties with those adumbrated at the meeting in Westminster Hall on 21 Aug.

[3] On the issues involved, see H. M. Chew, 'Mortmain in Medieval London', in *E.H.R.*, lx (1945), 1-15.

1392 questionarios ad hoc procuratos contigit contra unam parcium istarum sentenciam ferri super rebus predictis minus juste, pars altera senciit se gravari, vult agere ad reprobandum dicta questionariorum; numquid valeret processus dicte partis sic inceptus? Certe non. Istis vero consideratis dominus rex equa lance pensando vult quod isti questionarii tam bene London' de falsitate convincerentur sicut alibi extra in curiis suis aut sessionibus fieri consuevit libertate quacumque aut

p. 209 privilegio omnino cessante;[1] / item quod nullus nativus sit ibidem ita privilegiatus quod contra dominum suum illum calumpniantem quacumque libertate defenderet se in civitate ab illo, immo vult dominus rex quod tam plenum jus habeat dominus suus de illo in civitate sicut alibi extra, non obstante libertate quacumque.[2]

Tercio die Septembris mane fuit magna tempestas fulguris et tonitrui, ac adeo invaluit quod quendam hominem juxta Hampstede ejus ictu extinxit, vestes ejus et calciamenta et sotulares per minutas pecias dilacerando. Quo eciam anno circa festum Michaelis dominus papa cum sua curia transtulit se Perusium, ubi Perusienses eum satis stricte et caute custodierunt.[3] xiij.[a] die mensis Octobris Londonienses de more ad novi majoris eleccionem concorditer processerunt; et elegerunt Willelmum Staundon' in eorum majorem.[4] xj.[b] die Octobris dominus rex cum conventu Westmon' nudis pedibus processionaliter transivit, exeundo per portam de Toothull' usque Sanctum Jacobum,[5] et ab eo loco processit usque crucem de Charryng' et abhinc divertebat se per viam regiam usque ecclesiam Sancti Petri Westmon', factisque ibidem devocionibus suis in suum palacium illico est reversus. Transieruntque cum domino rege nudis pedibus quidam de suis clericis, perpauci tamen conventu Westmon' excepto, qui nudus eciam cum eo transivit. Sequenti vero die

---

[a] Written above duodecimo, which has not been deleted. [b] Written above nono, which has not been deleted.

---

[1] For the writ of attaint, see W. S. Holdsworth, *History of English Law* (7th edn., London, 1956), i. 340. Cf. *Cal. Select Pleas and Memoranda of the City of London, 1381–1412*, ed. Thomas, pp. 1, 18.

[2] For the privilege whereby a villein dwelling in the City for a year and a day acquired free status, see *Cal. Plea and Memoranda Rolls of the City of London, 1364–81*, ed. Thomas, pp. xxiv ff.

verdict on the issue is returned against one party by jurors 1392
suborned to that end, the defeated party feels aggrieved and
wants to take action to impugn the jury's verdict; but would
proceedings instituted by such a party be of any avail?
Certainly not. Taking these circumstances into account and
weighing the arguments impartially, the king decided that
any franchise or privilege should come to an end and that
jurors should be attainted for false verdicts as effectively in
London as is customarily the case in all his courts and
sessions elsewhere outside the city.[1] Thirdly, there was to be
no villein in London so privileged that within the city he
could invoke any franchise in his defence against his lord's
claim upon his person: on the contrary the king's will was
that the lord should have as full a right over him within the
city as elsewhere outside it, any franchise whatever notwithstanding.[2]

On the morning of 3 September there was a great storm
of thunder and lightning so violent that a man was struck
dead at Hampstead and his clothing, hose, and shoes ripped
to shreds. About Michaelmas [29 September] this year the
pope moved to Perugia, where the townspeople kept a pretty
close and careful eye on him.[3] On 13 October the Londoners
proceeded in a spirit of harmony to the usual election of a
new mayor, their choice for the office falling on William
Standon.[4] On 11 October the king walked barefoot in procession with the convent of Westminster, going out at the
Tothill Gate as far as St. James's,[5] from there to Charing
Cross and then turning into the highway to the church of St.
Peter, Westminster. Here he performed his devotions and
returned forthwith to his palace. Some of the king's clerks
walked barefoot with him, but they were very few, except
for the Westminster convent, who accompanied him with
their feet likewise bared. On the following day [12 October]

---

[3] Boniface IX took up residence in Perugia on 17 Oct. 1392, the Perugians
having made it a condition of their obedience (*Theoderici de Nyem de Scismate
Libri Tres*, ed. Erler, p. 146 and n.; Delaruelle, Labande, and Ourliac, *L'Église
au temps du grand schisme et de la crise conciliare (1378-1449)*, p. 70).

[4] Cf. *Letter Book H*, pp. 386-7.

[5] The Hospital of St. James was situated west of Charing. The Tothill Gate
was on the west side of the Abbey.

1392 dominus rex cum sua capella venit in chorum dicti monasterii ad vesperas, episcopo London' servicium officiante: ad matutinas quoque erat rex cum sua capella, et in crastino[1] ad processionem et ad magnam missam, qua finita perrexit in aulam abbatis, ubi splendide in maximo apparatu suos dominos et dominas qui tunc cum eo presentes extiterunt[a] et conventum totum pro majori parte laute refecit.

Circa hos dies obiit dominus Johannes Paule in partibus transmarinis miles utique strenuus et valens juvenis et formosus, qui egregie se habuit in terra barbarorum. Obiit eciam in Brabancia aput Lovayn' dominus Robertus de Veer quondam dux Hybernie et comes Oxon'; et quia non habuit heredem de corpore suo progenitum transivit comitatus ille ad patruum suum dominum Albericum de Veer.[2] In fine mensis Novembris cecidit magna copia nivis; et itidem circa festum Sancti Thome Apostoli fuit magna tempestas tam in mari quam in terra, tamque horribilis quod hominibus incussit timorem. Vicesimo tercio die Decembris obiit ducissa Eborac' soror ducisse Lancastr'.[3] Dominus rex tenuit suum

1393 Natale aput Eltham; ad quem circa festum Epiphanie venerunt Londonienses glorioso apparatu et presentarunt[b] sibi unum dromedarium cum uno puero sedente super eum: presentaruntque eciam domine regine unam magnam avem et mirabilem, habentem guttur latissimum.[4] Igitur post inmensa tripudia et solacia curiosa peracta dominus rex regraciatus est multum Londoniensibus ac ad instanciam domine regine aliorumque procerum perdonavit eisdem xx. milia librarum in quibus ei tenebantur pro forisfacto predicto, et adhuc debentur sibi pro eodem delicto alia xx. ⟨milia⟩[c] librarum.[5] Ad corroborandam vero perdonacionem suam confestim post solempnitatem peractam misit rex cancellarium et thesaurarium suos et alios de consilio suo ut eis palam intimarent perdonacionem suam; qui venientes ad Gildam Aulam[d] omnia eis exposuerunt secundum quod

---

[a] MS. extiterint.   [b] The letter s is expunged after this word.   [c] MS. om.
[d] MS. inserts et.

[1] The feast of the translation of St. Edward, king and confessor.
[2] Robert de Vere, until his forfeiture in 1388, 9th earl of Oxford and duke of Ireland, died on 22 Nov. 1392. Aubrey de Vere, 3rd and only surviving son of the 7th earl, received the earldom in the parliament of Jan.–Feb. 1393 (R.P., iii. 302–3; G.E.C., x. 233–4).

the king, together with his chapel, entered the choir of the 1392
monastery at Vespers, when the celebrant was the bishop of
London: the king was also present with his chapel at Matins
and on the day after [13 October][1] at the procession and at
High Mass, at the conclusion of which he passed into the
abbot's hall, where, with the utmost magnificence, the lords
and ladies then at court, as well as the whole convent, or the
greater part of it, were brilliantly and elegantly entertained.

At about this time the death took place overseas of Sir
John Paveley, a young and handsome knight of great vigour
and mettle, who distinguished himself by his conduct in
pagan lands. There also died, at Louvain in Brabant, Robert
de Vere, sometime duke of Ireland and earl of Oxford; and
since he had no issue the earldom passed to his uncle, Sir
Aubrey de Vere.[2] At the end of November there was a heavy
fall of snow; and then about the feast of St. Thomas the
Apostle [21 December] a great storm over both land and sea,
so dreadful that it struck terror into men's hearts. On 23
December came the death of the duchess of York, sister of
the duchess of Lancaster.[3] The king kept Christmas at
Eltham, where he was waited upon in great state about
Epiphany [6 January] by the Londoners and presented by 1393
them with a dromedary ridden by a boy: to the queen they
gave a large and remarkable bird with an enormously wide
gullet.[4] After a vast amount of merry-making and unusual
entertainment had taken place, the king heartily thanked the
Londoners and, prompted by the queen and by other persons
of rank, remitted £20,000 [of the sum] in which they stood
bound to him in respect of the forfeiture above described,
leaving a further £20,000 still owing to him in redemption
of their offence.[5] By way of ratifying this remission, as soon
as the festive season was over the king sent his chancellor
and his treasurer and other members of his council to
announce it publicly to the people of London. On their
arrival at the Guildhall these emissaries made a full statement

[3] Isabel, duchess of York, and her sister, Constance, duchess of Lancaster, were
daughters of Pedro the Cruel, king of Castile. For Isabel see *G.E.C.*, xii (2), p. 898.
[4] The description fits the pelican, about whose appearance there was considerable ignorance and confusion in England at this time. (I am indebted to Dr. Diana
Greenway for this note.)
[5] On 28 Feb. the king discharged the Londoners on payment of only £10,000
(*Cal. Pat. R., 1391-6*, p. 226); and see above, pp. 502-4 and n.).

1393 precepit eis rex, propter quod facta est leticia magna in populo.

Quartodecimo die Januarii aput Langeleye in Chilterne[1] fiebant solempnes exequie pro ducissa Eboracen'. Item xx. die Januarii dominus rex incepit suum parliamentum aput Wynton', et duravit usque decimum[a] diem Februarii; in quo dominus Aubricus de Veer factus est comes Oxon'.[2] Statutum eciam contra provisores promulgatum eo tempore confirmarunt, et alia plura fuerunt inibi tacta que per singula litteris exarare propter sui prolixitatem tedium legentibus[b] generaret, ideoque omissum est ea parte.[3] Septimo die Februarii fures quandam fenestram prope la Puwe fregerunt ex parte aque nocturno tempore et intrantes asportarunt jocalia ibi propter devocionem beate Virgini oblata ad valorem quingentarum marcarum.[4] Item xiiij. die Februarii idem fures vel alii nocte invaserunt ecclesiam Sancti Johannis Baptiste juxta Smethefeld'[5] et fregerunt unam fenestram dicte ecclesie et intrantes in vestibulum ejusdem crucem unam magni valoris, jocalia, pannos sericos et quosdam alios de velvetto abstulerunt ad valorem mille marcarum. Facto divulgato milites dicte domus celeriter ascenderunt eorum equos et per plura loca Anglie dictos latrones diligencius perquirentes et in tantum operam dabant quod infra quin-denam quinque comprehenderunt ex eis, quorum confes-sione innotuit eis ubi bona eorum ac eciam de la Puwe fuerint per eos furtive deducta: erant enim quedam ipsorum bonorum in quodam puteo profundo juxta Oxon' quem dicti latrones foderunt inventa, et circa principium mensis Marcii ad palacium domini regis fuerant reportata. Sicque pro majori parte dicta bona erant recuperata tam Sancti Johannis[c] quam Sancti Stephani, tamen mutilata in multis et lesa.

Item xxij. die Februarii obiit dominus Johannes Deverose miles egregius et seneschallus hospicii domini regis; in cujus

---

[a] decimum *repeated but deleted the second time.*   [b] *In the margin but marked for insertion at this point.*   [c] mu *deleted after this word.*

---

[1] In the Dominican church at King's Langley, Herts. (Walsingham, *Hist. Ang.*, ii. 215).

[2] See above, p. 510 and n.

[3] See *R.P.* iii. 300 ff. The Commons in this parliament agreed that the king

in pursuance of the king's instructions to them; and this set 1393 off great popular rejoicing.

On 14 January the funeral of the duchess of York took place with due ceremony at Langley in the Chilterns.[1] On 20 January the king opened at Winchester a parliament which lasted until 10 February; in the course of it Sir Aubrey de Vere was made earl of Oxford.[2] At this time, too, the statute published against provisors was confirmed; and several other topics were discussed in this parliament, but a detailed account of each of them would weary readers by its length and is consequently here omitted.[3] On the night of 7 February thieves who had broken a window by the 'Pew' on the side [of St. Stephen's Chapel] nearest the river got in and made off with 500 marks' worth of jewels offered there in devotion to the Blessed Virgin.[4] On 14 February the same, or other, thieves burgled the church of St. John the Baptist near Smithfield[5] at night; they broke a window and got into the vestry, from which they carried off a very valuable cross and jewels and fabrics, some of silk and others of velvet, worth altogether 1,000 marks. When the theft became known, the knights of the hospital were quickly mounted and off on a thorough search of many areas of England for the robbers, with such attention to their task that inside a fortnight they had laid five of them by the heels, from whose confessions they learned where their property, and that of the 'Pew' too, had been surreptitiously conveyed. Some of the stolen goods were found in a deep pit which the robbers had dug near Oxford and these were brought back to the king's palace about the beginning of March. And so the greater part of the property both of St. John's and St. Stephen's was recovered, though in many cases mutilated and damaged.

On 22 February occurred the death of Sir John Devereux, an outstanding knight who was steward of the king's household;

should continue to have a discretionary power, subject to the assent of the lords and the council, in the enforcement of the Statute of Provisors. See also *Diplomatic Correspondence of Richard II*, ed. Perroy, no. 158; and above, p. 482 and n.

[4] Cf. *Cal. Pat. R., 1391-6*, p. 244. The 'Pew' was the chapel or oratory of St. Mary the Pew on the south side of St. Stephen's Chapel in the Palace of Westminster; see *History of the King's Works*, ed. Colvin, i. 517.

[5] i.e. the church of the Hospital of St. John of Jerusalem in Clerkenwell (*Cal. Pat. R., 1391-6*, p. 241).

1393 loco dominus Thomas Percy fuit subrogatus.[1] Tunc dominus Willelmus Scrop' factus est camberlanus domini regis.[2] Item quinto die Marcii dux Lancastr', dux Gloucestr', episcopus Dunelm', magister Ricardus Rounhale, dominus Thomas Percy, dominus Johannes Harleston', dominus Lodowycus Clyfford' et alii electi ad tractandum de pace cum Francigenis transierunt Calesiam;[3] duravitque tractatus per annum et amplius, verumptamen modicum profuit Anglicis. Septimo die Junii aput Stafford' tres famosi latrones erant suspensi, de quibus unus fuit sacerdos decens persona et pulcher aspectu. Item xx. die Junii venerunt de tractatu duces Lancastr' et Gloucestr', fueruntque ad anniversarium patris eorum domini Edwardi tercii quondam regis Anglie.[4] Circa finem Julii proclamatum fuit London' quod inter Angliam et Franciam capta fuit treuga duratura a festo Sancti Michaelis usque idem festum anno revoluto.[5] Nam rex p. 210 Francorum gravi infirmitate detentus non vacabat / sibi circa tractatus occupari protunc, etenim fuit cessatum a tractatu inter duo regna usque festum Nativitatis beate Marie, in quo ex condicto Francigene venirent ad dominum nostrum regem aput Eltham; set venire parvipendebant.[6] Igitur deliberato ex utraque parte consilio iterato redierunt dicti duces ad Cales' et tractabant cum Francis diu usque festum Natalis Domini; redigeruntque in scriptis eorum acta utriusque partis sigillis auctenticis consignata.

[1] Cf. Rymer, *Foedera*, vii. 739, a reference to Percy as steward of the household on 22 Feb. 1393. For Devereux's death that day see also P.R.O., C. 136/80/18.

[2] Scrope was appointed under-chamberlain in the parliament which met at Winchester from 20 Jan. to 10 Feb. 1393 (*Vita Ricardi Secundi*, p. 133; Tout, *Chapters*, iii. 463).

[3] Sir John Harleston, a chamber knight lately returned from captivity in Prussia, is not named in the procuration dated 22 Feb. 1393 (Rymer, *Foedera*, vii. 738–9). The commission to Lancaster and Gloucester was renewed, with larger powers, on 12 Sept., 1393 and that to Lancaster renewed on 10 Mar. 1394, when the duke of York was named in place of Gloucester (ibid., pp. 753, 769–70). The negotiations, conducted throughout at Leulingham, were in two phases. The first conference, opening in Mar. 1393 and issuing in a draft treaty sealed on 13 June 1393, was interrupted by a month's adjournment beginning on 29 Apr. The accounts of Walter Skirlaw (bishop of Durham) and Lewis Clifford for this embassy show that they left London on, respectively, 27 and 28 Feb. The second phase began in late Mar. 1394 and lasted until the end of May or beginning of June. See P.R.O., E. 364/26, m. 53[v]; ibid., 27, m. 2[v]; ibid., E. 403/543, 10 May, 4 June, etc.; *Chronique du religieux de S. Denys*, ed. Bellaguet, ii. 75 ff.;

he was replaced by Sir Thomas Percy.[1] At the same time 1393
Sir William Scrope became the king's chamberlain.[2] On 5
March the dukes of Lancaster and Gloucester, the bishop of
Durham, Master Richard Ronhale, Sir Thomas Percy, Sir
John Harleston, Sir Lewis Clifford, and others who had been
chosen to treat with the French for peace crossed to Calais;[3]
the negotiations lasted for a year and more but brought
scanty profit to the English. Three notorious robbers were
hanged at Stafford on 7 June: one of them was a priest of
great physical grace and good looks. On 20 June the dukes of
Lancaster and Gloucester arrived from the conference-table
and attended the anniversary of their father, the late King
Edward the Third.[4] Proclamation was made in London about
the end of July that a truce had been struck between England
and France which was to last from Michaelmas [29 Septem-
ber] until the same feast in the following year.[5] The king of
France, handicapped by serious infirmity, was not free to
concern himself at this time with peace negotiations, and
talks between the two kingdoms were broken off until the
Nativity of the Virgin [8 September], when under the agreed
arrangements the French were to come to our king at
Eltham; this, however, they disregarded.[6] And so, after each
side had taken counsel, the two dukes returned once more to
Calais and remained in protracted negotiations with the
French until Christmas. The proceedings were drawn up in
writing and sealed with the authentic seals of the two parties.

Froissart, *Chroniques*, xv. 112-16.   [4] The anniversary was on 21 June.
    [5] The agreement to prolong the truce of Leulingham of 1389 until 29 Sept.
1394 was reached on 28 Apr. 1393; the order for its proclamation in London
and elsewhere is dated 26 June 1393 (Rymer, *Foedera*, vii. 748).
    [6] This sentence and the next contain a mixture of truth and error. The negotia-
tions of the spring and summer of 1393 were to have been consummated in a
meeting at Calais between Richard II and Charles VI, but the renewed insanity
of Charles VI in June of that year led to a postponement until Feb. 1394. It was
no doubt Richard II's residence in Kent in May and June, in preparation for the
crossing to France, that gave rise to a report that the French were to come to him
at Eltham. A renewal of negotiations between Lancaster and Gloucester, on the
English side, and Burgundy and Berry on the French, was planned for 29 Sept.
1393 but did not come about. Skirlaw was in Calais with a delegation of lawyers
from the 2nd week in Aug. to the 2nd week in Oct.; the negotiations between the
royal uncles were not resumed until March 1394. The sealed report referred to at
the end of this paragraph is the draft treaty of 13 June 1393. See P.R.O., E.
364/27, m. 2ᵛ; Palmer, in *T.R.H.S.*, 5th ser., xvi (1966), 81 ff.; and idem, *England, France and Christendom, 1377-99*, pp. 146 ff. and references given there.

1393   Item in mense Junii isto anno dominus rex fecit celebrari London' aput Sanctum Paulum unum solempne Placebo et Dirige cum missa die sequenti pro anima imperatricis et matris domine Anne regine Anglie;[1] ubi eciam regiis sumptibus erectum fuit imperiale feretrum valde curiosum quale in ecclesia Sancti Pauli nusquam[a] antea fuit visum. Item in mense Julii cognati Willelmi Bekwyth' de Thoma Blande, eo quod ipse recepit ab emulis dicti Willelmi quinquaginta marcas ut proderet eum illis nec pro ejus anima aliquid erogavit;[b][2] unde insidias ei paraverunt, quod ipse persenciens tucius se custodivit ab eis. Ipsi vero exasperati statuerunt finale colloquium cum illo habere, quare securitate hinc inde facta cum certis personis insimul convenerunt. Cognati vero dicti Willelmi pecierunt instanter ut aliquid de predicta summa quam ipse recepit pro interfeccione eorum cognati pro ejus anima erogaret; qui nequaquam adquievit votis eorum, propter quod unus illorum, qui erat audax et omnibus aliis forcior, irruit in predictum Thomam ense nudo et eum ac filium ejus unico ictu occidit; quod videns famulus dicti Thome, tenso arcu suo, sagitta eum percussit in capite, sic quod illico mortuus pervenit in terram. Veneruntque alii cognati sui, viderunt eum mortuum, contristati sunt valde: homines vero de patria eciam multum doluerunt super morte dicti Thome. Videatis bene quomodo sanguis clamat vindictam.

    Dominus rex tenuit suum Natale aput Westmon' magnis et profusis expensis; veneruntque Londonienses ad eum diverso apparatu, alii in diversis tripudiis, alii in variis concentibus ⟨et⟩[c] cantilenis, et quamplures alii venerunt ad eum in quadam navi conficta miro modo referta cum speciebus et aliis donariis pro rege et regina aliisque personis nobilibus largiendis. Major vero London' erat tunc Johannes Hadlee, vir sapiens et discretus.[3]

1394   *Parliamentum.* xxix. die ⟨Januarii⟩[c] aput Westmonasterium tenuit rex suum parliamentum, ubi protunc erant publicata[d]

---

[a] *Recte* numquam?   [b] *Some words, including a main verb, have been omitted from the MS.*   [c] *MS. om.*   [d] est *deleted after this word.*

---

[1] Elizabeth of Pomerania, widow of the Emperor Charles IV.
[2] See also above, p. 486 and n.
[3] Hadley, a grocer, was elected on 13 Oct. 1393 (*Letter Book H*, p. 401).

In June this year the king caused to be celebrated at St. 1393
Paul's, London, a solemn Placebo and Dirige, with a Mass on
the following day, for the soul of the empress, mother of
Anne, queen of England;[1] and a very unusual imperial
shrine, the like of which had nowhere been seen before in
the church of St. Paul, was also put up there at the king's
expense. In July the family of William Beckwith [exacted
retribution from] Thomas Bland, who had received 50 marks
as the price of betraying their kinsman to his enemies but
had spent nothing for the benefit of the dead man's soul.[2]
They accordingly made preparations to waylay him, but he
got wind of this and increased the means of safeguarding
himself against them. Losing their patience, they now
resolved to have a final interview with him, and when assurances had been exchanged, a meeting attended by certain
other persons took place between the parties. Beckwith's
family pressed their demand that out of the sum he had
received for his part in the killing of their kinsman Bland
should lay out something for the benefit of his soul; but he
flatly refused to fall in with their wishes, and in consequence
one of them, a reckless fellow tougher than any of the others,
hurled himself with his sword drawn upon Bland and with a
single blow killed him and his son. Seeing this, a servant of
Bland's bent his bow and hitting the assailant in the head
with an arrow dropped him dead on the spot. Others of
Bland's family now came up and were deeply grieved at the
sight of his corpse. His death was also much mourned by the
people of the surrounding countryside. You may clearly
see how blood cries out for vengeance.

The king lavished a great deal of expense on the Christmas
he celebrated at Westminster, where he was visited by the
Londoners with colourful pageantry, in which some engaged
in merry-making of various kinds, some rendered assorted
choruses and songs, and a large number arrived in a mock
ship remarkably crammed with spices and other gifts for
presentation to the king and queen and other persons of
rank. The mayor of London at this time was John Hadley,
a man of wisdom and judgement.[3]

Parliament. On 29 [January] the king held a parliament at 1394
Westminster during which an account of what was happening

1394 inter milites seniores et valenciores regni que fiebant in tractatu;[1] quibus perlectis et cunctis articulis seriatim patefactis eisdem displicuit enim eis in multis, primo quia absurdum esset quod rex Anglie faceret[a] regi Francorum homagium et fidelitatem pro Aquitannia et aliis terris suis ultramarinis ac tandem homoligius suus deveniret, sicque per hoc omnes Anglicos quotquot erant sub dominio regis Anglie rex Francorum suppeditaret ac sub servili jugo in posterum detineret; secundo non obstantibus predictis dux Berrye et dux Burgundie libere tenerent quasdam provincias peroptimas in Aquitannia ad totam vitam suam tantum, quarum reversio post mortem eorundem deveniret ad ducem Lancastr' vel suos heredes: et hec forent magnum prejudicium corone Anglie et exheredacio dampnosa regi Anglie imperpetuum.[2] Istis et aliis circumspecte pensatis noluerunt domini Anglie neque communitas ejusdem tali concordie assentire:[3] nam revera si mediocres hoc fecissent profecto ilico prodicionis notam non immerito incurrissent. Set dux Lancastr' facit quicquid libet absque nota. Circumvenit enim fratrem suum dominum ducem Gloucestr' promittendo sibi, ut dicitur, quasdam terras ut sue faveret opinioni nec sue contrariando perversissime intencioni. Hec fuit in vulgo crebra et quasi vera assercio confirmata, eaque dux Gloucestr' vocem populi deinceps amisit.

Finito parliamento sexto die Marcii dux Lancastr' cum aliquibus superius nominatis [b]⟨r⟩ediit Calesiis[b] significans Francigenis Anglorum ultimam voluntatem; confirmataque adhuc treuga inter duo regna per quatuor annos protunc et non amplius duratura.[4] Quo eciam tempore obiit ille miles

---

[a] Written above juraret, which has been expunged.   [b-b] In the margin but marked for insertion here.

[1] The draft treaty between England and France, agreed in June 1393, was rehearsed by the chancellor in his speech on 29 Jan.; for the text see J. J. N. Palmer, 'Articles for a Final Peace between England and France, 16 June 1393', in *B.I.H.R.*, xxxix (1966), 182–5. See also *R.P.*, iii. 315–16.

[2] Cf. Palmer, in *T.R.H.S.*, 5th ser., xvi (1966), 85 ff.; Vale, *English Gascony, 1399–1453*, p. 28 n., and above, pp. lxii–lxiii. For an earlier proposal of a usufruct for the duke of Berry, see above, p. 490.

[3] Cf. *R.P.*, iii. 315–16, recording the assent of the commons, provided that conditions prescribed by the lords and council for the proposed homage for Aquitaine were accepted. The conditions were that the homage should be simple and leave the king's other territories unaffected.

in the peace negotiations was given to the kingdom's more mature and substantial knights.[1] When this had been read through and each article in succession had been disclosed to them, there were many respects in which they were dissatisfied with it: first in that it would be ludicrous for the king of England to do homage and fealty to the French king for Aquitaine and other overseas territories and in fine become his liegeman, with the corollary that every single Englishman having the king of England as his lord would pass under the heel of the French king and be kept for the future under the yoke of slavery; secondly, despite all this, the dukes of Berry and Burgundy were to have a life interest only in the freehold of some of the very best provinces of Aquitaine, of which the reversion after their deaths was to devolve upon the duke of Lancaster and his heirs: this would be highly injurious to the English Crown and a ruinous disherison of the kings of England for all time.[2] After carefully weighing these and other considerations, both the lords and the commons of England refused their consent to an agreement on such terms:[3] indeed, if it had been men of modest station who had propounded them, they would have been immediately, and deservedly, branded as traitors on the spot. But the duke of Lancaster does as he likes, and nobody brands him. He duped his own brother, the duke of Gloucester, by promising, it is said, to give him a reward in land in return for supporting his opinions and forbearing to oppose his sinister designs. Statements to this effect were common among the public at large, and their truth was regarded as proved; in consequence the duke of Gloucester from now on lost popular support.

The parliament having come to an end on 6 March the duke of Lancaster, accompanied by some of the persons named above, returned to Calais to inform the French of the English government's last word; and the truce between the two kingdoms was confirmed for a further period of four years and no more.[4] At this time the death occurred in

[4] On 27 May 1394 the truce of Leulingham of 1389 was further extended to 29 Sept. 1398 (Rymer, *Foedera*, vii. 769-76). The Monk refers to the list of envoys on p. 514 above, but none named there is known to have accompanied Lancaster on this later mission; for those who did see P.R.O., E. 364/27, mm. 5[V], 8. One name in the later list, that of Mr. Ralph Selby, is of singular interest, since 4 years later he became a monk at Westminster (*Monks*, pp. 128-9).

1394 famosus in Lombardia dominus Johannes Haukewode, qui de paupere apprenticio caligarii London' venit Lombardiam, ubi miraculose se habuit tam in actibus bellicis extrinsecis quam in armis intrinsecis, quod numquam in Lombardia similis illi fuit inventus.[1] Vicesimo quinto die Marcii obiit ducissa Lancastr' senior filia domini Petri quondam regis Hispanie, et aput Leycestr' sepelitur.[2] Septimo die Junii aput manerium de Shene obiit Anna regina Anglie et filia imperatoris; quam summo mane nono die Junii dominus Thomas de Arundell' archiepiscopus Eboracen' et cancellarius Anglie in ecclesia Sancti Petri Westmon' sepelivit.[3]

Vicesimo die Junii proclamatum fuit London' sub pena et forisfactura omnium bonorum mobilium et immobilium quod omnes Hibernici in terra illa procreati et nati atque hic in terra Anglie quoquomodo vel quacumque industria radicati sive possessionati sint in Hibernia xv. die Augusti ad conducendum dominum nostrum regem in Hibernia ubicumque se inibi divertere disposuerit.[4] Item circa principium mensis Julii obiit comitissa Derbeye in puerperio, et aput Leycestr' est sepulta.[5] Erat namque ista comitissa junior filia domini Umfredi de Bohoun quondam comitis Herefordie, cujus soror senior vivit desponsata duci Gloucestr'; et utraque istarum reliquit post se semen satis gloriosum:[6] istis quoque duabus sororibus hereditas duorum comitatuum, Herefordie videlicet et Northampton', inter se spectabat equaliter[a] dividenda.

[a] In the margin but marked for insertion here.

---

[1] Hawkwood died in Florence on 16-17 Mar. 1394. His origins were not humble (D.N.B., ix. 236).

[2] The obit for Constance, duchess of Lancaster, was kept on 24 March, and this is the probable date of her death; she was buried in the church of St. Mary's Abbey, Leicester (Armitage-Smith, John of Gaunt, p. 429).

[3] Anne of Bohemia was buried in Westminster Abbey on 3 Aug. 1394 (P.R.O., E. 101/402/20, p. 57; Rymer, Foedera, vii. 776). The chronicler's mistake will seem less surprising if we take into account the fact that after 1394 and until Richard II's own death Anne was commemorated at Westminster on the day of her death: the exact date of her burial would have been quickly forgotten.

[4] The writ ordering this proclamation is dated 16 June (Letter Book H, p. 412; see also Cal. Pat. R., 1391-6, pp. 451-2, 453 ff.).

Lombardy of the celebrated knight Sir John Hawkwood, 1394
who, having started life as the poor apprentice of a London
hosier, made his way to Lombardy, where his exploits, both
in foreign wars and in internal conflicts, were so marvellous
that his like had never been found there.[1] The duchess of
Lancaster, elder daughter of Pedro, sometime king of Spain,
died on 25 March and was buried at Leicester.[2] On 7 June
Anne, queen of England, and daughter of the emperor, died
at the manor of Sheen; and early in the morning of the 9th
Thomas Arundel, archbishop of York and chancellor of
England, conducted the burial in the church of St. Peter,
Westminster.[3]

Proclamation was made in London on 20 June that on
pain of forfeiture of all their goods, movable and immovable,
all Irishmen born and begotten in Ireland and in any way,
or by reason of any business, established or possessed of any
property here in England, were to be in Ireland on 15 August
to escort our lord the king wherever in that country he was
inclined to travel.[4] About the beginning of July the countess
of Derby died in childbed and was buried at Leicester.[5]
This countess was the younger daughter of Humphrey de
Bohun, sometime earl of Hereford; her elder sister, who
survives, is married to the duke of Gloucester; and each of
the sisters has left illustrious offspring behind her.[6] The
succession to two earldoms, Hereford and Northampton,
belonged to the two of them in equal proportions.

[5] Mary, younger daughter of Humphrey de Bohun, earl of Hereford and Essex
and of Northampton, and constable of England (d. 1373), married Henry earl of
Derby in 1380. She was buried in the college of the Newark, Leicester, on 6 July
(Knighton, *Chronicon*, ii. 321; *Issue Rolls of the Exchequer, Henry III to Henry
VI*, ed. Devon, p. 321; McFarlane, *Lancastrian Kings and Lollard Knights*, p. 16).

[6] Eleanor, elder daughter of Humphrey de Bohun, who married Thomas of
Woodstock, earl of Gloucester, between 1374 and 1376, bore him one son,
Humphrey, for whom see *G.E.C.*, v. 729. For the 5 sons of the marriage of Mary
de Bohun and Henry, earl of Derby, see *Handbook of British Chronology*, ed.
Powicke and Fryde, p. 37. In his next words the Monk alludes reticently to a
cause célèbre, the attempt of Thomas of Woodstock to frustrate the claims of
Mary de Bohun to a pourparty of the Bohun inheritance; see R. Somerville,
History of the Duchy of Lancaster, i (*1265-1603*) (London, 1953), pp. 67-8
and nn.; C. Rawcliffe, *The Staffords, Earls of Stafford and Dukes of Buckingham,
1394-1521* (Cambridge, 1978), pp. 12 ff.

APPENDIX

The following is the text of the passage deleted after the words *personaliter fuissent in Anglia* on p. 138 of the MS. (See above, p. 46.)

1383   Et taliter isti milites egerunt ut vita sua, immo bonis suis, fruerentur. Profecto istud dampnabile factum numquam ab Anglicis militibus gestum esse cognoscimus, ut cicius temporalia lucra et momentanea contenderent servare quam bonam famam accumulare, que universis*a* bonis*b* *c*fortuitis preminet et precellit . . . possumus*c* adaptare: 'Erubesce, Sydon, ait mare'? *c*. . . Anglicis. . . .*c* Utinam non*d* fuisset hec pecunia, pro qua tanto facinore se*e* involverent ut tam vili pacto villas domino regi virtute bellica conquisitas sic de facili redderent *f*in manus inimicorum suorum.*f* Interea dum hec infeliciter agerentur videns episcopus sibi et suis periculum imminere secessit in Gravenyngg' cum domino Hugone de Calveleye et suis; cogitavit enim illud fortilicium contra suos adversarios aliquandiu tenere; set deficientibus hominibus armorum cum victualibus et succursu solotenus illud destruxit, prout inter ipsum et Francigenas extitit concordatum. Ipse *c*modicum post festum sancti Michaelis*c* cum suis salvus in terram Anglie veniens ad ducem Lancastr' se contulit, qui per totum mensem Septembris cum suo retenemento in Cancia juxta mare jacebat, ostendens se quasi paratum succurrere episcopo, quod non perfecit; a quo statim discedens pervenit ad regem, quem leta fronte suscipiens in

---

a Written over an erasure.   *b* Added in the margin.   *c–c* An erased marginale, still partly legible.   *d* numquam interlined as an alternative; cf. p. 46.   *e* Interlined.   *f–f* Interlind. There is a completely erased marginale opposite this point in the MS.

APPENDIX

The knights' motive in acting in this fashion was to enjoy 1383 their lives, or rather their possessions. English knights have never been known to do a deed so worthy of condemnation as their preferring to strive to preserve this world's ephemeral riches rather than to lay up for themselves that good name that outshines and overtops all fortune's favours. . . . Can we . . . apply . . . 'Be then ashamed, O Zidon, for the sea hath spoken'? . . . Englishmen . . . Would that that money had never existed for which they involved themselves in so great a crime that by a shabby bargain they tamely surrendered into the hands of his enemies towns which had been won for him by soldierly prowess. While these sorry doings were afoot, the bishop, seeing the danger that loomed over himself and his forces, withdrew into Gravelines, accompanied by Sir Hugh Calveley and his men; for he contemplated holding this stronghold for some time against his opponents; but for want of men-at-arms and food supplies to provide relief, he razed it to the ground in conformity with an agreement made between him and the French. Shortly after Michaelmas he arrived safely in England with his forces and betook himself to the duke of Lancaster, who throughout September had lain with his followers on the coast of Kent, ready, to all appearances, to go to the bishop's relief, though this he failed to do. Quickly leaving the duke, the bishop went to the king, who gave him a smiling welcome and laid himself out to do

1383 multis illum studuit honorare. *a*Ganenses vero deserta obsidione de Ipres paulo post quandam villam ceperunt vocatam Audonard, in qua inmensos thesauros et vina in maxima habundancia invenerunt; quibus ditati et referti ordinatis et positis capitaneis ad tutelam ville predicte ad propria sunt reversi: exultat nimium civitas Ganens' pro tantorum adquisicione bonorum; quare degentes in ea longe post erant opulenciores.*a*

*b*Septimo Kalendas Novembres tenuit rex suum parliamentum apud Westmonasterium; et duravit usque vigiliam Sancte Katerine, in quo concessa*c* fuit regi per viros ecclesiasticos *d*una decima,*d* et unam quintamdecimam concesserunt laici; et he*e* de difficili erant concesse et sub condicione, scilicet quod si rex haberet pacem cum Francigenis et Scotis tunc*f* sit contentus habere medietatem concessorum, alias concessa plene*g* haberet ad ultimum persoluta in festo Paschatis proximo futuro.*b* Incepto parliamento, ut proxime dictum est, misit rex Francie domino nostro regi et ad suum consilium ut mitteret aliquos nobiles ac viros discretos apud Cales' ad tractandum de pace; et ibidem prope quasi in confinio regni sui ea de causa statuit aliquos de suis nobilibus expectare; quod factum pluribus mirum videtur scilicet*h* quod rex Francie pro tractatu pacis nobis mitteret ex quo de nostris manum validiorem insolite reportavit et illos ad terram Anglie redire coegit. Diriguntur tamen ex parte nostra ad tractandum cum eis dux Lancastr', episcopus Hereforden', magister Walterus Skyrlowe doctor legum et portitor privati sigilli, magister Johannes Shepeye doctor legum et dominus Willelmus Nevyle miles,*h* qui de mense Novembris venerunt Cales' et fuerunt ibi per totum Natale et diu*i* post. Circa principium mensis Novembris Scoti invadebant partes Northumbranas, homines occiderunt, spoliarunt et totam patriam more hostili dampnis gravissimis consumebant: quapropter consilium regis super hoc informatum ordinavit ut domini habentes terras et redditus in partibus illis transirent

---

a-a The order of this sentence and the one that here succeeds it is reversed in the MS., but they are marked for transposition by the insertion in the margin of the letters b and a. *b-b See previous note.* *c Altered in MS. from concessum.* *d-d Interlined.* *e he Winterbottom; hoc MS.* *f Written over an erasure.* *g In the margin but marked for insertion here.* *h Interlined.* *i Written above longo tempore, which has been deleted.*

him numerous courtesies. The men of Ghent abandoned 1383
the siege of Ypres and a little later captured a town
called Oudenarde, in which they found untold treasure
and wine in the greatest abundance. Gorged and enriched,
they returned to their homes, having appointed and
posted captains to safeguard the town: the city of Ghent
was overjoyed at the accession of so much property, in
consequence of which the inhabitants for a long time
afterwards enjoyed increased affluence. On 26 October
the king held at Westminster a parliament which lasted
until St. Katherine's Eve and in which the king was
granted a tenth by the clergy and a fifteenth by the
laity; these grants were made with reluctance and subject
to the condition that, if the king made peace with the
French and the Scots, he was to be satisfied to have half
of the subsidies granted; otherwise he was to have the
grants in full to be paid at the following Easter at the
latest. When, as has just been reported, the parliament
opened, the king of France sent to our king and his
council to suggest that they should send men of rank and
judgement to Calais to conduct negotiations for peace; he
himself had laid it down that certain members of his own
nobility should, with the same purpose in view, wait near
by, on the very edge, as it were, of his kingdom. It
seemed to many people a surprising move that the king of
France should send to suggest peace-negotiations when for
once he had gained the upper hand of our troops and
forced them to return to England. Representatives were
however sent on our behalf to treat with the French:
they were the duke of Lancaster, the bishop of Hereford,
Master Walter Skirlaw LL.D. and keeper of the privy seal,
Master John Sheppey LL.D., and Sir William Nevill. They
reached Calais in November and remained there over the
whole of the Christmas season and for a long time after.
About the beginning of November the Scots attacked
Northumberland, slaughtering and pillaging and inflicting
very severe damage by their hostile devastation of the
entire countryside. The king's council, apprised of this,
consequently gave orders that gentry owning lands or
revenues in those parts should go there and protect their

1383 illinc,*a* terras et dominia eorum regisque a talibus invasionibus
custodirent, ac illi eo pacto ab omni tallagio sive taxacione
prorsus*b* forent immunes *c*cum suis.*c* Unde provide statuit
consilium predictum custodes patrie et plage predicte viros
prospicuos et preclaros, scilicet archiepiscopum Eboracen',
episcopum Carlien', dominum de Nevyll', dominum Fitz
Watre, dominum Ricardum Scrop', cum aliis dominis inibi
in partibus commorantibus et vasallis, concedensque eis
plenariam potestatem omnia faciendi que ad regni comodum
et honorem cedere poterunt quousque ea duxerit revocanda.

a Sic MS.; *recte* illuc.   *b* Interlined.   *c-c* Interlined.

own and the king's lands and domains from aggression of this
sort: on this condition they and their dependents would
henceforward be quite exempt from all tallage and other
taxation. The council thereupon in its wisdom appointed as
wardens of the countryside and area concerned certain
persons of prominence and renown, namely the archbishop
of York, the bishop of Carlisle, Lord Nevill, Lord Fitz Walter,
Sir Richard Scrope, and also other gentry living in those
parts and their vassals, granting them full power to do
everything that might tend to the profit and honour of the
kingdom until the council should see fit to rescind the
commission.

CONCORDANCE

In this concordance the page in the present edition is that on which the first word of the page in *Higden* will be found.

Higden	This Edn.	Higden	This Edn.	Higden	This Edn.
1	2	40	80	79	158
2	2	41	82	80	160
3	4	42	84	81	162
4	6	43	86	82	164
5	10	44	88	83	166
6	10	45	90	84	168
7	12	46	92	85	170
8	14	47	92	86	170
9	16	48	94	87	172
10	18	49	96	88	174
11	20	50	98	89	176
12	22	51	102	90	176
13	24	52	102	91	180
14	26	53	104	92	182
15	30	54	106	93	184
16	32	55	108	94	186
17	34	56	110	95	188
18	36	57	112	96	190
19	38	58	114	97	192
20	40	59	116	98	194
21	42	60	118	99	196
22	44	61	120	100	198
23	46	62	122	101	200
24	48	63	124	102	202
25	50	64	126	103	204
26	52	65	128	104	206
27	54	66	130	105	208
28	56	67	132	106	210
29	58	68	134	107	212
30	60	69	136	108	214
31	62	70	138	109	216
32	64	71	140	110	218
33	66	72	142	111	220
34	68	73	144	112	222
35	72	74	148	113	224
36	72	75	148	114	226
37	74	76	150	115	228
38	76	77	154	116	228
39	78	78	156	117	232

Higden	This Edn.	Higden	This Edn.	Higden	This Edn.
118	234	169	314	220	408
119	236	170	316	221	410
120	238	171	318	222	412
121	238	172	320	223	414
122	240	173	322	224	416
123	242	174	324	225	418
124	242	175	326	226	420
125	244	176	328	227	420
126	246	177	330	228	422
127	248	178	332	229	424
128	250	179	334	230	424
129	250	180	336	231	426
130	252	181	338	232	428
131	254	182	340	233	428
132	254	183	342	234	430
133	256	184	344	235	432
134	258	185	344	236	434
135	260	186	346	237	436
136	262	187	348	238	438
137	262	188	350	239	440
138	264	189	352	240	442
139	266	190	354	241	450
140	266	191	356	242	452
141	268	192	358	243	454
142	270	193	360	244	444
143	272	194	360	245	446
144	274	195	362	246	448
145	274	196	364	247	456
146	276	197	364	248	458
147	278	198	366	249	460
148	280	199	368	250	462
149	282	200	370	251	462
150	282	201	374	252	464
151	284	202	374	253	466
152	286	203	376	254	468
153	288	204	380	255	468
154	288	205	382	256	470
155	290	206	384	257	472
156	292	207	384	258	472
157	294	208	386	259	474
158	294	209	388	260	476
159	296	210	390	261	478
160	298	211	392	262	480
161	298	212	394	263	482
162	302	213	396	264	484
163	302	214	396	265	486
164	304	215	398	266	488
165	306	216	400	267	490
166	308	217	402	268	492
167	310	218	404	269	494
168	312	219	406	270	494

Higden	This Edn.	Higden	This Edn.	Higden	This Edn.
271	496	276	506	281	516
272	498	277	508	282	518
273	500	278	510	283	520
274	502	279	512		
275	504	280	512		

INDEX OF QUOTATIONS AND ALLUSIONS

A. THE BIBLE

	page		page
Genesis:		Hosea:	
vi. 6	186	x. 9	492
1 Kings (1 Samuel):		Zechariah:	
iii. 11	492	i. 21	208
vii. 10	476	Matthew:	
2 Kings (2 Samuel):		iv. 5	26
iii. 34	492	xxiv. 2	340
vii. 10	492	xxv. 25	384
xxii. 6	184	Mark:	
4 Kings (2 Kings):		xiii. 2	340
xxi. 12	492	Luke:	
1 Chronicles:		xix. 20	384
xvii. 9	492	xix. 44	340
Psalms:		xxi. 6	340
xvii. 6 (xviii. 5)	184	xxii. 15	462
lvi. 7 (lvii. 6)	118	John:	
cxxxviii. 12 (cxxxix. 12)	84	i. 1	34
Proverbs:		i. 14	34
xxi. 6	184	Acts:	
Wisdom:		i. 3, 9–10	388
vii. 14	386	Romans:	
Ecclesiasticus:		v. 20	14
xxviii. 22 (xxviii. 18)	348	1 Corinthians:	
Isaiah:		i. 30	384
i. 6	384	Galatians:	
xxiii. 4	46	iv. 4–5	384
lvi. 10	84	Hebrews:	
Jeremiah:		ix. 12	384
xviii. 18	8	1 Peter:	
xix. 3	492	i. 18–19	384

B. LITURGY AND OFFICE

— Exultet	388	— other	386, 388
— Pange lingua	388		

C. CLASSICAL AND MEDIEVAL SOURCES

Archpoet, x. 1	464	Ovid, *Ex Ponto*, II. ix. 3	190
Horace, *Ars Poetica*, 294	12	Pseudo-Isidore	138

GENERAL INDEX

Abberbury, Sir Richard, chamber knight, 230 and n.

Abingdon (Oxon., formerly Berks.), 234

Albret, Arnand-Amanieu, lord of (1358-1401), 142 and n.

Albuquerque, Fernando Afonso de, 142 n.

Alessandria (Italy), 476 n.

Alfred, king of Wessex, d. 899, xiii, xiv n., 416 n.

Alien priories, 148 and n., 168

Aljubarrota, battle of (1385), 132 and n., 142 n.

Almain, 476; see also Germany

Alps, the, 100, 118

Alvarez, Diego, see Pereira, Diego Alvarez

Amiens (Somme, Fr.), lxii, 487 n.

Anjou, Louis I, duke of (1356-84), 98-100, 100 n.

Anjou, Louis II, duke of (1384-1417), 466 and n.

Anne of Bohemia, queen of Richard II (1382-94), xxviii, 42, 86, 88, 92, 140, 144, 154, 160, 188-90, 434, 502, 506, 510

— and Westminster Abbey, 32, 450

— arrival, 22

— dower, 24 n.

— funeral, xxix, 520 and n.

— marriage, 22-4

— mother of, see Elizabeth of Pomerania

Anonimalle Chronicle, lxx nn., lxxi, lxxii

Antiphons, 506 and n.

Anti-pope, see Clement VII

Antwerp, Lionel of, son of Edward III, earl of Ulster and duke of Clarence d. 1368, 192-4, 194 n.

— Elizabeth, wife of, see Burgh, Elizabeth de

— Philippa, daughter of, m. Edmund Mortimer, earl of March, 194 n.

Appeal of treason (1387-8), xlvii, lxii, 196 n., 210-12, 214, 222 n., 234 n., 236 ff., 255 n., 267 n., 280 ff., 296-8

— art. 10, 305 n.

— art. 22, 257 n.

— art. 27, 275 n.

— art. 39, lxiv, lxv

Appellants, 202 n., 212 n., 216 n., 242 n., 248 n., 261 n., 263 n., 266 and n., 272, 274-6, 280 ff., 308 ff., 320, 328 and n., 336, 338, 342, 370

— and Londoners, lxviii, lxix, 232-4

— dissension among, lxv, 328, 330

— propaganda of, lii ff., lxii, lxiii-iv, lxix

— rising of, lxi, lxiv-v, 204 ff., 218 ff.

— See also Beauchamp, Thomas, earl of Warwick (1370-97, 1399-1401); Bolingbroke, Henry, earl of Derby; Fitzalan, Richard, earl of Arundel; Mowbray, Thomas, earl of Nottingham; Woodstock, Thomas of, duke of Gloucester

Appleton, Br. William, O.F.M., 6 and n.

Apulia (Italy), 98

Aquitaine, duchy of, 378, 484, 490 and n.

— duke of, see Gaunt, John of

— homage for, lxi, 414 n., 490, 518 and n.

— lieutenant in, see Hastings, John; Percy, Henry

— men of, 484

— See also Gascony; Guyenne; Woodstock, Edward of

Aragon, 164

Aragon, Pedro de, 133 n.

Ardres (Pas de Calais, Fr.), 457 n.

Arewelle, see Orwell Haven

Armagnac, Jean III, count of (1384-91), 142 and n., 476 and n.

Armenia, 154 n., 161 n.
— king of, *see* Leo VI
Artevelde, James van, 26
— Philip, son of, 26, 30
Artois (Fr.), county, 490
— march, 262, 278
Arundel (Suss.), castle, 88
Arundel, earl of, *see* Fitzalan, Richard, earl of Arundel
Arundel, John, lord, d. 1379, 440 n.
— John, lord, son of, d. 1390, 440 and n.
Arundel, Thomas, bishop of Ely (1373-88); archbishop of York (1388-96); chancellor (1386-9, 1391-6), lii, 168 n., 210, 226 n., 232, 233 n., 238, 286, 303 n., 324 n., 334 n., 337 n., 355 n., 382, 480, 499 and n., 520
— and Westminster Abbey, 380
Ashton, Sir Robert, keeper of Dover castle, 56
Assize of Bread and Ale, 368 n., 453 n.
Aston, Robert, 28 and n.
Audley, Sir James de, 188 and n., 244 and n.
Aumale, duke of, *see* Woodstock, Thomas of
Auray, battle of (1364), 188 and n.
Aversa (Caserta, Italy), 110 n., 163 n.
Avignon (Vaucluse, Fr.), 36 n., 464 n.
Aviz (Alto Antejo, Port.), 192 n.
Ayton, truce of (1384), 86 and n.
Azeuedo, Gonçallo Vaasquez d', 132 n.

Bablock hythe (Oxon.), 223 n.
Bache, Alexander, bishop of St. Asaph (1390-4), xxix, 434, 435 n.
Bacon, John, 142, 144 n.
Badajoz, treaty of (1382), 29 n.
Badges, 186, 256, 354-6
Bal, John, 322 n.
Baldwin, Sir, *see* Raddington, Sir Baldwin
Ball, John, 14 and n., 15 n.
Balsio, Reimundello de, 110, 111 n.
Bamburgh (Northumb.), 484
Bamme, Adam, goldsmith of London, mayor (1390-1), lxviii, 404, 450, 452, 494
Bamme, Henry, goldsmith and alderman of London, 494
Banbury (Oxon.), 220

Bangor, bishop of, *see* Swaffham, John
Bar, duc de, 352
Barbary, 432, 440, 448
Barentin, Drew, goldsmith and alderman of London, 494
Bari (Lemurge, Italy), 100 n.
Barnard castle (Durham), 486
Barnwell, (Cantab.), 369 n.
— priory, 354 n.
Barret, William, grocer and alderman of London, 494
Basingstoke (Hants), 498
Basset, Ralph, lord, of Drayton, d. 1390, 340, 434, 435 n.
Bath, bishop of, *see* Bath and Wells, bishop of
Bath and Wells:
— bishop of, *see* Erghum, Ralph; Skirlaw, Walter
— see of, 334 and n.
Battle (Suss.):
— abbey, 34 and n.
— abbot of, *see* Crane, Craneforde, John; Offynton, Haymo de
Batz Island (Fr.), 350
Bavaria, Alberic, Albert, duke of, count of Hainault, Holland, and Zealand (1389-1404), 452 and n.
— son of, *see* Ostrevantz, William, count of
Bay, the, *see* Biscay, Bay of
Bayonne (Basses Pyr., Fr.), 194 n., 195 n., 322, 344, 370 n.
Bealknap, Sir Robert, chief justice of the King's Bench, lvii and n., 96, 196, 258, 306
— proceedings against, l, 284-6, 336 n.
Beatriz, Infanta of Portugal, 28 and n.
Beauchamp, Sir John, baron of Kidderminster, d. 1388, 178, 179 n., 228
— chamber knight, 230 n., 269 n.
— proceedings against, 234 n., 236, 268 ff., 288, 292, 293 n., 318
— sentence on, 332
— steward of the king's household, 178 and n., 228, 292
Beauchamp, Thomas, earl of Warwick (1315-69), 160 n.
— Philippa, daughter of, m. Hugh de Stafford, 2nd earl of Stafford, 160 n.

Beauchamp, Thomas, earl of Warwick (1370–97, 1399–1401), 124, 160, 215 n., 218, 263 n., 267 n., 268, 288, 294
— and rising of Appellants, lii, liii, liv, lxiii–iv, 208 ff., 296–8
— in Merciless parliament, 234 ff., 280 ff., 302, 328 n., 332
Beauchamp, Sir Thomas, 440
Beauchamp, Sir Thomas, of Ryme, 440 n.
Beauchamp, Sir William, captain of Calais, 50 n., 134 and n., 136, 214, 215 n., 352, 353 n., 354; constable of army in Portugal, 31 n.; keeper of Calais, 44 n.
Beaumont, John, lord, d. 1396, 230, 376, 454, 474, 486
Beckwith, John, 443 n.
Beckwith, William, 442, 443 n., 444, 516
Belle Isle (Fr.), 352 and n.
Beltoft, Sir John, 500, 502
Bereford, Sir Baldwin, 230 and n.
Berkhampstead castle (Berks.), 20
Bermondsey (Surr.), 322
Bernabò, lord of Milan, see Visconti, Bernabò
Berners, Sir James, d. 1388, lvi, 42, 228
— chamber knight, 230 n., 269 n.
— proceedings against, 234 n., 236, 268 ff., 288, 292 and n., 318
— sentence on, 332
Berry, duke of, see Berry, John, duke of
Berry, John, duke of (1360–1416), 371 n., 372, 487 n., 490 and n., 515 n., 518
Berwick-upon-Tweed, 20 n., 40 n., 124, 147 n., 148, 154, 370, 374, 396
— captain of, see Lomley, Ralph de; Redmayne, Matthew
— castle, 104
— — keeper of, see Percy, Henry, earl of Northumberland; and Percy, Sir Henry (Hotspur)
Bethlehem, bishop of, see Bottesham, William
Bettenham, William, 31 n.
Beverhoutsveld, battle of (1382), 24, 25 n., 26
Beverley (Yorks.), 122 n.

— St. John's College at, 178, 180 and n., 245 n.
Beza, Theodore, xiv
Billericay (Essx.), 12 n.
Bilton Park (Yorks.), bailiff of, 443 n.
Biscay, Bay of, 352
Bishop's Clyst (Devon), 85 n.
Blackheath (Surr.), 2 n.
Blake, John, 202, 230 and n., 231 n., 244, 260, 270, 285 n.
— proceedings against, l, li, 269 n., 284
— referendary, 258
— sentence on, 284, 285 n., 314
Blake, Robert, 322 n.
Bland, Thomas, 486, 516
Blockley (Worcs.), 220
Blois, Charles de, count of Penthièvre, d. 1364, 188 and n.
Blois, Jean de, see Bretagne, Jean de
Blount, Sir Thomas, 230, 456 n.
— chamber knight, 231 n.
Bohemia, Bohemians, 274, 290, 476
Bohun, Humphrey de, earl of Hereford, Essex, and Northampton, d. 1373, 192, 479 n., 521 and n.
— Eleanor, daughter of, m. Thomas of Woodstock, earl of Gloucester, see Woodstock, Thomas of
— Mary, daughter of, m. Henry Bolingbroke, earl of Derby, see Bolingbroke, Henry
Bolingbroke, Henry, earl of Derby (1377–99), later duke of Lancaster and Henry IV of England, 192, 268, 432, 434 n., 458, 521 n.
— and rising of Appellants, lxiv–lxv, 208 and n., 218, 298, 302
— crusade to Prussia, 440, 441 n., 444 and n., 446, 448
— in Merciless Parliament, 234 ff., 280 ff., 328 n.
— Mary, wife of (Mary de Bohun), 192, 520, 521 n.
Bologna, bishop of, see Megliorato, Cosmas Gentilis
Boniface VIII, pope (1294–1303), 386, 460 n.
Boniface IX, pope (1389–1404), 382 n., 390 n., 404, 405 n., 410, 411 n., 414, 462 ff., 464 n., 465 n., 466 n., 508, 509 n.
— and Statute of Provisors, 412, 460,

462, 464 and n.
— letter of Richard II to, 468 ff.
Bordeaux (Gironde, Fr.), 152, 196, 372, 374, 375 n., 402
— mayor of, see Craddock, David
— people of, 142
Borewell, John, monk of Westminster, 379 n., 395 n.
Boston (Lincs.), 441 n.
Bottesham, Bottlesham, William de, O.P., bishop of Llandaff (1386–9), bishop of Rochester (1389–1400), 144 and n., 164, 165 n., 318–20, 394 and n.
— bishop of Bethlehem, 144
Bouin Island (now Bouin, Vendée, Fr.), 352
Boulogne (Pas de Calais, Fr.), 88 n., 374 n., 457 n., 487 n.
— truce of, 1384, 98 and n.
Bourbon, duke of, see Bourbon, Louis II, duke of
Bourbon, Louis II, duke of (1356–1410), 448, 450 n., 456 n., 487 n.
Bourbourg (Nord, Fr., formerly Flanders), 38, 39 n., 44 and n., 46 n.
Bourgchier, John, lord, d. 1400, 474–6
Bourgneuf (Loire Inf., Fr.), 352
Bourton-on-the-Hill (Glos.), 220 and n.
Bourton-under-Cotswold, see Bourton-on-the-Hill
Bouteville (Charente, Fr.), 352 n.
Bowet, Henry, 300 and n.
Boys, Hugh, citizen of London, 494
Brabant, 309 n., 344 n., 371 n., 372 and n., 492, 510
Brabant, Wenzel, duke of, d. 1383, 370, 372 n.
— —, Joanna, wife of, 372 n.
Brailes (Warwicks.), 220
Brampton, William, stockfishmonger and alderman of London, 494
Brantingham, Thomas de, bishop of Exeter (1370–94), treasurer (1389), 168, 232, 392, 402 and n.
— quarrel with archbishop of Canterbury, xviii, 84 and n., 85 n., 86
Braybrooke, Robert, bishop of London (1381–1404), chancellor (1382–3), 23 and n., 28 and n., 32, 36, 37 n., 138, 158, 332, 333 n., 343 n., 436, 438 and n., 450, 510

Brembre, Nicholas, grocer of London, mayor (1377–8, 1383–6), lv, lxix, 212 n., 214, 234 n., 245 n., 248, 249 n., 260, 264, 266, 270, 296
— and John of Gaunt, 144, 145 n.
— arrest, 214 n., 228, 230 n.
— election (1383), xxiv, lvi, lxvii, lxviii, 60, 62 and n.; (1384), lxvii, 100–2; (1385), xxvii, 136
— proceedings against, xlvii, lxv, 210–12, 236 ff., 280 ff., 308 ff.
— sentence on, 284, 314
— widow of, 406
Brentwood (Essx.), xxiii, 2 n., 12, 406 n.
Brest (Finistere, Fr.), 184, 185 nn., 196 and n., 262
— captain of, see Fitzalan, Richard, earl of Arundel; Holland, John
— castle, 262
Bretagne, Guy de, 188 n.
Bretagne, Jean de, count of Penthièvre (Jean de Blois), 188 and n., 256, 257 n., 301 n.
Breynte, John, monk of Westminster, xxxvii n.
Bridford, William, abbot of St. Mary's, York (1382–9), 402
Brien, Sir Guy de, 438, 439 n.
Brinton, Thomas, bishop of Rochester (1373–89), 392, 393 n.
Bristol (Avon, formerly Glos.), 454
— castle, 230 n.
Brittany, duchess of, see Holland, Joan
—, duchy of, 189 n., 400 n.
—, duke of, see Montfort, John de
—, parlement of, 152 n.
Broadwell (Glos.), 220 n.
Bromfield, Mr. Edmund, O.S.B., monk of Bury St. Edmunds, bishop of Llandaff (1389–93), 394 and n.
— abbot of La Grande Sauve, 394 n.
Bromyard, John, O.P., Summa Praedicantium, xlii n.
Brounfeld, Edmund de, 42 n.; see also Bromfield, Edmund
Bruce, David, see David II, king of Scotland
Bruges (W. Flanders, Belg.), 24 and n., 26, 30 n., 32 and n., 124, 152 and n.
Buckingham, earl of, see Woodstock, Thomas of

Bulls, papal, 30, 34, 164 n., 178 n., 196, 204, 390 n., 404
— Antiquorum habet fida, 1300, 387 n.
— Dignum censemus, 1382, 30 n.
— Dudum cum filii Belial, 1381, 30 n.
— Dudum cum vinea Dei, 1381, 30 n.
— Ineffabile sacramentum, 1429, 395 n.
— Salvator noster, 1389, xxi, 384 ff.
— Transiturus, 1264, 395 n.
— Unigenitus Dei filius, 1343, 384 n., 387 n.
— — so-called bull, 1391, 458
Burford (Oxon.), lxiv n., 220 n.
Burgh, William de, earl of Ulster, d. 1333, 194 n.
— Elizabeth, daughter of, m. Lionel of Antwerp, 194 and n.
Burgh, Sir William, justice of the Common Bench, 196, 258, 306
— proceedings against, 284-6, 316, 336 n.
Burghersh, Bartholomew de, d. 1355, 231 n.
— Joan, daughter of, m. John, lord Mohun, 230, 231 n.
Burgundy, Philip the Bold, duke of (1363-1404), count of Flanders (1384-1404), 150, 152 and n., 328 n., 371 n., 372, 374 n., 464, 465 n., 466 n., 487 n., 515 n., 518
Burley, Sir Richard, 190 and n.
Burley, Sir Simon, d. 1388, xxvi, 160, 293 n., 414-16
— arrest, 228, 230 n.
— chamber knight, 269 n.
— chamberlain, 72, 274
— constable/keeper of Dover castle, 56, 228, 272, 273 n., 276 n.
— constable of Windsor castle, 272, 273 n.
— knight of Garter, 292
— proceedings against, xlviii, l, lxxiv, 234 n., 236, 268 ff., 286-8, 318, 328 and n.
— sentence on, 290-2, 330-2
— under-chamberlain, 275 n., 276 n.
— tutor to Richard II, 275 n., 276 n.
— warden of the Cinque Ports, 276 n.
Burnell, Hugh, lord, d. 1420, 230, 231 n.

— wife of, 231 n.
Burton, John, keeper of the rolls of Chancery, xlix, li, 234 n.
Bury St. Edmunds (Suff.), abbey, 42, 376, 394
— abbot of, see Cratfield, William; Timworth, John de
— Edmund, monk of, see Bromfield, Edmund

Calais (Pas de Calais, Fr.), lx, lxi, 24, 33, 38, 88, 98, 134-6, 140, 154, 158, 160, 164, 166, 180, 188 n., 262, 278, 322, 352, 374 and n., 376, 398, 430, 432, 434 n., 456, 514, 515 n., 518, 524
— captain of, see Beauchamp, William; Percy, Henry, earl of Northumberland
— castle, 214, 262, 278; keeper of, see Pole, Edmund de la
— 'crossing to Calais', lviii, 330, 374, 436, 486, 514
— harbour, 134
— keeper of, see Beauchamp, William; Devereux, John
— men of, 178, 184
— negotiations at, 24, 48-50, 58, 116
— siege of, 30
— wool staple at, 354, 454 n., 480, 481 n.
Calatrava, master of, see Pereira, Pedro Alvarez
— Order of, 192 n.
Calveley, Sir Hugh, 44 and n., 46, 522
Cambridge, 186, 344, 430
— parliament at (1388), 354 ff., 372
Cambridge, earl of, see Langley, Edmund of
Camois, Sir Thomas, 230
Campbernart, Hennart de, 399 n.
Campden, see Chipping Campden
Canterbury (Kent):
— archbishop of, see Courtenay, William; Sudbury, Simon
— archbishop's cross, 290, 320
— council at, 478 and n.
— diocese of, 438 n.
— 'duke of', see Langley, Edmund of
— St. Augustine's abbey, 180, 202-4, 384

— —, abbot of, *see* Pecham, Michael; Welde, William

Capua, duchy of (Italy), 108, 110 and n.

Carlisle (Cumb.), 132-4, 384, 418, 420

— bishop of, 50, 86, 526; *see also* Merks, Thomas

— castle, keeper of, *see* Scrope, Richard

Carlisle, Adam, grocer and alderman of London, 494

Carrión, count of, *see* Sánchez Manuel, Juan

Cary, Sir John, chief baron of the Exchequer, 197 n., 258, 306

— proceedings against, 284, 286, 336 n.

Castile:

— *adelantado* mayor of, 133 n.

— kingdom of, 164, 194, 195 n.

— king of, *see* Juan I

— prior of St. John of, *see* Diaz, Pedro

Chamberlain, the king's, 76, 80, 356, 418; *see also* Burley, Simon; Courtenay, Peter de; Holland, John; Vere, Aubrey de; Vere, Robert de

— under-chamberlain, 418; *see also* Burley, Simon; Percy, Thomas; Scrope, William

Chamberlain of the Exchequer, *see* Lincoln, John

Champerty, 358 n.

Chancellor, 42, 52 and n., 164 n., 168, 216; *see also* Arundel, Thomas; Braybrooke, Robert; Courtenay, William; Pole, Michael de la; Scrope, Richard; Wykeham, William of

Chancery, xlvi, xlviii, xlix, 170, 264, 272, 364-6, 418, 452

— clerk of rolls of, 234 n., 356

— court, 38 n.

— keeper of rolls of, *see* Burton, John

Chantries, 356

Charing, *see* London

Charles IV, emperor, d. 1378, 465 n.

— widow of, *see* Elizabeth of Pomerania

Charles V, king of France (1364-80), 142 n.

Charles VI, king of France (1380-1422), xxiv, 30, 32 and n., 44, 46, 48-50, 56, 124, 126 n., 134, 136,

166, 178, 179 n., 250, 261 n., 278, 301 n., 320, 328 and n., 370, 371 n., 372, 396, 398, 400, 406, 456 and n., 457 n., 464 and n., 466, 468, 470, 500, 501 n., 514, 515 n., 524

Charles III, king of Naples (1381-6) (Charles of Durazzo), 36 n., 100 n., 108, 109 n., 110 and nn., 111 n., 140 and n., 163 n.

— and throne of Hungary, 162 and n.

Charlton, Sir Robert, chief justice of Common Pleas, 308 and n.

Cherbourg (Manche, Fr.), 105 n., 262, 374

— captain of, 374

— castle, 24, 262

Chester (Chesh.), liii, 186 n., 214, 278

— bishop of, *see* Skirlaw, Walter; Stretton, Robert

— constable of castle, *see* Molyneux, Thomas

— county, lxiv, 268

— justice of, 257 n.; *and see* Vere, Robert de

— seal of, 256, 257 n.

Chesterton, Thomas, abbot of Tewkesbury, 408

Chesterton, de Chesterton, William, 302, 303 n., 337 n.

Cheviot Hills, 42

Cheyne, Sir John, 430 n.

Cheyne, William, 249 n., 313 n.

Chichester:

— bishop of, *see* Medford, Richard; Reade, William; and Rushock, Thomas

— bishopric, 412

Chiltern Hills, 122, 484, 512

Chipping Campden (Glos.), 220

Ciboule, Robert, xiv

Cinque Ports, 274-6

— warden of, *see* Burley, Simon

Cirencester, Richard, monk of Westminster, xxvii, xxxi, xxxii, xxxiii and n., xxxvii

— *Speculum Historiale* of, xxxi-ii, xxxiii, xxxvii

Clandon (Surr.), xlii

Clanvow, Sir John, d. 1391, 68 n., 70, 161 n., 374 and n., 398, 432, 480

— chamber knight, 432 n.

Clare (Suff.), lordship of, 194 and n.

Clarendon (Wilts.), council at, 1389, 402 n.

Clement I, pope, xxxv, 138 n.

Clement VI, pope (1342-52), 380 n., 386

Clement VII, anti-pope (1378-94) (Robert of Geneva), 34, 35 n., 100 n., 108 and n., 128, 142, 202, 203 n., 396, 464 and n., 465 n., 466 and n., 468, 470

Clifford, Sir Lewis, 456 and n., 514 and n.

Clifford, Richard, clerk of the king's chapel, 230 and n., 300, 301 n., 341 n., 370

— proceedings against, 286, 288

Clifford, Roger, lord, d. 1389, 124, 231 n., 400, 401 n.

— warden of the marches, 50 n., 376, 378 and n.

Clifford, Thomas, son of, d. 1391, 230, 454, 455 n., 474, 480, 481 n.

— chamber knight, 231 n.

Clifford, 'Thomas, lord', d. 1389, see Clifford, Roger, lord

Clisson, Olivier de, 134, 135 n.

Clopton, Sir Walter, chief justice of the King's Bench, 292, 294, 308 and n.

Clyst (Devon), see Bishop's Clyst

Cobham, John de, 3rd baron Cobham, d. 1408, 24, 168, 210, 232, 238, 276 n., 322, 330, 332

Colchester, de Colchester, William, abbot of Westminster (1386-1420), xxxiii n., liv, lvii, lix n., 176, 354 n., 484, 485 n.

Columna, Guido de, Historia de Troia, xlii and nn.

Commissions:

— of array, 350 n.

— of continual council (1386-7), 188 n., 198 and n., 200, 238, 252, 259 n., 260, 264, 268, 274, 276-7, 296, 297 n., 298, 304

— of oyer and terminer, 15 n., 383 n., 442 n., 502 n.

— of peace, 362 n., 368 n.

— trailbaston, 82, 382, 383 n., 406, 442 and n.

Constable and marshal, court of, 106

Constance of Castile, daughter of Pedro I of Castile, m. John of

Gaunt, d. 1394, 142 n., 192, 510, 511 n.

— death, 520 and n.

Constantinople, 480

Constantyn, John, 64 and n.

Constanza of Castile, see Constance of Castile

Convocation:

— northern: (1384), 48 n.; (1385), 102 n.

—, southern: (1382), 28 and n.; (1383), 33 n., 48 n.; (1384), 82 n., 102 n.; (1385), 148; (1388), 368 n.

Coquet Island (Northumb.), 397 n.

Corfe castle (Dorset), 62, 64 n., 94, 95 n., 96

Cork (Ireland), 22 n., 294 n.

Coronation oath, 242, 246, 247 n., 294, 295 n., 342

Coronation regalia, 414, 416 and n.

Cossons, Sir John, 36

Coucy, Enguerrand de, earl of Bedford, d. 1397, 276 and n.

— Isabel, wife of (daughter of Edward III), 28, 188

— Philippa, daughter of, m. Robert de Vere, 188 and n., 275 n., 404

Coudenberghe, William de, 30 n.

Council, the king's, xxii, xxiv, lviii, lx, lxiii, 30, 40, 50, 54, 70, 82, 92 n., 98, 110-12, 142, 146 and n., 166, 194, 204, 216, 218, 220, 238, 240, 250, 254, 266, 276, 300, 301 n., 302, 328, 356 and n., 374, 376, 382, 430, 440, 456, 462, 478, 481 n., 502, 510, 512 n., 518 n., 524, 526

— and parliament, 148

— clergy in, 420

— continual (1386-7), xxxix n., xliii, 167 n., 168-76, 180, 184-6, 188 n., 196, 210, 226 n., 232 n., 252, 253 n., 254, 256, 257 n.

— earl of Northumberland in, 396

— great, 102 n., 254, 255 n., 391 n., 457 n., 480-90

— lords of, 356

— meetings: (Aug. 1381), 18 and n.; (Oct. 1381), 20 and n.; (Mar. 1382), lix, 24; (Jan. 1383), 32, 33 n.; (Sept. 1383), 48 and n.; (Aug. 1384), lxvii, 90 and n., 316; (Sept. 1384), 94 n.; (Oct. 1384),

98 n.; (May 1385), 120 and n.; (Mar. 1386), 164; (Jan. 1387), 228; (Nov. 1387), 210, 301 n.; (Jan. 1388), 228; (Aug. 1388), 350 and n.; (Jan. 1389), xxviii, 376-8; (May 1389), 390, 391 nn., 392; (Aug. 1389), 402 and n.; (Sept. 1389), 402 n.; (Dec. 1389), 406, 407 n., 408; (Apr. 1390), 437 n., 457 n.; (June 1390), 436; (Apr. 1391), 457 n.; (Aug. 1391), 478 n.; (Feb. 1392), 484-6; (May 1392), lxii, lxiii, 488 and n.; 490; (June 1392), 494, 498
— privy, 404
— seating at, 164
Courtenay, Edward, earl of Devon, d. 1419, 432 and n.
— Sir Peter de, son of, 36, 436
— —, chamber knight, 333 n.
— —, chamberlain, 332, 333 n.
— Sir Philip, son of, 36, 72
Courtenay, William, bishop of London (1375-81), archbishop of Canterbury (1381-96), chancellor (1381), xxxiv, 18-20, 22, 24 and n., 28, 116, 138, 156, 158, 168, 226 n., 238, 326, 390 n., 434, 436
— and Appellants, 210, 232
— dispute with bishop of Exeter, xviii, 84 and n., 85 n., 86
— dispute with bishop of Salisbury, 438 and n.
— in Merciless Parliament, 286
Courts:
— Chancery, 38 n.
— King's Bench, 15 n., 54, 80, 144, 323 n., 406 and n., 496 and n.
— of constable and marshal, 237 n., 414, 415 n.
— marshalsea, 414
— removal from London, 492, 498
Cousin, John, grocer of London, 494
Coventry (Warwicks.), 14
— commons of, 70
Coventry and Lichfield, bishop of, see Skirlaw, Walter; Stretton, Robert
Craddock, Sir David, 440
— mayor of Bordeaux, 440 n.
Craddock, Sir Richard, 246
— keeper of Fronsac castle, 247 n.
Crane, Craneforde, John, abbot of Battle, 34, 35 n.

Cratfield, William, abbot of Bury St. Edmunds (1389-1415), 376, 394 and n.
Croydon (Surr.), 410
Crusade, 154 n.
— against Castile, 164 and n.
— against Charles of Durazzo, 110 n.
— Barbary, 448, 450 and n.
— 'taking the Cross', xxiii, 32 and n.
— See also Despenser, Henry

Dagworth, Nicholas, 144 n., 228, 338, 369 n., 374 and n., 376, 396, 399 n., 403 n., 456
— chamber knight, 230 n.
Dalkeith castle (Midlothian), 347 n.
Dallingbridge, Sir Edward, warden of the City of London, 500 and n., 502
— escheator, 500 n.
Damian de Cataneis, 415 n., 458, 468, 480, 482
Damme (W. Flanders, Belg.), 124, 126 and n., 132 and n.
Danzig (Poland), 444 and n.
Dartmouth (Devon), 320, 372, 374, 376
Daventry (Northants), 48 n.
David II, king of Scotland (1329-71), 403 n.
Dax, bishop of, see Gutiérrez, Juan
Denia, count of, and marquis of Villena, 132
Derby, Henry, earl of, see Bolingbroke, Henry
Derian, Yves, 401 n.
Despenser, Henry, bishop of Norwich (1370-1406), 30 n., 44 and n., 46 and n., 47 n., 50, 522
— crusade of, xix, xxiii, xxiv, 34, 35 n., 36 and n., 38 and n., 39 n., 40, 44 and n., 46 and n., 47 n., 300 n., 522
— trial of, xxiii, 40 n., 47 n., 52 n., 53 n., 54, 300 n.
Despenser, Sir Hugh, 147 n., 154, 451 n.
Despenser, Thomas, later (1397-9) earl of Gloucester, d. 1400, 352, 474
Despenser family, 38 n.
Devereux, Sir John, d. 1393, lxi n., 28, 116 and n., 161 n., 168, 210, 238, 322, 324, 374

Devereux, Sir John (*cont.*):
— constable of Dover castle, 232
— keeper of Calais, 44 and n.
— steward of the king's household, 232 and n., 280, 282, 284, 286, 512
Devon, earl of, *see* Courtenay, Edward
Diaz, Pedro, prior of Order of St. John of Jerusalem in Castile, 132, 133 n.
Diss, Walter (Carm.), 164, 165 n.
Distraint of knighthood, 492
Donnington (Glos.), 220 n.
Douglas, Sir Henry, 403 n.
Douglas, James, earl of Douglas (1358–88), 346 and n., 347 n., 348 and n.
Douglas, Sir William, 474
Dover (Kent), 22, 56, 122, 160
— castle, 56, 228, 230 n.; constable/keeper of, *see* Burley, Simon; Ashton, Robert; Devereux, John
— mayor, 274
Drayton, Sir William, 147 n., 154
Drogheda (Louth, Ireland), 336 n.
Dublin (Ireland), 336 n.
— archbishop of, *see* Wikeford, Robert
— marquis of, *see* Vere, Robert de
Dunbabin, Mrs. J., 138 n.
Dunbar, John, earl of Moray (1372–91/2), 350, 436 and n.
Dunkirk (Nord, Fr., formerly Flanders), 30, 38, 39 n.
Duque, Juan, 132, 133 n.
Durant, John, 288
Durham, 124, 156, 346 n.
— bishop of, *see* Fordham, John; Hatfield, Thomas; Skirlaw, Walter
Durazzo, Lewis, duke of, d. 1362, 109 n.

Easton, Adam, monk of Norwich cathedral priory, cardinal priest of St. Cecilia, d. 1397, 106 and n., 410, 411 n.
Edgar, king of England (957–75), 324 n.
Edinburgh (Lothian), 66, 128
Edward, prince of Wales (the Black Prince), *see* Woodstock, Edward of
Edward the Confessor, St., king of England (1042–66), 8, 10, 324 n., 480
— coronation, 416 n.
— *See also* feast days

Edward the martyr, St., king of England (975–978/9), 463 n.
Edward I, king of England (1272–1307), xv, 200, 418, 420, 460 n.
Edward II, king of England (1307–27), 158, 200, 201 n., 436
Edward III, king of England (1327–77), 30, 38 n., 170, 188, 194, 296, 356, 360, 380, 418, 439 n.
— anniversary, lvii, 514
— encomium on, xix and n.
— Edmund son of, *see* Langley, Edmund of
— Isabel, daughter of, *see* Coucy, Isabel, wife of Enguerrand de
— Lionel, son of, *see* Antwerp, Lionel of
Elizabeth of Pomerania, widow of Charles IV, 516
Ellis, Roger, wax-chandler of London, 494
El Mahadia (Tunisia), 432 n., 450 n.
Elmham, Rober, 161 n.
Elmham, William, 44 and n., 52 n., 72, 74, 228, 338, 369 n.
— chamber knight, 230 n.
Eltham (Kent), lv, lx, 56, 154, 253 n., 279 n., 374, 400, 454, 478 and n., 488, 510, 514, 515 n.
Ely (Cantab.), 42
— abbey, 42
— bishop of, *see* Arundel, Thomas; Fordham, John
— prior of, 354 n.
Emperor, the, 372, 470, 472; *and see* Wenzel IV
Empire, the, 464, 465 n., 466, 468, 470
Epidemics, 20, 28, 44, 56, 190 and n., 204, 402, 438, 476
Erghum, Ralph, bishop of Salisbury (1375–88), bishop of Bath and Wells (1388–1400), 334 and n., 355 n.
Ertevelde (W. Flanders, Belg.), 126 n.
Essex, peasants of, lxx, lxxi, 2 n., 4, 12
Essex, William, draper of London, lvii, 90 n., 94 and n., 96 n.
Estouteville, Jean d', 401 n.
Ethelred I, king of Wessex (865/6–871), xxxii
Eton (Bucks.), 502 n.
Ettrick forest (Borders), 126

Eulogium Historiarum, xvi n., xxx n.

Evesham (Oxon.), abbot of, 220

Evote, William, draper of London, 494

Exchequer, 324, 336, 364
— barons of, 364, 404
— chief baron of, 356

Exeter (Devon):
— bishop of, *see* Brantingham, Thomas de
— cathedral, 84
— dean and chapter of, 85 n.
— diocese of, 84 n.

Exeter, John, xl

Exeter, Richard, monk of Westminster, prior (1377–82), xl ff.

Exeter, Robert, prior of Holy Trinity, Aldgate (1391–1408), xl n., 494

Exeter, Thomas, xl

Exton, Nicholas, fishmonger of London, mayor (1386–8), lxviii, lxix, 206 and n., 217 n., 261 n., 313 n., 334–6

Farindon, Sir William, 430 n.

Faringdon, Sir William, 44 and n.

Favent, Thomas, xlviii, lxv, 285 n.

Feast days: Corpus Christi, 390, 394, 395 n.; St. Anne, 390 and n.; SS. Basilides and Cyrinus, xxii; St. Edward the Confessor, lv and n., lvi, 450, 506 n., 510 n.; St. Lucy, 408 n.; St. Mary the Virgin (Visitation), 390 and n.; St. Milburga, xxii, xxxiii; St. Paul, *see* SS. Peter and Paul; St. Peter in Cathedra, lv; St. Peter in Chains, lvi; SS. Peter and Paul, lv, lvi; SS. Processus and Martinianus, xxii, xxiii n.

Felbrigge, George, chamber knight, 473 n.

Fernando I, king of Portugal (1367–83), 133 n.

Ferrers, Sir Henry, lord of Groby, 300, 301 n.

Ferriers, Sir Henry, 52 n.

Fetherstanhalgh, Alexander de, keeper of Lochmaben castle, 58 and n.

Fife, earl of, *see* Stewart, Robert

Fitchet, Sir Thomas, 190, 191 n.

Fitzalan, Richard, earl of Arundel (1376–97), 40, 66–8, 124, 168, 196, 210 n., 220–2, 233 n., 263 n., 264, 266 n., 268, 285 n., 340 n., 352 n., 382, 392
— admiral, lxvi, 180 n., 394 n.
— and rising of Appellants, lii, liii, 208 ff., 296–8
— captain of Brest, 394 n.
— in Merciless Parliament, 234 ff., 280 ff., 302, 328 n.
— naval expeditions, 180 and n., 182 and n., 184, 286, 290, 314, 318, 340, 350 and n., 352 and n.
— Elizabeth, daughter of, m. (i) Sir William de Montague; and (ii) Thomas Mowbray, earl of Nottingham, 88, 89 n.
— John, brother of, *see* Arundel, John, lord, d. 1379
— *See also* Appellants

Fitz Martin, John, alias Taverner, 302, 303 n.

Fitz Ralph, Richard, archbishop of Armagh (1346–60), 158 and n.

Fitz Ralph, Robert, 52 n.

Fitz Walter, Fitzwalter, Walter, lord, d. 1386, 190 and n.
— warden of the marches, 50 and n., 526
— Philippa, wife of, 406, 407 n.

Fitz Walter, Walter, lord, d. 1406, 474

Flanders, xxiii, xxiv, 25 n., 30, 35 n., 38 n., 44, 140, 352
— Louis de Mâle, count of (1346–84), 25 n., 26
— *See also* Flemings; Philip the Bold

Flemings, 38, 134
— negotiations with, lxvi, 328 and n., 330, 406 and n.
— of London, 6–8, 16
— ships of, 182 and n.

Flint castle (Clwyd), 188

Florence (Italy), 476 n.

Flores Historiarum, xxxi

Fogaça, Lourenço Anes, 142 n.
— chancellor of Portugal, 30, 31 n.

Fordham, John, bishop of Durham (1381–8), bishop of Ely (1388–1425), treasurer (1386), 86 and n., 125 n., 156, 200 and n., 230 and n., 334 and n., 355 n., 452, 453 n.

Forster, John, citizen of London, 494

Forth, Firth of ('the Scottish Sea'), 66, 128, 374

Foul Oak (Kent), 98 and n., 248

Fowey (Corn.), 376

France, 450

— and Castile, 194

— king of, 146, 150, 152, 204, 256, 432; *see also* Charles V; Charles VI

— marshal of, *see* Sancerre, Louis de

— *See also* French

Francis, John, goldsmith and alderman of London, 494

Franklin, John, citizen of London, 494

French, 188, 452, 488

— and Despenser crusade, 36, 38–40, 46 and n., 47 n.

— and Italy, 464 and n.

— and Richard II, 260, 262

— and Scots, 56 and n., 88 and n., 90, 98 n., 128, 130 and n., 132

— capture Poil, 476

— English negotiations with, lx, lxi, lxii, 24 and n., 48, 50 and n., 58, 88 and n., 98, 116 and n., 154, 155 n., 160, 161 n., 164–6, 261 n., 262, 263 n., 301 n., 374 and n., 376, 396–8, 400, 402, 436, 437 n., 456, 458, 478 and n., 486, 490, 514 and n., 515 n., 518, 524

— fire coastal buildings, 344

— fleet, 180–2

— in Königsberg, 476

Frenyngham, William, citizen of London, 494

Fresh, John, mercer and alderman of London, 494

Fresnel, Mr. Peter, *see* Frisevell, Peter

Frisevell, Mr. Peter, 89 n., 399 n.

Froissart, Jean, lxii, 347 n., 375 n., 432 n., 451 n.

Fronsac castle (Gironde, Fr.), keeper of, *see* Craddock, Sir Richard; Harpeden, Sir John

Fulthorpe, Sir Roger, justice of the Common Bench, 196, 197 n., 258, 306, 308 n.

— proceedings against, 284–6, 336 n.

Furneaux, John, grocer of London, 494

Galicia (Spain), 190 and n.

— *adelantado* of, 133 n.

Garter, the, 292, 452

Gascons, *see* Gascony

Gascony, 164, 490

— mission to England, lx, 484

— seneschal of, *see* Harpeden, Sir

John; Scrope, Sir William

Gatierrez, Juan, *see* Gutiérrez, Juan

Gaunt, John of, duke of Lancaster (1362–99), duke of Aquitaine (1390–9), xxiv, 22, 24, 30, 36, 42, 48 and n., 58, 66, 67 n., 82, 104, 140, 144, 156, 160, 188, 260, 372, 374, 406–8, 442 and n., 444, 522

— and affair of Carmelite friar, 68–70, 76, 78–80

— and Aquitaine, xxix, lix, 378, 379 n., 414 and n., 484, 490, 518

— and John Northampton, lxvii, lxviii, 92 and n., 145 n., 148–50, 440

— and London, 492

— and Richard II, 110–14, 116, 128–30, 440

— and Spain, 34, 36 n., 140, 142 n., 149 n., 164 and n., 190, 194 and nn.

— and Westminster Abbey, lvi and n., lx, 408

— at La Neyte, lvi, lxviii

— Blanche, wife of, *see* Lancaster, Blanche of

— Catalina, daughter of, 193 n., 194, 370 and n.

— chamberlain of, 191 n.

— confessor of, 165 n.

— constable of, 193 n.

— Constance, wife of, *see* Constance of Castile

— embassies, lviii, lxii, 48 n., 50, 56–8, 88 and n., 98, 116, 322, 344, 456 n., 486, 490, 514 and n., 515 n., 518, 524

— expedition to Scotland, 120, 124, 128

— Henry, son of, *see* Bolingbroke, Henry

— Katherine, daughter of, *see* Catalina, daughter of

— lieutenant in march, 20 n.

— marriages, 192 and n.

— marshal of, 191 nn.

— Philippa, daughter of, *see* Lancaster, Philippa of

— quarrel with earl of Northumberland, xx, 20 and n., 22 and n., 408

— retinue, 191 n., 230 n.

— secretary of, 165 n.

— steward of, 124

— style, 146 and n.
— surgeon of, 6
— warden of marches, 42 n.
Gavelkind tenure, 365 n.
Gavere (E. Flanders, Belg.), 126 n.
Genoa (Italy), Genoese, 130, 131 n., 140, 142, 178 and n., 432 n., 448, 450 n., 458, 468
Germany, Germans, 450, 452, 466; see also Almain
Gervys, Thomas, xlii and n.
Ghent (E. Flanders, Belg.), 24 and n., 26, 30 n., 44, 126 and n., 146, 147 n., 149 n., 150 n.
— men of, 30, 46, 124, 126 n., 146, 150-2, 524
Gilbert, John, O.P., bishop of Hereford (1375-89), bishop of St. David's (1389-97), treasurer (1386-9), lx-lxi, 164, 165 n., 168 n., 226 n., 232, 233 n., 382 and n., 402 and n.
— embassies, 24 and n., 28 and n., 50, 88 n., 490 n., 524
Gilds, 356, 482 n.
Glendonwys, Sir Adam de, 403 n.
Glendower, Owen, 194 n.
Gloucester, 158, 436, 454
— castle, 214 n., 230 n.
— earl of, see Despenser, Thomas
— duke of, see Woodstock, Thomas of
Golafre, Sir John de, chamber knight, d. 1396, 406 and n.
Gomes, Diego, see Manrique, Diego Gomez
Gomez de Lira, Lopo, 132, 133 n.
Gonçalves, Joham, 132 and n.
Gravelines (Nord, Fr., formerly Flanders), 30, 38, 39 n., 44 and n., 46, 47 n., 134, 522
Gray, Thomas, of York, 368
Green, Sir Henry, 72
Greystoke, Ralph, lord, d. 1418, 124 and n.
Groby (Leics.), 301 n.
Grosmont, Henry of, duke of Lancaster (1351-61), 192
— Blanche, daughter of, see Lancaster, Blanche of
Guelders, duchy of, 371 n., 373 n., 476
—, duke of, see Guelders, William I, duke of

Guelders, William I, duke of (1371-1402), duke of Jülich (1393-1402), 370, 371 n., 372 and n., 373 nn., 434, 436 and n., 450, 488
Guines (Pas de Calais, Fr.), 136, 457 n.
Gutiérrez, Juan, bishop of Dax (1380-93), 164, 165 n.
Guyenne, lordship of, 246

Hadley, John, grocer and alderman of London, mayor (1379-80, 1393-4), 494, 516 and n.
Hainault, Albert, count of, see Bavaria, Albert duke of
Hales, Sir Robert, prior of Order of St. John of Jerusalem in England, treasurer (1381), lxxi, 2, 4, 6
Halton (Cheshire), 344 n.
Hammes (Pas de Calais, Fr.), 136
Hampstead (Midd.), 508
Hanneslegh, Sir John, 440
Hanse, the German, lxvi, 331 n.
Haringay Park (Midd.), liii, 210 and n., 222 n.
Harleston, Sir John, 514
— chamber knight, 514 n.
Harpeden, Sir John, 36, 37 n., 246
— captain of La Rochelle, 152
— keeper of Fronsac castle, 247 n.
— seneschal of Gascony, 152, 247 n., 402 and n.
Harringworth (Northants), 71 n., 184 n., 231 n.
Hastings (Suss.), 352
Hastings, Sir Hugh, 190 and n.
Hastings, John, 2nd earl of Pembroke (1348-75), 152 and n.
— lieutenant in Aquitaine, 153 n.
Hastings, John, 3rd earl of Pembroke (1375-89), 192, 193 n., 408 and n., 410
Hatfield, Thomas, bishop of Durham (1345-81), xvi
Haulton, 344; and see Halton
Hawkwood, Sir John, d. 1394, 156 and n., 476 and n., 520 and n.
Hawley, John, 372-4
Hende, John, draper and alderman of London, mayor (1391-2), 494, 498, 500 and n., 502 and n.
Henry I, king of England (1100-35), 336 n.

Henry II, king of England (1154-89), lord of Ireland, 248 n.

Henry III, king of England (1216-72), xxxviii, 418

Hereford, 410
— bishop of, see Gilbert, John; Trefnant, John
— Dominican church, 410 n.

Hertford, 114

Hexham (Northumb.), 138

Higden, Ranulph, monk of St. Werburgh's, Chester, xv, xvi

Highbury (Midd.), lxxi, lxxii, 4, 5 n.

High Wycombe (Bucks.), 406 n.

Holcote, John, 300, 301 n.

Holland, Albert, count of, see Bavaria, Albert, duke of

Holland, John, earl of Huntingdon (1388-1400), 72 and n., 122 and n., 144, 158, 160 nn., 192, 193 n., 294, 295 n., 342 and n., 451 n., 492
— admiral and captain of Brest, 392, 394 n.
— chamberlain, 412, 414 and n.
— embassies, 50 n., 88 n., 322 and n., 486 n.
— Elizabeth, wife of, see Lancaster, Elizabeth of

Holland, Thomas, earl of Kent, d. 1360, 101 n.
— Joan, wife of, see Kent, Joan of
— Joan, daughter of, m. John IV, duke of Brittany, 100, 101 n.
— Maud, daughter of, m. Waleran, count of Ligny and St. Pol, 450 and n., 488

Holland, Thomas, earl of Kent, d. 1397:
— constable of Tower, 280, 286
— in Merciless Parliament, 310
— Eleanor, daughter of, m. Roger Mortimer, d. 1398, 194 n.

Holt, Holte, Sir John, justice of the Common Bench, 196, 218, 258, 306
— proceedings against, l, 284-6, 336 n.

Holy Land, 372, 374, 392

Holyrood Abbey (Linlithgow), 128 and n.

Homes, John, keeper of gaol of Salisbury castle, 80 n.

Hornsey (formerly Haringay, Midd.), see Haringay

Hoselaw (Borders), 126 n.

Hostiensis, xli

Houghton, Adam, bishop of St. David's (1362-89), 382

Household, the king's, 166, 168, 170, 172, 228, 232
— steward of, see steward

Hull (Yorks.), see Kingston-upon-Hull

Hungary, king of, 108; see also Lewis the Great
—, queen of, see Mary, queen of Hungary

Huntingdon, earl of, see Holland, John

Hyams, Dr. P. R., 32 n.

Hyde (Midd.), lvi

Hyde, William, grocer of London, 494

Impeachment in 1388, 268 ff., 284 ff., 318, 328, 330

Imworth, Richard, steward of the marshalsea, 8

Innocent III, pope (1198-1216), 164 n.

Ireland, 336, 529
— dukedom of, xxviii, 378
— duke of, see Vere, Robert de
— 'king of', 248 and n.
— lieutenant in, see Mortimer, Edmund; Windsor, William; Woodstock, Thomas of
— lordship of, 144, 146 n., 188 n., 244 and n., 246, 248 and n.

Isabel of Castile, countess of Cambridge and duchess of York, d. 1392, 510 and n., 511 n., 512

Italy, 464, 466, 470

Jerusalem, 480
— kingdom of, 100 n.

Joanna I, queen of Naples (1343-81), 100 n., 106, 108 and n.

Joan of Arc, xiv

João I, king of Portugal (1385-1433) (John of Aviz), 128 and n., 132 and n., 142 n., 192 and nn., 194 and n.
— wife of, see Lancaster, Philippa of

John, king of England (1199-1216), lord of Ireland, 248 n.

Juan I, king of Castile (1379-90) (John of Trastamara), lviii, 30, 37 n., 132 and nn., 142 n., 194 and n., 195 n., 322, 370, 370 n.
— Henry, son of, 370 n.

Jubilee, papal, 384 ff.
Jülich, duchy of, 372 n.
Jülich, William III, duke of (1361-93), 372 n.; Marie, wife of, 372 n.; William, son of, *see* Guelders, William I, duke of
Justices, 14, 94, 174, 200, 278, 300 n., 356, 366, 416
— in north Wales, 188 n.
— in parliament, 254, 386
— of assize, 358
— of Chester, 188 and n.
— of Common Pleas, 176
— of King's Bench, 176, 406
— of peace, 358, 360, 362, 363 n., 366-8
— proceedings against, xlviii n., l, 284 and n., 285 n., 287 n., 316 and n., 336 and n.
— Richard II's consultations with, xxxiv, 186 n., 196 ff., 206 n., 258, 264, 285 n., 316
— *See also under names of the several justices*

Kennington (Surr.), xxxii, lxvii, 24, 314, 324, 325 n., 340 n., 504
Kent, 364, 522
— earl of, *see* Holland, Thomas, earl of Kent, d. 1360; Thomas, earl of Kent, d. 1397
— epidemics in, 56
— judicial proceedings in, 406
— peasants of, lxx, lxxi, 2 n., 4
— Richard II in, 515 n.
Kent, Joan of (1328-85), m. (i) Thomas Holland, earl of Kent; and (ii) Edward, prince of Wales, 101 n., 128 n., 231 n., 292, 450 n.
Kidderminster, baron of, *see* Beauchamp, Sir John
Kilmore (Ireland), bishop of, *see* Rushock, Thomas
Kimbolton (Herefs.), 498
King's Langley (Herts.), 122, 484, 512
— Dominican friary, 512 n.
Kingston-úpon-Hull (Yorks.), 214, 320, 458 n.
Kirkley Road, 344
Kirklington (Yorks.), 300 n.
Knaresborough (Yorks.):
— chase, 443 n.
— forest, 442

— lordship and liberty, 442 n.
Knighton, Henry, xiii, lxiv, lxv, 227 n., 239 n.
Knights of the shire, 218 n., 230 n., 266, 278, 288, 290, 364, 365 n.
Knolles, Thomas, grocer of London, 494
Königsberg (W. Germany, formerly Prussia), 444 and n., 448, 474
Körenzig, treaty of (1388), 371 n., 372 and n.
Krakow, king of, *see* Poland and Krakow

Ladislas of Durazzo, king of Naples (1386-1414), 345 n., 466 n.
La Grande Sauve, abbey of (Bordeaux dioc., Fr.), 394 n.
Lakingheath, John, monk of Westminster, xvii n., xxxviii, xxxix and nn., xl and n., 176
Lambeth (Surr.), 2, 116
Lancaster:
— county of, lxiv, 268
—, duchess of, *see* Constance of Castile
—, duchy of, 344 n.
—, dukes of, *see* Gaunt, John of; Bolingbroke, Henry; Grosmont, Henry
Lancaster, Blanche of, d. 1369, wife of John of Gaunt, 192 and n.
—, Elizabeth of, m. John Holland, 192, 295 n.
—, Philippa of, m. João I of Portugal, 192 and n., 194 n.
Lancaster, John, 262, 278, 300
Lancecron, Agnes, 188, 190 and n.
La Neyte (Midd.), lvi and n.
Langham, Simon, abbot of Westminster (1349-61), bishop of Ely (1362-6), archbishop of Canterbury (1366-8), cardinal priest, later cardinal bishop of St. Sisto, 36 n.
— library of, xli and n., xlii n.
Langley, *see* King's Langley
Langley, Edmund of, earl of Cambridge (1362-1402), duke of York (1385-1402), 28, 29 n., 30, 42, 82, 112 n., 124, 140 and n., 168, 188
— and rising of Appellants, 210, 226 and n.
— 'duke of Canterbury', 126 and n.

Langley, Edmund of (*cont.*):
— embassy of, 514 n.
— in Merciless Parliament, lxxiii, lxxiv, 284, 286, 292, 310, 328, 330
La Rochelle (Charente Mar., Fr.), 37 n., 134, 153 n., 180, 182 and n., 350, 352 and n., 353 n., 374
— captain of, *see* Harpeden, Sir John
Latimer, Br. John (Carm.), 66–80
Latimer, William, lord, d. 1381, 2 and n.
La Zouche, *see* Zouche
Leatherhead (Surr.), 498
Le Botiler, James, earl of Ormond (1382–1405), 140 and n.
Leeds castle (Kent), 22
Legg, John, 6 and n.
Le Havre (Seine Inf., Fr.), 351 n.
Leicester, 440, 442 n., 520
— council at, 440
— Newark College, 521 n.
— St. Mary's Abbey, lxv, 520 n.
Leo IV, pope (847–55), 416 n.
Leo VI, king of Armenia (1373–93), lv, 154 and n., 156, 158, 160, 161 n., 374 n., 398
León (Spain), 164, 190 n., 192 n.
Lescrop', Le Scrope, *see* Scrope
Lesnes (Kent), 2 n.
Lesparre, Florimund de, 36, 37 n.
'Le Trade', 350
Leulingham (Pas-de-Calais, Fr.), 457 n.
— negotiations at, lx, 374 n., 437 n., 514 n.
— truce of (1384), lx, 58 and n., 89 n.
— truce of (1389), 377 n., 398 and nn., 400 and n.
Lewis the Great, king of Hungary (1342–82), 109 n., 162 and n.
— Mary, daughter of, *see* Mary, queen of Hungary
Liazari, Paul, *Lectura super Clementinis*, xlii
Ligny, count of, *see* Ligny and St. Pol, Waleran, count of
Ligny and St. Pol, Waleran, count of, d. 1415, 400, 401 n., 402, 450 and n., 451 n.
— Maud, wife of, 450 and n., 488
Lincoln, 303 n.
— diocese, 337 n.
Lincoln, John, 230, 300, 301 n., 341 n., 370

— chamberlain of Exchequer, 230 n., 300 n.
— proceedings against, 286, 288
Lindsay, Sir James, of Crawford, d. 1396, 350 and n., 400, 434 and n.
Listrac (Gironde, Fr.), 301 n.
Lithuania, king of, 444, 446, 448
Litlington, de Litlington, Nicholas, abbot of Westminster (1362–86), xxxviii, xxxix, liv, lvii, lix n., 38 n., 176
Livonia, 446, 448
— master of, 448
Llandaff, bishop of, *see* Bottesham, William; Bromfield, Edmund; Rushock, Thomas
Lochmaben castle (Dumfries), 58, 59 n.
Lockton, John, sergeant-at-law and justice, 196, 200, 258, 306–8
— proceedings against, 284–6, 336 n.
Loire, R., 398 n.
Lollards, Lollardy, xxxvi, 318, 320 n., 326, 330
Lombard merchant, 496
Lombardy (Italy), xxviii, 156, 466 and n., 476, 500, 520
Lombartzyde (W. Flanders, Belg.), 38
Lomley, Sir Ralph de, captain of Berwick, 374, 375 n.
London, xxiv, lxvi ff., 14, 20, 28, 58–62, 64, 104, 116 n., 122, 130, 148–50, 154, 184, 206, 207 n., 208 and n., 216 n., 224, 251 n., 266, 292, 334, 344, 366, 368, 398, 399 n., 400, 403 n., 408, 430 n., 434 and n., 436, 438, 440, 442 n., 450, 454, 474, 488, 490 n., 498, 514 and n., 515 n., 520
— aldermen, 24, 90, 136, 184 n., 216, 217 n., 224, 226, 232 n., 234 n., 251 n., 282, 312, 492, 494, 502 and n.; *and see also under individual names*
— and Appellants, lxviii–lxix, 226, 232–4, 312
— and Peasants' Revolt, lxx, 4 n., 8, 12, 16 n.
— and Westminster Abbey, xxviii, lvi–lvii
— bishop of, *see* Braybrooke, Robert; Courtenay, William
— Bridge, 6, 504
— churches and religious houses: Grey

Friars, 28, 410 n.; Holy Trinity, Aldgate, 494; priory of St. John of Jerusalem, Clerkenwell, lxxi, lxii, 4, 512, 513 n.; St. Mary Graces ('New Abbey'), 292, 293 n., 332; St. Paul's, 32, 38, 148, 164, 354, 404, 408, 516; Whitefriars, 34, 62
— — citizens, 22, 70, 94, 128, 136, 206 and n., 232 n., 234, 264, 266, 270, 306, 307 n., 504 n., 516; called *Trinoventani*, xxiii, 20; commoners, commons among, 494, 498, 502; *see also under individual names*
— common council, 60 n.
— council at, 98 n., 147 n.
— court of aldermen, 64
— escheator, 500 n.
— gilds and companies, lii, lxv, lxvi-vii, lxviii, 24, 64, 216, 232-4, 264, 312, 504; bakers, 452; brewers, 452; drapers, lxviii, 334, 404; fishmongers, 60 and n., 62 and n., 96, 334, 335 n.; goldsmiths, lxviii, 334, 404; mercers, lxviii, 334, 404; victuallers, 452; vintners, 334, 335 n.
— heads of religious houses in, 24
— liberties, lvii-viii, lxvii-viii, 334, 336 n., 495 n., 496, 500, 501 n., 502, 506 and n., 508 and n.
— mayor, 24, 60 n., 64, 90, 94, 116, 136 n., 184 n., 206, 216, 217 n., 224, 226, 232 n., 234 n., 249 n., 250, 251 n., 252, 260, 264, 270, 282, 312, 408, 474, 492, 502 n.; *and see under individual names*
— mayoral elections, lvi, 60-2, 100, 101 n., 102, 136, 370, 404, 450, 508
— ordinances, 60 and n., 62 n., 136 and n., 335 n.
— quarrel with Richard II, lxxiv, 492, 494, 496, 498, 500
— recorder, 312, 314
— sheriffs, lvi, 90, 282, 492, 502 n.; *and see under individual names*
— streets, districts, etc.: Charing, 206, 207 n., 212, 509 n.; Cheapside, 7 n., 8, 16, 102; Clerkenwell, xxiii, 94 n., 224 n., 513 n.; Clerkenwell Fields, 12 and n.; Eastcheap, 504; Fish Street, 504; Fleet Prison, 301 n.; Guildhall, lii, liv, lxix, 102,

226, 232, 510; Ludgate, 354; Mile End, lxxii, 6; Newgate, 64, 284; Newgate prison, 98, 102, 248, 249 n.; Savoy Palace, lvi, lxxi, lxxii, 4 and n.; Skinners Well, 94 and n., 224 and n., 476; Smithfield, xxiii, lv, lxxiii, 10, 164, 432, 436, 450, 512; Temple, lxxi; Temple Bar, 506; Tower, liii, lxxii, 4-6, 52, 94 and n., 96, 136, 220 and n., 224, 226, 240, 280, 282, 284, 286, 288, 290-2, 306, 312, 316, 318, 322, 332, 338, 340, 344 and n., 402 and n., 498; Tower Hill, lxxi, lxxii, 6, 332
— under-sheriff, *see* Usk, Thomas
— warden, *see* Dallingbridge, Edward; Raddington, Baldwin
Lothian (Scotland), 128
Loudham, Sir John, 446, 447 n.
Louvain (Brabant, Belg.), 492, 510
Lovell, John, lord, d. 1408, 230
Lovey, John, mercer and alderman of London, 494
Lucca (Italy), 178, 179 n., 202, 203 n., 344 and n.
Lustrake, James, 300, 301 n.
Lyonshall, castle and lordship (Herefs.), 276, 277 n.

Maghfeld, Gilbert, ironmonger and alderman of London, sheriff (1392-3), 494, 500, 501 n.
Magna Carta (1215), 248, 249 n.
Maintenance, 245 n., 248, 249 n., 358 and n.
Malvern, John of, monk and prior of Worcester Cathedral priory:
— chronicle of, xv, xvi and n., xix, xxvii
Manfield, Robert, provost of St. John's College, Beverley, 244, 245 n.
Manrique, Diego Gomez ('Diego Gomes'), 132 and n.
Manuel II of Thessalonica, d. 1425, 159 n.
March, earl of, *see* Mortimer, Edmund, d. 1381
Marches towards Scotland, 149 n., 246, 394-6, 396 n.
— east march, 346 n., 376
— lieutenant in, *see* Gaunt, John of
— wardens, *see* Clifford, Roger; Fitz

Marches towards Scotland, wardens (*cont.*):
Walter, Walter; Gaunt, John of; Mowbray, Thomas; Nevill of Raby, John, lord; Nevill, Ralph, lord; Percy, Henry, earl of Northumberland; Percy, Henry (Hotspur); Roos, John; Scrope, Richard xli–ii

Marco Polo, xli–ii

Maresy, Guychard, 89 n.

Marmion, Sir John, 190, 191 n.

Marseilles (Bouches du Rhône, Fr.), 450 n.

Marshal, the, 282
— of the king's household, 415 n.

Marshalsea, 410
— steward of, *see* Imworth, Richard

Martigo, *see* Vynelef, Martyletto de

Martin V, pope (1417–31), 395 n.

Martin, Geoffrey, clerk of the Crown, 281 n.

Mary, queen of Hungary, d. 1395, 162 and n.

Maudith, John, xlii

Maxwell, Sir John, of Pollock, 348 n.

Mayfield (Suss.), said to be in Kent, 400

Mayorga, count of, *see* Tello de Meneses, Juan Alonso

Medford, Richard, bishop of Chichester (1389–95), 228–30, 300, 301 nn., 341 n., 370, 382, 412, 413 n.
— king's secretary, 230 n.
— proceedings against, 286, 288

Médoc (Gironde, Fr.), 37 n.

Megliorato, Cosmas Gentilis, archbishop of Ravenna (1387–9), bishop of Bologna (19 June 1389–27 Apr. 1390), later cardinal 'Bononiensis' and Pope Innocent VII, 394, 410, 411 n.
— papal collector in England, 202, 203 n.

Melrose (Borders) abbey, 66, 126–7

Memel, R., 444, 446 and n.

Merk, Richard, xxxv n.

Merks, Thomas, monk of Westminster, bishop of Carlisle (1397–9), xxxv–vi, lxi, 354 n.

Middelburg (W. Flanders, Belg.), wool staple at, 146 n., 178, 354

Milan (Italy), 118

Modena diocese (Italy), 460, 468

Mohun, John, lord, d. 1375, 231 n.
— Joan, wife of, 231 n.
— Philippa, daughter of, m. (i) Walter, lord Fitz Walter; and (ii) Sir John Golafre, 406, 407 n.

Mokkynge, John, fishmonger of London, 494

Moleyns, Sir William de, d. 1381, 231 n.
— Margery, wife of, 230, 231 n.

Molyneux, Sir Thomas, d. 1387, 220 n., 222
— constable of Chester castle, 222 n.

Monk of Evesham, the, xiii

Monk of Westminster, the, xiv, xxi, xxx, xxxviii, xlii, xliii, 28 n., 62 n., 92, 96 n., 108 n., 110 n., 120 n., 133 n., 142 n., 144 n., 146 n., 162 n., 184 n., 186 n., 188 n., 192 n., 194 n., 196 n., 202 n., 232 n., 234 n., 281 n., 307 n., 309 n., 318 n., 319 n., 336 n., 344 n., 350 n., 395 nn., 398 n., 446 n., 456 n., 476 n., 484 n., 504 n., 506 n., 518 n., 520 n., 521 n.
— as scribe, xvii, xviii, xix, xx, xxv, xxvi, xxxiii–iv
— interest in diplomacy, lviii ff.
— interest in London affairs, xxiv, xxv, xxvii, xxviii, lvii–viii, lxvii ff.
— Latin style, xxxv, xxxviii
— sources, xxxiv n., xliii ff., 68 n., 90 n., 126 n., 132 n., 134 n., 149 n., 164 n., 185 n., 208 n., 261 n., 297 n., 324 n., 346 n., 351 n., 377 n., 380 n., 384 n., 431 nn., 437 n., 444 n., 462 n., 481 n.
— views on Appellants, xxxiv, liii
— views on John of Gaunt, lxii–lxiii
— views on Richard II, xxviii, xxxiv, liii, lxxiii ff.
— views on Thomas of Woodstock, xxx, lxii

Monkton, William, 300 and n.

Montague, Sir John, steward of the king's household (1381–7), 40, 72, 96, 178, 179 n.

Montague, Thomas, dean of Salisbury, 438 and n.

Montague, William, earl of Salisbury, d. 1397, 114, 124, 294, 490 n.

— in Merciless Parliament, 310

Montague, Sir William, 89 n.

Monte Cassino (Frosinone, Italy), abbey, 346

— abbot of, *see* Tartaris, Peter de

Montfort, John de, IV, duke of Brittany (1364–99), 152 and n., 185 n., 188 and n., 340 n., 351 n.

— Joan, wife of (Joan Holland), 100, 101 n.

Montgomery, Sir John de, of Egglesham, 348 n.

Moray, earl of, *see* Dunbar, John, earl of Moray

More, John, mercer of London, sheriff (1383–4), 90 n., 94 and nn., 150 n., 307 n.

— pardon, 442 n.

More, William, vintner and alderman of London, sheriff (1386–7), 494

Morice, Nicholas, abbot of Waltham Holy Cross (1371–89), 168, 408, 409 n.

Morieux, Sir Thomas, chamber knight, 72 and n., 190, 191 n.

Mortimer, Edmund, earl of March, lieutenant in Ireland (1379–81), d. 1381, 22 and n., 194 and n.

— Philippa, wife of, 194 n.

— Roger, son of, earl of March, d. 1398, 194 n., 229 n.

— —, Edmund, son of, d. 1425, 194 n.

Mortimer, Roger, earl of March, d. 1360, 222 n.

—, —, Sir Thomas, son of, 222 and n.

Mowbray, John, lord, d. 1361, 231 n.

— Blanche, daughter of, 231 n.

Mowbray, John de, earl of Nottingham (1377–83), 34 and n., 62

Mowbray, Thomas, earl of Nottingham (1383–99), duke of Norfolk (1397–9), 62, 63 n., 88, 219 n., 268, 436 and n.

— and rising of Appellants, 298, 302

— in Merciless Parliament, 234 ff., 280 ff., 328 n.

— marshal, 124, 236, 237 n., 240, 288

— warden of east march, 378 nn., 396 n.

Mugello Dinus de, *Super titulum Sexti de regulis iuris*, xlii

Muirhouse, truce of (1383), 42 and n.

Murcia, *adelantado* of, 132 n.

Naples (Italy), 36 and n., 64, 66 and n., 346

— kingdom of, 100 n., 108, 110, 111 n., 162; *see also* Sicily, kingdom of

— king of, *see* Charles III, king of Naples

— queen of, *see* Joanna I, queen of

Naples and Sicily, kingdom of, *see* Naples, kingdom of

Neel, William, abbot of Waltham Holy Cross, 441 n.

Nevill, Alexander, archbishop of York (1373–88), lv, lxviii–lxix, 168, 186, 200, 206, 210, 245 n., 268, 270, 278, 296, 484–6

— death, 492 and n.

— dispute with St. John's College, Beverley, 178, 180 and n.

— escape, 214 and n., 342–4

— proceedings against, xlvii, 210–12, 236 ff., 280 ff.

— sentence on, 308, 309 n.

— translation to St. Andrews, 334 n.

Nevill, John, lord, of Raby, d. 1388, 86 n., 124, 372 and n.

— 'earl of Cumberland', 126 and n.

— warden of marches, 50 and n., 350 n., 526

Nevill, Ralph, lord, of Raby, earl of Westmorland (1397–1425), 396

— warden of west march, 378 nn., 396 n.

Nevill, Sir William, d. 1391, 50, 432, 480, 524

— chamber knight, 432 n.

Newbattle abbey (Lothian), 128

Newcastle-upon-Tyne (Northumb.), 58, 120 n., 130, 344, 346 and n., 348

Newerk, Alan de, 430 n.

Newmarket Heath (Suff.), 220

Newton, Thomas, mercer and alderman of London, sheriff (1392–3), 494, 500, 501 n.

Nieuport (W. Flanders, Belg.), 30, 38

Nocera (Salerno, Italy), 66 n., 110 and n., 111 n., 130, 131 n., 140 n.

Noirmoutier Island (Fr.), 352

Nola, count of, 110
Nonantola (Modena, Italy), abbot of, lix, 458, 460, 462, 468, 472, 482 and n.
Norfolk, epidemic in, 44
Normandy, 134, 182, 184
— duchy, 490
— and Seine, admiral of, 134
Northampton, 218, 350 and n.
Northampton, John, draper of London, mayor (1381-3), lvii, 64, 145 n., 184 and n., 307 n., 404, 440, 442 n.
— and John of Gaunt, lxvii, lxviii, lxxiii, 92 and n., 440
— annulment of proceedings against, 454 n.
— appeal of Thomas Usk against, 90 and n., 92, 94, 245 n., 314-16
— arrest, 62, 64 n.
— mayoralties, xxiv, xxv, lxvii, 58, 60 and n., 62 and n.
— pardon, 440, 442 and n., 454
— second trial, 94 and n., 96 and n.
— sentences on, 92 and n., 96, 97 n., 148, 150 and n.
Northbury, Richard, mercer of London, 90 n., 94 and n., 150 n., 307 n.
— pardon, 442 n.
Northumberland, earl of, see Percy, Henry
Northumbria, 86, 100
Norwich (Norf.), diocese, 42, 337 n.
— bishop of, 124; see also Despenser, Henry
— monk of, see Easton, Adam
Nottingham, 42, 44, 180, 278, 316, 442, 498, 500 and n., 502
— castle, 96, 196, 230 n.
— council at, 42, 186 and nn., 301 n., 494
— earl of, see Mowbray, John; Mowbray, Thomas

Oakham (Leics., formerly Rutl.), castle, 414 and n., 442 n.
— forest, see Rutland
— lordship, 244 and n., 414 n.
Obidos (Estremadura, Port.), 132 n.
Ockendon (Yorks.), 443 n.
Odiham castle (Hants), 500
Offynton, Haymo de, abbot of Battle (1364-83), 34 and n.
Ogle, Sir Robert (1353-1409), 397 n.

Ogle, 'Sir Thomas', 396
Oliver, William, skinner and alderman of London, 494
Oporto (Douro, Port.), 192 n.
Ordinance of Labourers (1349), 361 n.
Orense (Spain), 190 n.
Orléans, Lorens d', Somme le Roi, xlii n.
Ormond, earl of, see Le Botiler, James
Orwell, see Orwell Haven
Orwell Haven (Suff.), 182, 183 n., 184
Osney (Oxon.), abbot of, 326
Ostrevantz, William, count of, later William VI of Holland, d. 1417, 450, 451 nn., 452
Otterburn (Northumb.), battle at (1388), 346 and n., 348, 350
Ottery St. Mary (Devon), 498
Oudenarde (W. Flanders, Belg.), 46, 524
Oxford, xlii, 20, 28, 86, 224, 512
— council at, 344
— earl of, see Vere, Aubrey de; Vere, Robert de
— epidemic at, 20
— Gloucester College, xxxvii
— St. Frideswide's Priory, 28 n.
— university, xxxi, xxxvi, xxxvii, xl

Padua (Italy), 476 and n.
Palencia (Spain), 370 n.
Panton, Thomas, citizen of London, 494
Papal curia, lix, 38 and n., 54, 158, 178, 188, 202, 204 n., 248 n., 300 n., 309 n., 336, 366, 378, 380, 382, 394, 404, 412, 424, 426, 428, 441 n., 454 and n., 485 n.; see also pope; Rome
Paris, 372, 396, 404
— parlement of, 152 and n.
Parker, Matthew, archbishop of Canterbury (1559-75), xiv, xv, xvii n.
Parker, William, mercer of London, 494
Parliament, xxii, 212 and n., 216 and n., 217 n., 246, 248-50, 266, 300, 302, 470, 472
— assembly of, 198
— clerk of, xlvi, xlix, l
— Commons in, xlvii, 36, 52, 82, 138, 142, 146, 166, 168, 174, 198, 200,

250, 252, 254, 268, 269 n., 270, 273 n., 276-96 *passim*, 297 n., 304, 306, 307 n., 308, 318, 322, 328 and n., 354, 356 n., 364, 368 n., 416, 422, 454, 455 n., 486 n., 512 n., 518 n.
— dissolution, 200
— elections to, 266, 267 n.
— law of, 282 and n.
— lords and commons in, lxvi, 314, 316, 320, 332, 336, 338, 342
— lords in, lxv, 36 and n., 136, 140, 166, 168, 174, 198, 200, 236, 250, 252, 254, 257 n., 271 n., 275 n., 280-96 *passim*, 308, 309 n., 330, 342, 454
— lords spiritual in, xlviii n., 66, 168, 276, 278, 280, 281 n., 286, 287 n., 288, 294, 295 n., 302-4, 307 n., 316
— lords temporal in, xlviii, 54, 66, 236 n., 242 n., 276, 278, 280, 294 and n., 295 n., 307 n., 316, 416, 496
— seating in, 144
— sessions: (20 Jan. 1307), 418, 420, 422; (8 Feb. 1310), 200, 201 n.; (9 Feb. 1351), 418, 422; (20 Oct. 1378), 144 n., 324 n.; (16 Jan. 1380), 38 n.; (3 Nov. 1381), xlvi n., 18 n., 20, 21 n., 22 and nn.; (7 May 1382), xlvi n., 26 and n.; (6 Oct.), 1382, xlvi n., 28 and n., 164 n.; (23 Feb. 1383), xlvi n., 34, 35 n., 36 and n.; (26 Oct. 1383), xlvi, 48 and n., 50, 52 and n., 54, 62 n., 82, 138, 524; (29 Apr. 1384), xl, lxiii, 48 n., 66 ff., 86; (12 Nov., 1384), lvi, 102-4, 106; (20 Oct. 1385), 126 n., 136-8, 140, 142, 144-6, 148 and n.; (1 Oct. 1386), xlvi n., 166, 167 n., 169 n., 174, 176, 178 n., 184 n., 198, 199 n., 202 n., 230 n., 238, 250, 251 n., 252, 253 n., 254, 270-2, 274, 276, 278, 279 n., 297 n., 298; (3 Feb. 1388), *see* Parliament, the Merciless; (9 Sept. 1388), xlvi n., 354 ff., 368, 372, 412; (17 Jan. 1390), lvi, 408, 410, 412, 414 and n., 416, 426, 430; (12 Nov. 1390), xxix, xlvi n., lviii, 452, 454 and n., (3 Nov. 1391),

xxix, xlvi n., lviii, 454 n., 480-2, 483 n., 486 n.; (20 Jan. 1393), 481 n., 510 n., 512, 514 n.; (27 Jan. 1394), xlvi n., lxii, 516; (29 Jan. 1394), *see* 27 Jan. 1394
Parliament, the Merciless, xxi, xlvi n., lxv-vi, lxviii, lxxiii, lxxiv, 167 n., 196 n., 222 n., 301 n., 303 n., 355 n., 452, 498
— dissolution, 296, 342
— first session, 234 ff., 280 ff., 308 ff.
— pardons in, 297 n.
— 'Process' of, xlvi ff., 280 ff.
— prorogation, 290, 320 and n.
— second session, 290 ff., 322, 328 ff.
— summons, 214, 216, 218 and n.
Parys, Robert, cofferer of London, 40 and n.
Paule, John, xxvi, 496 and n.
Paveley, Sir John, 510
Peace treaties and truces:
— Anglo-Bohemian (1381), 23 n., 24 n., 275 n.
— Anglo-French (1384), 58 and n., 89 n., 98 and n.; (1389), 398 and nn., 400 and n., 440 n., 490 and n., 492, 514 and n., 515 n., 518; draft treaty (1393), 514 n., 515 n., 518 n.; rumour of (1387), 204, 205 n.
— Anglo-Prussian (1388), 368, 369 n.
— Anglo-Scottish (1380), 41 n.; (1381), 41 n., 42 n.; (1383), 42 and n., 54 n., 56, 100, 101 n.; (1384), 98 n., 100, 101 n.; (1386), 403 n.; (1389), 398 and n., 402
— between Castile and Portugal (1382), 29 n.
— *see also* Badajoz; Boulogne; Körenzig; Leulingham; Ponte do Mouro; Tournai
Peasants' Revolt, 1381, xx, xxiii, lxvii, lxix ff., 2 ff.
Pecham, Michael, abbot of St. Augustine's, Canterbury (1375-87), 180 and n.
Pedro I, king of Castile (1350-69) (Pedro the Cruel), 142 n., 192, 511 n., 520
— Constanza, daughter of, *see* Constance of Castile
— Isabel daughter of, *see* Isabel of Castile

Pembroke, earl of, *see* Hastings, John, 2nd earl of; and Hastings, John, 3rd earl of

Penthièvre, counts of, *see* Blois, Charles de; Bretagne, Jean de

Percy, Henry, earl of Northumberland, d. 1408, 124, 196 and n., 226, 310, 376, 396 and n., 454
— captain of Calais, 455 n.
— in council, 396
— keeper of Berwick-upon-Tweed, 104
— quarrel with John of Gaunt, xx, 20 and n., 22 and n., 408
— warden of marches, 50 and n., 66, 67 n., 350 n.
— Sir Henry, son of (Hotspur), d. 1403, 134, 138, 346 and n., 348 and n., 350, 400, 402
— — keeper of Berwick-upon-Tweed, 134 n.
— — — lieutenant in Aquitaine, xxix, 402 n.
— — — warden of east march, 134 n., 346 n.

Percy, Ralph, 348 and n., 400

Percy, Sir Thomas, steward of the king's household (1393-9), earl of Worcester (1397-1403), 12 n., 50 n., 88 and n., 322 n., 344, 456 and n., 486 n., 490 n., 514 and n.
— under-chamberlain, 414

Pereira, Diego Alvarez, 132, 133 n.

Pereira, Pedro Alvarez, master of Calatrava, 132, 133 n.

Perinus Tomacellus (Pope Boniface IX), *see* Boniface IX

Perrers, Alice, 98 n.

Perugia (Italy), 202, 203 n., 344 n., 508, 509 n.

Peter Comestor, *Scholastica Historia*, xlii

Peter Romanus, *see* Tartaris, Peter de

Philip the Bold, duke of Burgundy and count of Flanders, *see* Burgundy

Philippa of Hainault, queen of Edward III (1328-69), lvii

Picards, 320

Picardy (prov., Fr.), 136, 262, 278, 352, 406 n.

Pinchbeck, Robert, liii n., 220

Pipino, Francesco, *Marci Pauli de Venetiis* etc., xlii and nn.

Pleshey (Essx.), 154

Plymouth (Devon), 164, 406

Poil (Pas-de-Calais, Fr.), 320-2

Poitou, county of, 490 n.

Poland, king of, 448

Poland and Krakow, king of, 448

Pole, Sir Edmund de la, keeper of Calais castle, 214

Pole, Michael de la, earl of Suffolk (1385-8), d. 1389, lv, lxviii-lxix, 126 and n., 140 n., 160, 169 n., 178 and n., 186 and n., 200, 202, 206, 208, 268, 270, 278, 296
— chancellor (1383-6), 36, 37 n., 96, 140, 247 nn., 272 and n., 274 and n., 326, 380
— death, 402, 403 n.
— escapes, 214, 272 and n., 320, 321 n.
— impeachment (1386), 200 n., 252, 272 and n.
— proceedings against (1388), xlviii, 236 ff., 280
— sentence on, 280, 308

Pole, Michael de la, 2nd earl of Suffolk (1398-1415), 231 n.

Polychronicon of Ranulph Higden, xxxii, xl n., xli, xlii and n.
— continuations, xv, xvi n., xix n., xxxi n.

Pons, Sire de, 352

Ponte do Lima (Minho, Port.), 133 n.

Ponto do Mouro, treaty of (1386), 192 n.

Pontefract (Yorks.), 120

Pope, the, 192, 196 n., 204, 248 and n., 303 n., 308, 382, 390, 394, 420, 422, 428, 436, 438, 440, 454; *see also* papal curia; Rome; *and the names of the several popes*

Poperinghe (W. Flanders, Belg.), 38, 39 n., 44

Portsmouth (Hants), 344

Portugal, 128 and n., 133 n., 164, 190, 194
— chancellor of, *see* Fogaça, Lourenço Anes
— king of, 28, 30; *see also* João I

Poynings, Richard, lord, d. 1387, 190 and n.

—, Thomas, lord, d. 1375, 231 n.; Blanche, wife of, m. (ii) Sir John Worth, 230, 231 n.

Prata, Pileus de, archbishop of Ravenna

(1370–87), and (from 1385) cardinal bishop of Tusculan, 202, 203 n.

Prignano, Francis, 110 n.

Privy seal, clerk/keeper of, 44, 168, 253 n., 356, 404, 418
— See also Stafford, Edmund; Waltham, John

Prussia, Prussians, lv, 330, 368, 373 n., 444, 455 n., 478, 480, 482
— marshal of, 444, 446, 448

Pseudo-Isidore, 138 n.

Puy, Mr. Raymond Guilhem du, 88 n.

Queenborough castle (Kent), 224
— keeper of, 439 n.

Rabe, Engelhardt, 444 n.

Radcot Bridge (Oxon.), battle at, liii n., lxiv, lxv, lxix, 220 and nn., 222 and n., 268

Raddington, Sir Baldwin, 288, 406
— controller of the wardrobe, 289 n., 407 n.
— warden of the City of London, 502 and n., 506

Radwell, William, stockfishmonger of London, 494

Radyngton, John, master of the Hospital of St. John of Jerusalem (1381–95), 432 and n.

Ragenhull, John, fishmonger of London, 494

Ramirez de Arellano, Juan, 132, 133 n.

Rattlesden (Suff.), 302, 337 n.

Ravenna (Italy), archbishops of, see Megliorato, Cosmas Gentilis; Prata, Pileus de

Reade, William, bishop of Chichester (1368–85), 130 and n.

Reading (Berks.), 186 n.
— council at, lxvii, 18 and n., 90 and n., 92, 120, 186, 316, 406, 456

Reading, John de, monk of Westminster, xvi, xxxi

Redmayne, Sir Matthew, 346, 348 and n., 350 and n., 396
— captain of Berwick-upon-Tweed, 347 n.

Reigate castle (Surr.), 210 n.

Ré Island (Fr.), 352

Responsories, 408 and n., 506 and n.

Rhodes, 122, 123 n., 178 n., 432 n.

Rhône, R., 398 n.

Richard II, king of England (1377–99), xv, xxiv, xxxvi, 52–4, 66 ff., 82, 88, 98, 102 and n., 106, 116, 122, 140, 142, 144, 158–60, 184, 222–4, 228 n., 240, 256, 432, 434, 439 n., 520 n., and passim
— and Appellants, lii, liii, liv, lxxiii, 208 ff., 216, 224 ff., 400, 406–8
— and Aquitaine, lviii–ix, lxi ff., 204
— and Boniface IX, 458 ff.
— and Despenser crusade, 48, 522–4
— and Edward II, 158 and n., 438 n., 486
— and Ireland, xxxvi, 248 and n., 520
— and John Northampton, lxvii, lxxiii, 90 ff., 148–50
— and London, lv, lvii–viii, lxviii, lxix, lxxiv, 24, 62, 206, 216, 224, 234 n., 250, 251 n., 492–508 passim, 510, 516
— and Merciless Parliament, lxv, 234 ff., 280 ff., 310, 316, 328, 330, 340, 342
— and parliament of 1386, 250–2
— and parliament of Sept. 1388, 354–6
— and Peasants' Revolt, lv, lxxi n., lxxii, 2 ff.
— and Westminster Abbey, xiii, xxxvii, xxxix, xl, xlvii, l, lv and n., lxix, 8–10, 32, 38 n., 144, 154–6, 176, 178 and n., 206–8, 314, 324–6, 338–40, 350, 372 and n., 378–82, 384, 414, 450, 454, 488, 506, 508, 510
— assumes majority, xxviii, 390–2
— chapel of, 450
— character, lxxii ff.
— clerks of chapel of, 314
— confessor of, xxix, 130, 434, 435 n.
— consultations with judges, 186 n., 196 ff., 206 n.
— coronation, xxvi, 156, 170, 218
— expedition to Scotland, 120 and n., 124 and n., 126 and n., 128, 130
— itinerary, 12 n., 14 n., 32, 42–4, 48 and n., 56, 86, 106, 114, 124, 128, 130 and n., 154, 158, 178, 180, 186 and n., 220 and n., 224, 254, 276–8, 301 n., 374, 400, 402, 408, 436, 438, 440, 442 and n., 450, 454, 456, 478 and n., 488, 502, 504, 510, 512, 514, 516

Richard II (king of England) (*cont.*):
— and jousts and tournaments, 110, 432, 436, 450, 451 n.
— kinsman of, 231 n.
— marriage, 22-4
— mother of, 114, 128, 292, 450 n.
— negotiations with France, 204, 205 n., 260 and n., 262 and n., 278, 301 n., 396-8, 456 and n., 457 n., 472, 478, 490, 515 n.
— on pilgrimage, 42
— quarrel with archbishop of Canterbury, 116, 138
— sister of, 450, 488
— succession to, 194 and n.
— threatened with deposition, 218, 228, 235 n.
Rickhill, William, xlix
Ripon, John, 188, 202 and n., 260, 300, 344 and n., 402 and n., 404
— justice, 202 n.
Rixhöft (Rozewie cape, Poland), 444 n.
Robert of Geneva (Clement VII, anti-pope), *see* Clement VII
Robinson, J. Armitage, xxii, xxxviii, xxxix, xl
Rochester (Kent):
— bishop of, *see* Bottesham, William de
— Bridge, xvi, 2
— castle, 230 n.
'Rodeneye', Lopo de, 132
Rokeley, Sir Richard, 487 n.
Rome, xxxiii and n., 64, 100 and n., 345 n., 346, 386, 390, 404, 416 n., 430, 460, 464, 484; *see also* papal curia; pope
Ronhale, Mr. Richard, lxi, 161 n., 196, 374 and n., 396, 406 n., 486 n., 487 n., 490 n., 514
Roos, John, lord, d. 1393:
— warden of west march, 378 nn.
Roozebeke, battle of (1382), 32 n.
Roughton, Br. Richard, O.F.M., 302, 303 n.
Roughton, Br. Thomas, O.F.M., 302, 303 n.
Roxburgh (Scotland), 42 and n.
Rushock, Thomas, O.P., bishop of Llandaff (1383-5), Chichester (1385-8), Kilmore (1388-92):
— proceedings against, xlviii and n., l, 284, 286 and nn., 292, 294 and n.

— sentence on, 316, 332
— translated, 294 n.
Rutland:
— earl of, *see* York, Edward of
— forest of, 244 n.

St. Albans (Herts.), xxiii, 14 and n., 18 n.
— abbey, xxxi, lix, 14
St. Andrews, see of, 309 n., 334
St. Asaph, bishop of, *see* Bache, Alexander
St. Benedict of Nursia, 346
St. David's, bishop of, *see* Gilbert, John; Houghton, Adam
St. Edward the Confessor, *see* Edward the Confessor
St. Edward the martyr, *see* Edward the martyr
St. Etheldreda, tomb of, 42
St. George, 222
St. Ingelvert (nr. Calais, Fr.), 432 n.
St. Ives, Adam de, grocer and alderman of London, 494
St. John, John of, 408, 410, 411 n.
St. John of Castile, prior of, *see* Diaz, Pedro
St. Mary the Virgin, 512
— feast of Visitation, *see* feast days
— merits of, 386, 388
St. Omer (Pas-de-Calais, Fr.), lxii n., 457 n., 486, 487 n.
St. Pol, count of, *see* Ligny and St. Pol, Waleran, count of
St. Thomas Aquinas, xxxvii
St. Thomas the martyr, 138
Salisbury (Wilts.), 80, 86, 402
— bishop of, *see* Erghum, Ralph; Waltham, John
— castle, keeper of gaol in, 68 n., 72, 76, 78, 80; *see also* Homes, John
— cathedral, 70
— dean, *see* Montague, Thomas
— diocese, 438 n.
— earl of, *see* Montague, William, earl of Salisbury
— parliament at, xl, lxiii, 66 ff.
— St. Martin's church in, 80
Salisbury, Sir John, d. 1388, lvi, 228, 262
— chamber knight, 269 n.
— proceedings against, 234 n., 236,

268 ff., 288, 292, 293 n.
— sentence on, 292, 293 n.
— steward of king's household, 332
— usher of king's chamber, 230 n.
'Salmo', count, 100
Samogitia (Lithuania), 444 n.
Sancerre, Louis de, marshal of France (1369-1402), 352 and n., 353 n.
Sánchez Manuel, Juan ('count of Carrion'), 132 and n.
Sandhurst, John, citizen of London, 494
Sandwich (Kent), 166
San Severino, Giacopo de, 110, 111 n.
San Severino, Thomas de, 111 n.
Santarem (Ribatejo, Port.), 142 and n.
Saquainville, Jean de, lord of Blaru, 478
Saracens, 432 and n.
Sarmento, Diego Gomez, 133 n.
Sarnesfield, Sir Nicholas, 456
Savoy, Amadeus VI, count of (1343-83), 101 n.
Scales, Roger, lord, d. 1386, 190, 191 n.
Scarle, John, xlvi-vii, li, lvii n.
Schism, the Great, 100 n.
Scotland, 142, 147 n.
— diplomatic relations, 88, 89 n., 98 n., 376, 377 n., 398, 402
— Edward I and, xv
— English incursions into, 42, 66, 138, 396
— French expedition to, xxvii, 56, 120 and n.
— king of, 54-6; see also David II
— marches towards, see marches
— ships, 182
Scots, 40-2, 50, 58, 154, 474-6, 524
— incursions into England, 40, 50, 86, 100, 104, 132, 138, 344, 346 and n., 370, 382-4, 396, 524
Scottish Sea, see Forth, Firth of
Scrope, Richard, dean of Chichester (1384-6), bishop of Coventry and Lichfield (1386-98), archbishop of York (1398-1405), xiv, 130
Scrope, Sir Richard, 1st baron Scrope of Bolton, chancellor (1381-2), d. 1403, 28 and n., 124 and n., 168, 169 n., 210, 214, 232, 322, 332
— keeper of Carlisle castle, 50 n.
— warden of marches, 50 and n., 526

Scrope, le Scrope, Sir William, later (1397-9) 1st earl of Wiltshire:
— captain of Cherbourg, 375 n.
— seneschal of Gascony, 402 n.
— under-chamberlain, 514 and n.
Seal, the Great, 240, 272
— in Statute of Cambridge, 360
— of Chester, 256, 257 and n.
Segrave, Hugh, treasurer (1381-6), 20, 160, 178, 179 n.
Seine, R., 40, 178, 350; see also Normandy and Seine
Selby, Mr. Ralph, monk of Westminster, 519 n.
Selsey (Suss.), xxxiii n.
Serbia, 123 n.
Seys, Sir Digory, 438, 439 n.
Shadworth, John, mercer and alderman of London, sheriff (1391-2), 494, 498, 500 and n., 502 and n.
Sheen (now Richmond, Surr.), lxix, 12, 207 n., 274, 400, 402, 458, 504, 520
Sheppey (Kent), xxxiii n.
Sheppey, John, lxi and n., 28, 50, 88 n., 374 and n., 524
Sheriffs, 218 n., 240, 266, 267 n., 288, 358, 360, 362, 364, 366 and n., 404
Sheringham, William, mercer and alderman of London, 494
Shiryngham, Simon, 205 n., 302
Shrewsbury (Salop), council at, 186, 197 n.
Sibile, John, citizen of London, 494
Sibill, Sibyle, Walter, fishmonger and alderman of London, 245 n., 368
Sicily, kingdom of, 466 and n., 470; see also Naples, kingdom of
Skelton, Richard, liii n., 220
Skirgiello, regent in Poland-Lithuania, 444 n., 446 n.
— 'king of Lithuania', 446
Skirlaw, Walter, keeper of the privy seal (1382-6), bishop of Durham (1388-1406), bishop of Coventry and Lichfield (1385-6), Bath and Wells (1386-8), lxi, 118 and n., 156, 232 and n., 334 and n., 348 and n., 355 n., 515 n.
— embassies, 50, 88 n., 161 n., 374 and n., 406 and n., 436, 437 n., 486, 514 and n., 524

Skirlaw, Walter (*cont.*):
— styled bishop of Chester, 118, 156, 160
Slake, Nicholas, 230 n., 300, 301 nn., 341 n., 370
— proceedings against, 286, 288
Sluys (Netherl., formerly Flanders), 124, 134, 178, 182 and n., 183 n., 251 n.
Smithfield, *see* London
Somenour, Richard, of Stepney, 6 n.
Southam, Mr. Thomas, papal sub-collector, lvii and n., 318, 330
Southwark (Surr.), lxx
Southwell, Nicholas, 262, 300
Spain, 28, 36, 160, 182, 192 and n.; *see also* Castile; Galicia; León; Portugal; Spaniards
Spaniards, 64, 152, 180
Sprot, Hugh, citizen of London, 494
Stafford, Edmund, keeper of the privy seal (1389–96), 392 and n., 393 n.
Stafford, Hugh, 2nd earl of Stafford (1372–86), 122 and n., 124, 144, 160 and n., 176
— Philippa, wife of, *see* Beauchamp, Philippa
— Ralph, son of, 122 and n., 144, 158 n., 160 and n.
Stafford, Thomas de, 3rd earl of Stafford, d. 1392, 480, 481 n., 500, 501 n.
— Anne, wife of, 481 n.
Stamford (Lincs.), 494
— council at, lxii, 488, 490 and n.
— Greyfriars, 128
Stamford Bridge, xxxiii n.
Standon, William, grocer of London, mayor (1392–3), 500 and n., 508
Standyche, Ralph, 10 n.
Stanton, Robert, *see* Stretton, Robert
Statute, statutes, xlvi
— 3 Edward I, cap. 34, 364 n.
— 35 Edward I, caps. 1–4, 418, 422
— 9 Edward III, 1, cap. 1, 334 and n.
— 25 Edward III, 3, cap. 2, 334 n.
— 25 Edward III, 4, 418 ff., 426, 428
— 27 Edward III, 1, cap. 1, 464 n.
— 34 Edward III, cap. 9, 362 n.
— 38 Edward III, 2, caps. 1–4, 464 n.
— 2 Richard II, 1, cap. 5, 364 and n.;

cap. 8, 361 n.
— 5 Richard II, 1, cap. 2, 364 and n.
— 6 Richard II, 1, cap. 9, 335 n., 366 and n., 367 n.
— 6 Richard II, 1, caps. 10–11, 335 n.
— 7 Richard II, cap. 11, 62 n.
— 7 Richard II, cap. 14, 54 n.
— 11 Richard II, cap. 7, 322 n., 334 n.
— 12 Richard II, cap. 1, 368 n.
— 12 Richard II, cap. 2, 358 n.
— 12 Richard II, cap. 3, 361 nn., 363 n.; cap. 4, 364; cap. 5, 362 n.; cap. 6, 362 n., 363 n.; cap. 7, 361 n., 363 n.; cap. 8, 361 n.; cap. 9, 362 n.; cap. 10, 362 n.; 363 n.; cap. 11, 364 n.; cap. 12, 365 n.; caps. 13–14, 368 n.; cap. 15, 367 n., 430; cap. 16, 368 n.
— 13 Richard II, 1, cap. 2, 415 n.; cap. 3, 415 n.; cap. 8, 412 n.
— 13 Richard II, 2, cap. 1, 416, 417 n., 418, 430; caps. 2–3, 412, 418 ff., 430
— 15 Richard II, cap. 5, 482 n.
— 2 Henry IV, cap. 5, 364 n.
— and parliament, 470
— enacting ordinance on council (1386), 198, 199 n., 252–4, 258, 260, 264, 268, 274, 276, 296, 297 n., 298
— lost (1310), 200, 201 n.
— of Cambridge (1388), lxiii, 363 n.; *see also* 12 Richard II, caps. 2 ff.
— of Carlisle (1307), 418, 464 n.
— of Praemunire (1353), 464 n., 472 n.; *and see* 27 Edward III, 1, cap. 1
— of Provisors (1351), 460, 464 n., 470; *and see* 25 Edward III, 4
— of Provisors (1390), 412, 455 n., 460, 464 n., 470, 480, 482 n., 512 n.; *and see* 13 Richard II, 2, caps. 2–3
— of Staple (1354), 454 n.
— of Treasons (1351), 304, 305 n.
— on alien priories, 148 n.
Steward of the king's household, 76, 80, 174, 286, 356, 415 n.; *see also* Beauchamp, John; Devereux, John; Montague, John; Percy, Thomas; Salisbury, John
Stewart, Robert, earl of Fife (1371/2–1420), 346 n.

Stody, John, vintner of London, 407 n.
— Idonea, daughter of, m. (i) Nicholas Brembre; (ii) Baldwin Raddington, 406, 407 n.
Stonegrave, Thomas, abbot of St. Mary's, York, 402
Stow (Glos.), see Stow-on-the-Wold
Stow, John, monk of Westminster, xl n.
Stow-on-the-Wold (Glos.), lxiv, 220 and n.
Stretton, Robert (Robert Stanton), bishop of Coventry and Lichfield (1360-85), styled bishop of Chester, 116, 118 and n.
Stury, Sir Richard, chamber knight, lxii, 28
Sudbury, Henry, skinner of London, xxxvi
Sudbury, Simon, archbishop of Canterbury (1375-81), chancellor (1380-1), lxxi, lxxii, 2, 4, 6
Sudbury, William, monk of Westminster, xxxvi-viii, 34 n.; John, brother of, 34 n.
Suffolk, earl of, see Pole, Michael de la; Ufford, William de
Swaffham, John (Carm.), bishop of Bangor (1376-98), 200, 202 and n.
Swylyngton, Robert de, 442 n.
Symond, Sir Thomas, 190, 191 n.

Taranto (Italy), 98
Tartaris, Peter de (Peter Romanus), abbot of Monte Cassino (1374-95), 345 n.
Taverner, John, alias Fitz Martin, 302, 303 n.
Taxation, 50, 204, 244, 526
— clerical subsidies, 28 and n., 32, 33 n., 48 and n., 82 and n., 84, 102 and n., 148, 149 n., 320, 368 and n., 524
— cloth subsidy, 170
— lay subsidies, 28, 48 and n., 82 and n., 84, 102 and n., 142, 143 n., 148, 149 n., 286, 287 n., 290 and n., 316, 318 and n., 320, 368 and n., 524
— petty custom, 170, 295 n.
— poll tax (1380), 6 n.
— poundage, 290 and n., 294, 320, 454 and n.
— wine subsidy, 170, 290 and n., 294,

320, 454 n.
— wool custom and subsidy, 170, 290 and n., 294, 320, 321 n., 454 n.
Tello de Meneses, Juan Alonso ('count of Mayorga'), 132 and n.
Teutonic Order, 444 n., 479 n.
Tewkesbury, abbot of, see Chesterton, Thomas
Thames, R., 4, 6, 16, 112, 116, 220, 223 n., 234
Thaxted (Essx.), Henry, clerk of, 302, 303 n.
— chantry, 303 n.
Thouars, vicomte de, 352
Tiler, Walter, 10, 11 n.
Timworth, John de, abbot of Bury St. Edmunds (1379-89), 42 and n., 376
Tintagel castle (Corn.), 96
Tolleshunt Major (Essx.), xxxv n.
Tonworthe, Ralph, monk of Westminster, xxxvii n.
Topsham (Devon), 85 n.
Torres Vedras (Estremadura, Port.), 133 n.
Tottenham (Midd.), 114
Touraine, Louis, duke of (1386-92), later (1392-1407) duke of Orleans, 464, 465 n., 466 and n.
Tournai (Hainaut, Belg.), 30 n.
— treaty of (1385), 150 and n., 152
Tournaments and jousts, 110, 164, 430, 432 and n., 436, 437 n., 450
Tours (Indre-et-Loire, Fr.), 350
Treason, allegations and charges of, 70, 90-2, 94 and n., 96, 106, 198-200, 212, 214, 238, 240 ff., 242 n., 270 ff., 292 n., 316, 324, 416, 418
— imputed to John of Gaunt, 68 ff.
— misprision of, 59 n., 90 n., 177 n., 303 n.
— penalties for, 16 n., 214 and n., 308, 332
— petty, 323 n.
Treasurer of England, 42, 156, 168, 232, 233 n., 253 n., 324, 356, 392, 404, 482, 492, 510-12; see also Brantingham, Thomas; Fordham, John; Gilbert, John; Hales, Robert; Segrave, Hugh; Waltham, John
Trefnant, John, bishop of Hereford (1389-1404), 382 and n., 394

Tresilian, Sir Robert, chief justice of the King's Bench, d. 1388, lxix, 15 n., 18 n., 94-6, 196, 210, 214 and n., 258, 270, 296
— arrest, xxvi, lvi, 282, 310 and n., 312, 326, 332, 498
— proceedings against, xlviii, 210-12, 236 ff., 280 ff., 312
— sentence on, 280, 282, 283 n., 312, 314
Treviso, march of (Italy), 466 n.
Trezzo, see Trezzo d'Adda
Trezzo d'Adda (Milan, Italy), 119 n., 158 n.
Trivet, Sir Thomas, xxi, liii, 44 and n., 46 n., 52 and n., 116, 212 and n., 228, 230 n., 338, 368, 369 and n.
— chamber knight, 116 n.
Tunisia, 432 n.
Turkey, 430
Tuscany, 466
Tutbury (Staffs.), 344
Twyford, Nicholas, goldsmith of London, mayor (1388-9), 101 n., 102, 370
Tyburn (Midd.), 282, 284, 292, 312, 332, 498
Tynemouth (Northumb.), 344, 396, 397 n.
— prior of, 397 n.
— priory, 397 n.

Ufford, 'Thomas de', see Ufford, William de
Ufford, William de, earl of Suffolk (1369-82), 22 and n.
Ulster, earldom of, 194
Urban IV, pope (1261-4), 395 n.
Urban VI, pope (1378-89), 30, 38 n., 66 and n., 130, 131 n., 140 and n., 142, 144 n., 150 n., 158 n., 159 n., 162, 163 n., 164, 178 and n., 179 n., 202, 203 n., 204 n., 332, 334 and n., 344 and n., 346
— and cardinals, 106, 108 and n., 110
— and kingdom of Naples, 36 n., 100 n., 106, 108 and n., 109 n., 110
— and Westminster Abbey, 196
— bulls of, xxi, 334 n.
Usk, Thomas, xxvii n., 234 n., 244, 270, 285 n., 314, 315 n., 316

— appeal of, 90 and n., 92-4, 96
— arrest, 90 and n.
— proceedings against, l-li, 269 n., 284
— sentence on, 284, 285 n., 314
— under-sheriff of London and Midd., 90 n., 258, 259 n.

'Valasco, Gonçalo', 132 and n.
Valasco, Joham de, 132 n.
Valassco, Pedro de, 132 n.
Vanner, Henry, vintner and alderman of London, sheriff (1391-2), 494, 498, 500 and n., 502 and n.
Varese (Italy), 119 n.
Venice (Italy), 156
Venour, William, grocer and alderman of London, mayor (1389-90), 404, 494
Vere, Aubrey de, earl of Oxford (1393-1400), 230, 231 n., 510 and n., 512
— chamberlain, 231 n.
Vere, Robert de, earl of Oxford (1381-92), marquis of Dublin (1385-8), duke of Ireland (1386-8), xlvii, lv, lxix, 68, 184 and n., 188 and n., 190, 202, 206, 210, 214, 216, 218, 257 n., 262, 268, 270, 272-4, 276, 277 n., 278, 296, 301 n., 320
— and John of Gaunt, 114, 124
— and campaign of Radcot Bridge, lii, liii, lxiv, 220, 222, 223 n., 224, 266-8, 342
— and lordship of Ireland, 146 n., 244 and n., 248 and n., 379 n.
— chamberlain, 231 n., 275 n., 333 n.
— chief justice of Chester, 256, 257 n., 186, 188 and n., 257 n.
— confessor of, 303 n.
— created marquis, 144
— death, 510 and n.
— divorce, 404
— marriages, 188, 189 n., 190 and n.
— mother of, 190, 277 n.
— on Scottish expedition, 124
— Philippa, wife of, see Coucy, Philippa de
— proceedings against, 210-12, 236 ff., 280 ff.
— sentence on, 280, 484-6
Vertus, count of, 476; see also Visconti, Giangaleazzo

Vienne, Jean de, xxvii, 56 and n., 120 and n., 136

Villaines, Bègue de, 478 n.

Villalpando (Zamora, Spain), 190 n., 191 n.

Villena, marquis of, see Denia, count of

Vilna (Wilno, Poland, formerly Lithuania), 444 n., 446, 448

Visconti, Bernabò, lord of Milan, d. 1385, 118-20, 466 n., 476 n.

Visconti, Giangaleazzo ('count of Vertus'), lord of Piedmont, lord and subsequently duke of Milan, d. 1402: 118 and n., 120, 466 n., 476 n.

Visconti, Giovanni, archbishop of Milan (1339-54), 118 n.

Vissegrad (Hercegovina, Yugosl., formerly Hungary), 162 n.

Vitold ('king of Wytort'), 444 n.

Vivent, Thomas, mercer and alderman of London, 494

Vladyslav II, grand prince of Lithuania (1377-1434), king of Poland (1386-1434), 444 n.

Vynelef, Martyletto de, 104 and n., 106

Wade, John, fishmonger of London, 494

Wakefield, Henry de, bishop of Worcester (1375-95), lxiv and n.

Walcot, John, draper of London, 494

Wales, lxiv, 254, 268, 382, 383 n.

— prince of, 484

Wallingford (Berks.), 128

— castle, 500

Walsh, John, victualler at Cherbourg, 104, 105 n., 106

Walsingham, Thomas, xiii, xxxv, lix, lxxi, 14 n., 212 n., 230 n., 444 n., 462 n.

— Chronica Majora, xix n., xxxv

— Short History, xix, xix n., xxxv

Waltham, John, keeper of the privy seal (1386-9), bishop of Salisbury (1388-95), 142, 168 n., 210, 232 and n., 238, 334 and n., 354

— dispute with archbishop of Canterbury, 438 and n.

— keeper of rolls, 142-4

— treasurer, 458

Waltham, John, d. 1384, sub-dean of York, 86 n.

Waltham Abbey (Holy Cross) (Essx.), 169 n., 440

— abbots, see Morice, Nicholas; Neel, William

Waltham Cross (Herts.), 210, 238

Walworth, William, fishmonger of London, mayor (1380-1), 10-12, 16 n.

Wandsworth (Surr.), 504

Wanton, Andrew, 322 n.

— Elizabeth, 322 n.

Wark Castle (Northumb.), 41 n.

Warwick, earl of, see Beauchamp, Thomas, earl of Warwick (1315-69); and Beauchamp, Thomas, earl of Warwick (1370-97, 1399-1401)

Waterford (Ireland), 336 n.

Weather, xxii, xxxv, 32, 40, 42, 88, 120, 156, 190, 204, 220, 232, 400, 414, 438, 444, 476, 482, 508, 510

Welde, William, abbot of St. Augustine's, Canterbury (1387-1405), 180, 204, 384 and n.

Welles, John, lord, d. 1421, 434 and n.

Wenceslas of Bohemia, see Wenzel IV, king of Bohemia

Wenzel IV, king of Bohemia (1378-1419), king of the Romans (1376-1400), 465 n., 473 n.

Westminster (Midd.), 20, 22, 26, 32, 34, 48, 94, 102, 114, 140, 174, 207 n., 214 n., 216, 228, 238, 272, 274, 280, 290, 292, 310 n., 332, 400, 406 n., 434, 480, 504, 516, 524, 552

— archbishop of York's house in, 212 n.

— councils at, 24, 32, 94 n., 116, 228, 390, 402 nn., 436, 456

— Hall, 110, 212, 273, 504 n., 506

— Hospital of St. James in, 508, 509 n.

— king's court in, 278

— King Street, 438

— New Palace Yard, 310 n.

— Palace, xxvi, lxix, 4, 104, 116, 310 n., 380 n., 414-16, 506, 512

— —, Marcolf chamber in, 391 n.

— —, St. Stephen's Chapel in, xxix, xxxvii, 22, 38 and n., 378, 380 and n., 512; chapel of St. Mary the Pew in, 513 n.

— Tothill in, 458

— wool staple in, 310 n., 312

Westminster Abbey, lv, lvi, lxix, 18,
   32, 36 n., 132, 142, 144 n., 156,
   196 n., 294, 314, 342, 488, 496
—— archdeacon, 176
—— chamberlain, lvi
—— chapel of St. John the Baptist,
   lvi, 332
—— church, 8, 22, 32, 38, 208, 508,
   510, 520 and n.
—— convent, 8–10, 508
—— conventual treasurers, xxxii, xxxviii,
   xl n.
—— Customary, liv
—— foundation of Eleanor of Castile
   in, xxxviii, xxxix
—— gate, 8
—— High Mass in, 450, 454, 510
—— historical writing at, xxxi and n.
—— infirmarer, infirmary, xli
—— king's gate, 208 and n., 416
—— monastic office, 450, 454, 510
—— monks of, see under individual
   names
—— new work, xxxix
—— precentor, xxxii
—— prior, see Exeter, Richard
—— prior and convent, 176, 506
—— quarrel with St. Stephen's Westminster, xxix, xxxviii, 38 and n.,
   378–82
—— regalia, xxxvii, xxxix, lv, 90, 156,
   414, 416 and n.
—— relics, xxxvii–viii, lv, 132, 156
—— royal gate, see king's gate
—— sacrist, lv, 310 n., 438 n.
—— SS. Peter and Edward, patrons,
   480
—— sanctuary, xxiii, xxvii, xxxii, xxxvii,
   lvi, lvii, 8 n., 144 n., 310 and n.,
   312 and n., 324 and n., 326–8,
   332, 336–40, 458, 496 and n.
—— shrine of Edward the Confessor,
   lv, lxxii, 8, 10, 178, 338, 372, 506
—— temporalities, xxxix, 38 and n.,
   178 n., 380
—— Tothill gate, 408, 508, 509 n.
—— treasury of wardrobe in, 8 and n.
—— vestments, 478
—— vestry, xxxvii, 414, 416
Westminster, abbot of, lvi, 332, 338,
   340, 378; and king's council, lix
   and n., 24; attendance at parliament, xlvi and n.; hall of, 510;

liberty of, 496 n.; steward of house-
   hold of, xvii, xxxviii, lvi n.; see also
   Colchester, William; Litlington,
   Nicholas
Westminster, abbot and convent of, xv,
   38, 144, 208, 379 n., 380 n., 408,
   480 n.
Westminster, abbot-elect, 196, 202,
   204
Weyland, Thomas, citizen of London,
   494
Whittington, Richard, mercer of Lon-
   don, 494
Wikeford, Robert, archbishop of Dublin
   (1375–90), lxiii, 200, 201 n., 206,
   273 n.
Wilford, Thomas, fishmonger and alderman of London, 494
Wilia, R. (now R. Nerva), 446 n.
William I, king of England (1066–87),
   xv, xxxii
William Durandus, Rationale divinorum officiorum, xli and n.
Winchelsea (Suss.), 34 n., 40 n.
Winchester (Hants), parliament at, 512,
   514 n.
—— castle, 323 n.
Winchester, bishop of, see Wykeham,
   William of
Windsor (Berks.), xxxvii and n., 32,
   42, 106, 158, 178, 184, 220, 224,
   402, 450, 456, 502
—— castle, 94 n., 178 n., 180, 217 n.,
   272, 500, 502 n.; constable of,
   see Burley, Simon
—— councils at, 220 and n., 402 and n.
Windsor, Sir William, lieutenant in Ire-
   land, d. 1384, 98 and n.
Witney (Oxon.), lii, lxiv and n., 220
   and n.
Woodcock, John, mercer of London,
   494
Woodstock (Oxon.), 408, 438
—— council at, 28, 186 and nn.
Woodstock, Edward of, son of Edward
   III, prince of Wales, prince of
   Aquitaine (the Black Prince), d.
   1376, 101 n., 142 n., 152, 292,
   450 n.
—— Joan, wife of, see Kent, Joan of
Woodstock, Thomas of, earl of
   Buckingham (1377–97), duke of
   Gloucester (1385–97), xxii n., xxiv,

xxix–xxx, xxxiv, xlix, lxiii, lxiv n., 12 n., 48, 58, 66, 116, 124, 140 and n., 154, 168, 184, 186, 188, 206, 229 n., 231 n., 267 n., 272, 285 n., 288, 310, 378, 521 n.
— and John of Gaunt, lix, lxii–lxiii, 82, 112 and n.
— and rising of Appellants, lii, liii, liv, 208 ff., 296–8, 302
— and Westminster Abbey, xxii, lv–vi, lx, 156, 332, 380, 478, 480 and n.
— Anne, daughter of, m. Thomas, 3rd earl of Stafford, 480, 481 n.
— anniversary, 480 n.
— constable, 124, 236 and n., 240, 268, 280
— 'duke of Aumale', 126 and n.
— Eleanor, wife of (Eleanor de Bohun), xxii, xl n., 192, 479 n., 480 n., 520, 521 n.
— embassies, 88 and n., 98, 514 and n., 515 n.
— expedition to Prussia, 478, 479 n., 480, 482, 484
— Humphrey, son of, 521 n.
— in Merciless Parliament, lxxiii, lxxiv, 234 ff., 280 ff., 328 and n.
— king's lieutenant in parliament, 290
— lieutenant in Ireland, xxviii–xxix, 379 n., 486 and n.
— plots against, 260, 262, 266–8
— political decline, lix, 518
Wool staple, 146 and n., 354, 454 and n.; see also Calais; Middelburg; Westminster
Worcester:
— bishop of, see Wakefield, Henry de
— cathedral priory (St. Mary's Abbey), xvi, 332
Worth, Sir John, 230, 231 n.
— Blanche, wife of, 231 n.
Wotton, William, woolmonger and alderman of London, 494
Writs:
— attaint, 273 n., 508 n.
— exigent, 144 and n., 426
— praemunire facias, 464 and n., 470, 472

— prohibition, 38 and n., 326 n., 378
— quare impedit, 464 and n., 470, 472
— summoning Londoners to Nottingham, 492–4, 498
— summons to parliament, 216–18
Wycliffe, John, d. 1384:
— death, 106 and n.
— heresy of, xxxvi, 14 n., 28 nn.
Wycombe, see High Wycombe
Wykeham, William of, chancellor (1367–71), bishop of Winchester (1366–1404), 168, 210, 226 n., 232, 238, 324, 332, 333 n., 340 n., 392 and n.
'Wytort', king of, 444 n., 446

Yaxley (Hunts.), 337 n.
Yeu Island (Fr.), 352
Yevele, Henry, master mason and architect, of London, 494
York, xxxv, 44, 50, 120, 122, 245 n., 368, 442
— archbishop of, 50, 86, 156, 526; see also Nevill, Alexander
— archbishopric of, 334 and n., 337 n.
— Bishopthorpe in, 120
— duke of, see Langley, Edmund of
— epidemic in, 476
— removal of courts to, 492
— St. Mary's abbey, 402; abbot of, see Bridford, William
York, Edmund, duke of, see Langley, Edmund of
York, Edward of, earl of Rutland (1390–1415), duke of Aumale (1397–9), and duke of York (1402–15), 28, 29 n., 414 and n.
York, duchess of, see Isabel of Castile
Ypres (W. Flanders, Belg.), 30 n., 32 and n., 44 and n., 46, 152 and n., 524

Zealand, Alberic, count of, see Bavaria, Alberic, duke of
Zouche, La Zouche, William, lord, of Harringworth, 70, 74–6, 77 n., 78, 184 n., 230